June 1995. To Hannah.
Hope it will
be useful
Love Grandma.

AMERICAN RENAISSANCE

BY THE SAME AUTHOR

THE ACHIEVEMENT OF T. S. ELIOT, 1939

DONALD McKAY, Builder of the *Flying Cloud,* the *Sovereign of the Seas,* the *James Baines,* and the *Lightning.*

Daguerreotype by Southworth and Hawes (Boston)

American Renaissance

ART AND EXPRESSION

IN THE AGE OF EMERSON AND WHITMAN

>»» «<

F. O. MATTHIESSEN

LONDON   TORONTO

OXFORD UNIVERSITY PRESS

NEW YORK

FOR

HANNS CASPAR KOLLAR, *formerly of Vienna,*

and HARRY DORMAN, *of Santa Fe, New Mexico,*

WHO HAVE TAUGHT ME MOST
ABOUT THE POSSIBILITIES OF LIFE IN AMERICA

'There is a moment in the history of every nation, when, proceeding out of this brute youth, the perceptive powers reach their ripeness and have not yet become microscopic: so that man, at that instant, extends across the entire scale, and, with his feet still planted on the immense forces of night, converses by his eyes and brain with solar and stellar creation. That is the moment of adult health, the culmination of power.'

—EMERSON, *Representative Men.*

'Men must endure
Their going hence even as their coming hither:
Ripeness is all.'

—marked by Melville in his
copy of *King Lear.*

METHOD AND SCOPE

THE starting point for this book was my realization of how great a number of our past masterpieces were produced in one extraordinarily concentrated moment of expression. It may not seem precisely accurate to refer to our mid-nineteenth century as a *re-birth;* but that was how the writers themselves judged it. Not as a re-birth of values that had existed previously in America, but as America's way of producing a renaissance, by coming to its first maturity and affirming its rightful heritage in the whole expanse of art and culture.

The half-decade of 1850-55 saw the appearance of *Representative Men* (1850), *The Scarlet Letter* (1850), *The House of the Seven Gables* (1851), *Moby-Dick* (1851), *Pierre* (1852), *Walden* (1854), and *Leaves of Grass* (1855). You might search all the rest of American literature without being able to collect a group of books equal to these in imaginative vitality. That interesting fact could make the subject for several different kinds of investigation. You might be concerned with *how* this flowering came, with the descriptive narrative of literary history. Or you might dig into its sources in our life, and examine the economic, social, and religious causes *why* this flowering came in just these years. Or you might be primarily concerned with *what* these books were as works of art, with evaluating their fusions of form and content.

By choosing the last of these alternatives my main subject has become the conceptions held by five of our major writers concerning the function and nature of literature, and the degree to which their practice bore out their theories. That may make their process sound too deliberate, but Emerson, Thoreau, and Whitman all commented very explicitly on language as well as expression, and the creative intentions of Hawthorne and Melville can be readily discerned through scrutiny of their chief works. It has seemed to me that the literary accomplishment of those years could be judged most adequately if approached both in the light of its authors' purposes and in that of our own developing conceptions of literature. The double aim, therefore, has been to place these works both in their age and in ours.

In avowing that aim, I am aware of the important books I have not written. One way of understanding the concentrated abundance of our mid-nineteenth century would be through its intellectual history, particularly through a study of the breakdown of Puritan orthodoxy into Unitarianism, and of the quickening of the cool Unitarian strain into the spiritual and emotional fervor of transcendentalism. The first of those two developments has been best sketched by Joseph Haroutunian, *Piety versus Moralism: The Passing of New England Theology* (1932). The whole movement will be genetically traced in Perry Miller's monumental study of *The New England Mind,* the first volume of which (1939), dealing with the seventeenth century, has already extended the horizons of our cultural past. Another notable book could concentrate on how discerning an interpretation our great authors gave of the economic and social forces of the time. The orientation of such a book would not be with the religious and philosophical ramifications of the transcendental movement so much as with its voicing of fresh aspirations for the rise of the common man. Its method could be the one that Granville Hicks has inherited from Taine, and has already applied in *The Great Tradition* (1933) to our literature since the Civil War. An example of that method for the earlier period is Newton Arvin's detailed examination (1938) of Whitman's emergent socialism.

Swedenborg

The two books envisaged in the last paragraph might well be called *The Age of Swedenborg* and *The Age of Fourier.* Emerson said in 1854, 'The age is Swedenborg's,' by which he meant that it had embraced the subjective philosophy that 'the soul makes its own world.' That extreme development of idealism was what Emerson had found adumbrated in Channing's 'one sublime idea': the potential divinity of man. That religious assumption could also be social when it claimed the inalienable worth of the individual and his right to participate in whatever the community might produce. Thus the transition from transcendentalism to Fourierism was made by many at the time, as by Henry James, Sr., and

Fourier

George Ripley and his loyal followers at Brook Farm. *The Age of Fourier* could by license be extended to take up a wider subject than Utopian socialism; it could treat all the radical movements of the period; it would stress the fact that 1852 witnessed not only the appearance of *Pierre* but of *Uncle Tom's Cabin;* it would stress also what had been largely ignored until recently, the anticipation by Orestes Brownson of some of the Marxist analysis of the class controls of action.[1]

But the age was also that of Emerson and Melville. The one common denominator of my five writers, uniting even Hawthorne and Whitman, was their devotion to the possibilities of democracy. In dealing with their work I hope that I have not ignored the implications of such facts as that the farmer rather than the businessman was still the average American, and that the terminus to the agricultural era in our history falls somewhere between 1850 and 1865, since the railroad, the iron ship, the factory, and the national labor union all began to be dominant forces within those years, and forecast a new epoch. The forties probably gave rise to more movements of reform than any other decade in our history; they marked the last struggle of the liberal spirit of the eighteenth century in conflict with the rising forces of exploitation. The triumph of the new age was foreshadowed in the gold rush, in the full emergence of the acquisitive spirit.[2]

1840's

The older liberalism was the background from which my writers emerged. But I have concentrated entirely on the foreground, on the writing itself. I have not written formal literary history—a fact that should be of some relief to the reader, since if it required a volume of this length for five years of that record, the consequences of any extension of such a method would be appalling. Parrington stated in his *Main Currents of American Thought* (1927): 'With aesthetic judgments I have not been greatly concerned. I have not wished to evaluate reputations or weigh literary merits, but rather to understand what our fathers thought . . .' My concern has been opposite. Although I greatly admire Parrington's elucidation of our liberal tradition, I think the understanding of our literature has been retarded by the tendency of some of his followers to regard all criticism as 'belletristic trifling.' I am even more suspicious of the results of such historians as have declared that they were not discussing art, but 'simply using art, in a purpose of research.' Both our historical writing and our criticism have been greatly enriched during the past twenty years by the breaking down of arbitrary divisions between them, by the critic's realization of the necessity to master what he could of historical discipline, by the historian's desire to extend his

1. See A. M. Schlesinger, Jr., *Orestes A. Brownson* (1939), and Helen S. Mims, 'Early American Democratic Theory and Orestes Brownson' (*Science and Society*, Spring 1939).

2. See Norman Ware, *The Industrial Worker*, 1840-1860 (1924), and E. C. Kirkland, *A History of American Economic Life* (1936).

domain from politics to general culture. But you cannot 'use' a work of art unless you have comprehended its meaning. And it is well to remember that although literature reflects an age, it also illuminates it. Whatever the case may be for the historian, the quality of that illumination is the main concern for the common reader. He does not live by trends alone; he reads books, whether of the present or past, because they have an immediate life of their own.

What constitutes the secret of that life is the subject of this volume. It may be held that my choice of authors is arbitrary. These years were also those of Whittier's *Songs of Labor* (1850), of Longfellow's *Hiawatha* (1855), of work by Lowell and Holmes and Simms, of Baldwin's *Flush Times in Alabama and Mississippi,* of T. S. Arthur's *Ten Nights in a Bar-room*. Nor were any of my authors best sellers. The five hundred copies of Emerson's first book, *Nature* (1836), had been disposed of so slowly that a second edition was not called for until 1849; and though his lecturing had made him well known by then, the sales of none of his books ran far into the thousands. Thoreau recorded in his journal that four years after the appearance of his *Week on the Concord and Merrimack* (1849) only 219 copies had been sold; so he had the publisher ship the remainder back to him and said: 'I have now a library of nearly nine hundred volumes, over seven hundred of which I wrote myself. Is it not well that the author should behold the fruits of his labor?' After that *Walden* was considered a great risk, but it managed to go through an edition of two thousand. Whitman set up and printed *Leaves of Grass* for himself, and probably gave away more copies than were bought, whereas Longfellow could soon report (1857) that the total sales of his books had run to over three hundred thousand, and *Fern Leaves from Fanny's Portfolio* (1853), by the sister of N. P. Willis, sold a hundred thousand in its first year. Although *Typee* (1846) was more popular than Melville's subsequent work, it never came within miles of such figures. Hawthorne reported that six or seven hundred copies of *Twice-Told Tales* (1837) had been disposed of before the panic of that year descended. To reach a wider audience he had to wait until *The Scarlet Letter,* and reflecting on the triumphant vogue of Susan Warner's *The Wide, Wide World* (1850), Maria Cummins' *The Lamplighter* (1854), the ceaseless flux of Mrs. E. D. E. N. Southworth's sixty novels, he wrote to Ticknor in 1855: 'America is now wholly given over to a damned mob of scribbling women, and I should have no chance of success while the public taste is occupied with their trash—and should be ashamed of myself if I did succeed. What is the mystery of these innumerable editions of *The Lamplighter,* and other books neither better nor worse?—worse they could not be, and better they need not be, when they sell by the hundred thousand.'

Such material still offers a fertile field for the sociologist and for the historian of our taste. But I agree with Thoreau: 'Read the best books first, or you may not have a chance to read them at all.' And during the century that has ensued, the successive generations of common readers, who make the decisions, would seem finally to have agreed that the authors of the pre-Civil War era who bulk largest in stature are the five who are my subject. That being the case, a book about their value might seem particularly unnecessary. But 'the history of an art,' as Ezra Pound has affirmed, 'is the history of masterwork, not of failures or mediocrity.' And owing to our fondness for free generalization, even the masterworks of these authors have been largely taken for granted. The critic knows that any understanding of the subtle principle of life inherent in a work of art can be gained only by direct experience of it, again and again. The interpretation of what he has found demands close analysis, and plentiful instances from the works themselves. With a few notable exceptions, most of the criticism of our past masters has been perfunctorily tacked onto biographies. I have not yet seen in print an adequately detailed scrutiny even of 'When lilacs last in the dooryard bloom'd,' or of *Moby-Dick.* And such good criticism as has been written has ordinarily dealt with single writers; it has not examined many of the interrelations among the various works of the group.

My aim has been to follow these books through their implications, to observe them as the culmination of their authors' talents, to assess them in relation to one another and to the drift of our literature since, and, so far as possible, to evaluate them in accordance with the enduring requirements for great art. That last aim will seem to many only a pious phrase, but it describes the critic's chief responsibility. His obligation is to examine an author's resources of language and of genres, in a word, to be preoccupied with form. This means nothing rarefied, as Croce's description of De Sanctis' great *History of Italian Literature* can testify: form for De Sanctis 'was not the "form" pathologically felt by aesthetes and decadents: it was nothing else than the entire resolution of the intellectual, sentimental, and emotional material into the concrete reality of the poetic image and word, which alone has aesthetic value.'

The phases of my somewhat complex method of elucidating that concrete reality can be briefly described. The great attraction of my subject was its compactness: [3] for though I made no attempt to confine my study of these authors to the strait jacket of a five-year segment of their careers, the fact remained that Emerson's theory of expression was that on which Thoreau built, to which Whitman gave extension, and to which Hawthorne and Melville were indebted by being forced to react against its philosophical assumptions. The nature of Emerson's achievement has caused me to range more widely in my treatment of him than in that of the others. *Representative Men* has no more right to be called his masterpiece than *Nature* (1836) or *The Conduct of Life* (1860). He wrote no masterpiece, but his service to the development of our literature was enormous in that he made the first full examination of its potentialities. To apply to him his own words about Goethe: he was the cow from which the rest drew their milk. My discussion of his theory has always in view his practice of it, and its creative use by the others. My prime intention is not Sainte-Beuve's: to be 'a naturalist of minds,' to relate the authors' works to their lives. I have not drawn upon the circumstances of biography unless they seemed essential to place a given piece of writing; [4] and whenever necessary, especially in the case of Melville, I have tried to expose the modern fallacy that has come from the vulgarization of Sainte-Beuve's subtle method—the direct reading of an author's personal life into his works.

The types of interrelation that have seemed most productive to understanding the literature itself were first of all the obvious debts, of Thoreau to Emerson, or Melville to Hawthorne. In the next place there were

3. I have avoided, therefore, the temptation to include a full length treatment of Poe. The reason is more fundamental than that his work fell mainly in the decade of 1835-45; for it relates at very few points to the main assumptions about literature that were held by any of my group. Poe was bitterly hostile to democracy, and in that respect could serve as a revelatory contrast. But the chief interest in treating his work would be to examine the effect of his narrow but intense theories of poetry and the short story, and the account of the first of these alone could be the subject for another book: the development from Poe to Baudelaire, through the French symbolists, to modern American and English poetry. My reluctance at not dealing with Poe here is tempered by the fact that his value, even more than Emerson's, is now seen to consist in his influence rather than in the body of his own work. No group of his poems seems as enduring as *Drum-Taps;* and his stories, less harrowing upon the nerves than they were, seem relatively factitious when contrasted with the moral depth of Hawthorne or Melville.

4. I have provided a Chronology of the principal events in the five authors' lives on pages 657-61.

certain patterns of taste and aspiration: the intimate kinship to the seventeenth-century metaphysical strain that was felt by Emerson, Thoreau, and Melville; the desire for a functional style wherein Thoreau and Whitman especially were forerunners of our modern interest. That last fact again suggests one of my chief convictions: that works of art can be best perceived if we do not approach them only through the influences that shaped them, but if we also make use of what we inevitably bring from our own lives. That is an unorthodox postulate for literary history. But if we can see *Moby-Dick* and *Pierre* much more accurately by uncovering Melville's extraordinary debt to Shakespeare, and come closer to Hawthorne's intentions by observing that his psychological assumptions were still fundamentally the same as Milton's, it seems equally clear that Henry James and Eliot can cast light back on Hawthorne, and that one way of judging *Leaves of Grass* is by juxtaposing it with the deliberate counterstatement made by Whitman's polar opposite, Hopkins. I have, therefore, utilized whatever interrelations of this type have seemed to grow organically from my subject. I do not expect the reader to be willing at this point to grant any relevance to the juxtaposition of Whitman with the painters Millet and Eakins, or to that of Thoreau with the theories of the forgotten sculptor Horatio Greenough. It will be my responsibility to demonstrate those relevances.

The phase of my subject in which I am most interested is its challenge to pass beyond such interrelations to basic formulations about the nature of literature. In the chapter, 'Allegory and Symbolism,' Hawthorne and Melville have been its center, but I have attempted, so far as I was able, to write also an account of these two fundamental modes of apprehending reality. In the concluding chapter, 'Man in the Open Air,' the concern was to bring all five writers together through their subject matter, through their varied responses to the myth of the common man. But these serious responses can be better defined if set into contrast with the comic myth of the frontier, especially in its richest expression by George Washington Harris' *Sut Lovingood*. And the function of myth in literature can be clarified by the rediscovery of its necessity by the age of Joyce and Mann. As a final descriptive instance of my method, I have conceived of the two central books on Hawthorne and Melville as composing a single unit in which the chief value would be the aspects of tragedy that could be discerned through its representative practice by these two writers. I have made no pretence of abstracting a general theory of tragedy, but have crystallized out certain indispensable attributes that are common also to the practice of both Shakespeare and Milton.

After this description of my method, it is obvious that the division into four books is merely to indicate the central emphasis of each. This division, with the index, should make it easy for a reader particularly concerned with a single writer to concentrate on his work alone. Since volumes of criticism are now conventionally supposed to be short, I might have concealed the length of mine by printing it as four separate books, spaced, say, a year apart. But that would have defeated one of my main purposes: to make each writer cast as much light as possible on all the others. Moreover, our chief critical need would seem to be that of full-length estimates. I saw no use in adding further partial portraits to those of Parrington and Van Wyck Brooks, but wanted to deal in both analysis and synthesis. That required extensive quotation, since a critic, to be of any use, must back up his definitions with some of the evidence through which he has reached them. Only thus can the reader share in the process of testing the critic's judgments, and thereby reach his own. I trust that the further division into sixty-odd short essays will help the reader to skip wherever he wants. However, when dealing with the work of one writer, I have made as many transitions as practicable to that of the others.

It may be of some help to the reader to know from the start that the structure of the volume is based on recurrent themes. In addition to the types of interrelation I have mentioned, the most dominant of these themes are: the adequacy of the different writers' conceptions of the relation of the individual to society, and of the nature of good and evil— these two themes rising to their fullest development in the treatment of tragedy; the stimulus that lay in the transcendental conviction that the word must become one with the thing; the effect produced by the fact that when these writers began their careers, the one branch of literature in which America had a developed tradition was oratory; the effect of the nineteenth century's stress on seeing, of its identification of the poet with the prophet or seer; the connection, real if somewhat intangible, between this emphasis on vision and that put on light by the advancing arts of photography and open-air painting; the inevitability of the symbol as a means of expression for an age that was determined to make a fusion between appearance and what lay behind it; the major desire on the part of all five writers that there should be no split between art and the other functions of the community, that there should be an organic union between labor and culture.

The avenue of approach to all these themes is the same, through attention to the writers' use of their own tools, their diction and rhetoric, and to what they could make with them. An artist's use of language is the most sensitive index to cultural history, since a man can articulate only what he is, and what he has been made by the society of which he is a willing or an unwilling part. Emerson, Hawthorne, Thoreau, Whitman, and Melville all wrote literature for democracy in a double sense. They felt that it was incumbent upon their generation to give fulfilment to the potentialities freed by the Revolution, to provide a culture commensurate with America's political opportunity. Their tones were sometimes optimistic, sometimes blatantly, even dangerously expansive, sometimes disillusioned, even despairing, but what emerges from the total pattern of their achievement—if we will make the effort to repossess it [5]— is literature for our democracy. In reading the lyric, heroic, and tragic expression of our first great age, we can feel the challenge of our still undiminished resources. In my own writing about that age, I have kept in mind the demands made on the scholar by Louis Sullivan, who found a great stimulus for his architecture in the functionalism of Whitman. 'If, as I hold,' Sullivan wrote, 'true scholarship is of the highest usefulness because it implies the possession and application of the highest type of thought, imagination, and sympathy, his works must so reflect his scholarship as to prove that it has drawn him toward his people, not away from them; that his scholarship has been used as a means toward attaining their end, hence his. That his scholarship has been applied for the good and the enlightenment of all the people, not for the pampering of a class. His works must prove, in short (and the burden of proof is on him), that he is a citizen, not a lackey, a true exponent of democracy, not a tool of the most insidious form of anarchy . . . In a democracy there

5. Santayana has said that the American mind does not oppose tradition, it forgets it. The kind of repossession that is essential has been described by André Malraux in an essay on 'The Cultural Heritage' (1936): 'Every civilization is like the Renaissance, and creates its own heritage out of everything in the past that helps it to surpass itself. *A heritage is not transmitted; it must be conquered;* and moreover it is conquered slowly and unpredictably. We do not demand a civilization made to order any more than we demand masterpieces made to order. But let us demand of ourselves a full consciousness that the choice made by each of us out of the past—out of the boundless hopes of the men who came before us—is measured by our thirst for greatness and by our wills.'

can be but one fundamental test of citizenship, namely: Are you using such gifts as you possess for or against the people?' These standards are the inevitable and right extension of Emerson's demands in *The American Scholar*. The ensuing volume has value only to the extent that it comes anywhere near measuring up to them.

ACKNOWLEDGMENTS

ALL my reading of American literature has been done during the era of Van Wyck Brooks and Parrington. It was hardly an accident that when I graduated from college in the early nineteen-twenties, I knew very little of our own literature except some contemporary poetry that I had read with my friends. The now encouraging, if tardy, attention that is being paid by our universities to our cultural past dates in most instances since that time. Consequently, the appearance of Lewis Mumford's *The Golden Day* (1926) was a major event in my experience. Through Mumford I became aware of the body of ideas he was popularizing, with their first expression in Brooks' *America's Coming of Age* (1915); and Brooks' stringent demands for a culture adequate to our needs were the strongest influence on my own first work, a critical biography of Sarah Orne Jewett (1929). These statements of my debts to Brooks and Mumford should be as explicit as possible, since when I come to discuss Melville, I am forced to take issue with the accuracy of Mumford's interpretation (1929). And by the time Brooks wrote *The Flowering of New England* (1936), he had relaxed his standards. He was no longer concerned with ideas, or with critical discriminations, but with describing the surfaces of the milieu that had produced the writing, good or bad. His picture is charming but sentimental. His method is most successful in its vignettes of minor and forgotten figures, but it has robbed the period of most of its clash and struggle, it has so diluted Thoreau that it is hard to tell him from Bronson Alcott, and, as I shall have to show when dealing with Hawthorne, it has deprived one of our few tragic writers of his chief significance.

The two critics who have helped me draw a circle of definition around my subject are Coleridge and Eliot. The leading practitioners in their respective times of the type of criticism that is always fertile—the artist's comment on the principles of his craft—these two have had a particular value for my purposes. Coleridge was the immediate stimulus to Emerson's organic theory of language and expression, and has given me many of the formulations for the creative aims of the whole transcendental age. Eliot, in turn, through his reaction against Emerson and his admiration for Hawthorne, has served both to put a period and to suggest an extension. He has typified the fundamental shift in our way of regarding the artist: from inspired seer to trained craftsman. He has also illuminated our deepening concern with tragedy.

Among my advantages nearer at hand, I probably owe even more than I am aware to those friends who have been engaged in the same field, especially to Perry Miller, Newton Arvin, Charles Olson, John Finch, and Howard Schomer. Olson's generosity in letting me make use of what he has tracked down in his investigation of Melville's reading, particularly Melville's markings in his volumes of Hawthorne, alone made possible my study of that interrelation. The three readers whom I have had in mind as the kind of audience I most wanted to satisfy are C. L. Barber, Harry Levin, and Howard Baker. Nearly every page has been improved by one (or more) of their blue pencils, as well as by the persistent scrutiny of my assistant, Stanley Geist, whose own first published work, his Harvard honors essay on Melville (1939), has already shown his devotion to style.

During the ten years that I have been working towards this volume I have received kindnesses from many scholars, and have become grateful to the staffs of many libraries, especially to those of Harvard and Yale, the New York Public Library, the Library of Congress, the Huntington Library in San Marino, the Morgan Library in New York, and the Library of Portsmouth, N. H. Whenever I have used unpublished material, I have made my acknowledgments in a note. A detailed bibliography would have been supererogatory, since during the past few years the *American Writers Series* (published by the American Book Company) has included volumes of representative selections from all five of my authors, in each case with a careful critical bibliography of the important work that has been done on the texts, and in biography and criticism. Two of these volumes are particularly notable: *Hawthorne,* edited by Austin Warren, especially for the section of the introduction dealing with Hawthorne's theology, by far the most searching treatment that has been made of that difficult subject; and *Melville,* edited by Willard Thorp, for its useful work in straightening out some of the badly confused details of Melville's biography.

I should like to hope that I am indebted to everyone who has worked with perception on any of the five authors, but there are undoubtedly some veins that I have missed. Among the older studies, George Edward Woodberry's critical biographies of Hawthorne (1902) and Emerson (1907) stand up the best, for Woodberry, a student of both Henry Adams and Charles Eliot Norton, strove for a synthesis of the intellectual rigor of the one with the aesthetic sensibility of the other. Mark Van Doren's *Thoreau: A Critical Study* (1916)—his first published work, done when he was hardly out of college—is still the most discerning treatment, and is rivalled only by two of Paul Elmer More's earlier *Shelburne Essays.* I have recorded in the notes my many other major obligations. Three books lying for the most part outside my particular subject that have been a stimulus through the skill of their respective methods are J. W. Beach, *The Method of Henry James* (1918), H. L. Mencken, *The American Language* (1919, revised edition 1936), and Constance Rourke, *American Humor: A Study of the National Character* (1931)—the most successful instance of her sensitive kind of cultural and folk history. I have also been indebted to, even when I have found myself in disagreement with, the challenging views of Yvor Winters in *Primitivism and Decadence: A Study of American Experimental Poetry* (1937) and in *Maule's Curse: Seven Studies in the History of Amercian Obscurantism* (1938).

For quotations from copyrighted material I have been granted permission by the following: Doubleday, Doran for the *Uncollected Poetry and Prose* of Walt Whitman, edited by Emory Holloway; Harcourt, Brace and Company for T. S. Eliot's poems and essays, for T. E. Hulme, *Speculations,* and for I. A. Richards, *Coleridge on Imagination;* Harper and Brothers for Mark Twain's *Autobiography;* Harvard University Press for T. S. Eliot, *The Use of Poetry;* Houghton Mifflin Company for Emerson's *Journals,* for *The Education of Henry Adams,* and for Charles Eliot Norton's letters; Little, Brown and Company for Newton Arvin, *Hawthorne,* and for Bronson Alcott's *Journals,* edited by Odell Shepard; Liveright Publishing Corporation for Hart Crane's poems; The Macmillan Company for W. B. Yeats, *A Vision;* The Macmillan Company and Lloyd Goodrich, Research Curator of the Whitney Museum of American Art, for letters by Thomas Eakins; Random House and Professor Emory Holloway for letters by Walt Whitman; Charles Scribner's Sons for Henry James, *The Golden Bowl, The Middle Years,* and *The*

Sense of the Past; Yale University Press for Hawthorne's *American Notebooks,* edited by Randall Stewart, and for Ezra Pound, *The ABC of Reading.*

During the course of this long volume I have undoubtedly plagiarized from many sources—to use the ugly term that did not bother Shakespeare's age. I doubt whether any criticism or cultural history has. ever been written without such plagiary, which inevitably results from assimilating the contributions of your countless fellow-workers, past and present. The true function of scholarship as of society is not to stake out claims on which others must not trespass, but to provide a community of knowledge in which others may share.

F. O. M.

Kittery, Maine
April 1941

CONTENTS

BOOK ONE: FROM EMERSON TO THOREAU

BOOK TWO: HAWTHORNE

BOOK THREE: MELVILLE

BOOK FOUR: WHITMAN

ILLUSTRATIONS

NOTE ON THE ILLUSTRATIONS

CONCERNED as he was with every possibility of *seeing,* Emerson was fascinated with the developing art of photography from the time of the invention of the daguerreotype in the late eighteen-thirties. He conceived of the camera as a powerful symbol for his age's scrutiny of character, just as Hawthorne was to do in making his hero in *The House of the Seven Gables* a practitioner in the new technique, and thus a searcher into the traits and motives behind men's faces. The great master of the photographic portrait in our mid-nineteenth century was Matthew Brady, who recorded both Hawthorne and Whitman at the time of the Civil War. Rather than add to these portraits any of the already well-known likenesses of my other writers, I have chosen to reproduce the finest daguerreotype I have ever seen, the portrait by Southworth and Hawes (1854) of Donald McKay (1810-1880), the master shipbuilder of the clipper era, a farmer's son who reached his full fame when, in the same year as *Moby-Dick,* he built at East Boston the *Flying Cloud.* McKay's portrait makes the most fitting frontispiece, since it reveals the type of character with which the writers of the age were most concerned, the common man in his heroic stature, or as Whitman called the new type, 'Man in the Open Air.'

My primary purpose in including the pictures by W. S. Mount, the most sensitive of our nineteenth-century genre painters, and by the great realist Eakins was to suggest that the advance of open-air painting came from a response to nature analogous to that expressed in *Walden* and *Leaves of Grass.* I give an analysis of all these paintings in the section dealing with Whitman.

BOOK ONE

⫸ ⫷

From Emerson to Thoreau

✺ I ✺

IN THE OPTATIVE MOOD

'Our American literature and spiritual history are, we confess, in the optative mood.'
—EMERSON, 'The Transcendentalist' (1842)

THE PROBLEM that confronts us in dealing with Emerson is the hardest we shall have to meet, because of his inveterate habit of stating things in opposites. The representative man whom he most revered was Plato. For Plato had been able to bridge the gap between the two poles of thought, to reconcile fact and abstraction, the many and the One, society and solitude. Emerson wanted a like method for himself, but he had to confess, in words that throw a bar of light across his whole career: 'The worst feature of this double consciousness is, that the two lives, of the understanding and of the soul, which we lead, really show very little relation to each other; never meet and measure each other: one prevails now, all buzz and din; and the other prevails then, all infinitude and paradise; and, with the progress of life, the two discover no greater disposition to reconcile themselves.' Accepting thus Kant's distinction between the Reason and the Understanding, he felt himself secure in the realm of the higher laws. To-day he has been overtaken by the paradox that 'The Over-Soul' proves generally unreadable; whereas, on the level of the Understanding, which he regarded as mere appearance, his tenacious perception has left us the best intellectual history that we have of his age.

We tend to take at its face value another of his lucidly objective self-estimates: 'My contribution will be simply historical. I write anecdotes of the intellect; a sort of Farmer's Almanac of mental moods.' Philosophers have long since abandoned the futile pursuit of trying to reduce such moods into a system. But the danger now is that in the multiplicity of his conflicting statements, we shall miss the wholeness of character lying behind them. He was in reaction against the formal logic of the eighteenth century, since he believed it not merely to confine but to distort; yet he insisted that 'we want in every man a logic, we cannot pardon the

3

absence of it.' What he wanted could not be measured by propositions: it was to be 'a silent method,' 'the proportionate unfolding of the intuition.' In strong opposition to the usual academic dismissal of Emerson's thought, John Dewey has recognized the sustained tone through his whole production and has called him 'the one citizen of the New World fit to have his name uttered in the same breath with that of Plato.' Dwelling also on the importance of Emerson's restoration to the common man of all the rights of art and culture, which always tend to be per-verted to mere sectarian and class uses, Dewey has found him the philoso-pher of democracy.

This estimate can be held only as Dewey made it, on the basis of a pervasive tendency. That is not to deny its being supported by a great number of such trenchant distinctions as that 'Bancroft and Bryant are historical democrats who are interested in dead or organized, but not in organizing, liberty.' When Emerson confined himself thus to observing phenomena as they were, his value can hardly be exaggerated for those who believe now in the dynamic extension of democracy on economic as well as political levels. But when he swam away into generalizations about the ideal, he showed at once the devastating consequences of the split between his Reason and his Understanding, between the two halves of his nature, which Lowell shrewdly epitomized in the seemingly off-hand characterization of him as 'a Plotinus-Montaigne.' When the first half was in the ascendant, Emerson could commit himself to such re-marks as that 'Money . . . is, in its effects and laws, as beautiful as roses. Property keeps the accounts of the world, and is always moral. The prop-erty will be found where the labor, the wisdom and the virtue have been in nations, in classes, and (the whole life-time considered, with the com-pensations) in the individual also.' So staggeringly innocent an idea makes clear what Henry James, Sr., meant by speaking of Emerson as his 'un-fallen friend,' who always kept astonishing him by his 'unconsciousness of evil.' The sentiments of such essays as those on 'Wealth' and 'Power,' working on temperaments less unworldly than their author's, have pro-vided a vicious reinforcement to the most ruthless elements in our eco-nomic life.

Neither the religious nor the social philosophy of Emerson is to be under detailed consideration here, but equally drastic paradoxes assert themselves in his theory and practice of art. When Henry James, Jr., wrote about him half a dozen years after his death, he took it as a sign of

Emerson's 'singular power' that he was 'a striking exception to the general rule that writings live in the last resort by their form.' This fell in with the estimate that Matthew Arnold had just made, that though Emerson was neither a great poet, nor a great master of prose, nor a great philosophy-maker, he was 'the friend and aider of those who would live in the spirit.' Sixty years later such a judgment helps us not at all. We have witnessed altogether too many vague efforts to 'live in the spirit,' following in the ruck of transcendentalism and disappearing in the sands of the latest theosophy. If Emerson is judged as a writer, he will not be found to have been favored by any exceptions, since time does not grant them. At the threshold of this volume, therefore, we are faced with a different problem from those we shall encounter in its later divisions. We can hardly assess Emerson's work in the light of his theory of language and art, since there is such disproportion between this theory and any practice of it. Yet we can come at once to the major problem that the artist must solve. For Emerson made one of the most challenging quests for a form that would express his deepest convictions, and that would bring him at the same time into vital communication with his society.

1. Consciousness

'Peculiarities of the Present Age . . . It is said to be the age of the first person singular.'

—EMERSON's *Journal* (1827)

RATHER than to give a bare formulation of Emerson's theory of expression,[1] it is more interesting to share in its development at crucial points, largely by recourse to his journal. By that means we can recapture something of his feeling of discovery as new horizons opened out. The quickest way to remind ourselves of what a different atmosphere from our own Emerson thought in is to note a remark made by Alexis de Tocqueville. Writing of the America that was just about to produce Emerson's work, the French critic began his chapter, 'Of Individualism in Democratic Countries,' by remarking, '*Individualism* is a novel expression, to which

---

1. A thorough summary of it was made by Norman Foerster in his chapter on Emerson in *American Criticism* (1928).

a novel idea has given birth.'[2] No wonder that Emerson believed that he was asserting a truth of cardinal importance for human development when he said in 1840: 'In all my lectures, I have taught one doctrine, namely, the infinitude of the private man.' Such a statement is the point from which any consideration of Emerson as an artist must start. For the aspect he dwelt on most was not form but content.

Shortly after the close of the Civil War he set down his 'Historic Notes of Life and Letters in New England,' his reminiscences of the transcendental era, probably the most illuminating account of the intellectual movements of our eighteen-thirties and -forties which has yet been written.[3] Reconsidering that period, he found the key to it in the fact that 'the mind had become aware of itself. Men grew reflective and intellectual. There was a new consciousness. The former generations acted under the belief that a shining social prosperity was the beatitude of man, and sacrificed uniformly the citizen to the State. The modern mind believed that the nation existed for the individual, for the guardianship and education of every man. This idea, roughly written in revolutions and national movements, in the mind of the philosopher had far more precision; the individual is the world.' That consciousness, an expansion of what Tocqueville had found to be 'a new idea,' was Emerson's subject matter. Near the outset of his career (1839) he asserted, 'Ours is the Revolutionary age, when man is coming back to Consciousness.' For the full expression of such an age he kept saying that what was needed most was a great *reflective* poet.

The most immediate force behind American transcendentalism was Coleridge, who gained many ardent readers in New England following the edition of *Aids to Reflection* that was brought out in 1829 by President Marsh of the University of Vermont. The far-reaching effects of his contribution to general critical vocabulary and thus to modes of thinking can be epitomized by a few of the terms which he coined or put into re-

2. The first English translator of *Democracy in America* (1840), which was based on Tocqueville's visit to this country in 1831-2, commented on this word: 'I adopt the expression of the original, however strange it may seem to the English ear, partly because it illustrates . . . the introduction of general terms into democratic language . . . and partly because I know of no English word exactly equivalent.' This is the first usage recorded by the Oxford English Dictionary. For Tocqueville's views concerning democratic language, see below in relation to Whitman, pp. 532-4.

3. Other comparable narratives which supplement Emerson's are Theodore Parker's *Experiences as a Minister* (1859) and Orestes Brownson's *The Convert* (1857).

newed currency.[4] This brief exercise in semantics is another shorthand way of recalling what things were fresh for Emerson that we take for granted. We could hardly get a sharper impression of the new centers of interest for Coleridge's day than in his remark that he had found it necessary to borrow back from scholasticism *subjective* and *objective:* 'because I could not so briefly or conveniently by any more familiar terms distinguish the *percipere* from the *percipi.*' We see more of the age's drift of interest in the need that Coleridge felt to introduce *psychological,*[5] as a supplement to Hartley's borrowing of *psychology* from the German, half a century before. Other Coleridgean terms, some of which he transferred to criticism by analogy with other branches of thought, and all of which are so familiar to us that it is hard to conceive how anyone ever discussed literature without them, are *aesthetic, intuitive, idealize, intellectualize, organic, organization,* and *self-conscious.* Though Emerson was no such daring coiner as Coleridge—indeed, there has been none to equal Coleridge in the whole course of criticism in English—he participated to the full in the new processes of mind which had demanded such means of expression.

The revolution in which Emerson shared was primarily the one that was waged against the formulas of eighteenth-century rationalism in the name of the fuller resources of man. Coleridge had stressed what was to be one of Emerson's recurrent themes, 'the *all in each* of human nature,' —how a single man contains within himself, through his intuition, the whole range of experience. Coleridge, in turn, had quoted from Schelling: 'On the IMMEDIATE which dwells in every man, and on the original intuition, or absolute affirmation of it . . . all the *certainty* of our knowledge depends.' Such a doctrine of knowledge lay behind the main developments of romantic literature, and naturally made a particular appeal to isolated, provincial America. As Henry James was to remark in his study of Hawthorne, introspection, thanks to the want of other entertainment, played almost the part of a social resource for lonely men and women in

4. I am indebted here to J. Isaacs' 'Coleridge's Critical Terminology' (*Essays and Studies by Members of the English Association,* 1936), which is a product of his work for a much-needed historical dictionary of critical terms in both literature and the fine arts.

5. His footnote to 'psychological' in his *Treatise on Method:* 'We beg pardon for the use of this *insolens verbum;* but it is one of which our language stands in great need. We have no single term to express the Philosophy of the Human Mind: and what is worse, the Principles of that Philosophy are commonly called *Metaphysical,* a word of very different meaning.'

New England. 'Our private theater is ourselves' might be the opening line of a lyric by Emily Dickinson as well as the drift of a passage in Emerson's journal. An even more characteristic saying for him is, 'Life consists in what a man is thinking of all day.' To his cheerful temperament, the turning of the individual upon his own inner life was a matter not for resignation but for exuberance. The possible tragic consequences of isolation, the haunted reverberations of the soul locked into its prison, though not envisaged by his optimism,[6] were the burdens of Hawthorne and Poe.

It is necessary to mark off more accurately the kind of consciousness that Emerson celebrated, if we are to understand what it was he wanted to express by saying, 'The individual is the world.' In 'Self-Reliance' he declared, 'Nothing is at last sacred but the integrity of your own mind,' a conclusion which, out of its context, may seem so extreme in its individualism as to involve finally the destruction of any valid individuality.[7] For, as John MacMurray has argued in *The Philosophy of Communism,* the 'last effort to preserve one's precious self' can lead only to the loss 'of everything that gives selfhood a positive significance.' What saved Emerson from the extremes of rugged Emersonianism was the presence not merely of egoism but also of a universal breadth in his doctrine that all souls are equal. What stirred him most deeply was not man's separateness from man, but his capacity to share directly in the divine superabundance. One of the first beliefs that he affirmed as he cut himself loose from the clergy was: 'The highest revelation is that God is in every man.'

Emerson agreed with Coleridge that the subjectivity which was the most fundamental distinction between modern and classic poetry was owing to the effect of Christianity in bending the mind inward on its own essence. He felt likewise the need for distinguishing between what he considered the true and false subjective. He was occupied with consciousness, not with self-consciousness. He wanted to study the laws of

6. An occasional somber qualification of this appears in the period before he had found his positive gospel, for instance in 1831, shortly after his first wife had died and the year before he resigned from the pulpit: 'One of the arguments which nature furnishes us for the Immortality of the Soul is, it always seemed to me, the awful solitude in which here a soul lives. Few men communicate their highest thoughts to any person. To many they cannot, for they are unfit receivers. Perhaps they cannot to any . . . Here I sit alone from month to month filled with a deep desire to exchange thoughts with a friend who does not appear. Yet shall I find, or refind, that friend.'

7. Poe carried such a thought even farther: 'My whole nature revolts at the idea that there is any being in the universe superior to myself.' He reached the desperate conclusion in *Eureka* that no one can believe 'that anything exists *greater than his own soul.'*

the mind, what he called throughout life the natural history of the intellect, but he always felt a repugnance to self-centered introversion. At the time when he was the target of the most direct personal attacks that were ever made upon him, after Andrews Norton had pronounced his Divinity School Address 'the latest form of Infidelity,' he wrote 'in his journal (1838): 'My prayer is that I may never be deprived of a fact, but be always so rich in objects of study as never to feel this impoverishment of remembering myself.' In the course of his 'Thoughts on Modern Literature' a couple of years later, he developed this distinction. He held that there was 'a pernicious ambiguity in the use of the term *subjective.*' On the one hand, it could simply mean that a man had no interest in anything save as it related to his own personality, a morbid self-indulgence. On the other hand, 'a man may say I, and never refer to himself as an individual'—such is the valid subjectivity that arises from the perception that 'there is One Mind, and that all the powers and privileges which lie in any, lie in all.' That was the beacon that Emerson believed could dispel the fogs of the romantic cultivation of the ego, for 'the great always introduce us to facts; small men introduce us always to themselves.'

Another distinction that will help disclose how much he implied by the 'integrity' of the mind is furnished in his contrast between *perception* and *notion:* 'Thoughtless people contradict as readily the statement of perceptions as of opinions, or rather much more readily; for they do not distinguish between perception and notion. They fancy that I choose to see this or that thing. But perception is not whimsical, but fatal.' [8] The doctrine hinted there is what Thoreau and Whitman also relied on. It involves a mystical acceptance of intuition as final, and demands an unswerving loyalty to its dictates. It discloses what Emerson meant by his frequent remark that he felt more kinship with the inner light of the Quakers than with any formal creed. It suggests also how his conception of consciousness extended beyond the grasp of analysis: 'There are no fixtures to men, if we appeal to consciousness. Every man supposes himself not to be fully understood; and if there is any truth in him, if he rests at last on the divine soul, I see not how it can be otherwise. The last

8. Cf. Coleridge: 'My opinion is this: that deep thinking is attainable only by a man of deep feeling, and all truth is a species of revelation . . . It is *insolent* to *differ* from the public *opinion* in *opinion*, if it be only *opinion*. It is sticking up little *i by itself*, i against the whole alphabet. But one word with *meaning* in it is worth the whole alphabet together. Such is a sound argument, an incontrovertible fact.'

chamber, the last closet, he must feel was never opened; there is always a residuum unknown, unanalyzable.' Again the tone conveys what Emerson discovered in himself. Similar investigations led to very different conclusions for Melville, to fluctuating ambiguity as door after door was opened onto dark truths in *Pierre,* and the last chamber was contemplated only with horror. But in Emerson, with all his alertness and receptivity, there remained what the elder Henry James found himself baffled by, a serenity that had grown from no depth of experience but seemed to be constitutional, 'like a woman's beauty or charm of manners.' Nevertheless his extension of the meaning of the inner life relates him to the dominant strain in modern art that leads from Hawthorne through the younger James to Proust, from Poe through the symbolists to Eliot.

One factor that separates Emerson's work from that of all these others, even from Hawthorne's, is that his initial preoccupation with Unitarian and transcendental thought made the origin of his conception of art almost exclusively intellectual. Those of his associates who were concerned with poetry felt the limitation in approaching it so purely through the mind. Margaret Fuller, after one of their interminable conversations, which, it must be added, she forced upon him, urged him to 'forego these tedious, tedious attempts to learn the universe by thought alone.' Thoreau seems instinctively to have agreed with a remark in Carlyle's *Characteristics,* that 'the sign of health is unconsciousness,' by which he meant that a lack of awareness of the processes of mind was the best way to realize the deeply spontaneous life. Carlyle himself grew increasingly indifferent to poetry, but he kept demanding of Emerson more concreteness in all his work. He had rejoiced in 'the sphere-music' of his friend's first book, his 'azure-colored' *Nature* (1836); but five years later he was saying of the *Essays* that they seemed like '*un*embodied' voices, whereas what he wanted was 'a stalwart Yankee man . . . with a coat on his back.' The image that was emerging from his impression of each successive volume, as from the second *Essays* (1844), was that of 'a *Soliloquizer* on the eternal mountain tops . . . only the *man* and the stars and earth are visible.'

Emerson knew such a charge to be fundamental. When Carlyle was constructing *Past and Present* (1842), he had protested against Emerson's separating himself 'from the Fact of this Present Universe . . . Surely I could wish you *returned* into your own poor nineteenth century.' He took the position that there was no use writing about things past unless they could be made things present. But that, emphatically, Emerson felt to be *his* position as well. Even when he had been a divinity student in Cambridge, he had confided to his journal, 'My business is with the living'; and now he answered the charge against his *Essays:* 'But of what you say now and heretofore respecting the remoteness of my writing and thinking from real life . . . I do not know what it means. If I can at any time express the law and the ideal right, that should satisfy me without measuring the divergence from it of the last act of Congress.'

A good deal hinges on what he meant by 'real.' In lamenting, over and again, that transcendental New England was too imaginative and intellectual, lacking in male vigor and earthiness, he was painfully aware of how much he shared in its defects. He did not, like Poe, conceive his content as being 'out of space—out of time.' When he said, 'I embrace absolute life,' he did not want to escape into the empyrean. He did not want his idealism to be divorced from the material facts of his age. How deeply involved with and dependent upon its tendencies he felt himself to be can be read throughout his journals, especially during the eighteen-thirties when he was finding his way. No matter what Carlyle might judge of the result, it seemed to Emerson that he could write both about Universal Man and about man as a democratic citizen. The kind of harmony he tried to effect between the Now and the Eternal may serve to reveal why he could believe that consciousness was a subject that deserved the devotion of all his mature years.

On his way home from Europe in the fall of 1833, when asked what he meant by morals, his only answer was, 'I cannot define, and care not to define. It is man's business to observe, and the definition of moral nature must be the slow result of years, of lives, of states, perhaps of being.' But he was not at all unsure of the drift of his inner existence: 'Milton describes himself in his letter to Diodati as enamored of moral perfection. He did not love it more than I. That which I cannot yet declare has been my angel from childhood until now . . . What is this they say about wanting mathematical certainty for moral truths? I have always affirmed they had it. Yet they ask me whether I know the soul immortal. No. But do I not know the Now to be eternal? . . . I believe in this life . . .'

No passages in Emerson are likely to stand up against searching .neological analysis. He cast overboard so much ballast of tradition that his buoyant expansiveness is like one of Whitman's lines—'Purpos'd I know not whither, yet ever full of faith'; or, even more like—'All bound as is befitting each—all surely going somewhere.' In the light of a further century of scientific development no one now is apt to be very impressed by his assertion of simple correspondence between scientific laws and moral rules. Nevertheless, these sentences embrace the heart of Emerson's discovery as he turned his back on the 'pale negations' of Unitarianism, and began to utter what, after long and quiet listening to himself, he knew that he really believed. The first and recurrent upsurge of his conviction was that 'life is an ecstasy,' that the moment was an almost unbelievable miracle, which he wanted, more than anything else, to catch and to record. And the Now did not remain a figment of the mind; it was drenched with local surroundings. He could rejoice that his advantages were 'the total New England,' and the promise of American life in its first years of mature fulfilment gave him his special tone: 'Of every storied bay and cliff and plain, we will make something infinitely nobler than Salamis or Marathon. This pale Massachusetts sky, this sandy soil and raw wind, all shall nurture us. Unlike all the world before us, our own age and land shall be classic to ourselves.'

Those whose ears are attuned to the more exact and delicate verbal harmonies of *Nature* and *The American Scholar* may find these sentences still a bit clumsy. The hackneyed 'infinitely nobler' might well have been pared away in revision. But the fact is that this passage is not by Emerson at all; it occurs in the Master's oration of Robert Bartlett of Plymouth at the Harvard Commencement of 1839. Bartlett could catch these accents because he had been listening to Emerson; and the more you read in the literature of the years just preceding Emerson's own appearance, the more you realize his dependence in turn upon a converging group of New England thinkers. You encounter especially in Channing (1780-1842), whom Emerson called 'our Bishop,' passages very close to Emerson's luminous eloquence.[9] In the same year as *Nature*, which contains in embryo nearly all his cardinal assumptions, five other books-appeared in Boston with kindred views of religion.[10] And Emerson was fully cogni-

Channing

9. E.g. Channing's statement: 'The grand truth which pervades poetry is that the beautiful is not confined to the rare, the new, the distant—to scenery and modes of life open only to the few; but that it is poured forth profusely on the common earth and sky.'

10. The titles of the others, all by men who were at that time identified with the transcendental movement, are more formally religious than Emerson's: George Ripley, *Discourses on the Philosophy of Religion;* Convers Francis, *Christianity as a Purely Internal Principle;* Orestes Brownson, *New Views of Christianity, Society, and the Church;* Bronson Alcott, *Conversations with Children on the Gospels;* W. H. Furness, *Remarks on the Four Gospels.* It is hardly surprising that, according to his enemies, Andrews Norton sat in his room with the blinds drawn, and meditated on the forms of infidelity.

zant of the measure in which he was simply rephrasing the position of Sampson Reed, the Swedenborgian druggist, whose little book, *Observations on the Growth of the Mind,* had been issued a decade before.

But Emerson's growth was fostered not merely by the renascence of idealistic philosophy, but likewise by his eager apprehension of the possibilities of American democracy. Only a few days after *Nature* was printed, he formulated in his journal a brief outline of literature since the Middle Ages. As he interpreted it, the line of development had tended to bring literature ever closer to the life which men know, to 'the Necessary, the Plain, the True, the Human.' He regarded that tendency in a double light. On the one hand, he spoke of its truth in transcendental terms, and found that whereas the eighteenth-century writers treated 'only of the life of common sense, the Apparent,' men like Wordsworth and Coleridge 'perceive the dependence of that on the life of the Reason, or the Real.' On the other hand, his belief in the infinitude of the private man was also a democratic doctrine. He shared in that revolution too, and held it responsible for the great extension of the scope of literature:

What is good that is said or written now lies nearer to men's business and bosoms than of old. What is good goes now to all. What was good a century ago is written under the manifest belief that it was as safe from the eye of the common people as from the Tartars . . . Tamerlane and the Buccaneers vanish before Texas, Oregon territory, the Reform Bill, the abolition of slavery and of capital punishment, questions of education, and the Reading of Reviews; and in all these all men take part. The human race have got possession, and it is all questions that pertain to their interest, outward or inward, that are now discussed, and many words leap out alive from bar-rooms, Lyceums, Committee Rooms, that escape out of doors and fill the world with their thunder.[11]

11. Many others were feeling the same promise in the air as Margaret Fuller did when launching *The Dial* in 1840: 'It is for dear New England that I want this review.' Longfellow had stressed the importance of native themes in the 'Defence of Poetry,' which he wrote five years before *The American Scholar* and six years before his own first volume of verse. Thoreau rejoiced that he had been 'born in the most estimable place in all the world, and in the very nick of time.'

A passage at the furthest extreme from Henry James' later recital of the liabilities encountered by an author of Hawthorne's day is this in Sylvester Judd's *Margaret* (1845): 'There are no fairies in our meadows, and no elves to spirit away our children. Our wells are drugged by no saint, and of St. Winifred we have never heard . . . The Valley of the Housatonic is beautiful as the Vale of Tempe, or of Cashmere, and as oracular. We have no resorts for pilgrims, no shrines for the devout, no summits looking into Paradise. We have no traditions, legends, fables, and scarcely a history . . . no chapels or abbeys, no broken arches or castled crags. You find these woods as inspiring as those of Etruria or

To do justice to that new interest as well as to the thinker's consciousness was the problem he set himself in trying to reconcile the claims of the One and the many, of the individual and his world. His unending concern with those claims caused his immediate response to the poet who was to declare:

> One's-self I sing, a simple separate person,
> Yet utter the word Democratic, the word En-Masse.

2. Eloquence

'I say to Lidian that in composition the *What* is of no importance compared with the *How*. The most tedious of all discourses are on the subject of the Supreme Being.'

—EMERSON's *Journal* (1837)

ONE OF the most absorbing themes to follow through the early volumes of Emerson's journal is his search for a form that would express the content ever latent in his mind. In a long passage of self-examination, written a month before his twenty-first birthday, he reached the decision to enter the ministry, despite his realization that, compared with his 'strong imagination' and 'keen relish for the beauties of poetry,' his reasoning faculty was 'proportionably weak,' and that he could never 'hope to write a Butler's Analogy.' A few pages later he was composing a 'Letter to Plato,' further to justify his decision by recounting what revelation had added to pagan philosophy.[1] Only a little farther on he tried, somewhat stiffly, to describe the kind of book that appealed to him most, the kind

Mamre. Robin-Good-Fellow is unknown, and the Devil haunts our theology, not our houses, and I see in the last edition of the Primer his tail is entirely abridged . . . NEW ENGLAND! my birthplace, my chosen pilgrimage, I love it.'

1. Its tone shows what a ready convert he had been for the doctrine of Channing's 'Moral Argument Against Calvinism' (1820): 'It is a favorite point, Plato, with our divines, to argue from the misery and vice anciently prevalent in the world, a certain necessity of the Revelation. Of this Revelation I am the ardent friend . . . But I confess it has not for me the same exclusive and extraordinary claims it has for many. I hold Reason to be a prior Revelation, and that they do not contradict each other . . . I need not inform you in all its depraved details of the theology under whose chains Calvin of Geneva bound Europe down; but this opinion, that the Revelation had become necessary to the salvation of men through some conjunction of events in heaven, is one of its vagaries . . .'

'which appears now and then in the world, once in two or three centuries perhaps, and which soon or late gets a foothold in popular esteem. I allude to those books which collect and embody the wisdom of their times, and so mark the stages of human improvement. Such are the Proverbs of Solomon, the Essays of Montaigne, and eminently the Essays of Bacon.' Although he declared that he was not 'so foolhardy' as to write *Sequel to Bacon* on his title page, the two strains alternating through his mind in these passages were never to be absent from it. They emerge repeatedly through the pattern of his reading. The dominant strain is the Christian, exhaling into Neo-Platonism; this is the element that attracted him to the seventeenth-century devotional and mystical poets, to Berkeley, to Swedenborg, to Coleridge; and later, through Coleridge and Carlyle, to German philosophy; and, later still, to the Oriental poetry and scriptures. In comparison, the strain that celebrates earthly wisdom is subordinate, but is continually cropping up in his lifelong delight in Montaigne's racy concreteness, in the fact that the Frenchman possessed 'the *de quoi* which the French cherubs had not when the courteous archbishop implored them to sit down.' [2] When Alcott proposed 'a historical record of conversations' held by a transcendental group, Emerson said, how joyful rather would be 'some Montaigne's book': 'full of fun, poetry, business, divinity, philosophy, anecdote, smut,' which would treat 'of bone and marrow, of cornbarn and flour barrel, of wife, and friend, and valet, of things nearest and next.' Emerson found this closeness to reality in Plutarch's 'sharp, objective eyes,' almost everywhere in the writers of the seventeenth century, in Carlyle's concentrated vigor, in Whitman's embrace of common humanity. The reconciliation of the two strains, of untrammelled speculation with Yankee practicality, was what he wanted most in his own writing.

Nine years subsequent to his resolve to become a minister, he reached a fresh decision, after hovering over the cabinets of Natural History in the Jardin des Plantes in Paris. He concluded: 'I am moved by strange sympathies; I say continually "I will be a naturalist."' [3] In what sense he

2. According to Emerson, the prelate said, 'Asseyez-vous, mes enfants,' and the fluttering cherubs answered, 'Monseigneur, nous n'avons pas de quoi.'

3. Bliss Perry made the interesting point, in *Emerson To-day* (1931), that Balzac, in consequence of his visits to the same museum in the same summer, arrived at his idea for *La Comédie Humaine* 'in a comparison between Humanity and Animality.' The effect of natural history on two such widely different temperaments is an indication of the kind of interest in science that became increasingly common for writers in the nineteenth cen-

was using that term becomes clearer when we remember that the subject of his first public lecture upon his return from Europe that fall was 'The Uses of Natural History,' and that he stated there: 'It is in my judgment the greatest office of natural science (and one which as yet is only begun to be discharged) to explain man to himself.' To explain man to himself, to be a naturalist of the soul, remained henceforward his resolve.

Such an explanation, as he conceived it, demanded both moral ·philosophy and the most exacting scrutiny of his own experience. But he felt himself still far away from the requisite form. On the voyage home he had noted, 'I like my book about Nature,' a book which he was not to write for nearly three years. Thereupon, in his detachment on seeing it in print, he wrote to Carlyle: 'This is only a naming of topics on which I would gladly speak and gladlier hear.' Within the months while his short chapters had been shaping, he set down a passage on form that put the issue as he was always to feel it: 'Read yesterday Goethe's Iphigenia. A pleasing, moving, even heroic work, yet with the great deduction of being an imitation of the antique . . . Yet when in the evening we read Sophocles, the shadow of a like criticism fell broad over almost all that is called modern literature. The words of Electra and Orestes are like actions. So live the thoughts of Shakespeare. They have a necessary being.' Then, having observed how the form of the Elizabethan play was determined by a living theater, he continued to glance through later history:

Sermons were thus a living form to Taylor, Barrow, South and Donne; novels and parliamentary speeches since Fielding and Burke . . . But thus it always must happen that the true work of genius should proceed out of the wants and deeds of the age as well as the writer, and so be the first form with which his genius combines, as sculpture was perfect in Phidias's age . . . Homer is the only true epic. Milton is to him what Michel Angelo is to Phidias. But Shakespeare is like Homer or Phidias himself. Do that which lies next you, O Man!

He thought he knew what lay next him when he had based his decision to be a minister partly on the grounds that he burned with 'a passionate love for the strains of eloquence.' That love was never to desert him; it wooed him under many guises, and invariably wove itself into his

tury. That both Balzac and Emerson found correspondences between human and animal life is probably owing also to the fact that both had been influenced by Swedenborg. The wide divergence between their conclusions is that Balzac was aware of the decay of society, and laid stress upon cruelty and brutality in his analogies with the animal kingdom.

conception of the highest art. He never forgot the thrill of his undergraduate response to the magic of Everett's rhetoric, through which his eyes had been opened 'to a new perception of Grecian beauty.' He went to listen to Webster whenever he could. He heard him deliver his funeral oration on Jefferson and Adams, who had died within a few hours of each other on the Fourth of July, fifty years after the Declaration. Emerson fell completely under Webster's spell, and remained so long after he recognized the chasm between the politician's aims and his own. He wrote Carlyle (1839) that he had followed after that 'great forehead' all his youthful days, 'from court-house to senate-chamber, from caucus to street . . . I owe to him a hundred fine hours and two or three moments of Eloquence.' So high a rating did Emerson put on that quality. His first recorded remarks on 'pulpit eloquence' come near the opening of his earliest journal. Already, at sixteen, his accent was hieratic when he spoke of 'the lips which the archangel hath purified and hallowed with fire.' Throughout life, an exquisitely modulated human voice, uttering man's convictions, seemed to him, as it did to Whitman, the greatest of God's gifts. Against such a background we can realize how much he implied when in 1834, the year after he had begun to try his skill as a lecturer, he advanced the hope that 'the high prize of eloquence may be mine, the joy of uttering what no other can utter, and what all must receive.'

He believed that the orator could speak both most directly and most deeply to men, breaking down their reserves, tugging them through the barriers of themselves, bringing to articulation their own confused thoughts, flooding them with sudden surprise that the moment of their life was so rich. In his comments on this art he came nearest to describing the kind of form he envisaged for himself. He did not want to speak about it soberly, for he believed the truly eloquent man to be 'inwardly and desperately drunk' with conviction. Looking back through history, it seemed to him that with the coming of the orator societies first arrived at civilization. A man speaking to men first unlocked their primitive awareness of themselves—in such a conception of consciousness Emerson broke through the mere intellectualizing with which he was often charged, to at least a glimpse of the deep subconscious forces that remain buried in men unless quickened to life. Through the inspired orator, 'a man possessed with mania and yet as firm as marble,' the hearer loses any sense of dualism, of hearing from another. He enters immediately into universal truth.

Emerson realized that such moments were as rare as they were sublime, and came to doubt his own powers to awaken them. But he did not conceive their possibility only in mythical antiquity; he knew that they could also be born in the stuffy air of the Lyceum. The hope of kindling such a blaze sustained him through all his appearances on the platform, waveringly vague and uncertain as the effects on his audiences often were. In a wistful note late in his journal he was asking, 'Why has never the poorest country college offered me a professorship of rhetoric? I think I could have taught an orator, though I am none.' Two of his essays are devoted to giving an account of this art. When he declared that it is eminently the one that flourishes in democracies, since it calls out the highest resources of character, his bond with one of the fundamental tenets of our early republic, obscured as it may have been by some of his cloudier flights, becomes unmistakable.

Oratory in America

Oratory, moving with the Revolution from the pulpit to the political forum, was, as Emerson recognized while still a boy, the one branch of literature in which America then had a formed tradition. It stemmed in part from the periods of Burke and the eighteenth-century conception of the sublime; and had been stimulated by the introduction into college education of such books as Hugh Blair's *Lectures on Rhetoric* (1783), a summary of late neo-classic opinion.[4] Moreover, our more dignified senators consciously modelled their public speech directly upon the examples of

Classical models

Greece and Rome, since a strong desire to profit from the analogies with classical experience had permeated every phase of our taste. John Adams, reading each year *De Senectute;* Colonel William Prescott, the hero of Bunker Hill, returning like Cincinnatus to his farm at Pepperell; the younger Josiah Quincy seeing his father's career mirrored in Pope's *Homer*—such figures might equally well have been chiselled as Roman

4. William Charvat, *The Origins of American Critical Thought, 1810-1835* (1936), examines the effect of such other imported works then current as Kames, *Elements of Criticism* (1762), Alison, *On the Nature and Principles of Taste* (1791), and Whately, *Elements of Rhetoric* (1823) in forming American principles of criticism.

As Emerson also perceived, the general tendency of the rhetoricians was to encourage correctness and formality rather than suppleness, and to delay the development of native idiom. Holmes, after letting himself go for a florid paragraph in *The Autocrat,* said that no man ever talked so, but 'in reporting one's conversation, one cannot help *Blair*-ing it up more or less.'

busts or have had their lives written by Plutarch.[5] In such classical qualities as their solid devotion to their land, their notion of public duty as sharply cut as their profiles, their belief in themselves and their descendants, we find the conditioning forces for Webster's balanced periods. We find too some of the reasons why Jefferson could lead the way in making the Greek revival in architecture our early national style, and why, in turn, settlers insisted on dotting the opening West with Troys and Carthages.

John Quincy Adams, in his Inaugural Oration in 1806 as the first Boylston Professor of Rhetoric and Oratory at Harvard, dwelt on the permanence of the form that had kept the ancient life available for our use: 'At Athens and Rome a town meeting could scarcely be held, without being destined to immortality; a question of property between individual citizens could scarcely be litigated, without occupying the attention, and engaging the studies of the remotest nations and the most distant posterity.' Adams' lectures, published four years later, would have been studied by Emerson as an undergraduate, and, despite their difference from his tone, may well have contributed to his desire to give lasting shape to the worth of the democratic present.

In an age when the vogue of the modern newspaper had not yet quite begun and libraries were relatively scarce,[6] public addresses were still a chief means of popular education: witness the rapid emergence of the Lyceum movement in the eighteen-thirties. They provided also one of the few sources of general diversion, whether in the Fourth of July oral fireworks [7] or the revival meeting. More than one European visitor noted

5. One of Van Wyck Brooks' happiest conceptions in *The Flowering of New England, 1815-1865*, was to call his opening chapter 'The Boston of Gilbert Stuart,' and to group therein many of the worthies of the Revolution who sat for that glowing brush, and who still set the tone for the New England in which Emerson grew up.

6. Neither the Boston nor the New York Public Library was founded until 1854. In 1850, the Harvard College Library, with its 72,000 volumes, was, according to Justin Winsor, the largest in the country.

7. With his family's customary willingness to give credit where credit was due, Adams wrote in his diary in 1826 of having read aloud Everett's Fourth of July Oration: 'There is at this time in this Commonwealth a practical school of popular oratory, of which I believe myself to be the principal founder by my own orations and lectures, and which, with the blessing of Him who reigns, will redound to the honor and advantage of this nation and to the benefit of mankind.' Ten years later, speaking again of Everett's gifts, he added: 'The custom of delivering orations on public occasions was introduced into this country by the Boston massacre of 5th March, 1770, of which there were thirteen delivered successively till 1783, in Boston town-meeting. The 4th of July was then substituted for the

how unusually large a proportion of volumes issuing from our presses were speeches. Such a penetrating observer as Tocqueville, amazed by the number of meetings for any purpose, could only conclude: 'It is impossible to spend more effort in the pursuit of happiness.' He also anticipated Dickens' Jefferson Brick by remarking: 'Debating clubs are, to a certain extent, a substitute for theatrical entertainments: an American cannot converse, but he can discuss; and his talk falls into a dissertation. He speaks to you as if he was addressing a meeting; and if he should chance to become warm in the discussion, he will say "Gentlemen" to the person with whom he is conversing.' When Emerson pronounced Webster on Bunker Hill to be 'the representative of the American continent,' more expressive of our national history than any poet had yet been, he phrased the ambition of every contemporary orator.

Yet no one would have responded more cordially than Emerson to Tocqueville's depiction of the bathos to which oratory could descend. He declared his own hatred of American 'pleniloquence,' and wryly observed: 'It is odd that our people should have—not water on the brain, but a little gas there.' In maturity he saw that Everett was merely a plaster bust, that the two-hour address that, as orator of the day, he delivered at Gettysburg had no weight in the scales against the few words that the President had spoken just as the crowd was leaving.[8] In Emerson's final judgment Lincoln's speech there and the speech of John Brown before receiving his death-sentence were 'the two best specimens of eloquence we have had in this country.'

Thirty years after college he could still recall not only Everett's virtuosity, but even the cadences of some florid declamation by a Southern

yearly town oration, and these have been continued till the present time. Other towns and cities have followed the example, and other occasions have been taken for the delivery of similar discourses, till they have multiplied so that they now outnumber the days of the year.'

8. It was quite in the approved convention of the time that Everett should have begun thus: 'Standing beneath this serene sky, overlooking these broad fields now reposing from the labors of the waning year, the mighty Alleghenies dimly towering before us, the graves of our brethren beneath our feet, it is with hesitation that I raise my poor voice to break the eloquent silence of God and Nature.' His completely conscious, and, to modern tastes, wholly external manipulation of rhetoric can be judged from one prolonged figure in the peroration of his very popular and many times repeated address for Washington's Birthday: '. . . the name and the memory of Washington on that gracious night will travel with the silver queen of heaven through sixty degrees of longitude, nor part company with her till she walks in her brightness through the golden gate of California, and passes serenely on to hold midnight court with her Australian stars.'

student.[9] Yet he had lived long since by the truth he had inscribed as the motto for his journal of 1835: 'To think is to act.' And particularly when it came to such a form as oratory, it struck him that the energy of thought and of action were practically indistinguishable. In this view he agreed with Milton that great art depends upon the artist's character, and borrowed from him, as the epigraph for one of his essays on 'Eloquence,' the famous statement: 'True eloquence I find to be none but the serious and hearty love of truth; and that whose mind soever is fully possessed with a fervent desire to know good things, and with the dearest charity to infuse the knowledge of them into others, when such a man would speak, his words . . . trip about him at command and in well-ordered files, as he would wish, fall aptly into their own places.'[10]

Such entire subordination of the man to his conviction is what we find as the sign of Lincoln's growth away from the stock western rhetoric with which he started, to his final classic utterance. But Emerson, in his dislike of obtrusive formality, went even farther. He could appreciate Lincoln's patient skill, but his kindred desire to eliminate ornamentation had led him to abandon even such devices of rhetoric as give structure to the Gettysburg Address. In his belief that the moment of eloquence was the only thing to be sought, he threw over the means by which the rhetoricians had held that even sublimity could be prepared for. What links him most with his age is that he considered such luminous elo-

9. He wrote in his journal for 1850: 'I have often observed the priority of music to thought in young writers, and last night remembered what fools a few sounding sentences made of me and my mates at Cambridge . . . I still remember a sentence in Carter Lee's oration, "And there was a band of heroes, and round their mountain was a wreath of light, and in the midst, on the mountain-top, stood Liberty, feeding her eagle." '

10. The closeness of Emerson to some of the most characteristic recent thought on the difficult question of the relation between art and action can be seen in this summary of Malraux's position by Ralph Bates (*New Republic*, Nov. 16, 1938): 'Ferral, who presumably speaks for Malraux [in *Man's Fate*], says to the serene old Kama, the Japanese painter, "Action alone justifies life . . . What would we think if we were told of a painter who makes no pictures?" And differentiating his revolutionary position from that of those reactionaries who, as Jules Romains says, praise action because they detest thought, he puts into the mouth of Garcia, the intellectual communist [of *Man's Hope*], a sentence of exceeding lucidity. The question is put, how can a man best spend his life? Garcia replies, "By converting as wide a range of experience as possible into conscious thought." '

Some relevant sentences of Emerson's are in *The American Scholar*: 'Action is with the scholar subordinate, but it is essential . . . Only so much do I know, as I have lived . . . The true scholar grudges every opportunity of action past by, as a loss of power . . . experience is converted into thought.'

quence an essential property of all literature. He defined a prose writer
as 'an *orateur manqué.*' In certain moods when he was longing for more
expressive cadences than any yet found, he could say, 'I think now that
the very finest and sweetest closes and falls are not in our metres, but in
the measures of eloquence, which have greater variety and richness than
verse.' In declaring that the best prose becomes poetic, that the sublimest
speech is a poem, Emerson was voicing the special desire of the transcendentalists to break through all restricting divisions. But in his tendency to link poets and orators whenever he listed the various arts, he was
responding to a more common and widespread belief of his time.

To a degree that we have lost sight of, oratory was then the basis for
other forms of writing, and its modes of expression left a mark on theirs.
The ludicrous possibilities glimpsed by Tocqueville were by no means
unperceived at home. When a Kentuckian ejaculated, 'What orator can
deign to restrain his imagination within a vulgar and sterile state of
facts?' he was unwittingly leading his delighted auditors into the realm
of tall talk. As grandiloquent perorations kept the eagle in constant flight
from the Alleghenies to the Rockies, a folk-adage declared that its shadow
had worn a trail across the basin of the Mississippi. The distinction between rhetorical bombast and fantastic exaggeration had become practically invisible. But not only did our humorists discover one of their
richest gold mines in mimicry and burlesque of oratory; our poets,
whether they wanted to or not, found their ears attuned to its cadences.
A writer in Cincinnati argued in 1834, 'A people who have fresh and
lively feelings will always relish oratory . . . The literature of a young
and free people will of course be declamatory.' The same conviction was
going to be voiced in the preface to *Leaves of Grass.* And when we look
through Whitman's notebooks, and see how often his early drafts for
speeches became interchangeable with poems, it is clear that he, just as
much as Emerson, expected a similar vibration from both forms. Certainly neither of them would have made the distinction arrived at by
John Stuart Mill:

Poetry and eloquence are both alike the expression or utterance of feeling:
but, if we may be excused the antithesis, we should say that eloquence is
heard; poetry is *over*heard . . . Poetry is feeling confessing itself to itself in
moments of solitude, and embodying itself in symbols which are the nearest
possible representations of the feeling in the exact shape in which it exists in
the poet's mind. Eloquence is feeling pouring itself out to other minds, court-

ing their sympathy, or endeavoring to influence their belief, or move them to passion or to action.

This is kindred to Yeats' enunciation that from the struggle with others we make rhetoric, from the struggle with ourselves we make poetry. The blurring of that distinction by Emerson and Whitman did not result in a wider social appeal for their work. It meant, in many instances, a form that was neither quite one thing nor the other. In his immediate desire to persuade, Whitman often indulged in rhetorical assertion instead of building up the exact plastic shape of what he had felt. Emerson, longing to catch only the moment of eloquence, instead of taking his reader with him, often left him gasping. As he ruefully noted: 'I found when I had finished my new lecture that it was a very good house, only the architect had unfortunately omitted the stairs.' On a less sincere plane than Emerson's, a confusion between what was really felt and the desire to move an audience vitiated Lowell's 'Commemoration Ode,' and left a stain of factitious rhetoric as unmistakable as tobacco-juice for a token of the age's general failure to distinguish between the nature of the two arts.

In his quest for a form, Emerson might say, 'I am in all my theory, ethics and politics a poet,' but by his middle thirties he had settled down to the realization that the lecture, drawn from the daily harvest of his journals, and finally to be distilled into an essay, was to be his form, or lack of. With the exaggeration of friendship Alcott wrote in his journal in 1856: 'There was no lecture till Emerson made it . . . and a public to listen to the master . . . That were a victory worth a life, since the lecture is the American invention, serving the country with impulse and thought of an ideal cast.' Emerson advanced no such claims for himself, but simply rejoiced to share in what he believed to be the age's evolution: 'I look upon the Lecture-room as the true church of to-day, and as the home of a richer eloquence than Faneuil Hall or the Capitol ever knew.' He had turned away from the pulpit, but so far as structure is concerned, *Nature* and *The American Scholar* still make use of the formal logical divisions of his early sermons. From that point onward the formality is ever less apparent. He rejected the training that had conditioned his youth, since it had starved the resources of sensibility. He made the fullest statement of what the lecture could be in his journal for 1839:

Eloquence. Lyceum.—Here is all the true orator will ask, for here is a convertible audience, and here are no stiff conventions that prescribe a method, a style, a limited quotation of books and an exact respect to certain books, persons or opinions. No, here everything is admissible, philosophy, ethics, divinity, criticism, poetry, humor, fun, mimicry, anecdotes, jokes, ventriloquism, all the breadth and versatility of the most liberal conversation; highest, lowest, personal, local topics, all are permitted, and all may be combined in one speech;—it is a panharmonicon . . . Here is a pulpit that makes other pulpits tame and ineffectual—with their cold, mechanical preparation for a delivery the most decorous,—fine things, pretty things, wise things, but no arrows, no axes, no nectar, no growling, no transpiercing, no loving, no enchantment. Here he may lay himself out utterly, large, enormous, prodigal, on the subject of the hour. Here he may dare to hope for ecstacy and eloquence.

As Emerson's enthusiasm mounts, his tone, even his words, approach Whitman's, who, even more exhilarated with the magnificent variety of the earth, wanted to bring it to unity within the measure of his songs. As Emerson is caught up into this warm glow of delight in a form without boundaries, it becomes apparent that no matter in what guise he was speaking, whether as the scholar or the seer, or in his other incarnations as Bacchus or Saadi, his sole art was that of the rhapsode: 'Loose the knot of the heart, says Hafiz . . . Expression is all we want: not knowledge, but vent.'

3. Expression

'Everything has two handles . . . Transcendentalism says, the Man is all. The world can be reeled off any stick indifferently. Franklin says, the tools: riches, old age, land, health; the tools . . . A master *and* tools,—is the lesson I read in every shop and farm and library. There must be both.'
—EMERSON'S *Journal* (1847)

To ANYONE who is not a transcendentalist, a form without boundaries is a contradiction in terms; and in the effort now not merely to describe Emerson's conception of art, but to understand it, we are faced with considerable difficulty. As could be expected, his doctrine asserts the superiority both of nature over art, and of content over its vehicle. His belief in the idea as the essence of art followed naturally from the great stress he put on the sublime, for, as Blair held, the production of this quality 'lies in the thought, not in the words.' That was one tenet of the rhetoricians that Emerson did not reject; but when he went on to say that the Idea, the infinite Reason, always sweeps beyond its temporary incarnation, that 'nothing is so fleeting as form,' he reminds us that his doctrine of art is also one of religion, that it assumes the superiority of soul to matter, as in the characteristic credo: 'I believe in the existence of the material world as the expression of the spiritual or real.' Moreover, it is the doctrine of a revolutionary movement, of a period in religion that insisted that the living spirit had rendered forms hollow and unnecessary, of a period in social evolution that thought it imperative to throw over conventions in order that the inner man might be free. Emerson was clearly thinking about both religion and literature when he maintained that 'when we have lost our God of tradition and ceased from our God of rhetoric, then may God fire the heart with his presence.'

Lending his strength to this breakdown of the distinctions between poetry and belief, Carlyle had declared and Emerson agreed with him: 'Literature is but a branch of Religion and always participates in its character: however, in our time, it is the only branch that still shows any greenness; and, as some think, must one day become the main stem.' They both were following Herder's *Spirit of Hebrew Poetry,* which abolished the distinction between sacred and secular, and held that the true poet shares in the same inspiration as the prophet. As Emerson put it, with his special accent on perception, 'Always the seer is a sayer.' Throughout his life he believed that if literature 'is resorted to as consolation, not as decalogue, then is literature defamed and disguised.'

Assumptions of the superiority of the spirit to the letter, of the vision to the words, of the soul that lies behind all expression to any embodiment of it, characterize the conception of art as inspiration, which is in sharp opposition to that of art as craftsmanship. The best writers of our own day, Joyce, Yeats, Eliot, have lived so thoroughly by the latter conception that the loose view against which they reacted has been regarded with salutary suspicion. Certainly Emerson, in his repudiation of tradition, could go to the most destructive extremes. His belief that the artist was simply the mouthpiece of the soul, that he 'sought his model . . . in his own mind,' led him to declare that all performances should be extempore, that 'it seems not worth while to execute with too much pains some one intellectual, or aesthetical, or civil feat, when presently the dream will scatter, and we shall burst into universal power.' He did not stop short of announcing that criticism too 'must be transcendental, that is, must consider literature ephemeral, and easily entertain the supposition of its entire disappearance.' It is hardly surprising that the complacence with which he reflected that all art is illusion should have contributed to the insubstantiality of his own. Indeed, the wonder of such views is that any art at all resulted from them.

But no misgivings about that possibility bothered Emerson as he turned to celebrating the positive element, the upwelling of genius. His shortest definition of it was 'that redundancy or excess of life which in conscious beings we call *ecstasy.*' Only through its plenitude, through the upthrust of male energy, could liberation be given to the spontaneous life within. But genius was not merely the affirmation of superabundant personal force; it was likewise reception, the openness of man to his deepest impulse, the maximum influx of the divine mind into his own. That was implied by Emerson's assertion that man, in the act of expression, became a facet of the Over-Soul, that genius did not 'increase the individuality, but the community' of his mind. His conception of genius as emanation makes as clear as it can be made why the sacredness of content seemed to dwarf its embodiment into insignificance. As he conceived the creative process, expression was inseparable from intuition, which came in turn from a reality beyond the reach of the understanding.

Consequently, he held that the one thing that could be demanded from a writer was obedience to his genius, that 'we need not much mind what people please to say, but what they must say.' With his habit of stating things in opposites, his religious veneration of genius led him into a scorn of talent as a trivial impertinence. He took over this dichotomy from Coleridge, as he did that between reason and understanding, but he carried it much farther, as far even as Blake had in his *Prophetic Books.* It caused him to say many things as reckless as that only those can write well 'who do not respect the writing.' Such indifference to the tools of the artist would make Emerson a leading exemplar of Tocqueville's conclusion that 'democratic nations naturally stand more in need of forms than other nations, and they naturally respect them less.'

But Emerson was also the man who wrote a sentence that Sarah Jewett underlined: 'I value qualities more and magnitudes less.' And if we are not goaded to exasperation by his recurrent mistiness and by overstatements as blithe as they are blind, we can find scattered through his work, and especially in his journals, a considerable body of observations that pose, with a fullness we will not encounter elsewhere, the problems of the artist as they were faced by Emerson and his contemporaries. Many of these observations also possess a continuing validity. In this respect Emerson is comparable to Coleridge, though the comparison would show wherein he is by no means the Englishman's equal. For Coleridge, with all his capacity for drifting away into the metaphysical fog, almost invariably gives you the sense, when he is talking about poetry, that he is keeping his attention on the nature of actual poems. He is too richly familiar with specific plastic objects to make the mistake of the practical American idealist who can rarely rest content with the aesthetic surfaces of a given poem, but is always wanting to go beyond those appearances to a hypostatized reality of all poems. How much this difference is owing to Coleridge's unique tenacity in observing the exact processes of his own mind, how much to the thinness of poetic tradition in America, would be hard to say.

Emerson himself saw with acumen the special situation of the artist in this country. When he remarked, 'How many young geniuses we have known, and none but ourselves will ever hear of them for want in them of a little talent,' he had come out of the cloud-land of his exaggerated dichotomy, and was speaking a language that bears on the arts as we can observe them. He continued to describe the New England character in art: 'Perhaps I value power of achievement a little more because in America there seems to be a certain indigence in this respect. I think there is no more intellectual people than ours. They are very apprehensive and curious. But there is a sterility of talent.' The diffusion of the theoretical mind into discussion was what Emerson called 'the American blight.' And he held it particularly necessary in the expanse of our 'naked, unatmospheric land,' that genius should come to condensed expression.

But to be sure whether he was capable of discerning the detailed process by which talent functions, we must probe a little further. In coming into Boston by the Concord coach, he often enjoyed most the ride through the North End, because, seeing men and women engaged there in hard work, or in the unrestrained attitudes of common life, he quickened to the sense of being near the very source of art—as he did not at the formality on Tremont Street—and felt the painter in him. 'But the painter is only *in* me; it does not come to the fingers' ends . . . I feel that genius organizes, or it is lost.' He could condense that feeling into a single sentence, 'Order is matter subdued by mind.' But there you can be doubtful whether Emerson's attention was simply fixed in contemplation of the ethereal force that could so magnificently subdue, or whether he was likewise aware of the step by step process required for the conquest. He gave better evidence of that awareness when, in reading Ben Jonson or Herbert, he was struck most by the completeness of even their shortest poems; or when, still fresh from such aesthetic experience, he said, 'Imagination is not good for anything unless there be enough. That a man can make a verse or have a poetic thought avails not, unless he has such a flow of these that he can construct a poem, a play, a discourse. Symmetry, proportion we demand, and what are these but the faculty in such intensity or amount as to avail to create some whole.' He dwelt frequently on his conviction that that man alone was an artist whose hands could execute what his mind had conceived. He could make it much more graphic: 'As a talent Dante's imagination is the nearest to hands and feet that we have seen.'

Therefore when he declared, in his essay on 'Intellect,' that 'to genius must always go two gifts, the thought and the publication,' he implied more in that last word than the merely spontaneous outpouring of the revelation with which the mind had been flooded. A cognate passage in his journal develops and extends what he meant: 'There are two powers of the imagination, one that of knowing the symbolic character of things and treating them as representative; and the other . . . is practically the tenaciousness of an image, cleaving unto it and letting it not go, and, by the treatment, demonstrating that this figment of thought is as palpable and objective to the poet as is the ground on which he stands, or the walls of houses about him.' This knowledge that talent consists in the poet's control over his experience, in his ability to seize both the thought and the image, shows that Emerson, at his most poised, could reconcile the claims of opposites in his view of art as 'an habitual respect to the whole by an eye loving beauty in detail.'

In his most adequate account of expression he recognized that it was not enough to proclaim the radiance of the vision he had had, but that he must compose a structure that would bring that radiance to a point of concentration. Organic wholeness was what he admired most; he could suggest it metaphorically by saying that writers like Montaigne or Browne, 'when they had put down their thoughts, jumped into their book bodily themselves.' When he turned to his contemporaries and himself, he missed this ability to do justice to the solid as well as to the ethereal:

'Mr. Knowall, the American, has no concentration: he sees the artists of fame, the Raffaelles and Cellinis with despair. He is up to Nature and the First Cause in his consciousness; but that wondrous power to collect and swing his whole vital energy into one act, and leave the product there for the despair of posterity, he cannot approach.' When Emerson wrote those sentences in 1847, Thoreau had just been making the experiment of living at Walden Pond, but the product of that experience, as concentrated as a hickory nut, was still seven years in the future.

Emerson's fecundity in perceptions of the nature of art was very great; every quotation in the foregoing paragraphs could be reinforced by a dozen others. Yet he also knew his own dilemma: 'I think I have material enough to serve my countrymen with thought and music, if only it was not scraps. But men do not want handfuls of gold-dust, but ingots.' In 1842, the same winter that he drew his portrait of 'The Transcendentalist,' he sketched the American poet whom he wanted:

We have yet had no genius in America, with tyrannous eye, which knew the value of our incomparable materials, and saw, in the barbarism and materialism of the times, another carnival of the same gods whose picture he so much admires in Homer . . . Banks and tariffs, the newspaper and caucus, Methodism and Unitarianism, are flat and dull to dull people, but rest on the same foundations of wonder as the town of Troy and the temple of Delphi, and are as swiftly passing away. Our log-rolling, our stumps and their politics, our fisheries, our Negroes and Indians . . . the northern trade, the southern planting, the western clearing, Oregon and Texas, are yet unsung. Yet America is a poem in our eyes; its ample geography dazzles the imagination, and it will not wait long for metres.

Whitman was to feel an even more electric attraction in such catalogues of materials; they swept him beyond metre altogether.

4. The Word One with the Thing

'Words and deeds are quite indifferent modes of the divine energy.
Words are also actions, and actions are a kind of words.'
—EMERSON, 'The Poet'

THE AIM is not merely to understand Emerson's conception of art, but
also to consider whether that conception was capable of bearing good
fruit. Therefore, instead of rehearsing any more of his contradictory generalizations, it is more useful to come directly to his specific observations
on language. Since language is the material in which the writer must
work, the only clay he can model, his theory of what its potentialities
are, of how it can be shaped, does not remain an abstraction but enters
inevitably into his practice. No American writer before Emerson had devoted such searching attention to his medium. A Franklin or an Irving
had taken considerable pains to develop a style, but had not desired to
pass beyond current models or usage. Emerson was concerned not merely
with choosing his words and arranging them, but with probing to the
origins of speech in order to find out the sources of its mysterious powers.
Such an attitude led to rich extensions in the possibilities of expression,
as Thoreau and Whitman were soon to realize. Never does one come
closer to the age's sense of the enormous fertility of life than when these
men are discovering the fresh resources of words.

The epitome of Emerson's belief is that 'in good writing, words become
one with things.' He reached that formulation as early as 1831, in a passage in his journal where he had just been discussing Schlegel, and at a
period when he was making frequent references to Coleridge. Coleridge
had declared, 'I would endeavor to destroy the old antithesis of Words
and Things: elevating, as it were Words into Things and living things
too.' That is an explicit statement about semantics, whereas Emerson's
variant (in which Coleridge also indulged on occasion) is really hyperbole, stimulating to the poet but with ambiguous possibilities.

My purpose in this section is to elucidate wherein this dramatic hyperbole served to challenge the writers of Emerson's day to bring their art
as close as possible to nature. It is not necessary here to follow very far

into Coleridge's difficult observations on the mind, but an indication of their main appeal to Emerson is imperative. Coleridge's statement announces his determination to reinstate the Logos as a living power, to demonstrate in poetry itself the word made flesh. Thus we are confronted again with the fact that the transcendental theory of art is a theory of knowledge and religion as well.

What impressed Emerson most in Coleridge was his affirmation of the wholeness of man's nature, as in the famous passage in the *Biographia* that declared how man might know himself: 'For as philosophy is neither a science of the reason or understanding only, nor merely a science of morals, but the science of Being altogether, its primary ground can be neither merely speculative, nor merely practical, but both in one. All knowledge rests on the coincidence of an object with a subject.' The American Scholar likewise insisted on a type of thought which should do justice alike to the contemplative and active sides of man. Moreover, Emerson followed Coleridge to the heart of his conception of the act of knowing. Coleridge held that 'the truth is universally placed in the coincidence of the thought with the thing, of the representation with the object represented.' As Emerson phrased it in 'The Over-Soul': 'The act of seeing and the thing seen, the seer and the spectacle, the subject and the object are one.' Richards' elucidation of Coleridge's meaning would also fit Emerson's at this point: his '*Subject* is the Self or the Intelligence, the sentient knowing Mind; his *Object* is Nature, what is known by the mind in the act of knowing.' From that instant of coalescence stemmed the conviction that adequate expression in words of such knowing would have to possess a similar organic unity.

Wordsworth, in many passages of his criticism, brought such an idea of coalescence to bear directly upon the language of poetry. He could tell DeQuincey that this language 'should not be "the dress of thoughts," but "the incarnation of thoughts," the thought itself made concrete.' For he believed that the poet 'will feel that there is no necessity to trick out or to elevate nature: and, the more industriously he applies this principle, the deeper will be his faith that no words, which *his* fancy or imagination can suggest, will be to be compared with those which are the emanations of reality and truth.' Such phrases would have come naturally to Emerson. He would have agreed that when the poet is receptive to the divine effluence, his mind is endowed directly with the word that embodies the thing. Carlyle also enunciated this phase of the doctrine: 'Poetic creation, what is this but *seeing* the thing sufficiently? The *word* that will describe the thing, follows of itself from such clear intense sight of the thing.' Emerson declared, shortly after the outset of his career: 'Adam in the garden, I am to new-name all the beasts in the field and all the gods in the sky.' To name a thing exactly was somehow magically to evoke it, as it had been for the primitive conjuror. That belief produced such lines as Wordsworth's

> The single sheep and the one blasted tree,

or Whitman's

> Night of south winds—night of the large few stars.

These several writers thus share in the general transcendental conception of language, though there are naturally many shades of difference between them. Emerson's particular development of the theory starts with the remark, 'The basis of poetry is language, which is material only on one side. It is a demi-God.' This accentuates his double approach. Under one aspect he regarded language as the vehicle for concrete facts, as, by license of analogy, the substantial material that could be handled by rhetoric and built into style. Under the other aspect language was symbol, the bridge that enabled man to pass from concrete appearance to spiritual reality. To both aspects he gave some of his most suggestive thought.

His most concise treatment of the subject is the dozen pages on 'Language' in his book *Nature,* where he starts out by listing three propositions:

1. Words are signs of natural facts.
2. Particular natural facts are symbols of particular spiritual facts.
3. Nature is the symbol of spirit.

In developing the first of these he goes back to the origins of language, for he holds that 'every word which is used to express a moral or intellectual fact, if traced to its root, is found to be borrowed from some material appearance. *Right* means *straight, wrong* means *twisted. Spirit* primarily means *wind; transgression,* the *crossing of a line; supercilious,* the *raising of the eyebrow.'* In such a view Emerson is still following Locke and the succession of eighteenth-century rhetoricians who for the most part simply echoed the brief section on 'Words' in the *Essay concerning Human Understanding,* where Locke stated that words are 'ultimately de-

rived from such as signify sensible ideas . . . Spirit, in its primary sig-
nification, is breath.' Emerson's handling of this material soon shows his
primary concern to be with the language of poetry, with what Robert
Frost has called 'the renewal of words.' As a result of realizing the physical origins of abstractions, Emerson was to declare in his essay on 'The
Poet': 'The etymologist finds the deadest word to have been once a brilliant picture. Language is fossil poetry.' In pursuing this metaphor Emerson could also discern that language was the briefest index to history,
packed to the full with the spoils of all man's occupations, his trades and
arts and games, and thus a kind of highly charged action in itself.

Such hidden dynamite was buried under abstraction in the educated
speech that surrounded him, in the formal correctness of the pulpit and
the reviews, in the polite usage of his period, which was on its way from
the palely elegant to the denatured genteel. Yet Emerson was sure that the
'immediate dependence of language upon nature, this conversion of an
outward phenomenon into a type of somewhat in human life, never loses
its power to affect us. It is this which gives that piquancy to the conversation of a strong-natured farmer or backwoodsman, which all men
relish.' It became the function of the contemporary artist, therefore, to
'pierce this rotten diction and fasten words again to visible things.' It was
incumbent upon him to release the charge, which he could do only if
he was aware that 'the artist still goes back for materials and begins again
with the first elements.' To such a degree could Emerson perceive the
primitive element in all great art.

In his criticism, he demanded it repeatedly, this power of the writer
to keep 'the truth at once to the senses and to the intellect.' He found
it in the English at their best, particularly in the era from Donne to
Bunyan, in their 'delight in strong earthy expression, not mistakable,
coarsely true to the human body, and, though spoken among princes,
equally fit and welcome to the mob.' In a characteristic reflection in his
journal he said: 'I think, if I were professor of Rhetoric—teacher of the
art of writing well to young men—I should use Dante for my text-
book . . . Dante knew how to throw the weight of his body into each act,
and is, like Byron, Burke, and Carlyle, the Rhetorician. I find him full of
the *nobil volgare eloquenza;* that he knows "God damn," and can be
rowdy if he please, and he does please.' What Dante could teach also
was that your daily surroundings 'are the very best basis of poetry, and
the material which you must work up.'

English folk-songs delighted Emerson by the homespun veracity of their plain style; and his own voice broke into eloquence just in declaring: 'I embrace the common, I explore and sit at the feet of the familiar, the low . . . What would we really know the meaning of? The meal in the firkin; the milk in the pan; the ballad in the street; the news of the boat; the glance of the eye; the form and gait of the body.' In this and many similar ejaculations he reminds the reader of Lessing's re-affirmation of the sources from which Luther had taken the language for his Bible: 'the mother in the house, the children in the street, the man in the market-place.' By Emerson's time, Lessing's insistence that the springs for a living literature are to be found in the speech and art of the folk had not merely shattered the thin restraints of German neo-classicism, but had proved one of the great factors in stimulating the romantic movement everywhere. Yet this doctrine was destined in many quarters to provide only another set of literary artifices. For instance, when Longfellow borrowed the metre of the Finnish folk-epic for *Hiawatha,* it served him to provide what Whitman called 'a pleasing, ripply poem,' but it hardly caught the energy of the primitive.

Yet that was Longfellow's hope in composing native ballads like 'The Wreck of the Hesperus,' as it was Whittier's in his homelier 'Skipper Ireson's Ride.' The measure to which they succeeded might be reckoned by their approximation to what Lowell, in his moment of greatest gusto, discovered in *The Biglow Papers* (1848): 'There is death in the dictionary . . . No language after it has faded into *diction,* none that cannot suck up the feeding juices secreted for it in the rich mother-earth of common folk, can bring forth a sound and lusty book. True vigor and heartiness of phrase do not pass from page to page, but from man to man.' Yet Longfellow's language tended to remain gracefully decorous, while the honesty of Whittier's effort was somewhat vitiated by the tone-deafness that robbed his verse of any full variety of cadences. But at the very time when Whittier was making his first attempts to tap the sources of our rural life in his *Legends of New England* (1831), Emerson was more directly concerned with the problem of language itself. Unlike Longfellow he was at no point simply sharing in a literary convention. He was moved by Luther's coarse vigor, and knew that Dante had declared the vernacular 'noble' because it was in common human usage.

During the years of his experience as a minister, he had grown increasingly aware of the need to break through the conventional style of writing, so trite and poor, so little idiomatic, to the language of conversation. He responded instinctively to 'the vigorous Saxon' of men working in the fields or swapping stories in the barn, men wholly uneducated, but whose words had roots in their own experience. But it was not until the period of *The American Scholar* that he began to make articulate the connection between his belief that 'the education of a mind consists of a continual substitution of facts for words,' and his belief that such grasping of facts was what he heard in the speech of men in the barber shop or in Bigelowe and Wesson's barroom. His ripest enunciation of that knowledge came in his journal for 1840, when he had been thinking also about Montaigne:

The language of the street is always strong. What can describe the folly and emptiness of scolding like the word *jawing?* I feel too the force of the double negative, though clean contrary to our grammar rules. And I confess to some pleasure from the stinging rhetoric of a rattling oath in the mouth of truckmen and teamsters. How laconic and brisk it is by the side of a page of the *North American Review.* Cut these words and they would bleed; they are vascular and alive; they walk and run. Moreover, they who speak them have this elegancy, that they do not trip in their speech. It is a shower of bullets, whilst Cambridge men and Yale men correct themselves and begin again at every half sentence.

When in that strain he could quickly kindle to incandescence and say: 'Give me initiative, spermatic, prophesying, man-making words.' You might well mistake that for a sentence in the preface to *Leaves of Grass;* and, to be sure, Emerson himself, in a lecture on 'Art and Criticism' (1859), while affirming that 'the key to every country' is 'command of the language of the common people,' and citing such different authorities as Rabelais and Borrow, Swift and Patrick Henry, declared Whitman to be 'our American master' in this vein. But by then, having felt that his enthusiasm for the first *Leaves* had perhaps gone too far, he was constrained to add the qualification that Whitman 'has not yet got out of the Fire-Club and gained the *entrée* of the sitting-rooms.'

In turning his ear to the strong accents of daily talk, Emerson was not alone. The rediscovery of the loamy subsoil of literature was fundamental to the best art of the time, and recognitions similar to his became widespread even in New England. The fact is worth dwelling on, particularly in view of the general suspicion of the vapidity and squeamishness of transcendental writers. Theodore Parker, whom Emerson called the Savonarola of the movement, was certainly no artist. Indeed, when he set out to make his *Massachusetts Quarterly Review* 'the *Dial* with a beard,' he was determined to rescue its thought from the twaddle about 'the absence of art' in America, which was being currently delivered by 'gawky girls and long-haired young men.' His answer was that 'we have cattle shows, and mechanics' fairs,' that the fine arts did not interest him 'so much as the coarse arts which feed, clothe, house, and comfort a people,' that he would rather be 'such a great man as Franklin than a Michelangelo.' The hard practicality of his idealism bore its best fruit in his love of the simple and concrete. It could at times endow his otherwise bare style with the words that he 'always preferred to use, when fit, the everyday words in which men think and talk, scold, make love, and pray, so that generous-hearted philosophy, clad in a common dress, might more easily become familiar to plain-clad men.'

Bronson Alcott's *Orphic Sayings,* and, indeed, nearly all his published works, seem about as remote as possible from colloquial idioms, the pure instance of transcendental genius without talent. Yet he posed the question of what constitutes living language as searchingly as anyone at the time. In 1837, near the end of the brief career of his experimental school in Boston, he recorded in his journal his increasing dissatisfaction with the artificiality of cultivated city speech. Its worst defect was its utter separation from the surrounding life. Such had not been the case with the people with whom Alcott had grown up at Spindle Hill, Connecticut. They 'put themselves into their speech . . . Words are things with them.' As the years passed, Alcott continued to observe the dilemma created by the fact that all our higher education tried to keep the writer on the plane of English literary diction, which was bleached to atrophy by being cut off from the sustaining juices of his childhood memories and of the native locutions that he could hear every day in the street or workshop. Alcott made his own connections between primitive life and great literature. Reading the seventeenth-century writers, whom he enjoyed as much as Emerson did, he was refreshed at their admitting him 'into an intimacy so entire with the thoughts and manners and speech of their day.' He went on to reflect:

I remember hearing the same words, and was indeed accustomed to use them, in my boyhood and native village, into which the refinements of the

brisk town had not found the way. It lay so remote and secluded there on
the mountains; neither was there a scholar to modify the homely speech of
the people. They spoke the speech of Shakespeare and Beaumont and Ben
Jonson. But now, if I would enjoy that pleasure of hearing my native tongue
in its riancy and exuberance I must listen to the boys about our school-houses,
or cast my eyes along the columns of the dictionary, there to recover the
animal spirit which once sparkled and pranked itself forth in the buxomness
and proud motions of our mother-tongue. What we have gained in elegance
we have lost in thought and expression.

He knew that the feeble pallor of his contemporaries was the result of
their having been trained to forget that 'the human body is itself the
richest and raciest phrase-book'; and that it was 'at once a proof of the
shallowness and indelicacy of our American authors that our rhetoric is
so seldom drawn from this armory, and our speech partakes so little of
the blood-warmth and flesh-colors of nature.'

By the time Alcott wrote those sentences he was almost fifty. He had
been largely self-educated, and during his formative years he had himself
been indelibly marked by the theory—whose viciousness he now understood—that separated written style wholly from common idiom. Emerson
kept urging him to bridge the gap, to use in his writing the same words
that he used in his house; but he could manage to only intermittently. In
the same year in which Alcott stated the problem so thoroughly in his
journal, Lowell, who as an undergraduate had listened eagerly to *The
American Scholar,* created the figure of Hosea Biglow and thus made substantial his own conviction that 'poets and peasants please us in the same
way by translating words back again to their primal freshness.' He had
chosen what he was half-inclined to call not a dialect but 'the Yankee
lingo,' in the hope that he might thus escape 'that faint perfume of musk
which Mr. Tennyson has left behind him . . . by turning into one of our
narrow New England lanes, shut in though it were by bleak stone walls
on either hand, and where no better flowers were to be gathered than
goldenrod and hardhack.' However, his real subject was not nature, but
the qualities of character that emerge through speech, especially the
Yankee's 'sour-faced humor' and shrewd satire, or, as Lowell phrased it
more imaginatively, 'a certain wild, puckery, acidulous (sometimes even
verging toward that point which, in our rustic phrase, is termed *shut-eye*)
flavor.' Still another writer to unearth at just this time some of the richness in the sort of village life Alcott remembered was Sylvester Judd,

many chapters of whose novel *Margaret* (1845) brought into print the authentic twists of folk-speech by recounting the customs of 'A Husking Bee' or of 'A Night at the Still.'

Such various but related approaches were being made to Emerson's proposition that 'Words are signs of natural facts.' His own practice of his theory may seem disappointingly mild. His difficulty was not exactly Alcott's, of having too heavy a weight to unlearn, for he had come to his full understanding of the indispensable fusion of abstract thought with concrete body somewhat earlier in his career. Nor did he veer like Lowell back into stock rhetoric as soon as he began to express a deep emotion. But though he could relish in the writing of others the 'coarse but warm blood' of daily circulation, it never became the major element in his own. His liberation from intellectualized formalism did not become complete, a thin residue of Puritan thought checked the more spontaneous life of his senses. But there is no gainsaying his continual joy in the homeliest speech, whether in the city slang that said 'Honey-pie' when there was any flattery, or in the understatements of the farmers who referred to mountain peaks not by their sometimes grandiloquent names, but simply as 'them 'ere rises.' He praised in his poem 'Monadnoc':

> Rude poets of the tavern hearth,
> Squandering your unquoted mirth,
> Which keeps the ground and never soars,
> While Jake retorts and Reuben roars.

Many of the bullet-like words they fired lodged in his journals, if fewer in the finished essays. But even there he was always injecting the surprise of a sudden colloquialism: 'the potluck of the day,' 'man in nature is surrounded by a gang of friendly giants,' Brook Farm is 'an Age of Reason in a patty-pan.' And he carried into his most serious passages what the critics in both the English and American reviews objected to as appalling Americanisms—as 'Truth is such a fly-away, such an untransportable and unbarrelable commodity that it is as bad to catch as light'; or 'It seems as if Deity dressed each soul, which he sent into nature, in certain virtues and powers not communicable, and . . . wrote *not transferable,* and *good for this trip only,* on these garments of the soul.' [1]

1. The disturbed tone even of the American critics can be heard in the review of *Nature* by Professor Francis Bowen, who was presently to translate Tocqueville: Emerson 'is in love with the old Saxon idiom, yet there is a spice of affectation in his mode of

We are often able to hear an actual speaking voice behind Emerson's words,[2] notably in such directness as that 'on affairs in Kansas' (1856): *'Manifest Destiny, Democracy, Freedom,* fine names for an ugly thing. They call it otto of rose and lavender,—I call it bilge-water.' But his steadiest gift is not the concretion that he so much admired; it is what William James had in mind when he declared Emerson's greatness to be pre-eminently that of a verbal artist: his delicate and subtle attention to the resources of the word. Having discovered the strength of primitive language, he tried to avoid learned and latinate terms whenever it was possible to return to a Saxon equivalent, or, at least, to interweave the Roman only sparingly, to alternate the two threads in a richer texture. Moreover, by his recognition that 'it is a rule of Rhetoric always to have an eye to the primary sense of the words we use,' he was frequently able to add a fragile piquancy to some Latin derivations by calling them back to their original meaning. Such was the case when he said in *Nature:* 'I dilate and *conspire* with the morning wind'; and 'Every heroic act is also *decent,* and causes the place and the bystanders to shine.'[3] Still another aspect of his interest was excited by books of modern science that yielded him the vocabulary of new discoveries, as in Humboldt's 'volcanic paps,' 'magnetic storms,' and 'veins inosculate,' or in that electric phrase, 'arrested development,' in Chambers's *Vestiges of Creation.*

Yet by far the strongest emotional impetus behind his desire to make

using it. He is sometimes coarse and blunt, that he may avoid the imputation of sickly refinement, and writes bathos with malice prepense, because he abhors forced dignity and unnatural elevation.' Bowen cited, as examples of what he disapproved: 'Whilst we use this grand cipher to expedite the affairs of our pot and kettle, we feel that we have not put it to its use, neither are able'; 'I expand and live in the warm day like corn and melons.' Most modern readers would consider the last sentence the very signature of Emerson's style, of his authentic freshness.

2. As good an instance as any in his verse is the speech of his old Concord farmers in 'Hamatreya':

> 'This suits me for a pasture; that's my park;
> We must have clay, lime, gravel, granite-ledge,
> And misty lowland, where to go for peat.
> The land is well,—lies fairly to the south.
> 'Tis good, when you have crossed the sea and back,
> To find the sitfast acres where you left them.'

3. He was less successful when, instead of keeping both the original and derived senses before the reader, he insisted on the former alone and spoke of great men as 'flagrant,' meaning that they were 'flaming beacons'; or in such occasional Pickwickian uses as 'eliminate' in the sense of 'bring out,' not 'leave out': 'we shall at last eliminate the true biography of Shakespeare.'

the word cover the thing was his perpetually fresh experience of the sublime in the commonplace. He wrote in his journal for 1831: 'When I stamp through the mud in dirty boots, I hug myself with the feeling of my immortality.' Already the accent is close to the passages in *Nature* that announce the ecstasy of the humblest moment of life. He had been reading Madame de Staël at that time, and may have unconsciously borrowed his image from her: 'I tramp in the mire with wooden shoes whenever they would force me into the clouds.' He remembered her sentence a quarter of a century later, and quoted it at the opening of his chapter on literature in *English Traits,* to drive home his conviction that great art must unite the solid with the ethereal.

If, in spite of this conviction, his own writing was always in danger of gliding away into the void, this was owing mainly to the lengths to which he developed the other two propositions that he listed in his treatment of 'Language': 'Particular natural facts are symbols of particular spiritual facts. Nature is the symbol of spirit.' He instinctively inclined towards the point that he reached in his long essay on 'Poetry and Imagination': 'The poet accounts all productions and changes of Nature as the nouns of language, uses them representatively, too well pleased with their ulterior to value much their primary meaning.' The representation he is thinking of is Swedenborg's, the correspondence between the physical world of appearance and the real world of spirit. The prospect of expressing the ulterior meanings is what caused Emerson to value literature above the other arts, since its medium is less material, and, for that reason, 'the finest tool of all' in being 'nearest to the mind.' A single statement like that can suggest the long background of Puritan distrust of plastic richness as a snare for the eye; it can remind you of the bias of provincial New England, whose higher culture had been so exclusively one of books that it had grown incapable even of appraising the worth of other modes of expression. Another remark of Emerson's shows how completely he could fall under the sway of that tradition: 'The art of writing is the highest of those permitted to man as drawing directly from the soul, and the means or material it uses are also of the soul.' Consequently, when Emerson says that the syllables of genius 'are an emanation of that very thing or reality they tell of, and not merely an echo or picture of it,' he is only carrying to the extreme his belief that the real words come directly from God. And we recall that he had been impressed not only by Coleridge, but also, and no less, by the pages on language in

Sampson Reed's *Growth of the Mind* (1826). In Reed's Swedenborgian view our language is merely a veil of illusion that will be withdrawn in the immortal state where the word will become one with Being itself.

Although Emerson agreed that 'there is somewhat in all life untranslatable into language,' yet the necessity of trying to make a translation, of approximating that reality in words, remained urgent. And as he developed his second proposition about language, he indicated the very way in which he himself worked:

A man conversing in earnest, if he watch his intellectual processes, will find that a material image more or less luminous arises in his mind, contemporaneous with every thought, which furnishes the vestment of the thought. Hence, good writing and brilliant discourse are perpetual allegories. This imagery is spontaneous. It is the blending of experience with the present action of the mind. It is proper creation. It is the working of the Original Cause through the instruments he has already made.

In these curt sentences Emerson is virtually recounting his own creative process. They correspond to a passage in his journal for the previous year, which is worth quoting since it reveals the extent to which his abstractions could fuse with visual images. Among the various examples he cites is a conversation that had turned to the popularity of Thomas à Kempis, whereupon Emerson had wanted to remark how, through time, 'the exact value of every book is determined, maugre all hindrance or furtherance.' Then he saw, as he spoke, 'the old pail in the Summer Street kitchen [in the house where he had lived as a child] with potatoes swimming in it, some at the top, some in the midst, and some lying at the bottom; and I spoiled my fine thought by saying that books take their place according to specific gravity "as surely as potatoes in a tub."' But instead of spoiling his thoughts, his intermittent and partial skill in thus fitting them with emblems served to make them viable. He does not often speak of this process as 'allegory'; indeed, he is generally explicit in his dislike of that device as being mechanical, and comes nearer to describing what he wants in saying, 'I like that poetry which, without aiming to be allegorical, is so. Which, sticking close to its subject, and that perhaps trivial, can yet be applied to the life of man and the government of God and be found to hold.' His desire for a quality of expression that cleaves to the fact and yet stands for something larger than itself, which suggests more than it can denote, led him to the symbol.

The state of belief in Emerson's age made the need for the symbol especially pressing. As a result of the decay of the church, Christianity itself was true to Emerson only symbolically, as were all other religions. Even Hawthorne who, with his stricter reliance on the New England past, did not follow the transcendentalists in asserting the equivalences between the Hebrew and Oriental scriptures, could himself express the truth of dogma not directly, but only obliquely, through a pattern of allegory.[4] It seemed to Emerson that the best way to express what he most wanted to—his consciousness of the infinite within the moment of experience—was by means of the symbol as Carlyle had described it in *Sartor*: 'In the symbol the Infinite is made to blend itself with the Finite, to stand visible, and as it were, attainable there.'

Emerson's own most extended definition of the symbol, in 'Poetry and Imagination,' insists on its inevitability. He introduces a quotation from Swedenborg to reinforce what had been his own reflection: '"There is nothing existing in human thought, even though relating to the most mysterious tenet of faith, but has combined with it a natural and sensuous image."' He extends this as follows: 'This power is in the image because this power is in Nature. It so affects, because it so is. All that is wondrous in Swedenborg is not his invention, but his extraordinary perception;— that he was necessitated so to see.—The selection of the image is no more arbitrary than the power and significance of the image. The selection must follow fate. Poetry, if perfected, is the only verity; is the speech of man after the real, and not after the apparent.' This definition will presently be seen to have the closest bearing on the peculiar qualities of Emerson's own poetry. It is worth recalling here that he insisted on the necessary character of consciousness in similar terms; and that he seems to equate imagination with this deepest intuition: an act of perception that penetrates through the show of things.[5] But he stopped short of

4. See the fuller treatment below in Chapter VII, 'Allegory and Symbolism.'

5. The typical breakdown of distinctions in America is indicated by Emerson's inclusive conception of intuition. Emerson's idealism passed beyond Kant's. He refused to rest content with the Kantian assertion that nature, as we perceive it, falls into patterns predetermined by consciousness, that we find nature orderly because we see only the forms of our own mind. For Emerson the mind does not create what it perceives: through intuition it knows the truth, the divine, directly. This immediate intuition into the divine mind became indistinguishable in Emerson from the imagination. Therein he goes farther than Coleridge who, closer to fundamental theology, restricts the faculty of intuition, the participation of the individual mind in divine Reason, to the religious and moral sphere, and distinguishes it from poetic imagination.

Swedenborg's type of mysticism that nailed one fixed symbol to each truth, and thus attempted to reduce it to a mathematical sign. For Emerson this was the error of all founders of systems, that they mistook accidental and individual symbols for universal ones. They were thus like Jacob Boehme, who, having seen his image of faith in the morning-redness, expected that this would mean the same thing to everyone, quite apart from the process of discovery that had made it come to life for him. Emerson was sure that the chief value of the symbol for the poet, in contrast to the mystic, consisted in its compelling the reader to share in the very process, in its rousing him to escape from all frozen limitations of dogma to an ever fresh awareness of the multiple facets of the single Truth.

Melville came to believe no less than Emerson that 'Nature is the symbol of spirit.' He made Ahab exclaim in his soliloquy on the whale's skull: 'O Nature, and O soul of man! how far beyond all utterance are your linked analogies! not the smallest atom stirs or lives on matter, but has its cunning duplicate in mind.' But Melville's greater ballast in facts never let the existence of matter slip away, as it could for Emerson when he went on to treat his third proposition about language. In veering into the idea that not only words are emblematic but things as well, he could carelessly toss language aside as being insufficient to encompass the reality that lay beyond it. At this point the thing that the word should cover is no longer the natural object that can give body to the thought; it has become the process of thought itself, by which the poet's mind shares in the divine mind. For the expression of such vision words are always inadequate, the merest reflection of the substance. In following his proposition to its vaguest conclusions, Emerson's approach to language becomes completely that of the transcendental idealist, as Shelley's did when he remarked that 'language is arbitrarily produced by the imagination, and has relation to thoughts alone.' It is not surprising, therefore, that the conception of poetry that rose out of Emerson's account of the symbol is at the opposite pole from Wordsworth's more experienced comprehension that 'the appropriate business of poetry . . . and her *duty,* is to treat of things not as they *are,* but as they *appear;* not as they exist in themselves, but as they *seem* to exist to the *senses,* and to the *passions.*' To be sure, Emerson had no taste for Shelley, and the Yankee in his make-up kept pulling him back to a grounding in common fact. Nevertheless, his characteristic bias can be seen in his development of the sentence from

Parmenides that he copied into his journal in 1830—'Thought and the object of thought are but one.' This sentence, the epitome of Emerson's own theory of knowledge as well as of his theory of language, gave rise finally to 'Brahma' (1856) where the object is lost in the thought. In Whitman the thought is lost in the object. Whitman was the new Adam whose words became one with the things he named, as he declared in 'There was a child went forth':

> the first object he look'd upon, that object he became,
> And that object became part of him . . .

> The early lilacs became part of this child,
> And grass and white and red morning-glories, and white and red clover, and
> the song of the phoebe-bird,
> And the Third-month lambs and the sow's pink-faint litter, and the mare's
> foal and the cow's calf,
> And the noisy brood of the barnyard or by the mire of the pondside,
> And the fish suspending themselves so curiously below there, and the beauti-
> ful curious liquid,
> And the water-plants with their graceful flat heads, all became part of him.

In contrast, Emerson's type of identity between word and thing was expressed in those stanzas in which all the severing details of man's existence, all the distinctions between shadow and sunlight, between the Brahmin and his hymn, indeed, between life and death, are caught up and reconciled and obliterated in the sweep of the divine mind.

5. 'The light of the body is the eye'

'The genius is a genius by the first look he casts on any object. Is his eye creative?'

—*Representative Men*

WE HAVE proceeded from the content Emerson wanted to convey, to his search for the form that could best convey it; and from his generalizations about the nature of art, to an examination of the specific tools of his own craft. Our survey of his theory of expression is now complete. It remains for the final sections of this chapter to see what he could do with his tools, to test his theory by some of the best examples of what he created.

One symbol recurs so often in both his poetry and prose that it must have had a particular significance for him: the tiny sea-shell. Its fragile, yet intricate form repeatedly rose to his consciousness as the aptest illustration for his belief that the secret of the universe could be read in a single manifestation, that the whole code of its laws might be written 'on the thumbnail.' When he declared himself a naturalist that summer in Paris, he could discern the very principle of organic development in each knot and spine and swelling volute. Likewise, when he turned to art, he held it the poet's function to cast enchantment over just such seemingly humble and trivial objects. As he looked at the shells on the edge of the beach and named them with fresh eyes, their pale tints appeared to glow and dilate. Buoyed by the rhythm of the waves, they became an instant revelation of how

> Being's tide
> Swells hitherward, and myriads of forms
> Live robed with beauty, painted by the sun;
> Their dust, pervaded by the nerves of God,
> Throbs with an overmastering energy
> Knowing and doing.

His imagination was carried from the radiance of the shells to the rising fullness of man's moments of inspiration, for he knew in both cases that once

> ebbs the tide, they lie
> White hollow shells upon the desert shore.

He had meditated on a related aspect of this fact: 'I remember when I was a boy going upon the beach and being charmed with the colors and forms of the shells. I picked up many and put them in my pocket. When I got home I could find nothing that I gathered—nothing but some dry, ugly mussel and snail shells. Thence I learned that composition was more important than the beauty of individual forms to effect. On the shore they lay wet and social by the sea and under the sky.' This passage was to reappear in his verse, in 'Each and All,' where it underscores his desire to live in every moment to a sense of 'the perfect whole.' What the shell symbolized to him can represent his problem as a poet. He had perceptions of the most delicate and poignant beauty, he was continually being flooded by the fullness of the moment. But when he came to set it down on paper, the rhythmical wholeness of the experience slipped away from him, and the residue seemed to turn to a lifeless gray. He could manage only seldom to build an organic form of his own.

Melville scored with approval in his copy of the *Essays* the passage declaring that poets are 'liberating gods,' that their role is to give exhilaration and abandonment to men, to make them drunk with the unquenchable wonder of life. Emerson prayed for this power in his hymn to Bacchus, as eloquent lines as he ever wrote. Many passages in his prose vibrate with similar cadences: 'Rhyme; not tinkling rhyme, but grand Pindaric strokes, as firm as the tread of a horse. Rhyme that vindicates itself as an art, the stroke of the bell of a cathedral. Rhyme which knocks at prose and dullness with the stroke of a cannon ball. Rhyme which builds . . . a splendid architecture to bridge the impassable, and call aloud on all the children of morning that the Creation is recommencing.' In such sentences you can share in his effort to hypnotize himself into rhapsody, the only state in which he believed that he could possess a sustained poetic power, or rather be possessed by it.[1] He wanted 'the wildest freedom,' the strain that he admired from afar in primitive poetry, in the irregular songs of the Norsemen and of the Welsh bards. But his forms never came very close to those of any folk-poetry. The irregularity with which he tried to

> mount to paradise
> By the stairway of surprise,[2]

was not Merlin's, but more nearly an echo of what Herbert and Donne had suggested to him. But lacking their dramatic concentration, his conceits could often run to seed, as in the dizzy waywardness of 'The Humble Bee.' In the act of his own best poetry he felt himself more essentially akin to the Oriental poets, though, characteristically, his analogies were

1. If such rhythms are like those of Emerson's free verse, they are also not unlike the oratory that could mount to tall talk. It may not be too ludicrous to find a kindred incantation, aiming to intoxicate both the speaker and his audience, in the virtuosity that Mark Twain heard as a boy on the river: 'Whoo-oop! bow your neck and spread, for the kingdom of sorrow's a-coming! Hold me down to the earth, for I feel my powers a-working . . . When I'm playful I use the meridians of longitude and parallels of latitude for a seine, and drag the Atlantic Ocean for whales! I scratch my head with the lightning and purr myself to sleep with the thunder! When I'm cold, I bile the Gulf of Mexico and bathe in it; when I'm hot I fan myself with an equinoctial storm . . . Whoooop! bow your neck and spread, for the Pet Child of Calamity's a-coming!'

2. The initial draft of these lines on a stray lecture-sheet reveals the conviction of the rhapsode: 'Do not the great always live *extempore*, mounting to heaven by the stairs of surprise?'

with their thought and not with their form, since he knew them only in translation. Yet such analogies with the Hindu gave him the structure for two of his most fully composed poems, 'Brahma' and 'Hamatreya'; [3] while some verses of Hafiz provided the immediate stimulus for 'Bacchus.' Moreover, Emerson might well have been describing most of his own work when writing this sentence in his essay on Persian poetry: 'Gnomic verses, rules of life conveyed in a lively image, especially in an image addressed to the eye and contained in a single stanza, were always current in the East; and if the poem is long, it is only a string of unconnected verses.'

For the utterance of like spiritual truths he knew himself fated to be a poet. As he wrote to Lydia Jackson shortly before their marriage in 1835: 'I am born a poet,—of a low class without doubt, yet a poet. That is my nature and vocation. My singing, be sure, is very husky, and is for the most part in prose. Still I am a poet in the sense of a perceiver and dear lover of the harmonies that are in the soul and in matter, and specially of the correspondences between these and those.' He was impelled to his vocation also by other harmonies than those of thought. He said, 'I remember any beautiful verse for twenty years.' That was true also of the most eloquent sentences that he had heard in speeches while at college, but, as we have seen, he was deeply interested in oratory only in so far as it approximated the poetic, the only medium where he felt really at home. The novel meant practically nothing to him. He could so utterly misconceive Hawthorne as to say, 'I never read his books with pleasure; they are too young.' And although he declared in 1848 that 'the novel will find the way to our interiors, one day, and will not always be novel of costume merely,' he seems not even to have glanced into *Moby-Dick*. Owing partly to the limited opportunities of the New England of his youth, he was even farther afield in the other arts. He had no developed ear for music, and accepted the romantic exaltation of the Aeolian

3. Passages copied by Emerson in 1845 from the *Vishnu Purana* and the *Bhagvat-Geeta* were quickened by others eleven years later from the *Katha Upanishad* to form the doctrine for 'Brahma.' The structure of 'Hamatreya' corresponds almost point for point to a passage from the *Vishnu Purana*, which he also copied in 1845, in this case only shortly before composing his poem. 'Hamatreya' is probably his best instance of acclimatizing Oriental doctrine in a Yankee setting; but it should be remembered that its doctrine is also substantially that of 'The Over-Soul,' which he had written before reading the Orientals. (A thoughtful examination of the sources of these poems was made by F. I. Carpenter, in *Emerson and Asia*, 1930.)

harp as the one instrument that could catch the sad and triumphant melodies of nature: 'Tie a couple of strings across a board and set it in your window, and you have an instrument which no artist's harp can rival.' More alive to the beauty of form than of color, sculpture appealed to him more than painting, though he was sublimely indifferent to its technique.

But these handicaps could disappear when he approached poetry. He said once, 'If I don't know what poetry is, I don't know anything'; and he could talk about it in ways that prove he was no outsider to its process. He knew how seemingly trivial a stimulus can set the poet in motion, for 'poetry seems to begin in the slightest change of name, or, detecting identity under variety of surface.' He could also feel how poetry can exist only by clinging fast to this variety; how its writer must not lose himself in the bare ideal, but must continue to 'expand and live in the warm day like corn and melons'; how the authenticity of his art depends on his being convinced 'that the great moments of life are those in which his own house, his own body, the tritest and nearest ways and words and things have been illuminated into prophets and teachers. What else is it to be a poet? What are his garland and singing-robes? What but a sensibility so keen that the scent of an elder-blow, or the timberyard and corporation works of a nest of pismires is event enough for him,—all emblems and personal appeals to him.'

But these are perishable materials, and Emerson's grasp even on them was tenuous, as he was only too aware in a letter to Carlyle (1839) that gives the counterstatement to the one to his wife, the counterstatement without which he could hardly approach any subject: 'I do not belong to the poets, but only to a low department of literature, the reporters; suburban men.' And he added a year or two later: 'When I see how much work is to be done, what room for a poet—for any spiritualist—in this great, intelligent, sensual, and avaricious America, I lament my fumbling fingers and stammering tongue.' His problem, as he faced it in his essay on 'Inspiration,' was how to control his insecure possession and avoid the quick ebb of power. ' 'Tis with us a flash of light, then a long darkness, then a flash again . . . What we want is consecutiveness.'

When he could achieve some roundness of composition, as in the early 'Rhodora' (1834), he was perhaps more indebted than he realized to a residue of eighteenth-century formalism, in the way that Bryant also had

profited by it. Emerson's deliberate assumption of the singing-robes is not
unlike that in 'To a Waterfowl':

> In May, when sea-winds pierced our solitudes,
> I found the fresh Rhodora in the woods,
> Spreading its leafless blooms in a damp nook,
> To please the desert and the sluggish brook.
> The purple petals, fallen in the pool,
> Made the black water with their beauty gay;
> Here might the red-bird come his plumes to cool,
> And court the flower that cheapens his array.
> Rhodora! if the sages ask thee why
> This charm is wasted on the earth and sky,
> Tell them, dear, that if eyes were made for seeing,
> Then Beauty is its own excuse for being:
> Why thou wert there, O rival of the rose!
> I never thought to ask, I never knew:
> But, in my simple ignorance, suppose
> The self-same Power that brought me there brought you.

This poem could stand as an illustration of the chapter in *Nature* that
deals with 'Beauty,' and which starts with the declaration that 'the simple
perception of natural forms is a delight.' In the poem his love for the
common, his shy fondness for native details, is just breaking through the
stiff chrysalis of a set rhetorical address, and is still impeded by such
vestiges of generalized diction as 'plumes' and 'array.' But there is no
mistaking the New England flavor; nowhere else would one begin a
poem about May with the raw East wind. Into this atmosphere flashes
the delight in sudden color, in the wild azalea, in the scarlet tanager,
contrasting sharply with the black pool. But the glimpse is not developed
and is hardly reinforced by any of the other senses, by the sounds and
smells and touch that would have added body to the sharp airiness of
the vision.

That vision is, of course, not merely of the scene. He was to end his
short chapter by affirming that 'beauty in nature is not ultimate, it is the
herald of inward and eternal beauty'; and 'The Rhodora' sprang from
what he realized in saying: 'For other things, I make poetry of them,
but the moral sentiment makes poetry of me.' He did not want this sentiment to be tacked onto a poem obtrusively, but to blend with and pervade
the whole. Beauty could express it, without apology; yet even in saying

that, he betrays his background. A lingering trace of doubt causes him to make an excuse in the very act of saying that one is not needed. Every detail in his later essay on 'Beauty,' in *The Conduct of Life* (1860), shows the same weight of that background, both its limitations and strength. By then he was aware enough of his own aptitudes no longer to try a definition but merely a recital of beauty's qualities. He found proportion and harmony to be its basis, but he threw his particular emphasis on the necessity of economy, on the avoidance, for the sake of organic structure, of all surface embellishment, since 'the tint of the flower proceeds from its root, and the lustres of the sea-shell begin with its existence.' He carried his understanding of the value of the functional to the point of saying that all productive labor, the carpenter building a ship, the smith at his forge, 'is becoming to the wise eye'; and he insisted that 'beauty must come back to the useful arts, and the distinction between the fine and useful arts be forgotten.'[4] The beauty that is its own excuse is Puritan in its simplicity and bareness, Yankee in its insistence on fitness and utility, Neo-Platonic in Emerson's typical quotation from Proclus, 'It swims on the light of forms.'

This last fugitive quality hardly appears in the grave lines about the rhodora, but all Emerson's other main convictions about beauty are there in embryo. It is hardly accidental that all the senses except the eye are slighted; this is the natural result of his almost exclusive absorption with seeing. That fact can provide us with a more adequate clue to his conception of poetry than we have had so far. He said himself that though he did not have a musical ear, he had 'musical eyes.' The opening pages of *Nature* reverberate with his pure joy in the discovery that there is no object that intense light will not make beautiful. He thrilled not only at what the eye saw, but at the organ itself. He wrote in his journal: 'There are some occult facts in human nature that are natural magic. The chief of these is the glance (*oeillade*).' This prepares us for the exalted climax of *Nature's* first chapter, the exaggerated image of which was caricatured even by faithful transcendentalists: 'Standing on the bare ground,—my head bathed by the blithe air and uplifted into infinite space,—all mean egotism vanishes. I become a transparent eyeball; I am nothing; I see all; the currents of the Universal Being circulate through me; I am part or parcel of God.'[5]

4. See the fuller treatment of this seminal idea in Chapter IV, 'The Organic Principle.'
5. Another rhapsody on the eye, running to four pages, is in the essay on 'Behavior.'

He held it the first responsibility of the artist to record adequately what he had observed; and he was reassured by the thought that 'our American character is marked by a more than average delight in accurate perception.' When he could believe himself to be not merely a reporter but a poet, he could phrase his conviction more intensely: the poet is the man 'whose eye can integrate all the parts.' Against the background of these reiterated views, several of his beliefs that we have considered separately are found to coalesce. In view of his unswerving trust in what, to adopt Blake's terms, could be seen not merely with but through the eye, it is no wonder that he made his cardinal distinction between perception and notion. In his chief passage on symbols, he took for granted the inevitability of what is perceived. His peculiar development of the Coleridgean theory of knowledge starts with the implications that he packs into his key-words: 'The act of seeing and the thing seen, the seer and the spectacle . . . are one.' With his belief that imagination itself is simply the highest perception, he naturally insisted on using the word 'seer' in its primary as well as in its figurative sense. This wider context gives point to an isolated sentence in his journal, 'Our age is ocular.'

The special stress that the nineteenth century put on sight is evinced by some of its outstanding creations, the perfection of Herschel's telescope, the invention of photography, the development of open-air painting, the advancing power of the microscope. But Emerson's emphasis, which has a special relevance to the poetry of the century, is on the identity between poet and prophet. The problems created by this assumption will confront us particularly in Whitman. Both conceptions of the eye—as the organ of realistic observation, and as a religious symbol, as what St. Matthew called 'the light of the body,' [6]—will be found fundamental to the best qualities in. *Leaves of Grass.*

Horace Gregory has remarked that D. H. Lawrence, 'like Emerson before him, accepted the task of reviving Adam in himself and renaming the beasts of creation.' One reason why it is so hard to-day to feel the freshness of much that Emerson saw is suggested by Lawrence himself. He reacted fiercely against our 'endless, objective curiosity. Sight is the least sensual of all the senses. And we strain ourselves to see, see, see—everything, everything . . .' Emerson was hardly objective, but his delight in

6. Cf. Coleridge's ninth aphorism in *Aids to Reflection,* on the theme, 'and man became a living soul': 'Nothing is wanted but the eye, which is the light of this house, the light which is the eye of this soul. This *seeing* light, this *enlightening* eye, is Reflection.'

the eye above the other senses, since it could pass most readily into the realm of inner light, aspired to the disembodied. It was true for him as for the Vedantist that the veil of Maya must be pierced, that man's salvation was in his spiritual eye, which was not to be deluded by the mirage of phenomena.[7] His delicate pleasure in his senses, and his even greater pleasure in soaring beyond them, caused him to say of the method of the artist that 'the sensual man conforms thoughts to things; the poet conforms things to his thoughts.' That oracular sentence could be interpreted variously, but the drift of Emerson's meaning is shown by his acceptance of Bacon's formula for poetry, an acceptance that for once he did not contradict elsewhere but recurred to as a touchstone, as 'our best definition': 'Poetry, not finding the actual world exactly conformed to its idea of good and fair, seeks to accommodate the shows of things to the desires of the mind, and to create an ideal world better than the world of experience.'[8]

That is in fundamental opposition to the view that holds that the greatest art comes from immersion in the complexities of experience. This latter view, which prevails in major tragedy, maintains that the potential world that art can envisage must be sought by wrestling with the actual, and not by evading it. The Baconian formula, an over-simplified debasement of Aristotle, is the limitation made by the narrowly scientific mind, which conceives of poetry as escape.[9]

As refracted by Emerson's idealism, this formula encouraged him to ignore experience whenever it was in harsh or ugly conflict with his optimism. He held that 'every thing is beautiful seen from the point of the intellect, or as truth. But all is sour if seen as experience. Details are melancholy; the plan is seemly and noble.' The ease with which he could abandon the details for the plan, in both life and art, is a symptom of why, in spite of all the scattered evidence of his close appreciation of

7. This is Arthur Christy's conclusion, in his excellent study of *The Orient in American Transcendentalism* (1932), p. 123.

8. Emerson is paraphrasing Bacon: 'And therefore it [poesy] was ever thought to have some participation of divineness, because it doth raise and erect the mind, by submitting the shows of things to the desires of the mind; whereas reason doth buckle and bow the mind into the nature of things.'

9. Cf. two related remarks of Bacon's: 'For as for Poesy, it is rather a pleasure or play of Imagination, than a work or duty thereof'; and 'History is the best of all the liberal arts—I had almost said of only use; for poets I can commend none, being resolved to be ever a stranger to them.'

poetry, he so generally failed to write sustained poems. At one point in his journal he mentioned a habit which, as measured by his own results, proved disastrous: 'I amuse myself often, as I walk, with humming the rhythm of the decasyllabic quatrain . . . or other rhythms . . . Ah, happy! if one could fill these small measures with words approaching to the power of these beats!' The defect that you are continually bumping against in his verse is that the metre, especially his four-beat couplet, seems to be pounding on monotonously, endlessly, not fused with the phrases that are brought to fit it so imperfectly. Even Thoreau, despite the drastic shortcomings of his own verse, could discern this fault in Emerson's 'Ode to Beauty': 'The tune is altogether unworthy of the thoughts. You slope too quickly to the rhyme, as if that trick had better be performed as soon as possible, or as if you stood over the line with a hatchet, and chopped off the verses as they came out . . . It sounds like parody. "Thee knew I of old," "Remediless thirst," are some of those stereotyped lines . . . Yet I love your poetry as I do little else that is near and recent, especially when you get fairly round the end of the line, and are not thrown back upon the rocks.' Such lines were to give John Jay Chapman the curious impression that he was reading a translation. The awkward split between form and content no doubt resulted in part from Emerson's too mechanical conception of Platonic forms waiting to be filled. Another way of accounting for it is by his equally dangerous fallacy that in order to poetize anything, 'its feet must be just lifted from the ground.' There again is his deviation from the actual world, the tendency that caused him to say: 'And what is Genius but a finer love, a love impersonal, a love of the flower and perfection of things, and a desire to draw a new picture or copy of the same?' But as William James was to write in the margin of his copy: 'There is no such flower, and love and genius both cleave to the particular objects which are precious because at the moment they seem unique.' [10]

10. Nine volumes by Emerson, which were owned by James, and which contain his markings and frequent annotations, are now in the Harvard College Library. If you judged James's opinion of Emerson by one remark in *The Varieties of Religious Experience*, you might conclude that he found little value in him. For he said there: 'Modern transcendental idealism, Emersonianism, for instance, also seems to let God evaporate into abstract Ideality.' But his markings show that he read with attention nearly everything that Emerson wrote; and even without his tribute at the centenary in 1903 to 'my beloved master,' there is ample evidence that Emerson's idealism provided a more central root for pragmatism than has generally been assumed. Even in *The Varieties* James went on to

The method by which a poet can mediate between the actual and the ideal may be suggested in an image that does justice to both poles: 'The poet, like the electric rod, must reach from a point nearer the sky than all surrounding objects, down to the earth, and into the dark wet soil, or neither is of use. The poet must not only converse with pure thought, but he must demonstrate it almost to the senses. His words must be pictures, his verses must be spheres and cubes, to be seen and smelled and handled.' There could hardly be a more exact description of what Emerson's poetry was not than this, which was, of course, written by himself. The briefest way, finally, to cut through to an understanding of the confusing divergence between so many of his perceptions and his practice is to remember where he always threw his last emphasis. He believed that 'this age is Swedenborg's' because it had accepted the philosophy that 'the soul makes its own world.' It could be called more widely 'the age of Hegel,' and though Emerson did not read that philosopher until long after his own thought was formed, he was attracted by Hegel's type of evolution, since its 'unfolding' of nature was from the mind. Or as Emerson paraphrased it, 'Nature always the effect; Mind the flowing cause.' That being the case, though Emerson liked to call nature the 'metaphor of the divine mind,' he was always brushing it aside to come to the very source of truth. He was incapable of being restrained within the hard actuality of experience, for he held that the deeper insight of the poet, 'who re-attaches things to nature and the Whole . . . disposes very easily of the most disagreeable facts.' Melville marked that with scorn: 'So it

say about the Over-Soul: 'Whatever it is, though, it is active. As much as if it were a God, we can trust it to protect all ideal interests, and keep the world's balance straight.' He once found 'a motto' for his own philosophy in the famous paragraph of 'Self-Reliance' which begins 'Trust thyself: every heart vibrates to that iron string,' and which ends, 'we are now men . . . and not minors and invalids in a protected corner, not cowards fleeing before a revolution, but guides, redeemers and benefactors, obeying the Almighty effort and advancing on Chaos and the Dark.' Yet the aspect of Emerson that James liked least was also to be found in that essay, where Emerson declared that the highest truth 'shall exclude example and experience.' James called this 'the anaesthetic revelation'; and reading it again, 'the tasteless water of souls.' It was this strain that caused him to declare 'The Method of Nature' (which contains the sentence on the flower of Genius) 'the weakest' in its volume, and 'Education' 'the poorest of all Emerson's essays.' The strain that recommended itself most highly to James celebrated the value of action; and it is significant that he marked the passage, 'Words and deeds are quite indifferent modes of the divine energy. Words are also actions, and actions are a kind of words.' (F. I. Carpenter's 'William James and Emerson' [*American Literature*, March 1939] has treated some of the leading issues presented by James's annotations.)

would seem. In this sense Mr. E. is a great poet.' That was only too true of the Emerson who could envisage the seer

> Without halting, without rest,
> Lifting better up to best.

That was the course of onward and upward, and its sterile separation from the springs of vitality could hardly be witnessed by more strained or barren lines. Yet that course was followed by many other nineteenth-century poets who were equally determined to build ideal worlds, though their structure seems now the hollowest rhetoric. Their misconception of their role can be defined by Eliot's distinction: 'In one's prose reflections one may be legitimately occupied with ideals, whereas in the writing of verse one can only deal with actuality.' That is a complete reversal, a reassertion that the function of the poet is to present experience, all of experience as he has known it, and not merely the refined sector of his hopes.

6. A Few Herbs and Apples

'Heaven walks among us ordinarily muffled in such triple or tenfold disguises that the wisest are deceived and no one suspects the days to be gods.'
—Emerson to Margaret Fuller, October 2, 1840.

With Emerson's worst lines in our ears, it might seem hardly profitable to consider him as a poet any further. Yet he himself persisted in that view, and, nearly thirty years after that letter to his wife, still wrote in almost the same terms of his vocation, with no pretension but with quiet certainty: 'I am a bard least of bards. I cannot, like them, make lofty arguments in stately, continuous verse, constraining the rocks, trees, animals, and the periodic stars to say my thoughts,—for that is the gift of great poets; but I am a bard because I stand near them, and apprehend all they utter, and with pure joy hear that which I also would say, and, moreover, I speak interruptedly words and half stanzas which have the like scope and aim:—What I cannot declare, yet cannot all withhold.'

Emerson, Thoreau, and Whitman all conceived of themselves primarily as poets, though, judged strictly by form, none of them was. All of them would have agreed with Emerson's decree that 'it is not metres, but a metre-making argument that makes a poem'; for, with the release of energy in which they shared, they were sure that their content outran the boundaries of earlier conventions of expression. But the writing of poetry becomes inordinately difficult without a living tradition to draw upon and modify. Thoreau and Melville both evolved richly modulated harmonies in their prose rhythms but were able to command far less music when they tried to borrow the more exacting medium of verse, which had hardly yet become acclimated in America.

The want of continuity in Emerson's form was a natural product of what we have seen, the confusing alternation in his experience. The reasons for the cleavage between his 'two lives, of the understanding and of the soul,' would require a book to establish, a book that could start with the breakdown after Edwards of the Puritan synthesis. Edwards had managed to reunite the two chief strains from the seventeenth century, its logic and its emotion, its hard grasp of fact and its deep capacity for mysticism, but after his death they split apart. The mysticism was caught up into Methodism and the evangelical movement, and was proportionately discredited in the cool eyes of the rationalists, who were Emerson's forerunners in the Unitarianism which he grew to find so inadequate. But with his fresh insistence on idealism, he no longer shared, or wanted to share, in the older dogma. He was a symptom of his age's expansiveness—but here would have to come another chapter, which would deal with the increasingly violent divergence between the world of transcendentalism and that of the industrial revolution. Emerson understood some of the consequences of this latter split, and dwelt on the acute difficulties of the thinker in making vital contact with a rapidly changing society.[1] He declared, 'Our relations to each other are oblique and casual,' a condition that Hawthorne regarded far more seriously as he examined the tragic effects of isolation. Emerson went on to say, in the same essay on 'Experience': 'Well, souls never touch their objects . . . There is an optical illusion about every person we meet . . . The individual is always mistaken. It turns out somewhat new and very unlike what he promised himself.' Even here he was still serene in his confidence in ultimate truth; but Melville saw in those very facts the sources of ambiguity that so goaded and tormented him in *Pierre*.

1. See his comment on the problem of the artist in an age of Property, p. 143, below.

Emerson concluded that a frontal attack could not overcome the discrepancy between the world of fact and the world that man thinks. For that reason in particular the symbol came to possess supreme value for him, since it enabled him to transcend the gap between these worlds. The quality that he continually ascribed to its power was that of 'indirection.' As he expressed it in a favorite figure, 'The gods like indirect names and dislike to be named directly.' [2] A similar feeling is frequent in Whitman. Contemplating the overwhelming variety of the continent, he said in his first preface: 'For such the expression of the American poet is to be transcendent and new. It is to be indirect and not direct or descriptive or epic.' [3] This feeling was due in part to the realization by both poets that the word was finally inadequate to cover the thing, that there always remained a revelation beyond. Their exaltation of content over form, their belief that expression was, to use Shelley's phrase, but 'a fading coal' in comparison with the moment of inspiration, inevitably led them to affirm that reality could be caught only tangentially, and conveyed obliquely.[4]

In Emerson's case the value of indirection was more heavily weighted still, since he secured by means of it the one kind of continuity that he knew. When he said, 'Everything in the universe goes by indirection,' he proceeded to develop his conviction that the only way in which his mind could gain knowledge from experience was not by worrying it with analysis, but by unquestioning immersion in the flow of every day, thus penetrating the mystery by living it. This process was what he meant in saying that 'we learn nothing rightly until we learn the symbolical char-

2. He found one of his chief texts for indirection in Zoroaster: 'It is not proper to understand the Intelligible with vehemence, but if you incline your mind, you will apprehend it: not too earnestly, but bringing a pure and inquiring eye. You will not understand it as when understanding some particular thing, but with the flower of the mind.' Emerson pronounced this a statement of fact 'which every lover and seeker of truth will recognize.'

3. See the fuller discussion of Whitman's indirection, pp. 519, 575.

4. The excesses of vagueness and obscurity into which this transcendental doctrine can run are only too apparent. They are mocked thus by Poe: 'Above all, study innuendo. Hint everything—assert nothing. If you feel inclined to say "bread and butter," do not by any means say it outright. You may say any and every thing *approaching* to "bread and butter." You may hint at buckwheat cake, or you may even go so far as to insinuate oatmeal porridge, but if bread and butter be your real meaning, be cautious, my *dear* Miss Psyche, not on any account to say "bread and butter." '

acter of life.' [5] Only by such knowledge could he bring the two separated halves of his consciousness into unity. He tried again and again to recount his actual steps. The first movement was to lie open and fallow, responding to the belief that man 'is great only by being passive to the super-incumbent spirit.' He described this state under many guises, for instance in these sentences in a letter, the relaxed rhythm of which suggests what the sensation gave him: 'Gray clouds, short days, moonless nights, a drowsy sense of being dragged easily somewhere by that locomotive Destiny, which, never seen, we yet know must be hitched on to the cars wherein we sit,—that is all that appears in these November weeks. Let us hope that, as often as we have defamed days which turned out to be bene-factors, and were whispering oracles . . so this may prove a profitable time.' Only through thus yielding himself to a trust in the hours as they pass could a man then 'put his ear close by himself and hold his breath and listen.' [6] And in that way only could he come finally to share in the active element, to escape the limitations of his private self and feel that he was swept by a force beyond his will, that he obeyed 'that redundancy or excess of life which in conscious beings we call *ecstasy.*' Such ecstasy in its flood-tide of abandonment was, as we have seen, Emerson's conception of genius. His process of entering into possession of its power has been re-garded by many as an incomplete pseudo-mysticism, and the conception itself may be judged a specially innocent kind of romantic spontaneity. It may cause some readers to take at its face value his observation to Mar-garet Fuller that he could discern no essential difference between the experience of his boyhood and that of his maturity, that he 'had never been otherwise than indolent, never strained a muscle, and only saw a difference in the circumstance, not in the man; at first a circle of boys—my brothers at home, with aunt and cousins, or the schoolroom; all agreed that my verses were obscure nonsense; and now a larger public say the same thing, "obscure nonsense," and yet both conceded that the boy had wit. A little more excitement now, but the fact identical, both in my consciousness and in my relations.'

5. The passage continues: 'Day creeps after day, each full of facts, dull, strange, despised things, that we cannot enough despise,—call heavy, prosaic and desert. The time we seek to kill: the attention it is elegant to divert from things around us. And presently the aroused intellect finds gold and gems in one of these scorned facts,—then finds that the day of facts is a rock of diamonds; that a fact is an Epiphany of God.'

6. This aim of Montaigne's was quoted admiringly by Emerson in his first letter to Carlyle.

Yet that unchanging identity beneath all seeming contradictions and inconsistencies is also Emerson's peculiar integrity, and gives the chief value to the life recorded in his journals. Its essential quality came to indirect expression in 'Days' (1851), which, as he himself thought, is the best of his poems: *Days"*

> Daughters of Time, the hypocritic Days,
> Muffled and dumb like barefoot dervishes,
> And marching single in an endless file,
> Bring diadems and fagots in their hands.
> To each they offer gifts after his will,
> Bread, kingdoms, stars, and sky that holds them all.
> I, in my pleached garden, watched the pomp,
> Forgot my morning wishes, hastily
> Took a few herbs and apples, and the Day
> Turned and departed silent. I, too late,
> Under her solemn fillet saw the scorn.

This vision of an Oriental procession through his Concord garden rose into words with such singular completeness that he commented upon it: 'I find one state of mind does not remember or conceive of another state. Thus I have written within a twelvemonth verses ('Days') which I do not remember the composition or correction of, and could not write the like to-day, and have only, for proof of their being mine, various external evidences, as the MS. in which I find them . . .' To be thus caught up and possessed was what he believed the sign of the real poet. He repeated often, and, indeed, wrote in his own copy of his *Poems,* as a motto to 'Bacchus,' Plato's saying that 'the man who is his own master knocks in vain at the doors of poetry.' He went so far in his belief in the selfless release of creation as to say, 'The muse may be defined, *Supervoluntary ends effected by supervoluntary means'*—a theory to be developed, in ways unforeseen by Emerson, by modern poets of the unconscious.

Supervoluntary or not, what he said here in a single sustained paragraph of blank verse corresponds to what he tried to say on literally dozens of other occasions. He had even made an approach to the central image of the poem more than a decade earlier, in the sentence to Margaret Fuller quoted as the epigraph to this section.[7] Four years before he composed the

---

7. A letter to his wife in 1846 contained this variant: 'But though days go smoothly enough they do not bring me in their fine timely wallets the alms I incessantly beg of them. Where are the melodies, where the unattainable words . . . ?' This suggests a partial source

poem, he wrote on the eve of his birthday: 'The days come and go like muffled and veiled figures sent from a distant friendly party, but they say nothing, and if we do not use the gifts they bring, they carry them as silently away.' Six years after the poem he not only used its metaphor in 'Works and Days,' but actually developed it into the theme of that entire essay. Looser variations of the image appear in verse in the final lines of 'Saadi' (1842), as well as in 'May-Day' (1865), and can be traced to an earliest version in a quatrain in the journal for 1831.[8]

What distinguishes 'Days' from all these and other partial efforts is that Emerson's gift for swift and fragile images has for once been reinforced by the extension and enlargement of his metaphor into a parable. The poem possesses more concentrated clarity than the essay, though exactly what it enunciates, and the importance of that content for Emerson, can be seen most adequately against the long background of its preparation. In one sense that may be held a limitation, since the best poetry speaks most fully for itself, without need of support from biography. But the point is not that 'Days' is obscure, but simply that it will shine more luminously in its proper setting. One reason why Emerson managed here to create a rounded and abiding form is that the thought and feeling of the parable rose from the central dilemma in his way of life. You could arrange under the rubric of its theme a thick anthology from his work, for it expresses the rhythm of his existence from at least his twentieth year, when he tried to voice it: 'The worst is, that the ebb is certain, long and frequent, while the flow comes transiently and seldom.' This mood could impinge with much greater intensity. In his hunger for abundance he could feel, as Thoreau was also to do, that life wastes itself while we are preparing to live, that 'on the brink of the waters of life and truth, we are miserably dying.'

He cast this conviction into several different images. At times he felt that he and his contemporaries were re-enacting the myth of Tantalus,

---

for Emerson's procession in Shakespeare's *Troilus and Cressida*, in the magnificent personification of Time with

> a wallet at his back,
> Wherein he puts alms for oblivion.

8. The days pass over me
   And I am still the same;
   The aroma of my life is gone
   Like the flower with which it came.

again that they were like millers on the lower levels of a stream where the factories above had diverted the water. His only solution was to accept whole-heartedly the potentiality of what each day might bring. Shortly after his year in Europe and with the future still uncertain before him, he wrote to Carlyle that he rejoiced in his example, in the fact that 'one living scholar is self-centered, and will be true to himself.' He also said, 'Possessing my liberty, I am determined to keep it, at the risk of uselessness (which God can very well abide).' Such a course was sufficiently rare in America with its press of competition and its demand for conformity to some practical occupation. As Cooper had pointed out with irony, his countrymen found no room for a class of 'learned idlers.' Carlyle knew the hazards involved for his friend, and was struck by his quiet tenacity: 'It is not one of your smallest qualities in my mind, that you *can* wait so quietly and let the years do their hest . . . Sit still at Concord.' [9]

From the time of his very earliest passages of self-analysis we can see him feeling his way to the realization that his kind of truth was to come through inaction and hope, through waiting for moments of illumination. But he sometimes regarded this tendency with misgiving: 'There is a dreaminess about my mode of life (which may be a depravity) which loosens the tenacity of what should be most tenacious—this my grasp on heaven and earth. I am the servant more than the master of my fates.' Ten years later than this entry he was writing to his brother Edward (1834): 'Here we sit, always learning, and never coming to the knowledge of.' Yet the 'apathy' and 'indolence' which he so often bewailed may well

9. The view taken of Emerson by the respectable was summed up by John Quincy Adams in 1840: 'The sentiment of religion is at this time, perhaps, more potent and prevailing in New England than in any other portion of the Christian world. For many years since the establishment of the theological school at Andover, the Calvinists and Unitarians have been battling with each other upon the atonement, the divinity of Jesus Christ and the Trinity. This has now very much subsided; but other wandering of mind takes the place of that, and equally lets the wolf into the fold. A young man, named Ralph Waldo Emerson, and a classmate of my lamented son George, after failing in the everyday avocations of a Unitarian preacher and schoolmaster, starts a new doctrine of transcendentalism, declares all the old revelations superannuated and worn out, and announces the approach of new revelations and prophecies. Garrison and the non-resistant abolitionists, Brownson and the Marat democrats, phrenology and animal magnetism, all come in, furnishing each some plausible rascality as an ingredient for the bubbling cauldron of religion and politics.' After the scandal of the Divinity School Address, Emerson was not invited to lecture in Harvard's halls again for thirty years. Following the Civil War, when transcendentalism could no longer be thought dangerous, he was chosen one of the Harvard Board of Overseers.

have been his unconscious protection against the terrible stimulus of nervous Yankee life. And even in the midst of his moods of regret that the days were slipping past without fulfilment, he did not doubt that his course was right. Out of the depth of his consent to his lot welled up the opposite mood, his dilation in response to the flux. His enunciation of this mood is very like some of Melville's passages about standing the mast-head. Particularly in a letter that Emerson wrote from Nantasket in the summer of 1841 do his rhythms seem affected by the soothing monotonous movement of the waves as well as by his having just been rereading Plato: 'But is it the picture of the unbounded sea, or is it the lassitude of the Syrian summer, that more and more draws the cords of Will out of my thought and leaves me nothing but perpetual observation, perpetual acquiescence and perpetual thankfulness. Shall I not be Turk and fatalist before to-day's sun shall set? and in this thriving New England too, full of din and snappish activity and invention and wilfulness.'

His positive doctrine could thus be reduced to the single command, 'Hear what the morning says and believe that.' But he was always alternating back to the other mood. He declared that a man has not learned anything until he knows that 'every day is Doomsday'—but what of the judgment upon him if it has dragged by with nothing done? He was ever being distracted by the disproportion between the means and the end, by the feeling that 'we are always getting ready to live, but never living.' There were so many years of education and earning a livelihood, of routine and sickness and travel, but 'very little life in a lifetime . . . a few, few hours in the longest.' In that state of mind all of existence seemed a disguise that he could not penetrate. Moreover, even when he was flooded with power, he had to confess to an inability to handle it. He continued in his letter from Nantasket: 'Can you not save me, dip me into ice water, find me some girding belt, that I glide not away into a stream or a gas, and decease in infinite diffusion?' For no less than Melville did he recognize the peril of being drowned in the 'honey-head of Plato,' as he went on to say: 'Noah's flood and the striae which the good geologist finds on every mountain and rock seem to me the records of a calamity less universal than this metaphysical flux which threatens every enterprise, every thought and every thinker. How high will this Nile, this Mississippi, this Ocean, rise, and will ever the waters be stayed?'

Thus he could alternate his metaphor that 'we are always on the brink of an ocean of thought into which we do not yet swim,' with this other metaphor, which expresses his realization that, even on the rare occasions when he was immersed, he was swept by currents beyond his control. Inundated by a new revelation, he felt that he lacked the ability to articulate it. His escape from the practical restrictions of his age had been so complete, the freedom of his consciousness was so absolute, that he sensed the need of some strict challenge to bring him back into manageable dimensions. Put in terms of artistic expression, the want of coherence between his understanding and his reason, his feeling that he was either parched or drowned, meant that he lacked the tension between form and liberation, between abandon and restraint. Coleridge knew that the power of art lay in reconciliation of these very opposites. Margaret Fuller was commenting on the absence of this dynamic struggle in Emerson when she said: 'It is a fine day for composition, were it not in Concord. But I trow the fates which gave this place Concord, took away the animating influences of Discord. Life here slumbers and steals on like the river. A very good place for a sage, but not for the lyrist or the orator.'

Emerson's belief in the ballast of experience and his belief that experience is illusory; his trust in the fullness of the moment and his sense that the moment eluded him, and his Puritanic scruple at the waste; his sense of being on the verge of a great discovery and of being inadequate to grasp it—all lie behind 'Days.' One weakness of his poems that he deplored was that they did not contain sufficient evidence of the 'polarity' of existence, of how its inevitable law is action and reaction, of how every statement contains the seed of its opposite. He said: 'I am always insincere, as always knowing there are other moods.' But in this poem there is for once set up the implication of counterstatement, which adds the density of real experience. These lines express his misgiving at his failure to rise to his opportunity, to enter into possession of the transcendent kingdom of stars and sky that has been stretched out before him. This feeling deepens into guilt as hieratic scorn confronts him for penetrating too late the disguise of appearance, for blindly neglecting to abandon himself at once to the mysteries of the Reason. But if this was his conscious intention in the poem, its undertone conveys something else. The symbol that he uses for the choice he made does not share in the ugliness of wrong. His instinctive taking of the few herbs and apples is the fitting expression for his spontaneous trust in the amplitude to man's needs of his immediate surroundings. The beauty that he sees is again in the commonest forms of nature. His clinging to this frail harvest, even though he regrets it, is what empowers him here to suggest the poignant complexity of his existence. By means of his parable he has been true to both halves of his consciousness and has set going a dynamic tension between them. In recompense he has received a gift: not of asserting the final Unity through dozens of monotonous lines, but of creating a variegated, if delicate, poetic whole.

7. The Flowing

'Mr. Coleridge has written well on this matter of Theory in his *Friend* . . . A true method has no more need of firstly, secondly, etc., than a perfect sentence has of punctuation. It tells its own story, makes its own feet, creates its own form. It is its own apology.'

—EMERSON's *Journal* (1834)

'In a fortnight or three weeks my little raft will be afloat. Expect nothing more of my powers of construction,—no ship-building, no clipper, smack, nor skiff even, only boards and logs tied together.'

—Emerson to Carlyle just before the appearance of his first *Essays* (1841)

ALL OF Emerson's books can be reduced to the same underlying pattern. They are hardly constructed as wholes. Even *Representative Men* (1850) and *English Traits* (1856) are collections of essays, written originally as lectures. Every lecture in turn, from *The American Scholar* to those published after his death, was made up by grouping together sentences from his journals. If his longer poems, 'Woodnotes,' 'Monadnoc' and 'May-Day,' are really strings of loosely connected verses, his constructive skills in prose were limited, as Woodberry saw, to the 'simple combination of the minister's old pulpit sermon and the man-of-letters' *pensée.'*

His work corresponds so naturally to his life that it constitutes the purest example of what individualism could produce. The sentence was his unit, as he recognized when confessing sadly to Carlyle (1838) that his paragraphs were only collections of 'infinitely repellent particles.' It is significant that he said the same thing when reflecting on society as 'an imperfect union': 'Every man is an infinitely repellent orb, and holds his individual being on that condition.' The sentence was the inevitable unit for the man who could say, 'A single thought has no limit to its value.' He was at his best when he could give both release and embodiment to one of his thoughts in a plastic image; but though he talked about the unexampled resources of metaphor and symbol, his staple device was analogy. As he said, 'All thinking is analogizing, and it is the use of life to learn metonymy.' His method was not induction, or logical persuasion of any kind, as even the relative infrequency of conjunctions in his paragraphs can show. In spite of his fondness for Montaigne, he had not a trace of skepticism in his being; and in spite of his profession of being a seeker, all his mature work proceeded from *a priori* deductive assertion. This would necessarily rely more on analogy than on the fresh discovery of metaphor; and the fact that Emerson seems to equate the value of the two modes is another instance of his concern with the idea to the partial neglect of its created vehicle.

His early attraction to Bacon was in keeping with his taste for the maxim, or as Bacon's age called it the 'sententia,' with its swift pithy compression of a thought. Such intensification of the moment in literature would be the natural instrument of the man for whom the intensification of the moment was the meaning of life.[1] He expressed a kindred enthusiasm for proverbs, which he conceived differently from Franklin as 'the literature of reason, or the statements of an absolute truth without qualification. Proverbs, like the sacred books of each nation, are the sanctuary of the intuitions.' This definition has much in common with Coleridge's conception of the aphorism. One of Coleridge's main purposes in writing *Aids to Reflection* was 'to direct the reader's attention to the value of the Science of Words . . . and the incalculable advantages attached to the habit of using them appropriately, and with a distinct knowledge of their primary, derivative, and metaphorical senses.' In furtherance of this aim he provided his aphorisms, since 'exclusive of the abstract sciences, the largest and worthiest portion of our knowledge consists of *aphorisms:* and the greatest and best of men is but an *aphorism.*' This conception of the identity of the man with his work was integrally related to that of the word with the thing. It might be said that the sentences by which

1. I am indebted for this formulation to O. W. Firkins, *Ralph Waldo Emerson* (1915). Though marred by some eccentric mannerisms, Firkins' chapter on 'Emerson as Prose-Writer' contains the closest technical analysis that has yet been made of his style.

Emerson has become a living part of our language, the ones in which he showed a poet's delicate attention to the word and an equally poetic gift of phrase and of rhythmical balance, still contain a residue of the Yankee's respect for Franklin.[2]

The problem of Emerson's prose was the same as that of his philosophy, how to reconcile the individual with society, how to join his sentences into a paragraph. Since his chief preoccupation was to demonstrate identity beneath all manner of variety, his formula for an essay was an abstraction instanced by an indefinite number of embodiments. His desire to get his whole philosophy into each essay led 'toward sameness and promiscuity at once; it made the sentences similar and the paragraphs diverse.' Firkins was not thinking in social terms in that remark, but it corresponds with what many observers have noted as the consequences of our American theory of the self-sufficient individual—our double tendency towards standardization and anarchy. It was the philosophic anarchists among Emerson's contemporaries to whom his essays were principally addressed, though most of his audience, less daring than Thoreau, would hardly have recognized themselves under that description. They knew simply that they found the old conformities of their environment intolerable; and in an era when the abolitionists were attacking the state as morally defective, it was natural that the radicalism of the transcendentalists should have demanded the fullest freedom from

2. Perhaps the most balanced epitome that Emerson ever made of his philosophy was that which placed him between the transcendentalists and Franklin. I have already quoted this as an epigraph to the section on 'Expression.'

Poor Richard brought a racy concreteness to the proverb, which it had not often possessed in the almanacs before him. Near the outset of his career as a journalist Franklin had written an essay on the text, 'Withdraw thy Foot from the House of thy Neighbor, lest he grow weary of thee, and so hate thee.' A few years later Poor Richard could say it thus: 'Fish and visitors smell after three days.' In like fashion, though by a very different route, Emerson's quality depended on the growth of his power to make his words a mirror of his personality. A dozen years of maturing life were necessary before the rhetorical diction in the following reflection of the divinity student could be liberated in *Nature:* 'He who frequents these scenes, where Nature discloses her magnificence to silence and solitude, will have his mind occupied often by trains of thought of a peculiarly solemn tone, which never interrupted the profligacy of libertines, the money-getting of the miser, or the glory-getting of the ambitious.' It was equally essential for Emerson to cultivate his aphoristic gift, if the sentiment, 'A portion of truth, bright and sublime, lives in every moment to every man'—which he expressed in a letter to his Aunt Mary in 1827—was to be clothed as 'the meal in the firkin, the milk in the pan.' Thus, as in Franklin, the physical and mental realms are fused.

"American Scholar"

all restraints. Emerson himself visualized his solitary reader in his journal for 1839:

In Massachusetts a number of young and adult persons are at this moment the subject of a revolution. They are not organized into any conspiracy: they do not vote, or print, or meet together. They do not know each others' faces or names. They are united only in a common love of truth and love of its work. They are of all conditions and natures. They are, some of them, mean in attire, and some mean in station, and some mean in body, having inherited from their parents faces and forms scrawled with the traits of every vice. Not in churches, or in courts, or in large assemblies; not in solemn holidays, where men were met in festal dress, have these pledged themselves to new life, but in lonely and obscure places, in servitude, in solitude, in solitary compunctions and shames and fears, in disappointments, in diseases, trudging beside the team in the dusty road, or drudging, a hireling in other men's cornfields, schoolmasters who teach a few children rudiments for a pittance, ministers of small parishes of the obscurer sects, lone women in dependent condition, matrons and young maidens, rich and poor, beautiful and hard-favored, without conceit or proclamation of any kind, have silently given in their several adherence to a new hope.

That hope itself was so sustaining that in Emerson's case at least it deferred the necessity of further radical action. He was uneasy at times in his detachment, as he was over his restricted audience when he compared the response of his few hundreds or thousands to the mass that greeted *Uncle Tom's Cabin.* He perceived also how it was that book's distinction to have been 'read equally in the parlor and the kitchen and the nursery.' But, as Eliot has observed, there are 'four ways of thinking: to talk to others, or to one other, or to talk to oneself, or to talk to God.' In the journals of Emerson and Thoreau we can participate in the shift from the fourth of those modes to the third. All of Emerson's work is illustrative of his early remark to Carlyle that 'the best poem of the Poet is his own mind.' That conviction put him in fundamental opposition to the norm of the previous century, as it had been made explicit, for instance, by Shaftesbury: 'I hold it very indecent that a man should publish his meditations or solitary thoughts. These are the froth and scum of writing, which should be unburdened in private and consigned to oblivion, before the writer comes before the world as good company.'

Nature was a Meditation, with some kinship to what the seventeenth century recognized as such, or at least to what Vaughan and Traherne had so recognized. Emerson gave its structure logical divisions, but they were somewhat stiff and arbitrary in contrast to his lyric unity of tone. Never again was he to succeed so well in clothing his abstractions in the colors of the visible world; or to sustain for so long the art of the rhapsode. No one could demand a composition more satisfactory for its purpose than that of *The American Scholar;* and the early essays still rely on the ordered skills of the preacher. In fact, at no time did Emerson lose his joy in such a device as the rhetorician's 'principle of iteration.' But, to paraphrase Firkins once more, Emerson's later work will sustain analysis better than perusal. With the inevitable loss of freshness in his repeated eloquence, the unity of tone—the method to which Coleridge had stimulated him—was no longer imaginatively compelling. Life remained for him primarily a flux and a becoming, and that flux and becoming were often carried over into his work. His essays tended to deliquesce, like that on the Over-Soul, which is compared to water no less than a dozen times.

As was the case with 'Days,' the paragraphs of his prose that assume wholeness in the reader's mind are those that grew from a pervasive theme. One of the most notable examples is the last paragraph of 'Illusions,' the concluding essay in *The Conduct of Life* (1860). The theme of this essay can be traced to the conviction of Plotinus that appealed to Emerson most: 'This, therefore, is the life of the Gods, and of divine and happy men; a liberation from all terrene concerns, a life unaccompanied with human pleasures, and a flight of the alone to the alone.' He quoted the final image in his letters, and echoed it in 'The Over-Soul' ('The soul gives itself, alone, original and pure, to the Lonely, Original and Pure'). He came back to it again when describing Swedenborg's mysticism, and developed his understanding of the flight as follows: 'This path is difficult, secret and beset with terror. The ancients called it *ecstasy* or absence—a getting out of their bodies to think.' That was also how Donne had described the process in his poem 'The Extasie,' which Emerson greatly admired, though he doubtless passed over Donne's insistence on the need to return to the body. Plotinus' image, transformed to Emerson's own usage and repeated at the beginning and the end of the paragraph in 'Illusions,' helped to provide a frame for his Neo-Platonic thought and to condense it, as 'Days' had been condensed, into an effective parable:

There is no chance and no anarchy in the universe. All is system and gradation. Every god is there sitting in his sphere. The young mortal enters the hall of the firmament; there is he alone with them alone, they pouring on him benedictions and gifts, and beckoning him up to their thrones. On the instant, and incessantly, fall snow-storms of illusions. He fancies himself in a vast crowd which sways this way and that and whose movement and doings he must obey: he fancies himself poor, orphaned, insignificant. The mad crowd drives hither and thither, now furiously commanding this thing to be done, now that. What is he that he should resist their will, and think or act for himself? Every moment new changes and new showers of deceptions to baffle and distract him. And when, by and by, for an instant, the air clears and the cloud lifts a little, there are the gods still sitting around him on their thrones,—they alone with him alone.

Without such condensation Emerson's writing was only too liable to exemplify the consequences of what he deemed the prevailing thought of his century, its reassertion of the Heraclitean doctrine of the Flowing. He saw himself, in a recurrent image, standing on the bank of a river watching the endless current upon which floated past him objects of all shapes and colors. He did not know whence they came or where they went, and he could not detain them as they passed, except by running beside them a little way along the bank. Similar images were the special signatures of nineteenth-century poets. Wordsworth felt that he escaped from uncertainty and understood the purpose of his own life by thus watching a river flow to the sea. By the time of Arnold the purpose was less clear, and his dominant thought was that the calm of the earlier stream was now lost in the incessant line of cities that crowded its edge. For Whitman these cities, as well as the river and the ocean itself, were all symbols for the movement that so exhilarated him while crossing Brooklyn ferry. For Baudelaire movement was more difficult, and the oppressiveness of the city overwhelming: a ship, with its white sails poised for flight, was his image of escape from the boredom and the horror. By the time of Rimbaud the ship had become *bateau ivre* whose pilot had lost all control and awaited the end in despair.

Emerson's work is as permeated with images of flowing as you would expect from his declaration that 'the philosophy we want is one of fluxions and mobility.' In *Nature* the earth becomes 'this green ball which floats him through the heavens.' Nothing solid is left secure, since all matter has been infiltrated and dissolved by thought. He noted himself how such images were the fitting expression of a mind most of whose values were continually varying, as in his estimate of America, 'which sometimes runs very low, sometimes to ideal prophetic proportions.' But unlike most poets who have contemplated mutability, Emerson found no cause for anguish even when he went to the length of saying that men's lives 'are spinning like bubbles in a river.' He was delighted that Swedenborg was 'a man who saw God . . . for a fluid moment.' Emerson's unshaken confidence lay in the river's progression onward, in the fact that 'God is a substance, and his method is illusion.' Consequently, when his images of flowing culminated in a paragraph of his 'Lecture on the Times' (1841), he intended it to convey a hopeful tone. But out of its context and a century later than those times, the undertones now seem somber. This paragraph can serve as a final instance of how his strongest writing emerged from his recurrent themes:

The main interest which any aspects of the Times can have for us, is the great spirit which gazes through them, the light which they can shed on the wonderful questions, What we are? and Whither we tend? We do not wish to be deceived. Here we drift, like white sail across the wild ocean, now bright on the wave, now darkling in the trough of the sea;—but from what port did we sail? Who knows? Or to what port are we bound? Who knows! There is no one to tell us but such poor weather-tossed mariners as ourselves, whom we speak as we pass, or who have hoisted some signal, or floated to us some letter in a bottle from far. But what know they more than we? They also found themselves on this wondrous sea. No; from the older sailors, nothing. Over all their speaking-trumpets, the gray sea and the loud winds answer, Not in us; not in Time . . .

The poignance of such isolation from any coherent community faded away in Emerson's sureness that he could step immediately out of time into the living moment of eternity.[3] He could therefore delight in the flow, except when he tried to catch the meaning of the objects and events that drifted past him, and found himself alone with lonely fragments.

3. Cf. his statement in 'Works and Days': 'In stripping time of its illusions, in seeking to find out what is the heart of the day, we come to the quality of the moment and drop the duration altogether.' This conception of time is akin to Thoreau's:

I moments live, who lived but years.

8. Self-Portrait of Saadi

'Let theist, atheist, pantheist,
Define and wrangle how they list,
Fierce conserver, fierce destroyer,—
But thou, joy-giver and enjoyer,
Unknowing war, unknowing crime,
Gentle Saadi, mind thy rhyme;
Heed not what the brawlers say,
Heed thou only Saadi's·lay.'

In this very 'Lecture on the Times' Emerson resolved to take a firm hold on the many: 'Why not draw for these times a portrait gallery? Let us paint the painters. Whilst the Daguerreotypist, with camera-obscura and silver plate, begins now to traverse the land, let us set up our Camera also, and let the sun paint the people.'[1] Emerson's resolve went back to his early desire (1824) to be another Montaigne, which he had rounded out with the sentence, 'My business is with the living.' It went back also to his feeling (1832) that the modern Plutarch was still to be written, and that in making the effort to write it, he would 'draw characters, not write lives.' That is certainly what he did in the thumbnail sketches scattered throughout his journals—in his recurrent absorption with Alcott as 'the highest genius of the time,' and yet as 'a tedious archangel' and 'a pail without a bottom'; in his unexpected flash of humor when epitomizing some pious old Calvinists: 'they had to hold on hard to the huckleberry bushes to hinder themselves from being translated.' He profited from his fondness for the seventeenth century's mode of presenting type-characters when he came to prepare a commemorative address for his step-grandfather, the Reverend Ezra Ripley (1751-1841), who had been the minister in Concord for more than sixty years. Emerson seized upon the details that could be made to count: 'Some of those around me will remember one occasion of severe drought in this vicinity, when the late Rev. Mr. Goodwin offered to relieve the Doctor of the duty of leading in prayer; but the Doctor suddenly remembering the

1. Cf. the Note on the Illustrations.

season, rejected his offer with some humor, as with an air that said to all the congregation, "This is no time for you young Cambridge men; the affair, sir, is getting serious. I will pray myself." One August afternoon, when I was in his hayfield helping him with his man to rake up his hay, I well remember his pleading, almost reproachful looks at the sky, when the thunder-gust was coming up to spoil his hay. He raked very fast, then looked at the cloud, and said, "We are in the Lord's hand; mind your rake, George! We are in the Lord's hand"; and seemed to say, "You know me; this field is mine,—Dr. Ripley's,—thine own servant!" '

Emerson's best product in this genre was his tribute to Thoreau, one of the finest brief biographies in the language. But that was called forth by the most concentrated character of the age; in his other attempts he showed flashes of brilliant brush-work, yet no final organization. His fascination with Webster kept him making sketches over a period of thirty years, but he never brought them together in a definitive portrait. And a single paragraph from Carlyle, who had met Webster at breakfast in London (1839), caused Emerson to praise the Scotchman's 'thirsty eyes, those portrait-eating, portrait-painting eyes,' and to regret again his own lack of the 'potent concentration,' the 'strong executive talent' without which he knew himself to have produced nothing but scraps.

A distinguishing greatness of English literature from Chaucer to Carlyle had been its ability to create character. This gift has often been attributed to the fact that England, even from the Middle Ages, was a nation built on dissent, on the exploits of strong individuals rather than on a corporate catholic tradition. In America the protestant drive had carried to further extremes, and both Emerson and Hawthorne showed the results of the long Puritan conditioning in habits of inward scrutiny. Neither of them had marked ability in representing outward solidness. Neither Hawthorne nor any other American novelist was to come near to rivalling Dickens' variety of types any more than Emerson could create a group of portraits to rank beside Carlyle's many heroes. Carlyle was more than just to *Representative Men* when he noted its want of third dimension by calling it a 'perfect set of Engravings in the line manner.'

The only character that Emerson succeeded in portraying at full-length was his own. If he could not represent the many, he gave the most faithful likeness of the one. The poets of the Irish movement, particularly

Yeats and Æ, in their own reassertion of a living tradition, cast a great deal of light on Emerson's problem. They thought primarily about Whitman, but what they said of him would fit Emerson and Thoreau as well. They believed that their own search for ideal types in the Irish myths had an aim similar to Whitman's, but that Whitman, lacking the ennobling influence of an ancient folk-lore, had been compelled to create a myth out of himself, to project what he called a 'stock personality' as a means of elevating and harmonizing the conception of an American. This may take Whitman farther into anthropology than he was himself conscious of going; but without attributing to Emerson the Frazer approach to primitive myth, we can observe him also feeling the necessity to rediscover the hero who should release the energies of his people. When he rejected the conventional New England occupations, he knew it incumbent upon him to present the ideal that he believed worth pursuing, and he did so under many guises.[2] He said, 'The path which the hero travels alone is the highway of health and benefit to mankind.' He saw that hero variously as the reflective man, the genius, the seer, the torch-bearer, the radical, and the spiritualist. Most of these types were subsumed under his broad conception of the American Scholar; but even after he had made that embodiment Emerson continued to sketch these others through many pages of his journals.

He recognized that his problem in such sketches was not that of the thinker but of the artist. He must objectify these aspirations of his consciousness. All too often the faint lineaments of his heroes recall Coleridge's apt remark about the imperfectly dramatic character of some of Wordsworth's poems: the style 'presents a species of ventriloquism,' since 'two are represented as talking, while in truth one man only speaks.' Emerson came closest to giving plastic incarnation to one of his heroes in his presentation of Saadi as the ideal poet. In the poem (1842) which he called by the Persian's name, he used him to symbolize the theme that the poet must dwell alone, that, no matter what the distractions and demands of the world, he must heed only what he knows himself born to say. Yet Saadi was not severe in his isolation. He thirsted for beauty, and was charmed by the occasional presence of men. His cheerful temper was expressed by a sentence that Emerson rejoiced to quote: 'It was rumored

2. See Henry N. Smith, 'Emerson's Problem of Vocation: A Note on *The American Scholar*' (*New England Quarterly*, March 1939). See also my final chapter, 'Man in the Open Air,' for the widespread myth-making faculty of the age.

abroad that I was penitent; but what had I to do with repentance?' Nothing could have phrased more aptly Emerson's liberation from his background, and he translated it thus into his verse:

> And yet it seemeth not to me
> That the high gods love tragedy;
> For Saadi sat in the sun,
> And thanks was his contrition.

Thoreau was to sound the same note: 'If you would know aught, be gay before it.' Emerson found Saadi a comforting *alter ego* on many occasions, as when he set down these sentences as part of the other's character: 'The poet is always awaited by the people. He has only the overdose of that quality whereof they have the underdose.'

He had an opportunity to sum up Saadi's nature when he agreed to write an introduction for a translation of *The Gulistan, or Rose Garden* (1865). When he began to sketch this in his journal, he said: 'Saadi is the poet of friendship, of love, of heroism, self-devotion, joy, bounty, serenity, and of the divine Providence.' On reconsideration he may have thought that some of these qualities applied more to his own aspirations than to his subject's. At any rate he left out of the published essay 'heroism,' 'joy,' 'bounty,' and 'the divine Providence.' But he was able to project a characterization that would bear likeness to both the Persian and himself: 'The word *Saadi* means *fortunate*. In him the trait is no result of levity, much less of convivial habit, but first of a happy nature, to which victory is habitual, easily shedding mishaps, with sensibility to pleasure, and with resources against pain. But it also results from the habitual perception of the beneficent laws that control the world. He inspires in the reader a good hope. What a contrast between the cynical tone of Byron and the benevolent wisdom of Saadi!'

The limitations of Emerson's ideal poet can be measured by the self-conscious if not quite self-righteous assurance that obtrudes itself into his voice here. These limitations could be dramatized by a comparison between 'Uriel' and 'Israfel,' poems in which Emerson and Poe give symbolic expression to their understanding of the poet's role. What is insistent through Poe's disjointed stanzas is his intense suffering. Emerson, who is making a parable out of his reaction to the storm over his Divinity School Address, is as serene as Saadi could wish, and speaks with the 'low tones that decide.' His doctrine in 'Uriel,' as throughout his poetry, affirms the increasing greatness of man. Yet he regarded himself as a prophet, not a Messiah—a distinction by no means so clearly maintained by Whitman or Hugo, by Nietzsche or D. H. Lawrence. Emerson's diffident blandness was hardly satanic pride, but his complete acceptance of himself showed little knowledge of humility. He himself remarked on the reason for his expansiveness, 'Least of all do we need any suggestion of checks and measures; as if New England were anything else.' As Henry James was to observe, Emerson felt his American society to be 'too sparse for synthesis.' But if our own inevitable concern with synthesis finds his delight in the flux and his celebration of the private individual to be exaggerated, reckless, or even meaningless, the fact of his genius remains as uncontestable as it did at his death. James described it then as 'the genius for seeing character as a real and supreme thing.' And if Emerson never created a form great enough to insure that his books will continue to be read, his whole career lived up to the resolve that he had made when he first settled in Concord (1834): 'Henceforth I design not to utter any speech, poem or book that is not entirely and peculiarly my work.'

II

THE ACTUAL GLORY

'I see, smell, taste, hear, feel that everlasting Something to which we
are allied . . . the actual glory of the universe.'
                    —*A Week on the Concord and Merrimack Rivers*

1. Expected Unexpectedness

'Methinks my own soul must be a bright invisible green.'
                                        —THOREAU

Thoreau

THOREAU has not ordinarily been approached primarily as an artist. His
first disciples tended to think of him as a naturalist, with the result that
later scientists have criticized him for his want of severe method and his
crotchety inaccuracies. He gave enough warnings against this interpretation. He said that he did not want too exact knowledge: the poet and the
botanist look very differently at the same object, since 'a man sees only
what concerns him.' He described the balance he sought (1851): 'See not
with the eye of science, which is barren, nor of youthful poetry, which is
impotent. But taste the world and digest it.' The shift of senses from sight
to taste was fundamental to his organic grasp of life. He was resolved that
maturity should not involve the loss of wonder at the ever fresh mystery
the years brought. He continued to affirm that natural phenomena interested him only as they 'may have lain in the experience of a human
being.' This thought became even more trenchant: 'Man is all in all,
Nature nothing, but as she draws him out and reflects him.'

Individualism Though he often talked in paradoxes, he was still more explicit in warning readers against taking *Walden* as a reformer's manual.[1] Yet his vitality

---

1. As in these statements in the chapter, 'Economy': 'I would not have any one
adopt *my* mode of living on any account; for beside that before he has fairly learned it
I may have found out another for myself, I desire that there may be as many different
persons in the world as possible; but I would have each one be very careful to find out
and pursue *his own* way, and not his father's or his mother's or his neighbor's instead.'
Also: 'As for Doing-good, that is one of the professions which are full. Moreover, I have

as a revolutionary is still unexhausted. Emerson said that 'Thoreau was in his own person a practical answer, almost a refutation, to the theories of the socialists.' But though he found no need for one of Fourier's phalanxes to enable him to live as he wanted, his essay on 'Civil Disobedience' has affected a mass movement. It was the chief basis upon which Gandhi built his doctrine of passive resistance. However, in spite of Emerson's prophecies, socialism rather than anarchism became the main radical drift of the succeeding century in the Occident; and in that drift Thoreau may seem reduced to the position that Whitehead has described: 'The self-sufficing independent man, with his peculiar property which concerns no one else, is a concept without any validity for modern civilization.'

Before beginning to assess the meaning and value of the *Week* and *Walden,* it is therefore imperative to remind ourselves of Thoreau's political context, to see why his natural direction was that of left-wing individualism.[2] He is generally remembered for his two most extreme acts: that he went to live in a hut in the woods, and that, as a protest against the Mexican War, he once refused to pay his poll-tax to a corrupt state. But both these acts were frankly imitative. Alcott had taken a similar stand, four years previously, against the immorality of the state, and had thus instanced the millennial strain that was widespread in our early forties. Among Thoreau's other friends, Stearns Wheeler had already built a shanty on Flint's Pond for the sake of economy, and Ellery Channing had gone more romantically to live on the prairie in Illinois. They had thus both made their responses to the *Zeitgeist,* as it was evidenced by the long popularity of such a book as Zimmermann's *Solitude.* Thoreau's radical value does not lie in his gestures of protest, the shock of both of which, incidentally, was cushioned by his circumstances, since he could build his hut on land borrowed from Emerson, and friends saw to it that his tax was paid and so got him out of jail after one night. His contribution

tried it fairly, and, strange as it may seem, am satisfied that it does not agree with my constitution.'

2. See Eunice M. Shuster, *Native American Anarchism: A Study of Left-Wing American Individualism (Smith College Studies in History,* 1932). This study reminds us that among Thoreau's older contemporaries were Josiah Warren (1798-1874), who was the founder of our first anarchist colonies, 'Utopia' (at Clermont, Ohio, 1847-51) and 'Modern Times' (at Brentwood, Long Island, 1850-c.1862), and whose labor and land theories anticipated respectively those of Proudhon and of Henry George; Stephen Pearl Andrews (1812-86), whose book *The Science of Society* (1852) called wider attention to Warren's philosophy; and Adin Ballou (1803-90), whose doctrine of Non-Resistance influenced Tolstoy.

to our social thought lies in his thoroughgoing criticism of the narrow materialism of his day. It is important to remember that when he objected to the division of labor, he was writing from an agrarian and craft economy where the forces of industrialism were still an encroaching minority. But his human values were so clear that they remain substantially unaltered by our changed conditions.

He objected to the division of labor since it divided the worker, not merely the work, reduced him from a man to an operative, and enriched the few at the expense of the many. As a critic of society he had the advantage of being close to its primary levels. The son of a man who had failed as a small merchant and had then set up as a pencil-maker, signpainter, and jack-of-all-trades, Thoreau came about as close to the status of proletarian writer as was possible in his simple environment.[3] Of the writers treated in this volume, only Whitman, the son of a Long Island farmer and carpenter, was to belong more completely to the life of the common man. However, the families of all the others, as it happens, were in declining circumstances. Emerson, the scion of a long line of ministers, grew up in virtual poverty after the death of his father when Waldo was seven. Hawthorne's family went into eclipse in Salem after the death of his sea-captain father when Nathaniel, his only son, was four. And Melville, the descendant of New York patroons, had no better prospects than to go to sea as a common sailor in the year of the panic of 1837. These facts undoubtedly helped cause them all to scrutinize the world of which they were part.

The social standards that Thoreau knew and protested against were those dominated by New England mercantilism. He granted that the life

3. Writing out of their knowledge of a society that had already undergone industrialization, Marx and Engels were equally opposed to the division of man, but made their solution depend on utilizing the possibilities of the new economy. They believed that 'la concentration exclusive du talent artistique dans quelques individus et son étouffement dans les grandes masses, qui en découle, est un effet de la division du travail . . . Dans une société communiste, il n'y a pas de peintres, mais tout au plus des hommes qui, entre autres, font de la peinture.' Their grounds for believing that the division of labor might be thus solved were: 'C'est seulement l'accroissement énorme des forces productives atteint grâce à la grande industrie qui permet de répartir le travail sur tous les membres de la société sans exception, et, par là, de restreindre le temps de travail de chacun de telle manière que tous aient assez de temps libre pour prendre part aux affaires générales—théoriques et pratiques,—de la société.' (I have used here the French translation in the useful series, Les Grands Textes du Marxisme. The volume collecting the opinions of Marx and Engels, Sur la littérature et l'art, was selected and translated by Jean Fréville, Paris, 1936.)

of a civilized people is *'an institution,* in which the life of the individual is to a great extent absorbed, in order to preserve and perfect that of the race.' But he insisted that it was essential to re-examine the terms under which that absorption was being made, to see whether the individual was not being ruthlessly sacrificed to the dictates of a mean-spirited commercialism. On the economic level it might be true that the degraded poor were only a minority of immigrants in the North—though in the South the laborers themselves were 'a staple production.' But whether a group like the Irishmen working on the railroad across Walden Pond were a minority or not, Thoreau held it only fair in judging society 'to look at that class by whose labor the works which distinguish this generation are accomplished.' Even waiving the special problem that these new groups presented, he declared that hardly any kind of workingman in the country had the 'leisure for a true integrity day by day . . . He has no time to be anything but a machine.'

The heart of Thoreau's revolt was his continual assertion that the only true America is that country where you are able to pursue life without encumbrances.[4] He did not want that freedom for his private self alone. His deepest reason for disliking the pinched Yankee standardization was its starvation of the minds and spirits of the citizens. One strain of his thought that has not yet been given due attention [5] was summed up by him thus: 'To act collectively is according to the spirit of our institutions.' The context of that remark in *Walden* is where he is maintaining that the community is responsible for providing a more adequate cultural life, good libraries, distinguished lecturers at the lyceums, encouragement for the practice of all the arts. He was as opposed to private hoarding of our spiritual resources as he was to the lust for ownership in our rapacious economy. He believed that all great values should be as public as light.

In estimating his particular value to our culture, I do not want to be deflected any further into appraising the vigorous paradoxes of his social thought. For it is my contention that we can judge his contribution most adequately if we heed his single remark, 'My work is writing,' and come

4. Cf. Alcott's characterization of him in 1851: 'This man is the independent of independents—is, indeed, the sole signer of the Declaration, and a Revolution in himself—a more than '76—having got beyond the signing to the doing it out fully.'

5. It has been emphasized, however, by Lewis Mumford in *The Golden Day,* and by Max Lerner in his article on Thoreau in the *Encyclopedia of the Social Sciences.*

to *what* he created through examining his own *process of creation*. Not that he ever thought of himself as a stylist in search of material, which he could then work up. His conception was just the reverse. He believed that the best works of art spring out of man's struggle for freedom, out of the effort to apprehend and control the forces that shape his life. In that spirit he turned, as did Whitman, to the open road of untried experience. But he was much more of a craftsman than Whitman, much more aware of the necessity of sacrificing himself to the work to be performed. In fact he came to realize, when occupied with *Walden,* that no 'valuable work' is accomplished except 'at the expense of a life.'

Emerson's consciousness of the exceptional accord of Thoreau's main convictions with his own may have caused him to envisage this other character too completely in his own image. Certainly it was natural for him to remark in 1841, when the younger man, only four years out of college, seemed to others also to be unreservedly his disciple: 'I told Henry Thoreau that his freedom is in the form, but he does not disclose new matter. I am very familiar with all his thoughts,—they are my own quite originally drest.' He was on less solid ground when he added: 'But if the question be, what new ideas he has thrown into circulation, he has not yet told what that is which he was created to say.' Thoreau's distinction was that he had few 'ideas.' In an era of theorizing run to seed, 'metaphysics was his aversion,' as his close friend Ellery Channing knew. 'Speculations on the special faculties of the mind, or whether the Not-Me comes out of the "I," or the All out of the infinite Nothing, he could not entertain.' What others were preaching he proved on his pulses, and when the implications of a doctrine were thus found to be true, he set himself to live them. But even the action became secondary. When he asked, 'How can we expect a harvest of thought who have not had a seed time of character?' he indicated what he wanted to garner. Emerson could foresee the value of that harvest right at the outset, in another notation in his journal for 1841, which does not mention Thoreau by name but seems to have full bearing upon him: 'What you owe to me—you will vary the phrase—but I shall still recognize my thought. But what you say from the same idea, will have to me also the expected unexpectedness which belongs to every new work of Nature.'

But in his final estimate, in the percipient and generous tribute at Thoreau's death, he did him one disservice. He was not really concerned with what Thoreau had written but with what he had done, and, in the one note of disappointment, with what he had failed to do. Emerson still visualized him in the guise of his own scholar in action, and could therefore regret that he had not turned his rare powers of 'energy and practical ability' to great enterprise and command. He could not help 'counting it a fault in him that he had no ambition. Wanting this, instead of engineering for all America, he was the captain of a huckleberry-party. Pounding beans is good to the end of pounding empires one of these days; but if, at the end of years, it is still only beans!'

With our understanding of the role played by even the most constructive of the empire-builders, we are less likely to believe that Thoreau's talents could have been spent valuably among them. Emerson had written the first draft of that observation eleven years before Thoreau's death, even three years before the appearance of *Walden,* which may help to account for his failure to concentrate squarely on the fact that here, among all his followers, was the rare artist for whom he had been looking. Emerson had said of himself: 'I am a natural reader, and only a writer in the absence of natural writers. In a true time, I should never have written.' This was not the case with Thoreau, as he grasped very soon in his career. The fourteen years' difference in age between the two meant that Thoreau could come immediately into his birthright. He was not faced with the necessity of the long anxious search, or with the struggle to crystallize his assumptions, or to determine his proper vocation. The fruits of the New England renaissance were already ripening. When *Nature* appeared at the opening of his senior year at Harvard, he could start at once to build his life upon it. His Commencement part, delivered two weeks before Emerson's Phi Beta Kappa Address, already developed the theme that 'the characteristic of our epoch is perfect freedom,—freedom of thought and action.'

The one thing that Thoreau said he got from college was the ability to express himself. He wrote essays for Edward Channing, who had been appointed Boylston Professor in Emerson's senior year, and whose sensitive concern was no longer with the formal ornaments of oratory, but with a clear and natural style. It must be added, however, that another requirement of the college, that of 'Forensics,' the preparation and support of an arbitrary side of a question, probably encouraged Thoreau in his wilful habit of contrast and strained paradox. Many of his essays have been preserved,[6] and display, as in the title of one of them—'The Ways in which a Man's Style may be said to offend against Simplicity'— the tenor of Channing's teaching, and the degree to which Thoreau responded to it in his mastery of firm construction.

Beyond that they contain few traces of his later style, but are none the less significant as a guide for his maturing convictions. An essay on the use 'of Keeping a private Journal' seems to borrow from Bacon's sententious method and backs up its conclusions with a citation from him, conclusions that had become the correct ones for Thoreau's era—the importance of a record of spontaneous thoughts, the growth that can come only through self-scrutiny and self-expression. A 'forensic' maintaining that an author's nationality and individual genius may be fully manifested in a work on a foreign or ancient subject asserts the centrality of man—'Shakespeare is Shakespeare, whether at home or abroad.' But Thoreau's essential feeling seems to emerge at the end of an essay he wrote a few months before the appearance of *Nature*, on 'Advantages and Disadvantages of Foreign Influence on American Literature.' Here he affirms the need for more independence, and his words vibrate for the first time with his own tone when he protests that his countrymen are still 'prone to sing of skylarks and nightingales, perched on hedges, to the neglect of the homely robin redbreast, and the straggling rail-fence of their own native land.'

Thoreau had doubtless met Emerson before he returned to Concord after graduating, but their close acquaintance dates from that year. It was not long before Emerson was speaking proudly of his young friend as *'the* man of Concord.' Thoreau also began his journal in the fall after he left college, and opened it thus: ' "What are you doing now?" he asked. "Do you keep a journal?" So I make my first entry to-day.' But although that journal was sometimes to run to three thousand words a day, and was to be in the end considerably longer than Emerson's, it does not often enable us to mark the definite moments of Thoreau's resolutions. Unlike Emerson, he was not much given to that kind of analysis. It may be that he was hardly even aware of when he reached the decision to be a writer, and to support himself by whatever odd jobs were at hand. But within the next year or two he had grown impalpably to realize that he had no other purpose for his life than making its meaning articulate

6. F. B. Sanborn printed selections from twenty-seven of them in the final (1917) edition of his biography.

in words. The launching of *The Dial* in 1840 gave him his first channel for publication, and, to judge from the widening variety of his journal at just that time, acted also as an important stimulant to his development. The composition of most of his small sheaf of poems dates within its first year; and it was soon to include such solidly characteristic essays as his 'Natural History of Massachusetts' (1842) and 'A Winter Walk' (1843). The scope of his aims can be suggested by the most ambitious piece of work that he submitted to its pages, 'The Service,' an earlier essay that it rejected.

2. What Music Shall We Have?

'Talk about learning our *letters* and being *literate!* Why, the roots of *letters* are *things*. Natural objects and phenomena are the original symbols or types which express our thoughts and feelings; and yet American scholars, having little or no root in the soil, commonly strive with all their might to confine themselves to the imported symbols alone. All the true growth and experience, the living speech, they would fain reject as "Americanisms." '

—Thoreau's *Journal* (1859)

"The Service"
(1840)

In this rejected essay (1840), he was trying his wings in the cloudy air of transcendental symbolism. Margaret Fuller found it 'rich in thoughts,' but protested that these thoughts were 'so out of their natural order' that it could not be read without pain. She agreed with Emerson that 'essays not to be compared with this have found their way into *The Dial.*' But those had been more unassuming in their tone; Thoreau's attempted so much that it needed to be 'commanding.' It was not printed during his lifetime, or until long after his death.[1] And certainly most of it provides evidence for Lowell's gibe that when Thoreau ejaculated, in the *Week*, 'Give me a sentence which no intelligence can understand,' he received a plentiful award.

Yet this essay is of cardinal value since it lets us follow the very process by which Thoreau found what he wanted to do with language. It has been suggested that the title, underscored by those of its first and

1. It was issued separately by Sanborn in 1902.

last sections, 'Qualities of the Recruit' and 'Not how Many, but where the Enemy are,' was the product of Thoreau's private reaction to current discourses on pacifism. The repeated imagery of a crusade seems borrowed from Tasso's *Jerusalem Delivered,* which had been one of his favorites in college, and whose hero Godfrey is cited here. However, the campaign that Thoreau urges is quite other. The first section sounds the theme, 'For an impenetrable shield, stand inside yourself.' The final pages are a trumpet blast to rouse the soul hovering on the verge of life, to call man not to action against others, but to the realization of his submerged potentialities. All such passages are what Emerson found in Thoreau at this time, simply Emerson's own thoughts originally dressed. But the middle section, 'What Music shall we have?' hints, if somewhat obscurely, at Thoreau's special qualities, and at the way by which he was to arrive at them. One of its sentences, 'A man's life should be a stately march to an unheard music,' may seem a vague enough acceptance of the romantic belief in such melodies. But it meant something compelling to Thoreau, since it became a recurrent image throughout his work. He varied it a decade later in his journal: 'It is not so much the music as the marching to the music that I feel.' He picked it up again in the conclusion to *Walden*: 'Let him step to the music which he hears, however measured or far away.' He obviously did not mean merely the disembodied harmony of thought, and it is worth trying to see upon what he grounded his image since it came to epitomize for him the relation between his life and his writing.

Rhythm

In 'The Service' Thoreau seems groping to convey his recognition, which was to grow increasingly acute, that a deep response to rhythm was his primary experience. He tried to develop it in this fashion: 'To the sensitive soul the Universe has her own fixed measure, which is its measure also, and as this, expressed in the regularity of its pulse, is inseparable from a healthy body, so is its healthiness dependent on the regularity of its rhythm.' The first statement is the usual transcendental doctrine of the merging of the individual with the Over-Soul; the remainder of the sentence, blurred as it is by its loose pronouns, still adumbrates what is going to be Thoreau's particular forte, his grasp of the close correspondence, the organic harmony between body and spirit. Emerson perceived this trenchantly when he said: 'The length of his walk uniformly made the length of his writing. If shut up in the house he did not write at all.' The context of the demand that Lowell mocked is nearly always forgotten: 'Give me a sentence which no intelligence can understand. There must be a kind of life and palpitation to it, and under its words a kind of blood must circulate forever.' Thoreau's first conviction about the artist was that his words should speak not to the mind alone but to the whole being. He made himself more explicit (1852) in this distinction between the thinker and the artist: 'Poetry *implies* the whole truth. Philosophy *expresses* a particle of it.' He said in the *Week* that 'a true account of the actual is the rarest poetry, for common sense always takes a hasty and superficial view'—a remark not far from the strictness upon which modern poets have again insisted. While still at college Thoreau had noted the Greek poets' 'appetite for visible images' in contrast to the tendency of the northern imagination to 'the dark and mysterious' and its consequent 'neglect of the material.'[2] His admiration continued to develop for the type of writer who 'was satisfied with giving an exact description of things as they appeared to him, and their effect upon him.' He found this ability pre-eminently in Homer, in the way he could convey the physical sensation of action: 'If his messengers repair but to the tent of Achilles, we do not wonder how they got there but accompany them step by step along the shore of the resounding sea.'[3]

Thoreau's emergence from the cloud-land of 'The Service' onto similar solid earth was due in large part to his having clung fast to his perception

2. The manuscript of Thoreau's review of H. N. Coleridge's *Introductions to the Study of the Greek Classic Poets,* dated October 1, 1836, is in the Huntington Library. This library also possesses, among much other Thoreau material, the entire manuscript of *Walden.*

3. Thoreau's convictions about the nature of art look forward to Hemingway's. Compare the sentences quoted in the paragraph above with Hemingway's suggested tests for determining the difference between reporting and creating: 'When you describe something that has happened that day the timeliness makes people see it in their own imagination. A month later that element of time is gone and your account would be flat and they would not see it in their minds nor remember it. But if you can make it up instead of describe it you can make it round and whole and solid and give it life. You create it, for good or bad. It is made, not described. It is just as true as the extent of your ability to make it and the knowledge you put into it.' (*Esquire,* October 1935.) Also: 'All good books are alike in that they are truer than if they had really happened and after you are finished reading one you will feel that all that happened to you and afterwards it all belongs to you: the good and the bad, the ecstasy, the remorse and sorrow, the people and the places and how the weather was. If you can get so you can give that to people, then you are a writer.' (*Esquire,* December 1934.) Despite his wide divergence in philosophy, T. E. Hulme would also have agreed with the core of these passages. They are in line with what he implied by saying that 'Plain speech is essentially inaccurate. It is only by new metaphors . . . that it can be made precise.'

feeling for
language

that both language and rhythm have a physical basis. His theory of language, in so far as he recorded one, seems at first glance to approximate Emerson's. He held that the origin of words is in nature ('Is it not as language that all natural objects affect the poet?') and that they are symbols of the spiritual. He spoke of the difficulty in finding the word that will exactly name and so release the thing. But he had a more dogged respect for the thing than any of his companions, and limitless tenacity in waiting to find the word. He remarked, for instance, how Channing called their walks along the banks of the river 'riparial excursions. It is a pleasing epithet, but I mistrust such, even as good as this, in which the mere name is so agreeable, as if it would ring hollow ere long; and rather the thing should make the true name poetic at last. Alcott wished me to name my book Sylvania!'

Thoreau knew that the farmer's lingo surpassed the scholar's labored sentences. He had a relish for old sayings and for rural slang, and set down many fragments of conversation with his friends the woodchoppers and the farmers.[4] He hated writers who did not speak out of a full experience but used 'torpid words, wooden or lifeless words, such words as "humanitary," which have a paralysis in their tails.' To those who think of him only as the extreme individualist it may come as a surprise to find that from the beginning of his career he asserted the social foundations of language: 'What men say is so sifted and obliged to approve itself as answering to a common want, that nothing absolutely frivolous obtains currency . . . The analogies of words are never whimsical and meaning-

4. Examples crop up everywhere in his journals. 'When it snowed yesterday very large flakes, an inch in diameter, Aunt said, "They are picking geese." This, it seems, is an old saying.' Thoreau's conversations with his friends Minott and Therien could be arranged into type-characters of the Farmer and of the Lumberman. Minott in particular provided Thoreau's journal with many fresh turns of phrase. For instance, 'I asked M. about the Cold Friday. He said, "It was plaguy cold; it stung like a wasp." ' Or again, Minott 'says that some call the stake-driver "belcher-squelcher," and some, "wollerkertoot." I used to call them "pump-er-gor." Some say "slug-toot." '

Everyday idioms found readier access into Thoreau's writing than into Emerson's. Still he seems to have responded involuntarily to the age's tendency to refine, for he made a few excisions even from Walden. For example, in the description of the teamster, near the opening of 'Economy,' he left out 'He rolls out of his cradle into a Tom and Jerry and goes at once to look after his team.' In 'What I lived for' he eliminated an even more characteristic Yankee colloquialism by dropping an instance of how 'our life is frittered away by detail.' The omitted sentence read: 'Its dish consists almost entirely of "fixings," and very little of the chicken's meat.'

less, but stand for real likenesses. Only the ethics of mankind, and not of any particular man, give point and vigor to our speech.'

Thus far nothing has really differentiated his position from what Emerson developed with much greater wealth of detail. But while discussing the primitive sense of words he made a remark that suggests what carried his practice such a considerable distance from his master's: 'We reason from our hands to our head.' Thoreau was not inclined to rate language as superior to other mediums of expression on the ground that it was produced solely by the mind and thence could share more directly in the ideal. On the contrary, he insisted upon its double parentage: 'A word which may be translated into every dialect, and suggests a truth to every mind, is the most perfect work of human art; and as it may be breathed and taken on our lips, and, as it were, become the product of our physical organs, as its sense is of our intellectual, it is the nearest to life itself.'

Deeds ....

According to Channing, in much that Thoreau wrote 'there was a *philological* side,—this needs to be thoughtfully considered.' He was always eager to probe roots and etymologies, and in some passages we can find him doing something more dynamic than that ordinarily amounts to. Even in a few notes on Latin terminations he dwelt on their closeness to physical life and revealed the kind of movement he wanted to catch in his own writing:

and words

This termination *cious* adds force to a word, like the lips of browsing creatures, which greedily collect what the jaw holds; as in the word 'tenacious' the first half represents the kind of jaw which holds, the last the lips which collect. It can only be pronounced by a certain opening and protruding of the lips; so 'avaricious.' These words express the sense of their simple roots with the addition, as it were, of a certain lip greediness . . . When these expressive words are used, the hearer gets something to chew upon . . . What is *luscious* is especially enjoyed by the lips. The mastiff-mouthed are tenacious. To be edacious and voracious is to be not nibbling and swallowing merely, but eating and swallowing while the lips are greedily collecting more food.

What separates Thoreau most from Emerson is his interest in the varied play of all his senses, not merely of the eye, a rare enough attribute in New England and important to dwell on since it is the crucial factor in accounting for the greater density of Thoreau's style. You think first, to be sure, of his Indian accuracy of sight that could measure distances like the surveyor's instrument and tell time almost to the minute by

Senses

the opening of the flowers. This alertness remained constant. Indeed, the last notation in his journal, before it was broken off by the consumption from which he died, considers the precise shape of some furrows made by the rain and concludes: 'All this is perfectly distinct to an observant eye, and yet could easily pass unnoticed by most.' But usually he felt that sight alone was too remote for the kind of knowledge he wanted, that 'we do not learn with the eyes; they introduce us, and we learn after by converse with things.' He held that scent was 'a more primitive inquisition,' 'more oracular and trustworthy.' It showed what was concealed from the other senses: by it he detected earthiness. Taste meant less to him, though eating became a kind of sacrament and out in the berry field he could be thrilled to think that he owed a perception to this 'commonly gross sense,' that he had been inspired through the palate. Just what he implied by that needs a longer declaration: 'Let not your life be wholly without an object, though it be only to ascertain the flavor of a cranberry, for it will not be only the quality of an insignificant berry that you will have tasted, but the flavor of your life to that extent, and it will be such a sauce as no wealth can buy.' Even in this fragile instance we can see his determination never to record an abstraction, but to give himself and his reader the full impression of the event.

He became ecstatic as he talked about touch: 'My body is all sentient. As I go here or there, I am tickled by this or that I come in contact with, as if I touched the wires of a battery.' He knew, like Anteus, that his strength derived from ever renewed contact with the earth. But he wanted more than contact with nature, he wanted the deepest immersion, and his delight mounted at being drenched in the summer waters of the pond, or when he could wonder whether 'any Roman emperor ever indulged in such luxury as . . . walking up and down a river in torrid weather with only a hat on to shade the head.' But as his preoccupation in 'The Service' has told us, he gave his most rapt attention to sounds. These alone among his sense impressions were to have a chapter devoted to them in *Walden*. He can hardly find enough verbs of action to describe what they do to him. They melt and flow, and he feels himself bathed in their surge. The sharp scream of the jay rasps at him like steel; the first faint peep of the hyla leaks into his ear. The liquid notes of a bobolink are as refreshing 'as the first distant tinkling and gurgling of a rill to a thirsty man.' On hearing an Italian boy with his hand organ, he expresses an intensity of pleasure equal to what Whitman felt in the

opera: 'these delicious harmonies tear me to pieces while they charm me.'
The most exquisite flavor is not to be compared to the sweetness of the
note of the wood thrush. As he listens, it seems to take him out of himself: he leaves his body in a trance and has the freedom of all nature.
After such an experience he can say, measuring his words, 'The contact
of sound with a human ear whose hearing is pure and unimpaired is
coincident with an ecstasy.'

It is no wonder, therefore, that he often failed to convey what it meant
to him. One of his earliest essays, parts of which he used in the closing
pages of the *Week,* was on 'Sound and Silence,' wherein he made an
impossible effort to catch the evanescent rippling of the one into the
other, and added the Carlylean reflection that so the most excellent speech
finally falls away into the perfect stillness that it has disturbed and intensified. He kept returning to the theme that 'there is all the romance of my
youthfulest moment in music. Heaven lies about us, as in our infancy.'
But the articulation of such a theme could quickly vaporize into an exaltation of the vague, which Thoreau's age so often identified with the
essence of music. He can carry us with him much more surely when he
talks of his simple joy in playing the flute, of how its echo lends detachment and so enchantment to his life. He has much to say about the good
cheap music of nature, the hum of insects, the booming of ice, the fall of
a distant tree, or the voice of a neighbor singing. He recounts the endless
excitement that the humming of the telegraph wire brought him. It is his
Aeolian harp, and reminds him of Anacreon and will make him read the
Greek poets again. It is the poetry of the railroad, the heroic thoughts
that the Irishmen had at their toil now given expression. The frequency
of his concern with it is extraordinary. He writes about it at length no
less than thirty times; and when in contrast he says that 'one will lose no
music by not attending the oratorios and operas,' and that only in proportion as a man has a poor ear for music must he go to art for it, we are
faced, as so often in Thoreau, with the odd balance between the poverty
of the materials of his experience and the fertility of his resource.

He himself had no doubts on this score, either for his life or for his art:
'Men commonly exaggerate the theme . . . The theme is nothing, the life
is everything. All that interests the reader is the depth and intensity of
the life excited.' [5] He was therefore intent to study the exact evidence of

5. Again Thoreau approximates the kind of concentration Hulme has demanded:
'There are then two things to distinguish, first the particular faculty of mind to see things

his senses, since he believed that only through their concrete reports could he project his inner life. Sometimes he felt a danger involved in forming too exact habits of observation, for they could run to excess and yield him, instead of fresh knowledge, merely a flat repetition of what he already knew. His remedy for this was what he called a free 'sauntering of the eye.' The poetic knowledge he wanted would come only through something like Wordsworth's 'relaxed attention,' only if he was not a scientific naturalist, 'not prying, nor inquisitive, nor bent upon seeing things.' He described his desired attitude towards nature by calling it one of indirection, by repeating frequently that the most fruitful perception was 'with the unworn sides of your eye.' We remember Keats' delight in 'the sidelong glance,' and his feeling that his ripest intuitions came through indolence. Thus nonchalantly, almost unconsciously, Thoreau could catch the most familiar scene in new perspective, with possibilities hitherto untold to his direct scrutiny, and with a wholeness of impression that could give it composition in writing.

It is true that in the later volumes of the journals, increasingly in the years after *Walden,* he felt that his senses were less buoyant than when he was young, that his moments of inspiration were much rarer, and that, in spite of himself, he was being narrowed to a round of external facts. This forces the question, which he would not admit, of whether he had not exhausted a too limited range of experience. Thoreau's own answer would be what Emerson's was when reflecting on the description of the telegraph wire in *Walden:* 'The sensibility is all . . . To prize sensibility, see the subjects of the poet; they were insignificant until he raised them.' And to the end, even in his most sterile moods, he could respond to such never stale melodies as those of the wood thrush, though he could not recapture quite this earlier pitch: 'Where was that strain mixed into which this world was dropped but as a lump of sugar to sweeten the draught? I would be drunk, drunk, drunk, dead drunk to this world with it forever.'

In that moment Thoreau approached Keats, but, in the act of mak-

as they really are, and apart from the conventional ways in which you have been trained to see them. This is itself rare enough in all consciousness. Second, the concentrated state of mind, the grip over oneself which is necessary in the actual expression of what one sees. To prevent one falling into the conventional curves of ingrained technique, to hold on through infinite detail and trouble to the exact curve you want. Wherever you get this sincerity, you get the fundamental quality of good art without dragging in infinite or serious.'

ing the comparison, you recall that Thoreau's idea of luxury was to stand up to his chin in a retired swamp and be saturated with its summer juices. This man, who, unlike Whitman, hated to lie with the sun on his back, was constant in his dislike of sensuality. His desire was for 'no higher heaven than the pure senses can furnish, a *purely* sensuous life.' The double suggestion here of the need for clarified perception and of the vision into which it could lead him brings out the mystical element that always remained part of his experience. Yet even when he was swept beyond his moments of physical sensation he did not forget his debt to them. The triumphal strains to which he was set marching in 'The Service' were not a nebulous fancy. They were the imaginative transformation of a rhythm he had actually heard and which he was trying to symbolize in words: 'In our lonely chambers at night we are thrilled by some far-off serenade within the mind, and seem to hear the clarion sound and clang of corselet and buckler from many a silent hamlet of the soul, though actually it may be but the rattling of some farmer's waggon rolling to market against the morrow.'

The checkrein of his senses was what held even such a passage from gliding away into a romantic reverie of escape. Their vigilance constituted his chief asset as an artist. It brought his pages out of the fog into the sunlight in which he wanted them to be read. He came near to defining his own ideal of style when he objected to DeQuincey's as too diffuse and flowing in detail, not sufficiently 'concentrated and nutty.' What he wanted were 'sentences which suggest far more than they say, which have an atmosphere about them, which do not merely report an old, but make a new, impression; sentences which suggest as many things and are as durable as a Roman aqueduct.' These lines tend to soar beyond bounds, until their swaying looseness is fortunately given ballast by the concluding example. If Thoreau at his best achieved weight and permanence, it was because he was always being called back from thoughts to the miracle of surfaces, because he lived up to his resolve: 'Whatever things I perceive with my entire man, those let me record, and it will be poetry. The sounds which I hear with the consent and coincidence of all my senses, these are significant and musical; at least, they only are heard.'

His remarks about music all lead to this point. He is never really talking about the art of music, of which he knew next to nothing, but about this close co-ordination, which alone made him feel that his pulse was beating in unison with the pulse of nature and that he could therefore reproduce it in words. By this analogy of the pulses he also emphasized the fact that resilient rhythm comes only from restfulness. And so he preached a gospel of leisure to Yankees, telling them that 'the truly efficient laborer will not crowd his day with work, but will saunter to his task, surrounded by a wide halo of ease.' Agreeing with Emerson that the poet's work needs 'a frolic health,' he understood much more intimately how style is based on physical aplomb. He had learned by the time he was twenty-two that 'the wise man . . . abides there where he is, as some walkers actually rest the whole body at each step, while others never relax the muscles of the leg till the accumulated fatigue obliges them to stop short.' Melville was to master the same thing from his experience: 'To ensure the greatest efficiency in the dart, the harpooners of this world must start to their feet from out of idleness, and not from out of toil.'

3. Thinking in Images

'Her pure, and eloquent blood
Spoke in her cheeks, and so distinctly wrought
That one might almost say, her body thought.'
—DONNE

IN SPITE of his keenness in scrutinizing the reports of his senses, Thoreau remained wholly the child of his age in regarding the material world as a symbol of the spiritual. He who held that 'the poet writes the history of his body' declared in another mood that 'poetry is the mysticism of mankind.' He could even contradict his enunciation that it was not the subject but the roundness of treatment that mattered, by saying that 'a higher truth, though only dimly hinted at, thrills us more than a lower expressed.' He stated early and kept repeating that he was ever in pursuit of the ineffable: 'The other world is all my art; my pencils will draw no other; my jack-knife will cut nothing else; I do not use it as a means.'

Yet even in that affirmation of faith Thoreau does not disappear into the usual transcendental vapor.[1] He gives us the sense that he is a man

---

1. Consider by contrast the record of one of Alcott's periods of illumination: 'And this seems to be our Apotheosis. Shall we name fitlier by another name what we see and feel

whose grip remains firm on this world as well, whose hand can manage both his knife and his pencil. In fact, Thoreau's success as an artist is exactly in proportion to such balance between means and end. On the occasions when he attempts a direct approach to his end, when, that is to say, he voices his bare thoughts, as in his pages on ideal friendship, his mind is revealed as much less capacious and less elastic than Emerson's. On the other hand, when he simply heaps up facts, as in the later volumes of his journal, he himself recognizes that facts so stated are parched, that they 'must be the vehicle of some humanity in order to interest us,' that they 'must be warm, moist, incarnated—have been breathed on at least. A man has not seen a thing who has not felt it.' This is to remark again that Thoreau was not specially equipped either for abstract theorizing or for strictly scientific observation. But when he could base theory on his own sturdy practice, as in 'Life Without Principle' or 'Civil Disobedience,' the impact of his humanity was dynamic. And when, as a writer, he could fuse his thought and his observation by means of a symbol, which was not just suggested but designed in sharp detail, he was able, in Coleridge's phrase, to 'elicit truth as at a flash.'

Thoreau's own description of his most fertile process, in the chapter 2, 'What I lived for,' is that 'we are able to apprehend at all what is sublime and noble only by the perpetual instilling and drenching of the reality that surrounds us.' The gerunds are characteristic, drawn from verbs of touch that penetrate to his inner being. They show the kind of fusion he could make by training into his writing the alertness of his senses. A passage from the Week will instance this fusion further, and will reveal the degree to which he could practice his theory. He introduced some

as Ourselves? For now the mysterious meters and scales and planes are opened to us, and we view wonderingly the Crimson Tablets and report of them all the day long. It is no longer Many but One with us . . . I am drawn on by enchantment, and seem taking the leaves of the tree of life there plucked for me, and to sojourn I know not whither through regions of spirit—some Atlantides, perhaps, of the Mind and Seats of the Blessed . . .' Alcott's words betray themselves at once by their stock 'literary' echoes, by the looseness and abstractness that fail to convey the impression of a thing clearly seen or wholly experienced. In mystical literature, no less than in other types, the manner of writing is organically dependent upon the strength and lucidity of the vision. The concrete firmness of an Edwards or a Woolman even in communicating what lies beyond the senses is one indication of what the transcendentalist lost by giving up the modes of traditional piety in order to assert the divineness of himself. One thing that saved Thoreau was his awareness of the shift in the object of his worship. As he said in his Sunday morning service on the Concord, 'of all the gods of New England and of ancient Greece,' he was perhaps most constant at the shrine of Pan.

entries from the account book of an old Concord fisherman, whose occupation was gone when the shad were blocked out by the factory dams.
These entries ran mostly to the daily purchase of 'rum and sugar, sugar
and rum, N. E. and W. I., "one cod line," "one brown mug," and "a line
for the seine"; rum and sugar, sugar and rum . . . Rather a preponderance of the fluid elements; but such is the fisherman's nature. I can faintly
remember to have seen this same fisher in my earliest youth, still as near
the river as he could get, with uncertain, undulatory step, after so many
things had gone down-stream, swinging a scythe in the meadow, his
bottle like a serpent hid in the grass; himself as yet not cut down by the
Great Mower.'

The rhythm is a clear instance of what Thoreau meant by saying that
it was not so much the music as the marching to the music that he felt.
For here, as in many other typical passages, his eye is reinforced not by
varied sounds so much as by impressions of movement and of muscular
pressure. He catches the step of the fisher in unison with the sweep of
his scythe, though the word 'undulatory' blends too with the flow of the
river, merging the old man as closely as possible with the source of his
former pleasures. In that fashion Thoreau projected his conception of
the harmonious interaction between man and nature, without which he
did not believe that man could be adequately described.

But the river in which so many things have gone down stream is also
that of the fisherman's throat, of his drunken life, the disintegration of
which Thoreau conveys entirely in concrete terms, each suggesting a
significance beyond itself. The snake that the old man might encounter
while mowing is likewise that of his temptation; and his own figure with
its scythe calls up that of Time. The final metaphor may seem too literary,
the romantic stock-in-trade. Along with Thoreau's fondness for his whimsical pun on 'fluid,' it may be the kind of thing Carlyle objected to when
he called the *Week* 'too Jean Paulish.' However, 'the Great Mower' saves
itself, at least to a degree that most of Richter's self-conscious fancies do
not, by the fact that it has not been lugged in arbitrarily. It has grown
integrally out of the context, and that lends some freshness to it.

The organic structure of Thoreau's symbols became more marked in
Walden, as in the laconic: 'Having each some shingles of thought well
dried, we sat and whittled them, trying our knives, and admiring the
clear yellowish grain of the pumpkin pine.' The deft telescoping of sense
impression and thought allows full play to both. We can share in the

relish of what he has seen, since his delicate skill has evoked the very look of the wood at the moment of being cut into. But the desultory act of whittling becomes also the appropriate image for conversation between Alcott and Thoreau around the winter hearth in Thoreau's hut. The single sentence gives a condensed dramatic scene, the very way these two friends appeared while trying their minds on thoughts 'well dried' by use; and, in this case, Thoreau's double meaning is pungent, since it frees the air of the suspicion of solemnness that might be there without it.

A more extended example of thinking in images is the best-known passage in the book, the core of his declaration of purpose:

> I went to the woods because I wished to live deliberately, to front only the essential facts of life, and see if I could not learn what it had to teach, and not, when I came to die, discover that I had not lived. I did not wish to live what was not life, living is so dear; nor did I wish to practise resignation, unless it was quite necessary. I wanted to live deep and suck out all the marrow of life, to live so sturdily and Spartan-like as to put to rout all that was not life, to cut a broad swath and shave close, to drive life into a corner, and reduce it to its lowest terms, and, if it proved to be mean, why then to get the whole and genuine meanness of it, and publish its meanness to the world; or if it were sublime, to know it by experience, and be able to give a true account of it in my next excursion.

The measured pace seems in exact correspondence with his carefully measured thoughts, and serves, as effective rhythm always does, to direct the fullest attention to the most important words. The satisfaction that we have seen him taking in the feel of syllables in the muscles of his mouth and throat is carried across to us by the placing of 'deliberately': as the first long word in the sentence, followed by a marked pause, it compels us to speak it as slowly as possible, and thus to take in its full weight: deliberate = *de + librare,* to weigh. A kindred desire to bring out the closest possible relation between the sense of a word and its sound seems to operate in his placing of 'resignation,' for again the pause emphasizes its heavy finality. A clearer instance of his 'philological' interest is the pun on 'dear,' which is not distracting since its basic sense of 'beloved' is no less relevant than its transferred sense of 'expensive.' Hence it encompasses something of what Coleridge praised in the puns of the Elizabethans, a compressed and thereby heightened variety.

But the chief source of power here seems to lie in the verbs of action: 'front,' barer than the more usual 'confront,' is also more muscular.

Behind Thoreau's use of it is his conviction that the only frontier is where a man fronts a fact. The extension of its range is reserved for the third sentence, where his metaphors shift rapidly but not in a way to interfere with one another, not until each has released its condensed charge. For the primitive act of sucking out the marrow is not incompatible with the military image, appropriate to this Spartan intensity, of putting to rout life's adversaries. And as the campaign returns from the enemy to the pursuit of the essence, both the range and pressure of Thoreau's desire are given fuller statement by the widened image of harvesting and the contracted image of closing in on a hunted quarry. With that final dramatic concentration, we are able to feel what it would really mean to reduce life to its lowest terms. The phrase is no longer a conventional counter since we have arrived at it through a succession of severe and exhilarating kinesthetic tensions. After which a characteristic turn for Thoreau is not to leave the impression of anything grim, but, by mentioning his 'next excursion,' to suggest its relaxed pleasure.

Wholeness

By this method of presenting an experience instead of stating an abstraction, Thoreau himself has elucidated both the meaning and the value of his long preoccupation with 'wholeness.' From the time he announced in 'The Service' that 'the exploit of a brave life consists in its momentary completeness,' he continued to make brief definitions of that quality, and of how it might be gained. These have direct bearing on the skill he had mastered in such passages as have just been discussed. The year after 'The Service' he developed his sentence further: 'The best and bravest deed is that which the whole man—heart, lungs, hands, fingers, and toes—at any time prompts . . . This is the meaning of integrity; this is to be an integer, and not a fraction.' He subsequently shifted his symbols to correspond to his own mode of existence, and grouped them not around the warrior hero but around the scholar, who, if he is wise, 'will confine the observations of his mind as closely as possible to the experience or life of his senses. His thought must live with and be inspired with the life of the body . . . Dwell as near as possible to the channel in which your life flows.' In this respect more than in any other was the practice of Thoreau's scholar more thoroughgoing than Emerson's. He never wavered in his belief that 'steady labor with the hands, which engrosses the attention also, is unquestionably the best method of removing palaver and sentimentality out of one's style, both of speaking and writing.' Emerson also advocated work in the garden as a sanative balance for the thinker, but neither his temperament nor muscles were geared to it, as his small son observed when he shouted, 'Papa, I am afraid you will dig your leg.' Nor did these efforts serve to steady and release his skill in writing; like Hawthorne at Brook Farm, he merely found his energies exhausted by them.

But for Thoreau, as for Robert Frost, this gospel was a living act. The root of his hatred of the division of labor was that it destroyed the potential balance of his agrarian world, one of the main ideals of which was the union of labor and culture. As Dr. Channing said, 'I wish to see labor honored and united with the free development of the intellect and heart. Mr. Alcott, hiring himself out for day labor, and at the same time living in a region of high thought, is perhaps the most interesting object in our commonwealth. I do not care much for Orpheus in *The Dial*, but Orpheus at the plow is after my own heart.' Although Channing's enthusiasm might have cooled if he had watched Orpheus neglect the plow for conversations at Fruitlands,[2] his general position was subscribed to on every hand. As Julian Hawthorne said of the world to which his father and mother had belonged, 'The seed of democracy was bearing its first and (so far) its sweetest and most delicate fruit. Men and women of high refinement, education, and sensibilities thought it no derogation, not only to work for their living, but to tend a counter, sweep a room, or labor in the field.' But what might be accepted as a sensible necessity by some and degenerate into a monotonous routine for others was hailed by Thoreau. He always insisted that 'men should not labor foolishly like brutes, but the brain and the body should always, or as much as possible, work and rest together.' That doctrine merges with what he wanted his rhythm to possess, the concentration that rises out of repose. Only by such unity of experience might his speech be 'vascular.' He developed his physiological analogy when, playing with the old notion of the bowels as the seat of compassion and tenderness, he said that poetry must not pass through them alone lest it become 'mere diarrhoea.' The poet 'must have

2. Yet to be fair to Alcott it should be added that however perversely his actual ventures might turn out, he still believed, when sixty, that it was his good fortune to have been 'born in the country and brought up in the arts of husbandry under the eye of a skillful farmer, who gave me early to my hands and the uses of tools, so that from a child I have known what to do with them . . . I came as naturally to the spade, the plow, the scythe and sickle as to book and pen.' That early training may have been the reason why he was a pioneer in education through his insistence that it was necessary to develop children's bodies as well as their minds.

something pass his brain and heart and bowels, too, it may be, all to-gether.'

Such a violent analogy was necessary to startle his contemporaries out of their complacent dreaminess. Ellery Channing, irritated that Thoreau jotted down notes on their walks, said petulantly, 'I am universal; I have nothing to do with the particular and definite.' But Thoreau's answer was that he also wanted to record something beside details: 'Facts which the mind perceived, thoughts which the body thought,—with these I deal.' There could hardly be a better definition of the way whereby he spanned the gap between the idea and the object. This power to unite thought with sense impression, the immediate feeling with the reflection upon it, is what Eliot has discerned to be the distinguishing attribute of the English metaphysical poets, and has called—in a term now somewhat worn by his followers but still indispensable for its accuracy—their 'unified sensibility.' One of the analogies by which he defined this quality is as explosively physical as Thoreau's. The seventeenth-century writers knew that it was not enough to 'look in your heart and write.' 'Donne looked into a good deal more than the heart. One must look into the cerebral cortex, the nervous system, and the digestive tracts.'

There are not many points of contact between Thoreau and Eliot. But it belongs to the New England heritage of both to insist upon integrity; and each found one of the strongest reinforcements of his own aims in the seventeenth-century strain. Thoreau's most cogent application of Donne was when he rounded again (1859) upon his perennial theme: 'A man thinks as well through his legs and arms as his brain . . . The poet's words are, "You would almost say the body thought!" I quite say it.'

By following the course of Thoreau's own observations on language and rhythm in relation to sense experience, I have tried to define the distinctive qualities of his style. But these raise wider questions. His kinship with the seventeenth century is not a coincidence. His repeated affirmation of the organic correspondence between art and nature is not an analogy peculiar to Emerson and himself. By investigating the reasons why not only Thoreau but Melville felt as close to the work of Sir Thomas Browne as to that of their own contemporaries, we can hope to understand better the sources from which our mid-century renaissance sprang, and also to understand why we have felt again to-day the vitality

of the seventeenth-century tradition. By examining 'the organic principle' as it was understood by Coleridge, we can apprehend a major theory
of art, the theory that conditioned *Leaves of Grass* no less than *Walden,*
and that leads directly into modern functionalism. In the next two chapters, therefore, we shall be engaged in related experiments. In the first
of these we shall be concerned with appraising the art of Emerson's day
through what its writers valued most in the art of the past. In the second
we shall examine what these writers meant by the correspondence of art
to nature, and why they found such a stimulus for fresh art in their
rediscovery of this fundamental relationship. The first should throw most
light on Thoreau and Melville and the twentieth-century rebirth of metaphysical poetry; the second, on Thoreau and Whitman and recent developments in our architecture and the arts of design. In both chapters
Emerson will be found to have played a crucial role through his consciousness of the values involved.

III

THE METAPHYSICAL STRAIN

1. Man Thinking

'We carry with us the wonders we seek without us: there is all Africa and her prodigies in us; we are that bold and adventurous piece of Nature, which he that studies wisely learns in a *compendium* what others labour at in a divided piece and endless volume.'—*Religio Medici*. This passage on 'the cosmography of myself' spoke to Coleridge of his 'own make of mind.' Thoreau copied it into the commonplace book that he kept at college.

In *The Seventeenth-Century Background* (1934) Basil Willey developed the proposition that for Sir Thomas Browne a fact 'was something to be felt as well as thought about,' that the different realms of his experience —of observation and of poetry, of judgment and of fancy, of science and of faith—were not sundered but so close together that he could pass freely from one to another and make use of all in each. To dramatize the point Willey quoted: 'Every fact lay in glory in his mind.' That remark was not originally made by Browne or about him. It was made by Emerson when elucidating how Thoreau was concerned not with the isolated detail in nature, but with the effect it left upon his sensibility, and how, as a result, every fact became 'a type of the order and beauty of the whole.'

Emerson was not thinking of the seventeenth century in this context, though, as we know, he recognized the pre-eminence of that age in 'keeping the truth at once to the senses and to the intellect.' The art of that period remained throughout his life the standard of excellence against which he judged the work of his own day. While still a divinity student he had wondered if it would not be impossible for any age soon to vie with that of Shakespeare and Herbert and Herrick, of Milton and Jonson and Marvell. Their work was 'the head of human poetry' for which he confessed an affectionate admiration such as he felt for no other. Ten years later (1838) he stated that this was the era 'in which the English language has its teeth and bones and muscles largest and strongest.' He developed these views in the chapter on 'Literature' in *English Traits* (1856), where he said that he could 'cite from the seventeenth century sentences and phrases of edge not to be matched in the nineteenth.' And when he came to select the anthology *Parnassus,* which he published in 1874, all his early favorites, among whom was also Donne, were generously represented.

Thoreau seems likewise to have used the same epoch as a criterion, for, according to his friend Sanborn, he had 'so high an opinion of Sir Thomas Browne that he told me in his last illness that he thought Emerson would stand, a century or two hence, as Browne did then, in the spring of 1862.' It may seem an odd coincidence that Longfellow, on returning from a lecture of Emerson's in 1846, wrote in his journal that he had heard 'the Chrysostom and Sir Thomas Browne of the day.' It becomes more than a coincidence, and evidence of the deep kinship that the age felt with the long buried modes of thought and feeling of the metaphysical strain, when we find Alcott writing in his journal (1847), 'I am often reminded of Sir Thomas Browne as well as of Quarles when reading Emerson, and this not because of any very striking resemblance of thought or diction but chiefly, I believe, from like tendency.' We then find Melville adding independently, after his first experience of hearing Emerson (1849), 'Lay it down that had not Sir Thomas Browne lived, Emerson would not have mystified.' They saw their representative man as a reincarnation. Coleridge, who had delighted in Browne's conjoining of 'a feeling heart' with 'a mind of active curiosity,' had already said that *Religio Medici* 'paints certain parts of my moral and intellectual being, (the best parts, no doubt,) better than any other book I have ever met with.'

Before we try to find out what Thoreau and Melville meant by their comparisons, it is important to discern what qualities were common to the various seventeenth-century authors who fed the New England renaissance. We are not concerned with examining a 'literary influence' in the sense in which that term has been deadened by scholarly misuse. The conventional assumption that you can find what produced a writer by studying earlier writers was refuted, long before the Ph.D. thesis was stillborn, by *The American Scholar*. Emerson knew that each age turns to particular authors of the past, not because of the authors but because of its own needs and preoccupations that those authors help make articulate. As Thoreau said, 'The researcher is more memorable than the re-searched.'[1] Yet the writers whom an age most admires provide a frame of reference against which its own contours can be sharply defined. In the case of Emerson and Thoreau, to be sure, several other such frames could be set up in addition to the seventeenth century. The bent of their thought and the divergences between them could be seen by tracing their relations to Oriental philosophy, by considering, for instance, the degree to which Emerson was accurate in identifying Brahma with his Over-Soul, Maya with Illusion, Karma with Compensation; and by noting that what Thoreau responded to in the same body of scripture was something quite other, not the mystical speculation but the challenge of the Yogi's ascetic way of life. It is significant that both these New Eng-landers had a particular fondness for the *Bhagvat-Geeta,* for its union of the gospels of action and contemplation. Again, the two could be placed and at least partially measured by their tastes in the classics, by Emerson's devotion to Plato as against Thoreau's more severe concern with the Greek language itself. Emerson was generally content with translations, since he felt that 'what is really best in any book' could be so conveyed, but Thoreau sought deliberately during his formative years for some of the clear Greek strength by translating Pindar and the whole of *Prometheus Bound.* The effect of this discipline appears in his most skill-ful poem, 'Smoke,' which Emerson thought suggestive of Simonides but better.

However, the seventeenth-century frame is of greatest relevance for the practice of their art. In reading Herbert or Browne they were affected not only by ideas, or by form as an abstract pattern, but also by qualities of their own language which the eighteenth century had allowed to decay, and which they were determined to renew. This does not imply that—for Emerson in particular—the chief attraction did not reside in the thought. He agreed with Carlyle that the eighteenth century had been unheroic because it had lacked the springs of faith. Emerson found what he most wanted in the Platonists of the century previous. In his inter-pretation of the history of philosophy, the decline from the great period of imaginative power, 'the influx of decomposition and of prose,' had

---

1. Cf. the corroboration from a distinguished classical scholar of the present, T. R. Glover: 'The scholar for whom all facts are of significance and all of equal significance, never understands anything, though Nature is kind to him and conceals from him that there is anything to understand.'

begun with Locke. Locke, 'to whom the meaning of ideas was unknown,' had become the new type of thinker, his 'understanding' the inadequate measure of intellect. In utter contrast stood the 'disciples of Plato' in the seventeenth century, and Emerson included the widest possible range in this category—Bacon as well as Henry More, Chapman along with Crashaw, Donne no less than Cudworth. However different one from another, their minds all were expansive in their creative generalizations, they 'loved analogy, were cognizant of resemblances, and climbers on the staircase of unity.'

Emerson's judgments are sweeping, but our concern is not with their inaccuracy, but with the image of himself that he believed he found mirrored in these 'idealists.' [2] In spite of his rejection of Calvinism he had kept more of the Puritan strain than he was quite aware, and it was no less characteristic of him than it was of Dr. Channing to feel a special veneration for Milton, who still remained the archetype of the poet for New England. Margaret Fuller went so far as to declare him 'more emphatically American than any author who has lived in the United States.' Whitman was to voice his dissent: 'Paradise Lost is offensive to modern science and intelligence—it is a poetical fanaticism with a few great strong features but not a great poem.' Nevertheless, its author's conception of the struggle between passion and reason remained an integral part of American ethics, as we shall be able to observe in Hawthorne's deep indebtedness to it, and in Melville's as late as Billy Budd. That is not to say that Milton's elaborate diction could be a model for any writer who had responded to Emerson's ideal of the closeness of style to daily speech. Still, Emerson did not make the sharp distinction between Milton and the metaphysical poets that we see to-day. But though he praised Milton for the sublimity of his eloquence, it was the Puritan's ideas, especially his devotion to liberty and to moral perfection, that formed the central theme in Emerson's essay about him (1838). When Emerson said that 'Human nature in these ages is indebted to him for its best portrait,' the traits he dwelt on were Milton's hope, self-reverence, piety, and delight in beauty. In contrast, Emerson went on to say, 'the man of Locke is

2. For example, in discussing Bacon, Emerson dwells on his duality, on his concern with the realm of ideas as well as with that of facts. Emerson's self-revelatory comment is, 'Bacon's perfect law of inquiry after truth was that nothing should be in the globe of matter which was not also in the globe of crystal; that is, nothing should take place as event in life which did not also exist as truth in the mind.'

virtuous without enthusiasm, and intelligent without poetry,' while 'Franklin's man is a frugal, inoffensive, thrifty citizen, but savors of nothing heroic.'

Even from such brief sketches of contrasting types we can see the basis for the description of transcendentalism as 'romanticism in a Puritan setting.' When an Emerson broke through the barriers of rationalism, he could not escape to the Middle Ages as could Keats and even Coleridge, for the long distrust of Catholic ritual was too deeply engrained in his background. Nor could he be quite at ease with the Elizabethans, for notwithstanding his devotion to Shakespeare, he could not help coming back to his suspicion of the theater, to his regret that the poet had spent his prodigious powers in being 'master of the revels to mankind.' Where Emerson felt really at home was with the 'English transcendental genius,' and, in the sentence where he uses that phrase, his examples are not his contemporaries but, once again, Herbert, Henry More, Donne, and Browne. The literature of that age was peculiarly his own tradition, since it gave expression to spiritual aspirations of which the settlement and early life of New England had been another manifestation. Looking back, Emerson made choices that reveal what he wanted to restore to his own age. He said that Herbert and Jeremy Taylor had mastered 'a beautiful mean, equi-distant from the hard, sour, iron Puritan on one side, and the empty negation of the Unitarian on the other.' Such a mean, he believed, could produce a richer harvest than any New England had yet enjoyed; and its growth did not seem unlikely since the seeds were imbedded in our heritage. With such convictions, it is natural that Emerson and Alcott and others of the *Dial* group, although they did not have any keener appreciation of individual seventeenth-century writers than Coleridge possessed, were yet more exclusive than he was in their concern with that period as the great age. It became a much more important ingredient in the composition both of their characters and of their art.[3]

3. The extent of New England's interest in even the less conspicuous figures can be suggested by such details as that James Marsh included, in his introduction to *Aids to Reflection*, long quotations from Henry More to reinforce Coleridge's argument; that among Theodore Parker's earliest publications was an essay on Cudworth in *The Christian Examiner* (1840); that Margaret Fuller wrote a dialogue in the Landor vein between George Herbert and Lord Herbert of Cherbury, the recluse and the man of the world; that Alcott's favorite poets included not only Donne but the whole metaphysical line down to Cowley, and that on one occasion when a contribution was expected from him for *The Dial*, he sent instead Henry More's 'Cupid's Conflict.'

Lowell remarked this fact and generalized on it in the sketch of the Yankee character with which he introduced *The Biglow Papers*. After dilating on this angular hybrid with its hitherto unheard-of combinations of 'mystic-practicalism,' 'calculating-fanaticism,' and 'sour-faced-humor,' he concluded:

Yet, after all, thin speculative Jonathan is more like the Englishman of two centuries ago than John Bull himself is. He has lost somewhat in solidity, has become fluent and adaptable, but more of the original groundwork of character remains. He feels more at home with Fulke Greville, Herbert of Cherbury, Quarles, George Herbert, and Browne, than with his modern English cousins. He is nearer than John, by at least a hundred years, to Naseby, Marston Moor, Worcester, and the time when, if ever, there were true Englishmen. John Bull has suffered the idea of the Invisible to be very much fattened out of him. Jonathan is conscious still that he lives in the world of the Unseen as well as of the Seen. To move John you must make your fulcrum of solid beef and pudding; an abstract idea will do for Jonathan.[4]

The primary reason why Emerson read these seventeenth-century writers appears in the use he made of one of his earliest enthusiasms among them, Cudworth's *True Intellectual System of the Universe*. That highly abstruse work probably gave him while an undergraduate his first introduction to Plato, and it served again as one of the precipitants for *Nature*. But, as he wrote later (1845), he knew of no book so difficult to read, for after handling it for years he had to confess that its method still remained 'a profound secret.' What he discovered in it was 'a magazine of quotations' from Platonism; or, as he had said in the year when he was writing *Nature*, 'an armory for a poet to furnish himself withal.' The kind of material from the book proper that must have appealed to him was its protest against Hobbes' atheistical refusal to allow reality to anything except the body, which was met by Cudworth's insistence that there

---

4. A significant twist in the New England reaction to metaphysical poetry is indicated by this passage in Harriet Beecher Stowe's *Oldtown Folks* (1869): 'Esther looked to me, from the first, less like a warm, breathing, impulsive woman, less like ordinary flesh and blood, than some half-spiritual organization, every particle of which was a thought.

'Old Dr. Donne says of such a woman, "One might almost say her body thought"; and it often came in my mind when I watched the movements of intense yet repressed intellect and emotion in Esther's face.' This etherealization, no part of Donne's original context, was repeatedly stressed by Hawthorne as he contrasted the solid Elizabethan women who had settled New England, with their nervous and spindling descendants in his own day.

is 'as much reality in fancy and consciousness as there is in local motion' —a belief integral to Emerson's idealism.

It happens that Thoreau, turning to this same book in 1840, also read it for the attitude it produced in him rather than for any communication of specific doctrine, on the ground that 'it is so rare to find a man musing.' Emerson rejoiced equally that Browne did not insist on practical use for his meditations but entertained them, as he declared, for 'variety and delight.' Such musing, which was very different from what utilitarian Yankees insisted on in their schools, alone could give release to 'Man Thinking.' The conception of the scholar implied in this phrase demanded the same wholeness that Emerson found to be the common denominator between the Cambridge Platonists and the metaphysical poets. This is what he meant by saying that they were all 'analogy-loving.' Coleridge admired Browne for the same thing: 'his entireness in every subject.'

Emerson was most interested by the complex analogy they made between man and nature through the theory of the microcosm and macrocosm. He seems to have meditated about this theory as early as 1830, for he copied then Aristotle's sentence, 'Man is a microcosm,' and followed it with passages from Donne and Daniel and Herbert, these lines among them:

> As man is of the world, the Heart of man
> Is an epitome of God's great book
> Of creatures, and men need no further look.
>
> He is in little all the sphere.
>
> Oh mighty love! man is one world, and hath
> Another to attend him.

What drew Emerson most to Renaissance individualism was its increased awareness of the self. He did not pay much attention to the elaborately worked-out parallels between man and the body politic, as, for instance, between the functions of his various organs and the hierarchical structure of functions for the different classes in the state. Indeed, such exact parallels between microcosm and macrocosm had been based on the Ptolemaic centrality of man in the universe and on the medieval conception of social order. This order, already breaking down for Donne, could exist for Emerson only as a remote imaginative stimulus from a time when the individual was more integrally a part of society, when the many were also one. What did speak to his own experience was what made him declare about Browne: 'How inward he is.' He took delight in the *Religio* as a record of self-observation, or as Browne said in its preface, 'a private Exercise directed to myself.' Emerson came even nearer to his own likeness to Browne when he quoted this sentence: 'The severe schools shall never laugh me out of the philosophy of Hermes, that this visible world is but a picture of the invisible.' There could hardly be an apter expression of Emerson's own doctrine that the universe is a system of symbolical correspondences, that nature is to be studied by the method of analogy and each fact to be read for its spiritual meaning.

These are the common properties that made so many of Emerson's contemporaries link him with Browne. If we may judge from the evidence of the journals, Emerson felt the attraction of similar ideas even more compellingly in Herbert, whose poem 'Man' expresses Emerson's own view that 'man is only a piece of the universe made alive.' He outlined in *Nature* the role of the naturalist who must investigate the 'wonderful congruity' subsisting between man and the world, and find 'something of himself . . . in every mountain stratum, in every new law of color, fact of astronomy, or atmospheric influence.' A great variety of seventeenth-century authors could have furnished the stimulus for this doctrine: for example, Vaughan, in his insistence on the real and not merely casual analogies between natural and spiritual laws; or John Smith, the Cambridge Platonist, in his regret that the new science was making a false separation 'between Metaphysical Truths and the Truths of Nature.' But to drive home his point Emerson felt that there was no better means than to give at length Herbert's poem, from which he had already quoted, half a dozen years before, to illustrate the theory of the microcosm. Or rather, he now gave the bulk of the poem but omitted the last stanza and thus concluded with some of his favorite lines:

> More servants wait on man
> Than he'll take notice of. In every path,
> He treads down that which doth befriend him
> When sickness makes him pale and wan.
> Oh mighty love! Man is one world, and hath
> Another to attend him.

What he left out was Herbert's characteristic Christian ending:

> Since then, my God, thou hast
> So brave a palace built; O dwell in it,
>   That it may dwell with thee at last!
>   Till then, afford us so much wit,
> That, as the world serves us, we may serve thee,
>   And both thy servants be.

Emerson broke off the quotation at just the point where he and Thoreau unconsciously parted company with the metaphysical strain. The close subordination of man to God, the desire of 'making humility lovely in the eyes of all men,' which animated Herbert's work, have little counterpart in Emerson's expansive purpose. He wanted to awaken his reader to the truth of the myth with which he almost immediately followed Herbert's lines, and which he said had been sung to him by an Orphic poet (perhaps an allusion to Alcott): 'A man is a god in ruins . . . the dwarf of himself. Once he was permeated and dissolved by spirit. He filled nature with his overflowing currents. Out from him sprang the sun and the moon; from man the sun, from woman the moon.' This imaginative myth of man as the creative center whose power must now again be renewed possesses some of the energy of Blake and of Lawrence; it is mystical, but no longer Christian.

Emerson's abandonment of the final link in Herbert's chain of values ordinarily gave his own lines a very different tone from that of the seventeenth century. How different can be heard by contrast in the one poem of his that was ever mistaken for Herbert's. This was the early 'Grace,' which W. H. Channing wanted to use among the epigraphs for their collaborative memoir of Margaret Fuller. To this Emerson answered: 'For your mottoes to your chapter, I saw that the first had the infinite honor done it of being quoted to Herbert! The verses are mine, —"Preventing God, etc."—so I strike them out.' The mistake was natural:

> How much, preventing God, how much I owe
> To the defences thou hast round me set;
> Example, custom, fear, occasion slow,—
> These scorned bondmen were my parapet.
> I dare not peep over this parapet
> To gauge with glance the roaring gulf below,
> The depths of sin to which I had descended,
> Had not these me against myself defended.

These lines pursue the same type of argument as does Herbert's 'Sin' from its opening proposition, 'Lord, with what care hast thou begirt us round.'[5] The tone of Emerson's verse is also suggestive of that in Milton's sonnet on his twenty-third birthday; and it is appropriate that Emerson should have written these lines inside the front cover of his copy of Milton's prose.[6] For the doctrine of 'Grace' is not that of 'Spiritual Laws' (1841), whose author dismissed the problem of original sin as 'the soul's mumps and measles'; it is that of the younger minister who still felt at times that there was an overwhelming preponderance of evil, and who could reflect on 'the terrible freedom' of the individual left to his own devices. Only such a state of mind could have produced the concentrated dramatic gravity of these lines. This attribute is Herbert's. It is naturally not to be found in the later Emerson, for whom man's dazzling potentiality quite obscured any necessity for struggle against evil or for dependence on God as a protection against himself.

Despite the comparisons that Emerson's contemporaries made, his typical emphasis is equally distant from Browne's. Even when their words are similar their implications are often at opposite poles. When Browne says, 'The world is now as it was in Ages past,' this does not cause him to reflect that 'the sun shines to-day also,' that man in the present need not be retrospective but can share immediately in the same splendor that previous eras knew. Browne's preoccupation is not with fresh beginnings, but with a declining world; not with the presentness of the past, but with the closeness of both to eternity. What Emerson himself noted in an early reading of *Hydriotaphia* applies substantially to all its author's work: it 'smells in every word of the sepulchre.' Even the sentence in *Religio Medici* that would seem to furnish the most exact description of the aims of both Emerson and Thoreau—'The world that I regard is my self; it is the Microcosm of my own frame that I cast mine eye on'—even this is greatly altered by its context. It follows directly after: 'For the World, I count it not an Inn, but an Hospital; and a place not to live, but to dye in.'

The reiterated weariness and solemn renunciation that rise continually

5. This was cited in Coleridge's *Aids,* under the title, 'Graces vouchsafed in a Christian Land.'

6. The connections with Milton were emphasized by G. R. Elliott (*New England Quarterly,* January 1929), who also pointed out that Emerson's verses are similar to passages in his journal during his European trip of 1832-3, when he was still in considerable uncertainty about the course of his life.

from Browne's absorption with mortality could have spoken to Thoreau even less than to Emerson. This lends an additional interest to examining Thoreau's paradoxical admiration for the author of the *Religio*. To be sure, Thoreau might with equal relevance be juxtaposed with Herbert, whose mark is so distinct upon the structure of his earliest poems, such as 'Sic Vita' or 'Friendship.'[7] But Thoreau's poems are relatively unimportant, and it is on his prose style that Browne left an enduring impression, and one more pervasive than upon Emerson's.

The precise grounds on which any authors appealed to Thoreau are more conjectural than in the case of Emerson, since Thoreau's comment was generally sparing. Yet there can be no doubt about the strong fascination that the seventeenth century held for him from the time he began to pack his undergraduate commonplace book with passages not only from Milton and Browne, but from Crashaw, Herrick, and Beaumont and Fletcher. When he started his journal, he headed it with mottoes from Herbert, Burton, and Marvell, the theme of all of them being condensed in the couplet he chose from 'The Garden':

> Two Paradises are in one,
> To live in Paradise alone.

Other minor favorites soon followed, Drummond and Giles and Phineas Fletcher; Carew whose verses on 'The Pretensions of Poverty' he cited at the opening of the chapter, 'Where I lived, and What I lived for'; and especially Quarles, whom he praised for pressing 'able-bodied and strong-backed words into his service, which have a certain rustic fragrance and force, as if now first devoted to literature after having served sincere and stern uses'—a more accurate statement of Thoreau's own desire than of Quarles'!

7. The opening lines of the former,

> I am a parcel of vain strivings tied
> By a chance bond together,

might make you think of Herbert, or equally of Vaughan's

> But I am sadly loose and stray
> A giddy blast each way.

Vaughan's particular conviction that nature possessed the steadiness and constancy which man so sadly lacked is also one of Thoreau's favorite themes. However, the chief likeness of Thoreau's angular stanzas to those of the seventeenth-century poets is that they are, as Alcott observed, 'vigorous and rugged enough to defy Quarles or Donne.'

The only seventeenth-century writer upon whom he wrote in detail was, oddly enough, Raleigh, whose courtly and sophisticated career would seem at first glance at the farthest remove from Thoreau's taste. But in the course of a fairly long essay, which he prepared originally as a Lyceum lecture, he cut through to common ground. He liked Raleigh's conception of the correspondence between man and the forces of the natural world; he liked his *History,* because it was written with the vivacity that could make the past seem present; but he was stirred most by the challenge of Raleigh's heroic character. We recall that seventeenth-century Puritans kept Raleigh's name alive as one of the great champions against monarchy; but what absorbed Thoreau's attention was the kinship between great writing and great action. As he developed this theme, he was not thinking primarily of the courageous soldier in the Tower who wrote because he had been prevented from further shaping his age; he was thinking of his own effort 'to make his words deeds.'

Concerning Browne, Thoreau commented no more than to say in the *Week:* 'That is a superfluous wonder, which Dr. Johnson expresses at the assertion of Sir Thomas Browne that "his life has been a miracle of thirty years, which to relate were not history but a piece of poetry, and would sound like a fable." The wonder is, rather, that all men do not assert as much.' It is hardly necessary to discuss further Browne's conception of the microcosm and its potential stimulus to Thoreau's doctrine of the individual's 'sphericity,' and to his habit of seeking the most profound laws of nature by contemplation of the smallest fact. As Browne put it, 'What Reason may not go to School to the wisdom of Bees, Ants, and Spiders?' Another of Browne's most infectious charms lay in his famous declaration, 'I love to lose my self in a mystery, to pursue my Reason to an *O altitudo!'* Therein Browne's eagerness to pass beyond the limitations of the understanding vibrates with the emotionalism of music, which, as we have seen, was Thoreau's most thrilling release. But Browne managed to combine knowledge with his wonder, to return from brooding on the 'wingy Mysteries' to weighing the facts, and this 'constant dualism,' which Paul Elmer More considered Browne's essential quality, was likewise inherently Thoreau's. His concern with both the visible world and the invisible, with the one as symbol of the other, could receive passionate support in what Browne called the 'delightful truths' of *The Garden of Cyrus*—the way in which images could suggest demonstrations and analogies could lead into principles.

Thoreau's ambition was to be, like Browne, present with undivided being in every subject he embraced; yet the wholeness that he achieved is quite different. Notwithstanding the enthusiastic response he could make to so many sentences in *Religio Medici,* his own attitude seems even farther from Browne's than Emerson's from Herbert's. Browne was a Christian, although his sustained stoic note was seldom relieved by spiritual joy. Thoreau is clearly not a Christian, and though Emerson called him 'a perfect piece of stoicism,' he felt no weariness of the world. He wanted simplicity in order that he might savor undistracted the luxury of his sensations. He did not 'propose to write an ode to dejection, but to brag as lustily as chanticleer,' if only to wake his neighbors up. In the broad use of the terms, he is much more of an epicurean than a stoic, and the exultant final sentences of *Walden* can remind us how far he was from any resignation: 'There is more day to dawn. The sun is but a morning star.'

The verses from Daniel that Thoreau quoted near the end of the *Week* were—according to Channing—perhaps more frequently on his lips than any other lines:

> Unless above himself he can
> Erect himself, how poor a thing is man.

These were also included among the passages that Emerson grouped under the heading, 'Man is a microcosm.' They had been used by Coleridge with 'above' italicized to illustrate one of his aphorisms in *Aids to Reflection.* What Coleridge thus emphasized was the poem's expression of the need for humility; for it still spoke in something of the spirit that actuated St. Bernard when he said, 'We must retire inward if we would ascend upward.' But the inwardness that Emerson and Thoreau read into Daniel's lines had changed to something looser, something perilously easy to confuse with their own impulse and will. They were no longer held in check by any religious dogma, and in their further revolt against the eighteenth-century conclusions concerning 'the weakness of human reason and the narrow limits to which it is confined,' they had been carried so far as to deny any limitations whatsoever to the mind's potentialities. When Thoreau quotes Daniel, it is not to urge subordination to anything outside himself. He has been describing the clouds as a backdrop for man's scene, and considers their beauty too rich for his customary poor acting, a challenge to play a more splendid role. This is not to forget that Thoreau can sometimes suggest some of Vaughan's radiance, as in his bare remark, 'Dreamed of purity last night.' Occasionally he states that 'what is peculiar in the life of a man consists not in his obedience, but his opposition, to his instincts,' that thus man strives 'to live a supernatural life.' Nevertheless, Mark Van Doren's stricture does not falsify the general pattern: 'The "spirit of fine expectancy" of the seventeenth-century poets would not have owned New England in 1850. Herbert's face was turned upward; Emerson's and Thoreau's faces inward. Herbert pleaded with God for vision; Emerson and Thoreau only pricked themselves perpetually on to further spiritual adventures.'

2. The Mingling of Walden and Ganges

THE ONE aspect of the seventeenth century that neither Emerson nor Thoreau had to modify or foreshorten to fit their own ends was the metaphysical poets' use of language. Nearly all Emerson's most productive suggestions about words sprang from his appreciation of the 'grip and exactitude of mind' which enabled the writers of the great period to do equal justice to both their sense impressions and their intellectual subtleties. He believed that 'this mental materialism makes the value of English transcendental genius,' since it resulted in the union of what he called 'Saxon precision' with 'Oriental soaring.' In lecturing on Herbert the year before he wrote *Nature,* he had already remarked that this poet's merit lay 'in his power of glorifying common and base objects,' by introducing homely images into the most sacred surroundings. Even though Emerson disliked Dr. Johnson's 'mutton-headed' definitions, he valued that of wit in the life of Cowley. For Emerson's perception of the value of the *discordia concors*—the yoking together of unlikes by a fresh and vigorous mind—was akin to that of the modern poets who have reclaimed some of the method of Donne.

You look in vain for sustained practice of that method by Emerson, though it is not hard to find occasional lines that echo earlier voices. The end of 'Hamatreya' calls up either Donne or Marvell:

> My avarice cooled
> Like lust in the chill of the grave.

Emerson's customary use of the four-beat line may have been influenced most by Marvell, for there are some resemblances in theme between 'Upon Appleton House'· and 'Woodnotes,' or 'The Garden' and 'May-Day.'[1] It is amusing, if hardly important, to conjecture that Donne may have provided the suggestion for that authentic metaphysical conceit, 'Hitch your waggon to a star.' For Emerson quoted in his journal this passage from one of Donne's sermons: 'Look so far towards your way to Heaven, as to the Firmament, and consider . . . there the star by which we sail and make great voyages.' Less conjectural is Emerson's adaption of Herbert's practice in scattering such conceits in *Nature* as 'this zodiac of lights, this tent of dropping clouds, this striped coat of climates, this fourfold year.' That is the metaphysicals' way of bringing the abstract down to earth. Browne's power to hold in solution different realms of his experience and to suggest one in terms of another was realized by Emerson most sensitively in the chapter in *Nature* on 'Beauty': 'Give me health and a day, and I will make the pomp of emperors ridiculous. The dawn is my Assyria; the sunset and moonrise my Paphos, and unimaginable realms of faerie; broad noon shall be my England of the senses and the understanding; the night shall be my Germany of mystic philosophy and dreams.' That has caught Browne's ability to take the familiar and to give it an unexpected outreach. Starting to celebrate the beauty of the near as superior to that of the remote, of the human average to that of the exceptional, Emerson has managed to give an epitome of the magnificent unity between present and past, to show how the cycle of the immediate day can encompass the whole range of thought.

But Emerson was not ordinarily able to compete with the metaphysicals 'in keeping the truth at once to the senses and to the intellect.' There are only occasional passages in either his prose or his verse that approach their intense concentration. We have already heard one reason for his failure in his confession, 'I am always insincere, as always knowing there are other moods.' Their greatest triumphs, as 'The Extasie' or 'To his Coy Mistress,' were owing to their recognition of latent contrasting feelings

1. The strain in Marvell that spoke to Emerson most directly was his delight in rural retirement:

> What Rome, Greece, Palestine, ere said
> I in this light Mosaick read.
> Thrice happy he who, not mistook,
> Hath read in Nature's mystick Book.

in every mood, and to the skill with which their verse could express
these complex states without sacrificing one kind of feeling in building
up another. To this end they had mastered principles of structure that
were almost architectural in the syllogistic firmness which allowed the
writer to pass from one proposition to the next, and thus to bridge the
gaps between shifting states of emotion. By contrast Emerson's poems can
hardly be said to have any structure at all. He could capture the surprise
of a moment, but he could hardly hold onto it long enough to suggest its
density: his moments of expression follow one another like rain drops
down a window pane, each iridescent and vibrant, but fugitive and blurring into the one before. Or, to follow his lead and shift the image, he
could pick up some of the stones that these earlier poets used, and handle
a few of their tools, but he could not build in their style. This inability
was not due merely to his lack of their cohesive rhetoric. The wholeness
of poetic structure for which they strove corresponded to their sense of
wholeness in the cosmic structure, a very different sense in the age of
the baroque from that in the age of individualistic protest.

Moreover, the tensions of their religious belief, their struggles between
doubt and acceptance, made their utterance dramatic where his was simply ejaculatory. Emily Dickinson's poems, because they have such tension,
are much more authentically in the metaphysical tradition than Emerson's are. Not, however, that many of his values were not hers also—especially where they concerned the integrity of the mind and the sufficiency
of inner resources. Moreover, her ideals of language, indeed her very
tricks of phrase, seem indistinguishable from those in one of his quatrains:

> To clothe the fiery thought
> In simple words succeeds,
> For still the craft of genius is
> To mask a king in weeds.

She does not have any of his range as a social critic, but her best
poems display an excruciated awareness of the matching of good against
evil, which was foreign to Emerson's temperament. Their compressed
form resulted from her need to resolve conflicts, and her conceits, unlike
many of his, do not dissipate in every direction, since they are subordinated to a central issue.

If Thoreau mastered the metaphysicals' union of abstract and concrete
far more effectively than Emerson, it was certainly not because of any

greater tendency to think in seventeenth-century terms about the relation of man either to God or to society. Even more for him than for Emerson, evil had become identifiable with external restraint, with whatever false barriers in society kept man from fully realizing himself. But it should be added that he did not think the battle was won with the removal of the barriers, since the individual must then train himself with 'the highest and finest discipline.' To that end, despite his sustained indifference to any theology, he wanted what he called 'a Puritan toughness.' He admired that quality so greatly that he spoke of John Brown as a typical Puritan who might have died in Cromwell's England and reappeared in nineteenth-century America. He felt most kinship for the earlier period in a group of writers to whom Emerson paid little attention, the first explorers and historians of New England. He did not read them for their stories as Hawthorne read Cotton Mather, but because, as he remarked in commenting on John Smith, these pages let him think himself 'in a wilder country and a little nearer to primitive times.' Quoting Bradford's unforgettable sentence on the coming of the first winter to the settlers at Plymouth—'For summer being ended, all things stood in appearance with a weather-beaten face'—Thoreau declared that we are to look 'for standard English' only in the words of a man who has such a depth of feeling; and that this language does not spring from those who gaze upon nature from the gentlemanly vista of a countryseat, but 'from the peasant's horn windows.' Bradford's words were as close to things as were those of Thoreau's friends the farmers Minott and Pratt. Bradford spoke of a gun being 'out of kilter,' just as they did, proving it an old phrase despite its omission from the dictionaries. Thoreau took an equal relish in the words of Josselyn's *Voyages* and Wood's *New England's Prospect*, because 'the strong new soil speaks through them.'

What fascinated him in the even earlier volume, Edward Topsell's *History of Four-footed Beasts* (1607), were such details as that the antelopes near the river Euphrates 'delight much to drink of the cold water thereof,' whereas the animals of most modern naturalists or those of the agricultural report 'do not *delight* in anything, and their water is neither hot nor cold.' Topsell really saw what he reported, though in making that statement Thoreau was perfectly aware that this book is a translation from Conrad Gesner, and that many of the beasts of the original had no existence save in the imagination of its writer. The important point is that 'they really have an existence there, which is saying not a little, for most of our modern authors have not imagined the actual beasts which they presume to describe.' That is the kind of paradox that delighted Thoreau, though he reserved his fullest praise for the first reporters on the American scene, for the curiosity that enabled them to be 'so sensitive and sympathetic to nature that they could be surprised by the ordinary events of life. It was an incessant miracle to them, and therefore gorgons and flying dragons were not incredible to them. The greatest and saddest defect is not credulity, but our habitual forgetfulness that our science is ignorance.'

In desiring to push as near as possible to the boundaries between the visible and the invisible, to reassert the primitive quality of wonder, Thoreau again approached Browne, though by a different route. Attention to the objects around him, not intricate speculation, furnished him with his best analogies. He could define his most fruitful process quite succinctly: 'Improve the opportunity to draw analogies; there are innumerable avenues to a perception of the truth. Improve the suggestion of each object, however humble, however slight and transient the provocation; what else is there to be improved?' He was nearest the practice of the seventeenth-century poets when he insisted on the use of *all* materials that experience affords; but his experience was less complex if no less concentrated than Donne's. It approximated that of the explorers in its excited immediacy of discovery, though what he wanted to discover was himself. His ability to do whatever he did with his whole being was the product of an awakened scrutiny, not, as for them, an unconscious response of minds that had never conceived any arbitrary gap between thought and feeling and so reacted with equal directness to physical and spiritual adventures. So Thoreau's pages are inevitably more literary, a mixture of the cultivated and the wild. Indeed, one of his chief distinctions—and again he shares this with Browne—is the infusion of his reading into his perception, as in the last paragraph of 'The Pond in Winter.' He has given a detailed account of the work of the ice company, which engaged in the export trade to the East Indies, and concludes:

Thus it appears that the sweltering inhabitants of Charleston and New Orleans, of Madras and Bombay and Calcutta, drink at my well. In the morning I bathe my intellect in the stupendous and cosmogonal philosophy of the Bhagvat-Geeta, since whose composition years of the gods have elapsed, and in comparison with which our modern world and its literature seem puny and trivial; and I doubt if that philosophy is not to be referred to a previous state of existence, so remote is its sublimity from our conceptions. I lay down the book and go to my well for water, and lo! there I meet the servant of the Bramin, priest of Brahma and Vishnu and Indra, who still sits in his temple on the Ganges reading the Vedas, or dwells at the root of a tree with his crust and water jug. I meet his servant come to draw water for his master, and our buckets as it were grate together in the same well. The pure Walden water is mingled with the sacred water of the Ganges. With favoring winds it is wafted past the site of the fabulous islands of Atlantis and the Hesperides, makes the periplus of Hanno, and, floating by Ternate and Tidore and the mouth of the Persian Gulf, melts in the tropic gales of the Indian seas, and is landed in ports of which Alexander only heard the names.

The places to which the ice is carried in the holds of ships carry his mind from Concord to the Orient, and the transition to its philosophy is sustained by turning the refreshing water into a metaphor. But having thus passed from the near to the remote, to a point so far distant both in space and time that his own world seems trivial, Thoreau prolongs his metaphor still farther and brings to the present a comparable magnificence. For the man who draws his living water from the well of the *Bhagvat-Geeta* possesses the same dignity irrespective of whether his image is reflected in Walden or Ganges. The waters have become mingled in a double experience: as the ships of the ice company complete their route around Africa, a further chapter in the history of transportation, in the conquest of space which has been progressing since the Renaissance, Thoreau also affirms his conquest—that of time—which can empower the provincial New Englander, while firmly rooted by his own green pond, to make the remote near, to embrace the richness of antiquity and also to land 'in ports of which Alexander only heard the names.'

Channing once called this passage 'mimicry' of Browne, and certainly the rhythmical succession of these splendid names recalls the almost hynotic charm of the concluding lines to *The Garden of Cyrus:*

Though Somnus in Homer be sent to rowse up Agamemnon, I finde no such effects in these drowsie approaches of sleep. To keep our eyes open longer were but to act our Antipodes. The Huntsmen are up in America, and they are already past their first sleep in Persia. But who can be drowsie at that howr which freed us from everlasting sleep? or have slumbring thoughts at that time, when sleep it self must end, and as some conjecture all shall awake again?

By looking at these passages together, you become aware that although Browne also circles vastly over space and time, his intention is the reverse from providing Thoreau's widening vista of opportunity. The solemn final cadence brings his reader back to meditation on death.

The passage from *Walden* is undoubtedly 'bookish,' as Whitman found all of Thoreau, but Browne's antiquarian reflections are generally even more so. Emerson caught Thoreau's special flavor when he described the forthcoming *Week* as 'a seven days voyage in as many chapters, pastoral as Izaak Walton, spicy as flagroot, broad and deep as Menu.' The criterion for such writing is not what Whitman demanded, the sense of being 'smack out of doors,' but whether the writer has been able to assimilate his reading with his experience and make a fresh combination. That the nineteenth-century vogue for Browne could result merely in imitation is more than apparent in DeQuincey; that it could provide the stimulus for authentic creation is confirmed by some of the most triumphant passages in *Moby-Dick*. This is worth demonstrating since examples may serve to clarify the nature of a living tradition. A previous mode of expression can be made fertile use of only to the degree that the later writer does not merely run in the same course but, by adding the content of a highly charged life, channels a new direction of his own. To both Thoreau and Melville the reading of Browne was a more compelling event than to DeQuincey since it was backed up at more points by what they brought to it.

3. Ishmael's Loom of Time

WHEN Melville returned from the trip to England that he made in the year before starting on *Moby-Dick*, he had with him a rich hoard of books, among them the 1686 folio of Browne [1] and *Confessions of an Opium Eater*. The first became much the more pervasive ingredient in his own masterwork, though without Coleridge's and DeQuincey's rediscovery of the author of the *Religio,* Melville might never have heard of him. Certainly DeQuincey was second not even to Coleridge

---

1. He had bought other seventeenth-century books, folios of Ben Jonson, Beaumont and Fletcher, and Davenant, and an old copy of Butler's *Hudibras*.

in his devotion, as shown by the celebrated tribute in his essay on
'Rhetoric.' He thought of Browne, along with Jeremy Taylor, as the
most accomplished and dazzling of all rhetoricians, in whom 'the two
opposite forces of eloquent passion and rhetorical fancy' had been brought
'into an exquisite equilibrium.'[2] Like Coleridge, he held that Browne
spoke both to the 'affections' and the 'understanding,' and cited the opening bars of the last chapter of *Urn-Burial:* 'Now since these dead bones
have already out-lasted the living ones of Methuselah, and in a yard under
ground, and thin walls of clay, out-worn all the strong and specious
buildings above it, and quietly rested under the drums and tramplings of
three conquests . . .'

But as DeQuincey advances to the height of his virtuosity by composing a variation on this theme, something of Browne's combination of
qualities has been lost:

What a melodious ascent as of a prelude to some impassioned requiem
breathing from the pomps of earth, and from the sanctities of the grave! What
a *fluctus decumanus* of rhetoric! Time expounded, not by generations or centuries, but by the vast periods of conquests and dynasties; by cycles of Pharaohs
and Ptolemies, Antiochi and Arsacides! And these vast successions of time distinguished and figured by the uproars which revolve at their inaugurations;
by the drums and tramplings rolling overhead upon the chambers of forgotten dead—the trepidations of time and mortality vexing, at secular intervals,
the everlasting sabbaths of the grave! Show us, O pedant, such another strain
from the oratory of Greece or Rome . . . that will make a fit antiphony to
this sublime rapture.

This passage has been justly considered one of DeQuincey's show-
pieces, for few writers can match the magnificence of these periods in the
spacing of their rhythm, their exactitude of intonation, and their cumulative volume. Thoreau's rustic flute could not handle such orchestra-
tion; Melville's impetuosity never learned to control every syllable to
such a massive and studied effect. But Emerson would have been able to
note what has disappeared from Browne's original, for Emerson knew
that the secret of language is mixture, that 'the male principle is the

2. This essay, printed in *Blackwood's* in 1829, grew out of a review of Whately's *Elements of Rhetoric*. It is interesting that the only other writer whom DeQuincey believed to
have mastered something of Browne's peculiar reconciliation of opposites was Richter. Although Jean Paul's rhetoric now seems florid and his emotions artificial, to Melville and his
contemporaries he seemed to possess surprising contrasts of fantastic speculation and deep
feeling, akin to those that delighted them in the seventeenth century.

Saxon, the female, the Latin,' and that they are married in every great style. 'The children and laborers use the Saxon unmixed. The Latin unmixed is abandoned to the colleges and Parliament.' But no sentence is 'made of Roman words alone, without loss of strength.'

Browne's stately elevation is kept from being vitiated into the merely learned and remote by the startling reminder of 'a yard under ground, and thin walls of clay.' Such details in DeQuincey are muffled beneath the far heavier proportion of Latinisms. Moreover, they have become abstractions—'the pomps of earth,' 'the sanctities of the grave'—and have thus been shorn of the compelling vitality of sense impressions. Nor does DeQuincey have much of the skill, which fascinated Thoreau as much as Emerson, of surprising word-play with the possible shades of Latin meaning. He does recall 'secular' to its original sense; but he cannot like Browne inject a word from which both the primary and derived meanings open out: the 'specious buildings' are shiningly beautiful, though that appearance is falsely showy.[3] In addition, DeQuincey is capable of using a Latinism that has not even the merit of being descriptive, for the noise of the uproar is muted by 'revolve.' Or he adds a second borrowed word with no sharpened extension of the sense, 'distinguished and figured'—a clear proof of the soundness of Emerson's view that 'a good writer, if he has indulged in Roman roundness, makes haste to chasten and nerve his period by English monosyllables.' In all these cases, and in the resonant cadences of the whole, DeQuincey has rivalled Browne's resources of sound. But lacking the intensity of emotion that springs only out of continued reinvigoration from the common things of life, sublimity has become a surface ornament.

Melville could not have phrased anything like so subtle an appreciation of the intricacies of Browne's rhetoric as DeQuincey did, though they exercised a powerful spell over him. His own acquaintance with the seventeenth century dated back as early as the first piece of his work that we have, for the opening lines of 'Fragments from a Writing-Desk,' which he wrote at nineteen, contain an offhand mention of 'old Burton.' But the bulk of Melville's reading came in the reverse sequence from that of most writers: it followed rather than preceded his experience of the world. It did not result from any formal training, for a whale ship was

3. Cf. the description of Dalila by Milton's Samson: 'That specious monster, my accomplished snare.'

his Yale College and his Harvard. And only when, at twenty-five, he had come back from his wandering, could he turn to books with his whole attention, partly in the hope of finding answers to questions of belief that had absorbed him in endless hours at sea, partly with the huge gusto of the man who feels that he has long been starved of his rightful fare. His account of 'A Man-of-War Library' in *White Jacket* suggests the books that appealed to him most as he began his return to civilization: among its chance miscellany that ranged from Plutarch's *Lives* to Blair's *Rhetoric*, his enthusiasm was greatest for 'some odd volumes of plays, each of which was a precious casket of jewels of good things,' *The Jew of Malta, Old Fortunatus, The City Madam, Volpone*, and *The Alchemist*.

By the time he had come to narrate the indignities of White Jacket's career, he could draw on Fuller's *Holy State* for an ironic epigraph ('Conceive him now in a man-of-war: with his letters of mart, well armed, victualled, and appointed, and see how he acquits himself.'—'The Good Sea-Captain'). But Browne's effect upon him had been far more manifold. Indeed, in the extraordinary transformation of Melville's aims from the two straightforward accounts of his adventures in *Typee* and *Omoo*, to the philosophic ambitions of *Mardi*, Browne's speculations operated as one of the strongest agents. Melville had been making constant use of his friend Evert Duyckinck's library, whose more than sixteen thousand volumes—one of the best private collections of the day—provided an incalculable stimulus to the growth of Melville's catholic tastes. Evert wrote to his brother George in the spring of 1848, 'By the way Melville reads Old Books. He has borrowed Sir Thomas Browne of me and says finely of the speculations of the *Religio Medici* that Browne is a kind of "crack'd Archangel." Was ever anything of this sort said before by a sailor?'

A year later, near the beginning of his new voyage in *Mardi*, Melville announced, while reflecting on the wonders of the sea still unrecorded by naturalists: 'Be Sir Thomas Brown [*sic*] our ensample; who, while exploding *Vulgar Errors*, heartily hugged all the mysteries in the Pentateuch.' He followed that example to the farthest reach, reacting with an even fuller charge than Thoreau. The books that really spoke to Melville became an immediate part of him to a degree hardly matched by any other of our great writers in their maturity.[4] His first intense re-

---

4. The other books which played a major role in releasing Melville's creative energies will be dealt with in Book Three.

sponse to Browne went to the length of ventriloquism. It was hardly
Melville's own voice that spoke in these wide-sweeping images of space
and time: 'We glided on for hours in twilight; when, on those mountains'
farther side, the hunters must have been abroad, morning glories all
astir'; or, 'What shaft has yet been sunk to the antipodes? what under-
lieth the gold mines?' The chief reason why Melville re-echoed the music
of some of Browne's very phrases was that here he had found an author
who spoke to him of the 'wingy Mysteries in Divinity,' who spoke to his
own awakening sense of the complexity of truth, of the difficulty of faith,
since, as Browne said, 'God hath not made a Creature that can comprehend him.' The necessity to come to a reckoning with such problems became severe for Melville, as it could not be for the transcendentalists,
whose serene affirmations were never tested by as much suffering and
evil as he had seen. He could not avoid squaring faith with experience.
In *Mardi* the mood of excited discovery was still dominant over that
of despair; he was carried along by Browne's desire to believe, more often
than by his skepticism.

A curious mixture resulted from Melville's effort to formulate his
thoughts, since they were still so new to him that he had as yet no vocabulary to express them that was not at second-hand. He grew momentarily
fascinated by the scholastic strain in Browne, which asserted that a thing
may be incredible and none the less true. Melville was led thence into
conjectures about one of Browne's favorite topics, metempsychosis. When
Browne said, 'Men are liv'd over again, the world is now as it was in Ages
past,' his gaze was turned backward. But for Melville, in tune with the
aspirations of his own age, this doctrine could be a way of showing that
'all things form but one whole' through the reincarnation of the past in
the present:

In some universe-old truths, all mankind are disbelievers. Do you believe
that you lived three thousand years ago? That you were at the taking of Tyre,
were overwhelmed in Gomorrah? No. But for me, I was at the subsiding of
the Deluge, and helped swab the ground, and build the first house. With the
Israelites, I fainted in the wilderness; was in court when Solomon outdid all
the judges before him. I, it was, who suppressed the lost work of Manetho, on
the Egyptian theology, as containing mysteries not to be revealed to posterity,
and things at war with the canonical scriptures; I, who originated the conspiracy against that purple murderer, Domitian; I, who in the senate moved
that great and good Aurelian be emperor. I instigated the abdication of Dio-

cletian, and Charles the Fifth; I touched Isabella's heart that she hearkened to Columbus. I am he, that from the king's minions hid the Charter in the old oak at Hartford; I harbored Goffe and Whalley: I am the leader of the Mohawk masks, who in the Old Commonwealth's harbor, overboard threw the East India Company's Souchong; I am the Veiled Persian Prophet; I, the man in the iron mask; I, Junius.

As he passes from example to example, led on by Browne's range, it becomes apparent that, in spite of Melville's enthusiasm for discovery and revolt, no depth of feeling has fused his instances with his abstraction. He has borrowed Browne's idea too directly, and has dug for his instances too much at random in the grab-bag of history. Consequently, though some of them suggest the pressure of his widening interests, the series as a whole does not carry the conviction of standing for anything especially relevant or central for him. The difference is marked from Thoreau's close matching of thought and feeling in the passage on Ganges and Walden.

By the time he composed *Moby-Dick* Melville had integrated both the matter and the manner of Browne more authentically to his own use. The method of *Vulgar Errors* undoubtedly encouraged him in heaping up his antiquarian lore about whaling, though such robust discursiveness stemmed just as much from *The Anatomy of Melancholy*.[5] Browne also stimulated him in his tendency to find symbols everywhere, although this habit of Melville's cannot be set apart from many other confluent sources.[6] But when Melville reflects on the mystery of time or projects the grandeur of space, his utterance, if more firmly his own than in *Mardi,* still owes most to Browne's music, upon which it now makes splendid variations: 'Who can show a pedigree like Leviathan? Ahab's harpoon had shed older blood than the Pharaoh's. Methuselah seems a schoolboy. I look round to shake hands with Shem.' Or again, Ahab, oppressed by his dry anguish, feels the touch of a mild breeze and fancies that 'they have been making hay somewhere under the slopes of the Andes, Starbuck, and the mowers are sleeping among the new-mown hay.'

The interest in dwelling on such small examples is that we can now perceive Melville, through Browne's tutelage, growing into possession of

5. It is an interesting item that Melville bought a Burton in the spring of 1847 and subsequently discovered that this very copy had once belonged to his father.
6. See Chapter VII, 'Allegory and Symbolism.'

the secret of the metaphysical style, and so gaining the ability to create a version of his own. Both the day by day routine of a whale ship and an absorbed concern with philosophy have been parts of his life. With the instinctive wholeness of the man for whom reading has not been a polite refinement but an answer to immediate questions, he too can make one realm of his experience subserve another. As a result even the chapters on the anatomy of the whale do not remain merely external description, something apart from his own consciousness. Even while he gives the details of how the ship was sorely strained by the hoisting of whales' heads along both port and starboard, another tension occurs to him: 'So, when on one side you hoist in Locke's head, you go over that way; but now, on the other side, hoist in Kant's and you come back again; but in very poor plight. Thus, some minds forever keep trimming boat. Oh, ye foolish! throw all these thunder-heads overboard, and then you will float light and right.' That shows an ability similar to Thoreau's to think in images. You get two experiences at once, one in terms of the other. The effect is like that of Thoreau's question near the end of *Walden:* 'What does Africa,—what does the West stand for? Is not our own interior white on the chart?' There the incompleted map and the undiscovered heart of man are seen together.

Coleridge, in commenting on Browne's doctrine of the microcosm— 'We carry with us the wonders we seek without us'—affirmed that 'he is the man of genius who . . . perceiving the riddle and the mystery of all things even the commonest, needs no strange and out-of-the-way tales or images to stimulate him into wonder and a deep interest.' From the midst of the hard routine of the *Acushnet,* Melville can seize all the material that his imagination requires. Tashtego has been lowered into a whale's head for the exacting and dangerous work of bailing out the rich sperm, bucket by bucket. He slips, loses his hold, and plunges out of sight into the oily mass. Melville presents the horror of the moment and the excitement of the rescue. Then, when it is all over: 'Now, had Tashtego perished in that head, it had been a very precious perishing; smothered in the very whitest and daintiest of fragrant spermaceti; coffined, hearsed, and tombed in the secret inner chamber and sanctum sanctorum of the whale . . . How many, think ye, have likewise fallen into Plato's honey head, and sweetly perished there?' The horror may seem to be forgotten in the relaxed deliciousness of the imagery. But beneath this lovely white-ness lurks dread, as the symbolism of the book everywhere proclaims.

Oblivion to cruel reality through idealism does not end in the transcendentalists' sweet vagueness, but in suffocation and death—as Melville was soon to show at length in the annihilation of the young idealist Pierre.

A by-product of Melville's ability to unite the abstract and concrete in a single image is the bizarre surprise. He is recounting the process of burning down the blubber in the try-works, and adds that 'it smells like the left wing of the day of judgment.' That may well be nearer the fantasies of frontier humor than to the conceits of 'Go, and catch a falling star.' Thoreau is more akin to metaphysical wit in the carefully spaced distance between his general dignified proposition and the sudden shock of his homely instance: 'Some circumstantial evidence is very strong, as when you find a trout in the milk.'

But Melville's mastery of the metaphysical style, of being 'totus in illo,' extends beyond single passages to the construction of such a sustained unit as Father Mapple's Sermon. There, by the continuous interweaving of doctrine with illustration, by making immediate the problems of belief through dramatizing the events that are closest to the congregation, Melville has broken down the arid divisions between learning and ordinary existence. By telling the story of Jonah and letting his generalizations rise from that center, the preacher has combined—to a degree that even Melville may not have been fully conscious of—some of the locutions of everyday speech with a vocabulary that does not scant the resources of complex philosophical diction:

> Screwed at its axis against the side, a swinging lamp slightly oscillates in Jonah's room; and the ship, heeling over toward the wharf with the weight of the last bales received, the lamp, flame and all, though in slight motion, still maintains a permanent obliquity with reference to the room; though, in truth, infallibly straight itself, it but made obvious the false, lying levels among which it hung. The lamp alarms and frightens Jonah; as lying in his berth his tormented eyes roll round the place, and this thus far successful fugitive finds no refuge for his restless glance. But that contradiction in the lamp more and more appals him. The floor, the ceiling, and the side, are all awry. 'Oh! so my conscience hangs in me!' he groans, 'straight upward, so it burns; but the chambers of my soul are all in crookedness!'

The schemata of that rhetoric may seem at first reading uncomfortably elaborate. A phrase like 'alarms and frightens' may grate as a repetition that expands the rhythm without advancing the sense; but the words have really been controlled with an accuracy that our blurred usage obscures: 'alarm' designates the moment of the arousal of apprehension, which widens into a state of fear, and rises to its climax in 'more and more appals him.' A sequence like 'maintains a permanent obliquity with reference to the room' certainly supports the charge that even Coleridge brought against Browne, that he started the corruption of the language by being 'hyperlatinistic.' With the advance of nineteenth-century realism, such a Johnsonian flourish, together with the possibility of creating its sonority, were destined to be clipped out of our prose until Joyce's sensitive ear rediscovered the purer music of the seventeenth century. Taken as a whole, Melville's sermon has been designed to speak to both the most simple and the most subtle of its auditors. It possesses the imaginative inclusiveness that has caused Jeremy Taylor to be called 'the Shakespeare of divines.' Father Mapple also can provide at once for both the groundlings and the highly educated by perceiving 'the mystery of all things even the commonest.'

Such sermons were not to be heard in Melville's day from the thinly cultivated ministers of upper-class Broadway or Tremont Street. And when a Theodore Parker revolted, it was in the name of transcendental reform, not of old-fashioned dogma; when a Henry Ward Beecher restored the earlier Calvinistic vigor, the drive of his emotions hardly permitted much intellectual flexibility. The nearest approach in life to Father Mapple, and a likely stimulus for Melville's character, was Father Edward Taylor (1793-1871), the ex-seaman and Methodist preacher to the sailors in Boston's North End. Emerson always felt enriched by being in his presence, and never lost his admiration for the way that Taylor's inexhaustible humanity could keep 'fusing all the rude hearts of his auditory with the heat of his own love, and making the abstractions of the philosophers accessible and effectual to them also.' So compelling was this power that when Taylor came to the church at Concord in 1845, 'black and white, poet and grocer, contractor and lumberman, Methodist and preachers, joined with the regular congregation in rare union.' Emerson likened Taylor's images to 'a string of rockets,' and recorded the flash of many of them. Once he had heard the preacher pray that God 'bless the bleached sail, the white foam': 'May every deck be stamped by the hallowed feet of godly captains, and the first watch and the second watch be watchful for the Divine light.' Again, when he was about to leave his congregation for a while, he reassured them: 'He who takes care of every whale, and can give him a ton of herrings for a breakfast, will find food for my babes.' Either of these sentences might have been delivered by Father Mapple, who had been 'a harpooner in his youth,' but the first was spoken when Melville was still a boy in Albany, and the second after *Moby-Dick* had been written.

Emerson, delighted by the joyful eloquence that could visualize young ministers coming out of divinity schools as 'poor fellows hobbling out of Jerusalem,' was still aware that Taylor's discourse had no more method than he had quite accidentally and 'ludicrously copied and caricatured from the old style, as he found it in some Connecticut tubs.' In contrast, Melville's method in his one attempt could hardly have been more delicately poised from the opening words, 'Beloved shipmates, clinch the last verse of the first chapter of Jonah,' to the fervent peroration on the 'topgallant delight' in store for him whom 'all the seas of the boisterous mob can never shake from this sure Keel.' Yet it is highly unlikely that Melville had the least sense of trying to restore an older literary tradition. He had simply learned for himself some of the truths that the great seventeenth-century writers had also possessed. In his first books he had aimed only to give the substance of what he had seen; by the time of *Pierre* the oppression of his thoughts had swung him to the other extreme, and his writing became ambiguous through its want of concretion. But in *Moby-Dick* his sense impressions and his reflective mind were in equilibrium. He might have said what Montaigne—no less than Thoreau—had discovered of himself: 'What I do, I usually do with all my faculties, proceeding as one complete whole; I make no move that is hidden or withdrawn from my reason, or which does not take place, so to speak, with the consent of all parts of me.'

This equilibrium served Melville well, not merely in the virtuosity of a single sermon, but in every phase of his need to objectify the complex conceptions that were rising so rapidly to his consciousness. He was as close to events as the early explorers whom Thoreau admired, but the sensation of discovery that Melville affords finds its best prototype not in the racy externality of John Smith, but in the unexpected combinations that rose from the sensibility of a man who could participate with equal vigor in the intricacies of law and divinity and in the expedition to Cadiz. The range of sensations possible to an author in Donne's time had narrowed with the nineteenth-century's division of labor. The most learned Victorian author was not a man who had also been a bricklayer, had fought in the Low Countries, and had narrowly escaped the gallows for killing an actor in a duel, while all the time he was amassing the kind of knowledge that enabled him to approximate the most polished Roman poets and also to shape the plot of *The Alchemist*.

In a very real sense Melville, coming to literature from rough life, re-lived rapidly the earlier experience of the race. In many respects he re-mained primitive in contrast to Donne or Jonson, and therein nearer to John Smith, but with questions pressing upon him for resolution that never troubled that hearty adventurer. Some of Melville's most memorable passages are those in which you feel that you are sharing in the very process of his developing consciousness. Ishmael starts to describe how he was helping Queequeg weave a mat on a sultry, lazy afternoon:

As I kept passing and repassing the filling or woof of marline between the long yarns of the warp, using my own hand for the shuttle, and as Queequeg, standing sideways, ever and anon slid his heavy oaken sword between the threads, and idly looking off upon the water, carelessly and unthinkingly drove home every yarn: I say so strange a dreaminess did there then reign all over the ship and all over the sea, only broken by the intermitting dull sound of the sword, that it seemed as if this were the Loom of Time, and I myself were a shuttle mechanically weaving and weaving away at the Fates.

The stillness of the sea, the almost imperceptible motion of the ship, produce the dreamlike rhythm that is the matrix of this thought. Another writer might have left it at this, an observed experience pushed to the edge of an abstraction that it loosely symbolizes. But at this stage the rare availability of Melville's experience—what Richards has emphasized as the distinguishing attribute of the artist—comes into full play. He per-ceives that the action of weaving falls into a chain of events that can hold in the clarity of a prolonged image the interrelations of one of the most perplexing of philosophical problems. To describe it thus makes Melville's process sound far too studied, as though he were about to manufacture a mechanical allegory instead of creating a parable in which the narrative and its interpretation are as densely interwoven as the threads of the mat. In fact, the imaginative excitement for the reader in what follows comes from his participating in the very moment of Melville's discovery of the analogies, when the literal details were separating out in his con-sciousness into metaphors and yielding that extension of awareness which is metaphor's most valuable gift:

There lay the fixed threads of the warp subject to but one single, ever returning, unchanging vibration, and that vibration merely enough to admit of the crosswise interblending of other threads with its own. This warp seemed necessity; and here, thought I, with my own hand I ply my own shuttle and weave my own destiny into these unalterable threads. Meantime, Queequeg's impulsive, indifferent sword, sometimes hitting the woof slantingly, or crookedly, or strongly, or weakly, as the case might be; and by this difference in the concluding blow producing a corresponding contrast in the final aspect of the completed fabric; this savage's sword, thought I, which thus finally shapes and fashions both warp and woof; this easy, indifferent sword must be chance—ay, chance, free will, and necessity—no wise incompatible—all interweavingly working together. The straight warp of necessity, not to be swerved from its ultimate course—its every alternating vibration, indeed, only tending to that; free will still free to ply her shuttle between given threads; and chance, though restrained in its play within the right lines of necessity, and sideways in its motions directed by free will, though thus prescribed to by both, chance by turns rules either, and has the last featuring blow at events.

The abundant details have all been subordinated to their application; and the point by point correspondence establishes the interworking of 'chance, free will, and necessity' with a clarity more decisive than pages of argument. It is notable that even after the three abstractions have risen to the surface, and Melville advances to his conclusion by resuming each in turn, he does not abandon the physical structure. His parable is struck into its final shape by the 'featuring blow' of Queequeg's sword. Then, in the next moment, the 'wild and unearthly' cry, 'There she blows!' sounds so suddenly from aloft that 'the ball of free will' drops from Ishmael's hand, and he is caught up once more by the inexorable demands of the whaleman's occupation.

In this whole sequence Melville has furnished his own illustration of what Coleridge meant by saying that the entireness of Browne's mental action can be seen by the way 'he metamorphoses every thing, be it what it may, into the subject under consideration.' Melville's aim in this parable could also be characterized by a remark of Professor Croll's about the metaphysical prose-writers, of whose style he has been the most discerning critic: 'Their purpose was to portray, not a thought, but a mind thinking, or, in Pascal's words, *la peinture de la pensée*. They knew that an idea separated from the act of experiencing it is not the idea that was experienced.'[7] This description amounts to a more exact statement of the combination of intellect and senses, which Emerson praised so consistently even though he was its infrequent master. The same thing was amplified in Eliot's essay on 'The Metaphysical Poets' (1921), which made articulate our contemporary awareness of the still unspent resources of the seventeenth century.[8] Emerson would have agreed with Eliot that 'a thought to Donne was an experience.' Thoreau especially would have liked the physical analogy that the poets of that age 'could devour any kind of experience.' Melville proved that he could amalgamate into a new whole fragments certainly as disparate as falling in love and reading Spinoza, 'the noise of the typewriter' and 'the smell of the cooking.'

It was unlucky for Melville that *Typee* made such a stir that Hawthorne and Whitman reviewed it with enthusiasm, Emerson and Thoreau referred to it in their journals, Longfellow read it aloud, and Lowell ended by declaring himself heartily sick of the flurry over it. Its *réclame* so fixed Melville's image as a writer of adventure that none of this group except Hawthorne seems to have given any attention to his later work, to the book that fused the contrasting qualities which Emerson most desired. That Emerson was right in concluding that even the perception of the value of that fusion had largely disappeared from the England of his day was borne out by *Blackwood's* reviewer of *Omoo*. To that writer it was incredible that such a book could have been written by a man who had been a sailor: 'There is nothing improbable in his adventures, save their occurrence to himself, and that he should have been a man before the mast on board the South Sea traders, or whalers, or on any ship or ships whatever. His speech betrayeth him.' That particular objection was not raised by American reviewers. The jack-of-all-trades was one of our most familiar and most cherished types, and, in so far as democratic opportunity for varied life cut through the Victorian specialization of a narrowly educated class, the language of our writers could be more in-

7. See M. W. Croll, 'The Baroque Style in Prose' (*Studies . . . in honor of Frederick Klaeber,* 1929, pp. 427-56).

8. The following make an interesting series of steps in the Donne tradition. He was a favorite poet of Lowell's, who affirmed that Donne 'wrote more profound verses than any other poet save one only.' It was 'from the text of the edition of 1633 revised by James Russell Lowell' that Charles Eliot Norton prepared his edition of Donne in 1895. And although the great modern edition was made by a Scotchman, H. J. C. Grierson, in 1912, the contemporary revival of the taste for metaphysical poetry owes most to Eliot's early poems and essays.

clusive both in vigor and subtlety. It could be 'concentrated and nutty,' what Thoreau demanded and did not find in DeQuincey, language able to give 'the most faithful, natural, and lifelike account of . . . sensations, mental and physical.' But the type was not furthered by our own middle-class culture, which encouraged correct and bloodless gentility, as Emerson knew. Thoreau won his wholeness only by uniting practice with theory in a way that involved a truceless war on current standards. Melville won his partly by the accident of poverty, which kept him from going to college, and immersed him, like Whitman, in common life. But he brought to bear upon this immediate knowledge a curiosity for recondite thinkers, whose names alone usually satisfied Whitman, and so came under the spell of the metaphysical strain, a fresh metamorphosis of which he created in the image of his own undissevered experience.

IV

THE ORGANIC PRINCIPLE

'Such as the life is, such is the form.'

1. From Coleridge to Emerson

BOTH Emerson and Thoreau would have objected energetically to having their work evaluated by its approximation to other art instead of to nature. When Emerson said (1835) that in the seventeenth century the 'language of nature . . . appeared in every book,' he was recalling a sentence from Thomas Shepard's *New England's Lamentation* ('And to put finger in the eye and to renew their repentance, they think this is weakness'). He had just been reminded of Shepard's homeliness by the talk of a Vermont drover. Thoreau laid down the proposition that 'there are two classes of men called poets; the one cultivates life, the other art,' and left no doubt about which he wanted to be. Emerson said, 'Ask the fact for the form,' thereby enunciating his conviction that art must be based organically on nature. He believed that the tendency of an artificially refined society is always 'to detach the beautiful from the useful,' to lose sight of the functional in trivial and effeminate ornamentation. In affirming that the duty of the artist is continually to renew elemental experience, Emerson also subscribed to Coleridge's conception of how the artist creates his forms. Coleridge's key-passage on the organic principle, which arose from his discussion of Shakespeare, sums up the central idea that is to be developed in this chapter:

No work of true genius dares want its appropriate form, neither indeed is there any danger of this. As it must not, so genius can not, be lawless; for it is even this that constitutes it genius—the power of acting creatively under laws of its own origination . . . The form is mechanic, when on any given material we impress a pre-determined form, not necessarily arising out of the properties of the material;—as when to a mass of wet clay we give whatever shape we wish it to retain when hardened. The organic form, on the other hand, is innate; it shapes, as it develops, itself from within, and the fulness of its development is one and the same with the perfection of its outward form. Such as the life is, such is the form. Nature, the prime genial artist, inexhaustible in diverse powers, is equally inexhaustible in forms . . .

A similar train of thought had been developed by Schlegel, among other German leaders of romanticism, into the principle that just as the inner force of a phenomenon in nature determines its external structure, so the vitality of a poet's seminal idea or intuition determines its appropriate expression.[1] The manifest risks for art in such a doctrine is that its exclusive emphasis on the inner urge rather than on the created shape can quickly run to formlessness, particularly when it insists on the same spontaneous growth for a poem as for a plant. In fact, it could be argued that the various degrees of formlessness in Emerson, Thoreau, and Whitman were owing to the varying lengths to which they carried this analogy. On the other hand, they themselves felt the greatest release for their creative impulses when they could believe their work integrally subordinated to natural force, and beating in harmony with it.

The terms that the three used to express this conviction are remarkably similar. In developing his proposition that 'it is not metres, but a metre-making argument that makes a poem,' Emerson held that the essential thought from which a poem rises must be 'so passionate and alive that like the spirit of a plant or an animal it has an architecture of its own, and adorns nature with a new thing.' Thoreau said in the *Week*: 'As naturally as the oak bears an acorn, and the vine a gourd, man bears a poem . . . since his song is a vital function like breathing, and an integral result like weight.' Like Whitman, Thoreau generally used the language of biology, for both held that the poet 'generates poems,' though Thoreau added, as Whitman would not have, that 'by continence he rises to creation on a higher level.' Thoreau spoke of a poem as 'a natural fruit,' as 'one undivided, unimpeded expression fallen ripe into literature,' a sentence that found extension in the first preface to *Leaves of Grass*: 'The rhyme and uniformity of perfect poems show the free growth of metrical laws, and bud from them as unerringly and loosely as lilacs or roses on a bush, and take shapes as compact as the shapes of chestnuts

1. See F. W. Lorch, 'Thoreau and the Organic Principle in Poetry' (*Publications of the Modern Language Association*, March 1938).

EEL SPEARING AT SETAUKET, by W. S. Mount

and oranges, and melons and pears, and shed the perfume impalpable to form.'

Emerson rejoiced that in the strict reliance of art upon nature, the artist works not as he will but as he must: 'We feel, in seeing a noble building, which rhymes well, as we do in hearing a perfect song, that it is spiritually organic; that is, had a necessity, in Nature, for being; was one of the possible forms in the Divine mind, and is now only discovered and executed by the artist, not arbitrarily composed by him.' As Emerson's thought follows there its normal course into Neo-Platonism, we perceive how art is organic for him in a double sense: not merely is the appropriate form an expressive growth from the poet's intuition, but that intuition in turn is an outwelling from the universal mind. When Emerson shifted his attention to this second sense, he quickly passed to a realm beyond technical discussion. For he maintained that since the universal mind is the sole creator of both the useful and the beautiful, the only way for the individual to partake in the creative act is by submitting himself entirely to this primal source beyond the understanding.

But before losing himself in his vaguely luminous doctrine of divine inspiration, Emerson enumerated many of the broad hints that material nature has given to the receptive mind and eye of the artist. By the time he wrote his first book he had already found verification for another phase of the organic principle—that beauty in art springs from man's response to forms in nature. He had noted that formal decorative designs can be reduced to endlessly varied imitations of plant and animal life, such as the shapes of leaves, the wheat-ear, the pine-cone, the sea-shell, and the lion's claw. In his essay on 'History' he went further, affirming that if we surrounded ourselves with the circumstances of primitive peoples, we could relive the experience of inventing all the orders and ornaments of architecture: how the slope of the roof was determined by the weight of the snow, how all the elaborations of the Greek temple go back to the first raising of the lintel on a Doric hut, how the Gothic arcade 'plainly originated in a rude adaptation of the forest trees.' He never lost interest in picking up examples from modern as well as ancient sources [2] to illustrate his theory, as that Smeaton built Eddystone lighthouse on the form of an oak tree; or, turning to the human

2. Longfellow noted in his journal (1849) that Emerson had come to dinner and had 'brought with him a book by Mr. Hay, showing that all the beautiful forms of antique vases were created by the different combinations of the egg-form.'

body as the original model, that Dollond based his achromatic telescope on the structure of the human eye, and that Duhamel, in constructing a bridge, got his hint for letting in a piece of stronger timber
for the middle of the under-surface from the formation of the shinbone.

In the opening pages of *English Traits* he cited his friend the sculptor
Horatio Greenough as having anticipated Ruskin in his conception of a
functional basis for architecture. Many passages in Greenough's essays, of
which Emerson was an enthusiastic reader, were incisive confirmations
of the analogies between art and natural history that Emerson had been
pursuing ever since his first dissatisfaction with the eighteenth-century
rhetoricians' notion of beauty as 'outside embellishment.' In a paper on
'American Architecture' (1843) Greenough developed the conception that
'the law of adaptation is the fundamental law of nature in all structure.'
He started with a question that might just as well have been phrased by
Emerson: 'If, as the first step in our search after the great principles of
construction, we but observe the skeletons and skins of animals, through
all the varieties of beast and bird, of fish and insect, are we not forcibly
struck by their variety as by their beauty?' Greenough's grasp of technical details allowed him to carry the discussion of the organic nature of
architecture to ordered conclusions beyond Emerson's scope. The sculptor
drove home the point that 'the normal development of beauty is through
action to completeness. The invariable development of embellishment and
decoration is more embellishment and more decoration. The *reductio ad
absurdum* is palpable enough at last; but where was the first downward
step? I maintain that the first downward step was *the introduction of the
first inorganic, non-functional element, whether of shape or color.*' [3]

Emerson tried to speak in similar terms of the art he knew best. One
of the reasons why he liked Herbert and the other metaphysical poets
so much was their elimination of irrelevant ornament for the sake of the
articulation of their meaning. But he did not want to imitate their
technical secrets, since he believed that the only way to gain a like fitness
of expression was through an equally direct relation to basic forces. He
was uneasy with any display of mere virtuosity and thought of Poe as 'the

3. Another passage that might almost have been written by Emerson: 'Conceive now
that an entire building might grow up out of conditions as a plant grows up out of soil,
as free to be itself, to "live its own life according to nature" as is the tree. Dignified as a
tree in the midst of nature.' But this is Frank Lloyd Wright, talking in his *Autobiography*
about the plasticity he has wanted in architecture.

jingle man.' His connotations in that phrase are extended when Merlin
says that he wants

> No jingling serenader's art,
> Nor tinkle of piano strings,

a declaration that Whitman frequently echoed in his scorn for 'piano
tunes.' Rhythm and rhyme became meaningful for Emerson only when
he could trace them to their origins as Pythagoras had done in announcing that 'the world subsists by the rhythmical order of its elements,'
and had found thus a reason for 'the elementary opposites of the universe,
the odd and even, one and many, right and left, male and female . . .
light and darkness . . . good and bad.'

Emerson dwelt recurrently on the action and reaction of such pairs
in his eagerness to prove the organic relation of metrical forms to nature.
'Merlin' rings the changes on the theme that 'Nature beats in perfect
tune,' instances an equally exquisite balance between the eagle's wings
as between the two sides of man's body, and concludes that the poet
should find a constant challenge to build his own harmonies from the
diurnal sequence of morning and night,

> As the two twilights of the day
> Fold us music-drunken in.

Emerson strove deliberately to catch nature's power. One journal
entry reads: 'Yesterday in the woods I followed the fine humble bee with
rhymes and fancies fine.' Inspecting the zigzag result, or the inordinate
and so finally monotonous catalogue of 'natural rhymes' in 'Woodnotes,' [4]
you have ample confirmation of the dangers involved in Emerson's
doctrine if it is misconceived literally. Such misconception is what Yvor
Winters has aptly called 'the fallacy of imitative form.' Although the poet
regains primitive strength through recognizing the physical basis of
rhythm, he mistakes his end utterly if he forgets that the fact is not the
form, that no more than language is the sound of a bird or a waterfall,
is his poem a part of nature. The world of nature may well be his most
inspiring subject, but if he attempts merely to assert an identity with it

4. E.g. Come lift thine eyes to lofty rhymes,
    Of things with things, of times with times,
    Primal chimes of sun and shade,
    Of sound and echo, man and maid,
    The land reflected in the flood,
    Body with shadow still pursued . . .

instead of making an independent construction of his own, he fails as completely as, to use Winters' example, Whitman failed on those occasions when he tried to express a loose America simply by writing loosely.

The more characteristic danger for Emerson, as we know, was not his immersion in material nature, but the other extreme, leaving it behind altogether. His most fruitful work resulted from a poise in attitude between the two extremes, when the organic analogy between art and nature gave substance to his lines without causing him to lose sight of the fact that it was simply an analogy. He phrased the necessary distinction in remarking, 'When I see the waves of Lake Michigan toss in the bleak snowstorm, I see how small and inadequate the common poet is. But Tennyson with his eagle over the sea has shown his sufficiency.' That kind of sufficiency, to profit from nature's stimulus and yet to create his own form, can be observed in Emerson's poem, 'The Snow-Storm.'

His initial intention can probably be traced in the stiff resolve (1832), 'Instead of lectures on Architecture, I will make a lecture on God's architecture, one of his beautiful works . . . I will draw a sketch of a Winter's day.' But the sleet whirling through the pine woods stirred him far more inwardly than that: it struck him as the very symbol for free and ecstatic release. It caused him to think in 1841, the year in which he wrote the poem, that all his own work looked miserably constricted in comparison and that he would never write more, that 'it is pitiful to be an artist.' Yet his admiration for nature as Coleridge's 'prime genial artist' did not stop with his notion that a snowdrift along the sides of a stone wall 'obviously gave the idea of the common architectural scroll to abut a tower.' His humming response to the snow's rhythm shaped itself into verse:

> Announced by all the trumpets of the sky,
> Arrives the snow, and driving o'er the fields,
> Seems nowhere to alight: the whited air
> Hides hills and woods, the river, and the heaven,
> And veils the farm-house at the garden's end.
> The sled and traveller stopped, the courier's feet
> Delayed, all friends shut out, the housemates sit
> Around the radiant fireplace, enclosed
> In a tumultuous privacy of storm.

In that opening stanza the fact that Emerson is re-creating, if only in miniature, his sensation of something actually seen and heard has al-

lowed him to escape from the scratchy abstractness that so often over-
took him. The onset of the poem conveys breathless speed, but then, as
the snow itself delays actions, shuts out or encloses, the movement of the
verse also slows down. But the exciting sound of the storm still remains
uppermost, and in presenting it, Emerson's ear has been sensitive to his
impression. The trumpets are high pitched: the thin vowel in 'sky' is
dominant through the following lines, especially in the phrases, 'driving
o'er the fields' and 'the whited air hides hills.' And the echo of the piercing wind, which is itself nowhere directly named, is still heard in the
phrase 'tumultuous privacy,' wherein the full vowel-sounds again give
way to the piercing notes.

Emerson goes on to develop his most lucid and graceful expression of
the doctrine of organic form:

> Come see the north wind's masonry.
> Out of an unseen quarry evermore
> Furnished with tile, the fierce artificer
> Curves his white bastions with projected roof
> Round every windward stake, or tree, or door.
> Speeding, the myriad-handed, his wild work
> So fanciful, so savage, naught cares he
> For number or proportion. Mockingly,
> On coop or kennel he hangs Parian wreaths;
> A swan-like form invests the hidden thorn;
> Fills up the farmer's lane from wall to wall,
> Maugre the farmer's sighs; and at the gate
> A tapering turret overtops the work.
> And when his hours are numbered, and the world
> Is all his own, retiring, as he were not,
> Leaves, when the sun appears, astonished Art
> To mimic in slow structures, stone by stone,
> Built in an age, the mad wind's night-work,
> The frolic architecture of the snow.

The rhythm is not so successfully sustained as in the more immediately
descriptive stanza, and limps very badly in the next to last line, only to
rally, to recapture once more the vibrating excitement that the poem has
been designed to express. Emerson has suggested nature's inexhaustible
plenitude, but has recognized its want of 'number' and 'proportion,' the
very qualities with which any art of man must be concerned. In creating

them here he shows how he could avoid the fallacy of literal imitation. In the passage where he said, 'Ask the fact for the form,' he developed what he implied in that phrase by continuing: 'For a verse is not a vehicle to carry a sentence as a jewel is carried in a case: the verse must be alive, and inseparable from its contents, as the soul of man inspires and directs the body, and we measure the inspiration by the music.'

It could easily be argued that his insistence that there must be no severance between form and content in the created whole hardly finds adequate manifestation in 'The Snow-Storm,' the architecture of which is certainly loose enough, not merely in contrast with that of the metaphysicals but even with the best of Wordsworth and Keats. Yet the attitude towards art that Emerson takes in this poem is integral to the determination of the American writers of his day to speak out of a direct relationship to experience, and not through borrowed modes. Thoreau made the attitude more explicit when he voiced the satisfaction with which he read, in a report on farms by a group of Middlesex husbandmen, of the number of rods of stone wall and of bushels of corn and potatoes: 'I feel as if I had got my foot down on the solid and sunny earth, the basis of all philosophy, and poetry, and religion even.' The implication again is of art as a natural growth, and since the solidity of both *Walden* and *Leaves of Grass,* as well as the limitations of the one and the weaknesses of the other, can be charged to that conception, we may profitably carry our examination of it beyond Emerson's occasional remarks.

2. Horatio Greenough (1805-52)[1]

AT THIS point Greenough's essays can have a substantial value by their very lack of pretension. He said that he wrote his 'Artist's Creed' because, having read Winckelmann, Schiller, and Goethe, he found the air thin and cold and often so foggy that he could not see his way. Without denying these men mastery of their ideas, he confessed that he simply did not

1. Horatio Greenough collected some of his essays and lectures and published them pseudonymously as *The Travels, Observations, and Experiences of a Yankee Stonecutter* (1852) by Horace Bender. In the year after his death this volume was reissued, under the forbidding title *A Memorial of Horatio Greenough,* with omissions of some of the less valuable material and with a biographical introduction by its editor, H. T. Tuckerman. In 1887 the

have the antecedent training necessary to follow them and still find his road back to practice. In his paper on 'Social Theories' he declared, 'I love the concrete,' and expressed his hearty dislike of all transcendental schemes of life, since they clipped away the roots by which he clung to the common soil. To explain his dissatisfaction further he fell naturally into an architectural metaphor, 'We build our church up into the sky against the gravitation, but 'tis only the *downward tendency* that holds it *fast.*'

The creed he had to offer, therefore, was not vitiated by the weakness that Emerson was always deploring in the period, that its artists were too intellectual and nervous, and so broke off all their flowers and left none to ripen to fruit. As Greenough saw it in 'Aesthetics at Washington,' the peculiar problem for America was how to profit by aesthetic theory when we had not yet developed a substantial art of our own, and were continually being flooded by imported writings that became as 'sterile and impotent, as is all faith without works.' He spoke out of the strong feeling of experience, since his own career had been a case history of the handicaps borne by the American artist. He spoke also with the authority of a man whose energy had carried him beyond the mistakes and mediocrity of his own work to a final ripe recognition of the true basis for American style. What he said was so germane both to the nature of the fine arts generally and to their basis in a democratic society that it can serve to clarify the aims of our writers as well.

As the first American to choose sculpture for a profession he had gone directly from his undergraduate life at Harvard to study at Rome under Thorwaldsen. In later years he spoke of being a self-made man: 'Indeed, I graduated at Harvard in 1825, which they who knew the school will allow was near enough self-making to satisfy any reasonable ambition.' Writing to William Dunlap in 1833, in answer to his request for biographical material to be included in his history of *The Arts of Design in the United States,* Greenough stated frankly, 'I fear that the circumstances under which I began my career will ever prevent me realizing my

letters of Horatio to his brother Henry were published by the wife of the latter. Since then very little attention has been paid to Greenough except for brief treatments of him in the standard histories of American sculpture. Van Wyck Brooks rediscovered his essays with enthusiasm. The only other discussion of him I have seen is a short but discerning appraisal by Nancy Wynne and Beaumont Newhall in *The American Magazine of Art* (January 1939).

idea of what sculpture should be.' However, the Boston in which he had grown up was not quite the thinly ministerial one that Emerson's boyhood knew. An older brother was devoted to drawing and painting, and two other brothers were later to make some reputation in architecture and sculpture. He could date his own desire to create from his instant delight in a marble statue of the Athenian general Phocion, a copy of the antique, which his father, a wealthy dealer in real estate, had bought for their garden. His only possible recourse at first was to try, unsuccessfully, to learn how to model in clay by studying the principles as outlined in the *Edinburgh Encyclopedia*. But while still in his early teens he was initiated into the rudiments by Solomon Willard, the wood-carver and architect, and by Binon, an itinerant Frenchman who had done a bust of John Adams. When a local stonecutter had shown him how to carve in marble and had thus enabled him to complete a bust of Bacchus, the possibilities of his American instruction were exhausted.

Looking back, Greenough believed that the sole asset for his craft that he took with him to Europe was that clay and marble were familiar to his touch. While an undergraduate, though he was able to study drawing and anatomy, he had counted his friendship with Washington Allston the one important influence, since it was the middle-aged painter who first taught him how to discriminate and how to feel. For the rest he had to be content with the kind of knowledge he could get from examining the casts and engravings in the Atheneum: 'I *gazed* at the Apollo and Venus, and *learned* little by it . . . It was not till I had run through all the galleries of Rome, and had under my eye the genial forms of Italy that I began to feel Nature's value. I had before adored her, but as a Persian does the sun, with my face to the ground.' He then grew to realize what he had previously barely glimpsed, the nature of mass and volume. Their dynamic possibilities almost overwhelmed him. As he concluded his letter to Dunlap: 'When I went, the other morning, into the huge room in which I propose to execute my statue, I felt like a spoilt boy, who, after insisting upon riding on horseback, bawls aloud with fright at finding himself so far from the ground! I hope, however, that this will wear off.'

The order for this statue—the colossal Washington—had come through the influence of Fenimore Cooper who, as Greenough declared, had been a father to him in kindness. It was Cooper who had saved him from despair by giving him his first commission, that of the Chanting Cherubs based on some figures of Raphael's, the first group to be executed by the chisel of an American. It was Cooper also who had persuaded Lafayette to sit for the young sculptor; and Greenough had felt his courage grow when he heard a print of his bust pronounced 'very like and in a *beau style,*' by Ingres, 'a man who never flatters.' But long before he had settled to work on the Washington, which was to occupy most of eight years and finally to allow him to reflect that 'no man since Canova has undertaken more,' he had revealed, while still at college, a far surer instinct for the true nature of art. He had made a wooden model for an obelisk in the competition for the monument for Bunker Hill. This work of his twentieth year was first chosen by the committee but was later supplanted in favor of a similar design on larger proportions by Solomon Willard. Still Greenough had had his vision of the singular power of an obelisk to call attention to a memorable event. As Emerson remembered, in the year of Greenough's death, 'He said, "An obelisk says but one word, *Here!* but it speaks very loud." '

Emerson recorded in his journal (1852) several passages of Greenough's extraordinarily pungent conversation, and rejoiced in him as one of the best proofs of our native capability. Emerson had probably forgotten that years before, just after he had written *Nature,* he had taken this same man as an instance of his conviction that there is 'no genius in the Fine Arts in this country,' that they are all feminine, with no character. To be sure, Emerson was making his standards exacting and somewhat arbitrary. He dismissed along with Greenough as our representative in sculpture, not only Allston in painting, but Channing in eloquence, Bryant in poetry, Irving and Cooper in fiction. Nevertheless, the reasons he gave for the want of male principle in American genius were extremely cogent: the fatal imitation of Europe, and the fact that American arts 'are not called out by the necessity of the people.' In the periods of great flowering, all the arts were 'enlisted in the service of Patriotism and Religion. The statue was to be worshipped, the picture also. The poem was a confession of faith. A vital faith built the cathedrals of Europe.' But in America who cares to see the products of our artists? 'The people never see them. The mind of the race has taken another direction,—Property.' These reasons would have been heartily endorsed by the Greenough whom Emerson remembered most warmly—not the young sculptor with whom in 1833 he had called on Landor in Florence and whose work he had vaguely objected to as 'picturesque,' but the seasoned character who, after his final return from Italy in 1851, grew incandescent with his perception of the potential sources of our strength to produce functional beauty. He insisted that these had been obscured too long, and spent his force so prodigally in speaking and writing about them that he exhausted himself and died suddenly of brain fever within a year.

It makes a sharp paradox that the sculptor whose name has been kept alive primarily by his half-draped Washington, a virtually unsurpassable example of derivative neo-classicism, should also have articulated the principle and have used almost the same words with which Louis Sullivan, half a century later, pointed out the course that has been taken by modern architecture. How nearly Greenough anticipated the declaration of the Chicago architect that 'Form follows function,' can be read in his proposition that 'instead of forcing the functions of every sort of building into one general form, adopting an outward shape for the sake of the eye or of association, without reference to the inner distribution, let us begin from the heart as a nucleus, and work outwards.' He insisted always on the importance of the heart. This reminds us that Sullivan, who had doubtless never heard of Greenough's essays, found the way to break through the desiccated eclecticism of his time to an architecture 'plastic to the mind and hand of the designer' by his warm response to Whitman. *Leaves of Grass,* as Sullivan tells in his *Autobiography of an Idea,* gave him his most compelling suggestion of how art could grow organically from the forces of American life.

Greenough provides a further revision of the conventional notion of the American artist as an untutored improviser. Like Poe and Henry James, he was forced by the very absence of a living native tradition for his art to re-examine the essentials of both its technique and its purpose, and so to arrive at fundamental discoveries in advance of current European practice. Only in Greenough's case his own work could not keep pace with his theory. This cannot be blamed entirely on want of time. He had reached his main tenets as early as 1843, when, having come home for a visit in order to witness the installation of his Washington, he was outraged at the storm raised by its semi-nudity. This led him to ask the reasons for the chaotic lack of standards in our taste. His sensitively trained eye was turned on America after almost two decades of European experience. What he saw was not merely the disordered absence of a national style in the confusion of the art and architecture of the Capital. Many observers had noted that, but what Greenough was then almost unique in discerning was the beauty of objects that had sprung out of an adaptation of structure to the needs of common life—the New England farmhouse, the trotting-wagon, the clipper ship.[2]

But his later sculpture did not absorb that knowledge. The second work to which he sacrificed years was a monumental group, The Rescue, a portrayal of a pioneer hunter in a half-classic costume, saving his wife and infant from the upraised tomahawk of an Indian in a loin-cloth. It is as grandiose and as lifeless as the gesture of his Washington, whose left arm holds a Roman sword reversed and thus signifies him first in war, while the right arm raised stiffly if benevolently gives an equal and undynamic emphasis to his primacy in peace. Both these huge works are saved from absurdity only by the sculptor's manifest devotion to his subjects. His honesty did not empower him to avoid the danger he recognized, that 'the translation of rhetoric into stone' is 'a feat often fatal to the rhetoric, always fatal to the stone.' Even his portrait busts, like that of Cooper, where his simple intention was to record a character whom he greatly admired, hardly show a trace of the generous love of life which so struck Emerson and to which the sculptor gave characteristic expression in one of his last letters: 'I would not pass away and not leave a sign that I, for one, born by the grace of God in this land, found life a cheerful thing, and not that sad and dreadful task with whose prospect they scared my youth.' What found its way into stone was an almost uniformly dry appearance of the flesh, a meager and undernourished look, which resulted from his tight handling of the features.

It would be hard to specify how much of this inadequacy must be put down to the limitations of Greenough's talent, how much to those of the whole school of sculpture in which he had been trained and which it was to require a widespread revolution in taste to overthrow. Greenough himself sensed a specifically national factor in the problem: 'We forgot that though the country was young, yet the people were old, that as Americans we have no childhood, no half-fabulous, legendary wealth,

2. Among the few who asserted some of the same things was Cooper. He had written in 1828, under the guise of a travelling foreigner: 'Though there is scarce such a thing as a capital picture in this whole country, I have seen more beautiful, graceful, and convenient ploughs in positive use here, than are probably to be found in the whole of Europe united. In this single fact may be traced the history of the character of the people, and the germ of their future greatness. Their axe is admirable for form, for neatness, and precision of weight, and it is wielded with a skill that is next to incredible.' Emerson's journal for 1847 contained the observation: 'The modern architecture is shipbuilding; and the modern art is music; and the new power, steam.'

no misty, cloud-enveloped background . . . We forgot that reason had been the dry nurse of the giant offspring, and had fed her from the beginning with the strong bread and meat of fact; that every wry face the bantling ever made had been daguerreotyped, and all her words and deeds printed and labelled away in the pigeon-holes of official bureaux.'

Greenough was not fighting against reason, but was sharply aware of its boundaries and was determined to scrutinize the cultural effects of its having presided over our national birth:

> Reason can dissect, but cannot originate; she can adopt, but cannot create; she can modify, but cannot find. Give her but a cock-boat, and she will elaborate a line-of-battle ship; give her but a beam with its wooden tooth, and she turns out the patent plough. She is not young; and when her friends insist upon the phenomena of youth, then is she least attractive. She can imitate the flush of the young cheek, but where is the flash of the young eye? . . . Alas! She cannot buy the breath of childhood. The puny cathedral of Broadway, like an elephant dwindled to the size of a dog, measures her yearning for Gothic sublimity, while the roar of the Astor House, and the mammoth vase of the great reservoir, show how she works when she feels at home, and is in earnest.

The vigorous concern for our culture that brought Greenough to these examples allowed him to perceive and enunciate the social basis of art in the same year that Ruskin published his first volume of *Modern Painters* (1843). But he went beyond Ruskin because he was more solidly grounded in actual life: he did not yearn for a revival of the conditions that had produced the great cathedrals. Holding fast to his conviction that the adoption of forms for purposes for which they were not intended was always a sign of decay, he looked directly around him for healthy roots from which American art could grow. In that way he made his own approach to the organic style, insisting that whether he was examining the length of vertebrae in the necks of grazing quadrupeds, the dugout canoe, or the symmetry of a Doric temple, he learned everywhere 'that God's world has a distinct formula for every function, and that we shall seek in vain to borrow shapes; we must make the shapes, and can only effect this by mastering the principles.'

The normal way for an American to begin to gain that mastery is by the fullest acceptance of the possibilities of democracy. The force with which Greenough drives home that fact has immediate bearing on our particular development of the organic style, especially by Whitman. Emerson's mind also gave full assent to the connection that Greenough made between his belief that 'everything of beauty for beauty's sake' is 'non-functional embellishment,' false and moribund, and his belief that such dying always follows the separation of art from its source in the community. As Emerson set down his crowded recollections of Greenough's conversation—which revolved continually around these two beliefs— he was led to pronounce him 'the grandest of democrats,' magnanimous and philosophical.

Some proofs of Greenough's democracy in his letters are in the flamboyant vein. He told his brother how a diplomat asked him about a lady, ' "She belongs to one of your great American families, does she not?" I answered, "We have no great families in America. We have colossal men, but families remain in their natural greatness. The lady of whom you speak has certainly given many good servants to the republic." ' Other remarks were less self-conscious. Mentioning a sea captain who had put down a mutiny, he made a parallel instinctive to our early patriots by calling him a man 'of the Brutus and General Jackson stamp.' After working closely with a carpenter and a mason in setting his Washington in place, he declared that he wanted to see 'no better men than the mechanics of this country; they have high notions of honor, and no pretension.' The implications of that statement become political when we find Greenough adding that he would place 'magnates first in the list of obstacles to republican progress.' In the year of his death he wrote to Charles Sumner: 'It should never be forgotten that the English aristocracy, though not averse to all the liberty necessary for trade and manufactures still would prefer despotism to democracy. There is no aristocracy in history that has not preferred a master who would make them safe to a struggle with the masses.' [3]

Emerson noted the kind of connection Greenough developed between politics and art. The sculptor had been arguing that in a healthy society 'everything is generative, and everything connected.' He had used as an example of false division any religion that isolates the priestly function from ordinary life. 'If you take chastity apart, and make chastity a virtue, you create that sink of obscenity, a monk. The old ages, seeing that circumstances pinched them, and they got no divine man, tried to lift up one of their number out of the press, and so gain a right man. But it turned

3. Quoted from the manuscript in the Harvard College Library.

out that the new development really obtained was abnormal; they got a bloated belly.' Such consequences had always followed the theory that 'out of a prostrate humanity, as out of a bank and magazine' you can 'draw the materials for culture to a class. All a lie, and had the effect of a lie.' When Greenough came to his perception of such effects in contemporary life, he drew a picture that had not often disturbed the serenity of Concord: 'Whenever there is a wrong, the response is pain. The rowdy eyes that glare on you from the mob say plainly that they feel that you are doing them to death; you, you, have got the chain somewhere round their limbs, and, though they know not how,—War, internecine war, to the knife, is between us and you. Your six percent is as deadly a weapon as the old knife and tomahawk.'

It is no wonder that, demanding social and economic equality as the only right foundation for art, he saw in the architecture of Egypt and the Middle Ages merely 'cost to the constituency,' prodigious toil of oppressed peoples. 'In the Greek alone, beauty.' For Greenough believed that Greek art had been a product of free men, not working in isolation but co-operating in their crafts, and subordinated to the needs of the community. He does not appear to have reckoned with its basis in slave-labor that so disturbed Ruskin. Holding Athenian democracy to be the best society he knew, he cast around in his America for analogies that might produce an equal cultural vitality. He saw the most encouraging sign in the work that was being turned out by the foundries and machine-shops, where all the more important efforts, with a vigor born of our political institutions, tended 'towards simple and effective organization.' In their knowledge that 'the redundant must be pared down, the superfluous dropped, the necessary itself reduced to its simplest expression,' the mechanics of the United States had already outstripped the artists by throwing overboard any imitation of the English and working from their own bold inspirations. Unlike nearly all the aestheticians of his day, who recoiled in dismay from the vulgar squalor of industrialization, Greenough was clear in his insistence that notwithstanding the immediate ugliness, the meretricious by-products of scroll-work and brummagem, the right course for art was to accept the principles of the newly invented machines. If we compare the first form of one of these 'with the perfected type of the same instrument, we observe, as we trace it through the phases of improvement, how weight is shaken off where strength is less needed, how functions are made to approach without impeding each other, how the straight becomes curved, and the curve is straightened, till the struggling and cumbersome machine becomes the compact, effective, and beautiful engine.' Whitman's delight in 'A Locomotive in Winter' was hardly more abundant, and Greenough's more exacting concern with details pointed directly to the line that has been taken by Frank Lloyd Wright and the functional school.

Such a thoroughgoing dredging to fundamentals caused Greenough to see the recently built Houses of Parliament as 'a sort of *parvenu* nightmare, caused by the Middle Ages not being yet thoroughly digested by the British stomach.' His dislike of imitations became so uncompromising that he was also made uneasy by much of our Greek revival. Second to none in his admiration for the beauty of the Parthenon, he did not wonder 'at the greediness of the moderns to appropriate it,' but merely 'at the obtuseness which allowed them to persevere in trying to make it work in the towns.' He carried his standards to the logical conclusion of objecting to Jefferson's recommendation of the model of the Maison Carrée for the State House at Richmond. It was not enough, Greenough contended, to say that it was beautiful, for 'if such reasoning is to hold, why not translate one of Pindar's odes in memory of Washington, or set up in Carolina a colossal Osiris in honor of General Greene?' The point that he wanted to drive home was the unalterable need for 'the adaptation of the forms and magnitude of structures to the climate they are exposed to, and the offices for which they are intended.' By that kind of thoughtful and flexible study of ancient art, the American builder 'will learn of the Greeks to be American.'

It would be interesting to know whether Greenough's severity granted that in the buildings for the University of Virginia Jefferson had shown the ripe fruits of such knowledge. The inflation of our neo-classic Capital struck Greenough as setting an ever more malignant example, and he urged as an antidote those creations wherein the craftsman's rejection of borrowed authority, through the use of plain good sense, had produced something so like taste 'as scarce to require a distinctive title.' Pre-eminently, the men 'who have reduced locomotion to its simplest elements, in the trotting-wagon and the yacht America, are nearer to Athens at this moment than they who would bend the Greek temple to every use. I contend for Greek principles, not Greek things. If a flat sail goes nearest wind, a bellying sail, though picturesque, must be given up. The slender harness and tall gaunt wheels are not only effective, they are beautiful—

for they respect the beauty of a horse, and do not uselessly task him. The English span is a good one, but they lug along more pretension than beauty; they are stopped in their way to claim respect for wealth and station; they are stopped for this, and, therefore, easily passed by those who care not to seem, but are.'

By a train of like instances, by never relaxing his grip on the fact that 'the expression of life which is what we all crave, can only be obtained by *living*,' Greenough arrived at the formula that could describe his main concern, the phases by which intention grew organized and ripened to completeness: 'By beauty I mean the promise of function, by action I mean the presence of function, by character I mean the record of function.' Such abstractions can be very slippery to handle, but, except for occasional excited bursts of incoherence, Greenough's belief in the principle of organic growth for both man and his products was able to demonstrate the connection that he held to exist between art and action. He made this most explicit in arguing that there is no such thing as independent beauty: 'If the normal development of organized life be from beauty to action, from action to character, the progress is a progress upwards as well as forwards; and action will be higher than beauty, even as the summer is higher than the spring; and character will be higher than action, even as autumn is the résumé and result of spring and summer. If this be true, the attempt to prolong the phase of beauty into the epoch of action can only be made by non-performance; and false beauty or embellishment must be the result.' This kind of analogy would have recommended itself highly to Emerson who maintained, as we know, that the speech of the great orator is 'not to be distinguished from action.' And metaphors identifying the fulfilment of function with the season of ripeness were as characteristic of Melville as of Thoreau.

In the final extension of his three divisions, Greenough read into them a religious significance that mounted from 'faith of future action' and 'hope of future character' to 'the divinity of character' that gives itself 'in charity . . . to God, in sacrificing self to humanity.' What saved this identification from being merely verbal or from dissolving into uplift was Greenough's robust dislike of all transcendental millenniums. When he spoke of the potential divinity of man, he did not forget his artist's knowledge that the human body is 'a multiform command,' 'the most beautiful organization of earth.' When Alcott heard him talk, less than a month before the sculptor's death, he was amazed 'by the subtlety and mysticism of his distinctions, no less than by his great American sense and solidity of perception,' and particularly by his conception of 'the symbolism of man's body.' That symbol gave Greenough his central clue for his interpretation of life:

This stupendous form, towering as a lighthouse, commanding by its posture a wide horizon, standing in relation to the brutes where the spire stands in relation to the lowly colonnades of Greece and Egypt, touching earth with only one half the soles of its feet—it tells of majesty and dominion by that upreared spine, of duty by those unencumbered hands. Where is the ornament of this frame? It is all beauty, its motion is grace, no combination of harmony ever equalled, for expression and variety, its poised and stately gait; its voice is music . . .

What adds real fervor to Greenough's rhetoric is the perception, which unites him with Blake and Whitman, of man in his full revolutionary and democratic splendor as the base and measure of society. The main source for great art lies in following the body's command to create a comparably organic structure. Moreover, a healthy society can exist only if the magnificent and terrible energies of men can find through its organization their fulfilment. Holding such principles, Greenough mistrusted the current type of theorist of ideal communities, and was even cool to the abolitionist. He protested that nine times in ten the reformer had 'no wholesome, working, organic relation with God's ground or with his fellow men.' Even when he did not 'sit perched upon an income which is a dead branch of the living tree of industry,' still his virtue tended to remain a mere 'elevation on paper.' He did not realize that to plant it on earth demanded a much more full-blooded conception of the nature of man than any his reformer's zeal had comprehended—an understanding, for instance, that the savage's brute vitality cannot and should not be shaken off from civilized man, but 'must be assimilated and absorbed.' Greenough's welcoming acceptance of passion and belligerence, his view of social adjustment as the result of an inevitable struggle between warring forces, made him one of the spearheads of radical advance in the America of his day. His ardor sprang from his hatred of all attempts, whether in the social structure or in art, to divide man's wholeness and so to disperse and drain his vitality. The unity for which he fought was always 'the subordination of the parts to the whole, of the whole to the func-

tion,' terms which he applied to both aesthetic and political theory. In affirming that there can be a more healthful growth of art from republican
soil than from any hot-bed culture whatsoever, he did not relax his demand for expert training and critical discrimination. He simply insisted
that the artist must find his impulse and his completion in the community. If his rare seed is to flower, it must be 'consigned to the earth which
we all despise so truly—the hearts and heads of common men. There
must it find the soil and moisture, blood and tears, which burst its rind
and evolve the godhead within.'

As he looked around him for the best instance of this integral relationship, he found, like Emerson, that 'the modern architecture is ship-building.' This idea led Greenough to his most eloquent expression of the
possibilities of American art:

Observe a ship at sea! Mark the majestic form of her hull as she rushes
through the water, observe the graceful bend of her body, the gentle transition
from round to flat, the grasp of her keel, the leap of her bows, the symmetry
and rich tracery of her spars and rigging, and those grand wind muscles, her
sails. Behold an organization second only to that of an animal, obedient as
the horse, swift as the stag, and bearing the burden of a thousand camels from
pole to pole. What Academy of Design, what research of connoisseurship,
what imitation of the Greeks produced this marvel of construction? Here is
the result of the study of man upon the great deep, where Nature spake of
the laws of building, not in the feather and in the flower, but in winds and
waves, and he bent all his mind to hear and to obey. Could we carry into our
civil architecture the responsibilities that weigh upon our ship-building, we
should ere long have edifices as superior to the Parthenon, for the purposes
that we require, as the Constitution or the Pennsylvania is to the galley of
the Argonauts.

A final paradox lies in Greenough's belief that things would stay put in
stone but not in argument. For as Emerson wrote at his death, his 'tongue
was far cunninger in talk than his chisel to carve.' And his eye discerned
the basis and the value of our best craftsmanship.

3. Thoreau

'TRUE, there are architects so called in this country,' wrote Thoreau as he began the account of how he had built his cabin, 'and I have heard of one at least possessed with the idea of making architectural ornaments have a core of truth, a necessity, and hence a beauty, as if it were a revelation to him. All very well from his point of view, but only a little better than the common dilettantism. A sentimental reformer in architecture, he began at the cornice, not at the foundation.' This passage in *Walden* derives from a circumstance recorded in his journal for January 1852. Emerson had shown him with enthusiasm a letter he had just received from Greenough,[1] and Thoreau's one glimpse of the sculptor's theories drew out these hard remarks. In their context in *Walden* he is making his sharpest argument against the division of labor, which reduces not merely the tailor but the preacher and the merchant and the farmer to 'the ninth part of a man.' (A note in the manuscript added: 'That remark applies universally to the condition of men to-day.') He was so opposed to any complicating of life that did not correspond to a real need that he declared that no house should be painted except with the color of its builder's own blood and sweat. (This expression in his journal was softened in *Walden* to 'Better paint your house your own complexion.') His dislike of ornament finally carried him to the length of protesting against a nation's trying to commemorate itself by any architecture instead of by its powers of thought: 'How much more admirable the Bhagvat-Geeta than all the ruins of the East!'

It was too bad that Thoreau's prickly reaction against anything proposed by Emerson—an attitude that, following his first discipleship, seems to have grown habitual—should have kept him from appreciating that in Greenough he had a natural ally whose maturer thought could have

1. Though several short letters from Greenough are to be found among the Emerson papers, this one has not yet come to light. It may have been the same one from which Emerson quoted in *English Traits:* 'Here is my theory of structure: A scientific arrangement of spaces and forms to functions and to site; an emphasis of features proportioned to their *gradated* importance in function; color and ornament to be decided and arranged and varied by strictly organic laws, having a distinct reason for each decision; the entire and immediate banishment of all make-shift and make-believe.'

guided his own. In fancied disagreement with the sculptor's theories, he said that the only true architectural beauty 'has gradually grown from within outward, out of the necessities and character of the indweller.' Yet he was simply repeating, in looser, less technical language, one of Greenough's cardinal assumptions. And the radicalism that led Thoreau to declare that the most interesting dwellings in this country were commonly the most unpretending, the logger's hut and the cottages of the poor, found a fuller voice in Greenough's conviction that the genuine taste of the day would become 'enamored of the old, bald, neutral-toned Yankee farmhouse which seems to belong to the ground whereon it stands, as the caterpillar to the leaf that feeds him.'

Wherever Thoreau turned for fresh confirmation of his belief that true beauty reveals necessity, he saw that 'Nature is a greater and more perfect art,' and that there is a similarity between her operations and man's even in the details and trifles. He held, like Emerson, that 'man's art has wisely imitated those forms into which all matter is most inclined to run, as foliage and fruit.' But Thoreau studied more examples in detail than Emerson did. Any glance from his door could provide him with fresh evidence. The sumach and pine and hickory that surrounded his cabin reminded him of the most graceful sculptural forms. The tracery of frostwork suggested the intricate refinements of design; and when he wanted his basic lesson in Coleridge's distinction between mechanic and organic form, all he had to do was to mould a handful of earth and to note that however separately interesting its particles might be, their relation was one of mere lifeless juxtaposition. In marked contrast was the shape of even 'the simplest and most lumpish fungus,' and the reasons for its fascination crowded upon him: 'it is so obviously organic and related to ourselves . . . It is the expression of an idea; growth according to a law; matter not dormant, not raw, but inspired, appropriated by spirit.' With so many principles to be gleaned from the humblest growth, no wonder he held it 'monstrous when one cares but little about trees but much about Corinthian columns.'

When he tried to apply these principles to creation in literature, he sometimes was content with saying that 'true art is but the expression of our love of nature.' But he often pushed to a rigorous extreme not merely the supremacy of nature over art and of content over form, but also that of the artist's life over his work. He developed his own version of Milton's view that the heroic poem could be written only by the man who had lived a heroic life. As Thoreau put it, 'Nothing goes by luck in composition . . . The best you can write will be the best that you are.' His distrust of 'the *belles lettres* and the *beaux arts* and their professors' sprang from his desire to break down all artificial divisions between art and living. He often confronted the problem that 'it is not easy to write in a journal what interests us at any time, because to write it is not what interests us.'[2] His only solution for this dilemma was, as he said in a letter to one of his followers: 'As for style of writing, if one has anything to say, it drops from him simply and directly, as a stone falls to the ground.' He came to the same point when he praised the style of John Brown: 'The *art* of composition is as simple as the discharge of a bullet from a rifle, and its masterpieces imply an infinitely greater force behind them. This unlettered man's speaking and writing are standard English. Some words and phrases deemed vulgarisms and Americanisms before, he has made standard American.' Again Thoreau was much closer than he knew to Greenough, who had insisted that the style indicated by our mechanics was miscalled economical and cheap. On the contrary, Greenough said, 'It is the dearest of styles . . . Its simplicity is not the simplicity of emptiness or of poverty, its simplicity is that of justness, I had almost said, of justice.'

When Thoreau said, 'Give me simple, cheap, and homely themes,' he had no notion that their execution would prove easy. Even when he declared that the real poem is what the poet himself has become, he added that 'our whole life is taxed for the least thing well done.' In adopting the tenet that poetry consists in knowing the quality of a thing, he had realized by his early thirties that such knowledge could be arrived at only through the slowest unconscious process, for 'at first blush a man is not capable of reporting truth; he must be drenched and saturated with it first. What was *enthusiasm* in the young man must become *temperament* in the mature man.' We might compare this with Lawrence's realization that 'we have to know ourselves pretty thoroughly before we can break through the automatism of ideals and conventions . . . Only through fine delicate knowledge can we recognize and release our impulses.' Only in seasoned maturity, to shift back to Thoreau's imagery, will the poet's

---

2. Or as he phrased it in an awkward couplet in the *Week:*

> My life has been the poem I would have writ,
> But I could not both live and utter it.

truth exhale as naturally from him as 'the odor of the muskrat from the coat of the trapper.'

He often spoke of the organic style in an equally characteristic image—of its being a slow growth, unfolding under the care of the poet's patient hands. The degree to which his own practice lived up to that metaphor is also the degree to which his craftsmanship goes beyond Emerson's. He accepted the older man's view that genius is the abundance of health, but was less intermittent in his demand that talent must go with genius. To be sure, he hardly ever discusses specific forms. He apparently took it for granted that the artist's intuition will shape what is proper for it, and, in the course of objecting to some of Carlyle's extravagances, said little more than that the great writer works not by introducing new forms but by reinvigorating old ones. However, in his perception that this renewal comes through the fresh handling of words, he generally sensed a more integral connection between the words and the thought than Emerson did. That was why he regarded translations as an impossibility, and held that the classics could be read only after a training as rigorous 'as the athletes underwent.' Moreover, he made another discrimination, essentially foreign to Emerson, between the spoken and the written word. He held that 'what is called eloquence in the forum is commonly found to be rhetoric in the study,' that however much we may admire the orator's power, the style that lives beyond the emotion of the moment demands a much more exacting composition. When Thoreau said of the poet, almost in Frost's words, that 'the tone and pitch of his voice is the main thing,' he knew that 'a perfect expression requires a particular rhythm or measure for which no other can be substituted.' Such knowledge—the product, as we have seen, of his own sensitive organization—was his firmest defense against the formlessness that beset his desire to speak in harmony with nature. If it seldom rescued his immature verse—almost the type instance of mechanic form in its imitation of the surface tricks of the metaphysicals—it brought both precision and timbre to the movement of his ripened prose.

Only by the accumulation of such slight threads as those spun out in the last paragraph can we finally distinguish between Thoreau's and Emerson's understanding of the organic style. In Emerson's record of one of the early conversations between them (1838), it was Thoreau who was complaining that 'if the man took too much pains with the expression, he was not any longer the Idea himself.' Emerson agreed, but pointed out 'that this was the tragedy of Art that the artist was at the expense of the man.' However, as the years advanced, it was the younger writer who was to accept this inevitable fact. Observing, two decades later, that farmer Tarbell had at last got his barn built, he knew that the artist could make his structure only through an equally 'steady struggle, with alternate failure and success.' He must learn both endurance and detachment, for his work consists in performing '*post-mortem* examinations of himself before he is dead.' Or, in a different figure, he must have 'the cold skill' to quarry and carve a statue out of his own feelings. This subordination of himself to the work to be done reminds us, even in its phrasing, of what Eliot has valued in Hawthorne: 'the firmness, the true coldness, the hard coldness of the genuine artist.'

4. New England Landscapes

'Concord woods were more to me than my library, or Emerson even. They were more to him than they were to me, and still more to Thoreau than to either of us. Take the forest and skies from their pages, and they, E. and T., have faded and fallen clean out of their pictures.'

—Alcott's *Journal* (1851)

ONE reason why both Emerson and Thoreau thought instinctively of art as 'a natural fruit,' was that they had chosen visible nature for so much of their subject matter. To be sure, they both insisted that their interest in this was subordinate to their concern with man. Nevertheless, what drew man out in Concord, what constituted a major resource unknown to cities, was the beauty of his surroundings. One way, therefore, of distinguishing between Emerson's and Thoreau's handling of the organic style is by appraising the differing qualities of their landscapes.[1]

William James, who also loved New England landscapes, singled out as among Emerson's best things the opening of his second essay on 'Na- *
ture': 'There are days which occur in this climate, at almost any season of the year, wherein the world reaches its perfection.' These halcyons

1. Both Emerson and Thoreau were treated in great detail by Norman Foerster, *Nature in American Literature* (1923).

* My Everyman edition, p. 294

may be looked for with most assurance in that pure October weather called Indian summer, for then 'the day, immeasurably long, sleeps over the broad hills and warm wide fields,' then 'everything that has life gives signs of satisfaction, and the cattle that lie on the ground seem to have great and tranquil thoughts.' This buoyant tone bears out the fact that if 'the two most obvious characteristics of Nature are loveliness and power,' as Whitehead has suggested, the former was all that Emerson generally saw. This is curious, in view of his environment, for even though he was not hemmed in by the savage energies of the jungle, 'red in tooth and claw,' nevertheless two centuries of New England had provided enough lessons of the hardihood essential to wrest a living from the bare recalcitrant elements. However, by Emerson's time the struggle had relaxed in the self-subsisting villages that 'whitened the land.' His own assurance could lead him into such blind generalizations as this in 'Prudence,' which Melville marked: 'The terrors of the storm are chiefly confined to the parlor and the cabin. The drover, the sailor, buffets it all day, and his health renews itself at as vigorous a pulse under the sleet, as under the sun of June.' 'To one who has weathered Cape Horn as a common sailor,' said Melville, 'what stuff all this is.' His experience had taught him that primitive brutality was not gone out of the world—not out of nature, and not out of man, as he knew man in America: a conviction that actuated his bitter attack on transcendentalism in *Pierre*.

That Emerson was not wholly negligent of nature's power can be seen in his early (1838) detailed analysis of the task confronting any American who would record her. Notwithstanding his joy in the English poets, he felt that they had conversed with the mere surface and show, that whenever he went into the forest he would find all as new and undescribed as 'the honking of the wild geese flying by night.' Debating, three years later, whether he ought not call his first collection *Forest Essays,* he seized upon what was still the significant feature of the American landscape. For Harriet Martineau had recently reported that in her travels throughout the country she was never out of sight of the woods except when on the prairies of Illinois. Emerson had tried to describe his mixed sensation at seeing the day break in Concord—of pain at feeling himself in 'an alien world,' a world not yet subdued by thought, and of exultation as his soul broke down its narrow walls and ranged out to the very horizon. He came to the source of his sensation when he wrote:

The noonday darkness of the American forest, the deep, echoing, aboriginal woods, where the living columns of the oak and fir tower up from the ruins of the trees of the last millennium; where, from year to year, the eagle and the crow see no intruder; the pines, bearded with savage moss, yet touched with grace by the violets at their feet . . . where the traveller, amid the repulsive plants that are native in the swamp, thinks with pleasing terror of the distant town; this beauty,—haggard and desert beauty, which the sun and the moon, the snow and the rain, repaint and vary, has never been recorded by art . . .

In view of this desire to catch nature's very features, we are surprised at Emerson's early hostility towards Wordsworth. At his first discussion of him (1826), Emerson was bothered by his 'being too much a *poet*,' and could not read his 'mystic and unmeaning verses without feeling that if he had cultivated poetry less, and learning and society more, he would have gained more favor at the hands of the Muses'—an objection that you could readily imagine to have been written against the later Emerson by a survivor from the eighteenth century. Two years later he was still put off by Wordsworth's 'trying to distil the essence of poetry from poetic things . . . He mauls the moon and the waters and the bulrushes, as his main business.' He had a low opinion of *The Excursion* since it was wanting in fact, in coarse and tangible details, and was merely 'metaphysical and evanescent.' Such strictures are the sharpest reminder of how much inherited rationalism Emerson had to throw away before he could begin to feel (1831) that Wordsworth had written lines 'that are like outward nature, so fresh, so simple, so durable,' or could come to his final recognition (1840) that, in spite of the poet's many glaring lapses in talent, his genius was 'the exceptional fact of the period,' since he had done 'as much as any living man to restore sanity to cultivated society.'

Even then he would still have felt that no Englishman could speak to him adequately of the different nature he knew, not trim hedgerows but a great sloven continent, 'nature sleeping, overgrowing, almost conscious, too much by half for man in the picture, and so giving a certain *tristesse*, like the rank vegetation of swamps and forests seen at night'—for such remained one of his dominant images. But its sadness was only infrequently uppermost. In some lines that he wrote soon after his arrival in Naples (1833), he said that

> Not many men see beauty in the fogs
> Of close, low pinewoods in a river town.

But for him, as he looked back across the ocean, there was no happier vision than that of a morning walk by a moist roadside where

Peep the blue violets out of the black loam.

Ten years earlier the stiff abstractness of his poem, 'Good-bye, proud world! I'm going home,' had been relieved by the details that drew him to the country—the blackbird, the pines and the evening star. He liked to call himself 'the bantling of a country Muse,' and when he came to write 'Self-Reliance' he was still certain that 'My book should smell of pines and resound with the hum of insects.' The year before writing *Nature* he had played with the idea of composing a book of the seasons, which 'should contain the natural history of the woods around my shifting camp for every month in the year'—a partial description of what was fulfilled by *Walden*. In 1837, only a few months before the first mention in his journal of Thoreau, he said that 'the American artist who would carve a wood-god, and who was familiar with the forest in Maine where . . . huge mosses depending from the trees and the mass of timber give a savage and haggard [again those adjectives] strength to the grove, would produce a very different statue from the sculptor who only knew a European woodland—the tasteful Greek, for example.'

Yet when Emerson came to carve his own, even Alcott had to say that his Nature, 'caught, it is true, from our own woods,' was 'never American, nor New English, which were better, but some fancied realm, some Atlantides of this Columbia, very clearly discernible to him but not by us.' As Alcott conceived it, Emerson 'was forbidden pure companionship with Nature' because 'he dwelt rather in an intellectual grove.' Emerson himself declared (1849) that the characteristic of the Greek age was that 'men deified Nature'; of the Christian, that Nature was looked upon as evil and that the soul craved a heaven above it; of the modern age, that men have returned again to Nature, 'but now the tendency is to marry mind to Nature, and to put Nature under the mind.' The conclusion of scholarship, in J. W. Beach's *The Concept of Nature in Nineteenth-Century English Poetry* (1936), reinforces Alcott's perception by finding that 'Emerson almost invariably views nature all too blandly through the eyes of the "mind" . . . Almost never does it occur to him that the mind may have something to learn from nature, from the world which it finds given to it from without.'

Emerson phrased the relationship in two lines in 'Woodnotes':

> So waved the pine-tree through my thought
> And fanned the dreams it never brought.

The nature to which he gave utterance is far more etherealized than Wordsworth's since it has so little of the freshening that was produced by Wordsworth's delicate but full trust in the knowledge that came from his senses. Emerson approached nearest to such trust when he confessed that, although the realm of nature remained strictly subordinate to the ideal, he had no hostility towards it, but rather a child's love for its 'gypsy attraction.' In such moments of shy fondness he achieved the lyric grace of his 'Gardener,' who,

> True Brahmin, in the morning meadows wet,
> Expound[s] the Vedas of the violet.

The single blossom against the soil is again the apt symbol for his kind of beauty, as were the petals of the rhodora in the black waters of the pool. From these fragile details his eye always moved off to the horizon, since he believed that in its distant line 'man beholds somewhat as beautiful as his own nature.'

It is no wonder then that many of his landscapes were composed not out of tangible materials but from the evanescent light of reflections. He liked to recount his excursions with Henry, how 'with one stroke of the paddle I leave the village politics and personalities, yes, and the world of villages and personalities, behind, and pass into a delicate realm of sunset and moonlight, too bright almost for spotted man to enter without novitiate and probation. We penetrate bodily this incredible beauty; we dip our hands in this painted element; our eyes are bathed in these lights and forms.' Or, again, with Ellery: 'My eye rested on the charming play of light on the water which he was striking with his paddle. I fancied I had never seen such color, such transparency, such eddies; it was the hue of Rhine wines, it was jasper and verd-antique, topaz and chalcedony, it was gold and green and chestnut and hazel in bewitching succession . . .'[2]

2. It seems worth notice in passing that Hawthorne also described such an excursion with Channing. Although his language is more stiffly Latinate and unable to register Emerson's vibrancy, he arrives at a conception of beauty to which Emerson could have subscribed: 'The river sleeps along its course and dreams of the sky and of the clustering foliage, amid which fall showers of broken sunlight, imparting specks of vivid cheerfulness, in contrast

When Thoreau came to describe the course of his boat on the river, the impression is quite different, as a passage near the outset of the *Week,* a sample of his level style, can show:

Late in the afternoon we passed a man on the shore fishing with a long birch pole, its silvery bark left on, and a dog at his side, rowing so near as to agitate his cork with our oars, and drive away luck for a season; and when we had rowed a mile as straight as an arrow, with our faces turned towards him, and the bubbles in our wake still visible on the tranquil surface, there stood the fisher still with his dog, like statues under the other side of the heavens, the only objects to relieve the eye in the extended meadow; and there would he stand abiding his luck, till he took his way home through the fields at evening with his fish. Thus, by one bait or another, Nature allures inhabitants into all her recesses.

Unlike Emerson's series of ejaculations, the aim of Thoreau's passage is not just to suggest the diffused radiance that stimulated him, but to present by minute notations the record of a whole scene. Although the perceived details are the slightest—the silvery bark on the pole, the bubbles on the tranquil surface—their exactness carries you down that particular unswerving mile, and gives you the illusion of sharing in the lapse of space and time during which the fisherman was still standing still on the bank with his dog. The quality of Thoreau's landscapes depends on his belief that 'man identifies himself with earth or the material.' Yet he also remained clear that 'we are not wholly involved in Nature,' and, in the awareness of his partial detachment, felt that he associated with it as a soul with its body. Although he often contrasted nature's innocence and serenity with perturbable man, in *The Maine Woods,* at least, he declared

with the quiet depth of the prevailing tint. Of all this scene, the slumbering river has a dream picture in its bosom. Which, after all, was the most real—the picture, or the original? —the objects palpable to our grosser senses, or their apotheosis in the stream beneath? Surely the disembodied images stand in closer relation to the soul.' Notwithstanding such a transcendent flight, Hawthorne proceeds to a conclusion very different from the thoughts of liberation that Emerson rejoiced in: 'And yet how sweet, as we floated homeward adown the golden river at sunset,—how sweet was it to return within the system of human society, not as to a dungeon and a chain, but as to a stately edifice, whence we could go forth at will into statelier simplicity!' As he saw the Old Manse from the river, he thought 'how gently did its gray, homely aspect rebuke the speculative extravagances of the day! It had grown sacred in connection with the artificial life against which we inveighed; it had been a home for many years in spite of all.' And reflecting that it was his home too, he 'prayed that the upper influences might long protect the institutions that had grown out of the heart of mankind.'

that 'we have not seen pure Nature, unless we have seen her thus vast and drear and inhuman, though in the midst of cities. Nature was here something savage and awful, though beautiful.' It was 'Matter, vast, terrific,' not man's familiar Mother Earth but the realm 'of Necessity and Fate.'

Here Thoreau was most akin to the tradition of the pioneer settlers, who had regarded the lonely wilderness with awe that could mount to terror. But it was not in his temperament to dwell on the diabolic power of the unsubdued dark wastes; his more characteristic mood is that of the Sunday morning worshipper of Pan. He repeatedly asserted that 'in literature it is only the wild that attracts us.' On that ground he felt that the English poets had 'not seen the west side of any mountain,' that they had missed the sterner primeval aspects, that Wordsworth was 'too tame for the Chippeway.' And despite his pleasure in Gilpin's *Forest Scenery,* Thoreau decided that the limitations of its mild picturesqueness came from looking too much at nature with the eye of the artist instead of in the more normal way of the hunter or woodchopper. In saying, 'as Cowley loved a garden, so I a forest,' he implied just the relation that he wanted and that he developed in *Walden:* 'I found in myself, and still find, an instinct toward a higher, or, as it is named, spiritual life, as do most men, and another toward a primitive rank and savage one, and I reverence them both.' He could describe this second instinct with a dash of humor when he said he might learn some wisdom from the woodchuck, since 'his ancestors have lived here longer than mine'; or when he delivered the jeremiad of the huckleberry picker over the fact that 'the wild fruits of the earth' disappear before the encroachments of civilization; or when he veered for a moment into thinking of Concord as an effete and emasculated region with its nobler animals exterminated, and thanked God for New Hampshire 'everlasting and unfallen.' He spoke from his heart when he said that he had no greater satisfaction in America than when he reflected that what William Bradford saw he still could see, since 'aboriginal Nature' had not changed one iota. And one night at Chesuncook, listening to his guide talk to the other Indians, he felt that he had come as near to primitive man as any of the discoverers ever did.

He left at his death eleven manuscript notebooks, running to over half a million words, in which he had recorded what he had learned of the Indians, their customs and lore, and their enduring struggle with the elements. He believed it the duty of the poet to report the residual effects that this race had made on the life of his own white generation. He felt an untold debt to the example of their discipline as he trained himself to comparable alertness of eye and ear. When Emerson said that his friend had 'turned a face of bronze to expectations,' he symbolized the fact that the stoic strain in his behavior was owing far more to his veneration of the red men than to any study of Zeno. Certainly the lessons he had learned from them contributed to the firm reality that distinguishes his portrayal of nature. And they had helped him discover that beneath the bright surfaces of the civilized mind, 'the savage in man is never quite eradicated.' [3]

In contrasting Thoreau with Emerson, Alcott felt that the former revealed secrets of nature 'older than fields and gardens,' that 'he seems alone, of all the men I have known, to be a native New Englander.' Yet he could not help regretting at times that Thoreau was so earthbound, and wished that he might come out of the woods to the orchards, and so be pastoral instead of wild. It is doubtful whether most readers now sense in Thoreau more than a whiff of wildness. He wanted to bring into his writing 'muck from the meadows'; but what he really managed to bring finds an apter image in the delicate fragrance of the ferns or perhaps the ranker odor of the pines. His instinct towards the higher life was so inordinately encouraged by his contemporaries that it was only by the sturdiest action that he held fast to the soil. He described his most fertile process while saying why he went to the woods: 'Let us settle ourselves, and work and wedge our feet downward through the mud and slush of opinion, and prejudice, and tradition, and delusion, and appearance, that alluvion which covers the globe, through Paris and London, through New York and Boston and Concord, through Church and State, through poetry and

3. Although repelled by transcendentalism and by what he considered Thoreau's eccentricities, Parkman made a kindred response to the forest as the great feature of the American landscape. He said that at sixteen he had become 'enamored of the woods.' 'Before the end of the sophomore year my various schemes had crystallized into a plan of writing the story of what was then known as the "Old French War," that is, the war that ended in the conquest of Canada, for here, as it seemed to me, the forest drama was more stirring and the forest stage more thronged with appropriate actors than in any other passage of our history. It was not till some years later that I enlarged the plan to include the whole course of the American conflict between France and England, or, in other words, the history of the American forest; for this was the light in which I regarded it. My theme fascinated me, and I was haunted with wilderness images day and night.' Out of his lifelong devotion to that theme sprang the most imaginative work of history that we have yet had in America.

philosophy and religion, till we come to a hard bottom and rocks in place, which we can call *reality,* and say, This is, and no mistake.'

This positive dredging beat reminds us again of his awareness of the physical basis of rhythm. It can remind us also of what Lawrence felt, that 'the promised land, if it be anywhere, lies away beneath our feet. No more prancing upwards. No more uplift.' Lawrence's discovery was quickened by watching and almost identifying himself with the downward thrust into the earth of the feet of Indian dancers. But Thoreau's knowledge was owing less directly to the Indians than to his re-creation for himself of the conditions of primitive life. He approximated Lawrence's words when he said that in good writing, 'the poem is drawn out from under the feet of the poet, his whole weight has rested on this ground.' Emerson, by contrast, wanted to 'walk upon the ground, but not to sink.' What Thoreau's language gained from his closer contact can be read in his evocation of a river walk, where every phrase is expressive of acute sensation: 'Now your feet expand on a smooth sandy bottom, now contract timidly on pebbles, now slump in genial fatty mud, amid the pads.'

But as you think again of the prolonged sensuous and rhythmical experience that Lawrence was able to make out of his response to the New Mexican corn dance, or of Hemingway's account of fishing on Big Two-Hearted River, you realize that Thoreau's product was ordinarily somewhat less full-bodied. When he said, 'Heaven is under our feet as well as over our heads,' he was speaking of the luminous clarity of the pond. A characteristic example to put beside Emerson's 'Snow-Storm' is the poem 'Smoke':

> Light-winged Smoke, Icarian bird,
> Melting thy pinions in thy upward flight,
> Lark without song, and messenger of dawn,
> Circling above the hamlets as thy nest;
> Or else, departing dream, and shadowy form
> Of midnight vision, gathering up thy skirts;
> By night star-veiling, and by day
> Darkening the light and blotting out the sun;
> Go thou my incense upward from this hearth,
> And ask the gods to pardon this clear flame.

The delicacy of the wraith-like movement finds its articulation in the succession of predominantly high-pitched vowels in the opening two lines. The 'Icarian bird,' a neat image for the melting away of the smoke in the bright morning sky, may then lead into too many fanciful conceits, but any tendency to vagueness is checked by the accurate epithet, 'star-veiling.' With that the contrast between the 'shadowy form' and the rays of light, latent from the start, flowers exquisitely and prepares the way for the final statement, which makes the poem no mere descriptive exercise but Thoreau's declaration of his ever fresh renewal of purpose with the kindling of his fire in the morning. The 'clear flame' of his spirit is so distinct and firm that it needs his plea for pardon to keep him from verging on *hubris* as he confidently contrasts his life with a world which is obscure and desperate in its confusion. That full contrast, to be sure, emerges only through the poem's context in *Walden,* but enough of the human situation is implied in the verses themselves to let them serve as a rounded, if minute, instance of Coleridge's distinction between imitation and mere copying. Coleridge held that the artist must not try to make a surface reproduction of nature's details, but 'must imitate that which is within the thing . . . for so only can he hope to produce any work truly natural in the object and truly human in the effect.' That combination has been created in this poem, since the reader's pleasure does not spring from the specific recordings, however accurate, but from the imperceptible interfusion with these of the author's own knowledge and feeling, and of his skill in evolving an appropriate form.

5. *Walden:* Craftsmanship *vs.* Technique

'You can't read any genuine history—as that of Herodotus or the Venerable Bede—without perceiving that our interest depends not on the subject but on the man,—on the manner in which he treats the subject and the importance he gives it. A feeble writer . . . must have what he thinks a great theme, which we are already interested in through the accounts of others, but a genius—a Shakespeare, for instance—would make the history of his parish more interesting than another's history of the world.'

—THOREAU's *Journal* (March 1861)

IT IS apparent, in view of this last distinction of Coleridge's, that the real test of whether Thoreau mastered organic form can hardly be made on the basis of accounting for the differences in body and flavor between his portrayal of the natural world and Emerson's, revelatory as these differences are. Nor can it be made by considering one of the rare occasions when his verse was redeemed by virtue of his discipline in translating from the Greek Anthology. Nor is it enough to reckon with the excellence of individual passages of prose, since the frequent charge is that whereas Emerson was master of the sentence, Thoreau was master of the paragraph, but that he was unable to go farther and attain 'the highest or structural achievements of form in a whole book.' The only adequate way of answering that is by considering the structure of *Walden* as a whole, by asking to what extent it meets Coleridge's demand of shaping, 'as it develops, itself from within.'

On one level *Walden* is the record of a personal experience, yet even in making that remark we are aware that this book does not go rightfully into the category of *Two Years Before the Mast* or *The Oregon Trail.* Why it presents a richer accumulation than either of those vigorous pieces of contemporary history is explained by its process of composition. Although Thoreau said that the bulk of its pages were written during his two years of sojourn by the pond (1845-7), it was not ready for publication until seven years later, and ultimately included a distillation from his journals over the whole period from 1838. A similar process had helped to transform his week's boat trip with his brother from a private to a symbolical event, since the record was bathed in memory for a decade (1839-49) before it found its final shape in words. But the flow of the *Week* is as leisurely and discursive as the bends in the Concord river, and the casual pouring in of miscellaneous poems and essays that Thoreau had previously printed in *The Dial* tends to obscure the cyclical movement. Yet each day advances from dawn to the varied sounds of night, and Thoreau uses an effective device for putting a period to the whole by the shift of the final morning from lazy August to the first sharp forebodings of transforming frost.

The sequence of *Walden* is arranged a good deal more subtly, perhaps because its subject constituted a more central symbol for Thoreau's accruing knowledge of life. He remarked on how the pond itself was one of the earliest scenes in his recollection, dating from the occasion when he had been brought out there one day when he was four, and how thereafter 'that woodland vision for a long time made the drapery of my dreams.' By 1841 he had already announced, 'I want to go soon and live away by the pond,' and when pressed by friends about what he would do when he got there, he had asked in turn if it would not be employment enough 'to watch the progress of the seasons'? In that same year he had said: 'I think I could write a poem to be called "Concord." For argument I should have the River, the Woods, the Ponds, the Hills, the Fields, the Swamps and Meadows, the Streets and Buildings, and the Villagers.' In his completed 'poem' these last elements had receded into the background. What had come squarely to the fore, and made the opening chapter by far the longest of all, was the desire to record an experiment in 'Economy' as an antidote to the 'lives of quiet desperation' that he saw the mass of men leading. This essay on how he solved his basic needs of food and shelter might stand by itself, but also carries naturally forward to the more poignant condensation of the same theme in 'Where I lived, and What I lived for,' which reaches its conclusion in the passage on wedging down to reality.

At this point the skill with which Thoreau evolved his composition begins to come into play. On the one hand, the treatment of his material might simply have followed the chronological outline; on the other, it might have drifted into being loosely topical. At first glance it may appear that the latter is what happened, that there is no real cogency in the order of the chapters. That would have been Lowell's complaint, that Thoreau 'had no artistic power such as controls a great work to the serene balance of completeness.'[1] But so far as the opposite can be proved by the effective arrangement of his entire material, the firmness with which Thoreau binds his successive links is worth examining. The student and observer that he has settled himself to be at the end of his second chapter leads easily into his discussion of 'Reading,' but that in turn gives way to his concern with the more fundamental language, which all things speak, in the chapter on 'Sounds.' Then, after he has passed from the tantivy of

1. The don of Harvard was not entirely blind to the man of Concord. Even in his notorious essay on *Walden* in *My Study Windows* he perceived that Thoreau 'had caught his English at its living source, among the poets and prose-writers of its best days,' and compared him with Donne and Browne. When Lowell tried to dismiss Thoreau as a crank, he was really bothered, as Henry Canby has pointed out, by Thoreau's attack upon his own ideals of genteel living. How different from Emerson's is Lowell's tone when he says that while Thoreau 'studied with respectful attention the minks and woodchucks, his neighbors, he looked with utter contempt on the august drama of destiny of which his country was the scene, and on which the curtain had already risen.' As Mr. Canby has added: 'By destiny, Lowell clearly means the "manifest destiny" of the exploitation of the West, whose more sordid and unfortunate aspects Thoreau had prophesied two generations before their time of realization.'

wild pigeons to the whistle of the locomotive, he reflects that once the cars have gone by and the restless world with them, he is more alone than ever. That starts the transition to the chapter on 'Solitude,' in which the source of his joy is to live by himself in the midst of nature with his senses unimpaired. The natural contrast is made in the next chapter on 'Visitors,' which he opens by saying how he believes he loves society as much as most, and is ready enough to fasten himself 'like a bloodsucker for the time to any full-blooded man' who comes his way. But after he has talked enthusiastically about the French woodchopper, and other welcome friends from the village, he remembers 'restless committed men,' the self-styled reformers who felt it their duty to give him advice. At that he breaks away with 'Meanwhile my beans . . . were impatient to be hoed'; and that opening carries him back to the earlier transition to the chapter on 'Sounds': 'I did not read books the first summer; I hoed beans.'

The effect of that repetition is to remind the reader of the time sequence that is knitting together all these chapters after the building of the cabin in the spring. From 'The Bean Field' as the sphere of his main occupation, he moves on, in 'The Village,' to his strolls for gossip, which, 'taken in homeopathic doses, was really as refreshing in its way as the rustle of leaves and the peeping of frogs.' Whether designedly or not, this chapter is the shortest in the book, and yields to rambles even farther away from the community than Walden, to 'The Ponds' and to fishing beyond 'Baker Farm.' As he was returning through the woods with his catch, and glimpsed in the near dark a woodchuck stealing across his path, then came the moment when he 'felt a strange thrill of savage delight, and was strongly tempted to seize and devour him raw.' And in the flash of his realization of his double instinct towards the spiritual and the wild, he has the starting point for the next two contrasting chapters, 'Higher Laws' and 'Brute Neighbors,' in considering both of which he follows his rule of going far enough to please his imagination.

From here on the structure becomes cyclical, his poem of the seasons or myth of the year. The accounts of his varied excursions have brought him to the day when he felt that he could no longer warm himself by the embers of the sun, which 'summer, like a departed hunter, had left.' Consequently he set about finishing his cabin by building a chimney, and called that act 'House-Warming.' There follows a solid block of winter in the three chapters, 'Winter Visitors,' 'Winter Animals,' and 'The Pond in Winter,' that order suggesting the way in which the radius

of his experience contracted then more and more to his immediate surroundings. However, the last pages on the pond deal with the cutting of
the ice, and end with that sudden extraordinary expansion of his thought
which annihilates space and time.

The last movement is the advance to 'Spring.' The activity of the ice
company in opening its large tracts has hastened the break-up of the
rest of the pond; and, listening to its booming, he recalls that one attraction that brought him to the woods was the opportunity and leisure to
watch this renewal of the world. He has long felt in his observations that
a day is an epitome of a year, and now he knows that a year is likewise
symbolical of a life; and so, in presenting his experience by the pond, he
foreshortens and condenses the twenty-six months to the interval from the
beginning of one summer to the next. In the melting season he feels
more than ever the mood of expanding promise, and he catches the reader
up into this rich forward course by one of his most successful kinesthetic
images, which serves to round out his cycle: 'And so the seasons went
rolling on into summer, as one rambles into higher and higher grass.'
To that he adds only the bare statement of when he left the woods, and
a 'Conclusion,' which explains that he did so for as good a reason as he
had gone there. He had other lives to live, and he knew now that he
could find for himself 'a solid bottom everywhere.' That discovery gave
him his final serene assurance that 'There is more day to dawn,' and consequently he was not to be disturbed by the 'confused *tintinnabulum*' that
sometimes reached his midday repose. He recognized it for the noise of
his contemporaries.

The construction of the book involved deliberate rearrangement of
material. For instance, a single afternoon's return to the pond in the fall
of 1852 was capable of furnishing details that were woven into half a
dozen passages of the finished work, two of them separated by seventy
pages. Nevertheless, since no invention was demanded, since all the material was a *donnée* of Thoreau's memory, my assertion that *Walden* does
not belong with the simple records of experience may require more establishing. The chief clue to how it was transformed into something else lies
in Thoreau's extension of his remark that he did not believe himself to
be 'wholly involved in Nature.' He went on to say that in being aware
of himself as a human entity, he was 'sensible of a certain doubleness'
that made him both participant and spectator in any event. This ability
to stand 'as remote from myself as from another' is the indispensable

attribute of the dramatist. Thoreau makes you share in the excitement of his private scenes, for example, by the kind of generalized significance he can give to his purchase and demolishment of an old shanty for its boards:

I was informed treacherously by a young Patrick that neighbor Seeley, an Irishman, in the intervals of the carting, transferred the still tolerable, straight, and drivable nails, staples, and spikes to his pocket, and then stood when I came back to pass the time of day, and look freshly up, unconcerned, with spring thoughts, at the devastation; there being a dearth of work, as he said. He was there to represent spectatordom, and help make this seemingly insignificant event one with the removal of the gods of Troy.

The demands he made of great books are significant of his own intentions: 'They have no cause of their own to plead, but while they enlighten and sustain the reader his common sense will not refuse them.' Propaganda is not the source of the inner freedom they offer to the reader, for their relation to life is more inclusive than argument; or, as Thoreau described it, they are at once 'intimate' and 'universal.' He aimed unerringly to reconcile these two extremes in his own writing. His experience had been fundamental in that it had sprung from his determination to start from obedience to the rudimentary needs of a man who wanted to be free. Greenough had seen how, in that sense, 'Obedience is worship,' for by discerning and following the functional patterns of daily behavior, you could discover the proportions of beauty that would express and complete them. It was Thoreau's conviction that by reducing life to its primitive conditions, he had come to the roots from which healthy art must flower, whether in Thessaly or Concord. It was not just a figure of speech when he said that 'Olympus is but the outside of the earth everywhere.' The light touch of his detachment allows the comparison of his small things with great, and throughout the book enables him to possess the universe at home.

As a result *Walden* has spoken to men of widely differing convictions, who have in common only the intensity of their devotion to life. It became a bible for many of the leaders of the British labor movement after Morris. When the sound of a little fountain in a shop window in Fleet Street made him think suddenly of lake water, Yeats remembered also his boyhood enthusiasm for Thoreau. He did not leave London then and go and live on Innisfree. But out of his loneliness in the foreign city he did write the first of his poems that met with a wide response, and

'The Lake Isle'—despite its Pre-Raphaelite flavor—was reminiscent of *Walden* even to 'the small cabin' Yeats built and the 'bean rows' he planted in his imagination. *Walden* was also one of our books that bulked largest for Tolstoy when he addressed his brief message to America (1901) and urged us to rediscover the greatness of our writers of the fifties: 'And I should like to ask the American people why they do not pay more attention to these voices (hardly to be replaced by those of financial and industrial millionaires, or successful generals and admirals), and continue the good work in which they made such hopeful progress.' In 1904 Proust wrote to the Comtesse de Noailles: 'Lisez . . . les pages admirables de *Walden*. Il me semble qu'on les lise en soi-même tant elles sortent du fond de notre expérience intime.'

In his full utilization of his immediate resources Thoreau was the kind of native craftsman whom Greenough recognized as the harbinger of power for our arts. Craftsmanship in this sense involves the mastery of traditional modes and skills; it has been thought of more often in connection with Indian baskets or Yankee tankards and hearth-tools than with the so-called fine arts. In fact, until fairly lately, despite Greenough's pioneering, it has hardly been consistently thought of in relation to American products of any kind. The march of our experience has been so dominantly expansive, from one rapid disequilibrium to the next, that we have neglected to see what Constance Rourke, among others, has now pointed out so effectively: that notwithstanding the inevitable restlessness of our long era of pioneering, at many stages within that process the strong counter-effort of the settlers was for communal security and permanence. From such islands of realization and fulfilment within the onrushing torrent have come the objects, the order and balance of which now, when we most need them, we can recognize as among the most valuable possessions of our continent. The conspicuous manifestation of these qualities, as Greenough already knew, has been in architecture as the most social of forms, whether in the clipper, or on the New England green, or in the Shaker communities. But the artifacts of the cabinet maker, the potter and the founder, or whatever other utensils have been shaped patiently and devotedly for common service, are likewise a testimony of what Miss Rourke has called our classic art, recognizing that this term 'has nothing to do with grandeur, that it cannot be copied or imported, but is the outgrowth of a special mode of life and feeling.'

Thoreau's deep obligation to such traditional ways has been obscured by our thinking of him only as the extreme protestant. It is now clear that his revolt was bound up with a determination to do all he could to pre-vent the dignity of common labor from being degraded by the idle tastes of the rich. When he objected that 'the mason who finishes the cornice of the palace returns at night perchance to a hut not so good as a wig-wam,' he showed the identity of his social and aesthetic foundations. Although he did not use Greenough's terms, he was always requiring a functional relationship. What he responded to as beauty was the appli-cation of trained skill to the exigencies of existence. He made no arbitrary separation between arts, and admired the Indian's woodcraft or the farm-er's thorough care in building a barn on the same grounds that he ad-mired the workmanship of Homer.[2] The depth to which his ideals for fitness and beauty in writing were shaped, half unconsciously, by the modes of productive labor with which he was surrounded, or, in fact, by the work of his own hands in carpentry or pencil-making or gardening, can be read in his instinctive analogies. He knew that the only discipline for Channing's 'sublimo-slipshod style' would be to try to carve some truths as roundly and solidly as a stonecutter. He knew it was no good to write, 'unless you feel strong in the knees.' Or—a more unexpected ex-ample to find in him—he believed he had learned an important lesson in design from the fidelity with which the operative in the textile-factory had woven his piece of cloth.

The structural wholeness of *Walden* makes it stand as the firmest prod-uct in our literature of such life-giving analogies between the processes of art and daily work. Moreover, Thoreau's very lack of invention brings him closer to the essential attributes of craftsmanship, if by that term we mean the strict, even spare, almost impersonal 'revelation of the object,' in contrast to the 'elaborated skill,' the combinations of more variegated resources that we describe as technique. This contrast of terms is still Miss Rourke's, in distinguishing between kinds of painting, but it can serve equally to demonstrate why Thoreau's book possesses such solidity in con-trast, say, with *Hiawatha* or *Evangeline.* Longfellow was much the more obviously gifted in his available range of forms and subject matters. But

2. Emerson also said, 'I like a man who likes to see a fine barn as well as a good tragedy.' And Whitman added, as his reaction to the union of work and culture, 'I know that pleasure filters in and oozes out of me at the opera, but I know too that subtly and unaccountably my mind is sweet and odorous within while I clean up my boots and grease the pair that I reserve for stormy weather.'

his graceful derivations from his models—the versification and gentle tone of Goethe's *Hermann und Dorothea* for *Evangeline,* or the metre of the *Kalevala* for *Hiawatha*—were not brought into fusion with his native themes.[3] Any indigenous strength was lessened by the reader's always being conscious of the metrical dexterity as an ornamental exercise. It is certainly not to be argued that technical proficiency must result in such dilutions, but merely that, as Greenough saw, it was very hard for American artists of that day, who had no developed tradition of their own, not to be thus swamped by their contact with European influences. Their very aspiration for higher standards of art than those with which they were surrounded tended to make them think of form as a decorative refinement which could be imported.

The particular value of the organic principle for a provincial society thus comes into full relief. Thoreau's literal acceptance of Emerson's proposition that vital form 'is only discovered and executed by the artist, not arbitrarily composed by him,' impelled him to minute inspection of his own existence and of the intuitions that rose from it. Although this involved the restriction of his art to parochial limits, to the portrayal of man in terms only of the immediate nature that drew him out, his study of this interaction also brought him to fundamental human patterns unsuspected by Longfellow. Thoreau demonstrated what Emerson had merely observed, that the function of the artist in society is always to renew the primitive experience of the race, that he 'still goes back for materials and begins again on the most advanced stage.' Thoreau's scent for wildness ferreted beneath the merely conscious levels of cultivated man. It served him, in several pages of notes about a debauched muskrat hunter (1859), to uncover and unite once more the chief sources for his own art. He had found himself heartened by the seemingly inexhaustible vitality of this battered character, 'not despairing of life, but keeping the same rank and savage hold on it that his predecessors have for so many generations, while so many are sick and despairing.' Thoreau went on, therefore, half-playfully to speculate what it was that made this man become excited, indeed inspired by the January freshet in the meadows:

3. And as F. L. Pattee has said of *Hiawatha*, in *The Feminine Fifties* (1940): 'The only really Indian thing about the poem is the Indian summer haze that softens all its outlines, but even this atmosphere is Indian only in name: it was borrowed from German romantic poets.'

There are poets of all kinds and degrees, little known to each other. The Lake School is not the only or the principal one. They love various things. Some love beauty, and some love rum. Some go to Rome, and some go a-fishing, and are sent to the house of correction once a month . . . I meet these gods of the river and woods with sparkling faces (like Apollo's) late from the house of correction, it may be carrying whatever mystic and forbidden bottles or other vessels concealed, while the dull regular priests are steering their parish rafts in a prose mood. What care I to see galleries full of representatives of heathen gods, when I can see natural living ones by an infinitely superior artist, without perspective tube? If you read the Rig Veda, oldest of books, as it were, describing a very primitive people and condition of things, you hear in their prayers of a still older, more primitive and aboriginal race in their midst and round about, warring on them and seizing their flocks and herds, infesting their pastures. Thus is it in another sense in all communities, and hence the prisons and police.

The meandering course of Thoreau's reflections here should not obscure his full discovery that the uneradicated wildness of man is the anarchical basis both of all that is most dangerous and most valuable in him. That he could dig down to the roots of primitive poetry without going a mile from Concord accounts for his ability to create 'a true Homeric or Paphlagonian man' in the likeness of the French woodchopper. It also helps account for the fact that by following to its uncompromising conclusion his belief that great art can grow from the center of the simplest life, he was able to be universal. He had understood that in the act of expression a man's whole being, and his natural and social background as well, function organically together. He had mastered a definition of art akin to what Maritain has extracted from scholasticism: *Recta ratio factibilium,* the right ordering of the thing to be made, the right revelation of the material.

BOOK TWO

✦

Hawthorne

V

THE VISION OF EVIL

AT THIS point the natural sequence would be to consider Whitman, and his development of the organic style. That order would also give a dramatic structure to my volume, since it would offset the optimistic strain from Emerson to Whitman against the reaffirmation of tragedy by Hawthorne and Melville. But that white and black contrast would be too dramatic: it would tend to obscure the interrelations between the two groups, and it would make it sound as though the last word in this age lay with tragedy. Actually the pattern of the age's cultural achievement can be more accurately discerned by remembering that the impulse from Emerson was the most pervasive and far reaching, and that Whitman's extension of many of Emerson's values carried far down into the period after the Civil War. We may stay closest to the pressures of the age, as its creative imaginations responded to them, by going from the transcendental affirmation to its counterstatement by the tragic writers, and by then perceiving how Whitman rode through the years undisturbed by such deep and bitter truths as Melville had found. It would be neater to say that we have in Emerson and Thoreau a thesis, in Hawthorne and Melville its antithesis, and in Whitman a synthesis. But that description would distort especially the breadth and complexity of Melville.

The creation of tragedy demands of its author a mature understanding of the relation of the individual to society, and, more especially, of the nature of good and evil. He must have a coherent grasp of social forces, or, at least, of man as a social being; otherwise he will possess no frame of reference within which to make actual his dramatic conflicts. For the hero of tragedy is never merely an individual, he is a man in action, in conflict with other individuals in a definite social order. It is for such a reason that the most perceptive of recent critics of Shakespeare, Granville-Barker, has remarked that dramatic art in its most fully developed form 'is the working-out . . . not of the self-realization of the individual, but of society itself.'

And unless the author also has a profound comprehension of the mixed nature of life, of the fact that even the most perfect man cannot be wholly good, any conflicts that he creates will not give the illusion of human reality. Tragedy does not pose the situation of a faultless individual (or class) overwhelmed by an evil world, for it is built on the experienced realization that man is radically imperfect. Confronting this fact, tragedy must likewise contain a recognition that man, pitiful as he may be in his finite weakness, is still capable of apprehending perfection, and of becoming transfigured by that vision. But not only must the author of tragedy have accepted the inevitable co-existence of good and evil in man's nature, he must also possess the power to envisage some reconciliation between such opposites, and the control to hold an inexorable balance. He must be as far from the chaos of despair as he is from ill-founded optimism.

These are the considerations which lie behind my entire treatment of Hawthorne and Melville, and to which I shall frequently refer.

You might judge that the era least likely to have produced a tragic vision of life would have been that dominated by Emerson's doctrine of 'the infinitude of the private man.' The transcendentalists were few in number, but their convictions that human nature should not be regarded as corrupt, in continual need of discipline and rebuke, but should be heartily encouraged to trust itself, to embark on the opening road of limitless freedom, were being acted upon in the eighteen-thirties and forties by many Americans who had never heard Emerson's name. In the era of Jackson, with the prospects of the common man seemingly brighter than they had ever been, and with our economic life just at the outset of its century of confident and reckless expansion, it became increasingly assumed that, as Margaret Fuller said, 'Man is not made for society, but society is made for man.'

Although Emerson was able to recognize that such a centrifugal theory was oversimplified, and was to devote his whole career to trying to effect some adjustment between the claims of society and solitude,[1] his voice vibrated with his deepest conviction when he said that he could not find language of sufficient energy to convey his 'sense of the sacredness of private integrity. All men, all things, the state, the church, yea, the friends

1. Cf. such a passage of formulation as this in his journal of 1838: 'Solitude is naught and society is naught. Alternate them and the good of each is seen . . . Undulation, alternation is the condition of progress, of life.'

of the heart are phantasms and unreal beside the sanctuary of the heart.'
He conceived of the heart in such pure isolation that his speculations
now seem remote from violent actuality. And even when his belief
in the free individual was endowed with flesh and blood in the richest poetry yet to have sprung from American soil, in *Leaves of Grass,*
it was destined to call out from Yeats the characteristic view of our own
time. Yeats came to feel, in spite of a youthful devotion, that Whitman as
well as Emerson 'have begun to seem superficial, precisely because they
lack the Vision of Evil.'

Many texts could be cited from Emerson to prove that he was not
unconscious that evil existed, but, as always with him, the significant
thing to determine is his prevailing tone. The assumptions that stirred
emancipated New Englanders of his day were those of 'Spiritual Laws'
(1841): 'Our young people are diseased with the theological problems of
original sin, origin of evil, predestination and the like. These never presented a practical difficulty to any man,—never darkened across any man's
road who did not go out of his way to seek them. These are the soul's
mumps and measles . . .' At the time when he had graduated from college and was struggling to find his vocation, he had felt, to be sure, that
'there *is* a huge and disproportionate abundance of *evil* on earth. Indeed
the good that is here is but a little island of light amidst the unbounded
ocean.' But even then he hoped that America might prove a fresher field.
A few years later, shortly after he had been ordained, he noted how
Pascal had exposed the contradictions existing in human nature, the paradox of its being both vile and sublime. But Emerson felt that Pascal had
emphasized the wrong aspect; for if close to meanness lies grandeur, 'how,
then, can man be low? If, on one side, his feet are in the dust, on the
other there is nothing between his head and the infinite heavens.'

That is the Emerson who prevailed, who declared in his 'Lecture on
the Times' (1841) that the terrors of sin had lost their force: 'Our torment
is Unbelief, the Uncertainty as to what we ought to do.' Thinking of
Hamlet, he had a fleeting perception that poetry could spring out of
suffering, but then, in the disarming candor with which he always
acknowledged the limitations of his temperament, he said: 'I grieve that
grief can teach me nothing.' He could say this in spite of his ample
experience of it in the cumulating deaths of his first wife, his two most
talented brothers, and his oldest boy. Even this last, most bitter loss was
dissolved in the wistful flow of his 'Threnody'; only rarely, most notably

in his essay on 'Fate,' did he stick to his observation that 'no picture of
life can have any veracity that does not admit the odious facts,' that great
men have always been 'perceivers of the terror of life.'

He was sometimes perplexed, as we have seen, at the discrepancy between the world of fact and the world that man thinks. But even at such
moments he could feel little doubt which realm to choose as the true.
If details are melancholy, if everything is sour as 'seen from experience';
as seen from the vantage point of the mind, the plan of the whole 'is
seemly and noble.' He was sure that 'good is positive, evil is merely
privative, not absolute,' that in the physical and moral spheres alike, the
ugly facts are merely partial and can be transcended. Consequently, no
matter how black appearances might be, there could always be found 'a
small excess of good, a small balance in brute facts . . . favorable to the
side of reason.' All fragmentary sorrow and suffering would disappear
in the radiance of good, like mists before the sun over Concord meadows,
and Emerson was free to go on and declare that 'the soul refuses limits
and always affirms an Optimism, never a Pessimism.'

Henry James, Sr., was baffled by Emerson's habit of fluctuating thus
from shrewd observer to seer with so little compulsion to bring the contrasting roles into any coherent relation. James could explain it only by
concluding that Emerson 'had no conscience, in fact, and lived by perception, which is an altogether lower or less spiritual faculty.' He added
that this made him 'fundamentally treacherous to civilization, without
being at all aware himself of the fact.' Perhaps the surest way to sense
Emerson's tone on the problem of evil is to test the effect he had on
other sympathetic contemporaries who were seriously concerned with it.
For James, who was determined, by means of his pungent combination
of Swedenborg and Fourier, to break through the constrictions of selfhood into a warm community with all men, was not unique in finding
Emerson's response to life less satisfactory than that of 'any average old
dame in a horsecar.' He was joined in his objections by the orthodox,
both Presbyterian and Catholic, who were united in pronouncing Emerson's poems 'hymns to the devil,' since in their pride they gave no 'recognition of sin, as actual or even possible.' In addition, friends of Emerson's
as diverse as Father Taylor and fastidious Charles Eliot Norton spoke in
almost the same terms.

The ex-sailor's opinion of a transcendental sermon was that it would
take as many like that 'to convert a human soul as it would quarts of

skimmed milk to make a man drunk.' After hearing Emerson preach, he altered his tune only to the extent of saying: 'Mr. Emerson is one of the sweetest creatures God ever made; there is a screw loose somewhere in the machinery, yet I cannot tell where it is, for I never heard it jar. He must go to heaven when he dies, for if he went to hell, the devil would not know what to do with him. But he knows no more of the religion of the New Testament than Balaam's ass did of the principles of the Hebrew grammar.'

Norton, who was a quarter of a century Emerson's junior, came to know him best during the days when they crossed the Atlantic together on Emerson's return from his last visit to Europe in 1873. The younger man had already confessed to grave doubts 'whether our period of economic enterprise, unlimited competition, and unrestrained individualism, is the highest stage of human progress.' The existing conditions of the social order were bad 'for the mass alike of upper and lower classes'; and looking ahead he could envisage only 'outbreak after outbreak of passion and violence.' Thirty years later he had advanced no closer to a belief in any potential social order, for the world looked then as if it 'were entering upon a new stage of experience, unlike anything heretofore, in which there must be a new discipline of suffering to fit men for the new conditions.' Thus his accents anticipated Eliot's.

[margin annotation: Chas E. Norton]

To such a perturbed spirit Emerson's discourse, robbed of the freshness and surprise that had marked his earlier work, seemed nearly meaningless:

His serene sweetness, the pure whiteness of his soul, the reflection of his soul in his face, were never more apparent to me; but never before in intercourse with him had I been so impressed with the limits of his mind . . . He can accept nothing as a fact that tells against his dogma. His optimism becomes a bigotry, and, though of a nobler type than the common American conceit of the pre-eminent excellence of American things as they are, has hardly less of the quality of fatalism. To him this is the best of all possible worlds, and the best of all possible times. He refuses to believe in disorder or evil. Order is the absolute law; disorder is but a phenomenon; good is absolute, evil but good in the making . . . He is the most innocent, the most inexperienced of men who have lived in and reflected on the world.

Emerson's essay on 'The Tragic' is as unsatisfactory as these comments would lead you to suppose. He approached no subject with less sympathy, unless it was 'The Comic,' for he simply could not accept the confines of a single attitude. He knew that tragedy consists in division, and he was always striving for reconciliation. What Goethe said of himself, that he was incapable of writing tragedies because he could not tolerate discords unresolved, was far truer of Emerson. He started his essay with the firm proposition that no theory of life 'can have any right' if it leaves out of account the values of vice, pain, and fear. But presently he drifted into saying that all sorrow 'is superficial'; and he ended on the note that the intellect and the moral sense 'both ravish us into a region whereunto these passionate clouds . . . cannot rise.' He was confident that no such thing as 'pure malignity' can exist.

How an age in which Emerson's was the most articulate voice could also have given birth to *Moby-Dick* can be accounted for only through reaction. Fortunately it is not necessary to conjecture what Melville might have thought about Emerson, since he has left his own annotated copies of the *Essays*. His pencilled remarks hardly constitute finished criticism. Their value lies in the immediate contact they give with a mind that was instinctively unwilling to allow a gap between the spheres of thought and experience, but was determined to make each stand the scrutiny of the other. Melville reveals here a full glimpse of the forces against which his startling and profound imagination had to make a desperate stand before it could discover any meaning in the life that surrounded him. He felt a strong attraction in the transcendental beliefs; he frequently underscored Emerson's lines with that heavily-freighted nineteenth-century word 'noble.' Yet at the same time his untrained but keen thought was thrashing to get free from many of their implications. On the level of everyday life it was not hard to confute the philosopher, as we have seen in Melville's dismissal of the blithe remarks in 'Prudence' on the unreal 'terrors of the storm.'

Against the metaphysical assumptions of 'Spiritual Laws' Melville made his most determined onslaught. When Emerson tried to establish the merely negative nature of evil by stating: 'The good, compared to the evil' which man sees, 'is as his own good to his own evil,' Melville replied: 'A Perfectly Good being therefore would see no evil.—But what did Christ see? He saw what made him weep . . . To annihilate all this nonsense read the Sermon on the Mount, and consider what it implies.' Seeking for a clue that would enable him to articulate further the ground of his objection, Melville found it in the bland oversimplification that declared, in *The Conduct of Life:* 'The first lesson of history is the good of evil.' To that Melville retorted: 'He still bethinks himself of his optimism—he must make that good somehow against the eternal hell itself.' Melville had already been angered by the analogous pronouncement that the problem of ugliness is solved by the Poet who, 'by a deeper insight, disposes very easily of the most disagreeable facts.' Yet many of Emerson's perceptions about art evoked Melville's warmest assent, particularly the belief in organic expression. He marked the passage that declares how the Poet 'names the thing because he sees it, or comes one step nearer to it than any other. This expression, or naming, is not art, but a second nature, grown out of the first, as a leaf out of a tree.' At the end of that passage Melville wrote his most inclusive comment: 'This is admirable, as many other thoughts of Mr. Emerson's are. His gross and astonishing errors and illusions spring from a self-conceit so intensely intellectual and calm that at first one hesitates to call it by its right name. Another species of Mr. Emerson's errors, or rather, blindness, proceeds from a defect in the region of the heart.'

These annotations were not made until Melville was past forty, since he did not buy these particular volumes of the *Essays* until the first year of the Civil War.[2] But he had reacted with substantially the same mixture of attraction and repulsion at his first contact with Emerson, when he had heard him lecture a dozen years before. He wrote to his friend Duyckinck that he had been 'very agreeably disappointed.' Heretofore he had only glanced at a book of Emerson's once in a bookstore, but 'had heard of him as full of transcendentalisms, myths and oracular gibberish . . . Say what they will, he's a great man . . . I love all men who *dive.*' But as he followed Emerson in his plunge into ideas, he quickly felt himself being suffocated. This philosopher's element was so purely intellectual that it was death to a man who wanted to dilate his lungs and drink in the sustenance of life. In his letter, he got no closer to his objection to Emerson's pale asceticism than to say, 'His belly, Sir, is in his

2. These volumes, along with many other books that belonged to Melville, are now in the Harvard College Library, owing to the generosity of his granddaughter, Mrs. Eleanor Melville Metcalf. The copy of *Essays, First Series,* new edition (1847) was signed by Melville on March 22, 1862; that of *Essays, Second Series* (1844) was dated by him March 22, 1861, which suggests that one date or the other may possibly be a mistake. Melville's copy of *The Conduct of Life* (1860), was not acquired until November 1870.

chest, and his brains descend down into his neck.'[3] Melville knew that
there was 'a gaping flaw' in all the transcendental yea-sayers to life, that
these continual affirmers of perfection were 'all cracked right across the
brow.' If he had read it, he would not have considered F. H. Hedge's
tribute in *The Christian Examiner* to amount to praise: 'Mephistopheles
. . . designates himself as the spirit "that always denies." Mr. Emerson
is not one of these spirits. We should characterize him as the spirit that
always affirms.' What Melville wanted was a man who could 'say No! in
thunder,' who had experienced not merely the mystery of life, but also its
black tragedy. He had had 'enough of this Plato who talks thro' his nose.'

Melville & Hawthorne

It was crucially fortunate that, in the year after he heard Emerson
lecture, Melville encountered the work of a contemporary who seemed
to him to be richly endowed with the substance that the philosopher
lacked. At this time he had been back from his adventures in the Pacific
for less than six years, but, having married, he had rapidly turned out
five books in an attempt to support his family by his pen. His mental and
spiritual growth within that concentrated interval had been enormous.
As he was himself to reflect a year later: 'Until I was twenty-five, I had
no development at all. From my twenty-fifth year I date my life. Three
weeks have scarcely passed, at any time between then and now, that I
have not unfolded within myself.' He had never really read Shakespeare
until he was twenty-nine, in the same winter when he had listened to
Emerson. And now in the summer of 1850, when he was ready for a
far greater effort than any he had yet made, and was indeed already
preoccupied with the theme of The Whale, he felt the spell of Hawthorne. Shortly after settling at Pittsfield, Melville picked up *Mosses from
an Old Manse,* which, though published four years previously, he had
hitherto let slide. The fact that Hawthorne, having just emerged into
belated fame with *The Scarlet Letter,* was now a near neighbor at Lenox,
no doubt provided the stimulus for reading him, though at the time the
two had not yet met.

M's review of "Mosses"

Melville poured out his impressions at once. As he confesses part way
through his essay, he had begun to write before he had finished the book.
Hardly more than with his annotations on Emerson can the result be
reckoned as fully rounded criticism. It is something rarer: a creative mind

---

3. Emerson's characteristic misgivings about Whitman were that his great inspiration was
'choked by Titanic abdomen,' by 'too animal experience.'

disclosing its own ambitions and problems in response to the profound challenge that only a fellow artist can present.

What satisfied him in Hawthorne was the mark of unhurried completion on every page, the sustained maturity of thought and style, an Indian-summer mellowness. The pervasive charm seemed to be symbolized in one of Hawthorne's own sentences: 'In the stillest afternoon, if I listened, the thump of a great apple was audible, falling without a breath of wind, from the mere necessity of perfect ripeness.' In reading the *Mosses,* Melville had been stirred for the first time by the sense of living at a moment of ripeness for American life and art. He seized upon the truths for which Cooper, in his insistence on cultural independence, had been battling for a generation. The creator of Leatherstocking had protested angrily against the inaccurate description of himself as 'the American Scott.' Melville echoed almost his very words: 'We want no American Goldsmiths, nay, we want no American Miltons.' At the time of Cooper's death a year later, Melville wrote that his books were among the earliest he could remember from his boyhood as having produced 'a vivid and awakening power' upon his mind. But in the flush of his first experience of Hawthorne's greatness, Melville saw the drastic limitations of our 'appendix to Goldsmith'; and though he did not mention Irving by name, the reference was unmistakable as he went on to describe 'that graceful writer, who perhaps of all Americans has received the most plaudits from his own country for his productions,— that very popular and amiable writer' who, 'however good and self-reliant in many things, perhaps owes his chief reputation to the self-acknowledged imitation of a foreign model, and to the studied avoidance of all topics but smooth ones.' Such facile success meant that the author had not even perceived what Melville formulated now as an axiom: 'He who has never failed somewhere, that man cannot be great. Failure is the true test of greatness.'

He had said practically the same thing when he had pushed off from the safe shores of his narratives of experience and had made his first excited trial of his own creative depths in *Mardi* (1849). He had recently scored, in his copy of *Lear,* Edgar's profound affirmation, 'Ripeness is all.' He sensed now in Hawthorne 'the culmination of his powers,' and thus unconsciously used the very phrase that Emerson had formulated the winter before to characterize the age that had produced Plato, and to express at the same time his hopes for his own day: 'There is a moment in the history of every nation, when, proceeding out of this brute youth, the perceptive powers reach their ripeness and have not yet become microscopic: so that man, at that instant, extends across the entire scale . . . That is the moment of adult health, the culmination of power.'

Within a year after his essay on Hawthorne, Melville himself had grown so far from the young barbarian who had lived among cannibals that he could feel that he had 'come to the inmost leaf of the bulb, and that shortly the flower must fall to the mould.' But in the mixed elation and anguish of finishing *Moby-Dick* not even he could have been fully cognizant of the rare moment of flowering of which he was a part. In a span of a little more than two years there came into being *The Scarlet Letter* (winter, 1850), *The House of the Seven Gables* (spring, 1851), *Moby-Dick* (fall, 1851), *The Blithedale Romance* (spring, 1852), *Pierre* (summer, 1852). Owing partly to the long obscurity of Melville's reputation, the concentrated force of these books as a group and the possible interactions between them have scarcely yet been reckoned with.

Hawthorne's one period of great productivity, coming in his late forties, seems to have been due more than to anything else to the stimulus of finding, with the publication of *The Scarlet Letter,* that he had at last a sufficient audience to serve as a challenge to his fullest energies. At the time when he met Melville, Hawthorne's mind and style were too completely formed to be susceptible of direct influence, but both he and his wife were enormously pleased with the essay on 'Hawthorne and his Mosses' when they read it in Duyckinck's *Literary World*. They did not know who had written it, since Melville had adopted the fanciful anonymity of pretending to be 'a Virginian spending July in Vermont,' but as Mrs. Hawthorne wrote to the editor, here was 'the first person who has ever in *print* apprehended Mr. Hawthorne.'

Hawthorne had read *Typee* when it came out, had liked it 'uncommonly well,' and had written a short notice of it. Now Duyckinck, who arranged for the two to meet just before the essay appeared, played the cagey impresario by sending Hawthorne the rest of Melville's books, but not yet revealing him as the essay's author. Still in ignorance, Hawthorne wrote in the same letter in which he expressed his appreciation for the generous estimate of his *Mosses*: 'I have read Melville's works with a progressive appreciation of the author. No writer ever put the reality before his reader more unflinchingly than he does in *Redburn,* and *White Jacket. Mardi* is a rich book, with depths here and there that compel a man to swim for his life. It is so good that one scarcely pardons the writer for not having brooded long over it, so as to make it a great deal better.'

The reserved Hawthorne liked Melville so much on their very first meeting that he asked him to come and stay a few days with him. It would be strange if fervent admiration from the man who talked to him 'about time and eternity, things of this world and of the next,' had not been a contributing cause to the more abundant activity of Hawthorne's talent in these years. Then, after the rapid succession of his three long narratives, he may have felt that he had said his say for the time being. At any rate he knew that he was still unable to live entirely by his pen, so (in 1853) he accepted his friend Pierce's offer of the consulship at Liverpool, and did not write his next book, *The Marble Faun,* until seven years later.

Melville's efflorescence came as an immediate response of his imagination to the possibilities that Hawthorne's had opened before him. Stirred by this evidence of 'the increasing greatness' among American writers, he reflected on other moments of artistic awakening, on the number of dramatists who had surrounded Shakespeare, and wondered, 'Would it, indeed, appear so unreasonable to suppose, that this great fulness and overflowing may be, or may be destined to be, shared by a plurality of men of genius?'[4] His choice of the Elizabethan drama as an example was not accidental, for he had just begun to meditate on Shakespeare more creatively than any other American writer ever has. This meditation brought him to his first profound comprehension of the nature of tragedy. This was the charge that released *Moby-Dick,* and that carried him in *Pierre* to the unbearable desperation of a Hamlet.

With the burden of those books still ahead of him, he could already perceive in Hawthorne the same kind of 'short, quick probings at the very axis of reality' that had so impressed him in Shakespeare. He realized that some of his readers would start at seeing those two names on the same page, that they would say that a lesser comparison 'might have sufficed to elucidate this Hawthorne, this small man of yesterday.' But Melville knew that he could make his contention good. He had himself

4. Many years later he marked in his copy of Arnold's *Essays in Criticism* (1865), which he bought in 1869, the passage in 'The Function of Criticism' on why great literary epochs are so rare: 'Two powers must concur, the power of the man and the power of the moment, and the man is not enough without the moment.'

previously heard Hawthorne admired for his quietness, as 'a pleasant writer, with a pleasant style,—a sequestered harmless man, from whom any deep and weighty thing would hardly be anticipated—a man who means no meanings.' But Melville quickly found this to be false. As he became fixed and fascinated by the haunting blackness in these tales, he discovered that it is often 'the least part of genius' that attracts popular admiration. In fact, he made a whole series of discoveries about Hawthorne, which are of equal value in illuminating himself. He became fully aware that there can be no authentic style unless it has been created by a meaning, by a close response to the complexity of existence. He was sure that Hawthorne's sketches, with their delicate revelations of human nature, could not have been produced by any mere technical skill. 'They argue such a depth of tenderness, such a boundless sympathy with all forms of being, such an omnipresent love, that we must needs say that this Hawthorne is here almost alone in his generation—at least, in the artistic manifestation of these things.' And as Melville conceived it, this power to sympathize with humanity could not exist in the 'high form called genius' without 'the indispensable complement of . . . a great, deep intellect which drops down into the universe like a plummet.' The conception that he was feeling his way towards here was to remain his touchstone for major literature. Both for its creation and for its appreciation there must be such a union of thought and emotion as in Hawthorne, who was 'content with the still rich utterance of a great intellect in repose . . . which sends few thoughts into circulation, except they be arterialized at his large warm lungs and expanded in his honest heart.' When Melville added that 'the great beauty in such a mind is but the product of its strength,' he had already grasped the principle upon which he was to act in evolving the right form for the massive content of *Moby-Dick*.

What made Hawthorne's somber analysis even more compelling to him was his conviction that it must have been the product of personal suffering, since 'this only can enable any man to depict it in others.' Whether there really lurked in Hawthorne, 'perhaps unknown to himself, a touch of Puritanic gloom,' Melville could not altogether tell. But he was certain, in diametrical contrast with Emerson, that 'this great power of blackness in him derives its force from its appeals to that Calvinistic sense of Innate Depravity and Original Sin, from whose visitations, in some shape or other, no deeply thinking mind is always and wholly free . . . Perhaps

NATHANIEL HAWTHORNE, BY MATTHEW BRADY

no writer has ever wielded this terrific thought with greater terror than this same harmless Hawthorne.' And brooding over 'Young Goodman Brown,' which struck him as the strongest of all the tales, Melville believed it no exaggeration to call it as 'deep as Dante' in its penetration into the mystery of evil.

Such were the qualities that made Melville feel that America had at last found a native voice, and so led him to exult: 'The world is as young to-day as when it was created; and this Vermont morning dew is as wet to my feet, as Eden's dew to Adam's.' His tone of jubilation is quite like Emerson's in *The American Scholar,* though they were rejoicing in very different things. But Melville could enter fully into the satisfaction of self-reliance when it meant that his country was living no longer on borrowed experience, but belonging to itself. He also agreed with Emerson in affirming that 'it is not so much paucity as superabundance of material that seems to incapacitate modern authors.' Out of such a mood he declared, 'It is for the nation's sake, and not for her authors' sake, that I would have America be heedful of the increasing greatness among her writers.' And though he could go to the nationalistic extreme in shouting, 'Let us away with this leaven of literary flunkeyism toward England,'[5] he generally held to a sounder basis in humanity, urging that each of our authors should write first 'like a man, for then he will be sure to write like an American.'[6]

5. The chief source of Melville's irritation is indicated in the manuscript of his essay, now in the Duyckinck collection in the New York Public Library, where the word 'Bostonian' precedes 'leaven.'

6. Cf. Thoreau's conviction that we should be men first and Americans only at a late and convenient hour.

VI

PROBLEM OF THE ARTIST AS
NEW ENGLANDER

1. Starting Point

Nathaniel Hawthorne

THE ASPECTS of Hawthorne that were so fiery clear to Melville's enthusiasm have not frequently been apprehended in all their implications. Many have remarked his tragic depth, but very few have realized that his thought bore an immediate relation to the issues of his own day. He has been regarded most often as a dweller in the shadows of history, weaving his art out of the haunted memories of Puritanism, but scarcely conscious of real life in the nineteenth century. The pre-eminent reputation of *The Scarlet Letter* has obscured the fact that Hawthorne's three other novels all deal with contemporary material. It is important to correct the prevailing conception of him as the re-creator of a dim past, primarily because such a view usually carries with it the belief that he thus failed to fulfil the major obligation of the artist, the obligation to confront actual life and to make his art 'an act of possession,' in André Malraux's phrase, and not one of oblique evasion. It is worth pondering that what satisfied Melville most thoroughly in Hawthorne was just such a sense of actuality. In writing to him about *The Seven Gables,* Melville reiterated: 'There is a certain tragic phase of humanity which, in our opinion, was never more powerfully embodied than by Hawthorne.' But what stirred Melville in this unbiased record of the 'profounder workings' of thought was not any merely abstract speculation about the nature of man. On the contrary, it was Hawthorne's intense feeling of the usable truth,' an expression that Melville went on to make clear: 'By usable truth, we mean the apprehension of the absolute condition of present things as they strike the eye of the man who fears them not.'

Such steady inspection of life, which does not flinch from probing sinis-

ter recesses and is determined to make articulate the whole range of
what it finds, is indispensable for the great artist. Only thus can he cut
through conventional appearances, and come into possession of what Eliot
has called 'a sense of his own age.' It is significant that Eliot, in whose
own work the dark strain of Hawthorne is more visible than in the work
of any other writer of the present, has judged him by criteria analogous
to those in Melville's letter. Writing about the intellectual world to which
his own Unitarian grandfather had belonged, Eliot concluded, shortly
before starting *The Waste Land:*

Neither Emerson nor any of the others was a real observer of the moral
life. Hawthorne was, and was a realist . . . In consequence, the observation
of moral life in *The Scarlet Letter,* in *The House of the Seven Gables,* and
even in some of the tales and sketches, has solidity, has permanence, the
permanence of art. It will always be of use; the essays of Emerson are already
an encumbrance. The work of Hawthorne is truly a criticism—true because
a fidelity of the artist and not a mere conviction of the man—of the Puritan
morality, of the Transcendentalist morality, and of the world which Hawthorne knew. It is a criticism as Henry James' work is a criticism of the
America of his times, and as the work of Turgenev and Flaubert is a criticism of the Russia and the France of theirs.

In passing from Emerson and Thoreau to Hawthorne we have moved
to a life with very different orientation, to an artistic career that was
faced with far more difficult problems. How completely aware both sides
were of the distance between them comes out in a series of candid comments. Hawthorne expressed his view of Emerson in the account of his
life at the old Manse, where he lived during the first three years after his
marriage in 1842. He reflected that it was necessary to go only a little
way beyond its peaceful threshold before encountering stranger moral
cranks than might be found elsewhere 'in a circuit of a thousand miles.'
These had been drawn thither 'by the wide-spreading influence of a great
original thinker, who had his earthly abode at the opposite extremity of   *Emerson*
our village.' Hawthorne studied from a distance the delusions of these
warped disciples, but confessed that though he 'admired Emerson as a
poet of deep beauty and austere tenderness,' he 'sought nothing from him
as a philosopher.' Even this tribute is somewhat cooled by Hawthorne's
frequent assertion that he disliked poetry; and his notebooks give his reasons for passing by the philosophy. He speaks of Ellery Channing as 'one

of those queer and clever young men whom Mr. Emerson (that ever-lasting rejector of all that is, and seeker for he knows not what) is continually picking up by way of a genius.' He describes a few walks they took together, during which Emerson, on his side, was afraid that since Hawthorne said so little, he had himself made the mistake of talking too much. One time they called on farmer Hosmer, the untutored philosopher whose wisdom Emerson had praised in *The Dial*. Hawthorne was suspicious of the effect of this, as he had previously been of the self-conscious assumption of equality on the part of the intellectuals with the workers at Brook Farm; he wondered whether Emerson might not have done the yeoman harm by putting him in print, since his character seemed less natural than before. Yet the novelist was amused to sketch the contrast between this 'man of sturdy sense, all whose ideas seem to be dug out of his mind, hard and substantial, as he digs potatoes,' and his admirer, 'the mystic, stretching his hand out of cloud-land, in vain search for something real.' Hawthorne phrased his main ground for dissatisfaction with what Emerson had grasped, in a quiet sentence in his preface to the *Mosses:* 'In truth, the heart of many an ordinary man had, perchance, inscriptions which he could not read.'

Emerson, in turn, despite his attraction to Hawthorne's personality, recorded at this same time the estimate of his work which he never substantially altered: 'Nathaniel Hawthorne's reputation as a writer is a very pleasing fact, because his writing is not good for anything, and this is a tribute to the man.' [1] As Emerson's son was later to express it, his father 'could not read Hawthorne because of the gloom of his magic mirror.' In the almost complete separation, on all essential levels, between two of the few distinguished writers of their day living at the two ends of a village, you have a perfect symbol for the age of extreme individualism. The transcendental belief that, since all knowledge comes from the divinity within, a man can scarcely attain to any full relation with another, was voiced in Christopher Cranch's 'Gnosis':

> We are spirits clad in veils;
> Man by man was never seen.

1. Each found his way to his fixed opinion within a few weeks after Hawthorne had come to live in Concord in July 1842. Hawthorne's description of the visit to Hosmer is dated August 15; the entry in Emerson's journal is under September 4.

Only a life based on such a belief could have failed as utterly as Emerson's did to penetrate Hawthorne's significance. To be sure, the novelist's unconquerable reserve rendered it as difficult as possible. Emerson, whose fascination with the other's character continued to the end, could discern, at the time of Hawthorne's death, that there had been 'a tragic element . . . in the painful solitude of the man.' How strangely aloof Hawthorne could hold himself is to be read in the half-serious vow that he made when his wife went away for a visit, that he would pass the whole term of her absence 'without speaking a word to any human being.' And though that was broken the first afternoon by a call from Thoreau, who interrupted his effort to take a nap with *The Dial* in his hand as a soporific, he could record trips to the village made without uttering a syllable, and finally two entire days spent in such monastic silence. Yet, in turning away from his surroundings, he found no solace in the theology against which Emerson had rebelled.

The tomes that had belonged to Hawthorne's predecessor in the Manse, the Reverend Ezra Ripley, called out only the stricture, which Melville marked in his copy of the *Mosses*, that 'thought grows mouldy. What was good and nourishing food for the spirits of one generation affords no sustenance for the next.' This seemed to him especially true of books of religion, which could hardly be taken as 'a fair test of the enduring and vivacious properties of human thought,' since they so seldom touched upon their ostensible subject. He concluded that as long as 'an unlettered soul can attain to saving grace,' theological libraries might not unjustly be considered for the most part as accumulations of 'stupendous impertinence.'

In weighing the heavy folios and quartos of the past two centuries against modern pamphlets and the volumes of the liberal *Christian Examiner,* both struck him as equally frigid, but he made one distinction: the older books 'seemed to have been earnestly written, and might be conceived to have possessed warmth at some former period.' But the only things he found on the shelves that retained any sap were a few old almanacs and newspapers. Their secret of life was that they had been written by the interests of 'the age itself,' and to this fact he ascribed also the vitality of many a ballad in contrast with most stillborn literary epics. This conviction of Hawthorne's crops up very often, as when he decided that the only way to endure for posterity is to live truly 'for your own age,' or that 'all philosophy that would abstract mankind from the present is no more than words.' He voiced a heart-felt desire when he said, in the preface to *The Scarlet Letter,* that he wanted 'to live throughout the whole range of his faculties and sensibilities.'

Thoreau　　That is close to Thoreau's resolve, and, judging from the slender evidence, Hawthorne felt himself in fuller sympathy with him than with Emerson. The only discussion of Thoreau's work in the notebooks is an acute forecast of his qualities, based on the reading of a single early piece in *The Dial,* 'Natural History of Massachusetts' (1842). Hawthorne found it somewhat rambling, and clouded here and there by 'dreamy metaphysics, partly affected'; but for the most part he admired the firm writing, and enjoyed the 'real poetry in him,' since it had a healthy basis in 'good sense and moral truth.' Further acquaintance with Thoreau's conversation led Hawthorne to observe 'a certain iron-poker-ishness and uncompromising stiffness in his mental character.' But this hardly dimmed his pleasure in Thoreau's mixture of 'wild freedom' with 'high and classic cultivation,' though when writing to Duyckinck in 1845, he felt the future of such an eccentric nature still to hang in the balance:

As for Thoreau, there is one chance in a thousand that he might write a most excellent and readable book; but I should be sorry to take the responsibility, either towards you or him, of stirring him up to write anything . . . He is the most unmalleable fellow alive—the most tedious, tiresome, and intolerable—the narrowest and most notional—and yet, true as all this is, he has great qualities of intellect and character. The only way, however, in which he could ever approach the popular mind, would be by writing a book of simple observation of nature, somewhat in the vein of White's *History of Selborne.*

And when *Walden* turned out to be such a book *plus,* Hawthorne found it one of the few works he could recommend while in England as having original 'American characteristics.'

Shortly before his death Hawthorne had planned to write a memorial sketch of Thoreau as a preface to *The Dolliver Romance,* since 'from a tradition which he told me about this house of mine, I got the idea of a deathless man, which is now taking a shape very different from the original one. It seems the duty of a live literary man to perpetuate the memory of a dead one when there is such fair opportunity as in this case: but how Thoreau would scorn me for thinking that *I* could perpetuate him. And I don't think so.'

For his own part Thoreau was almost wholly non-committal. He seems
to have liked Hawthorne's occasional company, though he shared to the
full the transcendental prejudice against fiction, and his journals never
mention Hawthorne's work. They do not even record the occasions when
the novelist borrowed Thoreau's music box, or bought from him the boat
that he and his brother had used on their famous trip. There is just one
allusion, when Thoreau says that his genius finds it better to learn the
peculiar flavor of the cranberry, and thereby 'of *life* in New England,
than to go consul to Liverpool.' But on Hawthorne's return, Thoreau was
pleased to find that he had not changed. 'He is as simple and childlike
as ever.'

Small wonder that Hawthorne, while trying to characterize an acquaintance, spoke of him as having 'a taste for reading that seems to point
towards the writings of Emerson, Thoreau, and men of that class.' He
instinctively dissociated himself from their aims. The first volumes of
Emerson's journals form one of the most absorbing of New England
dramas, for we can follow there day by day his struggle for emancipation.
The dozen solitary years after Hawthorne's graduation from Bowdoin,
which he spent writing on the top floor of his mother's house in Salem,
furnish only the most indirect clues to his development. Emerson had
found himself by moving with the current of the new aspirations, but
Hawthorne, born a year later, seemed destined to go against the stream.
Van Wyck Brooks has popularized a view of ghost-haunted Salem that
would account for the difference by Emerson's having been reared in the
new freedom of Unitarianism, while Hawthorne's youth had been knotted
by the distortions of the older faith. But therein Brooks has made the common mistake of supposing the contents of Hawthorne's imagination to be
a literal copy of his surroundings, whereas the actual relation between a
novelist's work and his environment is sure to be much subtler. And in
point of fact the Salem into which Hawthorne was born was the city
whose trade in all the seas was just giving McIntire his opportunity to
compose one of the great chapters of American architecture in the man-
sions on Chestnut Street. Its solid energetic life provided a natural birthplace for a historian like Prescott (1796-1859), the opulent pages of whose
extraverted rhetoric belong to the tradition that stems from Burke. Such a
flourishing city, whose merchant princes had had plenty of opportunities
to study 'comparative religion' among the Oriental heathen, had been
among the very earliest in the commonwealth to respond to the reasonable

appeal of the Unitarian church, to which Hawthorne's family had belonged for some years before his birth. The modest circumstances in which the family found itself after Captain Hawthorne died in Dutch Guiana in 1808 may well have made his son feel estranged from the dominant world of gentility based on wealth. Even so, he might have followed the new road that was leading so many other inward spirits beyond the tame Unitarian confines.

" The
Celestial
Railroad"

How little disposed he ever was to do so may be read in 'The Celestial Railroad' (1843), a *tour de force* bringing Bunyan up to date. All except the old-fashioned pilgrims now start out from the City of Destruction on a newly built line, on which Apollyon, enveloped in the traditional smoke and flame, is the engineer. Having a little time on his hands, Hawthorne 'resolved to gratify a liberal curiosity,' and to make the trip. The word 'liberal' is double-edged in this context. The first bridge they have to cross, over the Slough of Despond, seems terrifyingly flimsy in spite of Mr. Smooth-it-away's assurance that a sufficient foundation had been obtained for it by means of some 'volumes of French philosophy and German rationalism; tracts, sermons, and essays of modern clergymen; extracts from Plato, Confucius, and various Hindoo sages, together with a few ingenious commentaries upon texts of Scripture,—all of which by some scientific process, have been converted into a mass like granite.' At the end of the dreaded Valley where Bunyan had said that there dwelt two cruel giants, Pope and Pagan, was now only one monster, 'a German by birth,' who was called Giant Transcendentalist, but no one had ever been able to give an exact description of him. As the train rushed by his cavern's mouth, his ill-proportioned form appeared to the passengers' hasty glimpse no more distinct than 'a heap of fog and duskiness. He shouted after us, but in so strange a phraseology that we knew not what he meant, nor whether to be encouraged or affrighted.'

There no longer existed the old hostility between the pilgrims and Vanity Fair, which Hawthorne was gratified to learn, since he proposed to make a considerable stay in that city. For now, 'as the new railroad brings with it a great trade and a constant influx of strangers, the lord of Vanity Fair is its chief patron, and the capitalists of the city are among the largest stockholders.' Melville marked that sentence, and also the observation that 'the Christian reader, if he have had no accounts of the city later than Bunyan's time, will be surprised to hear that almost every street has its church, and that the reverend clergy are nowhere held in higher respect.' In justification of the high praise accorded them, Hawthorne had only to mention such names as the Rev. Mr. Shallow-deep, 'that fine old clerical character the Rev. Mr. This-to-day, who expects shortly to resign his pulpit to the Rev. Mr. That-to-morrow,' and, the most famous of all, the Rev. Dr. Wind-of-doctrine. The labors of these eminent divines, 'aided by those of innumerable lecturers,' now enabled any man to acquire a vast erudition 'without the trouble of even learning to read.' No wonder that many of the most respectable of the pilgrims were so content with life there that they entirely forgot their intentions of going on to the Celestial City.

Hawthorne's sustained irony falls short of major satire only through the feebleness of a dream ending, which, unlike Bunyan's reiterated 'Now I saw in my dream,' does not transform the whole into a vision, but simply allows him to wake up from the urgency of the situation, and thus renders his effect merely fanciful. Still his imagination often returned to the same theme, as in his sharply outlined sketch of the miserable plight of a minister who, 'yielding to the speculative tendency of the age, had gone astray from the firm foundation of an ancient faith, and wandered into a cloud region, where everything was misty and deceptive, ever mocking him with a semblance of reality, but still dissolving when he flung himself upon it for support and rest.' To what extent Hawthorne himself believed any dogma would be hard to ascertain. Many passages in his notebooks indicate a reliance upon Providence, and he was explicit that Divine Intelligence is not merely a reflection of human reason. But the hard concreteness of his mind was indifferent if not hostile to all religious controversy; and he never even joined any church. Yet despite his rejection of formal theology, his brooding absorption in what was common to human experience revealed to him the kernel of reality beneath the decayed husks. No matter how much he criticized the cruel rigidity of Puritanism in its effect upon Hester Prynne, he possessed an insight that understood it. This means that 'he saw the empirical truth behind the Calvinist symbols. He recovered what Puritans professed but seldom practised—the spirit of piety, humility and tragedy in the face of the inscrutable ways of God.' [2]

2. This is Herbert Schneider's penetrating summary in *The Puritan Mind* (1930). The conclusion of Hawthorne's son seems justified by all the evidence: 'He had a deep and reverent religious faith, of what precise purport I am unable to say'; or again, 'Hawthorne's religious faith was of an almost childlike simplicity, though it was as deeply rooted as his life itself.'

" A writer of fiction"

Possessing, or rather, possessed by such views, Hawthorne went even more drastically against the New England stream by setting out to be a writer of fiction. For here the new dispensation was united with the old in finding no substance in such a pursuit. To be sure, the literary tone of the era was by no means entirely set by the Transcendental Club, which had some scruples even about admitting Bronson Alcott on the grounds that he was not an ordained minister. Moreover, Hawthorne could draw sustenance from the same broadening of tastes that was to respond to Prescott's *Ferdinand and Isabella* in the year after the first collection of *Twice-Told Tales,* and that was presently to call out his classmate Longfellow's verse-stories, in which Hawthorne found a rich charm.[3] Nevertheless, at the time he began to write, he had no indigenous example upon which he could build.

Earlier fiction writers

Fiction in New England had hardly advanced since Royall Tyler had sensed the stirring of a new audience for novels, at the end of the eighteenth century. Tyler had stepped away from the prejudice of his native Boston by writing a play for the New York stage, *The Contrast* (1786), which, though liberally seasoned with Sheridan, was authentic enough to remain the brightest comedy written by an American until the twentieth century. In issuing his novel, *The Algerine Captive,* in 1797, he purported to have been absent from this country for seven years, and to have noted an extraordinary change on his return. 'When he left New England, books of biography, travels, novels, and modern romances, were confined to our sea-ports; or, if known in the country, were read only in the families of clergymen, physicians, and lawyers: while certain funeral discourses, the last words and dying speeches of . . . Levi Ames, and some dreary somebody's Day of Doom, formed the most diverting part of the farmer's library.' But now he found an avid taste for books 'designed to amuse rather than to instruct,' for books of 'modern travels, and novels almost as incredible.' 'The worthy farmer no longer fatigued himself with Bunyan's Pilgrim up the "hill of difficulty" or through the "slough of despond"; but quaffed wine with Brydone in the hermitage of Vesuvius, or sported with Bruce on the fairy-land of Abyssinia: while Dolly the dairy maid, and Jonathan the hired man, threw aside the ballad

---

3. Hawthorne's final opinion on the subject of poetry was expressed in a letter to Longfellow in 1864: 'I take vast satisfaction in your poetry, and take very little in most other men's, except it be the grand old strains that have been sounding all through my life.' These great exceptions were Spenser, Milton, and Shakespeare.

of the cruel step-mother, over which they had so often wept in concert, and now amused themselves into so agreeable a terror with the haunted houses and the hobgoblins of Mrs. Radcliffe, that they were both afraid to sleep alone.'

Tyler deplored only that 'while so many books are vended, they are not of our own manufacture'; and that they consequently did not give a picture of New England manners. He had therefore set himself to provide his hero with a New Hampshire background before sending him to sea and having him captured by pirates. But the best response made by a New Englander to the new taste that Tyler had heralded had been no more substantial than the slipshod volumes of John Neal of Portland (1793-1876), a kind of cross between Byron and Cooper, 'the damned ranting stuff' that Hawthorne had relished so much on its appearance while he was an undergraduate. Cooper had started his career with *The Spy* just as Hawthorne was becoming a freshman; while Irving's *Sketch Book*, which Longfellow was to copy so faithfully in *Outre-Mer*, had appeared a year earlier. But notwithstanding the fact that Hawthorne joined in the memorial tribute at Cooper's death, on the basis of many years of 'unwavering admiration,' it is obvious that neither the form nor the content of Cooper's hastily improvised narratives bore any vital relation to his own. Irving's re-creations of the Hudson River legends undoubtedly helped open his eyes to possibilities afforded also by his local background. So did a single story by a Boston lawyer, William Austin (1778-1841), which appeared in Hawthorne's junior year—that of Peter Rugg, the missing man, who, while out driving half a century before, with a storm threatening, swore that he would get home to Boston that night or never see home again. The nemesis for his oath was that ever since then he had been galloping in vain, a Yankee Flying Dutchman hunting for a vanished past, the appearance of whose horses on a road, according to folk superstition, always presaged a downpour.

But the only earlier American writer whose work bore any inner resemblance to Hawthorne's was Brockden Brown (1771-1811), who had turned out his four chief novels in less than two years as the eighteenth century reached its close. Brown's turbulence was the product of a passionate imagination that transformed the mechanical horrors of the Gothic novel into something really felt, as he explored a mysterious borderland between fantasy and reality. This ability to take the stock trappings of romanticism and to endow them with the genuine horror of tortured nerves has been a peculiarly American combination, from Philip Freneau's remarkable poem 'The House of Night' through Poe to Ambrose Bierce and William Faulkner.

Prescott's tribute to Brown, in a long biographical essay, stressed the symbolic importance of this Philadelphian's repudiation of the study of law to become our first professional author, and thereby to hearten the young men of the next generation to test their own gifts. Hawthorne may also have shared in this feeling,[4] but it still struck him that a special onus was attached to practicing the craft of fiction in New England, at least for a man whose ancestors had taken part in the founding of Salem, and who had been resolute soldiers in the persecution of the Quakers and the witches. He dramatized their utter disapproval of him in the famous passage in the preface to *The Scarlet Letter:*

Doubtless, however, either of these stern and black-browed Puritans would have thought it quite a sufficient retribution for his sins, that, after so long a lapse of years, the old trunk of the family tree . . . should have borne, as its topmost bough, an idler like myself. No aim, that I have ever cherished, would they recognize as laudable; no success of mine—if my life, beyond its domestic scope, had ever been brightened by success—would they deem otherwise than worthless, if not positively disgraceful. 'What is he?' murmurs one gray shadow of my forefathers to the other. 'A writer of story books! What kind of a business in life,—what mode of glorifying God, or being serviceable to mankind in his day and generation,—may that be? Why the degenerate fellow might as well have been a fiddler!' . . . And yet, let them scorn me as they will, strong traits of their nature have intertwined themselves with mine.

2. The First *Tales*

WITH all these handicaps on his back, you might expect that Hawthorne's first years of writing would have involved a painfully slow evolution, or that, like Longfellow, he would not have begun to find a distinguishable

4. In 'The Hall of Fantasy,' after remarking that statues are erected there to those men 'who in every age have been rulers and demigods in the realms of imagination,' and mentioning that Fielding, Richardson, and Scott 'occupied conspicuous pedestals,' Hawthorne concluded that 'in an obscure and shadowy niche was deposited the bust of our countryman, the author of *Arthur Mervyn.*'

voice of his own until he was past thirty. The reverse is the case. Even in *Style*
Fanshawe (1828), his novel about undergraduate life, which he began
when hardly beyond that state, his style shows a remarkable finish. It is
almost as though he had set out to prove his mastery of the *Practical
System of Rhetoric*[1] wherein his Bowdoin professor, Samuel Newman,
had insisted that 'purity and propriety' were the essential qualities both
in 'the choice of words' and 'the construction of sentences,' and that the
triple basis of taste lay in 'refinement, delicacy, and correctness.' For
these qualities belonged to Hawthorne in the first pages that he printed
as well as in the last. In reviewing *The Marble Faun,* Edwin Whipple,
the critic of his work for whom Hawthorne had the greatest respect,
made the point that his language possessed the simple correctness that
would have satisfied a Blair or a Whately, and yet could give expression
to psychological subtleties that would almost have justified 'the verbal
extravagances' of a Carlyle. In *Fanshawe,* to be sure, the style is still all a
matter of surface skill, for the plot of a romantic love story, with an ab-
duction and pursuit, belongs to the school of Godwin, and had so little
to do with Hawthorne's maturing interests that, shortly after its publication, he called in all the remaining copies, the bulk of the small edition,
and burned them. So far as the construction of the book shows anything
of his later method, he seems to have learned it from Scott, the beginning *Scott*
of whose *Waverley* series had been one of the great events of Hawthorne's
boyhood. This master may have led him at first to place his stories in the
past, for though the settings for *Fanshawe* are clearly those around Bowdoin, Hawthorne stated that the events took place 'eighty years since.'
He was likewise indebted to Scott both here and later for many devices
that were in turn a far-off echo of Shakespearean drama: the habit of
dividing his characters into groups and of carrying along the actions of
each group separately; the way of developing his plot by means of a few
spot-lighted scenes, with speeches of an exalted pitch, as those between
Hester and the minister; the occasional interweaving of oddities of low
comedy, as in Uncle Venner and the frequenters of the cent-shop in *The
Seven Gables,* or in Silas Foster, the farmer whose 'great, broad, bottomless yawn' interrupted the evening conversations of the cultivated community at Blithedale.

1. This popular manual, which was to run through more than sixty editions, was first
published in 1827, but its author had been propounding its principles when Hawthorne
was a seemingly indifferent student in the class of 1825.

In *Fanshawe,* this comic strain called out his best efforts both in style and characterization. He had not belonged at college to the literary society with Longfellow, but the experience that had led to his being fined for playing cards may readily have included such a type as he tried to draw in Hugh Crombie, the landlord of the Hand and Bottle, the composer of rowdy ballads, whom the young writer pictured as presenting 'an enviable appearance of indolence . . . as he sat under the old tree, polluting the sweet air with his pipe, and taking occasional draughts from a brown jug that stood near at hand . . . The tip of his nose glowed with a Bardolphian fire,—a flame, indeed, which Hugh was so far a vestal as to supply with its necessary fuel at all seasons of the year.' The humor of this is not entirely derived from Hawthorne's reading, and the language is already unmistakably his in its peculiar mixture of so high a proportion of latinate words with a relaxed, if hardly colloquial manner.

The serious characters in the book have scarcely the thickness of cardboard, though the solitary scholar Fanshawe, 'independent of the beings that surrounded him,' is a faint sketch of the type that, as Hawthorne grew more aware of the falseness of such a position, was to take on tragic proportions in Arthur Dimmesdale. But none of the cleavage so apparent in the early novel between an achieved manner of writing and an unmatured content is to be seen in the other work that Hawthorne was doing during his first years out of college, his legends of the region. He seems to have projected them as a volume even before he had written *Fanshawe,* and in choosing the title *Seven Tales of My Native Land,* he was already moving with the tendency that caused Longfellow a couple of years later to turn his 'untravelled heart' home from Germany to a plan for a sketch book of life down east. And although Longfellow's book remained unwritten, and its place as his first volume was taken by a series of his European impressions, a kindred nativism was stirring other writers. It soon prompted Whittier to begin his work in this field with *Legends of New England* (1831), a volume in bare prose and honest doggerel verse, which took some hints from Cotton Mather for stories of a spectre ship and a haunted house by the Merrimack, but tapped new veins by using oral traditions of Indian customs and strange folklore about a fight with wolves and the rattlesnake's power of fascination.

Some years before Whittier's book made its unsuccessful appearance, Hawthorne had despaired of finding a publisher for his tales, and was later said by his sister to have destroyed them as he had *Fanshawe.* At least two or three, however, seem to have escaped this fate, and to have been the first that he printed in magazines (in 1828-30). The only one of these that he ever reprinted was 'The Hollow of the Three Hills,' a six-page sketch whose very opening clause introduces the particular approach that he was destined to make throughout his work to the relation between appearance and reality: 'In those strange old times, when fantastic dreams and madmen's reveries were realized among the actual circumstances of life . . .' The weird situation that he poses is one in which a lady has revealed to her, by means of necromancy, fragments from her life in England which she has deserted. But the sounds that come to her out of the air, the talk between desolate parents, the bell tolling for a child who has been left to die, the frenzied voice of a husband whose burning thoughts have become his 'exclusive world'—these needed no witch's magic to conjure them up, but could readily have been the fantasies of tortured conscience. Within his brief compass here Hawthorne could not make the kind of investigation that he was deliberately to avow in *The Seven Gables,* of trying to find the amount of human nature contained in the ancient superstitions. But he was already aware of the implications that were to lead him to say there that 'modern psychology' might well endeavor to reduce the alleged powers of sinister influence into 'a system, instead of rejecting them as altogether fabulous.' Through his own meditation he found a psychological equivalent for the witch's evil eye in the contemporary abuse of mesmerism; and at a climax in *The Blithedale Romance,* his disgust mounted to horror as he described the way in which the unscrupulous adept **Dr.** Westervelt, appealing to his audience's desire to be thrilled by any debased 'spiritualism,' could gain possession over the sanctity of Priscilla's being. As Hawthorne had said, in beseeching his fiancée not to dabble in the current fad: 'The view which I take of the matter is caused by no want of faith in mysteries, but from a deep reverence of the soul . . . Keep the imagination sane.' His desire to probe spiritual reality beneath all manner of guises made him willing to suspend disbelief concerning whatever human hearts had long held to be true; but his hard critical sense equipped him to see through not only the distortions and delusions of Puritanism, but likewise through the sleight-of-hand of contemporary 'sciences' like phrenology and mesmerism, and thus to occupy a more serious domain than Poe.

In praising *Twice-Told Tales* as the only work of this kind by an American, with the exception of Irving's *Tales of a Traveller,* to possess 'real merit,' Poe cited 'The Hollow of the Three Hills' as an instance of Hawthorne's exceptional skill in creating a *totality* of impression. The secret seems to consist in the degree to which the whole has been imagined, even to the slightest sensuous details of its fragile setting within the hollow, where 'there was nothing but the brown grass of October, and here and there a tree trunk that had fallen long ago, and lay mouldering with no green successor from its roots. One of these masses of decaying wood, formerly a majestic oak, rested close beside a pool of green and sluggish water at the bottom of the basin. Such scenes as this (so gray tradition tells) were once the resort of the Power of Evil and his plighted subjects; and here, at midnight or on the dim verge of evening, they were said to stand round the mantling pool, disturbing its putrid waters in the performance of an impious baptismal rite. The chill beauty of an autumnal sunset was now gilding the three hill-tops, whence a paler tint stole down their sides into the hollow.'

This is the style that Poe declared to be 'purity itself,' and can serve as an instance of what Whipple found in the work that its author was doing more than thirty years later. Compared with Thoreau, the diction seems archaic, and Hawthorne's way of describing nature, despite his sustained pattern of subdued colors, is highly artificial. It makes you think of Yeats' remark that whenever language has been 'the instrument of controversy,' it has inevitably grown abstract. For behind Hawthorne's formality you can sense several New England generations in which rhetoric had served for public uses, for sermons and political deliberation, but scarcely at all for literature. And though renouncing the role of preacher as Emerson never did, Hawthorne kept a taste for other aspects of the age just previous to his own, for the Augustan authors who had gradually stimulated New England's enlightenment, and whom Emerson and Thoreau had joined Carlyle in dismissing as superficial to man's soul.

From the occasion when he had joined with other students at Bowdoin in giving to the college library complete sets of Johnson and Swift, there seems to have been no period when his relish for the eighteenth century lapsed.[2] He often re-read Thomson's *Castle of Indolence,* and once com-

2. This taste had a sound tap-root in his discriminating admiration for a character like Benjamin Franklin's. When writing his hack Biographical Stories in 1842, he made the boy for whom they were supposedly designed remark that he had read some of Poor Richard's proverbs, and that he did not like them. 'They are all about getting money or

mended Sterne's sermons as 'the best ever written.' By the deft touches
with which he portrayed Hepzibah Pyncheon's old-fashioned fondness
for the 'tarnished brilliancy' of *The Rape of the Lock,* he showed such
familiarity with its author that we do not need the evidence of his
having enjoyed reading Pope's *Epistles* aloud to his wife. In his essay
about old local newspapers, he noted the paucity of American literature
in that era, yet found, in occasional columns of the press, wit and humor,
'which, for breadth and license, might have proceeded from the pen of
Fielding and Smollett.' When he finally went to London, what interested
him most was the city that had been mentioned by the writers from
Addison to Goldsmith, and he spoke of Hogarth as 'the only English
painter.' When he visited Johnson's birthplace at Lichfield, he recalled his
childhood intimacy with his pages, remembering that even then he had
been partly aware that the Doctor 'meddled only with the surface of life.'
Yet considering that his own 'native propensities were towards Fairy
Land, and also how much yeast is generally mixed up with the mental
sustenance of a New Englander,' he reflected that such a 'gross diet' as
Johnson 'may not have been altogether amiss,' and that 'it is wholesome
food even now.' And he added a tribute to those 'two stern and masculine poems,' *London* and *The Vanity of Human Wishes.*

The steady pressure of this undercurrent of taste was what held Hawthorne's style to standards of which the eighteenth-century rhetoricians
could have approved. That such a style persisted through the period of
Carlyle and Macaulay (of whom Emerson remarked that a notable green-
grocer was spoiled in his making) almost places Hawthorne with the
hypothetical author whom Landor said that he had known in his
youth: 'My friend wrote excellent English, a language now obsolete.'
Hawthorne's use of it may be accounted for only on the basis of the frequent American cultural lag. This phase of him reminds us how late the
eighteenth century lingered in America, that traces of its formalism make
Cooper often seem stilted in contrast with the easy naturalness of Scott;

saving it.' To that his father answered that they had been suited to the condition of the
country as it then was, 'although they teach men but a very small portion of their duties.'
Hawthorne came closer to the mature Franklin when, after seeing a miniature of him
in Paris in 1858, he said: 'I do not think we have produced a man so interesting to contemplate, in many points of view, as he. Most of our great men are of a character that
I find it impossible to warm into life by thought, or by lavishing any amount of sympathy
on them. Not so Franklin, who had a great deal of common and uncommon nature in
him.' Cf. Melville's portrait of Franklin in *Israel Potter* (p. 493 below).

that, as Melville observed, pages of Goldsmith might almost have been written by Irving; that Pope was still the great poet in the Cambridge that Holmes and Lowell knew as boys. But the consequence of Hawthorne's taste was very different from what resulted when Prescott, having determined to become a writer after an accident to his eyes had compelled him to abandon the law, followed up his courageous resolve by a systematic study of Johnson's *Dictionary* and Blair's *Rhetoric*. He became second to no modern historian in the dramatic composition of his materials, and the long-starved New England imagination could riot in his flair for the gorgeous and the spectacular. But the brilliance of his pictures, such as that of the hand-to-hand struggle between the followers of Cortez and Montezuma on the top of the temple of Tenochtitlan, always depends on obvious devices, on the studded adjective, the prolonged antithesis, the overwhelmingly elaborate parallel. The effect of his style is even more old-fashioned than Hawthorne's, for its magnificent rhetorical skill is wholly a matter of external manipulation. Its stately flow is undisturbed by any stirring of the psychological depths that are always troubling the seemingly tranquil surface of Hawthorne's pages, and thus making them a delicate register of his mind.

During the years when Hawthorne's work was known only through the anonymity of magazines and gift books—his name did not appear in print until 1836—he often signed his stories as by the author of 'Sights from a Steeple' or of 'The Gentle Boy.' These pieces had been written before 1830, and, after 'The Hollow of the Three Hills,' seem to be the earliest that he included in *Twice-Told Tales*.[3] They present between them the two chief aspects of that volume, and can form the center of our discussion of it. 'Sights from a Steeple,' as its title suggests, is no tale at all, but in the genre that so charmed Hawthorne's age, the sketch—in this case, of what he could observe from his point of vantage above the shaded streets and wharves of Salem, and of what he could conjecture about the lives of the passers-by: 'the full of hope, the happy, the miserable, and the desperate, dwell together within the circle of my glance.'

Once you have granted this sketch what Poe did, a harmony of tone, it seems so slight as to be almost imperceptible: and for once Emerson

3. In establishing the conjectural dates for some of Hawthorne's early work, I have made use of the chronology worked out by Elizabeth Chandler in 'A Study of the Sources of the Tales and Romances Written by Nathaniel Hawthorne before 1853' (*Smith College Studies in Modern Languages*, 1926).

seems entirely right in his criticism of Hawthorne when complaining of another similar sketch, 'Footprints on the Sea-Shore,' that 'there was no inside to it. Alcott and he together would make a man.' Nevertheless, this phase of Hawthorne's work had a special appeal for many of his first readers. When Longfellow reviewed the *Tales,* he was delighted not only with Hawthorne's use of native legends, but also with his discovery that there is beauty in the commonplace, that 'the heaven of poetry and romance still lies around us and within us.' In his warm response to the poet's praise, Hawthorne showed what considerable stock he himself put in these sketches: he spoke of his 'great difficulty in the lack of materials; for I have seen so little of the world that I have nothing but thin air to concoct my stories of, and it is not easy to give a lifelike semblance to such shadowy stuff. Sometimes through a peep-hole I have caught a glimpse of the real world, and the two or three articles in which I have portrayed these glimpses please me better than the others.'

They also pleased Melville greatly. He found 'Buds and Bird Voices' exquisite, and nothing less than 'most admirable' could express his satisfaction with 'Fire Worship,' the tiny fancy in which Hawthorne regretted the social revolution wherein the open hearth had been driven out by 'the cheerless and ungenial stove.' Melville's many pencillings [4] of 'Footprints on the Sea-Shore' point to his eager agreement with Hawthorne's account of his reinvigoration by the touch of earth. Without Melville's

4. The volumes of Hawthorne that were owned by Melville include *Mosses from an Old Manse* (1846) ('H. Melville from Aunt Mary. Pittsfield. July 18, 1850'); *Twice-Told Tales,* second edition, 1842 ('Herman Melville from Nath'l Hawthorne, Jan. 22, 1850,' which must be a slip for 1851 since the two men did not meet until August 1850 and Melville had not read any of Hawthorne carefully until just before then); *The House of the Seven Gables* (1851) ('Herman Melville from Nath'l Hawthorne, April 11, 1851'); *The Blithedale Romance* (1852) ('Herman Melville, November, 1852'—both the name and date have been erased, but are still legible though the latter may be 1853); *The Marble Faun* (1860) (from 'his friend and neighbor S.A.M.[orewood] Pittsfield. June 1860'); *Our Old Home* (1863) ('H. Melville. Jan. 8, 1868'); *American Notebooks* (1868) ('H. Melville. June 8, '70. N.Y.'); *English Notebooks* (1870) (no dating of acquisition); *The Scarlet Letter* (1850) ('H. Melville, July 1870. N.Y.'); *The Snow-Image* (1865) ('H. Melville. Jan. 6, '71. N.Y.'); *French and Italian Notebooks* (1872) ('H. Melville. Mar. 23, '72. N.Y.'); *Septimius Felton* (1872) ('Herman from Lizzie. [i.e. Mrs. Melville] Aug. 1, 1872').

Owing to the courtesy of Melville's granddaughters, Mrs. Frances Osborne and Mrs. Eleanor Melville Metcalf, and to the generosity of Charles Olson who first tracked all these volumes down, I have been able to make use of Melville's occasional comments in them, and to examine his numerous markings, which are by far the most extensive in the *Mosses,* and after that in *Twice-Told Tales* and *The Seven Gables.* These have proved of great value in helping to define Hawthorne as well as Melville.

emphases it would hardly be possible to discern anything fresh in Hawthorne's description of an eventless day, but with them we can sense something of the quiet delight of his contemporaries in finding their most ordinary surroundings and occupations reflected in the mirror of his words. The Hawthorne who devoted so many pages of his notebooks to painstakingly faithful records of such strolls through the countryside, the vacuity of which Henry James deplored, thought of calling his first collection *Provincial Tales,* and said many years later, 'New England is quite as large a lump of earth as my heart can really take in.' This feeling for his own place was what drew him to the most vital strain in Longfellow, in reviewing whose *Evangeline* (1847) he was to say: 'Let him stand, then, at the head of our list of native poets, until some one else shall break up the rude soil of our American life, as he has done.' The cultural value of the province is that, however restricted in its range, it has sent its roots far down, as Brooks discerned in calling Hawthorne the 'most deeply planted of American writers, who indicates more than any other the subterranean history of the American character.' [5]

But if you put any of his sketches beside the first that Thoreau was to make a decade later in revivifying the tradition from Izaak Walton, the difference is at once apparent between recording a homely setting and suggesting the ranker flavor of the soil. Such a comparison presents Hawthorne's command of language in its least favorable light.[6] This statement might seem belied by his notebooks, for there he could indulge his declared 'appetite for the brown bread and the tripe and sausages of life,' which were not included in the ethereal fare of nice society. When

5. This is one of the many insights that make Brooks' few pages on our mid-century writers in *America's Coming of Age* (1915) far more revelatory of their essential quality than all the diffuse evocation of atmosphere in *The Flowering of New England* (1936).

6. Another comparison that suggests itself is with the sketches of Sarah Orne Jewett. Take the concluding paragraphs of 'The Toll-Gatherer's Day' and 'The Hiltons' Holiday':

Hawthorne: 'Far westward now the reddening sun throws a broad sheet of splendor across the flood, and to the eyes of distant boatmen gleams brightly among the timbers of the bridge. Strollers come from the town to quaff the freshening breeze. One or two let down long lines, and haul up flapping flounders, or cunners, or small cod, or perhaps an eel. Others, and fair girls among them, with the flush of the hot day still on their cheeks, bend over the railing and watch the heaps of seaweed floating upward with the flowing tide. The horses now tramp heavily along the bridge, and wistfully bethink them of their stables. Rest, rest, thou weary world! for to-morrow's round of toil and pleasure will be as wearisome as to-day's has been; yet both shall bear thee onward a day's march of eternity. Now the old toll-gatherer looks seaward, and discerns the light-house kindling on a far island, and the stars, too, kindling in the sky, as if but a little way beyond; and mingling reveries

he said that he could have stood and listened 'all day long' to the lingo
of a wandering peddler in the Berkshires, he would appear wholly transformed from the recluse son of Madame Hawthorne who usually left the
house only for a stroll after nightfall. On the long summer trips that he
took through the outlying regions of his province, he was delighted that
the people 'show out their character much more strongly than they do
with us.' Instead of the quiet dull decency of Salem's streets, there were
'mirth, anger, eccentricity,' all pouring forth freely. He noted the unusual
fact, 'I talk with everybody,' and after sitting for many evenings on front
stoops of taverns and in their barrooms, he observed of one of his casual
companions, a blacksmith 'big in the belly, and enormous in the back-
sides,' that 'his conversation has much strong, unlettered sense, imbued
with humor, as everybody's talk is, in New England.' He also added: 'I
know no man who seems more like a man—more indescribably human.'

He tried to gain command of this essential material for his craft by
catching occasional phrases from the talk—from the driver of the Pittsfield stage who pronounced one of his bays 'a dreadful nice horse to go,
but if he could shirk off the work upon the others, he would'; or from the
peddler's 'queer humorous recitative' as he shouted to some boys who
had climbed upon his cart: 'Fall down, roll down, tumble down—only
get down.' Such flashes show that Hawthorne had quite as good an ear
for Yankee speech-rhythms as Thoreau had, or as Melville when he re-
created Stubb's 'soothing drawl' to his boat-crew: 'Pull, my children, pull,
my little ones. Why don't you break your backbones, my boys?' Yet Hawthorne's ripest work, to say nothing of his sketches, contains hardly a trace

of heaven with remembrances of earth, the whole procession of mortal travellers, all the
dusty pilgrimage which he has witnessed, seems like a flitting show of phantoms for his
thoughtful soul to muse upon.'

Jewett: 'It was evening again, the frogs were piping in the lower meadows, and in the
woods, higher up the great hill, a little owl began to hoot. The sea air, salt and heavy, was
blowing in over the country at the end of the hot bright day. A lamp was lighted in the
house, the happy children were talking together, and supper was waiting. The father and
mother lingered for a moment ouside and looked down over the shadowy fields; then they
went in, without speaking. The great day was over, and they shut the door.'

The intentions here are similar. In both cases the simple materials have been valued for
themselves, and the sentiments, though obvious, are genuine. But the difference between
them is the difference wrought by Wordsworth's revolution in poetic diction. Hawthorne,
not responding to that, depends on generalized statements that no longer have the power
to make us share in his sensations. Miss Jewett's paragraph still vibrates with the quality
that William James found in *The Country of the Pointed Firs:* 'that incommunicable clean-
ness of the salt air when one first leaves town.'

of conversational idioms. Except for the very few low-comedy characters, the others all phrase themselves alike, and like no one else outside the decorous confines of a book of rhetoric.

Nor does his finished style, for all its limpid grace, ever come quite as close to sensuous actuality as the matter-of-fact notes, typical of many that he made, of an operation by a country dentist. The patient 'seats himself in a chair on the stoop, with great heroism. The doctor produces a rusty pair of iron forceps; a man holds the patient's head; the doctor perceives, that it being a difficult tooth, wedged between the two largest in the head, he shall pull very moderate; and the forceps are introduced. A turn of the doctor's hand; the patient begins to utter a cry; but the tooth comes out first, all bloody, with four prongs. The patient gets up, half amazed, spits out a mouthful of blood, pays the doctor ninepence, pockets the tooth; and the spectators are in glee and admiration.'

One force that operated on Hawthorne to remove such blunt details from his printed pages can be felt strongly enough in what his wife did, after his death, when editing this passage. Sophia Hawthorne's taste, as her son wrote, 'was by nature highly refined, and was rendered exquisitely so by cultivation.' You would therefore expect that her sensitive nerves would not be able to endure 'all bloody' and 'spits out a mouthful of blood.' But just as damaging to Hawthorne's effect as these excisions was her tidying up the grammar of the doctor's realization that he must pull 'very moderate,' in which you share in the contrary phrasing of his thought, as you do not when it is altered to 'very hard.' Throughout her hundreds of changes in his notebooks (which included inking out the conclusion of the sentence that reported a talk with Melville on 'all possible and impossible matters, that lasted pretty deep into the night . . .'), she seems to have been guided even more by the determination to root out his 'ineradicable rusticity'[7] than his infrequent coarseness. Though the toning down of 'whores' into 'women,' and 'swilling' into 'drinking' would come under the latter head, most of her efforts were devoted to making sure that her husband should appear before the world only with elegance. At least that would seem to be the reason why 'smell' yields to 'odor,' 'pantaloons' to 'trousers,' 'phiz' to 'physiognomy,' 'swap' to 'exchange,' his finding some talk 'not witty to kill' to 'not very witty,' or his

7. The phrase is Randall Stewart's, whose careful edition of *The American Notebooks* (1932) has restored what Hawthorne wrote, in so far as Mrs. Hawthorne's tampering with the manuscripts left restoration possible.

writing at Brook Farm 'to-day is another scorcher' to the flaccidly point-less 'it scorches again.'

He showed his clear perception of the value of simplicity when he said that learned ministers possessed every gift save that of being able to speak 'the heart's native language' and so to convey 'the highest truths through the humblest medium of familiar words and images.' Neverthe-less, the elaboration of his finished sentences cannot be blamed wholly on Sophia, for the notebook passages that he revised for stories are marked by the exactions of his own tastes and standards. He seems frequently to have wanted to move away from the colloquial, as when 'small' is dressed up as 'diminutive,' 'good' as 'beneficent,' 'loud' as 'obstreperous.' When some impressions that he had gathered in the mountains emerged, ten years later, as the setting for 'Ethan Brand' and a 'great, old dog' be-came a 'grave and venerable quadruped,' you sense his relish for the rounded period, and for the heightened dignity that the eighteenth cen-tury had believed must characterize serious art. Sometimes his conscious artificiality was part of a witty intention, as where he said of the ad-ventist Father Miller—whose prediction of the end of the world in 1843 may have stimulated 'The Celestial Railroad'—that he appeared to have 'given himself up to despair at the tedious delay of the final conflagration.' Melville's underlining this would seem to indicate that he smacked his lips over such an Augustan flourish; but Hawthorne's device is not just a matter of vocabulary. He believed that he could bring out the full effect of an ironic perception by deliberate rhetorical expansion, as when he remarked of a young barkeeper that 'he had a good forehead, with a particularly large development just above the eyebrows; fine intellectual gifts, no doubt, which he had educated to this profitable end; being famous for nothing but gin-cocktails.' The prolongation of the tiny in-stance was designed to give the reader time to take in its mockery of phrenology and its 'chart of bumps,' a pseudoscience that both Poe and Whitman accepted at its professed value.

Too often, however, this expansion led to mere diffuseness of detail, as when 'all such trash' as he found in Dr. Ripley's library became 'other productions of a like fugitive nature.' Its effect is the tameness which Hawthorne himself recognized in his preface to the *Tales*, and which he rightly attributed to the lack of any critical challenge from his en-vironment, any sense that he was writing for an audience that cared enough for his work to demand his best. In such circumstances fancy can all too easily sprawl and run to seed. But when Emerson deprecated Ellery Channing's remark that 'he is the lucky man who can write in bulk . . . ten pages on a man's sitting down in a chair, like Hawthorne . . . that will go,' he was running counter to the dominant taste of his age. The chapter on the death of Judge Pyncheon was among its favorite show-pieces, while Melville singled it out as one of 'the deeper passages' that struck him most. We have gone so far to the other extreme in our contemporary distrust of rhetoric that we have left our prose almost without any vertebrae to grow around; at all events, it has become almost impossible for us to take any pleasure in a *tour de force* like Hawthorne's chapter.[8] We need to exercise historical imagination to overcome our distaste sufficiently even to perceive that, no matter how obvious its devices, the structure of this chapter required considerable virtuosity, not wholly unlike Daniel Webster's. Indeed, it is conceivable that with so few models of local fiction to serve as competition, Hawthorne's unusual effort may have been stimulated in part by the great lawyer's example. For the circumstances of the murder of Captain White of Salem, a case to which Webster had devoted the full resources of his theatrical imagination in doing his share for the entertainment of an age without an adequate drama, seem to have furnished Hawthorne with several hints for the supposed guilt of Clifford in *The Seven Gables*.[9]

8. One contemporary effort to re-create the dramatic effects of formal rhetoric, somewhat in Prescott's vein, with an infiltration of D. H. Lawrence, was made by William Carlos Williams in 'The Destruction of Tenochtitlan,' a chapter of his *In the American Grain* (1925).

9. The passage in which Webster's imagination relived, for his transfixed auditors, the scene of the murder (1830), also provides an interesting study in comparative rhetoric: 'Deep sleep had fallen on the destined victim, and on all beneath his roof. A healthful old man, to whom sleep was sweet, the first sound slumbers of the night held him in their soft but strong embrace. The assassin enters, through the window already prepared, into an unoccupied apartment. With noiseless foot he paces the lonely hall, half lighted by the moon; he winds up the ascent of the stairs, and reaches the door of the chamber. Of this, he moves the lock, by soft and continued pressure, till it turns on its hinges without noise; and he enters, and beholds his victim before him . . . The face of the innocent sleeper is turned from the murderer, and the beams of the moon, resting on the gray locks of his aged temple, show him where to strike. The fatal blow is given! and the victim passes, without a struggle or a motion, from the repose of sleep to the repose of death! . . . The deed is done. He retreats, retraces his steps to the window, passes out through it as he came in, and escapes. He has done the murder. No eye has seen him, no ear has heard him. The secret is his own, and it is safe!

'Ah! Gentlemen, that was a dreadful mistake. Such a secret can be safe nowhere. The whole creation of God has neither nook nor corner where the guilty can bestow it, and

To such lengths have we been carried by questions suggested by the style of 'Sights from a Steeple.' The other piece by which Hawthorne was first known is of much greater substance, and would have to be included in any selection of his best work. For 'The Gentle Boy' is not the product of a notebook, but of a tragic imagination, which, by Hawthorne's mid-twenties—and nearly a decade earlier than Emerson came to his maturity in *Nature*—had already worked out its balance of values and knew how to seize upon the right concrete details to project its vision. As in 'The Hollow of the Three Hills,' Hawthorne found his theme in seventeenth-century Massachusetts, this time in no unearthly borderland, but through his intensive knowledge of the central problems confronted by the history of the colony. In creating his story from the bitter consequences of the persecution of the Quakers, it is almost as though his unconscious mind was insisting on performing an atonement for his ancestors' part in what he calls here the Puritans' 'brutal cruelty.' The situation presents a Quaker child, whose father has just been hanged, and who has been abandoned to its own frail resources. The official code, through the voice of the preacher who had himself felt in England the rigorous hand of Laud, holds that there is great danger in pity, 'in some cases a commendable and Christian virtue, but inapplicable to this pernicious sect.' The posing of such white innocence against the repulsive black distortions of the world was to be Melville's theme from *Redburn* to *Billy Budd*. He underscored his own preoccupation with the theme of

say it is safe . . . A thousand eyes turn at once to explore every man, every thing, every circumstance, connected with the time and place; a thousand ears catch every whisper; a thousand excited minds intensely dwell on the scene, shedding all their light, and ready to kindle the slightest circumstance into a blaze of discovery. Meantime the guilty soul cannot keep its own secret. It is false to itself; or rather it feels an irresistible impulse of conscience to be true to itself . . . A vulture is devouring it, and it can ask no sympathy or assistance, either from heaven or earth. The secret which the murderer possesses soon comes to possess him; and, like the evil spirits of which we read, it overcomes him, and leads him whithersoever it will. He feels it beating at his heart, rising to his throat, and demanding disclosure . . . When suspicions from without begin to embarrass him, and the net of circumstance to entangle him, the fatal secret struggles with still greater violence to burst forth. It must be confessed, it will be confessed; there is no refuge from confession but suicide, and suicide is confession.'

Webster's vocabulary, more basically Anglo-Saxon than Hawthorne's, is built into the patterns of eloquence that so intoxicated the younger Emerson. But when not backed up by the orator's presence, the psychological observation is seen to be fairly standardized. It is hardly illuminated by the continual flicker of subtle penetration that is to be found even in the set-piece on Judge Pyncheon.

isolation by marking the passage where the little boy, hovering at night-fall by the spot where his father met his death, says to the incredulous passer-by, 'in a sweet though faltering voice, "Friend, they call me Ilbra-him, and my home is here."' In this case, as in that of Melville's Ishmael, the blank separation of the boy from his surroundings appears even in his outlandish name. This had been given him by his tortured parents in memory of the fact that they had found kindness once in their endless wanderings, in the land of the Sultan—a discovery comparable to Ishmael's that when the hands of all civilized Christendom seemed turned against him, life was redeemed by the comradeship of Queequeg, a pagan savage.

Hawthorne continued to show his penetration into human complexity by observing that Tobias Pearson, the one man who had compassion for the boy and gave him shelter, was no religious enthusiast of any sect, but one of 'unprosperous fortunes' to whom emigration to the colony had ap-peared to offer some worldly advantages. And as the story proceeds, its most remarkable feature is its young author's sensitively accurate scale of wrongs and rights. He does not defame the Puritans by romanticizing their adversaries. He points out that Ilbrahim's mother, by neglecting him for the work of prophecy, in which her inspiration was often no more than malignity induced by the outrages she had suffered, has ill performed her most sacred office. She comes to a perception of her guilt at the moment when her martyr's spirit has compelled her to return once more to defy the authorities, and when, at the height of her wild denunciation of them before the whole congregation, she suddenly feels Ilbrahim's timid arms around her. But she has gone too far in her revolt to turn back, and, sentenced to banishment again, she yields her son to the care of Pearson's wife. As this mild, sadfaced woman, who has lost her own children by death—a judgment, some think, for her husband's lack of zeal,—receives the boy from his desperate mother, Hawthorne presents it as a picture of 'rational piety and unbridled fanaticism contending for the empire of a young heart.'

The child showed in his oversensitiveness some traces of the strain that had been put upon him by the disordered imaginations of his parents, for though his 'tender and social nature' soon began to flower in attachments to everything about him, he could not bear to risk contact with the Puritan children for fear of their scorn. But an opportunity seemed to arise for him when a somewhat older boy, having been badly injured by falling from a tree near the Pearsons' house, was brought there to recover. This boy had always seemed sulleh and disagreeable, owing in part to an indefinable distortion in his features. But from the moment he had been carried in the door, Ilbrahim's heart had seized upon him: he sat constantly by his bed, anxious to satisfy every need, and lightened his convalescence by telling him endless stories of his own imagining. He felt that at last he had gained a friend, and watched with sadness the boy's final departure to his own home.

Ilbrahim did not visit him there, but one afternoon he saw him, leaning on his invalid's cane, among the group of children playing in the woods behind the meeting-house. The summer air was filled with their laughter so that grown men, 'as they journeyed by the spot, marvelled why life, beginning in such brightness, should proceed in gloom; and their hearts, or their imaginations, answered them and said, that the bliss of childhood gushes from its innocence. But it happened that an unexpected addition was made to the heavenly little band.' Ilbrahim, confident because his friend was there, stepped forward for the first time to join them. A hush settled over their mirth, and they stood whispering together while he approached; then, all at once, 'the devil of their fathers' entered into them, and, with a fierce shrill cry, they rushed upon the defenseless little Quaker. 'In an instant, he was the center of a brood of baby-fiends, who lifted sticks against him, pelted him with stones, and displayed an instinct of destruction far more loathsome than the bloodthirstiness of manhood.'

Thus far removed was Hawthorne from any of the transcendental variants of the romantic belief in the unspoiled innocence of children. His discernment may have opened a door for James, leading to *The Turn of the Screw;* for Hawthorne did not draw back from depicting the extremes of natural depravity. During the beating of the child, the invalid stood apart from the rest, 'crying out with a loud voice, "Fear not, Ilbrahim, come hither and take my hand." ' As his friend struggled to obey, he stood watching him with a calm smile, and, when he was near enough, lifted up his cane and struck him across the mouth. Until then the child's arms had been raised to guard his head from the blows, but now he dropped them at once, and let his persecutors beat him down and trample upon him at will. This crisis infects the reader with a terror of violence similar to what Alyosha felt at the unleashing of the brutality of the children, in *The Brothers Karamazov*. And although Hawthorne's meditative strain has not the dramatic shock of Dostoevsky's passionate clairvoyance, the New Englander's penetration of moral obliquity is no less profound.

At last a few neighbors, attracted by the uproar, 'put themselves to the trouble of rescuing the little heretic,' and carried his senseless body to Pearson's door. He rallied slowly from his injuries, but there was no renewal of his spirit. Its fragile equilibrium had sustained the shock of separation from his mother, but now possessed no further resilience. He drooped in a listless decline, in which his foster-mother's kindness could not seem to reach him, and then sank into a mortal sickness, the early victim of his own unworldly nature. Other elements are woven into the story's conclusion: Pearson's drifting into Quakerism as a result of his contempt for the Puritans' intolerance; and the final return of Ilbrahim's mother, whose grief-stricken spirit, once a new forbearance had prevented the persecution of her sect, took on something of the gentleness of her dead child.

It may be objected that Hawthorne introduced more material than can be adequately presented in a short story. He may have furnished a theme for a tragedy rather than actually have written one, but he did imagine a human situation in its entirety. And all the fundamentals of his craft, the kind of theme he chose, his peculiar way of handling it, his fascinated absorption not merely with the individual but with his intricate conditioning by environment and heritage, all remained substantially unchanged from this story to his latest work. How true that is we can be sure only when we have examined the development of one of his novels in as great detail as we have its complex embryo in 'The Gentle Boy.' But at this point, while completing our effort to place Hawthorne's work by evaluating the qualities that first emerged as he set himself against the prevailing tendencies of his tradition, it may be adequate to suggest that a comparison between this first of his real successes and 'Ethan Brand,' one of the last short pieces he was to write, will show no progress in essentials. Or if you take the volume of *Twice-Told Tales* by itself, the not very bulky harvest of a dozen years' effort, several of the other most memorable, including 'The Maypole of Merrymount,' 'The Shaker Bridal,' and 'The Gray Champion,' appear to have been composed early within that interval, whereas some of the most drearily innocuous sketches, 'Little Annie's Ramble' and 'A Rill from the Town Pump,' belong near its close. This apparent dwindling rather than growth shows what he meant by complaining to Longfellow about his difficulty in finding material; and the fact that most of his early manifestations of artistic skill deal with the seventeenth century might indicate that his imagination could gain release only when it gave up the problem of confronting the bare present. But 'The Shaker Bridal' was suggested by his visit to the community at Canterbury, New Hampshire; and 'Ethan Brand,' the deftly presented sensuous details of which are as evocative even as those in 'Young Goodman Brown,' was based on his observation of scenes and people near North Adams. The test for Hawthorne's success, therefore, would seem to be not whether his material was contemporary or from the past, but whether it could be impregnated with his kind of inner theme. The human problems that he scrutinized were the same in both settings.

3. 'To open an intercourse with the world'

WHEN Hawthorne made his own estimate of *Twice-Told Tales* from the vantage point of their reissue in 1851, he could detach himself and walk all around his work, just as Henry James was to do with his, in the prefaces which, incidentally, seem to have received their first hint from the laconic but devastating self-appraisal of his countryman. Even in the choice of his peculiar title Hawthorne had concealed an irony turned on himself, in a way foreshadowing Eliot's. His tales were twice-told, not merely because he had derived some of them from history and others from local legends he had picked up, or by virtue of the fact that he had printed them previously in magazines, which, as Poe meticulously noted, made some of them now thrice-told. Hawthorne would almost certainly have been thinking also of the line from *King John:*

> Life is as tedious as a twice-told tale.

But as he looked back now at what it had meant to be 'for a good many years, the obscurest man of letters in America,' he no longer hid his ironies. Observing that during this period he had had no incitement to effort beyond 'the pleasure itself of composition,' he concluded that 'to this total lack of sympathy, at the age when his mind would naturally have been most effervescent, the public owe it (and it is certainly an effect not to be regretted on either part) that the Author can show nothing for the thought and industry of that portion of his life,' save the pieces winnowed in this volume. At the time when he had issued his second collection,[1] the *Mosses,* nine years after his first, he had already said, 'Such trifles, I truly feel, afford no solid basis for a literary reputation.'

. Tales

But now, with *The Scarlet Letter* behind him and *The Seven Gables* about ready to appear, he let himself go in this preface to the *Tales,* and again in the fall of this year of his greatest production,[2] when he yielded to his publisher's desire to take advantage of his new popularity and reluctantly consented to a final gleaning from his fugitive pieces, in *The Snow-Image.* What he said in his preface there was hardly calculated to increase the sales. Some of the stories that he had resurrected had been among the very earliest he had written, which, 'after lying for years in manuscript . . . at last skulked into the Annuals.' As he looked at them once again, he was disposed to quarrel with them 'both because a mature judgment discerns so many faults, and still more because they come so nearly up to the standard of the best that I can achieve now.' But he had been even more drastic when he had returned to his *Tales,* and, in one full-breathed paragraph, had stated the case against them more effectively than any critic has ever done. He felt that there could be no harm in the author's remarking that he rather wondered how they

should have gained what vogue they did than that it was so little and so gradual. They have the pale tint of flowers that blossomed in too retired a shade,—the coolness of a meditative habit, which diffuses itself through the feeling and observation of every sketch. Instead of passion there is sentiment; and, even in what purport to be pictures of actual life, we have allegory, not always so warmly dressed in its habiliments of flesh and blood as to be taken into the reader's mind without a shiver. Whether from lack of power, or an unconquerable reserve, the Author's touches have often an effect of tameness; the merriest man can hardly contrive to laugh at his broadest humor; the tenderest woman, one would suppose, will hardly shed warm tears at his deepest pathos. The book, if you would see anything in it, requires to be read in the clear, brown, twilight atmosphere in which it was written; if opened in the sunshine, it is apt to look exceedingly like a volume of blank pages.

1. There had been a second, expanded edition of *Twice-Told Tales* in 1842.

2. He had also written that summer *A Wonder-Book,* retelling for children the classical myths.

Thus he announced his failure to meet the test which Thoreau had set up two years before in the *Week,* that a book should be so saturated with nature that it could stand the scrutiny of the unobstructed sun; to say nothing of what Whitman was soon to demand of his lines, that they should read as though they had been charactered in blood. Hawthorne had first made public his recognition of where his audience was or was not to be found, in the mock-introduction he wrote for M. de l'Aubépine, the alleged author of 'Rappaccini's Daughter' (1844): 'As a writer, he seems to occupy an unfortunate position between the Transcendentalists (who, under one name or another, have their share in all the current literature of the world) and the great body of pen-and-ink men who address the intellect and sympathies of the multitude.' If not 'too refined,' at any rate 'too remote, too shadowy, and unsubstantial' for popular appeal, he was yet 'too popular to satisfy the spiritual or metaphysical requisitions' of the new élite.[3] Such reflections had been borne in upon Hawthorne both at Brook Farm and as a resident in the Manse; and when he

3. The curve of Melville's reputation was finally destined to fall even more drastically between these two orbits. *Typee* had come near to being a best seller, and the high point of his popularity probably arrived when its many delighted readers sat down to its sequel in *Omoo* and were not disappointed. But neither of these books had been regarded as important literature. The tone of their notices may be suggested by the brief one that Whitman wrote of the two together for *The Brooklyn Eagle,* May 5, 1847: '. . . two well-printed volumes of the most readable sort of reading . . . One can revel in such richly good-natured style . . . We therefore recommend this "narrative of adventure in the south seas" as thorough entertainment—not so light as to be tossed aside for its flippancy, nor so profound as to be tiresome.' The only serious discussion of them was deflected to the question of their authenticity, and to the moral protest from the religious reviews over the picture that Melville had given of the missionaries. These journals took him to task for his 'cool voluptuousness' and his 'lapses from gentility.' They were later to shudder at his 'free-thinking' in *Mardi,* just as they were to wonder whether Hawthorne, in *The Scarlet Letter,* was 'making fun of all religion' in the choice of his sensual theme, and to ask, 'Is the French era actually begun in our literature?'

With the appearance of *Mardi,* Melville started to lose his hold over the audience for travel literature, but as he was later grimly to reflect, he had been so indelibly labelled as 'the man who lived among the cannibals' that he did not gain the attention of more discerning readers. In spite of a fairly widespread interest in *White Jacket,* owing largely to its humanitarian propaganda against current abuses in the navy, *Moby-Dick* was to call out even less interest and less praise than *Mardi.* With *Pierre* any discernible following had disappeared; and *The Confidence Man,* though attracting some attention in England for its exposure of Yankee hypocrisies, brought him the scantiest notice in this country. (I am indebted here to an unpublished thesis, *The Reputation of Herman Melville,* by H. W. Hetherington [University of Michigan, 1933]; and to Willard Thorp's introduction to his selections from Melville, 1938.)

came to write *Blithedale,* it amused him to make his hero Miles Coverdale a minor transcendental poet, an interminable reader in Mr. Emerson's *Essays, The Dial,* Carlyle, and George Sand's romances—all of which, if agreeing in little else, were 'like the cry of some solitary sentinel, whose station was on the outposts of the advance-guard of human progression.'

In utter contrast Hawthorne observed that his *Tales* had none of the profundity or abstruseness that characterize 'the written communications of a solitary mind with itself.' It is almost as though he was using Eliot's four categories of thinking and emphasizing his deliberate divergences from Emerson's mode.[4] Looking back now to the time when he had hardly been able to feel that, as a writer of fiction in New England, he was addressing 'any public at all,' Hawthorne still declared that his stories had never been 'the talk of a secluded man with his own mind and heart (had it been so, they could hardly have failed to be more deeply and permanently valuable), but his attempts, and very imperfectly successful ones, to open an intercourse with the world.' Yet this imperfection was due to no transcendental 'obscurity of expression.' His style, he was insistent, never needed translation. 'It is, in fact, the style of a man of society,' by which quiet assertion he bears out my contention that many of his hidden roots are in the Augustan age.

With the composition of his *Tales* now a long interval behind him, and with his clear decision that he would never do any more in this kind, that he would write either full-length romances or nothing, he could speak of his first volume as a memorial 'of very tranquil and not unhappy years.' But when he had been immersed in their flux, he had felt far less easy over the wastage involved in giving up his life to supplying stories for no discernible demand. To be sure, he made no direct discussion in print of the problems of his craft earlier than these prefaces,[5] written

4. See p. 67 above.

5. Their self-depreciatory tone was established in the note of a few lines which he wrote for a small edition of 'The Gentle Boy' in 1839. This story seems to have been a special favorite with his family and friends; and an outline drawing of Ilbrahim, designed as a frontispiece by Sophia, marked the occasion for its separate issue. But Hawthorne wrote: 'The tale, of which a new edition is now offered to the public, was among the earliest efforts of its author's pen . . . There are several among the *Twice-Told Tales* which, on reperusal, affect him less painfully with a sense of imperfect and ill-wrought conception than "The Gentle Boy." But the opinion of many . . . compels him to the conclusion that nature here led him deeper into the universal heart than art has been able to follow.'

when his ninety-odd tales and sketches were an accomplished, if not very large, fact to show for the occupation of almost a quarter of a century. Yet his imagination had been repeatedly absorbed by what was involved in being an artist in New England. This can be traced through a series of stories, hardly less significant for the interpretation of Hawthorne's aims than the much more fully wrought group, which includes 'The Lesson of the Master,' 'The Death of the Lion,' and 'The Figure in the Carpet,' are for those of James; or, for that matter, than 'Tonio Kröger' and 'A Weary Hour' are for those of Thomas Mann.

In 'The Prophetic Pictures' (1836) and 'Drowne's Wooden Image' (1844), Hawthorne projected the problems encountered by a painter and a woodcarver in colonial times, both of whom were surrounded by communities in which many held it an offence against the Mosiac law to bring into existence lively images of God's creatures, and some of whose superstitions went even to the point of fearing that such skill could have come to a man only through the practice of black magic.[6] But Hawthorne was not wholly sympathetic with his artists: he looked at the obverse side as well, pointing out that the painter was interested only in probing the hidden traits of his sitters, and was unconcerned by their fates, even when his eye could detect that one of them was headed towards insanity. In his cold indifference to everything except his art, 'like all other men around whom an engrossing purpose wreathes itself, he was insulated from the mass of human kind.'

Hawthorne made a more sympathetic sketch of the creative temperament in his parable of 'The Artist of the Beautiful' (1844). One direct statement there seemed so true to Melville that he triple-scored it: Hawthorne, speaking not through his sensitive carver but in his own person, declared it 'requisite for the ideal artist to possess a force of character that seems hardly compatible with its delicacy; he must keep his faith

6. That this superstition had not entirely disappeared from nineteenth-century America is attested by Melville. Only a few weeks after he had finished *Moby-Dick,* he received from Duyckinck a newspaper account of a ship's having just been sunk by the deliberate attack of a whale. To this he answered, in a tone not altogether jesting: 'Your letter received last night had a sort of stunning effect on me. For some days past being engaged in the woods . . . the Whale had almost completely slipped me for the time (and I was the merrier for it) when Crash! comes Moby-Dick . . . It is really and truly a surprising coincidence, to say the least. I make no doubt it *is* Moby-Dick himself, for there is no account of his capture after the sad fate of the Pequod . . . I wonder if my evil art has raised this monster.'

in himself while the incredulous world assails him with its utter disbelief.' Owen Warland's frame did not appear capable of sustaining that hair-trigger balance when faced with his townspeople's one comprehensive method of accounting for any mysteries beyond their comfortable scope of narrowness and dullness: their pronouncing them acts of madness. Perhaps, Hawthorne reflected, their judgment in Owen's case may have been correct by anticipation. 'The lack of sympathy—that contrast between himself and his neighbors which took away the restraint of example,' was enough to have driven him insane.[7] Owen felt his spirit particularly oppressed in the presence of 'the hard, brute force' of a young blacksmith, and in this Hawthorne foreshadows his more fully developed contrast of Clifford's gentle and helpless imagination with Judge Pyncheon's iron insistence on actuality. The perverseness of fate that denied Owen everything that his nature needed for sustenance called out from his creator the eloquent reflection that it made 'human existence appear too absurd and contradictory to be the scene of one other hope or one other fear.' Yet, steeled by something of that resignation, the suffering carver finally won his way to equilibrium by relying on his own resources, by accepting the fact that 'the reward of all high performance must be sought within itself, or sought in vain.'

This sketch is one of Hawthorne's barest statements of a profound theme, but Owen's traits, in differing mixtures, were to reappear in many of his other creations. Turning by instinct to the kind of life he knew most intimately, Hawthorne made the four heroes—though scarcely the most interesting characters—of his novels, all refractions of the artistic nature: Dimmesdale is a sensitive scholarly recluse; Coverdale, a poet; Kenyon, a young American sculptor in Rome (a type that James was to endow with passion in Roderick Hudson, but not even then to make very convincing); and Holgrave, not weak like the minister, less pale than the others, is a practitioner of the most up-to-date art of his day, that of the daguerreotype.[8] In none of these books is the problem of the

7. Melville marked this, as he did the comment, in 'Drowne's Wooden Image': 'A Yankee, and throw away the chance of making his fortune! He has gone mad; and thence has come this gleam of genius.' The narrow border line separating the artist from insanity seems to have preoccupied Melville from the time that he wrote Mardi.

8. A similar choice of heroes was made in Hawthorne's unfinished romances: Septimius Felton, not unlike Fanshawe, was a young scholar whose introspection finally divorced him fatally from normal pursuits. Dr. Dolliver and Dr. Grimshawe were again both variants of the scholar-type, the latter, like Roger Chillingworth, so segregated from other men as to have become a fiend.

artist Hawthorne's central theme, but he had treated that more directly, at the time when it was most urgent for him, in another series of sketches.

In 'Passages from a Relinquished Work' (1832), which he finally included in his *Mosses,* we have the remains of what appears to have been his last scheme for providing a structure that would have bound together his New England legends. He proposed, under the title of *The Story-Teller,* to localize each tale by sketching the circumstances under which it had been recited by a young writer who had determined to support himself by becoming an itinerant peddler of fiction. This plan led its narrator, whom Hawthorne deliberately tried not to make identical with himself, into the none the less Hawthornesque observation: 'Thus my airdrawn pictures will be set in frames perhaps more valuable than the pictures themselves, since they will be embossed with groups of characteristic figures, amid the lake and mountain scenery, the villages and fertile fields, of our native land.' The fact that this framework seems to have appealed to no publisher heightens the equally personal application of many of the story-teller's generalizations. For Hawthorne also 'piqued' himself on his 'penetration into people's characters,' as witness his recording in his notebook the remark of the ruined and desperate one-armed man at North Adams who, in the midst of deep degradation, still took pleasure in the acuteness of his mind: ' "My study is man," said he. And looking at me, "I do not know your name," said he, "but there is something of the hawk-eye about you too." ' Moreover, Hawthorne had every reason to know as well as his young hero that the resolution not to go into business, dangerous anywhere, 'was fatal in New England. There is a grossness in the conceptions of my countrymen; they will not be convinced that any good thing may consist with what they call idleness; they can anticipate nothing but evil of a young man who neither studies physic, law, nor gospel, nor opens a store, nor takes to farming.' Though still undeterred, he could not escape the thought that, in deciding to be a writer, he had made an 'irrevocable choice' of evil fate.

What that fate involved was voiced with increasing urgency in the years just before Hawthorne gained his first recognition. 'Fragments from the Journal of a Solitary Man' (1834), the purported work of another young writer who had died, dwelt on what it had meant to be divorced from the usual round of existence, since, never having known at first hand 'its deep and warm realities,' he could not feel as if he had lived at all. The author of 'The Devil in Manuscript' (1834), who is called

Oberon—the romantic nickname by which Hawthorne was known to his closest college friends—was even more bitter as he determined to burn his stories. 'Would you have me a damned author?'—a question that Melville scored. 'You cannot conceive what an effect the composition of these tales has had on me . . . I am surrounding myself with shadows, which bewilder me, by aping the realities of life. They have drawn me aside from the beaten path of the world, and led me into a strange sort of solitude,—a solitude in the midst of men,—where nobody wishes for what I do, nor thinks nor feels as I do . . . Oh, I have a horror of what was created in my own brain.'

It may be protested that I am taking far too seriously what can be regarded as mere exercises of the imagination. But Melville went even farther in the fascinated attention he gave to 'Monsieur du Miroir' (1836), which, out of its context in Hawthorne's development, might well seem no more than the flimsiest variation on the expected romantic theme of the double nature of reflections, those of the mirror's surface and those in the mind of the figure peering into it. But Melville, marking this short sketch more heavily than he did any other piece of Hawthorne's work, added such comments as 'What a revelation,' and 'This trenches upon the uncertain and the terrible.' Through his eyes we can at least see what he took to be depths, in, for example, a sentence describing how the author sat alone in his chamber while evening deepened into night. The phrase which Melville underlined, 'the key turned and withdrawn from the lock,' suddenly projects its theme of the isolated individual forward a century to *The Waste Land:*

> I have heard the key
> Turn in the door once and turn once only
> We think of the key, each in his prison
> Thinking of the key, each confirms a prison . . .

As Hawthorne's character lights a lamp, he has the strange sensation that the 'tranquil gloom' of his image in the glass is that of 'a fated man,' whose youth 'has been wasted in sluggishness for lack of hope and impulse, or equally thrown away in toil that had no wise motive and has accomplished no good end.'

It is not an unwarranted distortion to read in these repeated thoughts Hawthorne's own dilemma, for he expressed that dilemma, without a mask, in a letter to Longfellow, in gratitude for his praise of the *Tales.*

Longfellow

The two had not been intimate at college, and had not met in the interval since. But after this renewal of contact their amiable relationship remained unbroken. Henry James, Sr. was to note the paradoxical contrast between them, as he observed them once at the Saturday Club a few months before the Civil War. In such company Hawthorne looked uneasily like 'a rogue who suddenly finds himself in a company of detectives.' But he 'seemed to me to possess human substance and not to have dissipated it all away . . . like good inoffensive comforting Longfellow.' By then Hawthorne, even though he felt that the poet's work continued to grow 'richer and deeper,' had long since discerned the fundamental cleavage between them. Longfellow had confided to his journal that, in spite of 'passages of extremest beauty,' Hawthorne's books were not wholly congenial to him 'because of the old dull pain that runs through all.' And the novelist knew that his friend generally seemed 'no more conscious of any earthly or spiritual trouble than a sunflower is—of which lovely blossom he, I know not why, reminded me.'

But after his long years of writing in the void, it had been an inestimable encouragement to find appreciation from a contemporary whose imagination had also been moved by life in New England, and who was not making literature merely a branch of the ministry. In his review of the *Tales,* Longfellow had airily quoted from Jean Paul about 'the lark's nest' in which an author dwells. This had made Hawthorne smile.

You would have been much nearer the truth if you had pictured me as dwelling in an owl's nest; for mine is about as dismal . . . By some witchcraft or other—for I really cannot assign any reasonable why and wherefore— I have been carried apart from the main current of life, and find it impossible to get back again. Since we last met, which you remember was in Sawtell's room, where you read a farewell poem to the relics of the class,—ever since that time I have secluded myself from society; and yet I never meant any such thing, nor dreamed what sort of life I was going to lead. I have made a captive of myself, and put me into a dungeon, and now I cannot find the key to let myself out,—and if the door were open, I should be almost afraid to come out. You tell me that you have met with troubles and changes. I know not what these may have been, but I can assure you that trouble is the next best thing to enjoyment, and that there is no fate in this world so horrible as to have no share in either its joys or sorrows. For the last ten years, I have not lived, but only dreamed of living.

This passage may seem to be written up with some of the artificiality of his tales, but that serves to bear out that such a rhetorical mode was Hawthorne's norm. For the statements here could scarcely be more explicit, and their implications ran throughout his work and constituted its almost obsessive theme. When he created in 'Wakefield' (1834) his kind of Rip Van Winkle, the hero's disappearance for twenty years was caused by no external arts of enchantment, but by his own perverse act one day in detaching himself from his family with the half-formulated notion of a brief experiment in watching his life instead of being part of it. Yet no sooner had he started than he found himself entangled in an uncontrollable web of scruples and influences that prevented him from coming back; for so complex are human adjustments that 'by stepping aside for a moment, a man exposes himself to a fearful risk of losing his place forever.'

What terrified Hawthorne most about the isolated individual was the cold inability to respond to ordinary life, whether, as in the case of Gervayse Hastings in 'The Christmas Banquet,' it was owing to the fact that since he had never suffered, other people seemed to him only shadows; or whether, as with an unscrupulous scientist like Rappaccini or a self-centered reformer like Hollingsworth, it was because their minds had lost touch with 'the magnetic chain of humanity.' In 'Sights from a Steeple' Hawthorne had innocently concluded that 'the most desirable mode of existence might be that of a spiritualized Paul Pry, hovering invisible round man and woman, witnessing their deeds, searching into their hearts . . . and retaining no emotion peculiar to himself.' But twenty-five years later Coverdale, as narrator of *The Blithedale Romance,* was far less happy about his role of chronic observer, and kept asking himself uneasily whether it was a healthy occupation, or merely a transcendental brand of Yankee curiosity, whether it had dehumanized him and involved him in a self-conscious battening on others' lives.

Hawthorne finally made unmistakable that Coverdale possessed real sympathies, however delicate and ineffective; but the degree to which Coverdale's problem was also his creator's shows the consequences of the kind of existence Hawthorne had led. These consequences are among the frequently noted distortions of centrifugal American life, which, in its continual fierce thrusts outward from European civilization, had left its exceptional individuals no common ground for meeting, no apparent recourse other than exploration of themselves. Especially in Hawthorne's surroundings, in what, from the later vantage point of Rome, he could look back to as 'the dryness and meagreness of a New England village,' the human products could be desperately undernourished, subject to Coverdale's neurotic scrupulosity, or to the attenuated sensitiveness of Priscilla, for whom the hero did not confess his love until it was too late. Her flower-like innocence seems to have received many hints from Hawthorne's own Sophia; but in risking such parallels between his life and his art, we must remember that Coverdale is not Hawthorne [9] any more than Prufrock is Eliot, that in each case the author has exorcised a danger-ous part of his experience by treating it with irony, or, as Santayana observed of Henry James, has overcome the genteel tradition 'in the classic way, by understanding it.'

4. The Haunted Mind

IN GIVING here the final strokes to the inner portrait of our one major artist in fiction yet to have come out of New England,[1] we can see that Hawthorne's inordinate detachment could sometimes amount to an asset. If an artist is to exist in New England or anywhere else, he needs to

9. The repetition of types in his fiction indicates that, like James, Hawthorne knew only a limited range of life at first-hand. But it would be unwise to conclude from this that any of Hawthorne's characters are *literal* self-portraiture. As he said in his preface to *The Snow-Image:* 'You must make quite another kind of inquest, and look through the whole range of his [the author's] fictitious characters, good and evil, in order to detect any of his essential traits.'

1. The best-known names among our novelists since Hawthorne's time substantiate that fact to an extraordinary degree. Waiving the question of 'major' and taking a wide sweep through the figures who have been given the most serious attention, you find that Mark Twain was born in Missouri; Howells and Sherwood Anderson in Ohio; James and Edith Wharton in New York; Frank Norris, Hemingway, and Dos Passos in Illinois, though none of them made their homes there; Stephen Crane in New Jersey; Dreiser in Indiana; Ellen Glasgow and Willa Cather in Virginia, though the latter grew up in Nebraska; Jack London in California; Upton Sinclair in Maryland; Sinclair Lewis in Minnesota; Faulkner in Missis-sippi; Wolfe in North Carolina. That leaves New England with Harriet Beecher Stowe and Sylvester Judd and Edward Bellamy; with minor talents of great distinction like Sarah Orne Jewett, Mary Wilkins, and Thornton Wilder, who was not born there; with the recently rediscovered John W. DeForest of Connecticut, the author of *Miss Ravenel's Conversion* (1867), and with Robert Herrick, who was born in Cambridge, Massachusetts, but whose creative life was passed in Chicago.

possess some share of what Hawthorne recognized in himself when, fore-warning his fiancée that he might not be able to rise to her enthusiasm for Father Taylor, he declared: 'I am a most unmalleable man.'[2] His surface must have been practically adamant to have resisted the waves of her admiration for Emerson, whom, as she confided to her diary, she thought 'the greatest man that ever lived. *As a whole* he is satisfactory . . . Pure Tone.' Another means of self-protection, of rendering himself immune to the attritions of Yankee life, was Hawthorne's generous strain of indolence, which led him to the frank avowal, 'I hate all labor, but less that of the hands than of the head.' A more certain sign of his creative temperament was the tenderness mixed in with his strength, an almost feminine passivity, which many of his friends noted and Alcott expressed in his own way by asking: 'Was he some damsel imprisoned in that manly form pleading alway for release?'

Another phase of his indolence that aided his survival was his indifference, if not dullness, to nearly everything that did not concern the medium in which he lived. The late W. C. Brownell, writing from the standards of the genteel tradition at its best, deplored Hawthorne's insufficient culture, his aesthetic ignorance, his utter lack of trained eye or ear. Many of the statements in his *Italian Notebooks,* a record of his mid-fifties, are appalling enough. He made labored objections to the nude in contemporary sculpture on the ground that naked bodies were no longer a part of daily life. He kept repeating his determination not to allow himself to be 'bamboozled' by the new experience of going to art galleries into pretending that he liked what he didn't; and then came out plump for Guido's Beatrice Cenci as 'the most profoundly wrought picture in the world.' Faced with the worked-up guide-book descriptions in *The Marble Faun,* you might even prefer the reactionary attitude that was to produce a decade later the heavy smartiness of *The Innocents Abroad.*

Yet without being perverse, it seems possible to question what further values would have accrued to the author of *The Scarlet Letter* if he had been able to follow Brownell in becoming a high priest of international culture. Brownell, in spite of his long devotion to acclimatizing in America the cultural ideals of Arnold, sometimes betrayed the fatal cleavage between life and art that Santayana found common to the other new humanists, whom he called, in contradistinction to the generation of

2. Remember that this is what he also said about Thoreau.

Lowell, 'the genteel tradition at bay.' In spite of the hard intelligence and enormous learning with which Babbitt and More set up their standards, their utter inability to measure the literature of their own time sprang from the inadequate sensibility that is a sign of the divorce between mind and experience. Their conception of human nature was high principled, but arid and inadequate.

The bearing of the fate of the genteel tradition upon Hawthorne's stalwart preference for looking at landscapes by his American contemporaries Brown and Thompson instead of at one by Claude, on the ground that though 'not nearly so great' they are 'better suited to this very present time,' may well seem tangential. But the point is that within Hawthorne's provincial limitations, there was a wholeness, a desire to record whatever he knew of human nature both from observation and from thought, and not to let himself be distracted by the transcendentalists' frequent confusions between what life was and what they hoped it to be.[3] Eliot has established a similar point about James, in accounting for his seemingly miraculous escape from the reverse of Hawthorne's dilemma, an overdose of European culture, to which his apparently indiscriminate enthusiasm for anything with 'references,' whether breakfast in a Liverpool hotel or the lawns of great country houses, might well have made him fatally susceptible. Yet, inheriting the ethical discernment of his father, James became a critic 'who preyed not upon ideas, but upon living beings . . .

3. In noting the evidence for this as furnished by the transcendentalists' reading, Hawthorne believed that Thoreau's tastes were 'more exclusive than is desirable.' The catholicity of Hawthorne's own reading, in which his New England opportunities had let him be really educated as he was not in music and the plastic arts, shows how little he was swayed by any one school of thought. For though Ellery Channing may have been no more accurate than usual when he said that Hawthorne's 'favorite writers were "the English novelists," Boccaccio, Horace, and Johnson,' still the list of books that he borrowed from the Salem Atheneum during the decade 1828-38 reveals a range even farther afield. Glancing down the list, which included history, science, and philosophy, and which, counting volumes of magazines, sometimes ran as high as two hundred titles in a single year, you find, among many others, the following works that you might not have looked for in the apparently undernourished diet of the author of 'The Lily's Quest' or 'Edward Fane's Rosebud' or other of the more anemic *Tales:* Mandeville's *Fable of the Bees,* Schlegel on History, Sidney on Government, Burns' Works, Dryden's Poems, Machiavelli's Works, *Essais de Montaigne, Œuvres de Rousseau, Œuvres de Voltaire* (several times), *Memoires de Richelieu, Œuvres de Pascal,* Taylor's Sermons, Sowerby's *English Botany, Œuvres de Racine* (several times), Massinger, Coleridge's *Aids to Reflection, Elements of Technology,* Fuller's *Holy State,* Jefferson's Writings, Strutt's *Sports and Pastimes,* Babbage on the Economy of Machinery, Pliny's *Natural History.* In addition, many titles point, of course, to his continual reading in the history of New England.

His critical genius comes out most tellingly in his mastery over, his baffling escape from, Ideas; a mastery and an escape which are perhaps the last test of a superior intelligence. He had a mind so fine that no idea could violate it.' He 'was not, by Adams' standards, "educated," but particularly limited; it is the sensuous contributor to the intelligence that makes the difference.'

The way that even the ideas for his books came to James as concrete images led Eliot to characterize him as a metaphysical novelist. That separates him sharply from Hawthorne, in whose writing there is none of the amalgamation of sense and thought that places both Melville and Thoreau in the metaphysical strain. But Hawthorne's wholeness is none the less in the tradition from the seventeenth century. He was like the Unitarians only in that he shared Theodore Parker's concern to distinguish between the transient and the permanent in Christianity. But his interpretation of the latter element was much more akin to *Paradise Lost* than to 'The Over-Soul'; it provided his chief basis for tragedy, as we shall see.

Hawthorne diverged significantly from Emerson in not trying to make his work an act of will. It was not the product of a determination to lift 'better up to best,' but a record of unconscious depths whose source was beyond his control. 'The Haunted Mind' (1834) is another of those harm-less-looking six-page sketches, which not even Melville marked. It de-scribes the sensation of waking up at midnight, 'when the mind has a passive sensibility, but no active strength: when the imagination is a mirror, imparting vividness to all ideas, without the power of selecting or controlling them.' In those few words you share in Hawthorne's creative process, in his apprehension of the fertile state that Keats described as 'negative capability,' the relaxed indolence that alone is receptive to the inwelling of fresh impressions. At these moments between sleep and waking Hawthorne's imagination is thronged by a train of images, 'in which Passion and Feeling assume bodily shape.' In the paragraph in which they troop by in this sketch, Sorrow, Hope, Disappointment, iron Fatality, and Shame may seem no more than traits out of one of Spenser's processional masques. But they are the same traits that dominate all Hawthorne's work.

What he cast here into allegorical form would now be called hypna-gogic images, the images subsisting on the borderland of the unconscious which surrealism has seized for its peculiar domain. The Freudian analysis of the manner in which these images arise was foreshadowed by a remarkably accurate description in Poe's *Marginalia:*

There is . . . a class of fancies, of exquisite delicacy, which are *not* thoughts, and to which, *as yet,* I have found it absolutely impossible to adapt language. I use the word 'fancies' at random, and merely because I must use some word; but the idea commonly attached to the term is not even remotely applicable to the shadows of shadows in question. They seem to me rather psychal than intellectual. They arise in the soul (alas, how rarely!) only at its epochs of most intense tranquillity, . . . and at those mere points of time where the confines of the waking world blend with those of the world of dreams. I am aware of these 'fancies' only when I am upon the very brink of sleep, with the consciousness that I am so.[4]

To such a degree did the provincial American mind, driven in upon itself, point the way, through its intense self-consciousness, to the kind of material which the French symbolists were to explore, and even to something of the method by which modern psychology was to investigate this material further. The coincidence with Hawthorne's conception of the imaginative process is very close. That being the case it may not be fanciful to foresee another development of modern literature in two more of his observations. The first is his reflection about 'a terrible dream' that appalled the hero of 'The Birthmark,' a reflection that Melville

4. Poe's almost clinical analysis of his own process continues thus: 'Now, so entire is my faith in the *power of words,* that, at times, I have believed it possible to embody even the evanescence of fancies such as I have attempted to describe. In experiments with this end in view, I have proceeded so far as, first, to control (when the bodily and mental health are good) the existence of the condition: that is to say, I can now (unless when ill) be sure that the condition will supervene, if I so wish it, at the point of time already described:—of its supervention, until lately, I could never be certain, even under the most favorable circumstances . . .

'I have proceeded so far, secondly, as to prevent the lapse from *the point* of which I speak—the point of blending between wakefulness and sleep—as to prevent at will, I say, the lapse from this borderground into the dominion of sleep. Not that I can *continue* the condition—not that I can render the point more than a point—but that I can startle myself from the point into wakefulness, *and thus transfer the point itself into the realm of Memory;* convey its impressions, or more properly their recollections, to a situation where (although still for a very brief period) I can survey them with the eye of analysis. For these reasons—that is to say, because I have been enabled to accomplish thus much—I do not altogether despair of embodying in words at least enough of the fancies in question to convey to certain classes of intellect a shadowy conception of their character . . . Should I ever write a paper on this topic, the world will be compelled to acknowledge that, at last, I have done an original thing.'

scored: 'Truth often finds its way to the mind close muffled in robes of sleep, and then speaks with uncompromising directness of matters in regard to which we practise an unconscious self-deception during our waking moments.' The other is an apparently casual note for a story: 'To write a dream which shall resemble the real course of a dream, with all its inconsistency, its strange transformations, which are all taken as a matter of course; its eccentricities and aimlessness,—with nevertheless a leading idea running through the whole. Up to this old age of the world, no such thing has ever been written.' Hawthorne did not possess the psychological equipment to enable him to realize this fantastic aim. But unless men, following Coleridge's study of his own mind, had begun to dwell habitually on such thoughts as Poe's and Hawthorne's, *Finnegans Wake* would hardly have been conceived.

Hawthorne's half-waking sensations so possessed him that he could not help 'running a doubtful parallel' between them and the rest of human life, for 'in both you emerge from mystery, pass through a vicissitude that you can but imperfectly control, and are borne onward to another mystery.' Doubtful or not, his work never escaped for long from such parallels. This was not owing to any love of mystery for itself, since he declared emphatically that he 'abhorred' it, that he dreaded any 'unintelligible expression' as a clouding veil 'between the soul and the truth which it seeks.' But his haunted mind made him write not as he would, but as he must. Whipple saw him acutely when he said that 'his great books appear not so much created by him as through him. They have the character of revelations,—he, the instrument, being often troubled with the burden they impose upon his mind.' Hawthorne might contrast his forefathers' gloomy spirit with his own 'tropic-love of sunshine,' but he could rarely convey that light into his pages. In his preface to *The Scarlet Letter* he objected to that story's being too 'stern and sombre'; but his objection did little good even though it became chronic. After finishing *The Marble Faun* he wrote to his publisher: 'When I get home, I will try to write a more genial book; but the Devil himself always seems to get into my inkstand, and I can only exorcise him by pensful at a time.' And when he was about to start on the ill-fated *Dolliver Romance,* he wrote again to Fields: 'There is something preternatural in my reluctance to begin. I linger at the threshold, and have a perception of very disagreeable phantasms to be encountered if I enter. I wish God had given me the faculty of writing a sunshiny book.' Yet on the one occasion that he succeeded, at least to the satisfaction of his wife, who was pleased by the more cheerful tone of *Our Old Home,* his series of English sketches, his own more accurate judgment was: 'It is not a good nor a weighty book, nor does it deserve any great amount either of praise or censure.'

Undoubtedly his best-known comment on his work is his contrast between his tragedy of Hester Prynne and the daily life of the custom-house in which he had just been participating: 'A better book than I shall ever write was there; leaf after leaf presenting itself to me, just as it was written out by the reality of the flitting hour, and vanishing as fast as written, only because my brain wanted the insight and my hand the cunning to transcribe it.' This chimes in exactly with his opinion of Trollope, whose first books he was to read after meeting him in Rome: 'It is odd enough that my own individual taste is for quite another class of novels than those which I myself am able to write. If I were to meet with such books as mine by another writer, I don't believe I should be able to get through them. Have you ever read the novels of Anthony Trollope? They precisely suit my taste; solid and substantial, written on the strength of beef and through the inspiration of ale, and just as real as if some giant had hewn a great lump out of the earth.'

In the light of this full understanding of the role of the realistic novelist, most critics, in regretting that Hawthorne was not a Fielding or a Balzac, have believed that he failed to come to grips with the life of his age by not portraying such concrete facts as he encountered as an inspector on the docks. But if his art was to fulfil its function by remaining true to what his deepest intuitions had known, there must inevitably have been woven into the texture of his style some thinness and bleakness, the consequences of the long domination of Puritan thought, and of the lack of any developed artistic tradition from which he could start. With all the feverish activity of America around him, there was not the social solidity that Fielding knew, or the manifold gradations between classes that Balzac could analyze. The frequent disproportion between the weight of what Hawthorne wanted to say and the flimsiness of the vehicle he could devise to carry it suggests the nature of the problem to be met by a man of his time who was not content with taking over conclusions from Europe, but was determined to grasp 'the usable truth,' the actual meaning of civilization as it had existed in America. What Eliot called Hawthorne's 'realism' could not depend on a notation of rich surface details;

its very starvation made it a truer facing of the tragedy of provincial New England.

Even odder than Hawthorne's appreciation of Trollope may appear the seldom-noted essay on 'The Genius of Nathaniel Hawthorne,' which the matter-of-fact English novelist was to write fifteen years after the other's death. He had read Hawthorne's remarks about himself, and was equally aware of the strong divergence. He started out with a modestly accurate account of his own aims, how it had always been his object to draw his 'little pictures' in such a way that his readers 'should feel that they were dealing with people whom they might probably have known, but so to do it that the every-day good to be found among them should allure, and the every-day evil repel.' Such he took to be the scope of the novelist of manners. In his view Hawthorne had dealt with persons and incidents 'which were often but barely within the bounds of possibility.' He confessed that he was frequently depressed beyond measure by these 'weird' tales, and yet that, in the act of reading them, he had 'become conscious of a certain grandeur of nature in being susceptible of such suffering.' By the honesty of his reaction Trollope thus described the purgative effect of tragedy.

He was equally perceptive of the kinship between Hawthorne's traits and those of his nation: 'The creations of American literature generally are no doubt more given to the speculative,—less given to the realistic,—than are those of English literature. On our side of the water we deal more with beef and ale, and less with dreams.' He could see even in the broad humor of Artemus Ward and Mark Twain 'an undercurrent of melancholy, in which pathos and satire are intermingled.' He found the same three interwoven strands in Irving, and all except the last one in Longfellow. The notable thing about the American handling of the weird was that it was not the manufactured Gothic article of a 'Monk' Lewis, but something indigenous, something inescapably there. 'With Hawthorne we are made to think that he could not have been anything else if he would.' [5]

5. Trollope continued this comment in a charming personal sketch of the sort he was best qualified to give: 'It is as though he could certainly have been nothing else in his own inner life. We know that such was not actually the case.' Although 'a man singularly reticent,' Hawthorne 'could, when things went well with him, be argumentative, social, and cheery. I have seen him very happy over canvas-back ducks, and have heard him discuss, almost with violence, the superiority of American vegetables. Indeed, he once withered me with a scorn which was anything but mystic or melancholy because I expressed a patriotic

In dedicating *The Snow-Image* to Bridge, Hawthorne had looked back once more to the state from which this friend had rescued him by securing a publisher for *Twice-Told Tales*. Again he could describe it only by saying that he had been 'like a man under enchantment,' caught in the entangling depths of a forest that had apparently sprung up around him, and from the obscurity of which no escape had seemed possible. He was re-creating in that image what he had phrased more desperately at the time.[6] Then, in a mood of discouragement, he had written Bridge that he felt as though he was drifting helplessly towards a cataract: 'I'm a doomed man, and over I must go.' It was at this point that Bridge, worried lest such depression might even lead to suicide, had set himself resolutely to find someone who would bring out the tales as a volume;

preference for English peas. And yet his imagination was such that the creations of his brain could not have been other than such as I have described.'

The engaging, if fatuous question whether America needed a Trollope rather than a Hawthorne calls up Henry James' comments on the Englishman as they were expressed in a series of reviews. His estimate just after Trollope's death (1882) was that though he had been too prolific to the point of becoming mechanical, 'his great, his inestimable merit was a complete appreciation of the usual.' But James as a young reviewer had previously been more exacting in his standards. He had perceived (1865) that Trollope wrote his solidly commonplace novels by an easy recipe. He found him (1866) 'a good observer, but . . . literally nothing else.' All the possible incidents of society seemed to be 'of equal importance and interest' to him; therefore he overdid the small things, he evaded the great, and the result was a general mediocrity. James granted him (1868) the whole force of his plots: 'When you can add nothing to the story in the telling, you must rest your claim to the reader's gratitude on your taking away as little as possible.' In brief, Trollope wrote gloriously stupid books, 'prepared for minds unable to think.' (The most interesting material from James' reviews has been collected by Cornelia Pulsifer Kelley, in her study of *The Early Development of Henry James*, 1930.)

6. The persistence of a similar fantasy in his dream life was recorded by him in his notebook on December 25, 1854. He had been reflecting that he had 'been happier this Christmas then ever before,—by my own fireside, and with my wife and children about me,—more content to enjoy what I have,—less anxious for anything beyond it in this life. My early life was perhaps a good preparation for the declining half of life; it having been such a blank that any thereafter would compare favorably with it. For a long, long while, I have occasionally been visited with a singular dream; and I have an impression that I have dreamed it ever since I have been in England. It is, that I am still at college,—or, sometimes, even at school,—and there is a sense that I have been there unconscionably long, and have quite failed to make such progress as my contemporaries have done; and I seem to meet some of them with a feeling of shame and depression that broods over me as I think of it, even when awake. This dream, recurring all through these twenty or thirty years, must be one of the effects of that heavy seclusion in which I shut myself up for twelve years after leaving college, when everybody moved onward, and left me behind. How strange that it should come now, when I may call myself famous and prosperous!—when I am happy, too!'

and, trying to rouse Hawthorne into his own more cheerful view of the situation, had written, 'the bane of your life has been self-distrust.'

To escape from such moods Hawthorne did not have the recourse of Emerson, who could say good-bye to the 'proud world,' and go home to find himself in solitude. Hawthorne could never feel that a man became more human in this way. In the first number of his *Spectator,* with the composition of which he amused himself during the summer he was sixteen, he had anticipated, with amazing completeness, his mature position. He stated, in a brief essay 'On Solitude'—whose manner suggests again the extent to which the eighteenth century shaped his style: 'Man is naturally a sociable being . . . It is only in society that the full energy of his mind is aroused. Perhaps life may pass more tranquilly, estranged from the pursuits and vexations of the multitude, but all the hurry and whirl of passion is preferable to the cold calmness of indifference.' In spite of his lasting shyness, Hawthorne never saw any reason to alter this belief. He did not share Thoreau's unswerving confidence that man could find himself by studying nature; indeed, in no respect is his difference from all the transcendental writers more fundamental than in this. Hawthorne visited nature in order to return, refreshed, to the world of men.[7] Not that he ever thought himself to be master of that world, for, like his own Wakefield, he often felt caught up by influences beyond his determining. He came to know ever more deeply that life was larger than himself, as he tried to fathom denser complexities than the problem of the isolated man.

He was always concerned in his stories not merely with the individual, but with the collective existence. This may seem contradicted by his absorption with the inner life of his characters, with what Gervayse Hastings had missed, 'the deep warm secret—the life within the life.' But though this relates him to the main development of the novel of consciousness, and though like James he also found his dramatic contrasts in moments of moral crisis rather than in external events, he wanted none

7. He did not romanticize the harmony between nature and man. Such a passage as this, on nature's indifference, looks rather towards the attitude characteristic of the end of the nineteenth century than to that of its beginning: 'Nothing comes amiss to Nature—all is fish that comes to her net. If there be a living form of perfect beauty instinct with soul— why, it is all very well, and suits Nature well enough. But she would just as lief have that same beautiful, soul-illumined body, to make worm's meat of, and to manure the earth with.' These sentences, recorded in his notebook, were worked into his description, half a dozen years later, of the drowning of Zenobia.

the less to study not merely 'human character in its individual developments,' but also 'human nature in the mass.' He made this statement in
'The Intelligence Office,' one of a group including 'The Christmas Banquet,' 'The Hall of Fantasy,' 'The Celestial Railroad,' and 'Earth's Holocaust,' all of which belong to 1842-3 and show his particular emphasis as
he returned to writing after his stay at Brook Farm. The method common
to them all is suggested in the title of another, 'The Procession of Life,'
for in them Hawthorne was trying to encompass the range of society by
presenting a procession of types, grouped together not by the external accidents of their trades or professions, but by their hidden desires or their
deeper bond of suffering. These sketches, for the most part hardly more
than notes for undeveloped themes, at least show how he was feeling his
way from the short story towards the wider scope of the novel, which he
already thought, during these years at the Manse, would alone justify his
continuing to write. But as he pursued his researches into the heart 'for
the purposes of psychological romance,' he was never impelled to deal in
autobiography. He wrote from his 'old chamber' in Salem, to which he
had returned for a brief visit in 1843, a sentence that sums up an incalculable amount about his temperament, the intention of his art, and its
style. He had been reflecting again on what had happened to him when
he had been almost imprisoned in this room, and concluded: 'It is this involuntary reserve, I suppose, that has given the objectivity to my writings;
and when people think that I am pouring myself out in a tale or an
essay, I am merely telling what is common to human nature, not what
is peculiar to myself.' He repeated, in the preface to *The Snow-Image,*
that his researches were always directed 'into the depths of our common
nature.' And by that means he hoped to make his art a bridge between
man and society.

   We have thus arrived at the paradox that the man whom even Emerson, used though he was to Thoreau, found taciturn and tragically secluded, was also the man who, both in Boston and London, took an
interest 'in all the nooks and crannies and every development of cities.'
In all his sketches of the artistic type, Hawthorne stressed openness of
attention and curiosity as the writer's chief assets in gaining his indispensable 'varied knowledge.' Hawthorne's own share in these assets is partly
seen in his shy fondness for common existence and 'for vagrants of all
sorts.' When he portrayed the tragedy of the warping thought that could
lead to lunacy, he often pointed to contact with the life of the streets as

the source of renewed balance. He himself finally participated in the ordinary business of his age to a considerably greater degree than either Emerson or Thoreau—or Whitman, for that matter; for he held appointments in both the Boston and Salem customhouses, as well as the consul's position at Liverpool. Moreover, as a further twist to the paradox, though he was at no time sympathetic to transcendental philosophy, he—and none of the Concord group—took part in the transcendentalists' most positive gesture, the formation of Brook Farm. To be sure, he went there primarily in the hope of saving enough money to get married, but as treasurer of the community, he also started out by sharing, half quizzically, in their aspirations to the extent of wanting to escape from 'all the fopperies and flummeries which have their origin in a false state of society.'

Yet as he reviewed, at the end of his term as surveyor of Salem's revenue, a decade of his existence, his reckoning of the community was different, though shot through with irony: 'After my fellowship of toil and impracticable schemes with the dreamy brethren of Brook Farm; after living for three years within the subtle influence of an intellect like Emerson's . . . after talking with Thoreau about pine-trees and Indian relics, in his hermitage at Walden . . . after becoming imbued with poetic sentiment at Longfellow's hearth-stone,—it was time, at length, that I should exercise other faculties of my nature, and nourish myself with food for which I had hitherto had little appetite.' Even the old Inspector—whose one great advantage over 'his four-footed brethren' was his ability to recollect the good dinners which he had had—even he was healthy as a contrast for 'a man who had known Alcott.'[8] Hawthorne could regard it as evidence of 'a system naturally well balanced,' that 'with such associates to remember,' he had been able to mingle on the docks with men of altogether different qualities, and enjoy them in their fullness and variety.

Nevertheless, he could not manage to write during his hours of leisure from the customhouse. As he always found, he needed monotony, 'an eventless exterior life,' before he could 'live in the world within.' As a

---

8. Hawthorne's mock-heroic sketch of this patriarchal Inspector is his fulfilment of the strain of low-comedy that he had begun with the inn-keeper in *Fanshawe:* 'His gourmandism was a highly agreeable trait; and to hear him talk of roast meat was as appetizing as a pickle or an oyster . . . A tenderloin of beef, a hindquarter of veal, a sparerib of pork, a particular chicken, or a remarkably praiseworthy turkey, which had perhaps adorned his board in the days of the elder Adams, would be remembered; while all the subsequent experience of our race, and all the events that brightened or darkened his individual career, had gone over him with as little permanent effect as the passing breeze.'

result of such feeling it seemed to him only a few days after he had left Brook Farm as though the interval had been twenty years; and he took this for 'one proof that my life there was an unnatural and unsuitable, and therefore an unreal one. It already looks like a dream behind me. The real Me was never an associate of the community.' This was always the case with him after every period of active life: the years as customs surveyor, as consul, were to appear at the moment of their dissolution equally baseless and insubstantial. Even while he was still in the midst of his first job on the Boston waterfront, he could write to Sophia that he had a mind to send her someday a journal of all his doings, his 'whole external life,' from one morning till he closed his eyes at night. 'What a dry, dull history would it be! But then, apart from this, I would write another journal, of my inward life throughout the self-same day . . . Nobody would think that the same man could live two such different lives simultaneously. But then the grosser life is a dream, and the spiritual life is a reality.'

That presents, in its most damaging form, the evidence for those who find Hawthorne an escapist. In spite of his stated fondness for 'all the warm materialism of life,' such a dichotomy shows why he failed to maintain a tenacious hold on the surfaces from which the realistic novelist draws his sustenance. This fact forces consideration of the problem that I have so far finessed, what has served most to keep readers away from him to-day, what he himself deprecated as 'an inveterate love of allegory.'

⇒ VII ⇐

ALLEGORY AND SYMBOLISM

'Shakespeare led a life of Allegory: His works are the comments on it.'
                                                                    --KEATS

'We learn nothing rightly until we learn the symbolical character of life.'
                                                                    —EMERSON

'When a part so ptee does duty for the holos we soon grow to use of an allforabit.'
                                              —JOYCE, *Finnegans Wake*

THEORY

1. The American Bias and Background

HAWTHORNE described the way in which his own imagination worked when he made one of his characters say, 'Everything, you know, has its spiritual meaning, which to the literal meaning is what the soul is to the body.' This expressed the approach to reality that was made by many other writers of the age, who, notwithstanding wide divergences, took for granted the pre-eminence of spirit over matter. This formed common ground with the transcendentalists for Melville as well as Hawthorne. For, as we have seen, Emerson's proposition that 'every natural fact is a symbol of some spiritual fact,' was likewise the basis upon which Melville could build his 'cunningly linked analogies' in *Moby-Dick*. Moreover, Poe, in spite of his running fire of satire on the transcendentalists and his indifference if not hostility to all manifestations of the Christian tradition, continued to use 'purest ideality' as one of his chief tests for poetry. He thought of Tennyson as 'the noblest poet that ever lived' because his beauty was the most 'elevating' and 'ethereal.' This tendency of mind distinguishes Poe crucially from Baudelaire, and provides a measure of

242

the richer ingredients that frequently entered into the European composition. Although Baudelaire accepted the formulas of Poe's 'Poetic Principle' to as great a degree as one poet can profitably accept the logic of another, their unmistakably different work was owing to the fact that Poe always rarefied his matter, since his imagination never moved in the physical world but in the psychical. In the choice and development of his symbols, Baudelaire was more sensual, more plastic, more human.

No art that sprang from American roots in this period could fail to show the marks of abstraction. The first quotation that Melville made in his appreciation of the *Mosses* came from the climax of Owen Warland's realization that 'when the artist rose high enough to achieve the beautiful, the symbol by which he made it perceptible to mortal senses became of little value in his eyes, while his spirit possessed itself in the enjoyment of the reality.' The tendency of American idealism to see a spiritual significance in every natural fact was far more broadly diffused than transcendentalism. Loosely Platonic, it came specifically from the common background that lay behind Emerson and Hawthorne, from the Christian habit of mind that saw the hand of God in all manifestations of life, and which, in the intensity of the New England seventeenth century, had gone to the extreme of finding 'remarkable providences' even in the smallest phenomena, tokens of divine displeasure in every capsized dory or runaway cow.

Hawthorne was never inclined to the metaphysical speculation that absorbed Melville in his efforts to express the human tragedy involved in the doctrine of 'innate depravity' that he had inherited from his Presbyterian youth. Nevertheless, Hawthorne could not help being interested in ideas, if only on the level of meditation. He typified the process from which his art arose by describing what he found in the symbolical letter A. His attention had first fixed upon its possibilities when giving an account of various punishments inflicted in 'Endicott and the Red Cross' (1837). But a dozen years later when he purported to have found an actual letter of scarlet cloth among some old documents in the customhouse, his imagination pressed further: 'Certainly, there was some deep meaning in it, most worthy of interpretation, and which, as it were, streamed forth from the mystic symbol, subtly communicating itself to my sensibilities, but evading the analysis of my mind.'

With all the forces conditioning his art that we have noted—the scantiness of material and atmosphere, his lack of plastic experience, his steady moral preoccupation—it is no wonder that the favorites of his childhood, Spenser and Bunyan, rose again to the surface when he began to write, and helped determine his bias to allegory. In working out his allegorical patterns, he seems sometimes to have started from a physical object, the minister's black veil, the Faun of Praxiteles, and to have worried it for implications. On the other hand, he could also start with noting an idea— 'The Unpardonable Sin might consist in a want of love and reverence for the Human Soul'—and then work up an embodiment to fit it. In either case the method could very readily lose proportion. His idea might be promising enough, as in several of the processional sketches, but then the illustrations it suggested to him could be as ingeniously trivial as the crowd of impossible guests, the Oldest Inhabitant, Monsieur On-Dit, the Clerk of the Weather, Nobody, who clutter the party of the Man of Fancy, and obscure the telling portrait of the Master Genius of the age.[1] Or again, his idea might itself be hardly more than a nervous *tic,* some freakish notion that possessed him in his solitude: 'To personify If—But— And—Though, etc.' To be sure, this proved too unsubstantial even for Hawthorne, and got no further than his notebook, but some of the themes on which he spent his talents were hardly more rewarding, as when he determined 'to make a story of all strange and impossible things,—as the Salamander, the Phoenix,' and the result was 'A Virtuoso's Collection,' a prolonged enumeration of such oddities.

Yet even when he began with solid objects, he could transform them into something just as imponderable. One reason why is suggested in another note: 'Meditations about the main gas-pipe of a great city,—if the supply were to be stopped, what would happen? . . . It might be made emblematical of something.' That predetermined habit of looking for emblems everywhere seems finally to have revenged itself on him in his four unfinished romances, all variations on the theme of a search for some

1. Yet even here Melville was greatly stimulated by this description of 'a young man in poor attire, with no insignia of rank or acknowledged eminence,' who learned that the only way to reach posterity 'is to live truly and wisely for your own age.' This is the man 'for whom our country is looking anxiously into the mist of Time, as destined to fulfil the great mission of creating an American literature, hewing it, as it were, out of the un-wrought granite of our intellectual quarries. From him, whether moulded in the form of an epic poem or assuming a guise altogether new as the spirit itself may determine, we are to receive our first great original work.' These thoughts led directly into Melville's own hopes, and caused him to think that the sustained fancy of this sketch, 'A Select Party,' was surpassed by 'nothing in Spenser.'

elixir of life. He had an array of symbolical potions, symbolical spiders, symbolical footsteps, but he could no longer seem to find exactly what they symbolized. As a result he took material that might have served for a flimsy sketch, and spun it out to tenuities that never created any more serious illusion than that of a children's horror story. But by then he had fallen into the organic exhaustion from which he did not recover. With the outbreak of the Civil War he had told Bridge that he had not found it possible to occupy his mind 'with its usual trash and nonsense during these anxious times'; and he came to be haunted impotently by the theme of life as he felt death hanging over him. Yet it should be noted that his realistic grip on facts remained unshaken to the end. In his increasing awareness of his loss of imaginative vigor, he finally wrote to Fields in the winter of 1864 that he knew he would never finish *The Dolliver Romance,* that his 'literary faculty' seemed to have broken down. 'I am not low-spirited, nor fanciful, nor freakish, but look what seem to be realities in the face, and am ready to take whatever may come.' Four months later he was dead.

The real test of his methods naturally must be made on more representative examples than those of his broken strength. It quickly becomes clear that the difference involved in his two ways of starting is only apparent; [2] also, that even when he is not writing formal allegory, as in many of the historical tales, his method of clothing his ideas remains the same. And if the material world often becomes impalpable in his pages, abstractions can take on, not exactly flesh and blood, but enough intensity to make them imaginatively alive. Even in such a flatly named allegory as 'Egotism, or The Bosom Serpent,' which may have been suggested by

2. A different reading of Hawthorne is made by Yvor Winters in the opening chapter of *Maule's Curse: Seven Studies in the History of American Obscurantism* (1938). He believes Hawthorne's dilemma, a dilemma 'tragically characteristic of the history of this country and of its literature,' to have consisted in 'the choice between abstractions inadequate or irrelevant to experience on the one hand, and experience on the other as far as practicable unilluminated by understanding.' In working out this challenging idea Winters finds *The Scarlet Letter* a masterful overcoming of the difficulties inherent in the first alternative. But Winters' dichotomy causes him to oversimplify. It leads to the conclusion that 'Hawthorne, when he reversed his formula of alternative possibilities, and sought to grope his way blindly to significance, made the choice of the later Romantics; and his groping was met wherever he moved by the smooth and impassive surface of the intense inane.' Such a conclusion not only relies far too much on Hawthorne's unfinished work for the signs of his confused 'obscurantism'; it also ignores the bulk of the evidence which shows that Hawthorne's thought in *The Scarlet Letter* was not exceptional, but the mode habitual to him.

Spenser's personification of Envy, the anguished contortions of the man's body are so described as to heighten our dread of what has happened to his viciously possessed spirit. In Hawthorne's maturer handling of a similar theme, just enough details are given about Hollingsworth in *The Blithedale Romance,* the least allegorical—and yet the thinnest—of the novels, to enable him to embody the idea of the reformer blinded by a single thought. This idea is what interested Hawthorne most: he even considered entitling the novel by the reformer's name. On the other hand, Hawthorne's physical objects remain no more concrete than the scarlet letter, on which every conceivable change is rung. It is not left merely the badge for Hester's sin, since she herself makes incarnate in Pearl's bright dress 'an analogy between the object of her affection and the emblem of her guilt and torture.' Moreover, on one occasion a shape like the letter seems diffused through the sky as a spectral omen; and a similar shape is repeatedly hinted to have grown on the minister's breast, a stigma for his hidden complicity.

Melville is equally concerned with the spiritual significances that lie behind what Ahab called the 'pasteboard masks' of appearance; but a fundamental difference between his art and Hawthorne's may seem to be suggested in Cleanth Brooks' remark that allegory 'is perhaps the first attempt which man makes to unite the intellect and the emotions when they begin to fall apart—Spenser's *Faerie Queene,* for example.' That is expressive of the taste of our generation, which has been formed by the symbolism of Yeats and Eliot, and has rediscovered that of Melville. But though I share in Brooks' judgment that Donne is a more serious poet than Spenser, this account of the origin of the latter's allegory strikes me as misleading. For *The Faerie Queene* is in no sense a beginning; it is one of the latter stages of a process that stretches back at least as far as St. Augustine.[3] His *Confessions* are not allegory, but they show what happened as the classical world yielded to the Christian. His gaze was turned inward. He could not rest content with the level of external appearances, since he was obsessed by the drama of conflicting forces that was going on in his own heart. For the projection of this struggle, for the probing of hidden significances, allegory was to become the prevailing

3. Cf. C. S. Lewis, *The Allegory of Love* (1936). Symbolical modes of thought, which sometimes express themselves in allegory, have existed also in primitive societies; but I confine myself here to our western tradition from the Middle Ages.

means of expression, as the long popularity of *The Romance of the Rose* and of plays like *Everyman* can attest.

To-day, with our experience of the compact characters of realistic fiction, we instinctively shy away from the bare personifications that throng such works. Our objections to their form were already phrased by both Poe and Henry James when writing about Hawthorne. According to the former, 'In defence of allegory, however, or for whatever object employed, there is scarcely one respectable word to be said . . . The deepest emotion aroused in us by the happiest allegory *as* allegory, is a very, *very* imperfectly satisfied sense of the writer's ingenuity in overcoming a difficulty we should have preferred his not having attempted.' Poe carried his attack to the logical extreme that was characteristic of him by concluding that *Pilgrim's Progress* was 'a ludicrously overrated book.' James was in agreement up to the point of saying that 'allegory, to my sense, is quite one of the lighter exercises of the imagination,' that 'it is apt to spoil two good things—a story and a moral, a meaning and a form.'

But to-day we have felt an even greater necessity to be on guard against the abstractions of allegory. For after the ruminations of Tennyson, which allowed poetry to escape into mere idealization, it was imperative to get back to the poetry of sensation, of dramatic immediacy. This need called into being Eliot's work, as well as our revival of Donne and our increasing taste for Baudelaire. But in our satisfaction with the dramatic lyrics of these poets, there is the danger, as Eliot has already realized in his own later work, that in exalting the poetry of sensation, we may overlook that we are also prolonging the circumscription of poetry's scope which came in with Coleridge and Keats. With the romantic movement, poetry tended, in spite of Wordsworth's prefaces, to become divorced from 'knowledge,' which, with the drift of the nineteenth century, became more and more the special province of science. As a result we have lost living touch with the great poetry of contemplation; we have almost forgotten in our own practice that poetry can deal with epistemology, as Dante showed in his exposition of the soul in the *Purgatorio*. Dante has existed for us primarily as a poet of magnificent visual images, and of the dramatic scenes in the *Inferno*. We have ordinarily not bothered to realize that from the moment of his encounter with the leopard, the lion, and the she-wolf in the opening canto, Dante was projecting an allegory of man's soul, far stricter in its fourfold interpretation than Bunyan's. We also neglect to remember that when Milton called Spenser 'a better teacher than Scotus or Aquinas,' he was referring to the insight into human nature that could be gained through Spenser's 'continued Allegory or darke conceit.'

These remarks are not intended to obliterate the distinctions between allegory and symbolism, but merely to suggest that a refreshed understanding of both modes may be gained by examining here the real ground that they hold in common. That ground is not very solid in Spenser, whose surface efflorescence represents a fundamental decay from the hard central clarity of Dante, and demanded the reaction of Donne. The techtonic formlessness of Spenser stands in the same relation to Dante and Donne, as the irrelevant ornamentation of flamboyant Tudor architecture to the firmer principles of organization of the Gothic or the baroque. In carrying on and developing Spenser's great humanistic tradition of moral philosophy, Milton freed his use of allegory from diffuseness: witness his majestic handling of the personifications of Sin and Death. However, it might be said, parenthetically, that any revitalization in English of the poetry of contemplation is burdened by Milton's having been so much less catholic than Dante. He buried his thought beneath an extremely individual kind of Puritan theology. He also buried it beneath a vocabulary remote from common usage, a learned diction incapable of merging his thought and passion in symbols.

The mention of Milton at this point is not beside my purpose, for it would never have occurred to his younger friend Marvell, as he wrote his lines of unstinted tribute to *Paradise Lost,* that his own metaphysical strain was as far from Milton's kind of poetry as it has seemed to Eliot and to us. Marvell would have been aware of the similarities in their beliefs, of their preoccupation with many of the same ethical and social problems—a fact made clear by his choosing for the subject of one of his poems a debate between 'the Resolved Soul and Created Pleasure.' In comparable fashion, though to a much greater degree, Melville felt himself at one with Hawthorne, for the strain of thought that gave rise to Hawthorne's allegories was what Melville recognized as truth. Hawthorne's debt to Milton's moral philosophy was almost as great as Melville's to Thomas Browne's style, and that Melville did not regard these two seventeenth-century authors as antagonistic will become manifest when we see the extent of his debt, in *Billy Budd,* to Milton's way of mediating between passion and reason.

The point to be established here is that both allegory and symbolism can arise from the same thinking. In the case of Dante you might best regard symbolism as the generic type of his thought, and allegory as one of its species of expression. But as Huizinga saw in *The Waning of the Middle Ages,* Dante's lucid control over both modes in his poetry was not destined to endure in the hands of less imaginative followers. 'Symbolism expresses a mysterious connection between two ideas, allegory gives a visible form to the conception of such a connection.' Regarded in this way, allegory 'aids symbolic thought to express itself, but endangers it at the same time by substituting a figure for a living idea. The force of the symbol is easily lost in the allegory.' Croce has made almost the same fruitful distinctions in considering the deterioration involved when a symbol loses its freeness of suggestion. For the 'allegory from which we have to detach the secondary meaning by a purely intellectual process has no imaginative, no aesthetic value. So long as the allegory is what the old works on rhetoric used to define it, an extended metaphor . . . the effect is imaginative and emotional.' This formulation would separate *The Divine Comedy, Pilgrim's Progress,* and *Moby-Dick* from *The Faerie Queene, Mardi,* and *The Marble Faun,* with *The Scarlet Letter* somewhere between the two groups.

Coleridge, as we might expect, distinguished the symbolical from the allegorical by calling it a part of some whole that it represents. Allegory 'cannot be other than spoken consciously,' whereas in the symbol 'it is very possible that the general truth represented may be working unconsciously in the writer's mind . . . The advantage of symbolical writing over allegory is, that it presumes no disjunction of faculties, but simple predominance.' This emphasis on how the imagination operates beneath conscious levels is apposite to Hawthorne's remark concerning the way that 'the mystic symbol' of the scarlet letter had struck him, 'communicating itself to my sensibilities, but evading the analysis of my mind.' The denseness of that process suggests why the created result was subtly imaginative, and only occasionally blemished by the kind of mechanically obtrusive fancy that was inherent from the start in the conjecture whether Donatello, the simple child of nature, really had the pointed ears of a faun.

The differentiation between symbolism and allegory, between Melville and Hawthorne at their most typical, is thus seen to be allied to Coleridge's fundamental distinction between imagination and fancy. Using some of Coleridge's terms, it may be said that symbolism is esemplastic,

since it shapes new wholes; whereas allegory deals with fixities and defi-
nites that it does not basically modify. As a result *Moby-Dick* is, in its
main sweep, an example of the reconcilement of the general with the
concrete, of the fusion of idea and image; whereas, even in *The Scarlet
Letter,* the abstract, the idea, is often of greater interest than its concrete
expression.

Melville did not thus discriminate between the two modes. He described how Pierre, at his first awareness of the meaning of suffering, also
discovered those 'horrible allegorical meanings' of the *Inferno,* which 'lie
not on the surface.' Melville thus equated the term with profundity; and
he seems to have thought of its application to his own book when he
said again that Pierre's forebodings were 'allegorically verified by the
subsequent events.' Moreover, he introduced his handling of the Enceladus myth, the few pages in which the tangled miseries of his theme are
made luminous through a symbol, by an allusion to Bunyan and 'his
most marvellous book.' Thus though Melville passed beyond allegory, he
seems never to have denigrated the use of it in the way that Hawthorne
did even while engaged in its practice. Melville said jauntily in *Moby-
Dick* that 'without some hints touching the plain facts' of the fishery,
some readers might scout the white whale 'as a monstrous fable, or still
worse and more detestable, a hideous and intolerable allegory.' But in a
letter to Mrs. Hawthorne he made a simple statement of what his thoughts
about his form had been: 'I had some vague idea while writing it, that
the whole book was susceptible of an allegorical construction, and also
that parts of it were—but the specialty of many of the particular subordinate allegories were first revealed to me after reading Mr. Hawthorne's letter, which, without citing any particular examples, yet inti-
mated the part-and-parcel allegoricalness of the whole.' Here again we
have a token of the unconscious working of the creative mind, which, to
an even greater degree than in Hawthorne's remarks about his letter A,
shows 'no disjunction of faculties.'

But neither Melville nor Hawthorne give any evidence of having
thought in Coleridge's terms, or of having made use of his differentiation
between imagination and fancy. We do not know exactly what Hawthorne, to whom the book was dedicated, said about *Moby-Dick,* since
none of his letters to Melville have come to light.[4] But the quality of his

4. Julian Hawthorne's ambiguous comment (1884) on the correspondence was that
'Hawthorne's answers, if he wrote any, were unfortunately destroyed some years ago.'

admiration reveals itself in a note to Duyckinck: 'What a book Melville has written! It gives me an idea of much greater power than his preceding ones. It hardly seemed to me that the review of it in the *Literary World*, did justice to its best points'—an observation that takes on significance when we realize that this review, which called the book 'an intellectual chowder,' was still one of the two American notices of any discernment that it received.[5] What Hawthorne wrote directly to Melville pleased him so much that he called it 'your joy-giving and exultation-breeding letter.' His response poured out his sense of their close accord with such a flow of gratitude that at the end he pulled himself up short: 'What a pity, that, for your plain, bluff letter, you should get such gibberish!' But the experience of feeling that his aims had been understood was so beyond anything he had grown to hope for that it had swept him out of control: 'For not one man in five cycles, who is wise, will expect ap-

5. The other, which appeared in *Harper's* (December 1851), was very possibly by George Ripley, who had been one of the founders of this new monthly the year before. Ripley, who struggled to support himself by hack work in New York after the collapse of Brook Farm, possessed solid critical gifts that have not yet received their due assessment. He was, for instance, one of the first to gauge the importance of both *A Week on the Concord and Merrimack* and *The Scarlet Letter*. Whether from his hand or not, this review of *Moby-Dick* was the best piece of criticism that Melville was accorded during his lifetime. It considered the book the height of his achievement thus far, praised its rich variety, saw beneath the story—as Duyckinck also had—'a pregnant allegory, intended to illustrate the mystery of human life,' and believed Melville's 'moral analysis' to be 'scarcely surpassed by his wizard power of description.'

How out of keeping this was with the general run of comments can be briefly indicated. Five magazines, which had reviewed previous works of Melville's, omitted all mention of *Moby-Dick*. *The Democratic Review* pronounced it the worst of his books. Fitz-James O'Brien, who regarded himself as an admirer of Melville's and who went out of his way to write two essays about him in the next few years, had glowing tributes for his revivification of travel literature, but was otherwise so confused as to say that 'save for its greater reasonableness and moderation, *The Confidence Man* ought to be ranked with *Moby-Dick* and *Mardi*.'

The English notices were, if anything, less perceptive. Except for one in the London *Leader*, they appear to have been generally unfavorable, for the most part because they could not fit the book into any of the recognized categories of fiction. The violent extreme of the tradition from the older quarterly-reviewers was reached in *The New Monthly Magazine*, which honored Melville in July 1853 by including him as fourth in its series on American authors. It was sure that *White Jacket* was his best book, and urged him to throw off his worser self and to return to such accounts of what he had seen. It declared the style of *Moby-Dick* to be 'maniacal—mad as a March hare—mowing, gibbering, screaming, like an incurable Bedlamite, reckless of keeper or straight waistcoat.' Small wonder that Melville appears to have been haunted at this time by the nearness of genius to insanity.

preciative recognition from his fellows, or any one of them. Appreciation! Recognition! Is love appreciated? Why, ever since Adam, who has got to the meaning of his great allegory—the world? Then we pygmies must be content to have our paper allegories but ill comprehended. I say your appreciation is my glorious gratuity.'

It appears at no point to have occurred to Melville to object to what Hawthorne, rereading his *Mosses* in Liverpool, was to call his 'blasted allegories.' The nearest Melville came to this was in the winter after he had written his essay on the *Mosses,* the winter when he was in the midst of *Moby-Dick.* He had then read through *Twice-Told Tales,* and wrote to Duyckinck that they far exceeded the *Mosses* in being 'an earlier vintage from his vine. Some of these sketches are wonderfully subtle. Their deeper meanings are worthy of a Brahmin. Still there is something lacking—a good deal lacking—to the plump sphericity of the man. What is that?—He doesn't patronize the butcher—he needs roast-beef, done rare.' Nevertheless, Melville still regarded him 'as evincing a quality of genius immensely loftier, and more profound, too, than any other American has shown hitherto in the printed form.' That final phrase may betray how much Melville hoped for the manuscript then under his hand.

Although this objection to Hawthorne's lack of body might be construed as an awareness of the limitations of allegory, Melville continued to admire Hawthorne's methods. In the summer just after he had finished *Pierre,* he picked up, while on a visit to Nantucket, a story about a woman named Agatha, who had been deserted by her husband. He felt the details 'instinct with significance,' but then, thinking again, and noting some circumstances in the husband's unpremeditated drifting away which reminded him of the situation in 'Wakefield,' it occurred to him that the whole really lay in Hawthorne's vein. So he sent him the outline of the narrative with many suggestions of how its symbols might be developed. These possibilities were uppermost in his mind when he said, 'You have a skeleton of actual reality to build about with fulness and veins and beauty. And if I thought I could do it as well as you, why, I should not let you have it.' But Hawthorne was to keep his resolve of some years' standing not to write any more tales, and nothing came of the theme.

2. The Imagination as Mirror

WITH what sympathy Melville had followed Hawthorne's imaginative processes can be read in the pattern of his markings in the *Mosses*. These cast telling light on the conception common to them both of the relation between spirit and matter, and of the role of the imagination in mediating between them. This makes it worth while to dwell for a few pages on what might otherwise seem rather minor material; since nothing is minor if it can bring us closer to what two of our few major artists envisaged as the function of art.

Hawthorne's clear-sighted rendering of what was due to both matter and spirit emerges in 'The Birthmark,' at the end of which Melville wrote, 'The moral here is wonderfully fine.' Its theme is the search for perfection, dramatized in the determination of an idealistic scientist to remove a mark from the cheek of his beautiful young wife. Though indistinct, this ingrown defect tormented him increasingly as a sign of 'the fatal flaw of humanity,' a reminder that even 'the highest and purest of earthly mould' are degraded 'into kindred with the lowest, and even with the very brutes.' From the outset of his career he had aimed to prove that man had the power to spiritualize physical details, and thus to redeem himself 'from materialism by his strong and eager aspiration towards the infinite.'

Hawthorne points to the dangers involved in Aylmer's experiment, since Nature 'permits us, indeed, to mar, but seldom to mend, and . . . on no account to make.' This is in keeping with Hawthorne's recognition, more reserved but no less steady than Emerson's, of nature's organic wholeness, as expressed by the remark in his notebook (1837) that 'the reason of the minute superiority of Nature's work over man's is, that the former works from the innermost germ, while the latter works merely superficially.' But Aylmer, whose researches have converged towards those of the medieval necromancers,[1] persists in his resolve; and his wife, though not sharing in his desire and apprehensive of the consequences,

---

1. That Hawthorne cast his few scientists, like Rappaccini and Dr. Heidegger, in the same romantic mode is another, if minor, token of the fact that truth for him meant religious truth.

is stirred by the purity of his love, which will rest content with nothing less than perfection. She submits to his operation, which succeeds. But at the moment of his triumph, she says, 'with more than human tenderness, "My poor Aylmer, you have aimed loftily; you have done nobly. Do not repent that with so high and pure a feeling, you have rejected the best the earth could offer. Aylmer, dearest Aylmer, I am dying."' At that moment too he hears the hoarse chuckle of the begrimed attendant of his laboratory furnace, whose brute shagginess had 'seemed to represent man's physical nature,' as Aylmer's slender figure and pale, intellectual face were 'no less apt a type of the spiritual element.'

'Thus ever,' Hawthorne reflects, 'does the gross fatality of earth exult in its invariable triumph over the immortal essence which, in this dim sphere of half development, demands the completeness of a higher state.' But this is not the moral whose fineness impressed Melville, for the last words of the story are: 'Yet, had Aylmer reached a profounder wisdom, he need not have flung away the happiness which would have woven his mortal life of the self same texture with the celestial. The momentary circumstance was too strong for him; he failed to look beyond the shadowy scope of time, and, living once for all in eternity, to find the perfect future in the present.'

These distinctions, couched in their barest allegorical form, may not seem impressive. But they are fundamental to Hawthorne's and Melville's awareness both of the mixed nature of life, and of the sources of human good and evil. Their full implications, therefore, can be brought out only when we have examined representative tragedies by both men. At this point I want merely to elucidate the meaning of some of the terms that relate to the mediating role of the imagination.

The first notebook entry from which this story grew was made in 1837: 'A person to be in the possession of something as perfect as mortal man has a right to demand; he tries to make it better, and ruins it entirely.' But it is hardly accidental that 'The Birthmark,' written five years later, was one of the first tales composed by Hawthorne after his own marriage; for its final statement corresponds to many declarations in his letters to Sophia during their engagement: 'You will be the same to me, because we have met in Eternity, and there our intimacy was formed . . . I feel that there is a Now, and that Now must be always calm and happy.' That is the kind of statement which drew out D. H. Lawrence's wisecrack: 'Hawthorne's wife said she "never saw him in time," which doesn't mean she saw him too late.' But Hawthorne knew' what he meant. He felt that through his love for Sophia he had been rescued at last from his unsubstantial solitude: 'Indeed, we are but shadows; we are not endowed with real life, all that seems most real about us is but the thinnest substance of a dream,—till the heart be touched. That touch creates us,— then we begin to be—thereby we are beings of reality, and inheritors of eternity . . . Do you not feel, dearest, that we live above time and apart from time, even while we seem to be in the midst of time? Our affection diffuses eternity round about us.'

Hawthorne is sharing here in the basic recognition of Christianity that man can be both in time and out of it, part of the flux, yet penetrating to the eternal. For the heart that has been touched by love embraces the paradoxical, the true, conception of eternity—timeless existence within time and above it.[2] Failure to understand that paradox was particularly rife in the quests for Utopias that characterized the feverish religious movements of our eighteen-thirties and forties. Aylmer's inhumanity made him one type of the resulting unbalance which Hawthorne probed under several other guises. The tragic loss involved when a young man of generous heart, but with no experience of the world, plunged headlong into the resolve to live out an impossible ideal became the subject of *Pierre;* and Melville's deepest speculation in that book on the contrast between heavenly ideals and earthly practice, between God's time and Greenwich time, could well have received its impulse from Hawthorne's stories, as well as from their talk together 'about time and eternity, things of this world and of the next.'

The balance that Pierre failed to keep was pondered not only in 'The Birthmark'; it constitutes one of Hawthorne's most recurrent themes, and one which can drive home his conception of the relation between daily facts and man's imagining. Since it is possible to define the outlines of this conception entirely on the basis of passages noted by Melville, I shall restrict myself to these in order to bring out to the full the kinship

2. I am greatly indebted here to Howard Schomer's prize-winning undergraduate essay at Harvard, 'Human Destiny in Hawthorne' (1937). Observe also what Eliot's Thomas à Becket says at the moment of his final resolve to meet the Knights who have come to murder him:

> It is not in time that my death shall be known;
> It is out of time that my decision is taken
> If you call that decision
> To which my whole being gives entire consent.

between the two writers. And though checking a statement in the margin is not necessarily equivalent to accepting it, when scattered markings converge on the same point, the presumption of belief becomes more compelling.

'Rappaccini's Daughter,' one of the most affecting of all Hawthorne's fantasies, is a more incisively drawn companion piece to 'The Birthmark,' in that the father cares 'infinitely more for science than for mankind' and 'would sacrifice human life, his own among the rest, or whatever else was dearest to him, for the sake of adding so much as a grain of mustard seed to the great heap of his accumulated knowledge.' Fascinated by his power, he has gradually infiltrated his daughter's system with poisons, which have rendered her immune but have made her very touch deadly to anyone else.[3] Unaware of this fact, a young student falls in love with her beauty, and though bothered by ambiguous forebodings when it seems as though the flowers he has brought wither in her grasp, he waves aside such idle thoughts and perseveres in the conviction that 'there is something truer and more real than what we can see with the eyes and touch with the finger.' He is desperately wrong, but only because her innocent nature has been worked upon by a diabolic influence beyond her control.

The 'Virtuoso's Collection' presents the opposite extreme from such a conviction. The Virtuoso, a man of high cultivation but with no spiritual insight, takes leave of the narrator whom he has shown through his museum, 'with a smile of cold triumph. "My destiny is linked with the realities of earth. You are welcome to your visions and shadows of a future state; but give me what I can see, and touch, and understand, and I ask no more." ' Struggling 'between pity and horror' at the thought of this dead soul bound to earth, the narrator held out his hand, to which the Virtuoso gave his own, with the habitual courtesy of the man of the world, but without a single 'throb of human brotherhood.'

The normal balance between these two extremes is suggested in 'The Hall of Fantasy.' Bewildered by the conflicting variety of ideals and dreams that he finds there, the narrator still knows it to be true that

3. Hawthorne's suggestion came in part from a passage in Thomas Browne's *Vulgar Errors:* 'A story there passeth of an Indian King, that sent unto Alexander a fair woman fed with Aconites and other poysons, with this intent, either by converse or copulation complexionally to destroy him.' Mrs. Hawthorne was thoroughly consistent. She refined Sir Thomas as well as her husband. Her printed version expunged from the notebook 'either by converse or copulation.'

'there is but half a life—the meaner and earthlier half—for those who never find their way into the hall.' And though he prides himself on realizing that 'the white sunshine of actual life' is necessary to test the worth of all fantasies, he is answered by his friend the poet that his faith in the ideal may be deeper than he is aware: 'You are at least a democrat; and methinks no scanty share of such faith is essential to the adoption of that creed.' When confronted with Father Miller, who has gone to the other pole from the schemers of earthly paradises, and hopes only for the world to be destroyed, the narrator's own philosophy crystallizes. He feels this deluded hope 'ungrateful to our mother earth' whom, with all her faults, he cannot bear to have perish: 'Neither will it satisfy me to have her exist merely in idea. I want her great, round, solid self to endure interminably . . . Nevertheless, I confide the whole matter to Providence.'

Such was the equilibrium which Hawthorne strove for in his life, and which, when disregarded by his characters, brought about the tragic situations that were the burden of his art. In maintaining the equipoise of matter and spirit, he knew that 'beauty is never a delusion,' a sentence that Melville underlined in 'Buds and Bird Voices,' a pastoral celebration of Concord spring. What made Hawthorne sure of this was his conviction of 'the renewing power of the spirit.' Though dwelling 'in an old moss-covered mansion,' with the withered leaves and rotten branches of the past ever hovering over him, he knew that man's imagination, no less than the cycle of the year, could surge up in rebirth. His expression of his knowledge in this sketch may seem a very innocent and idyllic version of the major affirmation of the age, Goethe's 'Sterb und Werden,' repeated death and becoming as the law of man's creative powers.

But as even Lawrence saw, Hawthorne was seldom as innocent as he looked. The beauty that he discerned was not a will-o'-the-wisp to lead him astray from actuality. He had been surprised to find among those in the Hall of Fantasy a group whose 'shrewd, calculating glance' had marked them as men of business, 'trusted members of the Chamber of Commerce.' Yet their matter-of-fact talk concealed 'the wildest schemes,' which might lead their followers to destruction—visions of cities to be built 'in the heart of pathless forests,' a revival of 'the old dream of Eldorado.' These casual fancies hardly constitute Hawthorne a forerunner of the satire on the westward movement, such as Twain was to voice in *The Gilded Age* (1873); but, written half a dozen years before the gold rush, they are antennae in the wind. Hawthorne's acumen is dependent upon one of his fundamental beliefs, that in contrast with these romantic speculators, the creative writer whose business it is to be trained in the distinctions between fact and imagination will not confuse the two realms: he 'knows his whereabout, and therefore is less likely to make a fool of himself in real life'—an observation in accord with Keats' strictest separation between the poet and the dreamer.[4] It may be merely accidental that this passage was not marked by Melville; yet the ambiguities between the actual and the ideal were destined to torture him as they never did Hawthorne's steadier, if less adventurous mind.

Acute discrimination between the two realms was preserved by Hawthorne's 'artist of the beautiful' even when his contemplation passed, like Spenser's, from earthly beauty to the heavenly beauty of which it was a symbol. To this point we know that Melville followed Hawthorne. Moreover, what moved him most in 'Monsieur du Miroir' was the related contrast between superficial appearance and hidden truth, between the pale features of the man reflected in the mirror and the tormented life that was locked up in his heart. The same penetration beneath exteriors was likewise what caused Melville to pronounce 'The Intelligence Office,' another of Hawthorne's processional sketches, 'a wondrous symbolizing of the secret workings in men's souls.' Consequently we may assume Melville's sympathy with Hawthorne's detailed account of *how* his imagination was stirred into such action, even though the key passages were not marked by him. For they occur in *The Scarlet Letter,* Melville's only surviving copy of which he dated in 1870 and did not annotate at all. This imputed sympathy does not imply that when we come to the heart of Hawthorne's extraordinarily accurate recognition of *what* his imagination could do, we shall not also discern a fundamental difference from Melville.

Why Hawthorne constructed a whole sketch around the eerie play of

4. Cf. the famous lines in 'The Fall of Hyperion':

> The poet and the dreamer are distinct,
> Diverse, sheer opposite, antipodes.
> The one pours out a balm upon the world,
> The other vexes it.

Eliot, in making the point, in 'The Perfect Critic,' that the bad critic is the man who does not see the work of art as it is, but who simply uses it for the exploitation of his own ego, holds that such emotional romantics are often to be found among 'stockbrokers, politicians, men of science' and others 'who pride themselves on being unemotional.'

reflections in a twilight mirror is accounted for by many passages scattered through his work. As moonbeams touch the glass in the room where the dead Judge sits, Hawthorne, continuing to probe deeper into what had been the realities of this man's character, which had been masked so carefully from others, says that a mirror 'is always a kind of window or doorway into the spiritual world.' An element of escape seems bound up with this finding of imaginative release primarily in reflections, in fountains and the fluid mirrors of streams. Why these became such favorite symbols for Hawthorne is elaborated in the description, in 'The Old Manse,' of his excursions on the Concord with Ellery Channing. The original draft in his notebook was even more detailed:

I have never elsewhere had such an opportunity to observe how much more beautiful reflection is than what we call reality. The sky, and the clustering foliage on either hand, and the effect of sunlight as it found its way through the shade . . . all these seemed unsurpassably beautiful, when beheld in upper air. But, on gazing downward, there they were, the same even to the minutest particular, yet arrayed in ideal beauty, which satisfied the spirit incomparably more than the actual scene. I am half convinced that the reflection is indeed the reality—the real thing which Nature imperfectly images to our grosser sense. At all events, the disembodied shadow is nearest to the soul.

That passage is full of Neo-Platonic pitfalls for the artist. It recalls Shelley's similar preference for scenery imaged in water, because it was one remove further from what was actually seen and grasped; and the unfortunate results are apparent in the thinness of the texture of his lines when contrasted with the richer tactual imagery of Keats. Far worse, Hawthorne's terms seem here to converge with those of Sophia who, when her body had been sluggish about leaving the house on a fine day, announced that 'Ideality led me out.' Yet Hawthorne believed no deflection from the profoundest truth to be involved in his half-thoughts, since some years later, at Stratford, he remarked that the Avon may have thus held Shakespeare's 'gorgeous visions . . . in its bosom.'

As he repeated that memory too is a mirror, his habit of symbolizing extended that metaphor diversely. Most frequently it became the glass of introspection, as at several critical moments in *The Scarlet Letter*. When Hester stood on the scaffold in the opening scene, her spirit relieved itself from the pressure of the crowd's eyes by summoning into this 'dusky mirror' a succession of 'phantasmagoric forms' from her happier past. In the chapter called 'The Interior of a Heart,' Dimmesdale sometimes punctuated his long vigils by staring at his own face in a looking-glass under the strongest light that he could throw upon it, and 'thus typified the constant introspection wherewith he tortured, but could not purify himself.' Hawthorne seems to have been compelled, apparently unconsciously, to produce a variant of this same powerful image when dramatizing Chillingworth's harrowed admission to himself that he had become diabolically transformed through his relentless persecution of the minister. At this first glimpse of his true moral aspect, the old physician 'lifted his hands with a look of horror, as if he had beheld some frightful shape, which he could not recognize, usurping the place of his own image in a glass.'

Elsewhere, this 'mind's eye,' as Hawthorne calls it, extends its range and becomes equivalent to the universal memory. That extension is the function of the fountains that he used as a device for breaking through the restrictions of the given moment, by projecting into their bubbling life imaginative hints of both the past and the future. The signal instance is Maule's Well, the spring in the Pyncheon's garden, the name of which is a reminder that the land whereon the mansion stands was originally wrested from a poorer family. It may seem strange that Hawthorne thought at one time of calling the book by this name, for only passing attention is paid to the well. But one sentence of its first description shows the kind of significance it held for him: 'The play and slight agitation of the water, in its upward gush, wrought magically with these variegated pebbles, and made a continually shifting apparition of quaint figures, vanishing too suddenly to be definable.'

What is created from those images depends on the beholder. To Clifford's broken mind, as, with childish delight in the open air after his long imprisonment, he hangs over the fountain, 'the constantly shifting phantasmagoria of figures' seemed like faces looking up at him, beautiful faces, except when suddenly he would cry out in anguish, 'The dark face gazes at me.' Matter-of-fact Phoebe could see nothing of this, 'neither the beauty, nor the ugliness,' but only colored pebbles disarranged by the force of the water. Nor did she comprehend the meaning of the daguerreotypist, a descendant of the Maules, who, thinking of the traditional curse on the house, pronounced this dark spring, in the midst of a garden long since run to seed, to be 'water bewitched.' On the last page of the book, after they have all gone away from the house to more hopeful surroundings, Maule's Well, 'though left in solitude, was throwing up a succession of kaleidoscopic pictures, in which a gifted eye might have seen foreshadowed the coming fortunes.'

Thus the imagination, by merging itself with 'the universal memory' of events, can perform its function of projecting the past into the future. I deliberately repeat Yeats' term, for though there are many differences between his account of the imagination and Hawthorne's, they share the belief, which is common also to Emerson and other 'Platonists,' that the individual imagination, like the disembodied reflections in the stream, is part of the Divine Mind.

By detaching Hawthorne's descriptions of the well from their context, the delicate spell he designed by them may have been broken. He was himself always aware of the destructibility of his imaginative life. In the preface to *The Scarlet Letter,* where he showed his full understanding of his creative process, he remarked that the atmosphere of a custom-house was so little adapted 'to the delicate harvest of fancy and sensibility' that his imagination had become 'a tarnished mirror.'[5] 'It would not reflect, or only with miserable dimness, the figures with which I did my best to people it.' Nor did this torpor quit him when he left his office for the day, not even when, late at night, he 'sat in the deserted parlor, lighted only by the glimmering coal-fire and the moon, striving to picture forth imaginary scenes . . . If the imaginative faculty refused to act at such an hour, it might well be deemed a hopeless case. Moonlight, in a familiar room, falling so white upon the carpet, and showing all its

5. Hawthorne's instinctive use of this metaphor for the imagination is further evidence of what we have already seen, his lingering attachment to the eighteenth century. For M. H. Abrams has demonstrated in *The Mirror and the Lamp: A Study of the Transition to Romantic Theories of Poetry and Criticism,* a Harvard doctoral thesis (1940), that during the eighteenth century the old conception of the mimetic theory still obtained, and the role of the poet was to hold the mirror up to nature. With the romantic movement 'the basic metaphor shifted from that of reflection to that of projection: the underlying analogy shifted from the mirror to the lamp. This change in poetic theory was part of a contemporary change in the prevailing concepts of the mind. Men no longer spoke of the mind as a passive receptacle—a mirror, a *tabula rasa,* or a wax plate on which impressions stamp themselves. They spoke of it as an active, contributing agent—as a lamp, or a wind-harp, or a growing plant.' The wind-harp and the growing plant are analogies common to Emerson, Thoreau, and Whitman, and are also to be found in Melville. But Hawthorne, with all his delicacy of sensibility, remained nearer than any of these others to the Augustan age. Yet note that when Hawthorne spoke of the imagination as a mirror, he was so far unlike the Augustans that he did not conceive of it primarily as reflecting external reality, but rather as reflecting the fantasies that welled up in his 'haunted mind.'

figures so distinctly,—making every object so minutely visible, yet so un-like a morning or noontide visibility,—is a medium the most suitable for a romance-writer to get acquainted with his illusive guests.'

Every syllable of this account, which extends to several pages, is ger-mane to the interpretation of what Hawthorne wrote, and of why he wrote it as he did. No one could be more explicit: 'The somewhat dim coal-fire has an essential influence in producing the effect which I would describe. It throws its unobtrusive tinge throughout the room, with a faint ruddiness upon the walls and ceiling, and a reflected gleam from the polish of the furniture. This warmer light mingles itself with the cold spirituality of the moonbeams, and communicates, as it were, a heart and sensibilities of human tenderness to the forms which fancy summons up. It converts them from snow-images into men and women.' That sentence may suggest that he again hid an ironic confession of failure in choosing *The Snow-Image* as the title for his last collection of tales. Then comes the final ingredient in the circumstances that stimulated him most: 'Glanc-ing at the looking-glass, we behold—deep within its haunted verge—the smouldering glow of the half-extinguished anthracite, the white moonbeams on the floor, and a repetition of all the gleam and shadow of the picture, with one remove further from the actual, and nearer to the imaginative. Then, at such an hour, and with this scene before him, if a man, sitting all alone, cannot dream strange things, and make them look like truth, he need never try to write romances.'

For, under these conditions, all the ordinary objects—the center table with its work basket, the sofa, a child's shoe—suffered a remarkable change. Seen afresh by the unusual light, they seemed 'to lose their actual substance' and to be 'invested with a quality of strangeness and remote-ness,' to be so 'spiritualized' that they became figments of the mind, and thereby susceptible of fresh and unexpected combinations. 'Thus . . . the floor of our familiar room has become a neutral territory, somewhere between the real world and fairy-land, where the Actual and the Imaginary may meet, and each imbue itself with the nature of the other.'

This climax, with its juxtaposition of the terms 'actual' and 'imaginary,' compels consideration of what I may have seemed to pass by too easily in Hawthorne's description of the river, the question of what he meant by the more inclusive term 'reality.' The detachment from concrete surfaces could lead to Emerson's statement that in order to 'poetize' anything, 'its feet must be just lifted from the ground.' This corresponds to the weakest element in Hawthorne's 'ideality,' to the fancy that he developed to Sophia on a brilliant February day: 'How much mud and mire, how many pools of unclean water, how many slippery footsteps, and perchance heavy tumbles, might be avoided, if we could tread but six inches above the crust of this world.' By itself that would seem to justify Brownell's pronouncement that Hawthorne 'shrank from reality,' and Brownell's taste was trained on the great realistic novelists from Flaubert to Tolstoy. But Brownell's cultural standards also had much in common with those of our earliest native champion of realism.[6] Howells was to say that as a young man he had been dominated by Hawthorne as completely as by any author he had ever read, and that Hawthorne's handling of 'the problem of evil' had not seemed 'the less veritable' because it shone out of the region of romance. But as Howells found his own steady if restricted course of development, he insisted on the treatment of everyday material. His opinion that *The Blithedale Romance* was the best of Hawthorne's books was consistent with the belief, to which Brownell subscribed, that fiction must correspond with life even to the most faithful literalness of detail. Howells' quiet decorum, his assurance that, if realism was to be true to America, it must concern itself 'with the large cheerful average of health and success and happy life,' is evidence of how little he too had shared in Hawthorne's tragic vision, and of how limited a term realism can become.

Essential truths of the human situation are exactly what Hawthorne's imagination could not shrink from—not even, as we have seen, when he wanted it to. Nor does his matured conception of art neglect the 'real' for the 'ideal'; it posits the relation that he believed should exist between them. In the opening paragraph of *The Marble Faun,* before he had had a chance to adulterate his pages with any of his odd 'literary' notions about the fine arts, he voiced a fundamental conviction. In leading up to his description of the Faun of Praxiteles, he spoke of how the great figures of antique sculpture are 'still shining in the undiminished majesty and beauty of their ideal life.' That phrases the function of idealization in art in a way that marks it off sharply from romantic escapism; it reaffirms the truth that art, both in its intention and its lasting result, raises its material to the level of contemplation, freed from

6. Interesting comparisons between Howells and Brownell are traced by Morton Zabel, in the introduction to his anthology of *Literary Opinion in America* (1937).

accidents and irrelevancies.[7] But Hawthorne did not forget where the artist's material must be found. Even in the midst of one of his wrong-headed disputes 'about the propriety of adopting the costume of the day in modern sculpture,' he contended that 'either the art ought to be given up (which possibly would be the best course), or else should be used for idealizing the man of the day to himself.' That was not to be the doctrine of the naturalistic novelists, but it had been followed by many great artists from the Greeks to the eighteenth century. Hawthorne's idealization was never at the cost of distorting the 'usable truth' of his own surroundings; or of forgetting the superiority of nature over art. He expressed the contrast between what he believed to be the true attitude and the false one when he described how a sunset in Edinburgh had irradiated a cluster of old houses into a spelled realm of the picturesque, quite obliterating the fact that 'layer upon layer of unfortunate human-ity' were massed there in squalor. 'The change symbolized the difference between a poet's imagination of life in the past—or in a state which he looks at through a colored and illuminated medium—and the sad real-ity.' Save for his personal fondness for Longfellow, Hawthorne had no respect for that kind of poet. 'The ideal' that Hawthorne wanted to project in art was 'the real': not actuality transformed into an impos-sible perfection, but actuality disengaged from appearance.

3. The Crucial Definition of Romance

OTHER terms that Hawthorne used in the account of his imaginative life also demand attention. His desire to provide a neutral ground where the Actual and Imaginary may meet' happens to contrast significantly with a note of Whitman's that 'imagination and actuality must be united.' To most tastes to-day that difference in phrasing corresponds closely to the

7. Cf. Butcher's comment on the Aristotelian doctrine of how art discovers the uni-versal beneath the particular: 'It passes beyond the bare reality given by nature, and' ex-presses a purified form of reality disengaged from accident, and freed from conditions which thwart its development. The real and the ideal from this point of view are not opposites, as they are sometimes conceived to be. The ideal is the real, but rid of contradictions, unfolding itself according to the laws of its own being, apart from alien influences and the disturb-ances of chance.'

difference between the two men's ability to project in their pages human characters of flesh and blood. Of the five chief writers treated in this volume, Hawthorne and Whitman certainly stand farthest apart. At the time when the poet sent one of the first copies of *Leaves of Grass* to Emerson, and when Thoreau was reported to have carried another around Concord 'like a red flag,' Hawthorne was settled in England, and there is no evidence that he ever glanced within the book's covers. There are not many more signs of Whitman's acquaintance with Hawthorne's work. When Hawthorne was made surveyor of the port of Salem, Whitman greeted the appointment with great approval in *The Eagle,* not on the ground of enthusiasm for any specific tales, but because their author had always been a Democrat, and had graced the party by his talents. Forty years later when Whitman was ready to oblige Traubel with opinions on any subject, irrespective of the state of his knowledge, he volunteered that Hawthorne would prove more lasting than Howells, but that there was 'a morbid streak' in him to which the poet could not accommodate himself. When 'someone kicked,' Whitman granted that Hawthorne had been a genius, even 'a master, within certain limits. Still . . . I do not read him with pleasure.'

When Whitman wrote in an early notebook, 'Let facts and histories be properly told, there is no more need of romances,' he was probably not thinking especially about Hawthorne, whose use of the term was peculiar to his own practice. But the poet would have been highly suspicious of Hawthorne's 'neutral territory.' It would have struck him as too suggestive of a drawn battle, as a sign that its author had not completely absorbed and mastered his material. Melville, in his increasing desperation while trying to compose *Pierre,* felt that it was impossible to write 'without apparently throwing oneself helplessly open' to experience. That suggests his more passionate relation to life than Hawthorne's. It also shows his lack of the artist's 'hard coldness,' which would have prevented his becoming so involved in his personal suffering that *Pierre* turned out to be a gigantic failure. But by the same token it attests why Melville's exposure of himself to what Lawrence was to call 'the sheer naked slidings of the elements' carried all his work, from *Moby-Dick* on, into a realm of emotional forces quite out of Hawthorne's range.

As usual Hawthorne was the first to note his own limitations. At the end of his account of how all vividness of imagination had deserted him during his tenure in the customhouse, he made his statement that a better book than he would ever write had doubtless lain hidden in what had struck him as the 'dull and commonplace' routine. 'It was a folly, with the materiality of this daily life pressing so intrusively upon me, to attempt to fling myself back into another age . . . The wiser effort would have been to diffuse thought and imagination through the opaque substance of to-day, and thus to make it a bright transparency; to spiritualize the burden that began to weigh so heavily; to seek, resolutely, the true and indestructible value that lay hidden in the petty and wearisome incidents, and ordinary characters, with which I was now conversant.'

The resolve to do this was what caused him to choose, as the settings for his next two books, the existence with which he was most familiar, an old house in Salem and the dramatic interlude of his experience at Brook Farm. The prefaces to these books outline his definition of a romance, which bears only tangential relation to any of the other usages then current. This definition, which is the most important text for his conception of reality, needs to be read in strictest relation to his circumstances at the time. Out of that context, as it has usually been taken, a sentence like this from the preface to *The Blithedale Romance* would seem such an evasion of the artist's responsibility as to forfeit his book all serious consideration: 'In short, his present concern with the socialist community is merely to establish a theatre, a little removed from the highway of ordinary travel, where the creatures of his brain may play their phantasmagorical antics, without exposing them to too close a comparison with the actual events of real lives.'

But behind that remark lay an incident: the humorous sketch of his companions in the customhouse had called down upon Hawthorne's head a storm of vilification. Consequently, when he proceeded to draw far more extensively on things he had observed near at hand, he wanted to take every precaution to make clear that he was not copying actual people, not even Margaret Fuller in Zenobia. He begged for the license in creating atmosphere which the European reader took for granted, but which the too literal-minded American public denied. In making this plea he had already had a bitter encounter with the dilemma that Cooper, once he had set himself to be a social satirist in *Homeward Bound,* had found to be that of the American author. In contrast with Europe, where bitter personalities excited disgust and society was deemed fair game, the individual here was constantly assailed, but no word was tolerated against the existing order—as Hawthorne had quickly discovered as a result of his mildly ironic remarks on having been turned out of the surveyorship by the Whigs' resumption of power. No wonder that he ended his preface to *The Seven Gables* with the covering disclaimer that he 'would be glad . . . if, especially in the quarter to which he alludes,' his book might be read as 'having a great deal more to do with the clouds overhead than with any portion of the actual soil of the County of Essex.' These protective remarks had been necessitated by the fact that his relative weakness in invention had obliged him to borrow many suggestions, even though no whole character, from people he had observed. The nearest he came to a dangerous likeness was through using as a basis for Judge Pyncheon some traits of the politician who had been most instrumental in ousting him from his job.

But, more importantly, his prefaces also formulated his positive distinctions between the novel and the romance. The former, as Trollope was to reaffirm, 'is presumed to aim at a very minute fidelity, not merely to the possible, but to the probable and ordinary course of man's experience.' In contrast, Hawthorne went on to say, the writer of a romance could assume 'a certain latitude, both as to its fashion and material.' If he thought fit, he might 'so manage his atmospherical medium as to bring out or mellow the lights and deepen and enrich the shadows of the picture.' He might even, though he had best handle these ingredients sparingly, make some use of the strange and marvellous. This suggests Hawthorne's way of finding beauty in a moonlit room, beauty that could not exist 'without some strangeness in the proportion,' as the romantic movement had followed Bacon in affirming. Hawthorne's share of this feeling had come to him especially from his sense of the resistances that the artist's imagination had to overcome in a land where, as he was to say in the preface to *The Marble Faun*, actualities were so 'terribly insisted on.'

In his dedication of *Our Old Home* to Pierce in 1863, he had to admit that by then 'the Present, the Immediate, the Actual,' in the sense of the horrible fact of the war, had proved too potent for him. It had taken away not only his 'scanty faculty,' but even his 'desire for imaginative composition'—remarks that recall how James was to find it impossible to continue *The Ivory Tower* after August 1914. Hawthorne had previously hoped that the notebook sketches he had made of English life should serve merely as a background for 'a work of fiction . . . into which I ambitiously proposed to convey more of various modes of truth than I could have grasped by a direct effort.' The furthest he got with this 'abortive project' was in his notes for *The Ancestral Footstep,* the germ of whose idea, the return of an American to rediscover the older European life, bears a curious resemblance to that of the other book James was to leave unfinished at his death, *The Sense of the Past.*

The significant words in this last description of Hawthorne's aim are 'various modes of truth,' for these stem straight back to the crucial points he made about the romance in the preface to *The Seven Gables,* that 'as a work of art, it must rigidly subject itself to laws,' and that 'it sins unpardonably so far as it may swerve aside from the truth of the human heart.' Again in the context of the time, it must be remembered that though the major drift of fiction had set towards realism, the term had not yet been applied to the novel in English.[1] Hawthorne was therefore taking advantage of the unsettled standards of taste to make a plea for the assumptions that came to him from his past, for what could not be expressed by the 'direct effort,' for the freeing of the inner life through the mode of symbolizing. We have already seen how Emerson equated 'indirection' with the symbol, and Whitman was to follow Emerson's use of that word very closely. In one of the chapters of *The Confidence Man,* Melville was to tuck away a defense of his own method of heightening everyday life, which stemmed at least partly from Hawthorne. Melville found it strange that, in a work of fiction, 'severe fidelity to real life should be exacted by anyone.' In contrast, the readers for whom he aims will sit down as 'tolerantly as they sit at a play, and with much the same expectations and feelings. They look that fancy shall evoke scenes different from those of the same old crowd round the customhouse counter, and the same old dishes on the boarding-house table.' Was he thinking in that sentence of *The Scarlet Letter,* and even, possibly, of the contrast in *Moby-Dick* between the earth-bound scenes at Peter Coffin's Spouter Inn and the wild drama of Ahab?

And as, in real life, the proprieties will not allow people to act out themselves with that unreserve permitted to the stage; so, in books of fiction, they look not only for more entertainment, but, at bottom, even for more reality, than real life itself can show. Thus, though they want novelty, they want nature, too; but nature unfettered, exhilarated, in effect transformed. In this way of thinking, the people in a fiction, like the people in a play, must dress as

---

1. The earliest Oxford English Dictionary quotation for 'realism' in relation to art or literature is from Ruskin's *Modern Painters* (1856).

nobody exactly dresses, talk as nobody exactly talks, act as nobody exactly acts. It is with fiction as with religion; it should present another world, and yet one to which we feel the tie.

By this extension of the tendency of Hawthorne's prefaces, Melville formulated more exactly the kind of heightened reality they both wanted in their fiction. He also indicated how different their conceptions finally were from those, say, of the classic sculptors whom Hawthorne admired. Hawthorne himself, after a round of galleries, suggested the divergence: 'I am partly sensible that some unwritten rules of taste are making their way into my mind; that all this Greek beauty has done something towards refining me, though I am still, however, a very sturdy Goth.' (Incidentally, this was one of the two passages marked by Melville in *The French and Italian Notebooks,* which he acquired shortly after their publication, in 1872.) What Hawthorne implied by his contrast between Greek and Goth is subject to further definition, which will bring us even closer than we have yet come to the way his imagination apprehended reality. It will bring us also to the central reason why the mode of symbolizing, whether it remained richly allusive or whether it froze into a conventional and arbitrary allegory, was basic to the kind of Christian thought that conditioned Emerson and Thoreau as well as Hawthorne and Melville, and was still latent in Whitman's Quaker strain. That generalization does not mean that any of the group, except probably Melville, would have agreed with what Hawthorne experienced in his first full impression of a Gothic cathedral. When Emerson and Thoreau considered architecture, we have seen them primarily concerned with the primitive origin of its forms, with how man might have found the first hint for a nave in an aisle of trees. But Hawthorne, by the very fact of not looking for these universal analogies, but by remaining a provincial, uncovered the deeply buried and almost sole link between an American and the medieval world—a world that had still persevered in many of the folkways of our first settlers, as it had in the overhanging second story, leaded windows, and quaint carvings, 'conceived in the grotesqueness of a Gothic fancy,' of Hawthorne's house of the seven gables.

In visiting Lichfield Cathedral, he had not been the passionate pilgrim, since he had been drawn to the town chiefly by his interest in Johnson's birthplace. Nevertheless, as he looked at its bewilderingly varied form, it seemed, to his 'uninstructed vision' to be 'the object best worth gazing at in the whole world . . .'

A Gothic cathedral is surely the most wonderful work which mortal man has yet achieved, so vast, so intricate, and so profoundly simple, with such strange, delightful recesses in its grand figure, so difficult to comprehend within one idea, and yet all so consonant that it ultimately draws the beholder and his universe into its harmony. It is the only thing in the world that is vast enough and rich enough.

Not that I felt, or was worthy to feel, an unmingled enjoyment in gazing at this wonder. I could not elevate myself to its spiritual height . . . Ascending but a little way, I continually fell back and lay in a kind of despair, conscious that a flood of uncomprehended beauty was pouring down upon me, of which I could appropriate only the minutest portion. After a hundred years . . . I should still be a gazer from below and at an awful distance, as yet excluded from the interior mystery. But it was something gained, even to have that painful sense of my own limitations, and that half-smothered yearning to soar beyond them. The cathedral showed me how earthly I was, but yet whispered deeply of immortality.

Citing this passage, Herbert Read has remarked that 'this sense of an almost giddy vertiginous gulf between human finiteness and the infinity of the Absolute, whether in art or in religion, is the peculiar Northern or Gothic sensibility.' This cleavage, as it was felt by Hawthorne, and by Melville in pressing his analogy between the operations of art and religion, was not the vague desire of the moth for the star. In their shared conviction that art 'should present another world, and yet one to which we feel the tie,' their roots were in the deepest Christian experience. The essence of Hawthorne's greatness, as Melville saw it, was that he breathed 'that unshackled, democratic spirit of Christianity in all things.' The range of implications that Melville compressed into that phrase will emerge only as we examine the development of his own handling of tragedy; but the fact that he became a tragic writer was owing to his widening sense of the gulf between the ideal and actuality, between the professions and practice of both democracy and religion. This sense was what separated him, as much as Hawthorne, from the transcendentalists, who bridged the gap between the finite and the Absolute by their assurance of 'the infinitude of the private man.'

Perhaps the chief reason why both Hawthorne and Melville succeeded in creating so few living characters, in contrast with Fielding and Jane

Austen, or even with their own contemporaries Thackeray and Dickens, was that the Americans were more concerned with human destiny than with every man in his humor. Certainly it is true that long before he had seen a Gothic cathedral, Hawthorne had wanted to establish in the 'laws' of his romances a related manner of multiple symbolizing of spiritual meanings. He too had wanted 'strange, delightful recesses,' liberties from literal verisimilitude. For the main concern of the romance was not external details, exactly presented settings, turns of speech, or characterizing gestures. It was 'the life within the life.'

PRACTICE

From this point forward in this chapter the concern is no longer with elucidating why allegorical habits of mind were natural to Melville as to Hawthorne, but with appraising some of Hawthorne's most characteristic work by means of various comparisons, chiefly with Melville and James. No longer theory, but practice.

The briefest way of estimating the effectiveness of allegory is suggested by Brownell's declaration that the form 'justifies itself when the fiction is the fact and the moral the induction.' *Pilgrim's Progress* and *Gulliver's Travels* are created as such true stories, so absorbing in themselves that the allegorical machinery does not grate on us. Their analogies present themselves naturally, not with the labored ingenuity of Spenser's siege of the House of Alma, the attack of the forces of evil on the soul's domain in the body, the description of which is elaborated even to the 'twice sixteen' glistering warders who guard the gate of the mouth.

Hawthorne possessed little of Bunyan's common solidity. The difference between them runs curiously parallel to the American's own repeated comment on the change between the early Puritans and their nineteenth-century descendants, clearly observable in the less substantial frame, the alteration from the ruddy English complexion to Yankee sallowness, the increased nervous sensibility. Only occasionally is Hawthorne's procedure as matter-of-fact as when he introduces 'The Maypole of Merrymount,' one of the very earliest of his historical tales, with the remark that the events, 'recorded on the grave pages of our New England annalists, have wrought themselves, almost spontaneously, into a sort of allegory.'[1] His more usual, deliberately worked-up process is suggested at the opening of 'The Threefold Destiny' (1838), where he says that he has experimented with combining 'New England personages and scenery' with 'a fairy legend,' and hopes that he has not entirely obliterated thereby 'the sober hues of nature.' 'Rather than a story of events claiming to be real, it may be considered as an allegory, such as the writers of the last century would have expressed in the shape of an Eastern tale, but to which I have endeavored to give a more lifelike warmth than could be infused into those fanciful productions.'

That suggests an added ingredient in Hawthorne's mixture, which goes far to explain why, as he developed, he could not feel Bunyan's unquestioning belief in the serviceability of the allegorical form. For *Rasselas,* to whose Happy Valley Hawthorne alluded on the second page of *Fanshawe,* was an altogether less serious exercise of the imagination than *Pilgrim's Progress.* In Johnson's view, literature existed for both 'instruction' and 'amusement,' but he thought that the latter element could be provided by sugaring the pill, by dressing up his moral platitudes in fancy Oriental costume. Although Johnson was a devout man, whose moral depth was greater than Hawthorne apparently granted, no intensity of religious imagination remained in the *lettres persanes* or *contes philosophiques,* the minor French refinements on the allegorical strain which Johnson borrowed for the form of *Rasselas.* What this genre could produce was the skeptical brilliance of *Candide,* which bore no relation to Hawthorne's aims.

But for a young American growing up in the early nineteenth century, the adventures of the Abyssinian prince were likely to be still as much a part of his household as whale-oil lamps. When Melville cut his moorings from narratives of personal experience, and determined to write 'a romance of Polynesian adventure' based on a voyage around the world of Mardi, in the company of a king, a philosopher, an historian, and a poet, his quest for truth and happiness would have appalled Johnson by its excited lack of control. Nevertheless, the wanderings and conversa-

---

1. To note the American background once more: one reason why these events fell so naturally into allegorical form for Hawthorne was that the emphasis of the early historians had already leaned in that direction. In Bradford, for instance, the settlers = Christ's chosen; the Indians = devils; Morton and his cohorts at Merry Mount = agents of Satan. This systematic structure of spiritual values reinforced the coherence of *The Scarlet Letter.*

tion of Rasselas and Imlac must have played a part in suggesting to Melville his typical structure; and the chapter whose title might almost serve as a motto for the whole book, 'They Sail Round an Island without Landing, and Talk Round a Subject without Getting at It,' is reminiscent of Johnson's 'Conclusion, in which Nothing Is Concluded,' and of the mode of eighteenth-century reflections on the vanity of human wishes. Johnson had never been the intimate favorite with Hawthorne that Bunyan and Spenser were, but the degree to which the novelist could not take allegory seriously reflects the adulteration of his Puritan imagination by the elephantine fancies of the Augustan age.

Yet Hawthorne was compelled to use the form for deeper reasons than James seemed able to perceive in advancing the explanation that it was lack of conviction which had led Hawthorne to handle the Puritan beliefs themselves with curious and strained conceits. For evidence of how much more akin his imagination was to Bunyan's than to Johnson's, we have only to note the extraordinary frequency with which memories of *Pilgrim's Progress* asserted themselves at moments when Hawthorne was creating his own most intense crises. Chillingworth, warped from his former upright calm by the irresistible compulsion to prey upon the minister in revenge, looked as though he had been struck by 'one of those gleams of ghastly fire that darted from Bunyan's awful doorway in the hill-side, and quivered on the pilgrim's face.' Clifford, at the instant of his and Hepzibah's poignantly ineffectual flight from the house in which the Judge has just died, cries out—and the archaic allusion does not seem impossible for his unworldly mind—that they must make haste, 'or he will start up, like Giant Despair in pursuit of Christian and Hopeful, and catch us yet!' The symbol for the treachery of pride by which Hawthorne felt that he could best express the downfall of both Ethan Brand and Hollingsworth was again the small opening in the earth close by the Delectable Mountains, 'an exemplification of the most awful truth' that 'from the very gate of heaven there is a by-way to the pit.' These iterated allusions may again attest to Hawthorne's limited invention, but they also reveal how profoundly it struck him that Bunyan had grasped the truth.

Hawthorne's own imagination is of course freest when farthest from anyone else's set example, when its range is wider than that of a fixed allegory, when his literal meaning and his spiritual meaning are least disjunct. His fascinated use of fountains and mirrors often enabled him to bring his material to artistic concentration, as well as to endow his scenes with depth and liquidity. He set his stage for Endicott's grim act of cutting the red cross from an English flag to show that neither Pope nor Tyrant had further part in the colony, by describing the Salem green as it was mirrored in this soldier's polished breastplate. In another of his most affecting tales, 'Dr. Heidegger's Experiment' (1836), a grotesque search for the fountain of youth is dramatized by four old people drinking an ambiguous fluid, which sparkles like champagne and, in the half light of the doctor's room, seems to gleam with a moonlike splendor. But at the moment of their exhilarated transformation, when the three now young gentlemen dance in a circle around the girl-widow, enamored by the freshness of her charms, 'by a strange deception, owing to the duskiness of the chamber, and the antique dresses which they still wore, the tall mirror is said to have reflected the figures of the three old, gray, withered grandsires, ridiculously contending for the skinny ugliness of a shrivelled grandam.' No wonder that Melville, consumed with interest in any manifestation of the contrast between appearance and reality, marked this subtle instance where the reflection in a mirror, as well as in the glass of memory and imagination, kept the truth that had been lost by the characters' frantic delusion.

We are now in a better position to understand precisely what Hawthorne implied in another description of images that Melville checked, of how, in one of Aylmer's innocent experiments, 'the scenery and figures of actual life were perfectly represented, but with that bewitching, yet indescribable difference which always makes a picture, an image or a shadow so much more attractive than the original.' We have observed that it never occurred to Hawthorne that art is more fundamental than nature. What we can find in this sentence is the lead to the kind of discrimination he made—though he did not use these terms—between mechanical copying and imaginative imitation. He had that difference in mind when putting his finger on the secret of Thoreau's power. Hawthorne judged that 'Natural History of Massachusetts' was an accurate 'reflection of his character,' and that it conveyed too 'a very fair image of his mind . . . so true, minute, and literal in observation, yet giving the spirit as well as letter of what he sees, even as a lake reflects its wooded banks, showing every leaf, yet giving the wild beauty of the whole scene.' There could hardly be a more sensitive analogy for the enchanted wholeness of imaginative composition.

1. The Scarlet Letter

WHY HAWTHORNE came nearest to achieving that wholeness in *The Scarlet Letter* may be accounted for in various ways. The grounds on which, according to Trollope, its superiority was 'plain to anyone who had himself been concerned in the writing of novels' were that here Hawthorne had developed his most coherent plot. Its symmetrical design is built around the three scenes on the scaffold of the pillory. There Hester endures her public shaming in the opening chapter. There, midway through the book, the minister, who has been driven almost crazy by his guilt but has lacked the resolution to confess it, ascends one midnight for self-torture, and is joined by Hester, on her way home from watching at a deathbed, and there they are overseen by Chillingworth. There, also, at the end, just after his own knowledge of suffering has endowed his tongue with eloquence in his great election sermon, the exhausted and death-stricken Dimmesdale totters to confess his sin at last to the incredulous and only half-comprehending crowd, and to die in Hester's arms.

[margin note: Symmetry]

Moreover, Hawthorne has also managed here his utmost approach to the inseparability of elements that James insisted on when he said that 'character, in any sense in which we can get at it, is action, and action is plot.' Of his four romances, this one grows most organically out of the interactions between the characters, depends least on the backdrops of scenery that so often impede the action in *The Marble Faun*. Furthermore, his integrity of effect is due in part to the incisive contrasts among the human types he is presenting. The sin of Hester and the minister, a sin of passion not of principle, is not the worst in the world, as they are aware, even in the depths of their misery. She feels that what they did 'had a consecration of its own'; he knows that at least they have never 'violated, in cold blood, the sanctity of a human heart.' They are distinguished from the wronged husband in accordance with the theological doctrine that excessive love for things which should take only a secondary place in the affections, though leading to the sin of lust, is less grave than love distorted, love turned from God and from his creatures, into self-consuming envy and vengeful pride. The courses that these three run

[margin note: Integrity of effect]

are also in natural accord with their characters as worked upon by circumstance. The physician's native power in reading the human soul, when unsupported by any moral sympathies, leaves him open to degradation, step by step, from a man into a fiend. Dimmesdale, in his indecisive waverings, filled as he is with penance but no penitence, remains in touch with reality only in proportion to his anguish. The slower, richer movement of Hester is harder to characterize in a sentence. Even Chillingworth, who had married her as a young girl in the knowledge that she responded with no love for his old and slightly deformed frame, even he, after all that has happened, can still almost pity her 'for the good that has been wasted' in her nature. Her purgatorial course through the book is from desperate recklessness to a strong, placid acceptance of her suffering and retribution.

But beyond any interest in ordering of plot or in lucid discrimination between characters, Hawthorne's imaginative energy seems to have been called out to the full here by the continual correspondences that his theme allowed him to make between external events and inner significances. Once again his version of this transcendental habit took it straight back to the seventeenth century, and made it something more complex than the harmony between sunrise and a young poet's soul. In the realm of natural phenomena, Hawthorne examined the older world's common belief that great events were foreboded by supernatural omens, and remarked how 'it was, indeed, a majestic idea, that the destiny of nations should be revealed, in these awful hieroglyphics, on the cope of heaven.' But when Dimmesdale, in his vigil on the scaffold, beholds an immense dull red letter in the zenith, Hawthorne attributes it solely to his diseased imagination, which sees in everything his own morbid concerns. Hawthorne remarks that the strange light was 'doubtless caused' by a meteor 'burning out to waste'; and yet he also allows the sexton to ask the minister the next morning if he had heard of the portent, which had been interpreted to stand for Angel, since Governor Winthrop had died during the night.

Out of such variety of symbolical reference Hawthorne developed one of his most fertile resources, the device of multiple choice, which James was to carry so much further in his desire to present a sense of the intricacy of any situation for a perceptive being. One main source of Hawthorne's method lay in these remarkable providences, which his imagination felt challenged to search for the amount of emblematic truth that might lie hidden among their superstitions. He spoke at one point in this story of how 'individuals of wiser faith' in the colony, while recognizing God's Providence in human affairs, knew that it 'promotes its purposes without aiming at the stage-effect of what is called miraculous interposition.' But he could not resist experimenting with this dramatic value, and his imagination had become so accustomed to the weirdly lighted world of Cotton Mather that even the fanciful possibilities of the growth of the stigma on Dimmesdale did not strike him as grotesque. But when the minister 'unbreasts' his guilt at last, the literal correspondence of that metaphor to a scarlet letter in his flesh, in strict accord with medieval and Spenserian personifications, is apt to strike us as a mechanical delimitation of what would otherwise have freer symbolical range.

For Hawthorne its value consisted in the variety of explanations to which it gave rise. Some affirmed that the minister had begun a course of self-mortification on the very day on which Hester Prynne had first been compelled to wear her ignominious badge, and had thus inflicted this hideous scar. Others held that Roger Chillingworth, 'being a potent necromancer, had caused it to appear, through the agency of magic and poisonous drugs.' Still others, 'those best able to appreciate the minister's peculiar sensibility, and the wonderful operation of his spirit upon the body,' whispered that 'the awful symbol was the effect of the ever-active tooth of remorse,' gnawing from his inmost heart outward. With that Hawthorne leaves his reader to choose among these theories. He does not literally accept his own allegory, and yet he finds it symbolically valid because of its psychological exactitude. His most telling stroke comes when he adds that certain spectators of the whole scene denied that there was any mark whatever on Dimmesdale's breast. These witnesses were among the most respectable in the community, including his fellow-ministers who were determined to defend his spotless character. These maintained also that his dying confession was to be taken only in its general significance, that he 'had desired, by yielding up his breath in the arms of that fallen woman, to express to the world how utterly nugatory is the choicest of man's own righteousness.' But for this interpretation, so revelatory of its influential proponents, Hawthorne leaves not one shred of evidence.

It should not be thought that his deeply ingrained habit of apprehending truth through emblems needed any sign of miraculous intervention

Pearl

to set it into action. Another aspect of the intricate correspondences that absorbed him is provided by Pearl. She is worth dissecting as the purest type of Spenserian characterization, which starts with abstract qualities and hunts for their proper embodiment; worth murdering, most modern readers of fiction would hold, since the tedious reiteration of what she stands for betrays Hawthorne at his most barren.

When Hester returned to the prison after standing her time on the scaffold, the infant she had clasped so tightly to her breast suddenly writhed in convulsions of pain, 'a forcible type, in its little frame, of the moral agony' that its mother had borne throughout the day. As the story advances, Hawthorne sees in this child 'the freedom of a broken law.' In the perverseness of some of her antics, in the heartless mockery that can shine from her bright black eyes, she sometimes seems to her harassed mother almost a witch-baby. But Hester clings to the hope that her girl has capacity for strong affection, which needs only to be awakened by sympathy; and when there is some talk by the authorities of taking the wilful child's rearing into their own hands, Hester also clings to her possession of it as both her torture and happiness, her blessing and retribution, the one thing that has kept her soul alive in its hours of desperation.

Forest scene

Hawthorne's range of intention in this characterization comes out most fully in the scene where Hester and the minister have met in the woods, and are alone for the first time after so many years. Her resolution to save him from Chillingworth's spying, by flight together back to England, now sweeps his undermined spirit before it. In their moment of reunion, the one moment of released passion in the book, the beauty that has been hidden behind the frozen mask of her isolation reasserts itself. She takes off the formal cap that has confined the dark radiance of her hair and lets it stream down on her shoulders; she impulsively unfastens the badge of her shame and throws it to the ground. At that moment the minister sees Pearl, who has been playing by the brook, returning along the other side of it. Picked out by a beam of sunlight, with some wild flowers in her hair, she reminds Hester of 'one of the fairies, whom we left in our dear old England,' a sad reflection on the rich folklore that had been banished by the Puritans along with the maypoles. But as the two parents stand watching their child for the first time together, the graver thought comes to them that she is 'the living hieroglyphic' of all they have sought to hide, of their inseparably intertwined fate.

As Pearl sees her mother, she stops by a pool, and her reflected image seems to communicate to her something 'of its own shadowy and intangible quality.' Confronted with this double vision, dissevered from her by the brook, Hester feels, 'in some indistinct and tantalizing manner,' suddenly estranged from the child, who now fixes her eyes on her mother's breast. She refuses Hester's bidding to come to her. Instead she points her finger, and stamps her foot, and becomes all at once a little demon of extravagant protest, all of whose wild gestures are redoubled at her feet. Hester understands what the matter is, that the child is outraged by the unaccustomed change in her appearance. So she wearily picks up the letter, which had fallen just short of the brook, and hides her luxuriant hair once more beneath her cap. At that Pearl is mollified and bounds across to them. During the weeks leading up to this scene, she had begun to show an increasing curiosity about the letter, and had tormented her mother with questions. Now she asks whether the minister will walk back with them, hand in hand, to the village, and when he declines, she flings away from his kiss, because he is not 'bold' and 'true.' The question is increasingly raised for the reader, just how much of the situation this strange child understands.

Thus, when the stiff layers of allegory have been peeled away, even Hawthorne's conception of Pearl is seen to be based on exact psychological notation. She suggests something of the terrifying precocity which Edwards' acute dialectic of the feelings revealed in the children who came under his observation during the emotional strain of the Great Awakening. She suggests, even more directly, James' *What Maisie Knew,* though it is typical of the later writer's refinement of skill and sophistication that he would set himself the complicated problem of having both parents divorced and married again, of making the child the innocent meeting ground for a liaison between the step-parents, and of confining his report on the situation entirely to what could be glimpsed through the child's inscrutable eyes.

The symbolical intricacies of *The Scarlet Letter* open out on every fresh examination of the book, since there is hardly a scene where there are not to be found some subsidiary correspondences like those presented by the stream of separation, which just failed to carry with it the token of Hester's miserable past that she had tried in vain to fling from her. Again, the forest itself, with its straggling path, images to Hester 'the moral wilderness in which she had so long been wandering'; and while describing it Hawthorne may have taken a glance back at Spenser's Wood of Errour. The clue to the success or failure of such analogies seems to consist in the measure of sound doctrine, or of imaginative fitness, or of both, which lies behind them. When they require the first and are without it, the result can be as mawkish as when Kenyon's anxious eyes followed the flight of doves upward from Hilda's deserted window, in the hope that 'he might see her gentle and sweet face shining down upon him, midway towards heaven, as if she had flown thither for a day or two, just to visit her kindred, but had been drawn earthward again by the spell of unacknowledged love.' It is embarrassing even to quote such a sentence, which, however, would undoubtedly have pleased Mrs. Hawthorne, whom her husband sometimes called his 'Dove.' But having made out a case for Pearl, who, judging from other critics, may well be the most unpopular little girl in fiction, it seemed only fair to present Hawthorne at his worst.

His usually firm moral perception is vitiated very rarely by such overtones of the era of *Godey's Lady's Book* and the genteel female. His occasional extreme lapses from imaginative fitness seem even less necessary. It is impossible to see on what basis he could have thought it effective to remark that Judge Pyncheon's excessive warmth of manner, as he walked through the town just before the election for governor, required, 'such, at least, was the rumor about town, an extra passage of the watercarts . . . in order to lay the dust occasioned by so much extra sunshine.' There is no lack here of Hawthorne's shrewd observation of the Judge's sinister hypocrisy; and it is conceivable, that if this remark had been phrased as a gibe by some corner-store philosopher, its Yankee wryness might have succeeded. But woven as it is into the sober texture of Hawthorne's exposition, it seems the almost perfect instance of Coleridge's statement that the images of fancy 'have no cónnexion natural or moral, but are yoked together . . . by means of some accidental coincidence.' The way that Hawthorne's intrusive notion robs his narrative of all sustained illusion at this point is the kind of thing James objected to most. James insisted that the creator must regard his creation seriously, that he must respect its life with the strictest detachment, and keep out all traces of his own irrelevant comments on his characters. These convulsive outbreaks of Hawthorne's fancy might be attributed to the fact that he felt such an irresistible compulsion to look for correspondences that he could not check himself even when he turned up bad ones. His lack of a critical audience is again telling at this point, as is his sense of the difficulties he had to overcome if his imagination was to flow freely.

The ideal surroundings that he described for starting his imagination off enter again and again into its most successful products. He reiterated, in a sentence in *The Snow-Image* that Melville marked, his belief that the moon creates, 'like the imaginative power, a beautiful strangeness in familiar objects.' In some of his pale demonstrations of that truth he may seem merely to bear out another remark, which can be turned devastatingly against him, that 'feminine achievements in literature' are so many 'pretty fancies of snow and moonlight.' Yet it is also true that an extraordinary number of his major scenes are played out under these rays. Or rather, the light does not remain a dramatic property, but becomes itself a central actor. Such is the case with the meteoric exhalations that harrow Dimmesdale with the thought that knowledge of his hidden guilt is spread over the whole broad heavens; and an even more dynamic role is played by the rising moon during Judge Pyncheon's night watch, since, as it fingers its way through the windows, it is the only living thing in the room. And simply to mention, out of many more, the two most effectively presented crises in the other romances, we remember the midnight stream from which the dead-white body of Zenobia is recovered; and the maddened instant when Donatello, seeing Miriam's sinister model emerging from the shadows into the moonlight, cannot resist the impulse to hurl him off the Tarpeian rock.

In all these scenes Hawthorne draws on every possible contrast between lights and darks; and the way he invariably focuses attention on the thought-burdened faces of his characters justifies the frequent comparison between his kind of scrutiny and Rembrandt's. Moreover, despite his relative ignorance of painting, he deliberately created, throughout his work, sustained landscapes of low-pitched tones to heighten the effects of his foreground. He generally visualized his outdoor scenes in neutral 'gray and russet,' against which he projected such symbols as the brilliant crimson and purple blossoms that hang over the fountain in Rappaccini's garden, and hide deadly poison in their beauty. Or, again at night, the dark woods on the mountain side, where the final agony of Ethan Brand is enacted, are shot through not only by occasional moonbeams, but by streaks of firelight from the limeburner's roaring furnace. More complex than this effect, or that whereby the tragedy of Ilbrahim is begun in lingering twilight and ended on a night of violent storm, is the

continual manipulation of the lighting in both *The Scarlet Letter* and
The Seven Gables. From the opening description of the elm-clustered old
house, the sense that 'the shadow creeps and creeps, and is always looking
over the shoulder of the sunshine' on the great vertical dial on one of the
gables is raised to the level of a central theme, for it symbolizes how the
actions of the fragile present are oppressed with the darkness of the past.
At the very start of *The Scarlet Letter* Hawthorne calls it 'the darkening close of a tale of human frailty and sorrow,' and in nearly every scene
the somber values are underscored. For instance, the minister and Hester
are made to meet in 'the gray twilight' of the forest; and the single 'flood
of sunshine' in the book, which Hawthorne emphasizes by using these
words as the title of the chapter, falls first on Hester in her moment of
release, and then is shifted, like a spotlight, to the figure of the child at
the brook. Calling attention thus to these devices makes them sound
more theatrical than they are in their subdued operation; and one of the
most subtle effects of the tragedy derives from the way in which the
words 'shadowy' and 'shadowlike' are reiterated in the closing pages as a
means of building up to the final sentence. This sentence describes how
the heraldic device of the letter, which was carved even on Hester's
gravestone, might serve—through its dramatic contrast of a sable field
with the A, gules—as a motto for the whole legend, 'so somber is it, and
relieved only by one ever-glowing point of light gloomier than the
shadow.'

2. From 'Young Goodman Brown' to 'The Whiteness of the Whale'

ONE INTENSIVELY compressed instance of Hawthorne's imaginative power
at its best can provide the most effective basis for comparison with the
methods of Melville and James. When young goodman Brown leaves
his wife Faith at home, and is deluded into attending a witch's sabbath
in the forest, Hawthorne has the kind of situation where his moral perception and imaginative resources are able to coalesce. The conception of
the dark and evil-haunted wilderness came to him from the days of Cotton
Mather, who held that 'the New Englanders are a people of God settled

in those which were once the devil's territories.' The fact that so many other strained religious minds had thus dramatized the heroic act of colonizing, had contributed to leave traces of awe in the presence of the lonely Maine woods even for a Pan-worshipper like Thoreau. Hawthorne's main concern with this material is to use it to develop the theme that mere doubt of the existence of good, the thought that all other men are evil, can become such a corrosive force as to eat out the life of the heart. In handling the question of what the young man really saw during his night in the forest, Hawthorne's imagination is at its most delicately masterful. In the sound of the rising wind it seemed to Brown that he heard the tune of a familiar hymn, sung to the most blasphemous words. Then, to his horrified gaze, four tall pines suddenly sprang into flame at the top, like candles at an evening meeting. 'Each pendent twig and leafy festoon was in a blaze. As the red light arose and fell, a numerous congregation alternately shone forth, then disappeared in shadow, and again grew, as it were, out of the darkness, peopling the heart of the solitary woods at once.'

But when he had turned his eyes upward just before, doubting whether there was a heaven above him, yet lifting his hands to pray, 'there was the blue arch, and the stars brightening in it,' except where a 'black mass of cloud was sweeping swiftly northward.'

Aloft in the air, as if from the depths of the cloud, came a confused and doubtful sound of voices. Once the listener fancied that he could distinguish the accents of townspeople of his own, men and women, both pious and ungodly, many of whom he had met at the communion table, and had seen others rioting at the tavern. The next moment, so indistinct were the sounds, he doubted whether he had heard aught but the murmur of the old forest . . . Then came a stronger swell of those familiar tones, heard daily in the sunshine at Salem village, but never until now from a cloud of night. There was one voice, of a young woman, uttering lamentations, yet with an uncertain sorrow, and entreating for some favor, which, perhaps, it would grieve her to obtain; and all the unseen multitude, both saints and sinners, seemed to encourage her onward.

'Faith!' shouted Goodman Brown, in a voice of agony and desperation; and the echoes of the forest mocked him, crying 'Faith! Faith!' as if bewildered wretches were seeking her all through the wilderness.[1]

1. This sentence was quoted by Melville to illustrate this story's penetration into 'the deep mystery of sin.'

The cry of grief, rage, and terror was yet piercing the night, when the un-happy husband held his breath for a response. There was a scream, drowned immediately in a louder murmur of voices, fading into far-off laughter, as the dark cloud swept away, leaving the clear and silent sky above Goodman Brown. But something fluttered lightly down through the air and caught on the branch of a tree. The young man seized it, and beheld a pink ribbon.

'My Faith is gone!' cried he, after one stupefied moment. 'There is no good on earth; and sin is but a name. Come, devil, for to thee is this world given.'

The intensity of the situation is sustained by all the devices Hawthorne had learned from the seventeenth century, for just as the heavens groaned in Milton's fall of the angels, the winds are made to whisper sadly at the loss of this man's faith. As long as what Brown saw is left wholly in the realm of hallucination, Hawthorne's created illusion is compelling. For the symbolical truth of what the young man had conjured up in his bewildered vision is heightened by the fact that when he staggered against one of the burning trees, its twigs were cold with dew. The dram-atization of his spiritual loss in the form of the agonized struggle and disappearance of his wife allows the description of the inner experience to become concrete, and also doubles its application. Only the literal insist-ence on that damaging pink ribbon obtrudes the labels of a confining allegory, and short-circuits the range of association.

That ribbon operates on an entirely different plane from 'the ball of free will' that dropped from Ishmael's hand when, in the midst of his weaving with Queequeg, the fateful cry, 'There she blows!' sounded from mid-air.[2] Melville's prolonged image was so constructed as to en-compass a whole extension of consciousness. The ball of yarn was there from the start; but Melville's perception was reinforced with so much energy that it created a bridge of metaphor that carried us across from one mode of existence to another. It should be remarked in passing that only by discovering such metaphors can the writer suggest the actual complex-ity of experience; and consequently, the more of them he is able to per-ceive, the more comprehensive is his grasp of human life.[3]

The concrete basis may well be the crucial factor in separating not only

2. Cf. p. 130 above.

3. Middleton Murry dealt with this fact in his early brilliant book, *The Problem of Style* (1922), particularly in his discussion of Shakespeare's increased mastery of metaphor in the later plays.

Melville's effect from Hawthorne's, but also that of *Moby-Dick* from that of *Mardi* or of *The Confidence Man*. We are bothered by the ribbon because it is an abstraction pretending to be something else; and we remain relatively unmoved both by the romantically elaborate personifications of Yillah and Hautia, and by the bare ideas who try to pass for characters in that savage masquerade on the Mississippi steamer. Not that Melville was looking for symbols less in *Moby-Dick* than in *Mardi,* since his quest for them as a means of articulating truth had become even more manifold. The doubloon, which Ahab had nailed to the mast as a reward "*doubloon*" for the first man to sight the white whale, was used by Melville as a device for mirroring each of his chief characters through their varied reactions to it. And he remarked in this connection that some symbolical significance 'lurks in all things, else all things are little worth.' But he had learned what he had not grasped adequately in *Mardi,* that 'the visible world of experience' is 'that procreative thing which impregnates the muses.' He made this remark while commenting on the staggering amount that young Pierre had still to learn as an author; and another observation there also has some bearing on himself. When he said that some authors of first books are falsely called original since actually their 'instant success' is chiefly owing 'to some rich and peculiar experience in life,' he might well have been thinking of *Typee,* and the general lack of comprehension that had met his more ambitious creations.

The course of his development may be briefly charted. He began with specific re-creations of what he had seen—though the number of his sources in other south-sea travellers that have recently been turned up[4] makes it clear now that he was never writing anything like straight autobiography. In *Mardi* his material and his method of presentation shifted to the diametrical extreme: the voyage he recounted there sprang from the social and religious systems he had thought about, hardly at all from what he had apprehended through his senses. When he tried a pot-boiler in *Redburn,* he fell back on concrete narrative, though he could not keep out of it his growing sense of tragic humanity, any more than he could from *White Jacket.* But this latter, running close to a tract of protest, became the most circumstantial in method of all his books, the most heavy and diffuse through its number of surface details. It is hard to think that *Moby-Dick* was to be Melville's next work, but the miracle of

4. This material has been compiled by Charles R. Anderson, *Melville in the South Seas* (1939).

his growth took place during the less than two years that elapsed before its publication. His two contrasting methods, of reporting and of allegory, were fused through his discovery of what could be achieved by the symbol. Its possibilities for intricate correspondence between matter and spirit seem to have stimulated him to express the life of his senses with a greater abundance and variety than before, at the same time that they brought his philosophical speculations to a control more disciplined than that of the untrammeled rhapsodies of Babbalanja. The balance of the symbol is precarious; the tensions it had to support in Melville's mind were great. In *Pierre* his restless intelligence was to push beyond the confines of concrete art with a far greater pressure than in *Mardi*. In the short *Israel Potter* his dependence on a previous history of the revolutionary exile encouraged a recrudescence of specific skills, particularly in his robust sketch of Franklin. But by the time of *The Confidence Man* the split between his two tendencies had carried him virtually to diagrammatic abstraction. Anything like the fusion in *Moby-Dick* of the inner and the outer world was to be recovered only in two stories of about a hundred pages, *Benito Cereno* and, after a lapse of more than three decades, *Billy Budd*.

The symbols in *Moby-Dick,* therefore, come with the freshness of a new resource, just as, in spite of its great length, the book is the most compact expression of Melville's enormous imaginative range. In this latter respect a parallel again holds with *The Scarlet Letter,* though Hawthorne's greater compression of energy there than in his other three romances was the product of somewhat different causes. It was due in part to the liberation he felt in being able to turn his full attention to writing again; for only by launching at last on the bigger piece of work that he had wanted to try for so many years could he still the 'unquiet impulse' within him. But that phrase in his preface may have been given more urgency by the fact that, since he had suddenly lost his job, his family was near poverty, and he needed to publish a book; [5] and also by the circumstance that he

5. Hawthorne's standing with the solid community at this time may perhaps be gathered from two conflicting reports. On the one hand, the charge was brought by some of his political enemies when they wanted to oust him from the customhouse, that he was 'loafing round with hard drinkers.' On the other, Fields was rebuffed when he urged Hawthorne's reinstatement on the grounds that a gifted writer had some claims upon his country. His answer, from a local politician: 'Yes, yes, I see through it all, I see through it; this Hawthorne is one of them 'ere visionists, and we don't want no such man as him round.'

wrote it under the oppression of the final sickness and death of his mother, which he called 'the darkest hour I ever lived.' At all events he spoke with more emotion of *The Scarlet Letter* than he ever did of any of his other books. He wrote to Bridge: 'It is . . . positively a hell-fired story, into which I found it almost impossible to throw any cheering light.' It makes a very striking coincidence that Melville, in the midst of the final chapters of *Moby-Dick,* was to use almost the same phrase in writing to Hawthorne about 'the hell-fire in which the whole book is broiled.'

Both works justify the intensity of these phrases, since the chief use for which their symbolical correspondences were designed was to make a searching expression of the tragic dilemmas of the soul. Melville developed his basic contrasts between land and sea, and between calm and storm, both for their own dramatic force, and as his most powerful means of projecting man's inner struggle. The theme of the sea is preluded in the opening pages where Ishmael gives among his reasons for going whaling that 'meditation and water are wedded forever'; and then adds that the tormenting image of himself, which man sees even in fountains and rivers, 'is the image of the ungraspable phantom of life; and this is the key to it all.' That serves to explain in a flash why Melville could find so much in Hawthorne's 'Monsieur du Miroir,' for there also baffled self-scrutiny used the image of Narcissus.

The sea conveys primarily gigantic restless power and obscurity. It is thus placed in opposition to 'the blessed light of the evangelical land'; or, handled humorously, to the tug earthward of New Bedford and Salem, 'where they tell me the young girls breathe such musk, their sailor sweethearts smell them miles off shore, as though they were drawing nigh the odorous Moluccas instead of the Puritanic sands.' No wonder that this fundamental contrast gives Melville the very terms that he needs when, at the moment of the whaler's setting sail on its interminable voyage round the world, he wants to suggest also his kind of voyage, wherein 'all deep, earnest thinking is but the intrepid effort of the soul to keep the open independence of her sea; while the wildest winds of heaven and earth conspire to cast her on the treacherous, slavish shore.'

Midway through the book, when the ship has already reached the whale grounds, a whole chapter is built out of the conflict between these two elements, as a means of forecasting the climax, which both outer and inner worlds are moving towards inexorably. Employing to the full the rhetorical device of parallel iteration, Melville dwells on the aboriginal terrors of the ocean, which no veneer of civilization can gloss over to perceptive eyes. He stresses the elementary fact that no inhabitants of the sea have even the kindness of the dog, but that their very touch has always been repellent to human kind. He shifts the ground to society's furthest development, and declares that 'however baby man may brag of his science and skill, and however much, in a flattering future, that science and skill may augment; yet forever and forever, to the crack of doom, the sea will insult and murder him, and pulverise the stateliest, stiffest frigate he can make.' He asks the reader to consider the subtleness of the sea, how it masks its hidden perils beneath the loveliest azure; to consider its universal cannibalism, since its creatures have been preying on each other, carrying on continual war ever since the world began. 'Consider all this; and then turn to this green, gentle, and most docile earth; consider them both, the sea and the land; and do you not find a strange analogy to something in yourself? For as this appalling ocean surrounds the verdant land, so in the soul of man there lies one insular Tahiti, full of peace and joy, but encompassed by all the horrors of the half-known life. God keep thee! Push not off from that isle, thou canst never return!'

The problem that has been encountered in the preceding paragraphs, the virtual impossibility of conveying the complex applications of Melville's symbols except in their own words, is posed by the properties of the symbol itself. In discriminating between the truth of science and that of poetry and religion, Austin Warren has said that the abstractions of the former 'give a clearer but thinner knowledge, knowledge *about* reality; reality in itself is never known save through symbols, and the thing symbolized can never, finally, be separated from its vehicle.' That does not mean that there are not differing degrees of truth in what is expressed in symbols, and that a partial vitiation of Melville's analogies may not lie in his romantically idyllic view of the land. But no imaginative symbol can be judged out of its context, and it must be remembered that this contrast between the terms of peace and violence is being made from a deck in mid-ocean by a young man on his first whaling voyage. In addition, Melville partially protects himself by the selection of his 'insular Tahiti,' a primitive state of innocence in which developing mankind may not remain, as Melville knew even when he half envied it in *Typee,* and as he was to express with devastating thoroughness when he came, in *Pierre,* to examine actual life on land.

His richly varying contrasts between calm and storm are less open to any objections. On one level they are part of his dramatic equipment, for from the first lowering to the final three days' chase, the great actions of his tragedy are invariably made to spring from a quiet sea, as if to heighten the ferocity of Ahab's relentless pursuit. As another facet of Melville's effect, the calmness of the Pacific finds its way into the slow rise and fall of some of his most remarkably sustained prose rhythms; for hardly less than Joyce's pages on the Liffey does Melville's pattern of language become one with the flux and sound of what it describes. That, to be sure, is a short-hand account of the process, suggested by Emerson's terminology, for Melville's rare ability to convey a sense of the movement of the sea depends not on literal imitation, which would be impossible, but rather on his discovery that all rhythm has a physical basis, on his own intimate response to the rhythm of the sea, and on his skill in re-creating his impression in words.[6]

But the full meaning of the sea was not exhausted for Melville in the way its long-breathed undulations could give rise to his own tranquil, almost dreamlike thoughts. As Melville construes it, calm is but the fragile envelope of storm; it is mere delusive appearance, like the treacherous repose of Moby-Dick himself, for the truth is violent and tempestuous. Sometimes Melville varies his interpretation, as in 'The Grand Armada,' where he describes the formation of a vast herd of whales, which arranged itself in a circle of two or three miles, thus making a protected region for the mothers and young. Ishmael had seen it all, since, to his terror, the boat in which he was one of the crew was dragged by a harpooned whale to the very center of this circle. There, as the whale finally broke loose, they glided as on the bosom of a lake, though surrounded on all sides by ominously heaving forms. Ishmael suddenly reflected that 'even so, amid the tornadoed Atlantic of my being, do I myself still forever centrally disport in mute calm; and while ponderous planets of unwaning woe revolve round me, deep down and deep inland there I still bathe me in eternal mildness of joy.'

But even this masterly self-reliance, as Melville knows, is liable to be swept by forces far beyond its control, just as the whole shipful of men, bathed in the tranquillity of sunset, plunges ahead into the dark of Ahab's tyrannic will. This force is symbolized in another remarkable

6. See the account of Whitman's rhythms at pp. 564 ff. below.

chapter, 'The Try-Works,' where the act of burning down the blubber on the ship's deck at night becomes, in its lurid flame, 'the material counterpart of her monomaniac commander's soul.' It seemed then to Ishmael, in a rare symbol for individualistic recklessness—indeed for a whole era of American development—'that whatever swift, rushing thing I stood on was not so much bound to any haven ahead as rushing from all havens astern.'

The fact that Melville's most effective symbols expand thus from indicated analogies into the closely wrought experience of whole chapters, and that such a quality as whiteness can hold different contents at different times, or indeed at the same time, should emphasize the futility of the game which was so popular a decade ago, of trying to 'spot' in a paragraph exactly what the white whale stands for. To D. H. Lawrence, we remember, it was 'the last phallic being of the white man,' its blood-consciousness sought out for destruction by the thin intellect. Van Wyck Brooks was reminded of the monster Grendel in *Beowulf,* another record in the Northern consciousness of the hard fight against the savage elements. To the disciple of Jung, said Mumford, it could stand for the Unconscious itself, which torments man, and is yet the source of all his boldest efforts. There is no lack of critical challenge in these suggestions, and in so far as they stress Melville's penetration to the primitive forces of experience, to the element of the irrational, they possess a basic relevance to the book. But the only way to convey the intricate significances of the white whale would be to quote the two entire chapters wherein, after the ship has been some weeks at sea and Ahab has announced the real purpose of his voyage, this great phenomenon is described.

Melville's sequence here is noteworthy. He devotes the first of these chapters, 'Moby-Dick,' to making his readers suspend disbelief in the circumstantial account of this whale's unexampled, intelligent malignity, by emphasizing how the whalemen's own superstitions go much further in accepting him as ubiquitous, if not immortal. It is only when he has thus planted in our consciousness this mixture of professed observation, which shades off into folklore, that he risks developing his philosophical meditation on 'The Whiteness of the Whale.' This chapter brings us to another of his central themes, that despite the conventional pure and mild connotations of heavenly radiance, there is terror at the heart of worship —a theme which is underscored by his continual contrast between calm and storm. But thus to state the theme of this chapter is no more to give the meaning of the white whale than a paraphrase of the content of a poem reproduces your experience of it. A created symbol, in contrast with allegory, is dynamic; 'its components, not to be equated with anything else, function in their own right.' It is 'a total communication,' in which thought and feeling have become one.⁷ This is not, of course, to deny that, just as you appreciate a poem line by line as well as in its cumulative impression, you can also experience Melville's amazing union of opposites, the fleece of innocence with ferocity, in a single sentence that almost blinds you with its excess of whiteness: 'Judge, then, to what pitches of inflamed distracted fury the minds of his more desperate hunters were impelled, when amid the chips of chewed boats, and the sinking limbs of torn comrades, they swam out of the white curds of the whale's direful wrath into the serene exasperating sunlight, that smiled on, as if at a birth or a bridal.'

'The Whiteness of the Whale,' Melville's show-piece for tastes that have been developed by metaphysical poetry, could stand beside 'Governor Pyncheon'—the irony of which chapter heading is that the Judge has been robbed of that election by death—as a prolonged contrast of the differing operations of the Imagination and the Fancy. But the juxtaposition would also make us realize that Melville has moved here into a different genre from any attempted by Hawthorne. Nor are Melville's connections closer at this point to other practitioners of the novel; for such a chapter stems back to Burton and Rabelais. But though Melville borrowed a few details from the chapter, 'What Is Signified by the Colors Blue and White' in the livery of Gargantua, its author's happy insistence that while blue symbolizes celestial things, white stands for joy and pleasure, was greatly altered by Melville's tragic irony. Nor did Burton's heaped antiquarian lore, though it may well have encouraged Melville's handling of cetology, ever become condensed into anything like his imaginative richness of language. For the nearest analogy to a chapter like this it seems that, despite superficial points of comparison with German romantics like Richter and Hoffmann, we must look forward rather than back, to the extensions of the symbolical novel, particularly those made by Joyce, and to Mann's use of snow in *The Magic Mountain*.

7. The quotations are from Robert Penn Warren's definition of myth in an essay on John Crowe Ransom (*The Virginia Quarterly*, January 1935). My own discussion of the extension of symbols into myths is reserved for the final chapter of this volume.

3. Hawthorne and James

THE LINE from Hawthorne leads ultimately in the same direction, for he is the direct ancestor of *The Golden Bowl.* Up to this point I have skirted the connections between him and James, but they are so fundamental for throwing Hawthorne's contribution into its proper light that they demand explicit statement.

James himself struck the key of his indebtedness when he wrote, in *Notes of a Son and Brother,* of the strong impression Hawthorne's death had made on him when he was twenty-one: 'For the moral was that an American could be an artist, one of the finest, without "going outside" about it, as I liked to say; quite in fact as if Hawthorne had become one just by being American *enough.*' What James finally made of that thought belongs beyond my present province, as, indeed, does any close scrutiny of 'the Hawthorne aspect' of James,[1] except in so far as it throws reflections back on Hawthorne himself. But the value of an author cannot be wholly separated from the tradition to which he has given rise, especially when the presence or absence of an American example to build on was precisely the factor that differentiated the early developments of these two.

Since the Civil War cut between their careers, and since the final ripening that made James a part of twentieth-century literature did not come until the amazingly prolific sequence of the three books grouped around his sixtieth birthday—*The Wings of the Dove* (1902), *The Ambassadors* (1903), *The Golden Bowl* (1904)—it is not strange that readers to-day think of Hawthorne and James as belonging to wholly separate worlds. But that division ignores how very closely some of James' first experiments follow Hawthorne's model. Indeed, you can hardly see anything else in 'The Romance of Certain Old Clothes' (1868): it takes its setting from eighteenth-century New England, and even makes its climax depend on the supernatural, though James' ghost is handled very amateurishly and without conviction. To cite only one more story among several that could show how James found himself through Hawthorne's methods,

1. A book on this subject is now under preparation by John Finch.

'The Last of the Valerii' (1874) owes something in its plot and its neat surfaces to Mérimée; but the allegorical theme of an Italian count who falls in love with a pagan statue, which his young American wife has had excavated in their garden, can hardly have been developed without backward glances at *The Marble Faun*. You also tend to forget that *Roderick Hudson* (1875), James' first ambitious attempt at a novel, was also cast in the American art colony in Rome only fifteen years after Hawthorne's laborious breaking of the ground. James' somewhat vague discussion of aesthetic problems there might have been even worse if Hawthorne had not already occupied all the most damaging pitfalls.

Again, the setting of *The Europeans* (1878) in an old house near Boston suggests more than a little of the atmosphere of *The Seven Gables*;[2] and Eliot has wondered whether James also had Hawthorne in mind in the Northampton of the opening chapters of *Roderick Hudson*. In making the point in his critical biography of Hawthorne (1879) that *The Seven Gables* has more 'literal actuality' than Hawthorne's other novels, James said that 'it renders, to an initiated reader, the impression of a summer afternoon in an elm-shadowed New England town.' When he returned to *Roderick Hudson* to write its preface for his collected edition, he led up to its then regretted lack of intensity of presentation by remarking that 'what the early chapters of the book most "render" to me to-day is not the umbrageous air of their New England town.'[3]

The critical biography itself is tantalizing in what it omits to say, since it was written at the very period when James was most determined to abandon all traces of romance for realism. He took generously for granted all he had learned from Hawthorne, in much the same fashion as Emerson could take for granted how much he had been conditioned by Channing, or as Thoreau could in the case of Emerson. James' main concern

2. James' book is much slighter but much more fully 'done,' as in the exquisitely fresh picture of his house—the scene, like Hawthorne's, is about 1850: 'It was an ancient house—ancient in the sense of being eighty years old; it was built of wood, painted a clean, clear, faded grey, and adorned along the front, at intervals, with flat wooden pilasters, painted white . . . A large white door, furnished with a highly-polished brass knocker, presented itself to the rural-looking road, with which it was connected by a spacious pathway, paved with worn and cracked, but very clean, bricks. Behind it there were meadows and orchards, a barn and a pond . . . All this was shining in the morning air, through which the simple details of the picture addressed themselves to the eye as distinctly as the items of a "sum" in addition.'

3. Eliot's chief discussion of the relations between James and Hawthorne is in his uncollected essays in *The Little Review* (1918).

was to make an accurate tribute, but since he was primarily a novelist in his mid-thirties still somewhat slowly finding his way, he inevitably used this book also as a means of clarifying his own views by stating why the recent movement in fiction, which went back to Balzac for its directive, now seemed to him on much firmer ground than the provincial American had been. Consequently, there was to be no overt sign of Hawthorne in James' realistic middle period, no recrudescence of anything like his method until James had digested all the implications of his own discovery that in *Madame Bovary* the possibilities of realism seemed to have said their last word. Not until such a late series of stories as those dealing with the life of the artist did he return to allegory, or at least to parable; not until the surcharged atmosphere of a story like 'The Altar of the Dead' (1895) did he furnish, whether consciously or not, an instance of the definition of romance that he made while saying what he had not intended in *The American*. What he found to be this mode's distinguishing attribute also recalls Hawthorne's distinctions, since the kind of experience with which romance deals is 'experience liberated, so to speak; experience disengaged, disembroiled, disencumbered, exempt from the conditions that we usually know to attach to it.' The test of the validity of such a mode lay, therefore, in the degree to which it could sustain its high illusion. Hawthorne had spoken in similar terms of the difficulty of this feat when he had told Fields that 'in writing a romance a man is always, or always ought to be, careening on the verge of a precipitous absurdity, and the skill lies in coming as close as possible, without actually tumbling over.'

James undoubtedly did not think that he was calling for such a test in the closely woven surface details of his final great series of novels, but to most readers their success is in direct proportion to their liberation from the confines of an excessively special social milieu by means of their magnificently sustained symbolism. Certainly there is no question of any specific debts to Hawthorne at this point, but of a fundamental reassertion of kinship in moral values, which defied for both writers any merely realistic presentation. That being the case, it may be illuminating to uncover some of the links in the hidden chain that bound them together from the very start of James' career, or, indeed, from the time of his earlier unconscious immersion in the ethically rich world of his father.

Eliot has found their most important resemblance to lie in this remark in James' biography: 'the fine thing in Hawthorne is that he cared for the deeper psychology, and that, in his way, he tried to become familiar with it.' The charm which James could feel even in Hawthorne's slightest allegories, and which redeemed their stiffness for him, was that they gave 'glimpses of a great field, of the whole deep mystery of man's soul and conscience. They are moral, and their interest is moral; they deal with something more than the mere accidents and conventionalities, the surface occurrences of life.' How inwardly they had spoken to him is attested by the theme of 'The Beast in the Jungle' (1903), whose hero is finally crushed by realizing that he is 'to have been the one man in the world to whom nothing whatever was to happen.' That statement could very well have come from Hawthorne's notebook, and the story's peculiar intensity of horror, which Charles Demuth was to re-create so poignantly in his watercolor illustrations for it, reveals an endowment that was common to all three. For in his later period, as in *The Turn of the Screw* (1898), which Demuth also chose to illustrate, James no longer fumbled in his handling of the supernatural. He had formulated a means of treating it which satisfied him: the ghost-sense must be presented as it had grown into being in someone's consciousness; the failure to develop such connections with the normal was what left Poe's *Arthur Gordon Pym,* for example, without 'intrinsic values,' since lacking in human illusion. The contrast of what James wanted comes out in 'The Jolly Corner' (1908), whose design 'of the strange and sinister embroidered on the very type of the normal and easy' leads in turn to Eliot's effort in *The Family Reunion.*[4]

The many leads back to Hawthorne need hardly be underlined, espe-

4. That Eliot thought of this story while composing his play, is made clear by one of Agatha's speeches describing how Harry, like James' exile at his return to his old home on 'the jolly Corner,' will be confronted everywhere by his past:

> I mean that at Wishwood he will find another Harry.
> The man who returns will have to meet
> The boy who left. Round by the stables,
> In the coach-house, in the orchard,
> In the plantation, down the corridor
> That led to the nursery, round the corner
> Of the new wing, he will have to face him—
> And it will not be a very *jolly* corner.

The allusion was less hidden in the manuscript draft, which continued:

> I am sorry, Gerald, for making an allusion
> To an author whom you never heard of.

cially since the types of character that both novelists conceived have so
much in common. To the creator of Olive Chancellor, the feminist reformer of *The Bostonians* (1886), and of Gilbert Osmond, the selfish
dilettante in *The Portrait of a Lady* (1881), the evil nature was the cold
egoist who used or preyed upon other people, just as much as it was to
the creator of Hollingsworth or of Miriam's model. In view of this, you
may be struck also by other similarities. James' confession, in his preface
to 'The Beast in the Jungle,' 'My attested predilection for poor sensitive
gentlemen almost embarrasses me as I march,' reminds the reader that it
was scarcely more habitual for James than for Hawthorne to get very
far away from his own restricted path of experience in that of his heroes.
The characters who mark his greatest advance beyond anything in Hawthorne's scope, and who are, indeed, the unique signatures of his sensibility, are his heroines, particularly Isabel Archer and Milly Theale. But
even here his meditation over Hawthorne may have borne some fruit.

Zenobia struck him, in her sumptuous passion, as being 'the nearest
approach that Hawthorne has made to the complete creation of a *person';*
and though other readers might think of Hester Prynne in this connection, these two and Miriam are certainly more thoroughly imagined than
any of Hawthorne's men. It may also be remarked that they are as different as possible from Sophia, who suggested some traits for Priscilla
and Phoebe, and, almost explicitly, for the virginal heroine Hilda. Both
Zenobia and Miriam were marked for tragic ends by their restless and
reckless natures. Hawthorne was careful, perhaps too careful, in disso-
ciating Zenobia from Margaret Fuller; but whatever qualities they had
in common in their high-spirited feminism, the living woman's strained
angularity bore little resemblance to the dark beauty that the novelist,
through the eyes of Coverdale, dwelt on with great satisfaction. Fascinated by her free if not quite decorous behavior, Coverdale reflected—in
words that foreshadowed the protest of Henry Adams—that 'we seldom
meet with women nowadays, and in this country, who impress us as
being women at all,—their sex fades away, and goes for nothing.' The
narrator continued his scrutiny to the point of a realistic male sureness,
for which he half apologized, that Zenobia's unconstraint betrayed her
as no longer a virgin. He also went so far as almost to fancy himself
actually beholding her in 'Eve's earliest garment,' though that thought

in Hawthorne's manuscript was somewhat toned down in publication.[5] But he stressed, in Hester as much as in these others, a 'voluptuous, Oriental' taste for the gorgeous. In Miriam the touch of exotic splendor in her full-blooded, almost majestic appearance is accounted for by the hint that she is partly Jewish. It can hardly be altogether fortuitous that James' Miriam Rooth, whose magnificent presence separates her so signally from all the other characters in *The Tragic Muse,* is similar in her beauty and her race, if not her fate, to her earlier namesake.

We are on solider and more significant ground in James' development of his most characteristic device, that of a narrator through whose consciousness all the events are to be sifted and thus given the form of a complete impression. A long distance separates Miles Coverdale, who seemed unwittingly to contribute something of his own self-conscious coolness to the story he was reporting, and Lambert Strether, whose rich sense of all that was unfolding enabled James so to center the composition of *The Ambassadors* that he could consider it his best achievement. But the stages of development between these two are precisely those of James' experiments, for which a natural starting point was provided by Coverdale's own recognition of his role, midway through the action: 'It resembled that of the Chorus in a classic play, which seems to be set aloof from the possibility of personal concernment, and bestows the whole measure of its hope or fear, its exultation or sorrow, on the fortunes of others, between whom and itself this sympathy is the only bond.' Hawthorne was aware by the end of the book of the degree to which his device had not succeeded, for he then had Coverdale say: 'I have made but a poor and dim figure in my own narrative, establishing no separate interest, and suffering my colorless life to take its hue from other lives.' That very danger was what James, in his later period, was eager to circumvent by every resource of technical invention; for he had grown determined to give 'not my own personal account of the affair in hand,

5. In the manuscript, preserved in the Morgan Library, the passage reads: ' "As for the garb of Eden," added she, shivering playfully, "I shall not assume it till after Mayday!"
' Assuredly, Zenobia could not have intended it,—the fault must have been entirely in my imagination. But these last words, together with something in her manner, irresistibly brought up a picture of that fine, perfectly developed figure, in Eve's earliest garment. I almost fancied myself actually beholding it.' The last sentence was excised in the printed version.

but my account of somebody's impression of it . . . through the opportunity and the sensibility of some more or less detached, some not strictly involved, though thoroughly interested and intelligent witness or reporter.'

But what Coverdale had dreaded acutely, that he was becoming inhuman through his analytical detachment, became the increasingly inescapable situation for James' super-subtle observers. They grew obsessed with their author's own insatiable scrutiny of motive for motive's sake, until, in the case of the narrator of *The Sacred Fount* (1901), it was not possible for him to be sure whether his inquisitiveness was good or evil, or whether, indeed, he might not actually be insane. Only a shift in attitude was necessary, from James' inordinate excitement in the unfettered play of consciousness to Eliot's horrified perception of the pathic observer's inability to leave any effectual mark on the world, and the choric role has become that of Tiresias, that 'infinitely gentle, infinitely suffering thing,' who, both male and female, is doomed to foresuffer all that happens in *The Waste Land*. A related movement in recent European cultural history is similarly evinced by the shift in attitude between these three American writers. The change is from Hawthorne's ingenuous sense in Rome of a cultural complexity that was outside his understanding, to the breathless desire of the narrator of *The Aspern Papers* to be immersed in all the rich beauty of Venice, to Eliot's ironic comment on the rotting away of the economic and humanistic bases for that splendor, in 'Burbank with a Baedeker, Bleistein with a Cigar.'

Still nearer my present subject is the further evidence that James' technical development was a direct response to his sense of Hawthorne's limitations. James' dissatisfaction with allegory as a means of expressing what he valued so much in the earlier novelist's content—its penetration behind action and beneath appearance—would have been the strongest sort of stimulus to him to develop his own dense symbols. Balzac had not yet quite taught him in *Roderick Hudson* that 'the art of interesting us in things . . . can *only* be the art of representing them'; but by the time he came to write *The Ambassadors* he had learned long since that 'art deals with what we see, it must first contribute full-handed that ingredient.' He had completely mastered the fact that the best way to convey even spiritual relations was by their suggestive concretion into an image. As a result, he had arrived at the state where his themes themselves came to him as images, where persons or situations fixed his attention because

they 'would fall into a picture or a scene.' He gave many explicit accounts
of the process, of how, for instance, his imagination had been caught by
'the accidental mention' of the manner in which a luckless child had
been affected by the remarriage of a divorced parent. Even so sketchily
suggested, 'these elements gave out that vague pictorial glow which
forms the first appeal of a living "subject" to the painter's consciousness.'

The vocabulary of painting became habitual to him, primarily because
his stories are a record of seeing rather than of doing, or better as he
called them, a 'process of vision.' He wanted to catch 'the color of life
itself'; he saw his characters as elements of a composition, and planned
how their relations to one another could be established by means of deft
foreshortening of his narrative. What bothered him, even in *The Scarlet
Letter,* was that the characters were not adequately modelled in detail,
but remained mere 'representatives, very picturesquely arranged, of a
single state of mind.'

Yet Hawthorne also had spoken, in the preface to *The Seven Gables,*
of wanting so to manage 'his atmospherical medium as to bring out or
mellow the lights and deepen and enrich the shadows of the picture.'
To be sure, his stress on seeing pursues no sustained analogy with painting, but serves to remind us of Emerson's belief that sight is the most
spiritual of the senses. Impressionism was soon to become a natural mode
of expression for this assertion of the primacy of light, and that the stress
on seeing could be a latent force beyond the confines of painting is borne
out by the fact that Whitman, with even less knowledge of the plastic arts
than Hawthorne, spoke from first to last of his poems as 'pictures' and
'landscapes.' [6]

The portrait as a means of analyzing character was one of the possibilities that attracted Hawthorne to stories about early New England
artists. He pressed further his use of this device in *The Seven Gables,*
where much is made of the picture of the original Colonel Pyncheon. It
seems to Hepzibah that though its colors have almost faded from the
darkening canvas, the bare, hard traits of the sitter have now come out
in a boldness 'of spiritual relief.' The sly, imperious nature that is thus
revealed also strikes the daguerreotypist with another likeness; and when
he shows Phoebe a sample of his art, she recognizes the expression of her
Puritan ancestor. He tells her to look again, for it is a modern face that

6. Cf. p. 51 and the fuller discussion of this at pp. 596 f. below.

his uncompromising light has recorded; and even her unreflecting nature is startled by the thought that beneath Judge Pyncheon's mask of benevolence, this grasping meanness has persisted as the strongest element in his heritage, one thing in the shifting family fortunes that has not been altered by the transmutations of time. A similar, though minor use is made of the Malbone miniature of Clifford as a young man, a glance at which enables Phoebe also to perceive in his now ravaged face something of the delicate beauty which he had possessed before his years of disaster.

Melville could hardly have had a more impressive suggestion for his contrast between the formal portrait of Pierre's father and the early impromptu sketch of him as a gay and somewhat sensual bachelor. A great deal in Pierre's ambiguous relation to Isabel is made to depend on the fact that he discovers in her face so haunting a similarity to the features of this sketch that he is persuaded that she must be his sister. Equally related to Hawthorne's means for probing beneath conventional appearance is James' introduction of the likeness between Ralph Pendrel and the young man in the portrait of a century ago, which James manipulates as a frankly fantastic symbol for the way in which the history-ridden modern American actually steps across into the past.[7]

From what we have learned of the operations of Hawthorne's imagination, it seems most natural that when he wanted to express Hester's and Dimmesdale's moment of recognition of themselves, he would cast it in terms of a caught image: 'the crisis flung back to them their consciousness, and revealed to each heart its history and experience, as life never does, except at such breathless epochs. The soul beheld its features in the mirror of the passing moment.' This gives the lead to why Hawthorne built his important situations as pictures, or rather as tableaux, which were the closest the dramatic inexperience of his milieu could come to a scene. Such was the structure of the three pivotal encounters on the scaffold;

7. How conscious James was of this device of Hawthorne's is made explicit near the end of *The Tragic Muse,* when Gabriel Nash disappears after Nick Dormer has started to paint his portrait. Nick reflects that his eccentric friend somehow could not bear this scrutiny, and diverts himself by imagining that the picture itself is fading from the canvas: 'He couldn't catch it in the act, but he could have ever a suspicion on glancing at it that the hand of time was rubbing it away little by little—for all the world as in some delicate Hawthorne tale—and making the surface indistinct and bare of all resemblance to the model. Of course the moral of the Hawthorne tale would be that his personage would come back in quaint confidence on the day when his last projected shadow should have vanished.'

of Zenobia's theatrical denunciation of Hollingsworth's true character, while standing at the base of Eliot's Pulpit, the great rock in the woods from which the apostle had preached to the Indians; and especially, in its full symbolical treatment, of Miriam's and Donatello's acceptance of their sad union, as they met in the cathedral-square of Perugia, and the shadow of the bronze statue of Pope Julius seemed to cast his benediction upon them.

In all of these, Hawthorne's method of procedure would appear to have been the same. He started with a dominant moral idea, for which his picture, like Spenser's, was to be an illustration. He might advise himself, as in his notes for *The Ancestral Footstep,* that he should build 'a very carefully and highly wrought scene'; but the fact would remain, at least to eyes as acute as James', that Hawthorne had gained picturesque arrangement but not dynamic composition, that he had hardly shown himself more concerned in his writing than when he had looked at pictures, with anything except the sentiment which the artist had wanted to express. James, in a sense, started where Hawthorne left off. He seized first upon a dramatic image—Isabel's coming into the room and seeing Madame Merle standing while Osmond is sitting down, Strether's glimpse of Madame de Vionnet and Chad together on the river, the Prince's entrance at the moment when Fanny Assingham has dashed the golden bowl to the floor—and then carefully worked it into a climax of his action, or rather made it the concrete core of his range of feeling and thought. His sense of the inadequacy of Hawthorne's loosely finished sketches could again have furnished the stimulus for his reiterated imperative to himself, 'Dramatize, dramatize.' James used the terminology of the stage almost as often as that of the studio, but he came closest to self-definition when he spoke of aiming at 'richly summarised and foreshortened effects,' at 'the true grave close consistency in which parts hang together even as the interweavings of a tapestry.'

The perfect instance of James' development of a symbol to the point where it can bring into focus all the diverging rays of his intelligence as they play over a situation, is provided by the golden bowl, with its fatal flaw. But its meaning, which shifts impalpably from suggesting the character of the Italian Prince to the wider suggestion of the relation between him and his wife and whether it can be mended, is hardly capable of satisfactory apprehension short of an analysis of the whole book. A condensed example of James' symbolism to compare with that of Hawthorne and of Melville comes in the opening chapter, when the Prince, talking to Fanny Assingham, senses what lies ahead for him in the strange American world into which he is about to enter by his marriage with Maggie Verver:

These things, the motives of such people, were obscure—a little alarmingly so; they contributed to that element of the impenetrable which alone slightly qualified his sense of his good fortune. He remembered to have read as a boy a wonderful tale by Allan Poe, his prospective wife's countryman—which was a thing to show, by the way, what imagination Americans *could* have: the story of the shipwrecked Gordon Pym, who drifting in a small boat further toward the North Pole—or was it the South?—than anyone had ever done, found at a given moment before him a thickness of white air that was like a dazzling curtain of light, concealing as darkness conceals, yet of the color of milk or of snow. There were moments when he felt his own boat move upon some such mystery. The state of mind of his new friends, including Mrs. Assingham herself, had resemblances to a great white curtain. He had never known curtains but as purple even to blackness—but as producing where they hung a darkness intended and ominous. When they were so disposed as to shelter surprises the surprises were apt to be shocks.

While writing his biography of William Wetmore Story just the year before *The Golden Bowl,* James mentioned Hawthorne's use of the sculptor's Cleopatra in *The Marble Faun,* and characterized it as 'the phenomenon of a recognition, an assimilation, which is not as that of criticism, but something tenderer,' since Hawthorne's book, 'in its wandering amiability, holds up for a moment a mirror to another work, a little magic mirror from which the reflection, once caught, never fades.' That is precisely what James in turn has done with Poe's imaginary voyage of horror, thus giving a token of how deeply it had impressed him, notwithstanding his reasoned account of its limitations in presenting the supernatural. There seems to be no evidence that James ever read Melville. He had been a small boy in New York when *Moby-Dick* appeared, but he was to say of his earliest education, 'All our books in that age were English.' At the time he was starting to branch out in his reading for himself, he was at school in Geneva, and by 1860, when the family returned to America in order that William might study painting with Hunt at Newport, Melville's name had fallen into total eclipse in the critical world of which Henry was soon to become part.

These facts make it doubly interesting that James, as an American, should have felt the impenetrable mystery of whiteness. Emerson repeatedly deplored the bleached pallor of the culture in which he was involved, and thus anticipated Wyndham Lewis' attack on the art of the Paleface, whose predatory mind has made no contact with the aboriginal vitality which it has destroyed. This amounts to another way of symbolizing the genteel tradition, as does again Lawrence's revulsion from the terrifying purity of the American woman as foreshadowed in Hawthorne's Priscilla and in Cooper's 'females.'[8] These suggestions of sterility are hardly even latent in James' symbol here, for he was characteristically absorbed with the other side of the medal, with portraying, especially in people like Maggie Verver and her father, the Americans' uncorrupted innocence, their capacity for moral fineness, in contrast with the sophisticated products of an older civilization.

In the mirror that James has held up to Poe's narrative he has not caught the horror of its unrelieved light, which had been the main intention of Poe's climax. There is no indication, among the amplitude of Melville's allusions to other treatments of whiteness, that he was thinking of *Pym,* the voyage of the mind which Poe had published in 1838, the year after Melville had first gone to sea. But Melville included in his testimony one of Poe's chief sources: 'Bethink thee of the albatross, whence come those clouds of spiritual wonderment and pale dread, in which that white phantom sails in all imaginations? Not Coleridge first threw that spell; but God's great unflattering laureate, Nature.'[9] Even

8. Such were the images that these created in Lawrence's imagination: Priscilla became for him 'a sort of White Lily, a clinging little mediumistic sempstress who has been made use of in public séances. A sort of prostitute soul.' Eve Effingham, Cooper's unintentionally snobbish heroine of *Homeward Bound,* is 'a perfect American heroine, and I'm sure she wore the first smartly-tailored "suit" that ever woman wore. I'm sure she spoke several languages. I'm sure she was hopelessly competent. I'm sure she "adored" her husband, and spent masses of his money, and divorced him because he didn't understand LOVE.'

9. Melville's conviction of the essential dependence of art upon nature is amplified in his note describing his first sight of an albatross, 'during a prolonged gale, in waters hard upon the Antarctic seas. From my forenoon watch below, I ascended to the overclouded deck; and there, dashed upon the main hatches, I saw a regal, feathery thing of unspotted whiteness . . . At intervals, it arched forth its vast archangel wings, as if to embrace some holy ark . . . As Abraham before the angels, I bowed myself; the white thing was so white, its wings so wide, and in those forever exiled waters, I had lost the miserable warping memories of traditions and of towns. Long I gazed at that prodigy of plumage. I cannot tell, can only hint, the things that darted through me then. But at last I awoke; and turning, asked a sailor what bird was this. A goney, he replied. Goney! I never had heard that name before; is it conceivable that this glorious thing is utterly

in such a brief passage you can observe the greatly different treatment of symbols in the hands of Melville and of James. Whereas Melville's take his reader ever farther into the multitudinous seas of speculation, James' are more essentially those of a novelist, and are designed, like every other detail in his book, to illustrate character.

He could reduce this method to a formula: 'What is a picture or a novel that is *not* of character? What else do we seek in it and find in it? It is an incident for a woman to stand up with her hand resting on a table and look out at you in a certain way . . . At the same time it is an expression of character. If you say you don't see it (character in *that* . . .), this is exactly what the artist who has reasons of his own for thinking he *does* see it undertakes to show you.' Those sentences might, incidentally, stand as an epigraph for Eliot's 'La Figlia Che Piange,' standing at the top of the stairs 'with a fugitive resentment in her eyes.' They also go far to explain why, even in his latest, least realistic period, James' symbols are so effective, why as Rebecca West remarked, his metaphors and similes seem sometimes more vivid and more solid than his settings. For they still sprang from his long discipline in factual observation, from his final extraordinary mastery of pictorial surfaces, even when what he wanted most was to penetrate beyond them. He still held to the principle that he enunciated in the preface to *The Portrait of a Lady,* of 'the perfect dependence of the "moral" sense of a work of art on the amount of felt life concerned in producing it.' He would also have maintained that the amount of 'felt life' informing any work was equally dependent upon the adequate presentation of the subject; and that is why it had been essential for him to move so scrupulously, so painstakingly beyond the method of what he called the 'total vague intensity' of *The Marble Faun.*

Writing about the evolution of his scheme for *The Sense of the Past,* he also pointed in the direction of developments since, when he said, 'At once, withal, I see it in images, which I must put as they come, and which make for me thus, don't I seem to feel? one of the first, if not

unknown to men ashore! never! But some time after, I learned that goney was some seaman's name for albatross. So that by no possibility could Coleridge's wild Rhyme have had aught to do with those mystical impressions which were mine, when I saw that bird upon our deck. For neither had I then read the Rhyme, nor knew the bird to be an albatross. Yet, in saying this, I do but indirectly burnish a little brighter the noble merit of the poem and the poet.'

the very first passages of my action. An action, an action, an action must it thus insuperably be—as it has moreover so well started with being—from the first pulse to the last.' It was from James' example that Eliot and Pound, living among Georgians, learned 'that poetry ought to be as well written as prose'; and by extending and tightening up such a note as this of James', Eliot could have arrived at his formulation of the objective correlative,'[10] which now stands as one of the classic definitions of wholeness of composition.

4. Hawthorne and Milton

IN REACHING such levels of technical expertness, we may seem to have left Hawthorne far behind. But his trump cards still remain to be played. These are comprised in the consistent pattern into which he could fit his findings concerning what James called 'the deeper psychology.' Hawthorne's most valuable inheritance from the seventeenth-century tradition lay in his comprehension of the dependence of the body on the mind, especially of the power with which the ego can warp man's physical constitution to its own savage bent. In the degree of objective equivalence that he could devise to give external form to these inner workings, he was indebted to the greatest masters of allegory; but his understanding of the nature of interanimation also looks forward to some of the main postulates of modern psychiatry. These are most evident in his portrayal of the relation between Chillingworth and the minister, in the search-

10. 'The only way of expressing emotion in the form of art is by finding an "objective correlative"; in other words, a set of objects, a situation, a chain of events which shall be the formula of that *particular* emotion; such that when the external facts, which must terminate in sensory experience are given, the emotion is immediately evoked.' The third chapter of my book, *The Achievement of T. S. Eliot* (1935), tries to develop the implications of this formula, and to apply them as a measure of various kinds of poetry.

The extent to which James' type of image could stimulate Eliot's method may be suggested by this bit of characterization in *The Spoils of Poynton:* ' "You don't think I'm rough or hard, do you?" he asked of Fleda, his impatience shining in his idle eyes as the dining-hour shines in club-windows.' That is well on the way to the witty surprise of

> A small house agent's clerk, with one bold stare,
> One of the low on whom assurance sits
> As a silk hat on a Bradford millionaire.

ing analysis in such a chapter as 'The Leech and His Patient.' The irony of its title lies in the fact that though the old physician knows Dimmesdale's bodily weakness to be due to a deeper sickness of the spirit, and though he is determined to discover its cause, he is actuated not by the hope that he may suggest a cure, but that he may suck out his patient's very vitality.

The physician's own transformation is handled with strictest accord to the Puritans' belief in how an erring mind could become so divorced from God that it lapsed into a state of diabolic possession. There had been a calm dignity in the long years of Chillingworth's devotion to knowledge, but his uprightness had begun to wither away from the moment he undertook his investigation of the minister. Although he imagined that he was conducting it 'with the severe and equal integrity of a judge, desirous only of truth,' he failed to realize that the question could not be considered as coolly as a geometric problem, since it involved his passionate feeling about the wrong that he had suffered. His pursuit gradually stirred up fires of malice, hitherto unsuspected in him; and when Hester saw him once after a considerable interval, she was startled by the change that had come over his appearance. He seemed uglier than before, with his shoulders more misshapen, and a fierce and terrifying glow in his eyes.

Needless to say, from what we know of Hawthorne's methods, these suggestions are not left thus implicit, but are labored with as many details as those by which Cotton Mather tried to prove, in his *Memorable Providences,* that 'there are Devils and Witches; and that though those night-birds least appear where the Day-light of the Gospel comes, yet New England has had Examples of their existence and operation.' But Hawthorne's repeated emphasis on Chillingworth's lurid glare is no more imaginatively compelling than the allegorical devices by which Spenser's characters are invariably recognized. However, the portrayal of Chillingworth's behavior at the moment of his discovery of the mark on the sleeping minister's breast draws upon a profounder moralist than any of the Mathers. His face is distorted with a mixed 'look of wonder, joy, and horror. With what a ghastly rapture, as it were, too mighty to be expressed only by the eye and features, and therefore bursting forth through the whole ugliness of his figure, and making itself even riotously manifest by the extravagant gestures with which he threw up his arms towards the ceiling, and stamped his foot upon the floor! Had a man seen old Roger Chillingworth, at that moment of his ecstasy, he would have had no need to ask how Satan comports himself when a precious human soul is lost to heaven, and won into his kingdom.'

How integrally Hawthorne accepted Milton's analysis of the way the passions operate can be suggested by the passage where Uriel looked down upon the sudden unrestraint of Satan, and

> Saw him disfigured, more than could befall
> Spirit of happy sort: his gestures fierce
> He mark'd, and mad demeanour, then alone,
> As he supposed, all unobserved, unseen.[1]

Hawthorne had thought out the full psychological pattern of his conception, for he was careful to note in his final sentence that the one still potentially saving element that 'distinguished the physician's ecstasy from Satan's was the trait of wonder in it.'

To Brownell, Chillingworth was 'the one piece of machinery' in the book; but living in the age of Hitler, even the least religious can know and be terrified by what it means for a man to be possessed. And once you have discounted Hawthorne's mode of typifying, the stages of the physician's disintegration are no less psychologically real than those in the retribution of the less purely allegorical Hester. This is particularly true at the final crisis, where Hawthorne observes that, after Dimmesdale's death, all the old man's 'strength and energy—all his vital and intellectual force—seemed at once to desert him.' To be sure, Hawthorne then weakens his presentation of that state by falling into a description very close to what happened to Spenser's jealous husband, Malbecco, for he adds that Chillingworth 'shrivelled away, and almost vanished from mortal sight, like an uprooted weed that lies wilting in the sun.' But irritation at this inadequate fancy should not prevent us from seeing the profound accuracy in the novelist's assumption that once Chillingworth's malignity was deprived of its object to feed upon, its energy became merely self-destructive. Hawthorne had studied the closeness of pleasure to pain, and had been impressed by the fact that hatred

1. As Randall Stewart has pointed out, Hawthorne may likewise have had this scene in mind when he contrived the one where the seducer Butler catches sight of Fanshawe standing on the top of a precipice above him. The allusion is suggested when Hawthorne says that 'there was something awful,' to Butler's apprehension, 'in the slight form that stood so far above him, like a being from another sphere, looking down upon his wickedness.'

and love seemed in the force of their operation to be 'the same thing at bottom.'

The same firmness of elucidative pattern for his characters' actions runs throughout his work. In depicting both Hester's wild grief in prison and her almost mad joy of release in the forest, Hawthorne was again subscribing to Milton's understanding of the way in which passion could drive out the faculty of reason, and wrongfully usurp its place. Perry Miller has noted how this faculty-psychology, which stems back to Aquinas and Aristotle's *De Anima,* 'furnished the cast of mental characters' for exactly the kind of 'psychological drama of salvation' that Bunyan wanted to present in his embodied concepts.[2] And even though Hawthorne, after Locke's revolution, could not have accepted the faculty-psychology in all its schematic intricacies, its heritage served him well in controlling his dramatic crises.

When Miriam has grown unbearably oppressed by the ambiguous power that her model holds over her—the nature of which she has been unable to confide to anyone—he appears stalking behind her and her friends that night in the Coliseum. She can stand the tension no longer, and shrinking into the shadow of an arch, and 'fancying herself wholly unseen,' she begins 'to gesticulate extravagantly, gnashing her teeth, flinging her arms wildly abroad, stamping with her foot. It was as if she had stepped aside for an instant, solely to snatch the relief of a brief fit of madness.' The similarity to the description of Chillingworth may again attest to Hawthorne's lack of variety in invention, just as does the red gleam in Judge Pyncheon's eyes. But these iterations also demonstrate how thoroughly his view of human behavior was colored by the older moral and theological tradition. In devising the closely linked chain of events that follow, he had unquestionably brooded over the meaning of *Paradise Lost.*

Miriam has not been unobserved, since Donatello's inarticulate devotion to her is as faithful in its watch as that of a hound. Up to this point, even in the extremity of her solitude, she has felt that it would be a sin to stain his innocently joyous nature with the blackness of a woe like hers. But now, though perceiving how ironical it is that, in her utmost need, her beauty and gifts have brought her 'only this poor simple

2. See *The New England Mind: The Seventeenth Century* (1939), Chapter ix, 'The Nature of Man.'

boy,' she decides that since he has seen so much, to-morrow she will tell him all.

At this moment they are rejoined by Kenyon and Hilda and the rest of the group. As they resume their walk, the sculptor speculates about the exact location of the spot where, according to the legend, Curtius plunged himself into a chasm in the earth in the belief that he might save his countrymen by this act of expiation. But to Miriam, though she has re-gained her self-control, this legend comes with a special application. Hawthorne almost suggests the words of Pascal when he makes her say that this 'chasm was merely one of the orifices of that pit of blackness that lies beneath us, everywhere. The firmest substance of human happi-ness is but a thin crust spread over it, with just reality enough to bear up the illusive stage-scenery amid which we tread. It needs no earthquake to open the chasm. A footstep, a little heavier than ordinary, will serve; and we must step very daintily, not to break through the crust at any moment. By and by, we inevitably sink!' Conventional Hilda is horrified at such thoughts, for it seems to her that there is no 'hideous emptiness under our feet, except what the evil within us digs'; and if there should be such a chasm, the one thing to do would be to bridge it over 'with good thoughts and deeds.'

As they continue to talk, Miriam suddenly draws the girl close to her, whispering, 'Hilda, my religious Hilda, do you know how it is with me? I would give all I have or hope—my life, oh how freely—for one instant of your trust in God! You little guess my need of it.' Hilda is then doubly frightened by her friend's doubt of Providence. Hawthorne only mentions this doubt in glancing fashion, but it lies behind the tragic event that transpires.

They have come finally to the Tarpeian rock, for Kenyon, a good American, is a walking Baedeker. Without realizing that the others have gone on, Miriam and Donatello linger on the precipice, since he has be-gun to ask her, with unexpected earnestness, about the kind of men who were punished here. She tells him that they were those who 'cumbered the world . . . men who poisoned the air, which is the common breath of all, for their own selfish purposes.' When he asks her again whether it was well done to fling them from the edge, she answers yes, for 'inno-cent persons were saved by the destruction of a guilty one, who deserved his doom.'

What happened next remained indistinct in her mind. She could seem to remember that as a figure approached her from the shadows, she had fallen in desperation on her knees; but in the wild moment that followed she could hardly distinguish afterwards whether she had been an actor or a sufferer. Donatello, in the fierce energy that had suddenly kindled him from a boy into a man, insisted that he had done only what her eyes bade him do. And she could no more deny that a kind of joy had flamed up in her heart as she beheld her persecutor in mortal peril, than she could say whether this feeling had been one of horror, or of ecstasy, or of both. She pressed Donatello to her in a clinging embrace, and in their first minutes together, they experienced a kind of rapture, a drunkenness like that of Adam and Eve after the temptation, the insane sense of release that is 'the foremost result of a broken law.' As their spirits rose 'to the solemn madness of the occasion,' they went down into the city, not stealthily, or fearfully, but with a stately and majestic stride. 'Passion lent them (as it does to meaner shapes) its brief nobility of carriage.' Their first union seemed closer than a marriage bond, so intimate that it annihilated all other ties. They felt that they were liberated 'from the chain of humanity; a new sphere, a special law had been created for them alone. The world could not come near them; they were safe!'

But if Hawthorne understood thus the nature of *hubris,* the understanding of *nemesis* came always more instinctively to the descendant of Puritans. There 'exhaled upward (out of their dark sympathy, at the base of which lay a human corpse) a bliss, or an insanity, which the unhappy pair imagined to be well worth the sleepy innocence that was forever lost to them.' But just then they heard below them the singing of the group who had so recently been their companions, the rising and falling of voices that had accorded with theirs. Then they knew they were alone. And even though, as they passed the site of Pompey's forum, Miriam's bravery reminded Donatello that a great deed had been done there, 'a deed of blood like ours!' she also knew, once these words were spoken— and recoiled from the thought—that they two together were now likewise of the fraternity of all other murderers.

Against the background of these unmistakable implications, it seems strange that so many critics have taken out of its context one of Miriam's speculations near the end of the book, in order to assert that Hawthorne's theme here is that the fall of man was really his rise. She argues to Kenyon that since Donatello's crime seems to have been the means of educating his simple nature to a level of feeling and intelligence that it would not have reached under any other discipline, may it not be that Adam's sin 'was the destined means by which, over a long pathway of toil and sorrow, we are to attain a higher, brighter, and profounder happiness than any our lost birthright gave? Will not this idea account for the permitted existence of sin, as no other theory can?' 'O felix culpa,' declares the Exultet for the Holy Saturday Mass, 'quae talem et tantum meruit habere redemptorem.'

But hardly more than the Church does Hawthorne hold this to be the whole truth. Miriam herself trembles at these irrepressible thoughts on regeneration through sin. Hawthorne declares that Kenyon 'rightly felt' them to be too perilous. But the novelist did not need to make this open comment, for the whole course of his action bears out that hardly more than Milton was he 'of the Devil's party without knowing it.' That comment on Paradise Lost was made by the greatest of the English romantics, Blake, and was subscribed to by Shelley in his equal fascination with the character of Lucifer. But what this interpretation ignores is the cumulative effect of the whole poem, the gradual decay and final degradation of the former Prince of Heaven, as the consequences of his fall from grace work themselves out inevitably in debasing his nature.

In comparable fashion, an understanding of The Marble Faun depends on being aware of the work as a whole. We must not overlook the circumstances in which Miriam's speculation occurs, for it is during the Roman Carnival, with its vestiges of the old pagan rite of spring. Miriam and Donatello have seized on the disguise of a masquerade for a moment of gay forgetfulness of their destiny. But when they encounter Kenyon, this is brought again, unavoidably, to the fore. It strikes the sculptor that these two have reached 'a wayside paradise,' but to-morrow—and here the analogy with the closing lines of Paradise Lost could hardly be more marked—'a remorseful man and woman, linked by a marriage-bond of crime, they would set forth towards an inevitable goal.'[3] Nor is that

---

3. The romantic interpretation generally remembers, as an augury of happiness, this line:

The world was all before them where to choose.

It neglects the fact that Adam and Eve have just been driven out of Paradise, and that the following and final lines destroy any suggestion of the joy of the open road:

The world was all before them where to choose
Their place of rest, and Providence their guide:
They hand in hand with wandering steps and slow,
Through Eden took their solitary way.

goal left shrouded in any doubt, for it is made explicit at the end that her life is to be spent in penitence, his in prison.

Even here, in his one diffuse handling of the European scene, and in spite of what Eliot has called 'all its Walter Scott-Mysteries of Udolpho upholstery,' Hawthorne has again established a world of solid moral values. It is based on a conception of man as a being radically imperfect, destined to struggle through a long labyrinth of error, and to suffer harsh and cruel shocks. The contrast with the one-way optimism of most of Hawthorne's contemporaries could hardly be more striking, and runs parallel to the estimate that Perry Miller has made of the value of the Puritans for us to-day. The impossibility of accepting their explanation of the universe should not blind us, he contends, to the accuracy of their observations of man. In the hard light of Freudian psychology or of recent political history, it is scarcely useful to regard man as perfect, or even as naturally good. Notwithstanding the humaneness and toleration that make Franklin and Jefferson among the strongest bulwarks in our social heritage, it is forced inescapably upon us that their rationalism was too shallow to encompass the full complexity of man's nature. In sharpest opposition to this, as well as to the transcendental and Utopian strains, the Puritans' understanding of man's tragic fallibility, and their consequent preparation to face the worst, are salutary in their toughness. It should hardly need to be added that such a tragic sense has not been restricted in America to the Puritans or to the seventeenth century. For Lincoln, among whose favorite quotations was the line, 'Why should the spirit of mortal be proud?,' was broad enough to unite the furthest reach of the democratic ideal with Christian humility over man's weakness and awe before his inscrutable fate.

How far Hawthorne's treatment of tragedy is 'democratic' and 'Christian' will be examined in the next chapter; but it is already apparent that what Melville and Eliot considered his realism was the accurate reading of human nature, which he shared with Milton and Bunyan. Hawthorne's ability to relive in his imagination some of their dramatic conflicts between passion and reason, and to understand the validity of their traditional moral standards, gave him a principle, which, as Emerson said, is an eye to see with. It gave him what the artist most requires, the power not merely to record but likewise to interpret the significance of what he has observed.

CODA

THE ATTITUDE we take towards allegory to-day is different from that of 1900. The awareness of social disintegration, the dread of violence and brutality that had grown so deeply into the European consciousness at the end of the first World War, inevitably broke through the surfaces of the realistic tradition and demanded a mode that could again give fuller expression to inner struggle. The most intense, if limited, method to be devised was that of Kafka, whose temper was so symptomatic of the emerging era that he produced in *The Trial* an allegorical typification of the horror of unchecked authoritarianism even before the phenomenon of the Nazi state had come into being. Kafka is likewise, as has often been noted, the almost pure example of the Freudian novelist, for the compulsive neuroses that drive his characters are not something manufactured from a psycho-analytical handbook, as they often are, say, in the case of O'Neill, but give the sense of being the inescapable means of conveying Kafka's type of spiritual experience.

The Freudian schematization of man's inner life, to judge from its pervasive effects on, for instance, the typical spokesmen for two successive generations, Lawrence and Auden, has tended just as much as the old faculty-psychology to drive towards allegory, as in the latter's plays; or at least as far as parable, as in the former's late story, 'The Man Who Died.' Lawrence indicated why his content found only handicaps in the technique of realism, when he said: 'Somehow, that which is psychic—non-human in humanity, is more interesting to me than the old-fashioned human element, which causes one to conceive a character in a certain moral scheme and make him consistent. The certain moral scheme is what I object to.' The final part of that statement introduces another factor, and suggests why Lawrence, in his passionate rejection of all conventions in the name of psychological accuracy, was better at creating moments of tension than in building them into a structure of either plot or character. His statement likewise presents a parallel to the problem that Melville encountered when, having plunged into the fluctuating obscurities of his inner life, he could no longer keep Hawthorne's firmness of moral interpretation. Thinking no doubt of *Pierre,* where he had felt both the necessity and the difficulty for art to portray the bewildering contradictions of the spirit, Melville declared in *The Confidence Man:* 'That fiction, where every character can, by reason of its consistency, be comprehended at a glance, either exhibits but sections of character, making them appear for wholes, or else is very untrue to reality.'

The same conviction that realism is inadequate appears in Eliot, a writer as different as possible from Lawrence in content. Eliot has also been more concerned with formal excellence than nearly all other contemporary writers, and has approached drama through its origin in Christian ritual. You find him making this characteristic effort to clear away William Archer's brittle notion of a well-made realistic play in favor of a more severe and more imaginative convention: 'It is essential that a work of art should be self-consistent, that an artist should consciously or unconsciously draw a circle beyond which he does not trespass; on the one hand actual life is always the material, and on the other hand an abstraction from actual life is a necessary condition to the creation of the work of art.' The substance of his attack upon Archer's statement that the faults of Elizabethan drama lay in its artificial unrealistic conventions was that, unlike Racine, for instance, it had not been conventional enough, that 'in one play, *Everyman,* and perhaps in that one play only, we have a drama within the limitations of art.' The example may seem preposterous in its let-down from the rich, if confusing, world of *Hamlet;* but the consistency of Eliot's critical logic was to be supported creatively a decade later by an instance of what he meant, in *Murder in the Cathedral.* But even in his allegorical tempters Eliot has still profited from James, as Kafka did from the naturalistic novel: the abstractions of both have been clothed with so many vivid and subtle details that we have to remind ourselves that we are dealing with allegory at all.

The briefest way of describing what has happened is to remember how contemporary literature has advanced since Synge's remark that writers had been too willing to make a mutually exclusive choice between reality and richness, that is to say, between the methods of Zola and of Mallarmé, between naturalism and symbolism. With the example of Joyce to show how both modes can be carried to hitherto unattained limits by the same man,[1] we are aware of resources that make the kind of allegory

1. See Harry Levin's essay on *Finnegans Wake* in *New Directions* (1939), an essay that should prove to be one of the landmarks in modern criticism.

that Auden and Isherwood devised to carry their Marxist and Freudian personifications in a play like *The Ascent of F6* seem bare and amateurish. However, it must be added that despite Joyce's balance between the two modes in *Ulysses,* the obscurity of motivation and direction in *Finnegans Wake* has left that work a monument of virtuosity, but scarcely one of great value as an instrument of communication.

We thus come back, reinforced by many examples, to the basic distinctions with which we opened this long chapter; to the truth in Conrad's remark that a novel is very seldom fixed to one exclusive meaning, since, 'the nearer it approaches art, the more it acquires a symbolic character'; [2] and to Lawrence's intuitive recognition that 'symbols are organic units of consciousness with a life of their own, and you can never explain them away, because their value is dynamic, emotional, belonging to the sense-consciousness of the body and soul, and not simply mental. An allegorical image has a *meaning*. Mr. Facing-both-ways has a meaning. But I defy you to lay your finger on the full meaning of Janus, who is a symbol.'

2. Conrad went on to say: 'You . . . may imagine that I am alluding to the Symbolist School of poets or prose writers. Theirs, however, is only a literary proceeding against which I have nothing to say. I am concerned here with something much larger.'

⋙ VIII ⋘

A DARK NECESSITY

'Peace, Hester, peace!' replied the old man, with gloomy sternness.
. . . 'My old faith, long forgotten, comes back to me, and explains
all that we do, and all we suffer. By thy first step awry thou didst
plant the germ of evil; but since that moment, it has all been a dark
necessity.'

1. Hawthorne's Politics, with the Economic Structure of *The Seven Gables*

To SHIFT the foreground of our attention from form to content, we return
at last to explicit consideration of Hawthorne's fulfilment of the standards
for tragedy posited at the opening of this second book.[1] With regard to
the two chief demands that the creation of tragedy makes upon its author,
a firm conception of the relation of man to society and of the nature of
good and evil, Hawthorne's position on the former has been suggested,
at least, in his dissatisfaction with the transcendentalists' dichotomy between society and solitude. But it may clear the ground further if we
summarize his politics, since, unlike Emerson's or Thoreau's, they have
generally been ignored, or misunderstood, as in Paul Elmer More's remark
that, 'though he lived in the feverish ante-bellum days, he was singularly lacking in the political sense, and could look with indifference on the
slave question.' To write a campaign biography with one eye on a consular appointment can hardly be construed as an unpolitical act, and
though Hawthorne demurred in his preface that he was unqualified for
such a piece of work, and though Pierce's enemies called the book Hawthorne's latest romance, it still enabled him to express his own long-held
convictions on the subject of slavery. He felt its wrong, but he could not
see any wisdom in the violent view and remedies of the abolitionists. He
concluded that 'the theorist may take that view in his closet; the philan-

1. See pp. 179-80 above.

316

thropist by profession may strive to act upon it uncompromisingly, amid
the tumult and warfare of his life. But the statesman of practical sagacity
—who loves his country as it is, and evolves good from things as they
exist, and who demands to feel his firm grasp upon a better reality before he quits the one already gained—will be likely here, with all the
greatest statesmen of America, to stand in the attitude of a conservative.'

To holders of the opposite position, Hawthorne's distrust of purposive
action presents a wide-open target. It might be necessary even for believers in dialectical process to grant some truth in his statement that
'there is no instance, in all history, of the human will and intellect having
perfected any great moral reform by methods which it adapted to that
end,' since every step of progress seems to call into being some new,
not wholly foreseen evil, which has to be wrestled with in turn. But when
he took the line to which Coverdale tended, on being struck, in the picnic
spirit of Blithedale, by 'the folly of attempting to benefit the world,'
Hawthorne could lay himself open to the full charge of obscurantism. By
far his most extreme pronouncement was that a way of viewing slavery,
which was 'probably as wise' as that of the abolitionists, was to regard it
'as one of those evils which divine Providence does not leave to be reme-
died by human contrivances, but which, in its own good time, by some
means impossible to be anticipated, but of the simplest and easiest operation, when all its uses have been fulfilled, it causes to vanish like a
dream.'

Such a statement would be preposterous not only to a materialist, but
conceivably even to a practical politician of Pierce's limited scope, and
certainly to any Christian who could envisage a more dynamic role for
his faith. The characteristic Hawthorne twist to this position is that he
could affirm it, and yet possess the detachment to perceive the validity of
its opposite. In an essay, 'Chiefly about War Matters,' which he wrote
after a trip to Washington in 1862, he made certain observations, under
the pseudonym of 'a Peaceable Man,' which The Atlantic Monthly
thought it impossible to publish in that time of tension. It insisted, and
he agreed, that some disclaiming notes be added. What is more, he wrote
them himself. The result is that he sustained in the text his typical reflection that 'no human effort, on a grand scale, has ever yet resulted according to the purpose of its projectors. The advantages are always incidental. Man's accidents are God's purposes. We miss the good we sought,
and do the good we little cared for.' Then he added at the foot of the

page: 'The author seems to imagine that he has compressed a great deal of meaning into these little, hard, dry pellets of aphoristic wisdom. We disagree with him. The counsels of wise and good men are often coincident with the purposes of Providence; and the present war promises to illustrate our remark.'

Socio-political position

Such suspension of disbelief can be useful for a writer if it enables him to accept the contradictory aspects of any human situation; and without that acceptance he conceives of crises in simple contrasts of black and white, a serviceable position for the pamphleteer, but impossible for anyone who would create an impression of complex actuality. Therefore, the most significant thing about Hawthorne's politics for his interpretation of human destiny is not that he was a skeptical conservative in a setting of Emersonian liberals and Garrison radicals; it lies rather in the paradox that he was also a Democrat. For the Whigs were the party of respectability, to whom even Emerson granted, through his fascination with Webster, the aristocracy of talents. But Hawthorne was a lifelong admirer of Jackson, and had been so even at the time when one of Emerson's earliest examples of compensation had carried him no further from Brattle Street than to say, 'God is promoted by the worst. Don't despise even the Kneelands and Andrew Jacksons.'[2] Moreover, Hawthorne remarked, in 'A Book of Autographs,' a historical sketch which he wrote while at the Manse, that Hamilton, despite his high qualities that had made him the idol of the Federalists, shared all their 'distrust of the people, which so inevitably and so righteously brought about their ruin.' For though Hawthorne expressed nothing but contempt for the professional politicians he encountered at the customhouse, he was not entirely ironical when he spoke of himself as 'the Locofoco surveyor.' He had been drawn to the party of the common people through what we have already seen in his notebooks—his shy but sympathetic fondness for ordinary coarse life. It also may well have been that his consciousness of his family's loss of their former position in purse-proud Salem had conditioned his withdrawal from its tight world, and had led him instinctively to cast his lot with the humbler rising forces.

A peculiar kind of social understanding made Hawthorne hold to both the contrasting terms of this paradox of being at once a democrat

2. Abner Kneeland was the Boston free thinker who had just (1834) been sentenced to jail for blasphemy.

COMING TO THE POINT, BY W. S. MOUNT

and a conservative. It enabled him to give a clear impression of human dignity in his character sketches of common men like those in 'The Toll-Gatherer's Day' or of 'The Old Apple Dealer,' [3] and caused him also to praise Pierce for daring 'to love that great and sacred reality—his whole, united, native country—better than the mistiness of a philanthropic theory.' As a result Hawthorne's views outraged everyone on the left, and their depth of spiritual integrity was doubtless lost on most of Pierce's conservative supporters among the Southern planters and the Northern proponents of the cotton interest.

Moreover, Brownell was to back up his contention of the novelist's *Concord battlefield* unawakened indifference to the whole subject of social development by what he considered the telling instance of his having said even *à propos* of the Concord battlefield, 'I have never found my imagination much excited by this or any other scene of historic celebrity.' But Brownell ignored the context, for Hawthorne had just remarked on 'the one circumstance' that had borne more fruit for him 'than all that history tells us of the fight': the story of a problem of conscience, which had been suggested to him by his having heard that a hired-boy, who had been chopping wood in back of the manse on the morning of the skirmish, had rushed out with his axe just as the enemy was retreating, and coming to the spot where the two British soldiers lay on the ground, had been startled to see one stir; whereupon, acting from a nervous and involuntary impulse, he had dealt him a fatal blow on the head. The theme for Hawthorne's unwritten story, which he finally tried to weave into *Septimius Felton,* was 'to follow that poor youth through his subsequent career, and observe how his soul was tortured by the blood stain, contracted as it had been before the long custom of war had robbed human life of its sanctity, and while it still seemed murderous to slay a brother man.'

Then, as Hawthorne continued to reflect on the battle site, he found 'a wilder interest' in the fact that an Indian village had once stood there,

3. Hawthorne's characteristic concluding apostrophe to this old man was that 'many would say that you have hardly individuality enough to be the object of your own self-love. How, then, can a stranger's eye detect anything in your mind and heart to study and wonder at? Yet, could I read but a tithe of what is written there, it would be a volume of deeper and more comprehensive import than all that the wisest mortals have given to the world; for the soundless depths of the human soul and of eternity have an opening through your breast.' Melville marked this conclusion, and said that 'such touches' argued to him Hawthorne's 'boundless sympathy with all forms of being.'

and tried to reconstruct in his imagination, as Thoreau had stimulated him to do, its kind of primitive existence. These are not the remarks of a man indifferent to history, but of one solidly planted in the knowledge of his province, who wants to utilize, not its few spectacular events, but its deeper life, for creative ends. James recognized this in stating that Hawthorne possessed 'that faculty which is called now-a-days the historic consciousness,' and, what was more significant for an artist, that 'his vision of the past was filled with definite images.' As we have grown by now to expect, Eliot has pursued that perception further, for he holds that 'in one thing alone Hawthorne is more solid than James: he had a very acute historical sense. His erudition in the small field of American colonial history was extensive, and he made most fortunate use of it. Both men had that sense of the past which is peculiarly American, but in Hawthorne this sense exercised itself in a grip on the past itself; in James it is a sense of the sense.'

The importance of that sense for an artist is that by it alone can he escape from mere contemporaneity, from the superficial and journalistic aberrations of the moment, and come into possession of the primary attributes of man, through grasping the similarities of his problems beneath differing guises. The historical sense puts no premium on the past over the present; it betrays a writer if it lets him forget the tensions of his own day; its value lies in increasing his power to concentrate on what is essentially human.

Hawthorne held very accurate scales in judging the world of Hester Prynne. He observed the inevitable severity in a people 'amongst whom religion and law were almost identical.' He believed it to constitute the most intolerant society that ever lived. Yet he did not minimize its substantial achievements, which he found typified in 'the sombre sagacity' of Governor Bellingham, who was well fitted to be the head of a community that had accomplished so much, 'precisely because it imagined and hoped so little.' Nor did Hawthorne make the mistake of supposing that such characters as the governor, unfeignedly devoted to duty as they were, believed it necessary 'to reject such means of comfort, or even luxury, as lay fairly within their grasp.' The novelist went so far as to affirm that the first generation of settlers, the offspring of Elizabethans, though already in the initial stages of a new joyless conduct, would still compare favorably with their nineteenth-century descendants in the point of holiday-keeping. For the long succession of Puritans in between had left New England sadly needing 'to learn again the forgotten art of gayety.'

One of the last things Hawthorne wrote before *The Scarlet Letter* was 'Main Street,' a processional panorama of two centuries of Salem, which he was able to compile while a customs officer.[4] He made there his most explicit statement of the attitude from which he re-created the past, some sentences of which Melville double-checked: 'Happy are we, if for nothing else, yet because we did not live in those days . . . Such a life was sinister to the intellect, and sinister to the heart; especially when one generation had bequeathed its religious gloom, and the counterfeit of its religious ardor, to the next . . . The sons and grandchildren of the first settlers were a race of lower and narrower souls than their progenitors had been.' He thus revealed his full awareness of what recent historians have been so careful to point out, the crucial distinction between the solid piety of John Cotton and the neurotic exaggerations of his namesake Cotton Mather. Hawthorne could, therefore, only conclude with this sentence, the last half of which Melville underlined: 'Let us thank God for having given us such ancestors; and let each successive generation

4. This was Hawthorne's contribution to the volume edited by his sister-in-law, Elizabeth Peabody, under the title, *Aesthetic Papers* (1849). Other contributions included Thoreau's 'Civil Disobedience' and Emerson's essay on 'War,' which took the position that although necessary 'when seen in the remote past, in the infancy of society,' war begins to look 'to sane men at the present day . . . like an epidemic insanity.' The editor, whose contribution was an essay urging the cultivation of the body through music and dancing—radical doctrine then for New England—hoped that such an anthology of 'new work' might be annual; but the public did not respond.

She had already helped to bring Hawthorne to some attention, having issued 'Grandfather's Chair' from her own press, in the bookshop she had opened in Boston in 1839. Responsive to all the new social enthusiasms, she could apparently be far too enthusiastic for her brother-in-law, who was to write her from England this typical passage: 'I do not know what Sophia may have said about my conduct in the Consulate. I only know that I have done no good; none whatever. Vengeance and beneficence are things that God claims for Himself. His instruments have no consciousness of His purpose; if they imagine they have, it is a pretty sure token that they are *not* His instruments . . . God's ways are in nothing more mysterious than in this matter of trying to do good.'

Elizabeth Peabody outlived both Hawthorne and his wife by a generation, and became known as 'the grandmother of Boston.' She continued to attend every lecture, and William James declared that her perennial curiosity made her 'the most dissolute woman' in the city. Though Henry James denied that he had her in mind while creating Miss Birdseye in *The Bostonians,* Van Wyck Brooks maintains, in his charming thumbnail sketch of her, that the likeness exists none the less.

thank Him, not less fervently, for being one step further from them in the march of ages.'

It is small wonder, therefore, that turning away from what he considered the unrelieved gloom of *The Scarlet Letter,* he thought *The Seven Gables* 'more characteristic of my mind, and more proper and natural for me to write.' The measure in which he intended the latter book as a criticism of his own age is somewhat obscured by his treatment of time. Even while he was examining his changing New England, he felt the past weighing heavily on the present's back. Unlike virtually all the other spokesmen for his day, he could never feel that America was a new world. Looking back over the whole history of his province, he was more struck by decay than by potentiality, by the broken ends to which the Puritan effort had finally come, by the rigidity that had been integral to its thought at its best, by modes of life in which nothing beautiful had developed. Furthermore, his contemporaries seemed still to be branded with lasting marks from the weight and strain of such effort. He was often reflecting on the loss in vitality, on such facts as that the 'broad shoulders and well-developed busts' of the women of Hester Prynne's day had long since tended, along with their 'boldness and rotundity of speech,' to wither away like trees transplanted in too thin a soil. Even at Brook Farm, he had not been able to share in the declaration that the new age was the dawn of untried possibilities. Even there he had thought about how much old material enters into the freshest novelty, about the ages of experience that had passed over the world, about the fact that the very ground under their feet was 'fathom-deep with the dust of deluded generations, on every one of which, as on ourselves, the world had imposed itself as a hitherto unwedded bride.'

Consequently, as he meditated on time in this story of the old house with its 'mysterious and terrible past,' the present often seemed 'this visionary and impalpable Now, which, if you once look closely at it, is nothing.' He was not, however, in any doubt as to the focus of his plot; in fact, he held that the only basis for calling this book a romance rather than a novel was its attempt 'to connect a bygone time with the very present that is flitting away from us. It is a legend prolonging itself . . . down into our own broad daylight.' His treatment of this legend constituted his nearest approach to everyday contemporary life, since he did not cast it in the special circumstances of a Utopian community or of an art-colony, but chose materials more naturally at hand.

His attitude towards them was in no sense different from that in his other books. He was always concerned with the enduring elements in human nature, but the structure he devised here enabled him to disclose better than elsewhere how 'the Colonel Pyncheon of two centuries ago steps forward as the Judge of the passing moment.' As a result Lowell wrote at once to tell him that this book was 'the most valuable contribution to New England history that has been made,' since it typified the intimate connections between heredity and descent, which more mechanical historians had failed to establish. On the other hand, James, sending a letter half a century later to the celebration at Salem of its novelist's centenary, was impressed most by the 'presentness,' by Hawthorne's instinctive gift in finding his romance, 'the quaintness or the weirdness, the interest *behind* the interest of things, as continuous with the very life we are leading . . . round about him and under his eyes.' He saw it in *The Seven Gables* 'as something deeply within us, not as something infinitely disconnected from us,' and could consequently make this book a 'singularly fruitful' example 'of the real as distinguished from the artificial romantic note.' Therefore, it will serve better than any of his others to answer the first of our two main questions about his equipment for writing tragedy: to what degree could he conceive of individuals who were representative of a whole interrelated condition of society?

The seventeenth-century house, grown black in the prevailing east wind, itself took on the status of a major theme. Hawthorne wrote to Fields that 'many passages of this book ought to be finished with the minuteness of a Dutch picture, in order to give them their proper effect'; and that aim can be read in his careful drawing of the thick central chimney, the gigantic elm at the door, the long-since exhausted garden, the monotony of occurrences in the by-street in which the mansion now fronts, the faint stir of the outside world as heard in the church bells or the far whistle of a train.[5] As he dwelt on this example of 'the best and stateliest architecture' in a town whose houses, unaccountably to our eyes, generally struck him as having little pretense to varied beauty, he

5. In one of the passages discussing his slow progress in appreciating the beauties of Rome, Hawthorne added: 'It is the sign, I presume, of a taste still very defective, that I take singular pleasure in the elaborate imitations of Van Mieris, Gerard Dow, and other old Dutch wizards, who painted such brass pots that you can see your face in them, and such earthen pots that they will surely hold water; and who spent weeks and months in turning a foot or two of canvas into a perfect microscopic illusion of some homely scene.'

could feel that it had been 'the scene of events more full of human interest, perhaps, than those of a gray feudal castle.' This is worth noting since he seems to have forgotten it by the time he was writing the preface to *The Marble Faun,* where, developing the thought that romance needs ruin to make it grow, he took the conventional attitude about the thinness of material for the artist in America. Since this, in turn, gave the lead to James' famous enumeration of all 'the items of high civilization,' all the complexity of customs and manners that were left out of Hawthorne's scene, it is important that the Hawthorne of *The Seven Gables* believed that no matter how familiar and humble its incidents, 'they had the earth-smell in them.' He believed far more than that, for within the oak frame of the house, 'so much of mankind's varied experience had passed . . . so much had been suffered, and something, too, enjoyed, that . . . it was itself like a great human heart, with a life of its own, and full of rich and sombre reminiscences.'

These furnished him with several other themes that were central to American history. The old spinster Hepzibah Pyncheon, at the opening of the book the sole possessor of the dark recesses of the mansion, is the embodiment of decayed gentility, sustained only by her delusion of family importance, lacking any revivifying touch with outward existence. Hawthorne knew how fully her predicament corresponded to the movement of the age, since 'in this republican country, amid the fluctuating waves of our social life, somebody is always at the drowning-point.' He made the young reformer Holgrave confront her with the unreality of her existence by declaring that the names of gentleman and lady, though they had once had a meaning and had conferred a value on their owners, 'in the present—and still more in the future condition of society—they imply, not privilege, but restriction!' Indeed, by imprisoning herself so long in one place and in the unvarying round of a single chain of ideas, Hepzibah had grown to be a kind of lunatic, pathetic in her efforts to merge with human sympathies, since no longer capable of doing so. Hawthorne posed her genteel helplessness against the demurely charming self-reliance of her niece Phoebe. By pointing out that it was owing to her father's having married beneath his rank that Phoebe possessed such plebeian capabilities as being able to manage a kitchen or conduct a school, Hawthorne deliberately etched a contrast between the Pyncheon family and the rising democracy. This contrast is sustained even down to the inbred hens in the garden, who have a 'rusty, withered aspect, and a gouty kind of movement,' in consequence of too strict a watchfulness to maintain their purity of race. This accords again with Holgrave's statement to Phoebe that 'once in every half-century, at longest, a family should be merged into the great, obscure mass of humanity, and forget all about its ancestors. Human blood, in order to keep its freshness, should run in hidden streams.'

But there is more substance to Hawthorne's contrast than the tenuous if accurate notation of the gradual waning of the aristocracy, as against the solidly based energy of common life. He had observed in one of his early sketches of Salem that the influence of wealth and the sway of class 'had held firmer dominion here than in any other New England town'; and he now traced those abuses to their source. The original power of the Pyncheons had been founded on a great wrong: the very land on which the house was built had first been occupied by the thatched hut of Matthew Maule, who had settled there because of the spring of fresh water, 'a rare treasure on the sea-girt peninsula.' But as the town expanded during its first generation, this treasure took on the aspect of a desired asset in real estate to the eyes of Colonel Pyncheon. A man of iron energy of purpose in obtaining whatever he had set his mind upon, he asserted a plausible claim to Maule's lot and a large adjacent tract of land, on the strength of a prior grant.

Hawthorne's treatment of this material is characteristic of his effort to suggest social complexity. He stated that since no written record of the dispute remained in existence, he could merely enter the doubt as to whether the Colonel's claim had not been unduly stretched. What strengthened that suspicion was the fact that notwithstanding the inequality of the two antagonists, in a period when well-to-do personal influence had great hereditary weight, the dispute remained unsettled for years and came to a close only with the death of Maule, who had clung stubbornly to what he considered his right. Moreover, the manner of his death affected the mind differently than it had at the time, since he was executed as one of the obscure 'martyrs to that terrible delusion, which should teach us, among its other morals, that the influential classes, and those who take upon themselves to be leaders of the people, are fully liable to all the passionate error that has ever characterized the maddest mob.' In the general frenzy it was hardly noted that Colonel Pyncheon had applied his whole bitter force to the persecution of Maule, though by stressing this origin of the condemned man's curse upon his enemy—

'God will give him blood to drink'—Hawthorne recognized how economic motives could enter even into the charge of witchcraft.

By the time the justification for that curse began to be whispered around, the mansion was built, and 'there is something so massive, stable, and almost irresistibly imposing in the exterior presentment of established rank and great possessions, that their very existence seems to give them a right to exist; at least, so excellent a counterfeit of right, that few poor and humble men have moral force enough to question it.' The Maules, at any rate, kept their resentment to themselves; and as the generations went on, they were usually poverty-stricken, always plebeian. They worked with 'unsuccessful diligence' at handicrafts, labored on the wharves, or went to sea before the mast. They lived here and there about the town in tenements, and went to the almshouse 'as the natural home of their old age.' Finally they had taken 'the downright plunge' that awaits all families; and for the past thirty years no one of their name had appeared in the local directory.

The main theme that Hawthorne evolved from this history of the Pyncheons and the Maules was not the original curse on the house, but the curse that the Pyncheons have continued to bring upon themselves. Clifford may phrase it wildly in his sense of release at the Judge's death: 'What we call real estate—the solid ground to build a house on—is the broad foundation on which nearly all the guilt of this world rests. A man will commit almost any wrong,—he will heap up an immense pile of wickedness, as hard as granite, and which will weigh as heavily upon his soul, to eternal ages,—only to build a great gloomy, dark-chambered mansion, for himself to die in, and for his posterity to be miserable in.' But this also corresponds to Hawthorne's view in his preface, a view from which the dominating forces of his country had just begun to diverge most widely with the opening of California: 'the folly of tumbling down an avalanche of ill-gotten gold, or real estate, on the heads of an unfortunate posterity, thereby to maim and crush them, until the accumulated mass shall be scattered abroad in its original atoms.' Hawthorne's objections to the incumbrance of property often ran close to Thoreau's.

What Hawthorne set himself to analyze is this 'energy of disease,' this lust for wealth that has held the dominating Pyncheons in its inflexible grasp. After their original victory, their drive for power had long since shifted its ground, but had retained its form of oppressing the poor, for the present Judge steps forward to seize the property of his feeble cousins

Hepzibah and Clifford, with the same cold unscrupulousness that had actuated the original Colonel in his dealings with the Maules. The only variation is that, 'as is customary with the rich, when they aim at the honors of a republic,' he had learned the expediency, which had not been forced upon his freer ancestor, of masking his relentless will beneath a veneer of 'paternal benevolence.' Thus what Hawthorne saw handed down from one generation to another were not—and this paradoxical phrase was marked by Melville—'the big, heavy, solid unrealities' such as gold and hereditary position, but inescapable traits of character.

He did not, however, make the mistake of simplifying, by casting all his Pyncheons into one monotonous image. If the Judge typified the dominant strain in the family, Clifford, the most complex character in the book, could stand for the recessive. His gently sensuous, almost feminine face had received years ago its perfect recording in a Malbone miniature, since as a young man he had loved just such delicate charm. Hawthorne suggested the helplessness of his aesthetic temperament before the ruthless energy of the Judge, by saying that any conflict between them would be 'like flinging a porcelain vase, with already a crack in it, against a granite column.' By using that symbolic, almost Jamesian image, he gave further embodiment to the kind of contrast he had drawn between Owen Warland and his hostile environment. His implications also extended beyond the Pyncheon family, for the hard competitive drives that had crushed many potentialities of richer, less aggressive living, had been a distorting factor throughout the length of American experience.

But Hawthorne made no effort to idealize Clifford. Holgrave calls him an 'abortive lover of the beautiful,' and it is true that the fragile mainspring of his life has been shattered by his long imprisonment for the supposed murder of his uncle. This punishment had been especially cruel since the old man had actually died of an apoplectic seizure, the traditional Pyncheon disease, but under such suspicious circumstances that his other nephew Jaffrey, who coveted the whole inheritance, could cause it to appear an act of violence. As a result he had gained the fortune on which he was to build the career that led to the eminent respectability of a judgeship; and Hepzibah was left with only the life occupancy of the house. And to the house she clung tenaciously, though its proper maintenance was far beyond her impoverished means, in the hope that is finally realized, of welcoming home her brother after his belated release. But the man who returns no longer possesses any intellectual or moral fibre to control his sensibility. His tastes express themselves only in a selfish demand for luxuries and in an animal delight in food, an exaggeration of the defects that Hawthorne always felt to lie as a danger for the artistic temperament, whose too exclusive fondness for beauty might end by wearing away all human affections. Clifford has retrogressed until he is hardly more than an idiot, a spoiled child who takes a childish pleasure in any passing attraction that can divert him from the confused memories of his terrible years of gloom. But, occasionally, deeper forces stir within him, as one day when he is watching, from the arched window at the head of the stairs, a political procession of marching men with fifes and drums. With a sudden, irrepressible gesture, from which he is restrained just in time by Hepzibah and Phoebe, he starts forward as though to jump down into the street, in a kind of desperate effort at renewed contact with life outside himself, 'but whether impelled by the species of terror that sometimes urges its victim over the very precipice which he shrinks from, or by a natural magnetism, tending towards the great centre of humanity,' Hawthorne found it not easy to decide.

Melville considered this one of the two most impressive scenes in the book; and the currents that are stirring here rise to their climax in the chapter in which Hawthorne's imagination moves most freely, 'The Flight of Two Owls,' the poignant account of how Hepzibah is swept away by her brother's strange exhilaration at finding the Judge, who had come to threaten him, dead of a seizure. Clifford is now determined to leave the whole past behind, and impels Hepzibah to start off at once with him crazily in the rain. With no definite goal, his attention is suddenly attracted by a feature of the Salem scene unknown at the time of his imprisonment, a train at the depot. Before Hepzibah can protest, they are aboard and are started on a local towards Portsmouth. The fact that Hawthorne had made a record in his notebook, just the year before, of this very trip, seems to have helped him to catch the rhythm of kaleidoscopic impressions into which the two old people are caught up. With a giddy sense that he has finally merged with life, Clifford's excitement mounts in ever more reckless talk with a man across the aisle, in which Hawthorne ironically makes him develop the transcendental doctrine that evil is bound to disappear in the ascending spiral of human improvement. But just as the hard-eyed stranger's suspicions of his insanity are crystallizing into certitude, Clifford is seized by the impulse that he has now gone far enough. Taking advantage of the fact that the train has stopped for a moment, he again draws the bewildered Hepzibah after him and both get off. Another moment and they are alone on the open platform of a deserted way-station, under a sullen rain-swept sky. Clifford's unreal courage deserts him all at once, and he is once more helplessly dependent on his sister to get him home. The impression that Hawthorne has thus created of their solitude, of their decrepit inexperience in an uncomprehending and hostile world, may well have been part of the stimulus for the most effectively intense chapter in *Pierre,* where the adolescent couple arrive in New York at night, for the luridly brutal first impact of corruption upon innocence.

Still another theme is introduced through the role that is played by Holgrave. At the start of the book Hepzibah has taken him as her sole lodger, though she has become increasingly startled by his strange companions, 'men with long beards, and dressed in linen blouses, and other such new-fangled and ill-fitting garments; reformers, temperance lecturers, and all manner of cross-looking philanthropists; community-men, and come-outers, as Hepzibah believed, who acknowledged no law, and ate no solid food.' Moreover, she has read a paragraph in a paper accusing him of delivering a speech 'full of wild and disorganizing matter.' But though this has made her have misgivings whether she ought not send him away, she has to admit from her own contact with him that even by her formal standards he is a quiet and orderly young man. His first effect on Phoebe, after she has come to visit her aunt and really to take over the burden of running the house, is more disquieting, for his conversation seemed 'to unsettle everything around her, by his lack of reverence for what was fixed.'

In unrolling Holgrave's past history, which is made up in part from the histories of various characters whom Hawthorne had picked up in his country rambles, the novelist made clear that he believed he was tapping one of the richest sources of native material. He said at more explicit length than was customary to him: 'A romance on the plan of Gil Blas, adapted to American society and manners, would cease to be a romance. The experience of many individuals among us, who think it hardly worth the telling, would equal the vicissitudes of the Spaniard's earlier life; while their ultimate success, or the point whither they tend, may be incomparably higher than any that a novelist would imagine for his hero.' Holgrave himself told Phoebe somewhat proudly that he

. . . could not boast of his origin, unless as being exceedingly humble, nor of his education, except that it had been the scantiest possible, and obtained by a few winter-months' attendance at a district school. Left early to his own guidance, he had begun to be self-dependent while yet a boy; and it was a condition aptly suited to his natural force of will. Though now but twenty-two years old (lacking some months, which are years in such a life), he had already been, first, a country schoolmaster; next, a salesman in a country store; and either at the same time or afterwards, the political editor of a country newspaper. He had subsequently travelled New England and the Middle States, as a pedlar, in the employment of a Connecticut manufactory of cologne-water and other essences. In an episodical way he had studied and practiced dentistry, and with very flattering success, especially in many of the factory-towns along our inland streams. As a supernumerary official, of some kind or other, aboard a packet-ship, he had visited Europe, and found means, before his return, to see Italy, and part of France and Germany. At a later period he had spent some months in a community of Fourierists. Still more recently he had been a public lecturer on Mesmerism.

His present phase, as a daguerreotypist, was no more likely to be permanent than any of the preceding ones. He had taken it up 'with the careless alacrity of an adventurer, who had his bread to earn.'

Yet homeless as he had been, and continually changing his whereabouts, 'and, therefore, responsible neither to public opinion nor to individuals,' he had never violated his inner integrity of conscience, as Phoebe soon came to recognize. His hatred of the dead burden of the past was as thoroughgoing as possible; but he had read very little, and though he considered himself a thinker, with his own path to discover, he 'had perhaps hardly yet reached the point where an educated man begins to think.' 'Altogether in his culture and want of culture'—as Hawthorne summed him up, somewhat laboriously, but with telling accuracy—'in his crude, wild, and misty philosophy, and the practical experience that counteracted some of its tendencies; in his magnanimous zeal for man's welfare, and his recklessness of whatever the ages had established in man's behalf; in his faith, and in his infidelity; in what he had and in what he lacked,—the artist might fitly enough stand forth as the representative of many compeers in his native land.' His saving grace was the absence of arrogance in his ideas, which could otherwise have become those of a crank. He had learned enough of the world to be perplexed by it, and to begin to suspect 'that a man's bewilderment is

the measure of his wisdom.' Melville checked that, as he did also the reflection that it would be hard to prefigure Holgrave's future, since in this
country we are always meeting such jacks-of-all-trades, 'for whom we
anticipate wonderful things, but of whom, even after much and careful
inquiry, we never happen to hear another word.' In short, Hawthorne
has presented a detailed portrait of one of Emerson's promising Young ←
Americans.[6]

The course that is actually foreshadowed for him is devastating in its
limitations. In consequence of the awakening of his love for Phoebe and
her acceptance of him, society no longer looks hostile. When Phoebe is
afraid that he will lead her out of her own quiet path, he already knows
that the influence is likely to be all the other way. As he says, 'the world
owes all its onward impulses to men ill at ease,' and he has a presentiment that it will hereafter be his lot to set out trees and to make fences,
and to build a house for another generation. Thus he admits, with a half-
melancholy laugh, that he feels the traditional values already asserting
their power over him, even while he and Phoebe are still standing
under the gaze of the portrait of Colonel Pyncheon, whom Holgrave
recognizes as 'a model conservative, who, in that very character, rendered
himself so long the evil destiny of his race.'

The conclusion of this book has satisfied very few. Although Phoebe's   *Conclusion*
marriage with Holgrave, who discloses himself at length as a descendant

6. Even Emerson, glutton for punishment though he was, finally reached the point where
he refused to be excited by any more Charles Newcombs as potential Shakespeares. He
wrote in his journal for 1842: 'When I saw the sylvan youth, I said, "Very good promise,
but I cannot now watch any more buds": like the good Grandfather when they brought
him the twentieth babe, he declined the dandling, he had said "Kitty, Kitty," long enough.'
Hawthorne's analysis is also akin to the formulation which James made of the New
England character in one of his early reviews (of Guérin's *Letters*, 1866): 'A very good
man or a very good woman in New England is an extremely complex being. They are as
innocent as you please, but they are anything but ignorant. They travel; they hold political
opinions; they are accomplished Abolitionists; they read magazines and newspapers, and
write for them; they read novels and police reports; they subscribe to lyceum lectures and
to great libraries; in a word, they are enlightened. The result of this freedom of enquiry
is that they become profoundly self-conscious.' This formulation led in turn to the kind of
world James tried to project in *The Bostonians* (1886), where the mixture of reformers
and blue-stockings is a late aftershine of Brook Farm and *Blithedale*. The general quality
of mind common to both Holgrave and to James' New England type is the strain of exposed consciousness, which James could observe in his contemporaries just as Hawthorne
had in his. This gives the most explicit reason for the continuity between them in the
development of their inward subject-matter.

of the Maules, is meant finally to transcend the old brutal separation of classes that has hardened the poor family against its oppressors, the reconciliation is somewhat too lightly made. It is quite out of keeping with Hawthorne's seemingly deliberate answer in his preface to the new thought's doctrine of Compensation, of the way good arises out of evil. For Hawthorne said there that his book might illustrate the truth 'that the wrong-doing of one generation lives into the successive ones, and, divesting itself of every temporary advantage, becomes a pure and uncontrollable mischief.' That unrelenting strain was still at the fore in his final reflections about Clifford. Although his feeble spirits revived once the Judge's death had removed him from the sphere of that malevolent influence, 'after such wrong as he had suffered, there is no reparation . . . No great mistake, whether acted or endured, in our mortal sphere, is ever really set right. Time, the continual vicissitude of circumstances, and the invariable inopportunity of death, render it impossible. If, after long lapse of years, the right seems to be in our power, we find no niche to set it in.'

In contrast to that tragic thought, Hawthorne's comparatively flimsy interpretation of the young lovers derives from the fact that he has not visualized their future with any precision. Trollope objected to this on the basic level of plot: 'the hurrying up of the marriage, and all the dollars which they inherit from the wicked Judge, and the "handsome dark-green barouche" prepared for their departure, which is altogether unfitted to the ideas which the reader has formed respecting them, are quite unlike Hawthorne, and would seem almost to have been added by some every-day, beef-and-ale, realistic novelist, into whose hands the unfinished story had unfortunately fallen.' As they leave for the new country house that has tumbled into their hands, they seem to have made the successful gesture of renouncing the worst of the past. The tone of the last page could hardly be more different from that of the end of *The Cherry Orchard,* where Chekhov dwells not on what lies ahead, but on the mingled happiness and despair that have been interwoven with the old house. But the Russian was aware of the frustration and impending breakdown of a whole social class, whereas Hawthorne assumed with confidence the continuance of democratic opportunity. Yet in the poetic justice of bestowing opulence on all those who had previously been deprived of it by the Judge, Hawthorne overlooked the fact that he was sowing all over again the same seeds of evil.

The world that both Phoebe and Holgrave had previously belonged to, as conservative and radical manifestations, was the New England into which both Sophia and Hawthorne had been born. Julian Hawthorne suggested its engaging innocence in the same passage where he commented on the democratic closeness between work and culture: [7]

> Plain living and high thinking can seldom have been more fully united and exemplified than in certain circles of Boston and Salem during the first thirty or forty years of this century . . . Religious feeling was deep and earnest, owing in part to the recent schism between the severe and liberal interpretations of Christian destiny and obligations; and the development of commerce and other material interests had not more than foreshadowed its present proportions, nor distracted people's attention from less practical matters. Such a state of things can hardly be reproduced, and, in our brief annals, possesses some historic value.[8]

But the implications that lay ahead in the young couple's inheritance of several hundred thousand were equally beyond both Hawthorne's experience and imagination. He took for granted that in a democratic society the domineering influence of private wealth would not be able to hold the evil sway that it did in the narrowly autocratic era of Colonel Pyncheon. But the fact that he hardly cast a glance to examine what would prevail at the Holgraves' countryseat, prevented him from suggesting their participation in any definite state of existence, as, for instance, Tolstoy could suggest the Russia of which Pierre and Natasha had become part at the close of *War and Peace*.

Out of his savage revulsion from the America that had followed—the America of Sinclair Lewis' early satires, whose roots Veblen had probed with deeper thoroughness—Lawrence could make his free interpretation

7. See p. 97 above.

8. One thing apparently overlooked in this survey, and, despite Ripley's trenchant articles in *The Harbinger*, hardly seen in adequate proportion by most of the community at Brook Farm was the emerging labor movement, dating from the late eighteen-twenties. The falseness of Van Wyck Brooks' remark 'that there were not wanting well-informed observers who were to assert, in later years, that from the Farm had sprung the movement of organized labor in New England and throughout the nation,' can be easily demonstrated by Norman Ware's monograph, *The Industrial Worker*, 1840-60 (1924), one of the best studies we yet have of a period in our labor history. It is important to check the community's somewhat unfounded idealism by such a realistic resolution as that of the Laborers' Union of South Boston in 1845, passed with Brook Farm in mind: 'That as practical laborers who have not the means or the inclination to withdraw from society, we deem it incumbent on us to use all the means in our power to remove existing evils from the present state of society.'

of Hawthorne's conclusion: 'The new generation is having no ghosts
or cobwebs. It is setting up in the photography line, and is just going
to make a sound financial thing out of it.' With all the old hates swept
out of sight, 'the vendetta-born young couple effect a perfect understanding under the black cloth of a camera and prosperity. *Vivat industria!*
. . . How you'd have *hated* it if you'd had nothing but the prosperous,
"dear" young couple to write about! If you'd lived to the day when
America was nothing but a Main Street.'[9]

Hawthorne's inability, despite all his latent irony, to conceive any such
world, made Eliot reflect, when he was about to start *The Waste Land*,
that the thinness of the novelist's milieu was owing to no lack of intellectual life, but to the fact that 'it was not corrupt enough.' This circumstance involved also 'the difficult fact that the soil which produced him
with his essential flavor is the soil which produced, just as inevitably, the
environment which stunted him.' What that means in the evidence furnished by *The Seven Gables* is that Hawthorne could conceive evil in
the world, but not an evil world. As a result his final pages drift away
into unreal complacence. No such blindness is to be found in his direct

9. Lawrence, who could not bear any of Hawthorne's young girls, might have been
better pleased with this picture, in *Our Old Home,* of the typical British female: 'I have
heard a good deal of the tenacity with which English ladies retain their personal beauty to
a late period of life; but (not to suggest that an American eye needs use and cultivation
before it can quite appreciate the charm of English beauty at any age) it strikes me that
an English lady of fifty is apt to become a creature less refined and delicate, so far as her
physique goes, than anything that we Western people class under the name of woman.
She has an awful ponderosity of frame, not pulpy, like the looser development of our few
fat women, but massive with solid beef and streaky tallow; so that (though struggling
manfully against the idea) you inevitably think of her as made up of steaks and sirloins.
When she walks, her advance is elephantine. When she sits down, it is on a great round
space of her Maker's footstool, where she looks as if nothing could ever move her . . .
Without anything positively salient, or actively offensive, or, indeed, unjustly formidable
to her neighbors, she has the effect of a seventy-four gun-ship in time of peace; for, while
you assure yourself that there is no real danger, you cannot help thinking how tremendous
would be her onset if pugnaciously inclined, and how futile the effort to inflict any counter-
injury . . .
'You can meet this figure in the street, and live, and even smile at the recollection. But
conceive of her in a ballroom, with the bare, brawny arms that she invariably displays
there, and all the other corresponding development, such as is beautiful in the maiden blossom, but a spectacle to howl at in such an over-blown cabbage rose as this . . . I wonder
whether a middle-aged husband ought to be considered as legally married to all the accretions that have overgrown the slenderness of his bride, since he led her to the altar, and
which make her so much more than he ever bargained for!'

reckoning with the forces surrounding him and with the problem of embracing them in an imaginative construction. He never ceased to be acutely conscious of the difficulty in doing what he wanted most, of opening an intercourse with society. He was aware that he was presenting in *The Seven Gables* hardly more of society's larger movements than could be glimpsed in 'one of the retired streets of a not very populous city.' He knew how hard it was to make his slender store of homely details extend over the surfaces of a whole book, for, no matter how authentic, their poverty would be revealed by the diffuseness with which they were spun out. But his basic problem was even harder, and was always the same, no matter what his chosen material: how was he to bridge the gap between foreground and background, how to suggest the whole scene of which his characters were part?

He never really succeeded. Although he could see his characters in a definite environment, he could not give the sense of their being in continuous contact with that larger outside world. It seems in his pages more like a backdrop than an enfolding atmosphere. He spoke apologetically in *Blithedale* of his method of 'insulating' his few characters from other relations in order to keep them so long upon his 'mental stage, as actors in a drama.' The resulting isolation enforces itself in a double degree: not only do they seem to be cut off from any full participation in society beyond their immediate circle, but, in addition, with the absence of the usual novelist's filling of other people and events, you become conscious of how Hawthorne's customary four or five principals are separated one from another by wide, unoccupied spaces. They often seem to move in a void as lonely as that which, notwithstanding the smallness of their seventeenth-century village, kept Hester and Dimmesdale from meeting by themselves for seven years. Furthermore, when Hawthorne centers directly on the presentation of his individuals, he can ordinarily manage no more than to give a careful notation of their traits—as we have just seen with Holgrave—instead of revealing them gradually through significant incidents. Even in their conflicts with one another, description nearly always usurps the place of immediate action. Hawthorne tells us that Hepzibah has struggled through a scene 'of passion and terror' in confronting the Judge; we recognize it, but we hardly feel it directly. Drama, at least the highly realized form that Granville-Barker speaks of, was beyond him: he could not project individuals against a fully developed society. For no such thing had yet been evolved in the individualistic career of our democracy.

'zeitgeist'

What is too often neglected in the current demand that a work of art should be a criticism of its age is that it becomes so, not by a mere frontal attack, not by virtue of any abstract statements of right and wrong, nor by bare demonstrations of social and economic abuses, but by the degree to which it can create a sustained vision of man's existence. Such a vision possesses validity and urgency just in proportion as it corresponds to *felt* experience. Hawthorne recognized this fact, in remarking in his preface to *The Seven Gables* that 'when romances do really teach anything, or produce any effective operation, it is usually through a far more subtle process than the ostensible one.' By subscribing to Hawthorne's success in doing that very thing in this book, Melville arrived at his conception of the way in which the artist creates 'the usable truth,' 'the absolute condition of present things as they strike the eye of the man who fears them not.' Although neither Hawthorne nor Melville would have thought in such terms, they were not unaware of what Engels later formulated concerning the role of the artist in contrast to that of the social theorist: 'The father of tragedy, Aeschylus, and the father of comedy, Aristophanes, were both very clearly poets with a thesis, as were Dante and Cervantes . . . But I believe that the thesis must inhere in the situation and the action, without being explicitly formulated; and it is not the poet's duty to supply the reader in advance with the future historical solution of the conflict he describes.'

Measured by the standard of this reasoning, Hawthorne fulfilled his chief function, since his work was a mirror of its age by virtue both of its searching honesty and of its inevitable unconscious limitations. His relative satisfaction, looking home from Italy, with our 'peaceful hum of prosperity and content,' his innocence of what lay ahead, are comprehensible in the special circumstances of his province, whose main drive towards industrialization had only just been launched. When he wrote, a decade after *The Seven Gables,* about his European experiences, he ended his chapter on English poverty with a deepened awareness of what he had slurred over in his novel, and with at least a faint perception of the need for collectivism: 'Is, or is not, the system wrong that gives one married pair so immense a superfluity of luxurious home, and shuts out a million others from any home whatever? One day or another, safe as they deem themselves, and safe as the hereditary temper of the people really tends to make them, the gentlemen of England will be compelled to face this question.'

p. 322 – 336 are reproduced in "C.20 Views", ed. Kaul. p. 141 on

2. Hawthorne's Psychology: The Acceptance of Good and Evil

THAT there are aspects of art which can hardly be reached by the scalpels of economic and social analysis was maintained by Yeats' belief that poetry is not 'a criticism of life' but 'a revelation of a hidden life.' This belief would unquestionably have been accepted by Hawthorne, who declared in one of his processional sketches—in another sentence marked by Melville—that human nature can be more truly represented in the wishes of its heart than in its actions, since such a portrayal has 'more of good and more of evil in it; more redeeming points of the bad and more errors of the virtuous; higher upsoarings, and baser degradations of the soul; in short, a more perplexing amalgamation of vice and virtue than we witness in the outward world.'

Why Hawthorne held this has been explained in part by such circumstances of his biography as we have dwelt on; and those circumstances were conditioned in turn by the centrifugal movement of American society. In like fashion, his conception of good and evil, which drove him to take the tragic view of life, might also be accounted for by his background, by his relation to a particular phase of the decay of the Puritan tradition. But unless the explaining of such things be considered an explaining away, unless all religious belief is held to be merely deluded fantasy to be dealt with only by the psychoanalyst, the value of Hawthorne's portrayal of spiritual conflict still remains to be reckoned with. This reckoning can be made only if we start from inside, so to speak— only if, instead of discounting his views as part of a world gone by, we try to experience to the full what he thought and felt about human destiny. For only then will we be in a position to test his interpretation against others, and against what we ourselves may believe to be primary forces in the universe.

Everywhere he looked he was struck by what, he conjectured, even

confused Clifford might have seen, 'in the mirror of his deeper consciousness': how 'he was an example and representative of that great
class of people whom an inexplicable Providence is continually putting at
cross-purposes with the world: breaking what seems its own promise in
their nature; withholding their proper food, and setting poison before
them for a banquet: and thus—when it might so easily, as one would
think, have been adjusted otherwise—making their existence a strangeness, a solitude, and torment.' It is no wonder that Holgrave went still
farther in his conclusions about the perverse labyrinth of circumstances.
Observing, as the ultimate reach of Pyncheon domineering, a timid spinster and a degraded and shattered gentleman, and thinking too of how his
own poor family had been kept out of its only inheritance, he could
see all the life that had passed within the house reduced to the reiterated
pattern of 'perpetual remorse of conscience, a constantly defeated hope,
strife amongst kindred, various misery, a strange form of death, dark suspicion, unspeakable disgrace.'

Such an accumulation of oppressive evil upon the roof of one family
hardly falls short of the terrible imagination of Aeschylus. Speaking from
the great range of his reading, More held (1904) that *The Seven Gables*
was the one companion in modern literature 'to the Orestean conception
of satiety begetting insolence, and insolence calling down upon a family
the inherited curse of Ate.' This kinship in theme also throws into relief
Hawthorne's difference from the Greeks in conceiving the operation of
a curse: not in sudden violent disasters so much as in the prolonged
'disease of inner solitude.' More recognized this as a consequence of
Hawthorne's particular Christian tradition: 'Not with impunity had the
human race for ages dwelt on the eternal welfare of the soul; for from
such meditation the sense of personal importance had become exacerbated
to an extraordinary degree. What could result from such teaching as
that of Jonathan Edwards but an extravagant sense of individual existence, as if the moral governance of the world revolved about the action
of each mortal soul?' Continuing this development to Hawthorne's day,
More held that with the loss of Edwards' intensity, with the partial waning of the old faith attendant on the introspection, there could only be
left a great residue of anguish and bereavement, a loneliness of the individual of 'a poignancy altogether unexampled.' Thus the most compact
examination of theological history brings us to the very point that we
have already reached in noting the effect of American social forces on an

individual like Hawthorne, who was not content with Emerson's new freedom of solitude.

It must be mentioned in passing that since More wrote, two other Americans have deliberately set themselves to re-create the Orestes story. O'Neill seems to have been drawn to it primarily as a means of projecting his sense of the violent decay of the New England heritage, and Eliot by his desire to relive a fundamental pattern of sin and suffering. Neither *Mourning Becomes Electra* nor *The Family Reunion* is one of the best works of its author, the one being especially clouded by half-assimilated Freud, the other presenting as its characters such a neutral and devitalized group of English gentry that most of the energy of the evil is lost. But it is not accidental that our modern writers,[1] with their sense of what has been implied for our society by Edwards' excessive conscience and by the moral preoccupation of Hawthorne and James, should, whether impelled by O'Neill's feeling of chaotic disintegration or by Eliot's belief in the need for regeneration, still create characters whose inner torment makes them imagine that they are followed by the furies.

Unlike these others, Hawthorne gave no indication that he was thinking of the example of Greek tragedy. But he did envisage his romance as the end of a drama, which, according to Holgrave, has been dragging its slow length over this very ground for so long that now at last 'Destiny is arranging its fifth act for a catastrophe.' Moreover, Hawthorne went so far with this analogy as to provide his scene with a Chorus. This is composed of the two laborers who, as the harsh voice of the world, comment loudly at the outset on old maid Pyncheon's folly in having opened a cent-shop under the front gable. One of them dug up her garden once, and knows that her scowl is enough to frighten Old Nick; while the other adds that when even so good a hand as his wife tried such a shop, she lost five dollars on her outlay. To Hepzibah, cowering inside her window on the first morning of this desperate venture to which she has been driven by her determination to keep the house ready for Clifford, the blank indifference of Dixey and his friend to either her dignity or her degradation 'fell upon her half-dead hope like a clod into a grave.'

The pair turn up again on the morning after the great storm, and seeing the shop door closed, repeat their same lines, unaware of the gulf

1. Robinson Jeffers has also retold the Greek story in 'The Tower Beyond Tragedy' and has stressed its incest theme as one of his many symbols for the violent consequences that have been produced by men's minds having been turned inward upon themselves.

between the petty failure over which they are gloating and the real state
of the house: from it the old brother and sister have fled; inside, alone,
sits a corpse. To clinch for the imagination how public opinion drifts
with appearances, Hawthorne gave the final speeches in the book to
the same pair. Their refrain is now different as they watch the Pyncheons
go away in their carriage: 'Pretty good business, pretty good business!'
They can understand this change as luck, but they can't 'exactly fathom
it . . . as the will of Providence'—a faint sign, at least, of Hawthorne's
own dissatisfaction with his close.

Hawthorne's tragic vision is hardly attested by his adoption of a few
of the devices of drama, but rather by his ability to endow such a pathetic
character as Hepzibah with a measure of heroic dignity. He presents her
absurd confusion of feelings as she stands behind her counter: her desire
to be treated like a lady, and her recoil from expressions of sympathy; her
inability to suppress a sense of superiority to her customers, and her bitter
virulence against 'the idle aristocracy,' to which she had so recently been
proud to belong. She had lived so long alone in the house that its dry-rot
had begun to eat into her mind. 'She needed'—and we know how much
Hawthorne implied in such a remark—'a walk along the noonday street
to keep her sane.'

He was aware of the problem with which he had confronted himself
by choosing for one of his protagonists not 'even the stately remains of
beauty, storm-shattered by affliction—but a gaunt, sallow, rusty-jointed
maiden, in a long-waisted silk gown, and with the strange horror of a
turban on her head.' Her insignificance was not even redeemed by real
ugliness, and her great life-trial 'seems to be, that, after sixty years of idleness, she finds it convenient to earn comfortable bread.' Yet Hawthorne
held that if a writer looked 'through all the heroic fortunes of mankind,'
he would find this same mixture of the mean and ludicrous in 'the purest
pathos which life anywhere supplies to him.' This was particularly the
case for anyone who wanted to represent human nature as it was in a
democracy, a truth that Melville was to proclaim later in this very year,
in his eloquent statement of the 'august dignity' to be found in his *dramatis personae,* the miscellaneous crew of a whaler. Hawthorne's lead to
a similar discovery lay in his final remark in the chapter wherein Hepzibah opened her shop: 'What is called poetic insight is the gift of discerning, in this sphere of strangely mingled elements, the beauty and
majesty which are compelled to assume a garb so sordid.' Again this dis-

covery is significantly close to Eliot's that 'the essential advantage for a poet is not, to have a beautiful world with which to deal: it is to be able to see beneath both beauty and ugliness; to see the boredom, and the horror, and the glory.' Hawthorne's belief in the dramatic reality of the issues of conscience can also be phrased most concisely in Eliot's statement, in *After Strange Gods,* that in moments of intense 'moral and spiritual struggle . . . men and women come nearest to being real.' In no conviction are the novelist and the poet more akin.

What Hawthorne could see in Hepzibah, and what Melville checked, was 'the moral force of a deeply grounded antipathy,' the strength of conscience that enabled her to stand up against the Judge and confront him with what he really was beneath the oily layers of respectability. Yet Hawthorne's somewhat wavering effort to create the scene that builds up to Hepzibah's moment is an exact instance of Whipple's observation that he was more interested in the conflict of ideas and passions than in the individuals who embodied them, that his characters were introduced 'not as thinking, but as the illustration of thought,' that he used them in order to express 'the last results of patient moral perception.'

Yet it was primarily by virtue of that perception that he broke through the individualism of his day to a reassertion not of man's idiosyncrasies, but of his elemental traits. It is no exaggeration to say that his recognition of the general bond of sin brought him closest to universality. He believed that 'man must not disclaim his brotherhood, even with the guiltiest, since, though his hand be clean, his heart has surely been polluted by the flitting phantoms of iniquity.' That bare, somewhat conventional statement of innate depravity is from one of his early sketches, but it formulates the conviction from which he never swerved. He possessed it, not as a result of any mere observation of mankind against the background of Puritan thought, but more especially in consequence of the sense of personal guilt that sprang from his dread that such a detached observer as himself was failing to participate adequately in life. Yet even such an explanation is oversimplified, and we may better describe his essential state of mind by saying that he felt in himself the presence of both Pyncheons and Maules.

When Eliot said once that you cannot understand James' quality of horror without knowing Hawthorne, he extended both background and foreground by remarking that both Judge John Hathorne and his own first American ancestor, Andrew Eliot, had been among the witch hangers. Hawthorne's imagination had not been able to rest content with its atonement, in 'The Gentle Boy,' for his first ancestor, Major William Hathorne's cruelty to the Quakers. He also remembered that in the next generation Judge Hathorne's peculiar severity towards a woman in the witch trials had called out from her husband the prophecy that God would take revenge upon such persecutors. This clearly gave Hawthorne the hint for the curse pronounced by Maule, whose name, incidentally, he had found in Felt's *Annals of Salem,* where one Thomas Maule appears as a sympathizer with the Quakers and as the author of a tract called *Truth Held Forth,* whose career involved being flogged for saying that the Reverend Mr. Higginson 'preached lies.'

One aspect of Maule's curse in operation was the mysterious disappearance of the title to a vast estate in Waldo County, in the vain dream of recovering which many Pyncheons had wasted their lives. Such a refraction of the American dream had been intertwined with his own family's waning fortunes, in the tradition that his mother's kin had been deprived of many acres in Raymond, Maine, through the loss of a deed. This tradition may not seem to have much to do with Hawthorne's sense of sin, yet it entered into his separation from the dominant Salem world to which his ancestors had belonged. In this way he became partly identified with the dispossessed Maules, whom he describes as having been marked off from other men—'not strikingly,' but 'by an hereditary characteristic of reserve.' Moreover, as Holgrave recognizes his share in other traits of the Maules, some of them are likewise those which Hawthorne felt dangerous in himself. His cool habit of scrutinizing the characters of others, which is symbolized by his daguerreotype portraits, causes the young man to say to Phoebe that this tendency, taken together with his faculty of mesmerism, might have brought him to Gallows Hill in the old days. As far as Holgrave's own career is concerned, the novelist makes clear that his unscrupulous power of analysis, his seeming lack of reverence for anyone else, inculcated in him by his feeling that the world's hand is against him, is saved from hardening into fatal arrogance by the birth of his love for Phoebe—which was also one of Hawthorne's names for his bird-like Sophia.

Seen thus, the common denominator between Holgrave and Judge Pyncheon and even Hepzibah, as well as between Hollingsworth and Ethan Brand and a dozen others, consists in pride, the worst sin in Dante's theology as well as in Milton's and Edwards'. In his stress on this sin Hawthorne's sense of innate depravity and his sense of social isolation are united. Not sin, but its consequence for human lives is Hawthorne's major theme. Newton Arvin, whose study of him (1929) contains some of the most incisive social criticism to have been stimulated by the earlier work of Van Wyck Brooks, was the first to make the linkage between this theme and the major problem of American society, its continual dissidence and dispersion. In the most eloquent passage of his book, a declaration of our newer mutual dependence, Arvin summed up the significance of our historical drift:

What have been our grand national types of personality? The explorer, with his face turned toward the unknown; the adventurous colonist; the Protestant sectarian, determined to worship his own God even in the wilderness; the Baptist, the Quaker, the Methodist; the freebooter and the smuggler; the colonial revolutionary; the pioneer, with his chronic defections; the sectional patriot and the secessionist; the come-outer, the claim-jumper, the Mormon, the founder of communities; the Transcendentalist, preaching the gospel of self-reliance; the philosophic anarchist in his hut in the woods; the economic individualist and the captain of industry; the go-getter, the tax-dodger, the bootlegger. The best and the worst of humanity, not to be confounded in one gesture of repudiation, but united after all in their common distrust of centrality, their noble or their ignoble lawlessness, their domination by spiritual pride. United in their refusal to work together on any but a false basis. United, finally, in paying the penalty for disunion—in becoming partial and lopsided personalities, men and women of one dimension, august or vulgar cranks. How can we forget the Dimmesdales and Hollingsworths and Pyncheons who have divided our life among them?

That Arvin's words can rise to such a pitch of feeling is evidence of another function that has been fulfilled by Hawthorne's art. In recording the tragic implications for humane living of a whole phase of American development, the novelist has helped free us from our reckless individualism in pointing to the need for a new ethical and cultural community. By understanding him, the goals of our own society become more clear. Yet what Arvin has seemingly overlooked is that it was not primarily Hawthorne's social observation, but his initial religious conception of man's nature which gave coherence to his interpretation of life.

As Melville said in his essay, existence became real for Hawthorne only through suffering. He would have agreed with the statement of his younger contemporary Dostoevsky, in *Letters from the Underworld*

(1861): 'I am sure that man will never renounce the genuine suffering that comes of ruin and chaos. Why, suffering is the one and only source of knowledge.' Although Hawthorne had had no personal experience of the terrible godless freedom that became the Russian's most obsessive theme, he shared the belief that only those who can suffer intensely are fully alive, since, as he said, there are 'spiritual depths which no other spell can open.' Contemplating Donatello's transformation from innocence to experience, he came closer to Dostoevsky's words by saying that the faun had 'had glimpses of strange and subtle matters in those dark caverns, into which all men must descend, if they would know anything beneath the surface and illusive pleasures of existence.'

Hawthorne reached the same insights in all his books. Scrutinizing the sham that Dimmesdale had become by hiding his relationship with Hester from the world, he concluded that 'the only truth' that continued to give the minister 'a real existence on this earth was the anguish in his inmost soul.' What made Hollingsworth's notions of sin so entirely unreal in his philanthropic scheme for reforming criminals by an appeal to their 'higher instincts' was the incapacity of his stone-blind egotism to see any imperfections in himself. Hawthorne's own perceptions were at the farthest extreme from those of the self-confident reformer. He grew so absorbed with the lasting weight of misery in *The Seven Gables* that he even questioned whether good was as real as evil. With a penetration no less deep than Dostoevsky's into the discipline of suffering, he had none of the mystical fervor. He repeatedly described society as a tangled wilderness of cross-purposes, overwhelmed by which a man like Clifford became 'a ruin, a failure, as almost everybody is.'

That would seem to imply that Hawthorne was incapable of sustaining the balance of great tragedy, that he could portray the horror of existence but not its moments of transfigured glory. That would mean also that his imagination was stirred only by the subordination of his helpless characters to an iron necessity, and not by the courage of their awakened and resolute wills, or by the possibility of their regeneration. In that case his books would have to be placed in the literature of moral despair. Yet Melville's immediate response was not only to Hawthorne's blackness, but also to his 'depth of tenderness,' his 'boundless sympathy with all forms of being,' his 'omnipresent love,' to what he called Hawthorne's balance between mind and heart. Hawthorne had himself used similar terms when he stated that the Master Genius of the Age, that unknown whom the country was looking for so anxiously, must be such a one 'as never illuminates the earth save when a great heart burns as the household fire of a grand intellect.'

These terms are fundamental in the psychology with which both Hawthorne and Melville worked, but their conception of the relation between the two was less simplified than that of the head-and-heart conflict that was dramatized by the followers of Rousseau—the frustrated romantic conflict between irony and pity. For Hawthorne, and Melville after him, was primarily concerned with envisaging the kind of harmony that might be established between thought and emotion, or, as the seventeenth century would have said, between reason and passion. Both believed disequilibrium between the two to be the chief source of tragedy, so it is necessary to pin down further Hawthorne's use of the terms. We remember that at the time of his one great emotional experience, giving himself in love to Sophia Peabody, he was already in his middle thirties, and therefore felt with exceptional acuteness the release from the prison of himself. That was what caused him to declare, with a fervency so rare for him, 'We are not endowed with real life . . . till the heart is touched. That touch creates us,—then we begin to be.' The experience was no mere interlude of romantic passion: he had glimpsed the same truth long before, and had already elucidated some of its implications in 'The Maypole of Merrymount' (1829). There the Lord and Lady of the May, their hearts opening for each other, feel suddenly something vague and insubstantial in the surrounding gaiety. When the heart is touched, one is born into life, which, even at that moment of ecstasy, is sensed by the lovers as something deeper than jubilation, as the shared burden of joy and sorrow and inevitable change.

The polar opposite from such full sharing was represented in 'Ethan Brand,' Hawthorne's most intense working out of the consequences of yielding to pride, which struck Melville by its fearful revelation of what happens when 'the cultivation of the brain eats out the heart.' That was its root idea, so integral to Hawthorne's reading of human nature that he had formulated it in his journal some years before writing the story: 'The Unpardonable Sin might consist in a want of love and reverence for the Human Soul; in consequence of which, the investigator pried into its dark depths, not with a hope or purpose of making it better, but from a cold philosophical curiosity,—content that it should be wicked in whatever kind or degree, and only desiring to study it out. Would not this, in other words, be the separation of the intellect from the heart?' Such investigation was pursued by Roger Chillingworth as well as by Ethan Brand, who finally declared in a frenzy of tortured pride that he had found within himself 'the sin of an intellect that triumphed over the sense of brotherhood with man and reverence for God, and sacrificed everything to its own mighty claims! The only sin that deserves a recompense of immortal agony!'

But in determining Hawthorne's conception of the heart, it must not be supposed, though he often dramatized the tragedy of the man of adamant in whom this organ had withered, that he put any unqualified sentimental trust in its natural virtue. His most frequent way of symbolizing it was as a dark cavern. At the same period at the Manse when he articulated his view of the Unpardonable Sin, he developed this condensed allegory of the heart, an allegory which gave expression to his then prevailing vision of life:

At the entrance there is sunshine, and flowers growing about it. You step within, but a short distance, and begin to find yourself surrounded with a terrible gloom, and monsters of divers kinds; it seems like Hell itself. You are bewildered, and wander long without hope. At last a light strikes upon you. You peep towards it, and find yourself in a region that seems, in some sort, to reproduce the flowers and sunny beauty of the entrance, but all perfect. These are the depths of the heart, or of human nature, bright and peaceful; the gloom and terror may lie deep; but deeper still is the eternal beauty.

But though he felt himself irradiated by that beauty, especially during the first years of his marriage, he seldom neglected to point out how difficult it was for imperfect man to sustain this vision. His chief subject-matter remained the labyrinths in which man's desires became distorted; and he often wrote as though he had set himself to answer Lear's question, 'Is there any cause in nature that makes these hard hearts?' At the close of 'Earth's Holocaust' (1843), written when the activity of the Millerites had caused him to ponder how reforming zeal might bring to destruction all the age-old abuses and encumbrances of the world, he observed that 'there's one thing that these wiseacres have forgotten to throw into the fire,' without which all their efforts for perfectibility would still remain futile: 'What but the human heart itself? . . . And, unless they hit upon some method of purifying that foul cavern, forth from it will reissue all the shapes of wrong and misery—the same old shapes or worse ones . . . The heart, the heart,—there was the little yet boundless sphere wherein existed the original wrong of which the crime and misery of this outward world were merely types.' Then he added a concluding sentence in which he revealed his understanding that the act of regeneration must involve the whole man, and in what manner his conception of the heart included also the will: 'Purify that inward sphere, and the many shapes of evil that haunt the outward, and which now seem almost our only realities, will turn to shadowy phantoms and vanish of their own accord; but if we go no deeper than the intellect, and strive, with merely that feeble instrument, to discern and rectify what is wrong, our whole accomplishment will be a dream.'

Hawthorne seldom portrayed his characters in a state of grace, since he was too thoroughly aware of how the heart as well as the head could go perversely astray. Yet with his thorough skepticism of all improvement except inner purification, and with only a limited hope of that, he habitually stopped short of what the next age in New England conceived as tragedy, short of Robinson's quiet curbing of despair as the last glimmerings of transcendentalism died away for the isolated 'man against the sky.' Hawthorne was grounded in a more coherent social order than Robinson could be, in his era of decay. Still Hawthorne could seize his saving truth only at the core of a paradox. He sometimes went as far as Holgrave in a hatred of the dead oppression of the past. Exhausted by the British Museum, he could wish that even the Elgin Marbles 'were all burnt into lime,' since 'we have not time, in our earthly existence, to appreciate what is warm with life, and immediately around us . . . I do not see how future ages are to stagger onward under all this dead weight, with the additions that will be continually made to it.' Nevertheless, picturing his home in the Manse, he had prayed for a long endurance for 'the institutions that had grown out of the heart of mankind.' It continued to be one of his fundamental tenets that if men were all intellect, as the transcendental reformers struck him as being, 'they would be continually changing, so that one age would be entirely unlike another. The great conservative is the heart.' In other passages he came near to saying that the heart is the great democrat.

His chief stricture against early New England was that its feelings were less developed than its mind. As Hester stood on the pillory, he reflected that it would not have been easy to find anywhere in the world a group of judges less capable of disentangling the mesh of good and evil in a woman's nature than these rigidly virtuous founding fathers. Indeed, Hester herself seemed conscious that 'whatever sympathy she might expect lay in the larger and warmer heart of the multitude.' And so it actually proved in her gradual adjustment to the community in which she had been sentenced to live as an outcast. The rulers were longer in acknowledging her selfless work for the sick and poor than the people were. Both started with harsh prejudices, but those of the latter were not so reinforced by 'an iron framework of reasoning' as to keep their intuitions from breaking through. To this degree then does Hawthorne put trust in common humanity, since their closeness to fundamental experience has not permitted the drying up of their affections. But he does not make the romantic simplification of saying that love is enough. Hester's tragedy came upon her in consequence of excessive yielding to her heart; and that was to be even more true in the reckless careers of Zenobia and Miriam. The balance which prevents disaster is symbolized in the union of Holgrave and Phoebe. For the daguerreotypist learns, through the action of 'the one miracle . . . without which every human existence is a blank,' that his mere prying analysis can never reach the fullness of truth that comes from the insight of feeling; and that discovery gives him wholeness as a man, and keeps him from hardening into the slave of thought that Hollingsworth is.

In his essay on the *Mosses,* Melville seized upon another such balanced individual, who appears in 'The Intelligence Office,' as an image of Hawthorne himself, and quoted the following in confirmation:

A man now entered, in neglected attire, with the aspect of a thinker but somewhat too rough-hewn and brawny for a scholar. His face was full of sturdy vigor, with some finer and keener attribute beneath. Though harsh at first, it was tempered with the glow of a large, warm heart, which had force enough to heat his powerful intellect through and through. He advanced to the Intelligencer and looked at him with a glance of such stern sincerity that perhaps few secrets were beyond its scope. 'I seek for Truth,' said he.

It is entirely unlikely that Hawthorne had any intention of self-portraiture in drawing this figure. But one reason why Melville found it a satisfying symbol was the intimate correspondence between such a man and what he himself felt to be the major cultural aspirations of the age. Though again Hawthorne probably did not so intend it, this seeker for truth is an excellent likeness of Emerson's American Scholar. He is an embodiment of the belief in the possibility of a native culture, its thought grounded on the heart-felt acceptance of the homely facts and opportunities of our life, and therefore able to make its strength prevail.

Hawthorne's way of conceiving a rounded character thus demonstrates his own kind of response to the belief in the common man. It demonstrates likewise that the one-sided and broken figures who throng his most typical pages are seen against a human norm, that he was not so immersed in presenting distortion and defeat as to be incapable of imagining harmony. But his stature as a writer of tragedy cannot be attested even by this perception of the double nature of life, of the fact that there is no such thing as good unless there is also evil, or of evil unless there is good. For tragic power springs not from the mind's recognitions, but from the depth to which the writer's emotions have been stirred by what he has recognized, from the degree to which he has really been able to comprehend and accept what Edgar meant by saying,

> Men must endure
> Their going hence even as their coming hither:
> Ripeness is all.

The briefest description of the tragic attitude is the one Keats gave when he called it 'the love of good and ill'; and by virtue of his courageous acceptance of their inevitable mixture he also gave promise of possessing more of the Shakespearean type of imagination than any other poet of the romantic movement.

The testing of an author's possession of that attitude depends on your experience of one of his whole compositions. Its presence can be briefly scrutinized, however, in his ability to hold an undismayed control between the pressure of conflicting forces. The kind of poise that is demanded is what enabled Hawthorne to say in the opening scene of *The Scarlet Letter* that if there had been a Papist among these Puritans he might have been reminded by his first glimpse of this beautiful woman, with her baby at her breast, 'of that sacred image of sinless motherhood, whose infant was to redeem the world.' Yet he would have been quickly disabused, for here, in bitterest contrast, was 'the taint of deepest sin in the most sacred quality of human life, working such effect, that the world was only the darker for this woman's beauty, and the more lost for the infant she had borne.' Nevertheless, throughout the book Hawthorne emphasizes the self-righteousness of the Puritan leaders who pursue her with such relentless rigor. Her punishment and suffering are treated as inevitable; but you are never allowed to forget the loss involved in their sacrifice of her generosity and tenderness, by the lack of which their own lives are starved.

The purgative effect of such acceptance of tragic fate was reinforced in Greek drama by what Aristotle called the recognition scene, wherein the protagonist became aware of the inexorable course of the action and of his implication in it. Such is the scene where Iphigenia, a priestess at last in a foreign country, accepts a victim for sacrifice, and then beholds him to be her brother Orestes; such, even more terrifying, is that where Oedipus finally sees in his unwitting self the criminal who has brought destruction upon the state. These crises strike us now as affecting in proportion to their not merely being discoveries of the necessity of external events, but involving also Oedipus' kind of inner, moral recognition. And this latter strain was developed to the full by Hawthorne. For his protagonists finally face their evil and know it deserving of the sternest justice, and thus participate in the purgatorial movement, the movement towards regeneration.[2] These last phrases may seem an unwarranted transfer of the tragic catharsis from the audience to the protagonist, but though I would not presume that such a formula would fit all tragedies, what I mean by purgatorial movement can be observed most fully in Shakespeare in Lear's purification through suffering; it also forms the basis for the rising inner action of Milton's Samson. Such too is the slow, heroic course by which Hester arrives at a state of penitence; such is the crisis that at last brings the wavering minister to confess his guilt and beg for mercy; such even is the desperate recognition by Chillingworth that he, 'a mortal man, with a once human heart,' has become a fiend for Dimmesdale's 'especial torment'—though by then his will has become so depraved, so remote from divine grace that he can only feel a revulsion of horror from the 'dark necessity' that he cannot escape.

Moral recognition is equally central to the remorse of Miriam and

2. I have received some hints for this formulation from Maxwell Anderson's essay, 'The Essence of Tragedy' (1939). Meditation on the *Poetics* had taught him a primary rule for modern dramatic construction: 'A play should lead up to and away from a central crisis, and this crisis should consist in a discovery by the leading character which has an indelible effect on his thought and emotion and completely alters his course of action. The leading character, let me say again, must make the discovery; it must affect him emotionally; and it must alter his direction in the play.'

Donatello, which we have observed to be so closely analogous to that of the protagonists in *Paradise Lost*. Another of Hawthorne's most affecting scenes is that which follows Hollingsworth's icy rejection of Zenobia, when she declares with passion to Coverdale, 'The whole universe, her own sex and yours, and Providence, or Destiny, to boot, make common cause against the woman who swerves one hair's-breadth, out of the beaten track. Yes; and add (for I may as well own it, now) that, with that one hair's-breadth, she goes all astray, and never sees the world in its true aspect afterwards.' Hawthorne does not slur over the fact that many evils are irreparable, that Clifford and Hepzibah are too warped by their experience ever to merge again with the stream of outer life, that there is no release for Zenobia save in death. Yet in such a figure, as well as in Hester and Miriam, since he was able also to convey their sexual fascination, Hawthorne was most able to affirm the warmth and strength of the heart, and so to create a sense not merely of life's inexorability and sordidness, but of its possibilities of beauty and grandeur.

3. From Hawthorne to James to Eliot

A TOTAL impression of one of Hawthorne's tragedies, in its careful and subtle gradations, demands a closer reading than most critics have apparently been willing to give. Otherwise, so sensitive a reader as Van Wyck Brooks could hardly have confined his comment on *The Seven Gables* to saying that 'the story moved in a soft September light, melting like a happy dream of Shakespeare.' To be sure, one of Hawthorne's most skillful devices was the time-scheme into which he shaped his events. Hepzibah opens her little shop on a morning in mid-summer; then Phoebe's visit and Clifford's return occupy the ensuing weeks, so that the crisis of the Judge's death can be made to coincide naturally with the outer violence of the equinoctial storm; and the departure can take place while some of the autumn leaves are still on the great elm. But if you are to take the questionable risk of trying to suggest the tone of a whole book by a single atmospheric sentence, one of Hawthorne's own comes closer to what he has conveyed than Brooks' graceful dismissal of the entire problem of evil. The sentence characterizes Clifford's fitful pleasure after his return from prison: 'Coming so late as it did, it was a kind of Indian summer, with a mist in its balmiest sunshine, and decay and death in its gaudiest delight.'

The danger of Brooks' impressionism is even more marked in the half-paragraph, which, after all his evocation of memoirs, is the only space he has left for *The Marble Faun*. (*The Scarlet Letter* is dealt with in three short sentences similar to that on *The Seven Gables*.) When he says that Rome had provided Hawthorne 'with a fairy setting,' and speaks of 'the dusky Miriam of the shrouded past, the delicate wood-anemone of the Western forest,' the flowering that he envisages has virtually nothing to do with Hawthorne's maturely bitter fruit. He should not go unchallenged, since, as a result of letting his attention be deflected from the work itself, he has made one of our few major artists seem less male and robust, much less concerned with important issues than he was. Of all Hawthorne's heroines, Miriam leaves an impression least like the fragility Brooks describes. Her quick response to Kenyon's statue of Cleopatra (which is Hawthorne's response to Story's), is owing to her feeling within herself the operation of qualities equally fierce and turbulent. At times she is made to suggest something of the shattered majesty of a Lady Macbeth. She is more deeply involved in a background of ambiguous guilt than any other of Hawthorne's characters; and his method of conveying this should be observed as a final aspect of his tragic technique, since it leads directly into the practice of James and Eliot.

Hawthorne never specifies exactly what had made Miriam shroud herself under an assumed name, or what relationship enabled her much older model to possess his sinister hold upon her, and what made her desire his death. The novelist's lack of knowledge in such matters may have compelled him to leave his details indefinite; but it is equally true that his interest was always in the psychological effect rather than in the deed itself. Because of this emphasis, *The Scarlet Letter* has sacrificed its intensity even less than *The Golden Bowl*, as our attitude towards adultery has become less stringent. In the case of Miriam, Hawthorne did not want any fake mystery but seems to have felt that the horror could be heightened by a certain impalpability. The remoteness and strangeness of her background are brought into sharp enough light by Hilda's suddenly discovering in her friend's face the very expression of unfathomable sorrow that made Guido's Beatrice the 'saddest picture ever painted.' What Hilda saw corresponds closely to a passage in Hawthorne's notebook, which explains the fascination of this picture for him in its look 'of a being unhumanized by some terrible fate, and gazing at me out of a remote and inaccessible region, where she was frightened to be alone, but where no sympathy could reach her.' Hawthorne's concentration on the inevitability of suffering for Beatrice and Miriam contrasts with Shelley's more typically romantic handling of the theme of incest in *The Cenci,* with his passionate protest against the cruelties of justice and his acceptance of Beatrice's characterization of her act of parricide,

Which is or is not what men call a crime.

Hawthorne gives no evidence that his use of Guido's picture was suggested by Melville, but if he had read *Pierre,* he could hardly have failed to remember the way in which the incest theme is elaborated in its closing pages, when Pierre and Isabel see in a gallery, hung directly opposite a copy of the Beatrice, another portrait that looks startlingly to Pierre like the early sketch of his father, and to Isabel like herself. That Hawthorne had surely read this book cannot be established by any references that have yet come to light, but the presumption is that he had, since his continued interest in Melville's work led him to mention, in *Our Old Home,* the later *Israel Potter* as 'an excellent novel or biography' of the American astray in Europe. On his part, Melville gave as little sign, in his annotations in *The Marble Faun,* whether he saw there any kinship to his work. He took the novel with him on the voyage he made to San Francisco in 1860, on the clipper-ship *Meteor* of which his brother Thomas was captain; but his not very numerous markings passed over entirely the chapter dealing with Hilda's copy of the Beatrice. The only chapter on which they lingered in any detail was that describing 'the emptiness of picture galleries' for anyone harassed by the hard pressures of life. At the top Melville wrote, 'Most original and admirable, and, doubtless, too true.' Upon the remark that 'a taste for pictorial art is often no more than a polish upon the hard enamel of an artificial character,' he added 'excellent'; for his lack of aesthetic sophistication, like Hawthorne's, seems to have left him distressed by most art's want of fidelity to basic nature. The one exception that he took to anything in the chapter was to Hawthorne's saying 'Perugino was evidently a devout man.' Writing from 'Lat. 41° South Atlantic,' the more extensive traveller wrote: 'On the contrary, if I remember right, he is said, in "Lives of the Painters," to have been a jeerer at all religion, a —.'

But what attracted Melville in the very next paragraph was the sense of tragedy which we have been analyzing. Hawthorne was developing the view that Sodoma's portrayal of Christ bound to a pillar escaped the shallowness of most religious pictures by showing the Saviour in the lonely despair from which was wrung forth 'the saddest utterance man ever made, "Why hast Thou forsaken me?"' Yet even in this extremity of anguish his figure had been represented by the painter with 'a celestial majesty and beauty'; and by such union of opposites this picture had 'done more towards reconciling the incongruity of Divine Omnipotence and outraged, suffering Humanity, combined in one person, than the theologians ever did.' Thus the mingled strain of the divine and the commonly human, which both Hawthorne and Melville felt in tragedy, in its moments of heroic transfiguration, is given another symbolic expression.

But in their uses of the symbol of Beatrice Cenci we have a pointed instance of the divergence between the two novelists. Hawthorne was not obsessed by a sense of 'the ambiguities,' which became the sub-title of *Pierre,* and whose operation caused its hero, even while being struck by the likeness of the portrait in the gallery, to wonder whether this work by an unknown artist did not prove that all resemblance between Isabel and the sketch of his father had been only accidental, and that his desperate sacrifice on the assumption that she was his sister had been sheer delusion. Hawthorne's intention in suggesting through Miriam's likeness to Beatrice her unwilling entanglement in a criminal past was to emphasize the inescapability of destiny. What he was after was not uncertainty or obscurity, but breadth of effect. This is not to maintain that his indefiniteness of suggestion was not carried too far. It contributed to the 'total vague intensity' to which James demurred, and caused such dissatisfaction among Hawthorne's first readers that he was reluctantly compelled to the lame device of tacking on a conclusion of partial explanations. Nevertheless, he had been working in the direction of what James formulated in the preface to *The Turn of the Screw.* 'Only make the reader's general vision of evil intense enough, I said to myself . . . and his own experience, his own imagination, his own sympathy (with the children) and horror (of their false friends) will supply him quite sufficiently with all the particulars. Make him *think* the evil, make him think it for himself, and you are released from weak specifications.' Ignoring this, even

Edmund Wilson was led to think James' special brand of ambiguity unintentional rather than thus deliberate.

Hawthorne's 'general vision of evil' came to him directly from theological tradition, from the weight of which James was freed early by his father's insistence that the boys attend different churches in turn, and so have their ethics cleared from any restrictions of dogma. Another adjustment of Hawthorne to tradition, which links him more closely to Eliot, though also to the James of *The Sense of the Past,* is what we have observed in his work from the time of 'The Hollow of the Three Hills': his continual effort to suggest the symbolical equivalence, beneath whatever guises, of human traits in different ages. One of his most detailed instances was in *The Seven Gables,* where mesmerism, when used as a means of exploiting another's nature, impressed him as a modern manifestation of what had been meant by witchcraft, both being types of the separation of the analytic mind from the heart.

In Rome it was even more natural that he should sense the past in the present, its 'weight and density' pressing down upon the evanescent moment. This sense held such sway over his imagination that he saw not only Beatrice Cenci in Miriam; but the pagan Faun in Donatello; and the ugliness of Guido's demon, who had to be slain by Michael, in the face of Miriam's model. Thus perpetually for Hawthorne the shimmer of the now was merely the surface of the deep pool of history. But as an American he resented the massiveness of antiquity that made his moment seem less real in Rome than it did elsewhere. This attitude towards Europe was operating in his notes for *The Ancestral Footstep,* the most promising of his unfinished romances, where the cross-purposes and animosity that were engendered by his American hero's having returned to England to take up the inheritance of an estate led only to the conclusion: 'Let the past alone.' This is a conclusion more incisive than what would probably have emerged from the adventures of the historically infatuated hero of *The Sense of the Past,* where what is uppermost, so far as the book was finished, is the contrast between the vulgar vitality of the London Midmores and the finer consciousness, bought at the expense of attenuation, in their American descendant of a century later.

The presentness of the past is what Eliot has meant by tradition. Although casual readers of a poem like 'Sweeney Among the Nightingales' may have mistaken his irony and have believed that he was merely mocking the defeat and debasement of the modern world, his intention in such a poem was actually double: Sweeney may make an incongruous Agamemnon; nevertheless, he is a man whose plotted death enlists our sympathy, and the created atmosphere of foreboding thus stirs an undertone of pity and terror. The crucial factor, as Eliot observed when writing about the Ezra Pound of twenty years ago—the great translator in the Chaucerian sense, 'the inventor of Chinese poetry for our time,' the creator of our version of Propertius—is that he had seen aspects of their civilizations as 'contemporary with himself,' that he had grasped certain things there 'which are permanent in human nature . . . When he deals with antiquities, he extracts the essentially living; when he deals with contemporaries, he sometimes notes only the accidental . . . Time, in such connexions, does not matter; it is irrelevant whether what you see, really see, as a human being, is Arnaut Daniel or your green-grocer. It is merely a question of the means suited to the particular poet, and we are more concerned with the end than with the means.'

Irony was the chief instrument in Eliot's early work because his world had been savagely transformed from that of Hawthorne and James. He knew that the essential bond between the two novelists was 'their indifference to religious dogma at the same time as their exceptional awareness of spiritual reality.' Such awareness, when the springs of religion had dried up, could become the nightmare of *The Waste Land,* the agony of a society without belief. Before religious experience could have any meaning for him, Eliot had to free himself from the desiccated Christianity in which he had been brought up. He had first to rediscover the sources of religion in the vitality of primitive myth and ritual. The acuteness of his problem can be illustrated by the shallow waters into which Hawthorne and James had drifted, partly, at least, through their indifference to dogma.

By turning over some of Hawthorne's unexamined assumptions, especially in *The Marble Faun,* we can get an ugly glimpse of American spiritual life, as it was destined increasingly to become in the decades after the Civil War. He clearly intended Kenyon and Hilda to be attractive: an earnest young sculptor of promise and 'quick sensibility,' who, as the era deemed appropriate, believed reverently that the girl he loved was 'a little more than mortal.' In his treatment of their relationship Hawthorne has obviously interwoven many strands of his own relations with his wife; but the unintended impression of self-righteousness and priggishness that exudes from these characters brings to the fore some extreme limitations of the standards that Hawthorne took for granted.

We need look no farther than two critical scenes with Miriam, before and after the murder of her model. In the first she has been driven by her 'weary restlessness' to visit Kenyon in his studio, in the half-formed hope that he may be able to counsel her how to escape from her desperate situation. At the sight of his Cleopatra, she is so impressed by his intuitive grasp of woman's nature that she turns impulsively to him: 'Oh, my friend, will you be my friend indeed? I am lonely, lonely, lonely. There is a secret in my heart that burns me,—that tortures me! Sometimes I fear to go mad of it; sometimes I hope to die of it; but neither of the two happens. Ah, if I could but whisper it to only one human soul!' He bids her speak, but with a hidden reserve and alarm, which her suffering can detect. For his cool reasonableness knows that if she does pour out her heart, and he then fails to respond with just the sympathy she wants, it will be worse than if she had remained silent. ' "Ah, I shall hate you!" cried she, echoing the thought which he had not spoken; she was half choked with the gush of passion that was thus turned back upon her. "You are as cold and pitiless as your own marble." '

It does no good for him to protest, as Miles Coverdale might also have done, that he is 'full of sympathy, God knows,' for his ineffectual scrupulosity has driven her away. The very evening after this visit the terrible event takes place.

Of this event Hilda, who had turned back from the other walkers to rejoin Miriam and Donatello, became thus unwittingly the only observer. In deliberately creating in her the ideal innocence of a New England girl, Hawthorne set himself to examine a nature that, as Miriam recognizes, might endure a great burden of sorrow, but 'of sin, not a feather's weight.' One source of Hawthorne's knowledge of such a problem is suggested by Elizabeth Peabody's remark that with all her sister Sophia's bravery in the face of much suffering, 'there was one kind of thing she could not bear, and that was, moral evil.' The result in Hilda is terrifying: Kenyon's nature is broad as a barn in comparison. What is uppermost in the single interview she allows herself with Miriam after the murder is her dread that she, too, may be stained with guilt. Her dearest friend has 'no existence for her any more,' and she wonders if she can even talk to her 'without violating a spiritual law.'

Miriam urges, in her despair, that she is still a woman as she was yesterday, 'endowed with the same truth of nature, the same warmth of heart, the same genuine and earnest love, which you have always known in me. In any regard that concerns yourself, I am not changed . . . But, have I sinned against God and man, and deeply sinned? Then be more my friend than ever, for I need you more.' But as the girl recoils from her, Miriam adds: 'I always said, Hilda, that you were merciless; for I had a perception of it, even while you loved me best. You have no sin, nor any conception of what it is; and therefore you are so terribly severe! As an angel, you are not amiss; but as a human creature, and a woman among earthly men and women, you need a sin to soften you.'

To this Hilda's only answer is that she prays God may forgive her if she has spoken 'a needlessly cruel word,' for 'while there is a single guilty person in the universe, each innocent one must feel his innocence tortured by that guilt. Your deed, Miriam, has darkened the whole sky!'

To such a dazzling extreme does the daughter of the Puritans merit Kenyon's tribute to 'the white shining purity' of her nature as 'a thing apart.' At one point much later in the narrative she thinks remorsefully, 'Miriam loved me well, and I failed her at her sorest need.' But Kenyon, though observing that Hilda's unworldly separation between the good and the bad cuts like a steel blade, and that she is incapable of mercy since in need of none herself, still defends to Miriam her 'just severity.' Its justice is accepted by the novelist, and even by Miriam. Yet she repeats that if Kenyon had not been cold to her confidence, if she had obeyed her first impulse, 'all would have turned out differently.' She knows too that both her friends, by their lack of active sympathy, have allowed the unreleased energies of her heart to grind destructively on herself.

The dilemma that Hawthorne has run into here through his determination to keep the scales of justice exact is due to his limited ability to create characters instead of states of mind. We can accept the position that since Miriam has sinned, or has at least been implicated in Donatello's act, her retribution must run its course. For we know that moral laws, whether under the aegis of Destiny or of Providence, are by their nature relentlessly inhuman. But what we cannot accept is that Kenyon and Hilda should be such correct mouthpieces for justice. They become thereby appallingly conscious of the significance of events in which their own human fallibility would be more confusedly involved, and they thus take on an air of insufferable superiority.

Still worse things remain to be seen in Hilda. Chilled into torpor by the fact of having to bear the knowledge of Miriam's guilt, she feels utterly alone in the Rome which Kenyon has left for the summer. In this state she begins to be drawn by the magnet of Catholicism, by its apparent comfort on all occasions for the pent-up heart. She asks herself whether its universal blessings may not belong to her as well, whether the New England faith in which she was born and bred can be perfect, 'if it leave a weak girl like me to wander, desolate, with this great trouble crushing me down?' Her struggle brings her compellingly to St. Peter's, to a confessional booth, *Pro Anglica Lingua*. But when she has poured out her whole story, and the priest asks her in some perplexity, whether, though born a heretic, she is reconciled to the Church, her answer is 'Never.' ' "And, that being the case," demanded the old man, "on what ground, my daughter, have you sought to avail yourself of these blessed privileges, confined exclusively to members of the one true Church, of confession and absolution?"

' "Absolution, father?" exclaimed Hilda, shrinking back. "Oh no, no! I never dreamed of that! Only our Heavenly Father can forgive my sins . . ." ' This instinctive determination of Hilda's to eat her cake and have it too is, one must admit, as American as the strip-tease, of which it forms the spiritual counterpart.

To be sure, though Hilda tells the priest that she will never return to the confessional, she also says that she will hold the cathedral in 'loving remembrance' as long as she lives, as the spot where she found 'infinite peace after infinite trouble.' But by then she has decided that it was 'the sin of others that drove me thither; not my own, though it almost seemed so.' She has also finally begun to accept Kenyon's long hopeless love; and, at last, it is he who turns to her for guidance, since his mind has been entangling itself in the intricate problem of wherein Donatello has been educated and elevated by his sin. The sculptor feels that in his own lonely life and work his thought has wandered dangerously wide, and adds: 'Were you my guide, my counsellor, my inmost friend, with that white wisdom that clothes you as a celestial garment, all would go well. O Hilda, guide me home!'

She disclaims any such wisdom, but they start back to New England together, and though she wonders what Miriam's life is to be and where

Donatello is, still 'Hilda had a hopeful soul, and saw sunlight on the mountain-tops.' Those were the final words of the book until Hawthorne yielded to the demand for a more explicit account of the destinies of the two who remained in Rome. In its original form the end coincides curiously with the bright vision in the final sentence of *Walden,* and with the rising light that Whitman, even more than Emerson, envisaged as flooding his America.

But the America to which Hawthorne as well as Kenyon was to return in the year of the publication of *The Marble Faun* was soon to be at war. Thoreau was to die of consumption during the first year of that conflict, and shortly after its end Emerson was to write his poem 'Terminus,' in which he intuitively foresaw the waning of his creative powers. Hawthorne himself did not outlive the struggle, during which, lacking Whitman's expansive faith, his forebodings often were that 'our institutions may perish before we shall have discovered the most precious of the possibilities which they involve.'

The world that ensued was not one in which he could have imagined the future careers of brittle natures like Kenyon and Hilda, who would no doubt have been equally shocked by the success of the robber barons and by Whitman's frank avowal that the workers alone could overthrow this predatory domination. Hawthorne recognized, in *Our Old Home,* that 'those words, "genteel" and "ladylike," are terrible ones,' though he somewhat weakened this observation by the tone in which he remarked that 'fineness, subtlety, and grace' were 'that which the richest culture has heretofore tended to develop in the happier examples of American genius, and which (though I say it a little reluctantly) is perhaps what our future intellectual advancement may make general among us.' His lack of effective resistance to that tendency was what let him be caught off guard in his creation of these lovers, who are the perfect bleached prototypes of the genteel tradition. When he was creating the world of *The Scarlet Letter,* he understood the limitations of the seventeenth century, since he could see them against the opportunities for fuller development in the democracy in which he believed. But he was not able to take the more difficult step, and to pass across in imagination from his relatively simple time and province to the dynamic transformations of American society that were just beginning to emerge.

That is not to say that Hilda's voice remains dominant even at the end of *The Marble Faun*. Although she gets the last word, Kenyon's somber reflections just before are more in keeping with the prevailing tone of the whole. He thinks that such genial natures as the Faun's 'have no longer any business on earth . . . Life has grown so sadly serious, that such men must change their nature, or else perish, like the antediluvian creatures, that required, as the condition of their existence, a more summer-like atmosphere than ours.' Melville marked that and also double-scored a passage earlier in the book where Hawthorne was meditating likewise on the theme of cheerless decay. Hawthorne was always aware of how in his Yankee world, 'no life now wanders like an unfettered stream; there is a mill-wheel for the tiniest rivulet to turn. We go all wrong, by too strenuous a resolution to go all right.' It was that competitive America to which Hawthorne, with his usual startling frankness, told Ticknor that he had no desire to come back. After his long sojourn in Europe he declared that he still loved his country: 'The United States are fit for many excellent purposes, but they certainly are not fit to live in.'

No really integrated principles can be made out of his varying reflections on his social and economic milieu. What he was acutely conscious of, in the realm in which his thought was most at home, was the slow disintegration of the bases upon which the earlier moral values had depended. During his life at the Manse he had remarked that Dr. Ripley's successor 'labors with faith and confidence, as ministers did a hundred years ago, when they had really something to do in the world.' Mrs. Hawthorne omitted that last clause, and also these two sentences: 'I find that my respect for clerical people, as such, and my faith in the utility of their office, decreases daily. We certainly do need a new revelation—a new system—for there seems to be no life in the old one.'

Many passages in his European notebooks, even as issued by Mrs. Hawthorne, the only form in which they have yet appeared,[1] attest to his interest in Catholicism. His tenor frequently accords with that of his first impression of a service at the Madeleine in Paris, that the ceremonies of the Church 'were a superb work of art, or perhaps a true growth of man's religious nature; and so long as men felt their original meaning, they must have been full of awe and glory.' But like Kenyon he dwelt on the many corruptions of the visible church; and he gave the background for his belief that Hilda was right in her rejection when he

---

1. An edition of *The French and Italian Notebooks* from the original manuscripts is now being prepared by Norman H. Pearson, who with Stanley Williams, Randall Stewart, and Manning Hawthorne, is also engaged in editing Hawthorne's letters.

said, 'Generally, I suspect, when people throw off the faith they were born in, the best soil of their hearts is apt to cling to its roots.' Further evidence of how deeply Hilda's problem had absorbed his family circle is furnished by the fact that neither of his daughters was able to find peace in their father's indifference to dogma, and both, like many other troubled New Englanders of their day, took ·the solution opposite to Hilda's. Una, whose childish perversities had given some hints for Pearl, lived mainly in England after her mother's death in 1871, accepted the Anglican faith after a long struggle, and devoted herself to works of charity until she died while on a visit to a Protestant convent. Rose married George Parsons Lathrop, and both she and her husband were finally converted to Catholicism. After his death she became a nun under the name of Sister Alphonsa, and, haunted no less than her father by the existence of suffering, founded in New York a sisterhood for the relief of victims of incurable cancer.

But the America to which both girls had returned with their parents in 1860 was the one whose bleak dreariness depressed Kenyon, and of which they doubtless knew little more than their contemporary Henry James, to whose earliest schoolboy reflections in Washington Square it had appeared that the whole country was divided strictly into 'three classes, the busy, the tipsy, and Daniel Webster.' You might maintain that the only important difference in James' later knowledge of the active forces in America—to which, in 1860, he was also returning with his family—was that Daniel Webster was dead. There is no questioning James' growth into a more developed consciousness of social complexity than Hawthorne's, nor his belief that 'the province of art is all life, all feeling, all observation, all vision.' Yet his exemptions from ordinary existence are far more sweeping than those in the 'theatre, a little removed from the highway,' which Hawthorne had set up in *The Blithedale Romance*. His beautifully ample lawns and endless afternoons compose a kind of hanging garden in which his characters are forever being 'splendid' and 'brave' and 'wonderful' and 'extraordinary' and 'prodigious.' The length of 'sacrifice' that counts in this realm is 'of the opportunity of dressing' for dinner; the 'sacred' situation in which the Prince and Charlotte find themselves is owing to no less than the thoughtful care they have taken to spare their respective wife and husband from the pain of knowing of their adultery.

But James is always much easier to ridicule than to understand, since of all writers he is most susceptible to misrepresentation by words torn out of the charmed web of his special context. Even the most rigorous social critic would have to grant what Arvin called 'the deadly lucidity' with which James saw things that strictly speaking he did not comprehend. 'He made out no historic meaning in the corrupt life of the great bourgeoisie or the philistine morals of the small bourgeoisie of his time, but he saw that corruption, that philistinism, as few of his contemporaries saw them.'[2] His perception grew with his experience: in consequence of his visit to America in 1906 after so many years' absence, he projected, in the unfinished *Ivory Tower,* a study of the preoccupation with wealth— hardly less searching than those of Balzac. James knew then what tough Mr. Betterman, the dying millionaire, said about his contemporaries, 'Money is their life'; he knew also the truth of the remark that he gave to one of his Newport gentlemen: 'We're all . . . unspeakably corrupt.'

Yet the question remains whether James' social and moral values were at any period as solidly based as Hawthorne's. In *The Spoils of Poynton* (1897), for instance, he attributed an absolute worth to the accumulated property itself, to what he called in his preface 'the felt beauty and value of the . . . Things, always the splendid Things.' This aesthetic relish seems far less cognizant of the driving forces in society than Hawthorne's understanding of the crushing disaster produced by the greed for inheritance, even in his lesser New England house of half a century before. James' moral sense, exquisite as it could be, drew little direct nourishment from any widely accepted ethical system. One place where he gave himself away coincides with his last allusion to Hawthorne. At the opening of the third book of *The Sense of the Past,* he summed up the effect produced on his hero by having encountered in the darkened room the figure of the portrait of his ancestor, and by having discovered the face to be his own:

He wished he had been a Catholic, that he might go to confession; his desire, remarkably enough, being no less for secrecy than for relief. He recalled the chapter in Hawthorne's fine novel in which the young woman from New England kneels, for the lightening of her woe, to the old priest at St. Peter's, and felt that he sounded as never before the depth of that passage. *His* case in truth was worse than Hilda's and his burden much

2. Newton Arvin, 'Henry James and the Almighty Dollar,' *Hound and Horn,* Henry James number (Spring 1934).

greater, for she had been but a spectator of what weighed upon her, whereas he had been a close participant.

It does no good for James to maintain that 'it mattered little enough that his sense was not the sense of crime,' for the falseness of the whole analogy is that Hilda was at least oppressed by her knowledge of the mortal guilt of Donatello and Miriam, whereas Ralph Pendrel is involved in nothing more than his eerie sensation of having gained a private entrance into the past. He is an unattached young man who has written a 'remarkable volume,' *An Essay in Aid of the Reading of History;* but since his action here can hardly have great consequences for anyone save himself, James' drift away from central standards of value becomes ludicrous when he adds that his hero's first sense of identification with his forebears' world taught him that there were at least as many more things in life 'for one's philosophy than poor Hamlet himself was to have found in heaven and earth.'

The disproportion between means and end in James' work can frequently be thus marked. In his created realm of infinite leisure, which is rarely broken into by the irrelevances of practical existence, his characters finally became as breathlessly abandoned to idle curiosity as their author. He was sometimes aware of the morbid risks involved in what he termed his own 'irrepressible and insatiable, his extravagant and immoral, interest in personal character and in the "nature" of a mind.' He even knew, in his one suggestion of the 'sinister anarchic underworld' of militant socialism, in *The Princess Casamassima* (1886), that the overcharged weight of such 'treasures of reflexion' could bring about tragic collapse—though the destruction, you recall, is of the sensitive young radical whose convictions become so confused by the torture of his impossible love for the Princess that he can find no solution except suicide. It must be granted that James had not the slightest political intention in this novel; he was interested solely in the personal problem, in what would happen when 'a dingy little London bookbinder' with 'an aggressive, vindictive, destructive social faith' should establish 'a social—not less than a socialist —connexion.' The result is not so preposterous as these phrases from the preface may make it sound, since James devoted his full resources to bringing out the 'intrinsic fineness' of Hyacinth Robinson. But the young man's excessive sensibility is finally just as dangerous to his own welfare as is the even more extravagant development of this quality to that of the neurotic 'I' who narrates *The Sacred Fount*. By the time of the latter book, as we have noted, James had become excruciatingly conscious of how preoccupation with nothing but personal relations might pass into insanity.

Nevertheless, those relations composed his world. In most of his novels the characters are segregated from any but the most dimly implied connection with the social violence and chaos that the busy and the tipsy had been producing in the world of Ulysses Grant. On the other hand, in marked contrast with Hawthorne, there is not even the implication of any dependence upon a world overhead. The only intrusion of a Church is through a figure like Father Mitchell, 'good holy hungry man,' who 'prattled' undiscouraged over 'viands artfully iced' on a hot Sunday at Fawns, while Maggie Verver, from the resources of her inner reliance, knew that she had no need for him. This was the kind of world in which Henry Adams was oppressed by the terrifying drying-up of all springs of effectual faith. But James, suffused with fascination for the heroic courage of a Maggie Verver or a Milly Theale, was unaware that he had passed into a realm where the word 'sacred' no longer had a real meaning.

Against this background it is hardly surprising that Eliot felt himself increasingly stifled by the emphasis of his cultural milieu on nothing beyond such personal values. His first important essay, 'Tradition and the Individual Talent' (1917), was a reaction against the romantic exploitation of personality in poetry, and declared that 'the progress of an artist is a continual self-sacrifice,' the surrender of himself to the work to be performed. He was undoubtedly helped to that classic attitude by the example of James as well as of Flaubert, but fifteen years later he felt the necessity of extending its range from art into society and religion: 'What I have been leading up to is the following assertion: that when morals cease to be a matter of tradition and orthodoxy—that is, of the habits of the community formulated, corrected, and elevated by the continuous thought and direction of the Church—and when each man is to elaborate his own, then *personality* becomes a thing of alarming importance.'

In an early poem like his 'Portrait of a Lady,' he had already perceived the dead-end of Jamesian fastidiousness. In 'Gerontion' his tones deepened into terror at the spectacle of a life divided and lost in a cosmopolite world whose excessively complex fragments possessed no real coherence.[3] With the old man's ejaculation,

> After such knowledge, what forgiveness?

Eliot himself had come to the point where he could no longer endure the emptiness of life without belief. The slow course of his conversion cannot be followed here, but in completing our survey of the drift of influence from Hawthorne, it may be adequate to note Eliot's deepening comprehension of what, as expressed by Baudelaire, he called 'the greatest, the most difficult of the Christian virtues, the virtue of humility.' In meditating on the career of Pascal, Eliot came to the conclusion that he

3. Fragments from two lives, which, as is so often the case with Eliot's creative process, can be seen to have stimulated this poem, are recorded in *The Education of Henry Adams* and in A. C. Benson's biography of Edward Fitzgerald. The passage in Adams (which was pointed out to me by Robert G. Davis) comes at the beginning of the chapter describing his settling in Washington, and the richness of its spring so foreign to a New Englander: 'The Potomac and its tributaries squandered beauty . . . Here and there a negro log cabin alone disturbed the dogwood and the judas-tree . . . The tulip and the chestnut gave no sense of struggle against a stingy nature . . . The brooding heat of the profligate vegetation; the cool charm of the running water; the terrific splendor of the June thundergust in the deep and solitary woods, were all sensual, animal, elemental. No European spring had shown him the same intermixture of delicate grace and passionate depravity that marked the Maryland May. He loved it too much, as though it were Greek and half human.' That many of these phrases worked upon the formation of the following lines is unmistakable, though Eliot's theme is the loss of such ecstasy when cut off from the roots of faith:

> In the juvescence of the year
> Came Christ the tiger

> In depraved May, dogwood and chestnut, flowering judas,
> To be eaten, to be divided, to be drunk
> Among whispers . . .

The passage in Benson (which was discovered by M. D. Zabel) occurs where he is weaving together some excerpts from Fitzgerald's letters, and making interpolations of his own: 'Here he sits, in a dry month, old and blind, being read to by a country boy, longing for rain:—"Last night . . . we heard a Splash of Rain, and I had the book shut up, and sat listening to the Shower by myself—till it blew over, I am sorry to say, and no more of the sort all night. But we are thankful for that small mercy." ' Benson's words virtually compose the opening lines of the soliloquy of Eliot's old man; and as Zabel added in a letter to me, Benson's 'whole book, with its picture of Fitzgerald in his pathetic, charming, and impotent old age, pondering on the pessimism of Omar, and beating out the futility of his final years, may have crystallized in Eliot's mind the situation (already drawn in earlier poems, of course) not only of "Gerontion" but of other passages in his work of that time.' It is notable that both the Adams and Fitzgerald passages contain allusions to water, the absence of which life-giving source was to be one of the chief symbols of *The Waste Land*.

could think 'of no Christian writer, not Newman even, more to be commended . . . to those who doubt, but who have the mind to conceive, and the sensibility to feel, 'the disorder, the futility, the meaninglessness, the mystery of life and suffering, and who can only find peace through a satisfaction of the whole being.'

We could hardly be made more acutely aware of the urgency of issues that James could still ignore. Eliot's final step from such awareness into the Anglo-Catholic faith seems to have followed this chain of Hulme's reasoning, which Eliot quoted once against the humanism of Babbitt:

I have none of the feelings of *nostalgia,* the reverence for tradition, the desire to recapture the sentiment of Fra Angelico, which seems to animate most modern defenders of religion. All that seems to me bosh. What is important, is what nobody seems to realize—the dogmas like that of Original Sin, which are the closest expression of the categories of the religious attitude. That man is in no sense perfect, but a wretched creature, who can yet apprehend perfection. It is not, then, that I put up with the dogma for the sake of the sentiment, but that I may possibly swallow the sentiment for the sake of the dogma.

The solution accepted by Eliot has not proved popular, nor has he ever expected that it would be. In a period so overwhelmed by economic and social upheaval, so without roots in any living Christian tradition, religious experience has seemed meaningless, or a gesture of escape, to most thinkers and writers. Or, speaking more accurately, many have tended to substitute religions of their own. Eliot himself has observed how fatally easy it is, in the broken conditions of modern society, for 'a writer of genius to conceive of himself as a Messiah'; and we need look no farther than Lawrence for a leading example. Others, like Malraux and the younger radical poets and novelists, have tended to subsume the religious impulse under the breadth of their devotion to purposive social action. To Eliot, rightly or wrongly, this means a blurring of basic distinctions. He holds that if you deny religion as such, it is sure to break out in a political form. He insists that distortion can be prevented only if you render strictly what is due to each realm. He would undoubtedly agree with Hulme's definition that 'romanticism is spilt religion'; and owing to the observable effects of Emerson's green wine on natures less temperate than its maker's, we can understand what that means. When Saadi became Nietzsche's Zarathustra, the ideal man of self-reliant energy was transformed into the hard-willed *Übermensch,* whose image was again to be altered and degraded into the brutal man of Fascism.[4] But we do not have to trace this lineage so far afield for our example. From the weaker aspects of Emerson's thought, the rocking chair of Mary Baker Eddy, as has been observed, is only just around the corner; and it is no long step from his indiscriminate glorification of power to the predatory career of Henry Ford, who still declares Emerson's *Essays* to be his favorite reading.

By his revulsion from the effects of all such adulterated religions, by a sense of suffering more acute than that of Charles Eliot Norton, Eliot was driven to realize that man to-day could not continue to drift even with Hawthorne's and James' 'exceptional awareness of spiritual reality.' He came to believe that the choice lay between further disintegration of the sort that Hawthorne already foresaw, and a return to dogma upon which to base more adequate values than those of James. He has not increased the popularity of his choice by his reiterated awareness that our crisis may be a collapse and a return into the dark ages. The faith voiced in *Ash Wednesday* and *Murder in the Cathedral* is scarcely triumphant; it is often nearly obscured in doubt, and beset by the most subtle of temptations, that in which spiritual pride masks itself as humility. But Eliot has faced the dark necessity of what he believes to be true. He has known long since that in the realm of religious and cultural values 'we fight rather to keep something alive than in the expectation that anything will triumph.'

4. See p. 546 in the discussion of Whitman for further commentary on this descent.

BOOK THREE

⇒⇒⇒ ⇐⇐⇐

Melville

➤➤➤ IX ➤➤➤

MOMENT OF TRANSITION

1. 'Out of unhandselled savage nature'

THE AMERICAN with the richest natural gifts as a writer became one
largely by accident. In sharpest contrast to Hawthorne's deliberate resolve
to be an author of fiction, his embarrassed withdrawal of the still-born
Fanshawe, and his subsequent long apprenticeship to his craft before
collecting his *Tales,* Melville's first book was a record of experience.
Undertaken directly upon his return from nearly four years of adventure,
it was in print and making his reputation only a little more than a year
after he had been discharged from the frigate *United States* as a common
seaman. The writing he had done previously amounted to nothing more
substantial than two 'Fragments from a Writing-Desk,' which had been
printed in *The Democratic Press* of Lansingburgh, New York, when he
was a schoolteacher of nineteen. These are stock dilutions of the *Spectator* tradition, and show no more than that his own formal education,
broken off at fifteen by his family's upset finances, had subsequently
been extended to include allusions to *Romeo* and *Hamlet,* to Sheridan
and Burke and Coleridge, and that his taste was somewhat adulterated
by the sentiment of Tom Moore.

If *Typee* had not been an instant success, Melville might well have
stopped there, since he had his living to make. But its sequel *Omoo* was
clearly called for, and after he became aware of his talents through their
exercise, the thought next occurred to him that, having published two
narratives of travel that had been regarded with incredulity in many
quarters, he might try a romance and see if it could be made to pass for
truth. But by the time he had launched on *Mardi* he was married, and
his first child was born just before the book appeared. He was compelled,
therefore, to undertake a pot-boiler, and turned for his material to another segment of his adventures, his first voyage, the passage to Liverpool

he had made at seventeen. That led on naturally to a book about what had happened to him after his life among the cannibals and as a beach-comber in Tahiti; and so he based *White Jacket* on his months in the navy. The one large part of his experience that was still left untapped by all these was the knowledge he had acquired of the whaling industry before he had jumped ship at Typee. *Moby-Dick* ranged farther from his personal history than even *Mardi* had, since the turgid conversations of that romance had often been the debates of his own developing mind, whereas Ahab and his crew were more completely an imaginative pro-jection. When he decided at last to represent life in America, he was no longer writing autobiography even in the loose sense that *Redburn* can be so called; though because of the scantiness of information for Mel-ville's early years, *Pierre* has been unjustifiably so taken by most of his biographers. In the volumes that remained, *Israel Potter,* the bulk of *The Piazza Tales, The Confidence Man,* he was not drawing on his own actions at all.

The author of *Typee* was two years older than the author of *Fanshawe.* The author of *Pierre* was thirty-three, the same age as the author of *Twice-Told Tales,* a year older than Thoreau was when he issued the *Week,* three years younger than Whitman when he printed his first *Leaves,* four years younger than the Emerson of the first *Essays,* thirteen years younger than the author of *The Scarlet Letter.* The bursting of Melville's vitality gives the proof of what Emerson had proclaimed in *The American Scholar:* 'Not out of those on whom systems of education have exhausted their culture, comes the helpful giant to destroy the old or to build the new, but out of unhandselled savage nature.'

In his essay on Hawthorne, Melville exclaimed: 'Believe me, my friends, that men not very much inferior to Shakespeare are this day being born on the banks of the Ohio. And the day will come when you shall say, Who reads a book by an Englishman that is a modern?' This was the natural response to Sydney Smith's British arrogance of a genera-tion before: 'In the four quarters of the globe, who reads an American book?'[1] Melville's tone is akin here to Whitman's, and may strike us as

1. In *The Edinburgh Review,* January 1820. Smith was particularly unfortunate in the timing of his question, since Irving had just issued his *Sketch Book;* and with the appear-ance in the following year of Bryant's first volume of poems and especially of Cooper's *Spy,* the literature of the new nation, as distinct from colonial literature, had begun to find its voice.

the extreme of romantic extravagance, as the kind of recklessness that made Carlyle remark that Whitman thought he was a big man because he lived in a big country. Yet without this heady confidence there could hardly have been the renaissance of these years; and Melville and Whitman were right in their intuitions that they were living at the very hour of matured harvest. Emerson was more conscious, in his journal of 1847, of the precarious balance of such periods: 'In history, the great moment is when the savage is just ceasing to be a savage . . . that moment of transition,—the foam hangs but a moment on the wave; the sun himself does not pause on the meridian; literature becomes criticism, nervousness, and a gnawing when the first musical triumphant strain has waked the echoes.'

In the double excitement of his discovery of both Hawthorne and Shakespeare, Melville felt that other minds might go as far, that there was 'hardly a mortal man, who, at some time or other, has not felt as great thoughts in him as any you will find in Hamlet.' In the summer that he wrote this, he was responding far more to the abundance of Shakespeare's creative energy than to the corrosion of Hamlet's self-scrutiny. He had not yet lived through the experience of writing the tragedies of Ahab and Pierre. Only through the act of doing what he praised Hawthorne for, through dropping his mind 'down into the universe like a plummet,' was he to come to something like the fierceness of Hamlet's disillusion. Nervous attritions oppressed him when nearly all that resulted from his two major efforts was violent misunderstanding or neglect. Even during the tension of finishing *Moby-Dick,* he foresaw, in the letter to Hawthorne wherein he dated the beginning of his life from his twenty-fifth year, the year of his return from the sea, that the culmination of powers implied an end. 'I feel that I am now come to the inmost leaf of the bulb, and that shortly the flower must fall to the mould.'

Among *The Piazza Tales* was 'Benito Cereno,' one of the most sensitively poised pieces of writing he had ever done. However, by then Melville's more prevailing mood had become that of *The Confidence Man,* where his angrily frustrated satire broke off unfinished with, 'Something further may follow of this Masquerade.' When he wrote that sentence, he had had a full decade as a professional writer. He seems to have decided that was enough, for though he lived nearly thirty-five years more, he published no more prose.[2] The poems that formed his running commentary on the Civil War were issued in the year after its ending. By that year, too, he had given up any hope of a consular appointment, which, being very little of a party man, he had sought both through Hawthorne and later from the Lincoln administration. He had also had enough of a brief career of lecturing, in the years just prior to the War, on such subjects as 'The South Seas,' 'Travelling,' and 'Statuary in Rome,' as far afield as Chicago and Montreal. Consequently, he accepted the job of outdoor inspector of customs in New York. Unlike Hawthorne, he held his post for twenty years, during which he found time to produce his philosophical poem *Clarel,* finally published in 1876 on money provided by an uncle. Its interminable debates between doubt and faith used for their setting the trip to the Holy Land that he had made in 1856 after writing his last novel. With his retirement from the customhouse in 1885, he had sufficient leisure for issuing two more small volumes of verse, privately printed in only twenty-five copies; and for the final major recrudescence of his prose in *Billy Budd,* which was left in manuscript at his death, and not published until 1924.

In *Moby-Dick* Ishmael meditated, as Melville had in *Typee,* on the fact that 'long exile from Christendom and civilization inevitably restores a man to that condition in which God placed him, i.e. what is called savagery,' and added, 'I myself am a savage.' But there were many senses in which Melville was not. Of the same racial mixture as Whitman, English on his father's side, Dutch on his mother's, his ancestors had risen far above the Whitmans' plebeian class. There was a weight of wealth and aristocracy behind Melville much greater even than that behind Hawthorne, and he had suffered a much sharper personal experience of family decline. His mother's forebears had been good brewers in Albany from the era of Harmen Van Gansevoort, who had come to this country sometime before 1660, and whose descendants had given the name to Gansevoort Street in New York, at the foot of which, ironically, was the wharf where Melville worked for the government. Melville's grandfather, Peter

2. In his copy of Arnold's *Essays in Criticism,* which he acquired in 1869, he marked Maurice de Guérin's dictum, 'The literary career seems to me unreal, both in its own essence, and in the rewards which one seeks from it, and therefore fatally marred by a secret absurdity.' To this Melville added: 'This is the first verbal statement of a truth which everyone who thinks in these days must have felt.' He also scored a remark on the torture of having to produce: 'To a sensitive man like Guérin, to silence his genius is more tolerable than to hackney it.'

Gansevoort, had been a distinguished soldier in the Revolution, and his namesake, the uncle who was to provide for *Clarel,* graduated from Princeton, became a banker in Albany, and was an active public figure during the same period when an enterprising Irish Presbyterian immigrant, William James, was founding his family's fortune there in commerce and real estate. Melville's other grandfather, Major Thomas Melville, the subject of Holmes' 'The Last Leaf,' was, like so many Boston revolutionaries, conservative in everything except his opposition to unjust taxation, and wore his cocked-hat and knee-breeches until his death in 1832.

Melville's father died in that same year, his mind deranged by worry and overwork. He had been an importer of dry-goods, who had established himself first at Albany, and then, prospering, had moved to New York just before his third child, Herman, was born. He believed that 'money is the only solid substratum on which man can safely build in this world,' and was never deflected towards any other goal. But his business did not recover from a depression in the late twenties; he became deeply involved in debt and was forced to move back to Albany, badly beaten. Within two years after his death, his son Herman had to leave the Albany Academy and become a clerk in the bank. But even less promising prospects lay ahead. In the year of the panic of 1837 the boy shipped for Liverpool, for substantially the same reasons that he attributed to Redburn: 'Sad disappointments in several plans which I had sketched for my future life, the necessity of doing something for myself, united to a naturally roving disposition, had now conspired within me, to send me to sea as a sailor.'

Redburn's shocked horror at his first glimpse of the suffering and brutality of the world was intensified by the contrast with his family's former well-being. An equally strong contrast was borne in upon the narrator of *Typee,* who, in 1841, was 'forced by the united influences of Captain Marryat and hard times' to embark on a whaler. In *Typee* Melville's most serious scrutiny was given to the differences between civilized and savage life, to the frequently contaminating effect of the white man. Even in his relaxed days on the island, when Fayaway slipped off her robe and stood with it in the bow of the canoe as the prettiest mast and sail he had ever seen, another force was working beneath the happy surface of Melville's mind. He could never be a savage; his background of Presbyterian orthodoxy, though in abeyance now, was soon to reassert itself in his meditations on innate depravity.

Melville's early experience had thus compelled his attention to the essential problems of tragedy. The Albany in which he grew up was known as a rich man's town where 'the best families live extremely well, enjoying all the conveniences and luxuries of life; but the poor have scarcely the necessaries for subsistence.'[3] His rapid initiation into the contrast between aristocratic pretensions and the actual state of masses of people gave him much to ponder concerning the theory and practice of democracy in America. He next made the equally rapid discovery that all the pretensions of civilization might be no better grounded than those on which the French and English missionaries attempted to convert the Polynesians, while actually preparing their ruin at the hands of predatory commerce. This completed his education in skepticism, yet he was a skeptic with a religious and philosophic bias that would not let him rest, but drove him further into speculation on the nature of good and evil than any of his contemporaries had gone. When he demanded, in his essay on Hawthorne, recognition for 'those writers who breathe that unshackled, democratic spirit of Christianity in all things,' he was just coming to his own full stature. In his examination of both society and religion he became increasingly possessed by Hamlet's problem, by the difference between what seems and what is. What impressed him most in all Shakespeare's tragedies was this same probing 'at the very axis of reality.' He declared that, 'tormented into desperation, Lear, the frantic king, tears off the mask, and speaks the same madness of vital truth.' In *Moby-Dick* and *Pierre* he made his great attempt thus to unmask himself and his age.

3. Quoted from Dr. Morse's standard geography of the time by H. A. Larrabee, 'Herman Melville's Early Years in Albany' (*New York History,* April 1934). This is the most substantial study yet to be made of Melville's family background and boyhood environment. Larrabee's conclusion is that Christian Albany furnished a striking example of the typically American contrast between 'the *professed* creed, which was largely traditional, theological and imported; and the *practised* one which was native, commercial and opportunist.'

2. *Mardi:* A Source-Book for Plenitude

BUT, AGAIN unlike Hawthorne, he did not start as a writer with a tragic vision. We have found the tone of Hawthorne's earliest sketches to be virtually that of his latest novel; the tone of *Typee* may be suggested by one of Melville's remarks about the savage life, how it gave him 'that all-pervading sensation which Rousseau has told us he at one time experienced, the mere buoyant sense of a healthful physical existence.' The opening chapter—and a great deal can be told about a writer from the first note he strikes—brought a fresh quality to the polite American writing of that day, a hearty and full-blooded exuberance. Melville gave at once a picture of a native queen, with a Rabelaisian anecdote:

She was habited in a gaudy tissue of scarlet cloth, trimmed with yellow silk, which, descending a little below the knees, exposed to view her bare legs, embellished with spiral tattooing . . . Upon her head was a fanciful turban of purple velvet, figured with silver sprigs, and surmounted by a tuft of variegated feathers.

The ship's company crowding into the gangway to view the sight, soon arrested her majesty's attention. She singled out from their number an old *salt,* whose bare arms and feet and exposed breast were covered with as many inscriptions in India ink as the lid of an Egyptian sarcophagus. Notwithstanding all the sly hints and remonstrances of the French officers, she immediately approached the man, and pulling farther open the bosom of his duck frock, and rolling up the leg of his wide trousers, she gazed with admiration at the bright blue and vermilion pricking, thus disclosed to view. She hung over the fellow, caressing him, and expressing her delight in a variety of wild exclamations and gestures. The embarrassment of the polite Gauls at such an unlooked-for occurrence may be easily imagined; but picture their consternation, when all at once the royal lady, eager to display the hieroglyphics on her own sweet form, bent forward for a moment, and turning sharply round, threw up the skirts of her mantle, and revealed a sight from which the aghast Frenchmen retreated precipitately, and tumbling into their boat, fled the scene of so shocking a catastrophe.

Whether or not Falstaff's threat, 'I'll tickle your catastrophe!' was in Melville's mind as he wrote, it tends to spring to the reader's. The sustained pungency of such a passage reveals a writer fully in command of his material. The kind of life he relishes is epitomized in the portrait of Dr. Long Ghost in *Omoo:* for from whatever high estate this whaler's doctor 'might have fallen, he had certainly at some time or other spent money, drunk Burgundy, and associated with gentlemen. As for his learning, he quoted Virgil, and talked of Hobbes of Malmsbury, besides repeating poetry by the canto, especially "Hudibras." He was, moreover, a man who had seen the world. In the easiest way imaginable, he could refer to an amour he had in Palermo, his lion-hunting before breakfast among the Caffres, and the quality of the coffee to be drunk in Muscat.' The personality of the author, which radiates through both these books, suggests, in its self-possession and in its robust meeting of life, something of the 'great individual' whom Whitman's poems were to announce a decade later:

The great individual, fluid as Nature, chaste, affectionate, compassionate,
　　fully-armed . . .
A life that shall be copious, vehement, spiritual, bold.

Near the opening of *Mardi* Melville broke into a strain different from any that had belonged to his narratives of adventure. This might be Emerson speaking: 'All things form but one whole . . . No custom is strange; no creed is absurd; no foe, but who will in the end prove a friend.' A few chapters later, when he took Sir Thomas Browne as his witness for the magnificent variety of existence, he held that the only real infidelity was for 'a live man to vote himself dead.' *Mardi* could serve as source book for reconstructing the conflicting faiths and doubts that were sweeping this country at the end of the eighteen-forties. While the habit of writing had been growing on Melville, he had also become charged with many of the beliefs of his day: the potential magnitude of democratic man, his pride in his equal heritage of all philosophies and creeds, and yet, contrasting with this, a new awareness even in America, borne in upon us by the failure of the European revolutions of 1848, of the complex forces involved in the struggle for freedom.

In Melville's case the double discovery—of his inner self and of the social and intellectual world of which he was part—took place so swiftly during his first years back in America that it seemed to him like a new birth. Halfway through *Mardi* he tried to articulate his sense of what had happened to him, by a succession of images in a chapter called

'Dreams.' He now felt that 'many souls' were in him, as though he was undulating to the swell of a vast ocean, as though he was hearing also the call and response of all the instruments in an orchestra. He translated this music into a succession of great authors whom he had read or heard of, beginning with the phrase that, 'like a grand ground swell, Homer's old organ rolls its vast volumes under the light frothy wave-crests of Anacreon and Hafiz; and high over my ocean, sweet Shakespeare soars, like all the larks of the spring.' Again his image shifted to that of the Mississippi mustering all its tributary streams: 'so, with all the past and present pouring in me, I roll down my billow from afar.' Yet with his sense that this 'sort of sleep-walking of the mind' was a state of inspiration, he felt that his own powers had not originated it: 'not I, but another: God is my Lord.'

Shortly before this, Babbalanja,[1] Melville's philosophical mouthpiece in this voyage round the world, had formulated what he was trying to probe: "I am intent upon the essence of things, the mystery that lieth beyond . . . that which is beneath the seeming.' In the chapter immediately after Melville's symbolization of the birth of his own inner life in dreams, King Media pointed out to Babbalanja the dangers involved in his quest: 'if doubts distract you, in vain will you seek sympathy from your fellow men . . . you are ever unfixed.' That forecasts Melville's state at the time he was writing *Pierre,* the flux in which he felt himself helplessly tossed. But even here he was aware that his new fullness, Babbalanja's sense that 'in one lifetime we live a hundred lives,' was a far stronger force than he could handle. He projected Babbalanja's problem by the device of making the philosopher's utterance of dark truths come

1. The names in *Mardi* are a conglomeration of fragments of Polynesian dialects and of onomatopoeic sounds that Melville borrowed from other languages or invented for himself. Babbalanja suggests 'babbling angel' or perhaps merely 'babbling on,' your connotations depending on what you think of philosophers. Azzageddi, the philosopher's turbulent demon, may owe his name in part to the Italian word for battle-ax. King Media generally acts as a moderator. Taji is the name the islanders give to the narrator, since he seems to them an avatar of their White God. I presume that Yoomy and Yillah were meant to be lovely sounds for the lyric poet and the blonde.

Further investigation of Melville's background may turn up more particulars like those noted by Willard Thorp: that the account of surf-board riding in the chapter, 'Rare Sport at Ohonoo,' is based on what Melville observed at Waikiki Beach on Oahu; and that Monlova, the valley where the travellers feasted, is really Manoa. Melville, who lived for several months in Hawaii before being mustered into the navy, seems also to have made some use in *Mardi* of folk-tales of the islands.

through moments of possession by the demon Azzageddi. Only in that way could Melville convey his own mingled sense of plenitude and conflict. Thus, then, did Babbalanja express his crowded sensation of the promise and yet incompletion of man, in words again very like those in which Emerson had for a decade been posing the dilemma of his newly wakened country: 'Before a full-developed man, Mardi would fall down and worship . . . Giants are in our germs; but we are dwarfs, staggering under heads overgrown. Heaped, our measures burst. We die of too much life.'

Thoreau had been conscious of that plenitude as he settled down to keep his journal in Concord. He had written in 1840:

> The world is a fit theatre to-day in which any part may be acted. There is this moment proposed to me every kind of life that men lead anywhere, or that imagination can paint. By another spring I may be a mail carrier in Peru, or a South African planter, or a Siberian exile, or a Greenland whaler, or a settler on the Columbia River, or a Canton merchant, or a soldier in Florida, or a mackerel-fisher off Cape Sable, or a Robinson Crusoe in the Pacific, or a silent navigator of any sea. So wide is the choice of parts, what a pity if the part of Hamlet be left out!

This was Thoreau's version of Whitman's catalogues of endless possibilities for the new American. It provides a clear instance of what Professor Lovejoy, the most searching historian of romanticism, has found to be the enduring element in its ideal of diversity. Along with the individualism, which could so readily run to extremes, was the movement's equivalent for universality: the insistence that the great individual must possess a comprehensive knowledge of every activity of mankind and a sympathy to match his knowledge.[2] The great breadth of *Leaves of Grass,* as of *Moby-Dick,* is owing primarily to this desire to enter as fully as possible into the immensely varied range of experience.

Thoreau said that he had listed only a few of his chances, since he might, if he chose, 'repeat the adventures of Marco Polo or Mandeville.' In order not to be distracted and dispersed, he set himself the lifelong task of simplifying, to distill the essence of so much potentiality. Bab-

2. See especially 'Romanticism and the Principle of Plenitude,' Chapter x in A. O. Lovejoy, *The Great Chain of Being* (1936). By plenitude Lovejoy implies not merely fullness but potentiality of fulfilment.

balanja had no such self-possession, though he was the kind of nay-sayer whom Melville admired. When Babbalanja saw his fellow-men all grafting new vines and dwelling in flourishing arbors, he forever persisted in pruning his: 'I will not add, I will diminish; I will train myself down to the standard of what is unchangeably true.' Shortly after Azzageddi became articulate, the philosopher's tone grew even more intense. He insisted that during a long discourse he had not asserted any wisdom of his own: 'I but fight against the armed and crested lies of Mardi, that like a host assail me. I am stuck full of darts; but tearing them from out me, gasping, I discharge them whence they come.'

It is hardly surprising that Melville's efforts in this book are frequently turgid and confused. Here he was not in control; he possessed no disciplined knowledge of philosophy, and was often whirled about by his abstractions. You can hardly construct a coherent view of man and society from the many counterstatements that are made; but you can follow the urgent drives of his mind in the directions in which they were aiming. One conversation in the grove between the poet, the philosopher, and the historian constitutes virtually a handbook of current theory of art, no less typical for being somewhat disordered. Most of the chief Emersonian positions are scattered about here, though according to Melville's own statement, he had not yet read the *Essays.*[3] However, he could have picked up many similar ideas from Carlyle, at the same time as, responding to the *Zeitgeist* in much the same way as Whitman, he was finding out the others for himself. Babbalanja—who, like most philosophers, dominated the talk—gave utterance to all of the following: that 'the truest poets are but mouthpieces'; that the poet and the philosopher are ideally one; that the past and present are an organic whole, since 'in the books of the past we learn naught but of the present; in those of the present, the past'; that every man can be inspired if he heeds the one supreme autocrat—'his crowned and sceptred instinct'; that content bursts through form; that no finished work is more than 'a poor scrawled copy of something within'; that 'genius is full of trash,' which must tumble out with the purer element, since 'the way to heaven is through hell.' Judging from the tone of Melville's letters to Hawthorne, substantially

3. Cf. p. 185 above. Melville's statement to Duyckinck, 'I had only glanced at a book of his once in Putnam's store—that was all I knew of him, till I heard him lecture,' was dated March 1849, when *Mardi* had been finished for some time, and was just coming off the press.

these views seem to have been operating in the composition of *Moby-Dick*.

It would be harder to abstract from *Mardi* Melville's politics, since most of the relevant passages here are cast in the form of satire, somewhat in the vein of Cooper's *Monikins*. In the course of their voyage, King Media and his followers visit Porpheero (Europe) and Vivenza (the United States). Their criticisms of America must be taken as partly Melville's, partly as the warnings of a detached king and philosopher. Melville's own views at this time, as expressed outside this book, included an admiration for General Taylor, the hero of Palo Alto and the successful Whig candidate for the presidency in 1848. In the summer after the Mexican War, which had so properly outraged Emerson and Thoreau, Melville had written, in the short-lived *Yankee Doodle, or the American Punch,* a hearty series of 'Authentic Anecdotes of "Old Zack," ' celebrating among other things the legend of how 'Old Rough and Ready' had once had a tack on his saddle all day long without knowing it. These sketches make pretty flat reading now, since tall-tale humor was hardly Melville's forte. But despite his enthusiasm for Taylor, if we can judge from the account of a senatorial debate in Vivenza, Melville saw through the evils of imperialist expansion as expressed by the jingoistic oratory of Senator Allen of Ohio,[4] who made belligerent threats against the activities of the British in the Pacific Northwest.

As a result of the outbreaks of 1848 Melville had also become more critically aware of other dangers that might lie in store for this country. He gave an affecting picture of the suffering of the Chartists—'Bread, bread! or I die mid these sheaves!'—and of their abortive march on London, which he viewed as a case of a revolution betrayed by its leaders, in which 'down went the hammers and sickles.' Consequently, when his travellers reached America, they urged the new country not to ignore so recklessly the lessons of history. Some of the opinions they voiced might have come straight from Carlyle: 'Better be secure under one king, than exposed to violence from twenty millions of monarchs, though oneself be of the number.' But an anonymous proclamation by one of the party came much nearer to a problem which was to absorb Melville under many differing guises: to what extent could man be free? The proclamation pointed out that the chronicles of Vivenza might have told a dif-

---

4. The disguise of Alanno of Hio-Hio is even more transparent than that of Saturnina— 'Gall and Spurzheim! saw you ever such a brow?'—for Webster.

ferent story if its population had been 'pressed and packed' like that of its sire-land Dominora. Yet even Vivenza's western plains would be over-run at last, 'and then, the recoil must come.' Then turbulent forces would prove the inherent instability of a republic, which would not remain as liberal as it had been. For the rule often was that 'he who hated oppressors is become an oppressor himself.' Moreover, one fundamental lesson that the people of Vivenza had yet to learn was that 'it is not the prime end, and chief blessing, to be politically free.' This freedom is 'only good as a means,' and counts for little if the people are abased in poverty. Nor did it behoove Vivenza to be too complacent with its record thus far. 'Students of history are horror-struck at the massacres of old; but in the shambles men are being murdered to-day.'

This proclamation is torn into shreds by the crowd as an insult from 'an old tory and monarchist,' and is to be taken as Melville's acute awareness of the problem rather than his own certain conclusions. *The Southern Quarterly Review* objected to his 'loathsome picture of Mr. Calhoun, in the character of a slave driver'; but here again, though declaring that humanity was crying out against the 'vast enormity' of the institution, Melville had Babbalanja make a plea for moderation on the part of the North in order to preserve the Union. Though less skeptical of purposive action than Hawthorne, Melville had already learned, from observing the activities of the missionaries in the South Seas, that 'the object in view may be the achievement of much good,' and yet the 'agency may nevertheless be productive of evil.'

It would be even more difficult to say precisely what Melville believed on the basis of his treatment of religion in *Mardi.* So far as this book has a resolution, it lies in Babbalanja's finding peace at last in the ideal Christian state of Serenia. Although the church is corrupt in the rest of Mardi, here 'right reason' and Alma (Christ) are held to be the same. Here, though the people do not believe in man's perfection, they do not regard him as 'absolutely set' against all good. Here, too, the social state, though also imperfect, at least is not based on making 'the miserable many support the happy few.' But Taji, the narrator, cannot be reconciled to remaining in Serenia, or deflected from his hopeless quest of the maiden, Yillah. In a passage near the end, which strikes the note of intensity that became habitual with Melville in his pursuit of truth, Taji breaks out: 'Oh, reader, list! I've chartless voyaged . . . So, if after all these fearful, fainting trances, the verdict be, the golden haven was not gained;—yet, in bold quest thereof, better to sink in boundless deeps, than float on vulgar shoals; and give me, ye gods, an utter wreck, if wreck I do.'

The tediously elaborated allegory of Taji's thwarted love, which leads up to this wild conclusion, is at no point very lucid. It starts with Taji's rescue of the blonde girl from her captors, a rescue that involves the killing of a pagan priest. It is complicated by Yillah's disappearance as the result of the machinations of dark Hautia. In some passages the two girls seem to stand for Taji's good and evil angels; and the loss of Yillah seems to symbolize the fact that good based on an initial act of evil is doomed to end in disaster. Elsewhere, however, Hautia appears to suggest experience in contrast with Yillah's innocence, and Taji's rejection of the dark girl's advances thus to involve a denial of mature passion. The resulting impression is that good and evil can be inextricably and confusingly intermingled—a state that was to be one of Melville's chief sources of ambiguity. One reason why this theme is not very moving here is that the symbols he has chosen to convey it are artificial: these girls might have stepped out of any of the imitations of *Lalla Rookh*. Another, and more important reason has to do with the uncertainties of Melville's unformed style. It would be more accurate to speak of his styles, since this book, which contains enough allusions to the names of other authors to make the catalogue of a library, veers from opening passages of straight narrative energy to suggestions of Browne's music buried in Carlyle and in even more adulterated rhetoric.[5] Melville was aware of the transition he was going through, since he made Babbalanja say that 'there are those who falter in the common tongue, because they

5. Obvious marks of Carlyle's thought include King Media's scorn of juries: 'What! are twelve wise men more wise than one? or will twelve fools, put together, make one sage?'—questions that practically paraphrase, 'If nine out of ten men are fools, how look for wisdom in the ballot-box?' One of Babbalanja's 'discourses in the dark' runs close to Teufelsdröckh's courage of desperation: 'Sick with the spectacle of the madness of men, and broken with spontaneous doubts, I sometimes see but two things in all Mardi to believe:—that I myself exist, and that I can most happily, or at least miserably exist, by the practice of righteousness.' Consequently, it seems likely that Babbalanja's passage from 'the everlasting nay' to a state of spiritual acceptance may also have been suggested by the conversion of Carlyle's philosopher. The likelihood of this is increased by the fact that 'the clothes-philosophy' itself is drawn on for the chapters satirizing the Tapparians, a tribe whose social distinctions were entirely based on the quality of tappa each wore.

Carlyle's apostrophes continued to explode in *Moby-Dick*, where there is a hint of the method of *Sartor Resartus* in the introductory 'Etymology' and 'Extracts'; and more than

think in another; and these are accounted stutterers and stammerers.'

The chapter on 'Dreams' is a parable, not merely of the birth of his inner life, but of the way in which this fresh consciousness demanded new ranges of language for its expression. In this Dionysian state, as he called it, he turned instinctively, as Whitman was going to do, to analogies with music and with the sea; and the result, in a passage that tried to express his sense of abundance by means of the most recent allusions, was closer to poetry than to prose: 'Dreams! dreams! golden dreams: endless, and golden, as the flowery prairies, that stretch away from the Rio Sacramento, in whose waters Danae's shower was woven;—prairies like rounded eternities: jonquil leaves beaten out; and my dreams herd like buffaloes, browsing on to the horizon, and browsing on round the world; and among them, I dash with my lance, to spear one, ere they all flee.' The crowding alteration of the images, the way the sentence structure breaks in the middle into virtual incoherence, indicate how far Melville had gone in his 'sleep-walking of the mind.'

In the chapter that describes the island of Nora-Bamma, he may have been indebted to Tennyson's 'Lotos-Eaters' for his realm of endless afternoon, and here his writing breaks even farther from any norm of prose, almost provoking scansion into feet:

Who dwells in Nora-Bamma? Dreamers, hypochondriacs, somnambulists; who, from the cark and care of outer Mardi fleeing, in the poppy's jaded odors, seek oblivion for the past, and ecstasies to come.

Open-eyed, they sleep and dream; on their roof-trees, grapes unheeded drop. In Nora-Bamma, whispers are as shouts; and at a zephyr's breath, from the woodlands shake the leaves, as of humming-birds, a flight.

a hint in the exaggerated facetiousness of quoting from imaginary authors, such as 'the learned Fogo Von Slack, in his great work on smells, a text-book on that subject.' Another of Carlyle's doctrines, the celebration of Silence, is refracted in both *Moby-Dick* and *Pierre.* Some of the grammatical eccentricities of the latter, the use of the second person singular, the heavily compounded German adjective, the inordinate frequency of the dash, are probably owing to the same roiled source.

The sweep of Melville's continued interest in Carlyle is shown by his having borrowed from Duyckinck during 1850 all of the following: *Sartor, Heroes and Hero-Worship,* the translations of *German Romance* and of *Wilhelm Meister.* He went beyond Carlyle to at least one of his sources in also borrowing Richter's *Flower Pieces.* The torrent of allusions that was turned loose in the chapter on 'Dreams' includes mention of Ossian, Waller, Milton, Petrarch, Prior, St. Paul, Montaigne, Julian the Apostate, Augustine, Thomas à Kempis, Zeno, Democritus, Pyrrho, Plato, Proclus, Bacon, Zoroaster, Virgil, Sidney, Xenophon.

Such 'poetic' writing is not a medium that could possibly be sustained; nor is it very effective even for a short rhapsody. Melville falls into stock phrases ('cark and care,' 'zephyr's breath'); he is hypnotized by his own rhythm into images that are anything but exact, since the stirring of leaves in the slightest air would seem to have little in common with the intense concentrated whirr of a humming-bird. By following the transcendental denial of distinctions between prose and verse, not in theoretical discussion but in such practice, Melville raises questions that are even more relevant to Whitman. But Whitman, having rejected the forms of conventional verse in which he showed little talent, found, as we shall see, a base of his own by developing his interest in oratory into a new kind of lyrical speech. What base lies beneath these passages of Melville's is somewhat harder to discern. Compared with both Emerson and Whitman, he seems to have been relatively indifferent to the effects of spoken rhetoric. Although he said that Redburn had had 'vague thoughts of becoming a great orator like Patrick Henry,' when he rounded back upon this subject in *Pierre* he added that 'on the high-raised, stage platform of the Saddle Meadows Academy, the sons of the most indigent day-laborers were wont to drawl out the fiery revolutionary rhetoric,' and were thus instructed in 'that great American bulwark and bore—elocution.'

By the time of *Moby-Dick*, Melville's characters were delivering dramatic speeches based on Shakespeare's verse, but that profound influence had not yet begun to work on him in *Mardi*. Nor had he yet learned the truth that he was to recognize in Shakespeare's most mature pronouncement on the relation of art to nature. The passage comes in *The Winter's Tale,* where Polixenes is talking to Perdita about her garden. Melville double-scored it, and added the comment, 'a world here,' to its opening two lines:

> Yet nature is made better by no mean
> But nature makes that mean: so, over that art,
> Which you say adds to nature, is an art
> That nature makes. You see, sweet maid, we marry
> A gentler scion to the wildest stock,
> And make conceive a bark of baser kind
> By bud of nobler race: this is an art
> Which does mend nature, change it rather, but
> The art itself is nature.

Years later Melville was to triple-score, in Arnold's essay on Spinoza, the philosopher's statement that 'our desire is not that nature may obey us, but, on the contrary that we may obey nature.' But in *Mardi* he had hardly begun to think how this difficult end might be gained. In his first two books he could claim that his intention had been simply to describe what he had seen; and though we know now that the process of composition was more complex than he alleged, since he drew on many printed narratives to reinforce and rearrange his own memories, still his main problem there remained the organization of concrete events. In *Mardi* he had reached levels where he had no first-hand experience to support him, and he had not yet gained much notion of how to blend his abstractions into symbols by his own equivalent of the metaphysical style.[6] As a result, much of this romance was no more organically based either on observation of nature or on any norm of prose than this transport of Taji's at the height of his bliss with Yillah: 'High above me was Night's shadowy bower, traversed, vine-like, by the Milky Way, and heavy with golden clusterings. Oh stars! oh eyes, that see me, whereso'er I roam: serene, intent, inscrutable for aye, tell me, Sybils, what I am.—Wondrous worlds on worlds! Lo, round and round me, shining, awful spells: all-glorious, vivid constellations, God's diadem ye are! To you, ye stars, man owes his subtlest raptures, thoughts unspeakable, yet full of faith.'

As an example of emotion *not* conveyed, this quotation might well have been choked off at the end of the first sentence, but Melville's extraordinary if intermittent triumphs in *Moby-Dick* could hardly be thrown into higher relief than by realizing that only a couple of years earlier he could fall into a manner indistinguishable from that of hundreds of writers in the gift-books. This peculiarly American brand of minor romanticism failed of all vividness since, as a result of the cultural lag, our writers could still pour out the dregs of eighteenth-century generalized diction in their loose ejaculations over natural beauty. One remedy was furnished by Poe, who deliberately set out, as in his presentation of the vale of Arnheim, to make his effects depend on being as artificial as possible.

But Melville had none of Poe's equipment as a theorist. It is significant that his only passages of detailed discussion of the craft of fiction came in *The Confidence Man,* when his practice of it was virtually over. In

6. See above, pp. 119-32.

Mardi, in spite of his enthusiasm for various transcendental ideas about art, he was obviously not operating on any coherent theory at all. His excursions into elaborate rhythms were spontaneous improvisations, not controlled experiments to prove that prose could absorb some of the quality of poetry. His formal verse, in the songs of Yoomy, was wholly banal, and showed only that his knowledge of that medium was even more lacking in the mastery of any organic principles. What his problem came down to was this: He knew how to write effective surface narrative, and was to prove it again in *Redburn* and *White Jacket.* But he now wanted to produce more complex effects; yet when he tried to surpass the technique of the simplest realism, he had nothing at hand but the stagey trappings of romance. He had not yet studied Hawthorne, and had not even glimpsed the solution which, though he did not make it explicit until *The Confidence Man,* he would demonstrate in *Moby-Dick:* of how he could provide 'more reality, than real life itself can show.'[7]

This solution demanded the bringing together of the two halves of his interest: the immediate with the abstract, the concrete event with the thought rising from it, the scientifically accurate with the imaginatively free. These halves of man tended to become ever more widely dissevered in the increasing specialization of the nineteenth century, and it needed great breadth of character to unite them. A typical limitation of the romantic movement was that its imaginative writers did not possess adequate knowledge of their environment. For instance, when a writer said, 'I am one with the tempest,' the context generally showed him to be attitudinizing, or attributing his emotions—'Be thou me, impetuous one'—to natural forces whose impersonal violence he had imperfectly comprehended. Melville himself noted this weakness in the earliest piece of his criticism that has come to light, his review of J. Ross Browne's *Etchings of a Whaling Cruise,* which he wrote just as *Omoo* was about to appear.[8] He admired the book's 'disenchanting revelations' of sea life, its tonic antidote to such 'humbugging' as Barry Cornwall's popular

> The Sea! The Sea! the open Sea!
> The blue, the fresh, the ever free!

7. See the discussion of 'The Crucial Definition of Romance,' pp. 264-71 above.

8. In *The Literary World* (March 6, 1847). This was reprinted for the first time by Willard Thorp (*Melville: Representative Selections,* pp. 320-27), who found the holograph manuscript in the Duyckinck collection in the New York Public Library.

In his growing concern with reality Melville believed that any such poetry was 'very much on the wane,' that 'the perusal of Dana's *Two Years Before the Mast,* for instance, somewhat impairs the relish with which we read Byron's spiritual "Address to the Ocean."' Consequently, when Melville himself said, 'You become identified with the tempest, your insignificance is lost in the riot of the stormy universe around,' he was speaking out of such assimilated knowledge of a terrific event as enabled him to finish his account of this great storm in *White Jacket* with a symbolic reflection that gradually extended the event into a basic law of life: 'But how could we reach our long-promised homes without encountering Cape Horn? by what possibility avoid it? And though some ships have weathered it without these perils, yet by far the greater part must encounter them. Lucky it is that it comes about midway in the homeward-bound passage, so that the sailors have time to prepare for it, and time to recover from it after it is astern. But, sailor or landsman, there is some sort of a Cape Horn for all.' Melville had already tried to dramatize what this crisis might mean for the relentless seeker for truth, in the concluding lines of *Mardi,* where Taji, having thrown off the restraining hands of his friends the historian and the poet, turned his prow into the running tide, which seized him 'like a hand omnipotent,' and thus 'pursuers and pursued flew on, over an endless sea.' By the time of *Pierre* he had run straight against the brute power of the Cape, and needed every ounce of strength to survive.

We shall want later to give more attention to the way in which Melville's dominant symbols tended both to recur within a single work and also to extend their applications from book to book. But at this point, his growing perception of the symbol's value can serve to indicate why he was not content merely with reacting against the romantic poets. If the alternative to their imaginative fullness meant restricting your report of experience to what you could measure scientifically, that seemed to him even less true. Even at the period when his steady practice in writing had given him such control over specific detail that he could turn out both *Redburn* and *White Jacket* within a year, he was not satisfied with this kind of mastery. He had been enough impressed by Smollett's racy skill to sketch many of the characters and scenes in *White Jacket* under his tutelage, especially the brutal Captain Claret and the physical horrors of an operation as conducted by Dr. Cadwallader Cuticle. He also responded to his contemporary Dickens' manner of suggesting eccentric idioms, as in the fragments of the Dutch sailor's talk in *Redburn,* the lingo of Stubb and Flask, the Micawber-like locutions of Charlie Millthorpe in *Pierre.* But such devices were never more than an intermittent concern for Melville. The most perfected surfaces of verisimilitude could lead, he believed, only to the reproduction 'of the same old crowd round the customhouse counter.' They could give him realism, but not reality.

3. Autobiography and Art

WHAT he meant by this latter term is fully illustrated by only one passage prior to *Moby-Dick,* the chapter at the very end of *White Jacket,* which describes the fall from the yard-arm: the first extended instance when the two halves of his experience, his outer and inner life, are fused in expression. It merits scrutiny, for it is very different in texture from the rest of the book, which comes near to being overweighted by the accumulation of circumstantial particulars. It is equally different from the romantic effusions of *Mardi* for reasons which involve the innermost nature of Melville's developing power.

This chapter, 'The Last of the Jacket,' tells how this 'outlandish garment' of canvas, which he had had to devise for himself since no more regular pea-jackets were to be had, and which has stood from the outset as a token of bad luck and isolation, at last nearly causes his death. He had gone aloft to reef the halyards, when a deep plunge of the ship sent the heavy skirts of the jacket right over his head. Thinking it was the sail that had thus flapped, he threw up his hands to drag it down.

Just then the ship gave another sudden jerk, and, head foremost, I pitched from the yard. I knew where I was, from the rush of the air by my ears, but all else was a nightmare. A bloody film was before my eyes, through which, ghost-like, passed and repassed my father, mother, and sisters. An unutterable nausea oppressed me; I was conscious of gasping; there seemed no breath in my body. It was over one hundred feet that I fell—down, down, with lungs collapsed as in death.

From even these few sentences you can see what distinguishes this from all of Melville's previous recording of events. This is no longer an external description, but the evocation of an immediate moment. That evocation depends on his ability to present the life of his senses with a tenacity and fullness like that of Keats, in order to convey the actual oppression on his whole body. He has now also realized the physical sources of rhythm. No longer does he merely make analogies with music or with the sea; he has learned the way to create an experience by means of the most subtly varied movement of his prose. After the first gasp of horror, he prolonged the endless sensation of falling by adding, 'All I had seen, and read, and heard, and all I had thought and felt in my life, seemed intensified in one fixed idea in my soul. But dense as this idea was, it was made up of atoms. Having fallen from the projecting yard-arm end, I was conscious of a collected satisfaction in feeling that I should not be dashed on the deck, but would sink into the speechless profound of the sea.'

All sense of speed has now slackened off, and the rhythm of his sentences has itself become part of the trance-like balance he felt, hovering between life and death:

With the bloody, blind film before my eyes, there was a still stranger hum in my head, as if a hornet were there; and I thought to myself, Great God! this is Death! Yet these thoughts were unmixed with alarm. Like frost-work that flashes and shifts its scared hues in the sun, all my braided, blended emotions were in themselves icy cold and calm.

So protracted did my fall seem, that I can even now recall the feeling of wondering how much longer it would be, ere all was over and I struck. Time seemed to stand still, and all the worlds seemed poised on their poles, as I fell, soul-becalmed, through the eddying whirl and swirl of the maelstrom air.

The elaborate simile of the frost-work may seem too far-fetched to be an organic part of such an experience, yet it serves to develop what Melville wanted: the strange feeling of remoteness, where the coldness of fear itself was only a shifting tracery. Melville's use of whiteness for such an image had already become instinctive.

The impression of length of time is reinforced by breadth of space, since not only our world but all the other planets too seem poised in this utter calm. Then, when this suspension of movement has been carried to its extreme, the actual violence breaks in again with the 'whirl and swirl' of the maelstrom into which he is plunging. A few matter-of-fact sentences snap the spell of his trance, by describing how, having fallen head-first, he seemed to have partly recovered himself in the air, so that when he struck the water he felt a slanting blow across his shoulder and along his right side. The pace has changed again to breathlessness, which gradually yields to a luxurious relaxation, as the impressions of his eyes and ears and his muscular responses are all drawn upon to convey a new sensation:

As I gushed into the sea, a thunder-boom sounded in my ear; my soul seemed flying from my mouth. The feeling of death flooded over me with the billows. The blow from the sea must have turned me, so that I sank almost feet foremost through a soft, seething, foamy lull. Some current seemed hurrying me away; in a trance I yielded, and sank deeper down with a glide. Purple and pathless was the deep calm now around me, flecked by summer lightnings in an azure afar. The horrible nausea was gone; the bloody, blind film turned a pale green; I wondered whether I was yet dead, or still dying. But of a sudden some fashionless form brushed my side—some inert, soiled fish of the sea; the thrill of being alive again tingled in my nerves, and the strong shunning of death shocked me through.

This illusory calm is built up by resourceful gradations in his verbs of motion, by contrasting the crashing impact with the subsequent soft gliding. The colors, too, are no longer the bloody film of nightmare, or the white icy absence of feeling, but a lovely green, a purple that seems to shade into the azure of a summernight's sky. But then this second trance is shattered by a twist of imagery of the sort that was to become peculiarly Melville's. He is startled back into the sense of being alive by grazing an inert form; hardly anyone but Melville could have created the shudder that results from calling this frightening vagueness some 'soiled fish of the sea.' The *discordia concors,* the unexpected linking of the medium of cleanliness with filth, could only have sprung from an imagination that had apprehended the terrors of the deep, of the immaterial deep as well as the physical.

The reversal of direction which then follows is again dependent on the most skillful variations in rhythm. The moment of agony is protracted, then passes into a struggle of the tiny energy of life pitted against death's overwhelming force. This tension is resolved into a slow upwelling, a quickening of motion, and a final burst of release. But there is no need for further diagrammatic paraphrase:

For one instant an agonizing revulsion came over me as I found myself utterly sinking. Next moment the force of my fall was expended; and there I hung, vibrating in the mid-deep. What wild sounds then rang in my ear! One was a soft moaning, as of low waves on the beach; the other, wild and heartlessly jubilant, as of the sea in the height of a tempest. Oh soul! thou then heardest life and death: as he who stands upon the Corinthian shore hears both the Ionian and Aegean waves. The life-and-death poise soon passed; and then I found myself slowly ascending, and caught a dim glimmering of light.

Quicker and quicker I mounted; till at last I bounded up like a buoy, and my whole head was bathed in the blessed air.

Unlike the metaphysical conceit of the 'soiled fish,' the Homeric simile here is somewhat neutral, since, as they are presented, the Ionian and Aegean seas hardly suggest the terrifying difference between the two contrasted forces. However, the simile has added a kind of Homeric universality; and, taken in conjunction with the elaborate one of the frost-work, is a token of imaginative abundance. But what makes these two pages most notable in their entirety is Melville's extraordinary mastery of his material. On the level of accurate notation of a multiplicity of details, this goes far beyond any skill that he had possessed while writing *Typee* and *Omoo*. He has also succeeded in the more exacting task of telling 'the truth about his own feelings at the moment when they exist.' This is what Eliot has respected in Hemingway, and its difficulty consists in the great demands it makes both on integrity of sensibility and on expert command of language. Moreover, the thematic variations on the symbols of life and death are carefully subordinated to the concrete expression; they add their full pressure of emotion but do not obtrude themselves as abstractions.

This passage is one of the best examples in Melville for the critics who take all art to be autobiography. These pages out of his life have been used to prove the inevitable dependence of writing upon first-hand experience, since it has seemed obvious that only a man who had suffered such a thing could present it with this living fullness. But when the log of the frigate *United States* during the period when Melville was aboard came to light a few years ago, there was no mention, as there would have been if it had happened, of any such accident to him.[1] On the other hand,

1. See *Journal of a Cruise to the Pacific Ocean*, 1842-1844, *with Notes on Herman Melville*, ed. C. R. Anderson (1937).

Nathaniel Ames' *A Mariner's Sketches,* published in 1830, contains the following:

> I was going aloft and had got as far as the futtock shrouds, when a ratlin broke under my feet, and I fell backwards. My first sensation was surprise; I could not imagine where I was, but soon ascertained from the rushing of the air by my ears that I was falling and that head foremost.
>
> Dr. Johnson says that the near approach of death wonderfully concentrates a man's ideas. I am sure it did mine for I never thought so *fast* before or since, as I did during the few seconds that I was tumbling . . . There was a blood-red light before my eyes, through which a thousand horrible forms were constantly gliding. Then I thought of home, and the forms of all I hold dear on earth, and many others, 'strangers of distinction,' beside, floated before me. Then the recollection of the infernal gun and the consequent smash across the breech of it, put all these phantoms to flight, and I felt that peculiar sickness and distress at the stomach, which it is said one experiences when on the point of undergoing a sudden and violent and painful death, and I thought to myself 'surely it *must* be almost time for the shock.'
>
> A shock I certainly did receive, and that no very gentle one across the back of the head, neck and left shoulder, and in an instant all was dark and still. 'It is all over,' thought I, 'this is the state between death and resurrection.' I really thought I had passed the first and awaited with increased terror for the second, when to my utter dismay, I felt myself falling a second time, but the sensation was different; the blow that I had received turned me, and I was descending feet foremost.
>
> But no words can express my delight, my ecstasy, at finding myself *overboard,* instead of on the gun. I kept going down, down, till it appeared to me that the seven fathoms and a half, (the depth of water at our anchorage,) had more than doubled since we let go our anchor.
>
> After a while I became stationary and soon began slowly to ascend. When I looked up, I saw high, very high above me, a dim greenish light, which became brighter and brighter till at last I bounded on the surface like a cork.

That is a record of experience, faithful and informative, which could hardly have served Melville in better stead for his own creation. There could also hardly be a more revelatory instance of some differences between autobiography and art. Melville has borrowed from Ames not only details, but also the outline of his entire sequence. Yet his handling of this material is Shakespearean, since, relieved of the necessity of inventing, he has been able to release all his energy to imagine the sensation as a whole.

He has demonstrated once again his realization of what Donne knew and Tennyson's day had largely forgotten: that there should be no artificial separation between the life of the mind and of the body, that reading, to a quickened imagination, could be as much a part of assimilated experience as adventures. In order to write such a passage Melville did not need to have fallen from a yard-arm, any more than Rimbaud needed to have had disasters in navigation in order to compose *Bateau ivre*. What was essential has emerged in the various traits in Melville's passage: the maturing of thought and emotion that comes from intense living.

Another way of describing this is to call it the capacity for knowledge and sympathy, which, as we have seen, characterized the age's desire for plenitude. Goethe's robust curiosity about knowledge for its own sake took him farthest from the private worlds of merely romantic individualists. Melville had to possess a contagious share of this, if he was to demonstrate that a narrative of the whaling industry could be made the basis both for a tragic drama and for philosophical speculation. He also needed the gift of projecting himself into others' actions, the possession of which he showed by recognizing in Ames' clumsy narrative the very climax to bring to an end the symbol of the ill-starred white jacket. For as the sailor breathed again 'the blessed air,' he ripped off the water-logged garment, and let it sink, so that it would not drag him under once more. And shortly after this event the Capes of Virginia were off their bow. Such imaginative fellow-feeling with others' lives was to constitute Whitman's greatest asset, for it enabled him to range through the multifarious activities of Americans and to persuade his reader to accept the illusion when he said,

> I was the man, I suffered, I was there.

THE REVENGER'S TRAGEDY

'Life, seen from the distance which brings out the true proportion
of all its parts, is revealed as a tragedy—a long record of struggle and
pain, with the death of the hero as the final certainty.'—from the
Translator's Preface to Schopenhauer, *The Wisdom of Life* (1891),
scored by Melville in that year.

1. The Economic Factor

„Redburn"

THE WAKING of Melville's tragic sense is more apparent in *Redburn* and
White Jacket than in the wooden allegory of Yillah and Hautia. These
books reveal that the actual sufferings of mankind had been so impressed
upon his consciousness that none of the optimistic palliatives or compensa-
tions of his age could ever explain them away. As was the case with
Keats, the miseries of the world became misery for him, and would not
let him rest. The account of Redburn's first voyage is a study in disillusion, of innocence confronted with the world, of ideals shattered by facts.
It is the most moving of its author's books before *Moby-Dick,* since it
does not read like a journal of events. It has gained the quality that
comes when material is not written off the top of the mind but rises
to the surface through assimilated memories. Its opening seven chapters
in particular, which take its boyish hero from his upstate village to the
setting sail from New York, are more thematically arranged than anything Melville had heretofore attempted. The curve of each is a downward one from hope to despondency, as every new experience makes a
sharper break with Redburn's previous fancies of the joy of life at sea.
The way these fancies were woven into his childhood is expressed in
passages of idyllic charm, quite different again from any of Melville's
previous styles, and suggestive only of a more robust and more perceptive
Sketch Book.

The contrast between these happy pictures and even the first hours at sea is handled in a way calculated to bring out Redburn's recoil of horror. His encounter with the sailors while still in port had made him dread their roughness, but on the first night out, his romantic view of them begins to return, since they are unexpectedly friendly to him. It only gradually dawns on him that they are drunk. Then, at the height of their conviviality, a man with delirium tremens rushes shrieking up on deck, and before anyone can stop him, throws himself overboard. The men hide their own fright by cruelly abusing Redburn for showing his. From then on he feels himself absolutely alone in the ship, without a friend or companion, and dreads lest he become 'a sort of Ishmael.'

The rest of the book does not quite live up to the opening, since Melville becomes more discursive, and sometimes blurs his effect by neglecting to keep his center of consciousness in Redburn's inexperience, and by adding reflections that could only have occurred to someone much older. But the difference between anticipation and reality is brought to its height by the boy's first impressions of England. It is not the same Liverpool where, a generation later, Henry James descended at a hotel.[1] It is more like the city that Hawthorne knew about through having had to handle in his office many cases of the brutal treatment of seamen. Hawthorne recorded 'the universal testimony that there is a worse set of sailors in these short voyages between Liverpool and America than in any other trade whatever.' But the docks and dingy alleys were only a part of his picture of the city, whereas they formed the world to which Melville himself had belonged on his first voyage. Whether or not he actually saw the same desperate scenes that Redburn describes, the most unforgettable chapter is that which sets forth the boy's discovery of a woman and her two babies who have been left to die of starvation in an open areaway.

The theme of poverty is the most recurrent one through the entire

1. Cf. the account of his arrival in 1870: 'The small hour was just that of my having landed at Liverpool in the gusty, cloudy, overwhelmingly English morning, and pursued, with immediate intensities of appreciation, as I may call the muffled accompaniment for fear of almost indecently overnaming it, a course which had seated me at a late breakfast in the coffee-room of the old Adelphi Hotel ("Radley's" as I had to deplore its lately having ceased to be dubbed,) and handed me over without a scruple to my fate. This doom of inordinate exposure to appearances, aspects, images, every protrusive item almost . . . I regard in other words as having settled upon me once for all while I observed for instance that in England the plate of buttered muffin and its cover were sacredly set upon the slop-bowl after hot water had been ingeniously poured into the same, and had seen that circumstance in a perfect cloud of accompaniments.'

narrative. Redburn, in his misery, cannot bear to think 'of those delightful days, before my father became a bankrupt, and died, and we removed
from the city.' While at sea he tries to read the book that a grim friend
of his family's had given him, with the advice that it might teach him
how to retrieve their fortunes. But he finds *The Wealth of Nations* unreadable, and becomes even more wretched when he looks at the guide
book that had belonged to his father, and reflects that he is no traveller
but only 'a common carrier.' However, he gradually grows beyond self-
pity as he learns many things about the poor. He notices that when a collection is taken up for a stowaway boy, whose immigrant father had died
of drink in America, and who is trying to get back to Lancashire, the
officers lend it their best wishes, but fifteen dollars 'in cash and tobacco' is
contributed by the sailors and steerage passengers. On shore, he is struck
everywhere by the violently artificial separation between rich and poor,
and by the heartless injustices that result from it. In fact he has no chance
to observe much else as he wanders about the streets, and is even turned
out of the Lyceum because of his shabby clothes, just as though he had
been 'a strange dog, with a muddy hide, that had stolen out of the
gutter.' The last thing he saw in England, as the ship was pulling out of
the dock, was a policeman collaring a boy and dragging him off to the
guardhouse.

His study of society was advanced on the voyage home by the sharp
boundary line between the few cabin passengers and the mass of emigrants. The quitting of land was as tragic as it had been on the way out,
since to match the drunken suicide there was the discovery that one of the
newly impressed men, brought on board by a crimp, was not drunk, but
already a corpse. This horrible fact seemed to set the tone for what happened in the ensuing weeks. Jammed into inadequate quarters, the steerage passengers fell helplessly into squalor, of which the inevitable result
was a pestilence of malignant fever that killed them by dozens. When
the weather grew milder and the contagion subsided—since those who remained could go on deck and have decent air again—Redburn added to
his discoveries the fact that grief is subdued 'among the poor and desolate.' For it becomes 'no indulgence of mere sentiment, however sincere,
but a gnawing reality that eats into their vital beings.' They know 'they
must toil, though to-morrow be the burial, and their pall-bearers throw
down the hammer to lift up the coffin.'

THE SWIMMING HOLE, BY THOMAS EAKINS

Melville's avoidance of any sentimentalizing of the emigrants reveals that he has developed the balance that is indispensable for the writer of tragedy. He notes that the very hardships to which they are subjected, instead of uniting them, tend only, by embittering their tempers, to set them fighting against each other: 'and thus they themselves drive the strongest rivet into the chain by which their social superiors hold them subject.' At the time of the fever they are so ignorant and besotted that they cannot even be prevailed upon to take the rudimentary precautions, or to lift a hand in their own salvation. But this harsh realization did not drive Melville to the other extreme of cynicism. He concluded his account of steerage life by indicating his lack of agreement with the 'agitated national topic, as to whether such multitudes of foreign poor should be landed on our American shores.' His conviction, which was given practical weight by the existence of our widely unoccupied land, was that 'the whole world is the patrimony of the whole world.' But he waived the question of whether others would accept this, and concentrated on the necessity of better treatment for whatever emigrants did come. After noting the continual violations of the recent laws that had made minimum demands upon the shipowners for decent conditions, he broke out with the sympathy that was the rare counterpoise to his bitter knowledge: 'We may have civilized bodies and yet barbarous souls. We are blind to the real sights of this world; deaf to its voice; and dead to its death.'

There is no sign that Melville ever became thus insensible. Nor did he lose sight of the problems that oppressed Redburn. When he came to write about Israel Potter, the Revolutionary private who had been taken prisoner and who, though escaping, could not contrive to get back to this country until after a half-century of desperate hole-and-corner existence in England, Melville attributed this tragedy entirely to the man's poverty. He observed that Paul Jones was a hero—but the man Potter who had done this commander signal service—what advantages had he? Consequently his main theme in this story of the sufferings of a common man, was that 'while we revel in broadcloth, let us not forget what we owe to linsey-woolsey.' He could not adequately describe the London in which Potter was condemned to pass his tormented years short of calling it the City of Dis. The only faces among the 'uninvoked ghosts' drifting across London Bridge which struck the ex-soldier as having any earnestness of character were the mournful ones, a token that man 'succeeds better in life's tragedy than comedy.' [2]

The latent economic factor in tragedy remained part of Melville's vision at every subsequent stage of his writing. It may seem dwarfed into insignificance before the implacable power of Ahab's revenge; yet the reader is not meant to forget that the first reason Ishmael gave for going to sea was 'having little or no money in my purse.' The hard bargains that Captain Bildad, in spite of his nominal Quakerism, drives with the prospective members of the crew as to their tiny shares in the venture show the kind of system in which the men are caught. Ahab knows this well, though in his isolated pride, in his obsession with other ends, he has merely contempt for their dependence on cash, or as he says, for the fact that 'the permanent constitutional condition of the manufactured man . . . is sordidness.'

While Melville was trying to finish *Moby-Dick*, at the time when its first chapters were already driving through the press, he exclaimed to Hawthorne: 'Dollars damn me . . . What I feel most moved to write, that is banned,—it will not pay. Yet, altogether, write the *other* way I cannot. So the product is a final hash, and all my books are botches.' This sense of the distorting anguish involved in coining a serious book for bread was projected into the defeat of Pierre. During the next few years (1853-5), Melville wrote a series of sketches, which he never bothered to collect, dealing with other aspects of poverty. Among these were 'The Two Temples,' in which a cordial crowd in the gallery of a London theatre is contrasted with the frigid atmosphere of a fashionable New York church, where even a Madonna and child in a painting impressed Melville as being unwelcome strangers, as 'the true Hagar and her Ishmael.' [3] In 'Poor Man's Pudding and Rich Man's Crumbs,' and espe-

---

2. It is an interesting coincidence that the *Inferno* also suggested to Eliot the most striking way of presenting his London:

> Unreal City,
> Under the brown fog of a winter dawn,
> A crowd flowed over London Bridge, so many,
> I had not thought death had undone so many.

3. A letter to Melville from the editor of *Putnam's Monthly* in 1854 shows how hard it was even to get such material into print: 'I am very loth to reject the "Two Temples" as the article contains some exquisitely fine description, and some pungent satire, but my editorial experience compels me to be very careful in offending the religious sensibilities of the public, and the moral of the "Two Temples" would sway against us the whole power of the pulpit, to say nothing of Brown, and the congregation of Grace Church.'

cially in 'The Tartarus of Maids,' he went further in his detailed accounts of American poverty. In the day when the magazines had been giving idealized versions of the lot of the Lowell factory-girls, he tried to picture the actual conditions in a New England paper-mill where 'machinery— that vaunted slave of humanity—stood menially served by human beings.' His image of desolation was characteristic: 'At rows of blank-looking counters sat rows of blank-looking girls, with blank, white folders in their blank hands, all blankly folding blank paper.'

The whole bitter sequence of *The Confidence Man* is built around characters who are made fools or knaves by money; and as further token of how effectually Melville was stirred by the age's growing manifestations of greed, we have two of the relatively infrequent passages where his verse sprang into some life. He had commented in *Mardi* on how the starving miners of '49 were robbed by the merchants 'who toiled not, dug not, slaved not'; and this thought came to later fruition in

> Gold in the mountain,
> And gold in the glen,
> And greed in the heart,
> Heaven having no part,
> And unsatisfied men.

Though *Clarel* is practically unreadable because of Melville's inexplicable choice of rhymed tetrameter as the medium for philosophic meditation, its most pointed lines are cast in this question:

> How many Hughs of Lincoln, say,
> Does Mammon in his mills, to-day,
> Crook, if he do not crucify?

Yet Melville's main concern was not with studying the factory system, but with human suffering wherever he found it. He knew so much more about ordinary life than Emerson did that he never fell into the one-sided statements that he marked in his copy of a current book, William Alger's *The Solitudes of Nature and of Man* (1867). In a chapter on 'The Dangers of Solitude,' Alger observed that 'even the kindly Emerson illustrates the temptation of the great to scorn the commonalty, when he speaks of "enormous populations, like moving cheese,—the more, the worse"; "the guano-races of mankind"; "the worst of charity is, that the lives you are asked to preserve are not worth preserving"; "masses! the calamity is the masses; I do not wish any shovel-handed, narrow-brained, gin-drinking mass at all."' To this Melville added: 'These expressions attributed to the "kindly Emerson" are somewhat different from the words of Christ to the multitude on the Mount.—Abhor pride, abhor malignity, but not grief and poverty, and the natural vices these generate.'

2. 'The world's a ship on its passage out'

THE SUB-TITLE of *White Jacket* set forth Melville's deliberate intention to picture 'the world in a man-of-war,' to examine the nature of life in such a microcosm. Many different analogies suggested themselves to him: the regimentation made the existence something like that 'in a large manufactory.' It was also 'a continual theatre,' including among its cast of five hundred every possible shade of character. Basically, however, it composed 'a state in itself,' whose members would be quite able, if wrecked on a desert shore, to found an Alexandria and to fill it 'with all the things which go to make up a capital.' Melville's choice of city was not accidental, for he also believed the navy to be 'the asylum for the perverse, the home of the unfortunate.' He had seen that an 'almost incredible corruption' tended to pervade all ranks, and hopelessly to deprave any seamen of good habits.

Therefore he set himself to examine the system that had produced such results. It was a monarchy in which Captain Claret's voice was absolute. But in presenting this hard-drinking character, Melville states explicitly that his cruelties were not personal, but the inevitable results of his position. Melville concluded from experience that 'both the written and unwritten laws of the American Navy are as destitute of individual guarantees to the mass of seamen as the Statute Book of the despotic Empire of Russia.' His own assumptions of democratic justice come out in the unanswered question, 'Who put this great gulf between the American captain and the American sailor?' He believed that an incurable antagonism must result where two classes, the officers and the men, are in perpetual conflict, and where the smaller of the two groups is backed up by all the controls of power. He hardly thought that the system could be much alleviated by reforms, since so long as such a thing as a battleship exists, explicitly designed for the most 'barbarous and brutal' of man's activities, life on it 'must ever remain a picture of much that is tyrannical and repelling in human nature.'

Upon this basis he studied 'The Social State in a Man-of-War,' and found that its cog-wheels of authoritarian discipline kept 'systematically grinding up in one common hopper all that might minister to the moral well-being of the crew.' Separated from those above them by spiked barriers of rank, driven in upon themselves 'like pears closely packed,' the men decayed through this inescapable contact, since every vicious plague-spot thus became contagious. The only conclusion that Melville could draw, from the ship's spiritual corruption as well as from its lack of democratic rights, was that the general condition was 'the precise reverse of what any Christian could desire.'

His protest against specific abuses like flogging was that they were opposed 'to the essential dignity of man, which no legislator has a right to violate.' His fundamental objection to the system as a whole was that by exaggerating the inequalities between men it did violence to their common traits, since 'title, and rank, and wealth, and education cannot unmake human nature,' and men differ from one another only in the degrees of their development. But he did not sentimentalize the sailor any more than he did the emigrants in *Redburn.* He wanted it understood that he had no 'theoretic love' for him, 'no romantic belief in that peculiar noble-heartedness and exaggerated generosity of disposition fictitiously imputed to him in novels.' He thought that some improvement could be made by levelling downward, that in a country 'boasting of the political equality of all social conditions, it is a great reproach that such a thing as a common seaman rising to the rank of a commissioned officer in our Navy is nowadays almost unheard of.' Nevertheless he had learned, from observing men in action, the same hard truth that was to enable Mark Twain to create the most powerful scene in *Huck Finn,* where Colonel Sherburn's scorn withers the bravado of the mob. As Melville saw it, such influence could always be wrought 'by a powerful brain, and a determined, intrepid spirit over a miscellaneous rabble.' Moreover, he had learned things which prevented him even more effectually from regarding any class of men as innocent-hearted. Arraigned at the mast and sentenced to an unjust beating, White Jacket had discovered within himself hitherto unsuspected capacities for violence. Measuring with his eye the distance between the captain and the opening of the gangway, he could barely control himself from the fatal lunge that would have carried them both overboard, and that would have made him a murderer and a suicide.

Melville had thereby arrived at a more thoroughgoing conception of human evil than Hawthorne had embodied in the conclusion to *The Seven Gables,* since he knew that both individuals and contemporary society itself were tainted with it. In his final analogy between the world and a man-of-war, he stated that 'oppressed by illiberal laws, and partly oppressed by themselves, many of our people are wicked, unhappy, inefficient.' Nevertheless, his firm self-reliance asserted itself when he added that 'the worst of our evils we blindly inflict on ourselves,' 'there are no mysteries out of ourselves.' Consequently, though he said that 'we are all Fatalists at bottom,' he was emboldened also to add, with a confidence he would not have been able to summon by the time he wrote *Pierre,* 'Ourselves are Fate.'

His use of the word 'mysteries' is significant of what he had grown to regard as the essence of life. White Jacket made several remarks that could also characterize the author of *Moby-Dick.* Commenting on his contemplative nature, he said that 'a forced, interior quietude, in the midst of great outward commotion, breeds moody people.' He went further in describing the process that had become habitual for him when he stated that 'the inmates of a frigate are thrown upon themselves and each other, and all their ponderings are introspective.' Melville's own reflective gifts had been called out as he passed the night watches, 'serenely concocting information into wisdom.' He had been carried to the center of problems of whose dangerous implications he had hardly yet had time to be cognizant. He began by being struck with the paradox of having religious services on board a man-of-war, since the Gospels are so opposed to inequality; and, moreover, war itself is utterly unchristian, and capable only of bringing men 'down to the Feejee standard.' But he could hardly stop his thoughts there, and the book keeps coming back to his preoccupation with how so-called civilization itself is at war with Christianity.

How inescapably the bias of Melville's mind was determined by his religious background is disclosed in the predominant tendency of all his ponderings. When he had first begun to express his inner life in *Mardi,* he was driven to envisage the ideal state of Serenia. The test of great literature that he was to formulate in his essay on Hawthorne was to be as much religious as artistic. In the winter of 1849, when *Mardi* and *Redburn* were both about to appear and he had begun to read through Shakespeare, his first comment to Duyckinck was: 'Ah, he's full of sermons-on-the-mount, and gentle, aye, almost as Jesus.' Such a remark helps explain why Melville's tragedies are more concerned with spiritual and metaphysical issues even than with the economic and social.

With his Emersonian belief in the divinely inspired poet, he was naturally impelled to examine what Emerson and Thoreau had agreed upon as the chief subject on which that inspiration could feed, man's relation to nature. We have previously observed certain key-positions that he held in common with the transcendentalists, especially the doctrine of 'linked analogies' between nature and man's mind, and that of the symbolical significance of every natural fact.[1] He agreed that spirit is substance, but when he contemplated the mystery of the unseen, he began to diverge from the transcendental conclusion that its effect on man was necessarily beneficent. He voiced his divergence in many of the condensed parables of *Moby-Dick:* in one, for example, where he recounts how worthless a young sailor, 'with the Phaedon instead of Bowditch [2] in his head,' is for the business of sighting whales:

Lulled into such an opium-like listlessness of vacant, unconscious revery is this absent-minded youth by the blending cadence of waves with thoughts, that at last he loses his identity; takes the mystic ocean at his feet for the visible image of that deep, blue, bottomless soul, pervading mankind and nature, and every strange, half-seen, gliding, beautiful thing that eludes him; every dimly discovered, uprising fin of some undiscernible form, seems to him the embodiment of those elusive thoughts that only people the soul by continually flitting through it . . . But while this sleep, this dream is on ye, move your foot or hand an inch; slip your hold at all; and your identity comes back in horror. Over Descartian vortices you hover.[3] And perhaps, at mid-day, in the fairest weather, with one half-throttled shriek you drop through that transparent air into the summer sea, no more to rise forever. Heed it well, ye Pantheists!

1. See p. 43.

2. Nathaniel Bowditch (1773-1838), author of *The Practical Navigator,* was one of the worthies of the Salem in which Hawthorne grew up.

3. This is an instance of Melville's fondness for the taste of philosophy rather than for its exact terms, since he is obviously not referring in any strict sense to the vortex theory of motion which enabled Descartes to reconcile Copernicus with Biblical doctrine.

Melville could make this instinctive critique of transcendentalism, since he knew that these beautiful fins were part of cruel forms; and he also knew that no ideal philosophy could afford to neglect the facts of Bowditch. In projecting the character of Ahab, he concentrated on the obverse side of the transcendental dream. Emerson would have agreed with the captain that 'All visible objects, man, are but as pasteboard masks'; but he felt none of Ahab's torment at the demonic element in the unseen, at the hidden malignity which caused him to break out: 'That inscrutable thing is chiefly what I hate; and be the White Whale agent, or be the White Whale principal, I will wreak that hate upon him.'

The point, of course, is not that Ahab's thoughts represent the entirety of Melville's own. But he had gone farther than Emerson in his realization that what you find in nature, whether you consider a phenomenon angelic or diabolic, depends—as Coleridge knew in the 'Ode to Dejection' —greatly on your own mood. He had marked the passage where Hamlet tells Rosencrantz that 'there is nothing either good or bad, but thinking makes it so'; and had added, 'Here is forcibly shown the great Montaigneism of Hamlet.' Melville recurred frequently to this thought, and gave it most explicit expression when Pierre, driven desperate by his frustrated efforts to live a life of truth, saw only—instead of what an old Baptist farmer of Saddle Meadows had christened the Delectable Mountain—a stark Mount of Titans where a gigantic rock-formation took on the likeness of Enceladus in an unequal struggle against the gods. In introducing this prolonged symbol of Pierre's mental state, Melville remarked: 'Say what some poets will, Nature is not so much her own ever-sweet interpreter, as the mere supplier of that cunning alphabet, whereby selecting and combining as he pleases, each man reads his own peculiar lesson according to his own peculiar mind and mood.'

Already, in *Mardi,* he had made Babbalanja note the external world's indifference to man's concerns: 'Through all her provinces, nature seems to promise immortality to life, but destruction to beings . . . If not against us, nature is not for us.' Ishmael went farther than that. He was not only struck by nature's 'impersonal stolidity,' but, finding an emblem for the law of life in the way that the sharks and the gulls fed upon the body of a dead whale, he was revolted by the 'horrible vulturism of earth.' By the time he was facing such facts in the creation of *Moby-Dick,* Melville could only mock at the ease of Goethe's 'Live in the all' as a means of escape from the wretchedness of man's separate identity. He had come to believe that *Ecclesiastes* provided a surer guide to what he was likely to find in the world. Yet he granted, in a postscript to Hawthorne, that 'this "all" feeling though, there is some truth in. You must often have felt it, lying on the grass on a warm summer's day. Your legs seem to send out shoots into the earth. Your hair feels like leaves upon your head. This is the *all* feeling. But what plays the mischief with the truth is that men will insist upon the universal application of a temporary feeling or opinion.'

That reads like a comment in advance on what was to be Whitman's mood, 'I loafe and invite my soul,' in his mystical vision in 'Song of Myself.' What differentiates Melville most from Whitman is that he was never satisfied with what delighted the poet, with immersion in nature, in pure sensation, with the return to elemental life unblemished by the strivings of thought. Melville was never stirred by the advantages of 'living with the animals.' Even during his months in Typee, when he was impressed by the fact that the savage 'enjoyed an infinitely happier, though certainly a less intellectual existence, than the self-complacent European,' he had no idea that he could share permanently in it. It would mean denial of the mind, and consequently, although thought was painful,[4] a retrogression to an immature state.

Melville's concentration on the brutal energies in nature places him in the developing trend of scientific perception, which, so far as literature is concerned, was to culminate a generation later in Hardy's disillusion, and in the naturalists' worship of force. But Melville could at no point rest content with the kind of truth that was to be found in science. The questions that remained imperative for him to the end had come down from an older heritage. They had been the fundamental questions in Puritan theology: what constituted original sin, to what extent could man's will be free? The kind of reflection upon nature that still impressed him in the last year of his life was what he checked in Schopenhauer's *Religion and Other Essays* (1890): 'Taking an unprejudiced view of the world as it is, no one would dream of regarding it as a god. It would be more correct to identify the world with the devil, as the venerable author of the *Deutsche Theologie* has, in fact, done in a passage of his immortal work,

4. It is significant that he checked the note, in his edition of Shakespeare, on Enobarbus' answer to Cleopatra at the moment of the rout of her forces: 'What shall we do, Enobarbus?' 'Think, and die.' The note said: 'To *think* or *take thought,* was anciently synonymous with to *grieve.*'

where he says, "Wherefore the evil spirit and nature are one, and where nature is not overcome, neither is the evil adversary overcome." '

Speculations in this vein had carried him far from the daily routine in a man-of-war, though they had first begun to grow upon him on board the *Acushnet* as he took his turn looking for whales, perhaps no more effectually than the young Platonist. By the time he had finished *White Jacket*, he felt the need to allow fuller scope to some of this material. He was ever more sure that genius consisted in a superfluity of energy, and he sensed within himself resources that were still untapped. He also felt poised in a rare equilibrium between contending forces, and came closest to describing this state, the state of mind that produced *Moby-Dick*, at the end of one of its chapters, where he rejoiced in the intuitions that could irradiate the fog of his doubts: 'Many deny; but doubts or denials, few along with them have intuitions. Doubts of all things earthly, and intuitions of some things heavenly; this combination makes neither believer nor infidel, but makes a man who regards them both with equal eye.'

That harmony is reflected in the serene wave-like movement of many passages of the book, especially in the chapter describing the entrance into the Pacific, where his prose rhythms have found the organic principle that they were hunting for in *Mardi*. But he could not hold the wave at the crest. The deeper he searched his divine intuitions, the more uncertain they seemed. In *Mardi* he had been mainly concerned with exposing the deceits and hypocrisies of the world; in the struggle between Ahab and the white whale he embodied his growing sense that evil was an integral, if inexplicable, element of life itself. The torrential force of Ahab's long soliloquies often breaks into incoherence from the conflicting pressures of Melville's thoughts.

He could hardly have provided a stronger demonstration of his belief that 'to produce a mighty book, you must choose a mighty theme,' than by choosing the saga of the most exciting and dangerous of the basic American industries of his day. But if the release of his thought and feeling was not to flow confusedly in every direction, he must, as Emerson would have said, draw a circle around his experience. In other words, he must devise a structure that could combine the story of whaling, Ahab's tragedy, and his own speculations on human destiny.

3. Structure

'In prose, the character of the vehicle for the composer's thoughts is not determined beforehand; every composer has to make his own vehicle.'—marked by Melville in Arnold's *Essays in Criticism* (1865).

'If we examine with a critical view the manner of those painters whom we consider as patterns, we shall find that their great fame does not proceed from their works being more highly finished than those of other artists, or from a more minute attention to details, but from that enlarged comprehension which sees the whole object at once.'—marked by Melville in Joshua Reynolds' *Discourses,* which he acquired in 1870.

> 'In him who would evoke—create,
> Contraries must meet and mate.'
> —from the manuscript draft of Melville's poem, 'Art,' which
> was included, in a different form, in *Timoleon* (1891).

THE STRUCTURE Melville had hit upon in *White Jacket* was more useful to his purposes in *Moby-Dick* than was that of *Mardi*. There had been an arbitrary split in his Polynesian romance between the opening, which read like another matter-of-fact passage to the South Seas, and the bulk of the book, which, once Taji had jumped ship, took him into the allegorical realm of King Media. To be sure, Melville had thereby evolved a mythical world-voyage in the tradition of Rabelais and Swift, but he had not succeeded in endowing his satire with much of their devastating concreteness. His sense impressions and his abstractions seem divided into separate compartments. The structure of *White Jacket* permitted his thoughts on society and religion to develop directly out of an everyday matrix. The advantages of such a microcosm appealed to him again in *The Confidence Man,* where he stated that he found as much variety in the passengers on his Mississippi steamboat 'as among Chaucer's Canterbury pilgrims.'[1] In *Clarel* he chose as his cast a group of contemporary pilgrims to the Holy Land.

1. The multiple types he envisaged were of the material which the frontier humorists were already quarrying, and which the local colorists were to discover after the Civil War: 'Northern speculators and Eastern philosophers . . . Sante Fé traders in striped blankets,

In the chapter called 'Knights and Squires,' where he introduced the crew of the *Pequod,* another analogy struck Melville. These men of so many lands and races, now 'federated along one keel,' composed 'an Anacharsis Cloots deputation,' for they caused Melville to think of the German-born baron who appeared at the bar of the French assembly in 1790 at the head of thirty-six foreigners, and in the name of this 'embassy of the human race,' declared that the world adhered to the Declaration of the Rights of Man. This analogy occurred to him again near the opening of *The Confidence Man,* where the deck, as they leave St. Louis, is crowded with 'a piebald parliament, an Anacharsis Cloots congress of all kinds of that multiple pilgrim species, man.' That this thought is an integral part of Melville's conception of the world as 'a ship on its passage out' is underscored by its recurrence at the beginning of *Billy Budd.* It rises there, in practically the same form, out of his memory of a variegated group of sailors he had seen on the docks in Liverpool, 'now half a century ago.'

Unlike a whaler or a battleship, a river steamboat provided him in addition with a panorama of a commercial society, which he saw being increasingly corrupted by greed for money. But the weakness of *The Confidence Man* is due to the fatal ease with which Melville could get rid of his many characters by the mechanical device of having them disembark at the ends of chapters, and could thus dodge the necessity of sustaining the implications of any of them. This may furnish unconscious evidence on the side of Henry James' contention that, since 'it takes such an accumulation of history and custom, such a complexity of manners and types, to form a fund of suggestion for a novelist,' the American writer of Hawthorne's day must inevitably have been nearly starved.[2]

and Broadway bucks in cravats of cloth· of gold; fine-looking Kentucky boatmen, and Japanese-looking Mississippi cotton planters; Quakers in full drab, and United States soldiers in full regimentals; slaves, black, mulatto, quadroon; modish young Spanish Creoles, and old-fashioned French Jews; Mormons and Papists; Dives and Lazarus; jesters and mourners, teetotallers and convivialists, deacons and blacklegs; hard-shell Baptists and clay-eaters; grinning negroes, and Sioux chiefs solemn as high-priests.'

Melville declared that there was 'a sort of pagan abandonment and assurance' in this assemblage, and added: 'Here reigned the dashing and all-fusing spirit of the West, whose type is the Mississippi itself, which, uniting the streams of the most distant and opposite zones, pours them along, helter-skelter, in one cosmopolitan and confident tide.'

2. The context of this remark gives it—like so much else in James' critical study—more intimate bearing upon himself than upon Hawthorne. To be sure, James starts with the

For in spite of Melville's initial assertion of the abundance of life on the river, very little of it is to be seen in the successive mean-spirited incarnations of the confidence man: the crooked agent for the Seminole Widow and Orphan Asylum, the dispenser of the Samaritan Pain Dissuader, the seller of dubious stock, the ambiguous cosmopolitan, the various con-game artists who push themselves to the center of this two dimensional travelling-salesman's world. The discrepancy between what Melville said was to be found on the Mississippi and the bleak sense of existence that he managed to create there would suggest that he had no adequate grasp of this kind of society. That might very well be because it was in such a state of flux that no outsider like Melville could hope to generalize about it. What was required for its full portrayal was some intimate experience, like that of a pilot who knew every foot of the river in its vast sweep down to New Orleans, and who could re-create, too, its human richness as well as the meanness and distortions in the life of its plantations and frontier villages, as they had grown into his consciousness from the time he had drifted on rafts as a kid. But that was to be Twain's epic, not Melville's.

In the case of *The Confidence Man* the problem was further complicated by Melville's own state of mind at the period, since he was in such a mood of Timonism that he was driven into writing the whole book as a satiric comment on the text from *Corinthians,* 'Charity suffereth long and is kind.' He was too bitter, too distressed personally, to keep his satire under control, and so there is no progression to his theme, no sense of what he emphasized at the end of his introduction of 'Knights and Squires': that Ahab's crew composed a deputation of humanity, bound 'to lay the world's grievances' at some bar of judgment.

statement in the preface to *The Marble Faun,* that 'No author, without a trial, can conceive of the difficulty of writing a romance about a country where there is no shadow, no antiquity, no mystery, no picturesque and gloomy wrong, nor anything but a commonplace prosperity, in broad and simple daylight, as is happily the case with my dear native land.' But we know that Hawthorne's view had been something other at the time he wrote *The Scarlet Letter* and *The Seven Gables.* James also indicates the center of his own interest when he says that Hawthorne's sentence 'must have lingered in the minds of many Americans who have tried to write novels, and to lay the scene of them in the Western world.' James had himself just finished a novel laid in New England, *The Europeans* (1878), and was presently to compose *Washington Square* (1880). But with *The Portrait of a Lady* (1881), he turned again to what he had already tried in *Roderick Hudson* (1876) and *The American* (1877), and what was to prove his most fertile theme, the American in Europe.

Melville was so far from having imagined a conclusion for *The Confidence Man* that he could only break it off as a distended fragment. *Clarel* might have been formed into a whole, but again he let himself be swamped by too many indistinct characters; and their discussions of religion became as tediously abstract as the details in *White Jacket* had been heavily concrete. Women, necessarily excluded from the world in a man-of-war, might have brought more variety to both *The Confidence Man* and *Clarel,* but the exposé of commercial sharpers and the serious debate of ideas both tend to leave them far in the background. The only book in which Melville follows his primary structure without the reader's feeling a similar loss in variety is *Moby-Dick.* In *Pierre* he tried to work out a wholly different structure, but in *Moby-Dick,* in focusing on man's primitive struggle against nature, he solved the problem of plenitude by presenting a succession of levels of experience, distinct and yet skillfully integrated.

The means by which he accomplished this have never been examined in adequate detail. The nature of these levels can be suggested by a passage in Eliot's criticism, which also points to the source whence Melville received the greatest creative stimulus of his life:

> The most useful poetry, socially, would be one which could cut across all the present stratifications of public taste . . . The ideal medium for poetry, to my mind, and the most direct means of social 'usefulness' for poetry, is the theatre. In a play of Shakespeare you get several levels of significance. For the simplest auditors there is the plot, for the more thoughtful the character and conflict of character, for the more literary the words and phrasing, for the more musically sensitive the rhythm, and for auditors of greater sensitiveness and understanding a meaning which reveals itself gradually. And I do not believe that the classification of audience is so clear-cut as this; but rather that the sensitiveness of every auditor is acted upon by all these elements at once, though in different degrees of consciousness.

We know that Melville started to go through the whole of Shakespeare in the winter of 1849. And though some allusions in *Mardi* and *White Jacket,* as well as the pat quotations in 'Fragments from a Writing-Desk,' show that he exaggerated a little in telling Duyckinck that he had not read the plays hitherto, this was certainly his first thorough immersion in them.[3] He made the response of his era in considering Shakespeare primarily as a great voicer of truth. Emerson had followed Coleridge in holding that the 'speculative genius' of the nineteenth century was 'a sort of living Hamlet.' With his New England distrust of the stage, Emerson had of course gone farther, and had felt that Shakespeare had partly squandered his enormous gifts by resting content with being 'master of the revels to mankind.' He ended his account in *Representative Men* by declaring that 'the world still wants its poet-priest' who will reconcile Shakespeare and Swedenborg.

Melville had not been led thus astray by an abstraction. He subscribed to the opinion of an age which had been unable to create a significant theatre of its own, and believed that there was a hidden greatness in Shakespeare, which could not be seen 'on the tricky stage.' But he had no doubt that Shakespeare's 'blackness,' which surpassed even that of Hawthorne, made him 'the profoundest of thinkers.' He knew the taboos against voicing the resultant thought, and his markings show him attracted to such an honest speaker as Enobarbus, who confronts Antony with, 'That truth should be silent I had almost forgot'; and especially to Lear's Fool, who defies his master by insisting on the bitter realities of their situation. Melville had no notion that Shakespeare was being 'master of the revels' when he made Gloucester state,

> I shall see
> The winged vengeance overtake such children,

only to have Cornwall answer, 'See't shalt thou never,' as he prepared to put out his eyes. Melville wrote in the margin, 'terrific!,' weighting the word with its full value.

In writing to Duyckinck, he expressed the wish that Shakespeare might have been a contemporary, so that 'the muzzle which all men wore on their souls in the Elizabethan day,' might not have intercepted his 'free articulation.' Stimulated by having just heard Emerson lecture for the first time, he felt that even though truth was almost impossible 'in this

3. The edition of Shakespeare that Melville acquired at this time, and in whose 'glorious great type' he exulted, was the one issued by Hilliard and Gray (Boston, 1837). Owing again to the painstaking research of Charles Olson, these seven volumes were brought to light a few years ago, and are now in the Harvard College Library. The concentration with which Melville read them is apparent from his markings in all the volumes. These are heaviest in *Antony and Cleopatra* and *Lear.*

intolerant universe,' 'the Declaration of Independence makes a difference.'⁴ He had not yet realized how the price of that freedom might be anarchy. He returned to the same theme in his essay on Hawthorne, where he announced, as though prophesying the structure that he was then forming, 'You must have plenty of sea-room to tell the Truth in.' Only thus could you express—and we come closer to his expectations in this context—'that unshackled, democratic spirit of Christianity in all things.' He believed that one obstacle to the emergence of an American as great as Shakespeare was that the critics 'somehow fancy he will come in the costume of Queen Elizabeth's day; be a writer of dramas founded upon old English history or the tales of Boccaccio. Whereas, great geniuses are parts of the times, they themselves are the times, and possess a corresponding coloring.'

Melville had no Puritan prejudice against the dramatic form, but no more than to Hawthorne did it occur to him to try to write plays. The tradition of Elizabethan tragedy was dead except in a closet-drama like Shelley's *Cenci,* or in the many earnest but essentially imitative and 'literary' efforts to revive it on the stage, among which *Francesca da Rimini* (1855) by Melville's Philadelphia contemporary, George Henry Boker, was probably the best.⁵ The radical difference between Boker's verse and Melville's prose can be attributed in part to the former's dictum to his friend, R. H. Stoddard: 'Read Chaucer for strength, read Spenser for ease and sweetness, read Milton for sublimity and thought, read Shakespeare for all these things, and for something else which is his alone. Get out of your age as far as you can.' Melville understood much better the way a tradition stays alive when, suggesting how an American might equal Shakespeare, he concluded: 'All that has been said but multiplies the avenues to what remains to be said.'

4. These letters to Duyckinck from Boston, while Melville was visiting his father-in-law, the distinguished liberal Judge Lemuel Shaw, during the winter of 1849, have not been given adequate attention by any of Melville's biographers, though they are indispensable to interpreting this crucial period of his development. They were never even printed in full until Willard Thorp included them in his *Selections.* My reading of Melville's very crabbed hand differs at several points from Professor Thorp's. An edition of all Melville's letters is greatly to be desired.

5. On the other hand, such a play as R. T. Conrad's *Jack Cade, the Captain of the Commons* (1835, rewritten 1852), owed its popularity—much greater than that gained by any of Boker's plays—to the fact that it transformed the fifteenth-century revolt into the issues of Jacksonian democracy. But though this play was a favorite of Whitman's, Melville could hardly have learned much from its broken-down verse.

"Moby Dick"

He entered upon his broadest avenue of expression through an account of whaling. Modern critics have usually described *Moby-Dick* as an epic; and when Melville spoke of his 'narrative,' he meant his story of a heroic industry.[6] But if we are to establish the genre to which this book belongs, it is equally clear that Melville thought of Ahab's actions in dramatic terms. He made Ishmael step forth in an 'Epilogue' to say, 'The drama's done'; and from the moment of introducing his *dramatis personae,* he had reckoned with his problem as that of a 'tragic dramatist' who was trying to endow 'a poor old whale-hunter' with the dignity of a Shakespearean hero. Once he had presented his characters, he placed many of their situations by means of explicit stage-directions, as 'The Quarter Deck' (*Enter Ahab: Then all*); or 'Sunset' (*The cabin; by the stern windows; Ahab sitting alone, and gazing out*). What follows in that chapter of two pages may only be called a Shakespearean soliloquy. That mode became Melville's most effective means of expressing Ahab's development, since, isolated in his pride and madness, he tended to voice his thoughts to himself alone. To what extent Melville had meditated on the possibilities of this device is borne out by the fact that in 'The Sphinx' he made Ahab look over the side of the ship at the head of the dead whale suspended there, and re-enact a scene that had been an Elizabethan favorite from *Hamlet* to Tourneur—the soliloquy to the skull.[7] It is worth noting that Ahab's demand from this 'vast and venerable head' to yield up the hidden answer to life gave expression, at its climax, to what we have already found to be one of Melville's own recurring thoughts: 'O Nature, and O soul of man! how far beyond all utterance are your linked analogies.'

It is not my contention that Melville was deliberately trying to approximate Shakespeare's different levels by providing the story of whaling for the groundlings, and the study of Ahab's sense of evil, together with the metaphysical scrutiny of 'The Whiteness of the Whale,' for those who

6. E.g. the opening of 'The Affidavit,' where he assembled the evidence for the possibility of finding a particular whale in the vastness of the ocean: 'So far as what there may be of a narrative in this book; and, indeed, as indirectly touching one or two very interesting and curious particulars in the habits of sperm whales, the foregoing chapter, in its earlier part, is as important a one as will be found in this volume.' The 'foregoing chapter' was 'The Chart,' in which he had told how whales can be traced back to the spot where once seen, by knowledge of their seasonal habits.

7. For this point, as well as for several others in Melville's handling of Shakespeare, I am indebted to Charles Olson, *'Lear* and *Moby-Dick'* (*Twice a Year,* 1938, no. 1).

could follow him. But so far as we can trace the genesis of any creative process, we have an example here of how Melville's own sense of life had been so profoundly stirred by Shakespeare's that he was subconsciously impelled to emulation. Without the precipitant of Shakespeare, *Moby-Dick* might have been a superior *White Jacket*. With it, Melville entered into another realm, of different properties and proportions. This must have been what he had in mind when he finally articulated his theory of fiction in that page or two of *The Confidence Man,* and stressed the necessity for characters in a novel to be allowed the 'unfettered, exhilarated, in effect transformed' behavior of those 'in a play.' 'It is with fiction as with religion; it should present another world, and yet one to which we feel the tie.'

In considering the effectiveness of *Moby-Dick,* we can hardly exaggerate the importance of the elementary level, the accumulated lore of the whaleman's craft. It prevents the drama from gliding off into a world to which we would feel no normal tie whatever. As we have seen in Melville's handling of symbols,[8] he first accounted for the nature of the white whale by every circumstantial resource, lest it should seem, like so many symbols of romantic poetry, merely a figment of his hero's imagination. A similar procedure of nailing his drama to actuality served Melville well at many critical junctures, as the mention of 'The Affidavit' has just instanced. Or again, his method of suspending the reader's disbelief was to allude to such a legend of antiquity as that of the fountain Arethusa—which, as Melville probably knew, had entered into the inspiration for 'Kubla Khan'—and then to add that 'these fabulous narrations are almost fully equalled by the realities of the whaleman.' Thus juxtaposed with the incredible legend of a stream's flowing underground from the Holy Land and rising to the surface in Syracuse—which was nevertheless believed in for ages—the apparent ubiquity of Moby-Dick is put in the realm of reasonably credible facts. The extreme case is Fedallah, the fire-worshipping Parsee who possesses some secret hold over Ahab. He is the typically exaggerated product of romantic Satanism, but even his phantom appearance from below deck with his dusky crew, at the dramatic moment of the first lowering, is given some objective possibility by Melville's recounting the widespread superstition among 'honest mariners' that such Orientals are agents of the Devil. The wealth of traditional lore

8. See pp. 284-91 above.

that Melville picked up in the Pacific thus joined with his Goethean appetite for all knowledge for its own sake, and provided a solid context even for his most outlandish improbabilities.

He was indebted again to Shakespeare for his insistence that outer and inner facts correspond. Not only is Ahab's violence made to equal that of the typhoon that strikes the ship; but likewise, at such a crisis as the captain's first declaration to the assembled crew of his purpose to hunt down the white whale, Starbuck's 'foreboding invocation,' 'God keep me! —keep us all!' is put in tone with 'the presaging vibrations of the winds in the cordage,' 'the hollow flap of the sails,' and with a 'low laugh from the hold.' Even this theatrical admonition of Fedallah's presence is treated by Melville as being not so much a prediction from without as a verification of 'the innermost necessities' of Ahab's will.

The instinctive rightness with which he interrelated the levels in his structure can be seen only by a kind of slow moving-picture of the whole. Almost a fifth of it makes a first solid unit: the account of New Bedford and Nantucket, the meeting between Ishmael and Queequeg, and the departure from shore, which, as we have found, provided Melville with one of his key-symbols, the contrast between land and sea, between a life of safety and the search for truth. Then, at the launching of the voyage, he introduces, in quickly successive chapters, 'The Advocate' and 'Knights and Squires'—the first proclaiming the dignity of whaling in general, the second focusing on the composition of this particular crew. The first asserts the 'peaceful influence' of such a basic industry throughout the world during the previous sixty years, and goes to the length of maintaining that whalemen, in first breaking through the jealous policy of the Spanish crown regarding her South American colonies, led the way to their liberation, and to 'the establishment of the eternal democracy in those parts.' After endowing his subject with such rich legends, it is small wonder that he declares with pride that 'a whale ship was my Yale College and my Harvard,' or that he feels that he has drawn a background against which his cast of characters may assume heroic proportions.

As a means of heightening his dramatic effect, he delays Ahab's appearance until all the others have been seen, keeps him inscrutably in his cabin for several days after leaving Nantucket, until finally in this atmosphere of uncertainty, 'reality outran apprehension; Captain Ahab stood upon his quarter-deck.' After the captain's desperate and stricken character has been suggested in his very looks, and his will has been put into action in a scene with Stubb, Melville returns to his other main theme in a chapter called 'Cetology.' At this point he begins to heap up his antiquarian lore, in a manner suggestive of Burton's, but he keeps it from swamping him by the method adopted in the next three chapters, 'The Specksynder,' 'The Cabin-Table,' 'The Mast-Head,' where the general customs of the industry are instanced specifically by this voyage.

Now he is ready for his first sequence of scenes to be played on this deck, and the next five chapters develop from the occasion when Ahab calls the crew together in order to announce his purpose, to nail the doubloon to the mast as reward for the first man to sight the white whale, and, with grog drunk from the butt-ends of harpooning irons, to pledge their consent to his mad aim. The scenes progress through 'Sunset' and 'Dusk,' through the soliloquies of Starbuck's misgivings and Stubb's jocular acceptance to 'Midnight, Forecastle' (*Foresail rises and discovers the watch standing, lounging, leaning, and lying in various attitudes, all singing in chorus*). This last scene is akin to O'Neill's mood in *The Moon of the Caribbees,* for it is a loose atmospheric sequence in which the various sailors voice their thoughts and desires, and make sleepy Pip, the Negro cabin boy, amuse them with his tambourine, until a fight breaks out between a Spanish sailor and the enormous black Daggoo, with encouragement from a Belfast man: 'A row! arrah a row! The Virgin be blessed, a row!' Then a squall comes up, they are called to their posts, and Pip is left alone, with the final comment on the situation into which Ahab's intensity has swept them all: 'Oh, thou big white God aloft there somewhere in yon darkness, have mercy on this small black boy down here; preserve him from all men that have no bowels to feel fear!'

The next sequence is composed of the two masterful chapters, 'Moby-Dick' and 'The Whiteness of the Whale,' in the second of which, Ishmael, having told what this beast meant to Ahab, and what legends had risen concerning it, passes to Melville's philosophical level by dwelling upon the nameless horror that it aroused in him. We are now a good third of the way through the book, and the narrative and the drama are again closely interwoven, through 'The Chart,' 'The Affidavit,' 'The Mat-Maker,' to the episode of 'The First Lowering.' Shortly thereafter Melville introduces an important method of gaining variety by the first of nine encounters with other ships, with the *Albatross,* which they sight after a demon-driven Coleridgean storm, and from which they are parted by the wind before Ahab can learn whether it has any news of his quarry. Almost at once, since they are now in the region of the Cape of Good Hope, 'much like some noted four corners of a great highway,' they fall in with the *Town-Ho,* and gain their first tidings of Moby-Dick—that he has destroyed one of the *Town-Ho's* crew.

For almost the next two hundred pages, about a quarter of the whole, Melville delays the forward movement of his drama—though he thereby heightens suspense—by giving a detailed itemization of the trade. He makes this material immediate by following through the various stages in the dismemberment of a whale that Stubb killed, from the moment of harpooning to 'The Funeral,' when the stripped carcass is cut loose and allowed to drift astern, still attended by 'the mourners,' the gulls and the sharks. The saga of 'the honor and glory of whaling' is also punctuated by Ahab's soliloquy to the skull, by Tashtego's falling into a sperm whale's head, and by three well-spaced meetings with other vessels. These are the plague-ridden *Jeroboam,* on which a crazed sailor, Gabriel, believes the white whale to be the Shaker God, and shrieks at Ahab to beware the blasphemer's end; the luckless German *Virgin,* empty of both whale oil and of news; and the French *Rosebud,* with a high-smelling carcass alongside, but totally unaware of 'Cachalot Blanche.'

The drama now becomes tenser and more dominant, throughout the final quarter of the book, though at no time is it separated from the context of the everyday routine. 'The Castaway' recounts how Pip, who jumped out of Stubb's boat in terror at the first charge of a harpooned whale, was left floating for so long by the boat crew, bent inflexibly upon their hot pursuit, that he was made an idiot by the shock, and provided the 'predestinated' ship 'with a living and ever accompanying prophecy of whatever shattered sequel might prove her own.' The elements of foreboding are increased by the weird night scene of burning down the blubber, when it strikes Ishmael that 'whatever swift rushing thing I stood on was not so much bound to any haven ahead as rushing from all havens astern'; and by the meeting with the *Samuel Enderby,* of London, whose captain can match Ahab's experience by having lost his arm from a harpoon wound inflicted when his boat was upset by Moby-Dick. But his hearty reaction is simply to steer clear of that monster hereafter, and he can only think Ahab insane in declaring that 'he still will be hunted for all that. What is best let alone, that accursed thing is not always what least allures.'

At this juncture, twenty additional pages about the whale, passing from 'the marvels of his outer aspect' to the magnitude of his skeleton, may seem for once obtrusive padding, even though they give occasion for Melville's statement of the necessity of 'a mighty theme.' These are the last pages of cetology in the book. Then, after a scene between Ahab and Starbuck in the cabin, in which the mate's righteous protest against the increasingly reckless pursuit does not deflect the captain's will even for an instant, the drama advances ever more inexorably to its conclusion. The final movement opens with their entry into the Pacific, whose serenity is at once contrasted with the delirious mood in which Ahab, insisting that his specially forged steel must be sealed in blood from the harpooners' arms, shrieks out: 'Ego non baptizo te in nomine patris, sed in nomine diaboli!'

Melville also manipulates here a whole series of other telling contrasts. Laboring against the wind, the *Pequod* meets the *Bachelor,* scudding home to Nantucket, its hatches bursting with casks of oil, its happy captain not even believing in the existence of the white whale. A sun-drenched day comes to an end as Ahab watches a dying whale's head turn towards the fading light, and affirms that the dark half of the sphere rocks him 'with a prouder, if a darker faith.' This momentary lull is in keeping with the further symbolic fact that there were now 'times of dreamy quietude' even for the men afloat in the whale-boats, when, 'beholding the tranquil beauty and brilliancy of the ocean's skin,' they could forget 'the tiger heart that pants beneath it.'[9]

The frequency of dramatic omens is also skillfully increased as the climax approaches. The night of the typhoon is preluded by the sign of which the sailors stand most in awe, 'the corposants,'[10] the pallid fire that suddenly tips the masts. But the only effect this spectral flame has upon Ahab is to make him declare that its 'right worship is defiance.' With like inflexibility he brushes aside what the rest take for successive warn-

9. This seems a curious refraction of Shakespeare's line in *Henry VI:* 'O tiger's heart wrapp'd in a woman's hide,' the line which Greene mocked in his famous death-bed attack on his rivals: 'Yes trust them not: for there is an upstart Crow, beautified with our feathers, that with his *Tygers hart wrapt in a Players hyde* supposes he is as well able to bombast out a blanke verse as the best of you.' Melville had marked this passage in the 'Life of Shakespeare' prefaced to his edition.

10. So called from *corpo santo,* the holy body of Elmo, the sailors' patron saint.

ings, the fact that the compasses are turned by the storm, that the log-line breaks, the life buoy sinks, and a sailor is drowned. They meet the *Rachel,* which has sighted Moby-Dick the day before, and has lost sight of one of her boats that drifted apart in the vain chase. But though Captain Gardiner, whose son is in the lost boat, is a Nantucketer known to Ahab, the latter refuses to be swerved from his vengeance even long enough to help in the search.

Two short chapters later comes the ninth and final meeting, with the ill-named *Delight,* from which a boat with its entire crew has just been destroyed by the white whale's violence. The day is a transparent azure, the sea and air are hardly separable, yet out of this delicate 'symphony,' as Melville names it, spring the three days of the final chase, the longest and most sustained episode of the book, the finest piece of dramatic writing in American literature, though shaped with no reference to a stage. The skills that Melville depends on here will demand further analysis, but with regard to the completion of his structure, it is enough to remark that his narrative of the industry, which was not launched until after the opening fifth of the book, is confined mostly to the central third. Placed there it provides what Van Wyck Brooks has rightly described as 'ballast' for the whole. It gives solid grounding for what Ishmael calls 'the black tragedy of the melancholy ship,' but it does not encroach upon it, since the final fifth progresses at its ever more compelling speed, entirely unimpeded by further general material. Yet the elementary level is made to reinforce the drama so integrally that, even at the height of the chase, Melville can increase the credibility by insisting that 'this pertinacious pursuit of one particular whale, continued through day into night, and through night into day, is a thing by no means unprecedented in the South Sea fishery.'

4. 'A bold and nervous lofty language'

AT THE time of Melville's death, Richard Henry Stoddard, one of his few professed defenders, felt obliged to state that 'his vocabulary was large, fluent, eloquent, but it was excessive, inaccurate, and unliterary.' Some just application can be found for all the first five adjectives, for the fourth and fifth especially in *Pierre;* but the reaction of the modern reader to the last is that the Melville of *Mardi,* and, on occasion, even of *Moby-Dick,* could all too easily fall into the 'literary.' Stoddard's conventional standards betray themselves in his further remark that Melville's early books made him 'famous among his countrymen, who, less literary in their tastes and demands than at present, were easily captivated by stories of maritime life.' Actually Melville had felt himself constrained by just such genteel demands. In *White Jacket,* for instance, he said that his aim was to be a chronicler of the navy exactly as it was, of what might become obsolete, 'withholding nothing, inventing nothing.' Yet he found that he quickly reached the limits that were permitted him. When he wanted to present the scene of a flogging, the captain's abusive epithet had to be left blank, with the note, 'The phrase here used I have never seen either written or printed and should not like to be the first person to introduce it to the public.' His own modesty joined again with the taboos of his age when he came to probe the daily life of the men, for he skirted the subject with remote allusions to the *Oedipus* and to Shelley's *Cenci,* and with the remark that 'the sins for which the cities of the plain were overthrown still linger in some of these wooden-walled Gomorrahs of the deep.'

More fundamental than these evasions is the fact that Melville never felt impelled to the kind of discipline that was soon to actuate Flaubert in his desire to sacrifice everything to finding the word that would evoke the very look and gesture. Melville had a good ear for speech rhythms: in his review of Ross Browne's *Etchings of a Whaling Cruise,* his own memories of a mate's lingo, 'Pull, pull, you lubberly *hay makers!,'* foreshadowed his creation of Stubb and Flask. But even in *Moby-Dick* he was very intermittent in what would now be a main concern for many writers: to base the talk of their common men as closely as possible on American idioms. His deepest interest was other, as he had already phrased it in *White Jacket:* to 'dive into the souls' of men, even if that meant 'to bring up the mud from the bottom.' In *Mardi* he had attempted this by the device of Babbalanja's demon, but he had not yet developed a controlled heightening of diction that could make the reader accept the lack of verisimilitude. In *White Jacket* he fell between two goals. He was a master there neither of realism, nor of an intensified reality. The general level of honest but stiff writing, which had tended also to characterize his early travel books, can be briefly instanced by this description of a dying sailor:

'I could not help thinking, as I gazed, whether this man's fate had not been accelerated by his confinement in this heated furnace below; and whether many a sick man round me might not soon improve, if but permitted to swing his hammock in the airy vacancies of the half-deck above, open to the port-holes, but reserved for the promenade of the officers.' The defects need hardly be labored. The style is workmanlike enough, but its want of vividness comes from conventional rather than idiomatic phrasing ('if but permitted'), and from a diction still influenced ('accelerated by his confinement') by merely formal standards of correctness.

Melville suggests how he found the lead to the freedom of speech he needed, in a note on one of his war poems, 'Lee in the Capitol.' In trying to present, not what the General had actually said when summoned before the congressional Reconstruction Committee in 1866, but what might be imagined to have been his deepest feelings on that occasion, and in aiming to invest his words with heroic dignity, Melville was aware that he had taken 'a poetical liberty.' 'If for such freedom warrant be necessary, the speeches in ancient histories, not to speak of those in Shakespeare's historic plays, may not unfitly perhaps be cited.'

His liberation in *Moby-Dick* through the agency of Shakespeare was almost an unconscious reflex. Unlike Emerson he discussed at no point the origins and nature of language. The great philologian Jacob Grimm had, as Renan was to perceive, arrived at mythology through his investigation of speech.[1] Words and fables became finally inseparable for him, and he sought their common source in the most primitive and most profound instincts of the race, in its manner of feeling and imagining. It may be said of Melville that he intuitively grasped this connection. In his effort to endow the whaling industry with a mythology befitting a fundamental activity of man in his struggle to subdue nature, he came into possession of the primitive energies latent in words. He had already begun to realize in the dream-passages of *Mardi* that meaning had more than just a level of sense, that the arrangement of words in patterns of sound and rhythm enabled them to create feelings and tones that could not be included in a logical or scientific statement. But he did not find a valuable clue to how to express the hidden life of men, which had become his compelling absorption, until he encountered the unexampled vitality of Shakespeare's language.

1. See Renan's preface to the translation of Grimm, *De l'Origine du Langage* (1859).

We have already observed that other forces beside Shakespeare conditioned his liberation. Thomas Browne had taught him that musical properties of prose could help increase its symbolical richness. Carlyle's rhetoric may have drugged him into obscurities, but it had also the value of helping him rediscover what the Elizabethan dramatists had known, that rhetoric did not necessarily involve a mere barren formalism, but that it could be so constructed as to carry a full freight of emotion. But his possession by Shakespeare went far beyond all other influences, and, if Melville had been a man of less vigor, would have served to reduce him to the ranks of the dozens of stagey nineteenth-century imitators of the dramatist's stylistic mannerisms. What we actually find is something very different: a man of thirty awakening to his own full strength through the challenge of the most abundant imagination in history. Since Melville meditated more creatively on Shakespeare's meaning than any other American has done, it is absorbing to try to follow what the plays meant to him, from the superficial evidence of verbal echoes down through the profound transformation of all his previous styles.

Shakespeare's phrasing had so hynotized him that often he seems to have reproduced it involuntarily, even when there was no point to the allusion, as was the case with the 'tiger's heart.' [2] On other occasions he enjoyed a burlesque effect: in omitting from his account such dubious specimens as the Quog Whale or the Pudding-headed Whale, he says that he 'can hardly help suspecting them for mere sounds, full of leviathanism, but signifying nothing.' He came closer to the feeling of the original passage when he found an equivalent for the gravedigger in the ship's carpenter, at work on a new whale-bone leg for Ahab, who had broken his former one by jumping into his boat. Melville had marked Hamlet's answer to the King's demand for Polonius: 'But, indeed, if you find him not within this month, you shall nose him as you go up the stairs into the lobby.' Now he transferred that to the situation where the carpenter, sneezing over his job, since 'bone is rather dusty, sir,' is told by Ahab: 'Take the hint, then; and when thou art dead, never bury thyself under living people's noses.'

You could trace such kaleidoscopic variations of Shakespeare's patterns throughout this book, since, once you become aware of them, you find

2. In view of the enormous impression that *King Lear* made upon him, it is possible that even his chapter title 'Knights and Squires' was suggested by Goneril's 'Here do you keep a hundred knights and squires.'

fragments of his language on almost every page. Even Ishmael's opening remark about having 'no money in my purse' probably re-echoes *Othello*. 'The Spirit Spout,' that scene when a whale was sighted eerily by moonlight, and which, incidentally, was one of the episodes wherein Mrs. Hawthorne read an allegorical significance that Melville said he did not intend, seems to owe something of its enchanted atmosphere to the last act of *The Merchant of Venice,* if you can judge from the effect that is built up to by the phrase, 'on such a silent night a silvery jet was seen.' The end of *Othello* is more integral to the account of Moby-Dick's former assault upon Ahab; but, as an instance of how Melville's imagination instinctively reshaped its impressions to suit his own needs, it is to be noted that

> Where a malignant and a turban'd Turk
> Beat a Venetian and traduced the state,

is altered to: 'No turbaned Turk, no hired Venetian or Malay, could have smote him with more seeming malice.' On such levels, where the borrowed material has entered into the formation of Melville's own thought, the verbal reminiscences begin to be significant. What he implied by calling the crew 'an Anacharsis Cloots deputation' is made sharper by the addition that they are going 'to lay the world's grievances at the bar from which not very many of them ever come back.' The hidden allusion to Hamlet's 'bourn' from which 'no traveller returns,' serves to increase our awed uncertainty over what lies before them.

The most important effect of Shakespeare's use of language was to give Melville a range of vocabulary for expressing passion far beyond any that he had previously possessed. The voices of many characters help to intensify Ahab's. For instance, as he talks to the blacksmith about forging his harpoon, he finds the old man 'too calmly, sanely woeful . . . I am impatient of all misery . . . that is not mad.' This seems to have drawn upon the mood of Laertes' violent entrance, 'That drop of blood that's calm proclaims me bastard'; or since it has been remarked that 'Ahab has that that's bloody on his mind,' it probably links more closely to Hamlet's 'My thoughts be bloody, or be nothing worth.' The successive clauses, with their insistent repetitions, 'Thou shouldst go mad, blacksmith; say, why dost thou not go mad?' have built upon the cadences of Lear. Finally, as Ahab takes up the blacksmith's statement that he can smooth all dents, and sweeping his hand across his own scarred brow, demands,

'Canst thou smoothe this seam?,' Melville has mingled something of Lady Macbeth's anguish with her husband's demand to the physician, 'Canst thou not minister to a mind diseased?'

In view of Shakespeare's power over him, it is not surprising that in 'The Quarter Deck,' in the first long declaration from Ahab to the crew, Melville broke at times into what is virtually blank verse, and can be printed as such:

> But look ye, Starbuck, what is said in heat,
> That thing unsays itself. There are men
> From whom warm words are small indignity.
> I meant not to incense thee. Let it go.
> Look! see yonder Turkish cheeks of spotted tawn—
> Living, breathing pictures painted by the sun.
> The pagan leopards—the unrecking and
> Unworshipping things, that live; and seek and give
> No reasons for the torrid life they feel!

That division into lines has been made without alteration of a syllable, and though there are some clumsy sequences, there is no denying the essential pattern. Nor is this a solitary case. Ahab's first soliloquy begins:

> I leave a white and turbid wake;
> Pale waters, paler cheeks, where'er I sail.
> The envious billows sidelong swell to whelm
> My track; let them; but first I pass.

Starbuck's meditation opens the next chapter:

> My soul is more than matched; she's overmanned;
> And by a madman! Insufferable sting . . .

The danger of such unconsciously compelled verse is always evident. As it wavers and breaks down again into ejaculatory prose, it seems never to have belonged to the speaker, to have been at best a ventriloquist's trick. The weakness is similar in those speeches of Ahab's that show obvious allusions to a series of Shakespearean characters. The sum of the parts does not make a greater whole; each one distracts attention to itself and interferes with the singleness of Ahab's development.

Emerson had thought about this problem. Writing in his journal in 1838 about the experience of having re-read *Lear* and *Hamlet* on successive days, he did not feel obliged to assume his platform manner, and to call for the emergence of a super philosopher-poet. He was lost in wonder at 'the perfect mastery' of the architectural structure of these wholes. Yet they faced him as always with the question of the derivative literature of his own country, since he knew that, despite all his admiration, he could not construct 'anything comparable' even to one scene. 'Set me to producing a match for it, and I should instantly depart into mouthing rhetoric.'

That Melville so departed on many occasions may hardly be gainsaid. Yet *Moby-Dick* did not become another *Prince of Parthia*. This first tragedy by an American, composed in 1759 by Thomas Godfrey, a young Philadelphian, foreshadowed the romantic conventions that still were prevailing on the stage in Melville's day. It set its scene in a country of whose life its author knew nothing, at the beginning of the Christian era. It passed over contemporary themes, with which, as an officer in the militia shortly to undertake the expedition to Fort Duquesne, Godfrey was to become better acquainted. But even if he had written his tragedy after he had gone as a tobacco factor to North Carolina—where he was to die of a sunstroke at twenty-seven—it is improbable that he would have brought his poetry nearer home. For it resumed the debate between love and honor where Dryden had left off, and made its lines a pastiche of familiar quotations from Shakespeare, and of some less familiar from Beaumont and Fletcher. By the time of Boker the manner had been more subtly assimilated, but the main problem still remained unsolved. Emerson came near to suggesting its resolution in his journal of 1843:

Do not write modern antiques like Landor's *Pericles* or Goethe's *Iphigenia* . . . or Scott's *Lay of the Last Minstrel*. They are paste jewels. You may well take an ancient subject where the form is incidental merely, like Shakespeare's plays, and the treatment and dialogue is simple, and most modern. But do not make much of the costume. For such things have no verity; no man will live or die by them. The way to write is to throw your body at the mark when your arrows are spent, like Cupid in Anacreon. Shakespeare's speeches in *Lear* are in the very dialect of 1843.

No matter whether Shakespeare's language seems to us anything but 'simple,' Melville's feeling that such words spoke to him directly of life as he knew it called forth from him an almost physical response. The first result might be that he started to write high-flown speeches entirely under the dramatist's spell. But they did not remain mere posturing, since he was able 'to throw his body at the mark.' The weight of his experience backed up what he wanted to do with words. He knew what he was about in the way he prepared the reader for the improbability of Ahab's diction. He stated that there were instances, among the 'fighting Quakers' of Nantucket, of men who, 'named with Scripture names—a singularly common fashion on the island,' had in childhood naturally imbibed 'the stately dramatic thee and thou of the Quaker idiom.' Such men were substantially schooled in the 'daring and boundless adventure' of whaling; they were led, 'by the stillness and seclusion of many long night-watches in the remotest waters,' to think 'untraditionally and independently.' Moreover—and here is a telling factor that operated on Melville as well as on Ahab—they received 'all nature's sweet or savage impressions fresh from her own virgin voluntary and confiding breast,' and had come, 'thereby chiefly, but with some help from accidental advantages, to learn a bold and nervous lofty language.'

In Melville's case the accident of reading Shakespeare had been a catalytic agent, indispensable in releasing his work from limited reporting to the expression of profound natural forces. Lear's Fool had taught him what Starbuck was to remark about poor Pip, that even the exalted words of a lunatic could penetrate to the heavenly mysteries. But Melville came into full possession of his own idiom, not when he was half following Shakespeare, but when he had grasped the truth of the passage in *The Winter's Tale* that 'The art itself is nature,' [3] when, writing out of his own primary energy, he could end his description of his hero in language that suggests Shakespeare's, but is not an imitation of it: 'But Ahab, my captain, still moves before me in all his Nantucket grimness and shagginess; and in this episode touching emperors and kings, I must not conceal that I have only to do with a poor old whale-hunter like him; and, therefore, all outward majestical trappings and housings are denied me. Oh, Ahab! what shall be grand in thee, it must needs be plucked at from the skies, and dived for in the deep, and featured in the unbodied air!' The final phrase seems particularly Shakespearean in its imaginative richness, but its two key words appear only once each in the plays, 'featured' in *Much Ado* ('How wise, how noble, young, how rarely featured'), 'unbodied' in *Troilus and Cressida* ('And that unbodied figure of the thought That gave't surmised shape'), and to neither of these usages is

3. See above, p. 386.

Melville indebted for his fresh combination. The close concatenation of 'dived' and 'plucked' is probably dependent upon their presence in Hotspur's

> By heaven methinks it were an easy leap,
> To pluck bright honour from the pale-fac'd moon,
> Or dive into the bottom of the deep,
> Where fathom-line could never touch the ground,
> And pluck up drowned honour by the locks.

But Melville has adapted these verbs of action so entirely to his own usage that they have become his possession as well as Shakespeare's.

In driving through to his conception of a tragic hero who should be dependent upon neither rank nor costume, Melville showed his grasp of the kind of art 'that nature makes,' and fulfilled Emerson's organic principle. His practice of tragedy, though it gained force from Shakespeare, had real freedom; it did not base itself upon Shakespeare, but upon man and nature as Melville knew them. Therefore, he was able to handle, in his greatest scenes, a kind of diction that depended upon no source, and that could, as Lawrence noted, convey something 'almost superhuman or inhuman, bigger than life.' This quality could be illustrated at length from the language of 'The Grand Armada' or 'The Try-Works' or the final chase, or from Ishmael's declaration of what the white whale signified for him. One briefer example of how Melville had learned under Shakespeare's tutelage to master, at times, a dramatic speech that does not encroach upon verse, but draws upon a magnificent variety and flow of language, is Ahab's defiance of fire:

Oh! thou clear spirit of clear fire, whom on these seas I as Persian once did worship, till in the sacramental act so burned by thee, that to this hour I bear the scar; I now know thee, thou clear spirit, and I now know that thy right worship is defiance. To neither love nor reverence will thou be kind; and e'en for hate thou canst but kill; and all are killed. No fearless fool now fronts thee. I own thy speechless, placeless power; but to the last gasp of my earthquake life will dispute its unconditional, unintegral mastery in me. In the midst of the personified impersonal, a personality stands here. Though but a point at best; whenceso'er I came; whereso'er I go; yet while I earthly live, the queenly personality lives in me, and feels her royal rights. But war is pain, and hate is woe. Come in thy lowest form of love, and I will kneel and kiss thee; but at thy highest, come as mere supernal power; and though thou launchest navies of full-freighted worlds, there's that in here that still remains indifferent. Oh, thou clear spirit, of thy fire thou madest me, and like a true child of fire, I breathe it back to thee.

The full meaning of that speech can be apprehended only in its context in the tumultuous suddenness of the storm, and in relation to Ahab's diabolic bond with the fire-worshipping Parsee. Even in that context it is by no means clear exactly how much Melville meant to imply in making Ahab regard the fire as his father, and presently go on to say: 'But thou art my fiery father; my sweet mother, I know not. Oh, cruel! what hast thou done with her? There lies my puzzle.' Immersed in primitive forces in *Moby-Dick*, Melville soon learned that—as he made Ishmael remark concerning 'the gliding great demon of the seas of life'—there were 'subterranean' levels deeper than his understanding could explain or fathom. But whatever the latent radiations of intuition in this passage, they emanate from a core of articulated thought. Here, if Emerson's prejudice against the novel had only allowed him to see it, was the proof that the dialect of mid-nineteenth-century America could rise to dramatic heights. That does not mean that any American ever spoke like this, any more than Elizabethans talked like Lear; but it does mean that the progressions of Melville's prose are now based on a sense of speech rhythm, and not on anybody else's verse. The elaborate diction should not mislead us into thinking that the words have been chosen recklessly, or merely because they sounded well. For they are combined in a vital rhetoric, and thereby build up a defense of one of the chief doctrines of the age, the splendor of the single personality. The matching of the forces is tremendous: the 'placeless,' 'supernal power,' a symbol of the inscrutable mystery which Ahab so hates, is set over against his own integrity, which will admit the intrusion of nothing 'unintegral,' and which glories both in its 'queenly' magnificence and in the terrible violence of its 'earthquake life.' The resources of the isolated man, his courage and his staggering indifference to anything outside himself, have seldom been exalted so high.

The verbal resources demonstrate that Melville has now mastered Shakespeare's mature secret of how to make language itself dramatic. He has learned to depend more and more upon verbs of action, which lend their dynamic pressure to both movement and meaning. A highly effective tension is set up by the contrast between 'thou launchest navies of full-freighted worlds' and 'there's that in here that still remains indifferent.' The compulsion to strike the breast exerted by that last clause suggests how thoroughly the drama has come to inhere in the words. Melville has also gained something of the Shakespearean energy of verbal compounds ('full-freighted'); and something, too, of the quickened sense of life that comes from making one part of speech act as another—for example, 'earthquake' as an adjective, or the coining of 'placeless,' an adjective from a noun.

But Melville's new ripeness of power should not be thought of solely in relation to his drama. It is just as apparent in his narrative, as can be suggested very briefly by one of his many Biblical allusions, which for once he makes not for solemnity but to heighten humor. He is just finishing his chapter on 'The Tail': 'Dissect him how I may, then, I but go skin deep; I know him not, and never will. But if I know not even the tail of this whale, how understand his head? much more, how comprehend his face, when face he has none? Thou shalt see my back parts, my tail, he seems to say, but my face shall not be seen. But I cannot completely make out his back parts; and hint what he will about his face, I say again he has no face.'

The effect of that burlesque is to magnify rather than to lessen his theme, not to blaspheme Jehovah, but to add majesty to the whale. Melville's inner sureness was now such that it freed his language from the constrictions that had limited *White Jacket*. He had regained and reinforced the gusto of *Typee* on a level of greater complexity. Whether or not he consciously intended to symbolize sex in the elemental energies of fire or of the white whale, when he wanted to deal with the subject directly he did not resort to guarded hints, but handled very simply the Whitmanesque comradeship between Ishmael and Queequeg. In 'The Cassock' he could also write a chapter about the heroic phallus of the whale.

5. The Matching of the Forces

IN TRACING the effect of Shakespeare on Melville's language, perhaps not enough attention was given to the equally obvious marks left by the dramatist on the composition of scene after scene. Some of the results are

lumbering enough, particularly the interludes of 'comic relief': the char-
acter-part of the black cook Fleece; Stubb's account, in a chapter called
'Queen Mab,' of a queer dream in which he had been kicked by Ahab;
the scraps of talk between the crew to offset the outer and inner tempests.
All these seem so derivative in their conception that the humor runs
thin. Melville was much more adept at handling some of Shakespeare's
serious devices, since these were more in tune with his own temper.
Fedallah's elaboration of the seemingly impossible things that must happen before Ahab can die is reminiscent of Birnam wood and Dunsinane.
Ahab feels assured for this voyage when he is told that the Parsee will
perish before him, and will appear again after death, and that 'hemp
only' can kill Ahab. But it turns out that Fedallah, who is drowned by
Moby-Dick's onslaught on the second day of the chase, *is* seen again,
pinioned incredibly in the entangled lines on the whale's back. It also
happens that in Ahab's final darting of his harpoon into his enemy, the
line runs foul, catches him around the neck, and propels him instantly
to his grave.

A more effective since less labored derivation adds intensity to the
moment when Ahab pledges the crew to his purpose in the harpoon-cups.
For he also makes the three mates cross their lances before him, and
seizes them at their axis, 'meanwhile glancing intently from Starbuck to
Stubb, from Stubb to Flask.' The cellarage scene where Hamlet compelled Horatio and Marcellus to swear on his sword was operating on the
construction here. This is also the juncture when Fedallah's spectral laugh
is heard from the hold, a counterpart of Hamlet's father's Ghost. An
oddly transformed allusion, which shows again how deeply Shakespeare's
words had entered into Melville's unconscious, is added by Ahab. He
breaks off to say to the boy who has brought the grog, in a recombination of some of Hamlet's remarks to the Ghost: 'Ha! boy, come back?
bad pennies come not sooner.' An important contrast between such allusions and those of our age of more conscious craft, those in *The Waste
Land* or *Ulysses,* is that Melville did not intend part of his effect in this
scene to depend upon the reader's awareness of his source. Indeed, from
the way he handles that source here, he seems to have been only partly
aware himself of its pervasive presence. His attention was wholly taken
up with the effort to pour this energy into a new mould of his own.

But fascinating as the study of some of these configurations can be,
they still leave us on the periphery of Melville's interest. The reason why

his borrowings did not constitute a series of romantic tableaux was because they were only the by-product of the effort to engage in his own
terms with what he had perceived to be the central problems of tragedy.
The common denominator he found between Shakespeare and Hawthorne
is illuminating. He marked in *The Seven Gables* many of Hawthorne's
contrasts between the 'big, heavy, solid unrealities' of Judge Pyncheon's
wealth and power, and the core of his real nature. The same 'contraries,'
as Melville called them, struck him more than any other element in his
reading of Shakespeare: the incongruous and often heartrending discrep-
ancies between appearance and truth. An editor's note that he underlined
in *All's Well* suggests Hawthorne's attitude towards the Judge. Designed
to elucidate the remark,

> Good alone
> Is good without a name: vileness is so,

it concluded, 'and so vileness would be ever vile, did not rank, power, and
fortune, screen it from opprobrium.'

Melville followed Shakespeare's diverse treatments of these 'contraries'
through play after play. He noted them particularly in Timon's disillusioned discovery of the difference between the conduct of men towards
him when he was rich and when he was poor. To judge from his pencil
marks, he was absorbed by the theme of *Measure for Measure,* which is
made explicit on many occasions, as in the Duke's observation:

> O, what may man within him hide,
> Though angel on the outward side!

He also marked Othello's torture at the ambiguity of appearance:

> By the world,
> I think my wife be honest and think she is not,
> I think that thou art just and think thou art not.
> I'll have some proof.

He underlined Cordelia's statement to her sisters after her disastrous
truthfulness in the opening scene,

> Time shall unfold what plaited cunning hides.

But Melville was aware, in that play particularly, of the desperate odds
against which truth had to battle; and when Regan called Gloucester,
'Ingrateful fox!' he added, 'Here's a touch Shakespearean—*Regan* talks of
ingratitude.'

Such passages were in his mind when he stated in his essay on Hawthorne that 'through the mouths of the dark characters of Hamlet, Timon, Lear, and Iago, he craftily says, or sometimes insinuates the things which we feel to be so terrifically true, that it were all but madness for any good man, in his own proper character, to utter, or even hint of them.' Melville believed that 'the same madness of vital truth' was spoken also by Lear's Fool. Therefore, when dealing with the eerie wisdom in Pip's lunacy, he declared that 'man's insanity is heaven's sense,' words that practically state the theme of Emerson's 'Bacchus' or of Emily Dickinson's lyric which begins,

> Much madness is divinest sense
> To a discerning eye.

This insistence that what is hidden from common sense may be revealed to intuitive vision is the poetic mode of asserting the Kantian contrast between Understanding and Reason. Its most imaginative expression had been made by Blake, in whose work, significantly, Melville was to find a strong attraction in his later years, at a time when it was still not widely known in America. Emerson's madness always kept a gentle decorum; and though Emily Dickinson's comprehension of Shakespeare's treatment of good and evil was undoubtedly as keen as Melville's, her own drama, however intense, remained personal and lyric. Melville's greater horizon of experience, the vigorous thrust of his mind, and the strength of his passion carried him, as similar attributes had carried Blake, into wider and more dangerous waters.

It may be a coincidence that the four characters whom he linked together as the voicers of violent truth are the very four who left the most lasting mark on his own searching of experience. When the terror of the storm scenes is re-enacted on the *Pequod,* Ahab's fierceness owes something of its stature to Lear. Moreover, one of the crucial elements in the evolution of the old captain is his relation with Pip, a relation that, in its interplay of madness and wisdom, is endowed with the pathos of the bond between the King and his Fool. In *Pierre* Melville made his own kind of response to the view held by Coleridge and Emerson that this was the age of Man Thinking, and tried to create an American *Hamlet.* The misanthropic mood of *The Confidence Man,* exposing the mockery of all other 'trust' save that of the cash-nexus, is Melville's own realization of Timonism. And what we shall find to be his most recurrent type of evil character—from Jackson, the sailor whose sinister will so terrified young Redburn, to Claggart, the master-at-arms in *Billy Budd*—is one whose malignity seems to be stirred most by the envious sight of virtue in others, as Iago's was.

Even from such a brief summary it is clear that we have arrived at the point where we are no longer dealing with an ordinary 'influence,' but with a rare case, in which Shakespeare's conception of tragedy had so grown into the fibre of Melville's thought that much of his mature work became a re-creation of its themes in modern terms. But we can best approach the meaning of Ahab's tragedy if we leave the Shakespearean strain in abeyance for a while, and try to apprehend Melville's own awakening sense of the meaning of sin, of suffering, and of the 'boundless sympathy with all forms of being,' to which he had responded so eagerly in Hawthorne as well as in Shakespeare. As he wrote to Duyckinck after his first expression of enthusiasm at hearing Emerson lecture: 'Nay, I do not oscillate in Emerson's rainbow, but prefer rather to hang myself in mine own halter than swing in any other man's swing.' As he grew more dissatisfied with Emerson's inadequacy, he seized upon Shakespeare and Hawthorne as allies. Yet his 'sense of Innate Depravity and Original Sin' did not remain just what he found in Hawthorne. A fundamental reason for some transmutation was that, unlike Hawthorne, he did not confine himself to moral and psychological observation, but launched out into metaphysics. The background of Calvinistic thought over which Hawthorne's imagination played served to keep his brooding interpretation within a coherent frame. He dwelt on the contrast between appearance and reality, but his quiet disillusion accepted their inexplicability; he did not expect the hard facts of life to swerve one foot in the direction of the idealists' hopes. Melville could be neither so cool nor restrained. Though deeply impressed by the firmness of the Puritans' conception of evil, his mind had moved away from any fixed system of theology. Unchecked by formal education, a far more passionate temperament than Hawthorne's drove him to speculate. He felt compelled to search out the truth for himself, even while he recognized, in a growing wildness and turbulence, that it was as unfathomable as the sea.

The disasters of his course came full upon him in *Pierre,* but he was already aware of the danger signals in *Mardi* and *Moby-Dick.* He made Ishmael remark that 'clear Truth is a thing for salamander giants only to

encounter; how small the chances for the provincials then?' In ending
one of his chapters he felt his dilemma: 'This whole book is but a
draught—nay, but the draught of a draught. Oh, Time, Strength, Cash,
and Patience!' But although *Moby-Dick* is more notable for abundance
than for control or lucidity, Melville had managed to work out his
central assumptions about good and evil in ways that are fairly unmistakable. We have already traced some of his symbolic contrasts between
land and sea, between calm and storm. His reaction against transcendentalism and the other current optimisms is voiced in the opening chapter,
where Ishmael, who is to act as a kind of choric spectator to Ahab's tragedy, says: 'Not ignoring what is good, I am quick to perceive a horror.'

The preponderating stress on evil in this book is sometimes loosely romantic, as when Ishmael declares that all noble things are touched with
melancholy. But the ground is solider when he bases his belief that the
man 'who hath more of joy than sorrow in him . . . cannot be true—
not true, or undeveloped,' on the proposition that 'the truest of all men
was the Man of Sorrows,' and the truest of all books *Ecclesiastes*. Ishmael
finds evil in the violent forces of nature, in the 'horrible vulturism' of
animals; but he also knows that 'there is no folly of the beasts of the
earth which is not infinitely outdone by the madness of men.'

If Melville grants such width of range to unleashed evil, it is important
to determine what kind of discriminations he makes between it and
good. Some of the more extravagant of the symbolical interpretations of
his masterpiece could have been eliminated if the critics had paid stricter
attention to Melville's own text, notably to the two chapters where he
unfolds his basic conceptions of evil, 'Moby-Dick' and 'The Whiteness of
the Whale.' He clearly distinguishes between this whale and all others.
The whale in general is one of 'the interlinked terrors and wonders of
God,' majestic in its size, portentous in its 'unconscious power.' While
meditating on the prehistoric antiquity of fossil whales, unearthed by
geologists, Melville falls into the strains of *Hydriotaphia,* into something
like Browne's mystical awe before the sepulchral urns that had been ex-
humed in Norfolk: 'Who can show a pedigree like Leviathan? Ahab's
harpoon had shed older blood than the Pharaoh's. Methuselah seems a
schoolboy. I look round to shake hands with Shem. I am horror-struck
at this antemosaic, unsourced existence of the unspeakable terrors of the
whale, which, having been before all time, must needs exist after all humane ages are over.'

That conceit may be half playful, but Melville keeps coming back to
the primitive, pre-human energies that are represented by the whale. He
also urges on the reader a recognition of the ever-present perils involved
in the whaling industry: 'For God's sake, be economical with your lamps
and candles! not a gallon you burn, but at least one drop of man's blood
was spilled for it.' But, aware of the mixed nature of life, he does not
make the oversimplification of considering man good, and the whale evil.
In describing the capture of a diseased and decrepit whale, he adds that
'for all his old age . . . and his blind eyes, he must die the death and be
murdered, in order to light the gay bridals and other merry-makings of
men, and also to illuminate the solemn churches that preach unconditional inoffensiveness by all to all.' He dwells on the want of pity in callous Flask, who, noting an ulcerous wound on the flank of the still-living
creature, cries out, 'A nice spot, just let me prick him there once.' And
though Starbuck shouts, 'Avast! there's no need of that!' his humaneness
comes too late to stop the needless cruelty. Such a brutal act thus becomes
a contributing factor to our sense that though whaling is necessary to
civilization, still this crew may deserve something of the retribution that
overtakes it.

But before hazarding any such generalizations, it is essential to comprehend just what the conflict is here between the forces of good and
evil. In telling what Moby-Dick had signified for other mariners before
Ahab, Melville reiterates that what separates him from the rest of the
species is 'that unexampled, intelligent malignity which, according to
specific accounts, he had over and over again evinced in his assaults.'
How such a creature can be made to symbolize evil in Melville's drama
becomes manifest in the long declaration of what the white whale grew
to mean for Ahab after that first savage encounter in which he had lost
his leg. Ever since then Ahab had cherished 'a wild vindictiveness' against
this whale,

all the more fell for that in his frantic morbidness he at last came to identify
with him, not only all his bodily woes, but all his intellectual and spiritual
exasperations. The White Whale swam before him as the monomaniac incarnation of all those malicious agencies which some deep men feel eating
in them, till they are left living on with half a heart and half a lung. That
intangible malignity which has been from the beginning; to whose dominion
even the modern Christians ascribe one half of the worlds; which the ancient Ophites of the East reverenced in their statue devil;—Ahab did not

fall down and worship it like them; but deliriously transferring its idea to the abhorred White Whale, he pitted himself, all mutilated, against it. All that most maddens and torments; all that stirs up the lees of things; all truth with malice in it; all that cracks the sinews and cakes the brain; all the subtle demonisms of life and thought; all evil, to crazy Ahab, were visibly personified, and made practically assailable in Moby-Dick. He piled upon the whale's white hump the sum of all the general rage and hate felt by his whole race from Adam down; and then, as if his chest had been a mortar, he burst his heart's hot shell upon it.

The verbal action, which has become Melville's signature as well as Shakespeare's, is able to carry forward all the burden of abstract thought with which he has loaded it here; and rises to a climax in that final image, which is as like the compressed conceits of metaphysical poetry as is that one in Enobarbus' death speech that Melville marked:

> Throw my heart
> Against the flint and hardness of my fault,
> Which, being dried with grief, will break to powder,
> And finish all foul thoughts.

Before commenting on the thought in Ahab's declaration, we must re- member how Melville goes on to emphasize that in the captain's mono- mania, 'not one jot of his great natural intellect had perished,' but had been sharpened rather into a deadly weapon for executing the demands of his inflexible will. At this point Melville shows again his awareness that he is dealing with primitive human drives far beyond the scope of the cultivated mind. He expresses this in a remarkable image for Ahab's nature, an image that originated in Melville's having visited the Hotel de Cluny in Paris, and having seen, after 'winding far down' within it, the much earlier remains of 'those vast Roman halls of Thermes; where far beneath the fantastic towers of man's upper earth, his root of gran- deur, his whole awful essence sits in bearded state.' In that kind of image Melville asserts the mystery of the elemental forces in man, the instincts that lie deep below his later consciousness.

His emphasis on these forces is an important element in making cred- ible his insistence on malignity. By presenting such a character as Ahab, Melville breaks through the veneer of civilization and reminds the reader that the shallow light of his educated consciousness really penetrates only a very short way into the profundity of the universe. He raises the question—to return to Ahab's declaration—whether the savage may not have been instinctively right in feeling the necessity to exorcise the powers of evil, whether the Ophites, one of the Gnostic sects of the second century, may have been not merely perverse in their veneration for the serpent that tempted Eve. The extent of Melville's acquaintance with primitive religions is hard to determine, but his allusions show the quality of his interest. He wrote to Duyckinck, a month after his letters about Shakespeare and Emerson, at the moment when his horizons were opening in all directions, that he had just bought a set of Bayle's *Philosophical Dictionary,* and intended, on his return to New York, 'to lay the great old folios side by side and go to sleep on them through the summer,' with the *Phaedo* in one hand, and Thomas Browne in the other. He presumably read in Bayle (1647-1706) the article about the Gnostics, to whom he made a passing reference in *White Jacket,* which he was writing that summer. If Melville read far in the *Dictionary,* he must also have noted its author's hardly veiled bias to Manicheism. This may have something to do with Melville's loose remark that 'the modern Christians ascribe one half of the worlds' to the dominion of evil, a position that most theologians would hold to be based on the Manichean heresy. Melville may have meant to imply that, no matter how strenuously the theologians, especially the Calvinists in his own background, defended themselves from the charge of that heresy by insisting that evil was allowed to exist only by Providence; nevertheless, the dark battleground of sin with which their believers were faced admitted in fact evil's partial dominion. The Manichean doctrine that the whole world was divided between the independent principles of good and evil had derived from Zoroaster. By making Fedallah a Parsee, one of the fire-worshipping followers of Zoroastrianism, and thereby preserving, as he said, a link with 'earth's primal generations'; and by stating that Ahab's livid scar had come from his participation in their sacramental rites, Melville revealed the strong impression which their myth had left upon his imagination. According to the Zoroastrian account, the world has emanated from Ormazd, the spirit of light and fire, who wills the good. Yet his spirit is not free in this temporal epoch, but restricted by its antagonist and own twin brother, Ahriman, the spirit of darkness and evil. Zoroaster stresses the ultimate triumph of the good spirit, but the history of these brothers' conflict is the history of the world.

Emerson had reflected in 1847 that 'any journal would be incomplete that did not admit the Zoroastrian element,' but it is not possible to tell from the context whether he was thinking simply of the sentences of wisdom that he found in the *Zend-Avesta*, or of this dynamic struggle of opposed forces, which Nietzsche was later to dramatize through his own Zarathustra. Emerson often enjoyed the metaphor of such struggle, but he weighted the odds so heavily on the good that the victory became a rout. On the other hand, Melville was deeply attracted by any philosophy that inclined to the other side. That was one of the reasons why he was so affected by Shakespeare's villains. He marked one of the notes to his *Julius Caesar,* which said that 'envy,' as used by Brutus in urging that the acts of the conspirators should be free from all suspicions of its taint, was, 'as almost always by Shakespeare . . . used for "malice." ' However true that may be, the character of Edmund crystallized Melville's general impression into the remark that 'the infernal nature has a valor often denied to innocence.' He had thus rediscovered for himself what the tragic poet of the next generation, Hopkins, was to feel that Keats had missed in 'Lamia': 'some lesson of the terrible malice of evil, which, when it is checked, drags down innocence in its own ruin.'

In projecting Ahab's belief that he had been a victim of 'that intangible malignity,' Melville set the terms for a tragedy of revenge. But it is significant that he did not allow this sense of Moby-Dick's evil to be developed in Ahab's brain alone. Starbuck may protest, 'I came here to hunt whales, not my commander's vengeance.' The crew may be swept along by the magnet of Ahab's irresistible will without really understanding what they are about. But Ishmael is explicit: 'What the White Whale was to Ahab has been hinted; what, at times, he was to me, as yet remains unsaid.' Caught up into the reckless mood that followed Ahab's first announcement of his quest, he 'could see naught in that brute but the deadliest ill.' Subsequently that feeling grew upon him, and grew wider in its connotations. He found it almost impossible to put 'in a comprehensible form' why the whiteness of the whale 'above all things appalled me . . . Yet, in some dim, random way, explain myself I must, else all these chapters might be naught.'

To such a depth and breadth does the whiteness become a symbol. All its extraordinary ramifications stem from an assumption antipodal to Emerson's, from what Melville calls the instinctive 'knowledge of the demonism in the world.' Thus, despite even the radiant hue of 'the very veil of the Christian's Deity,' Ishmael is driven to the knowledge that 'though in many of its aspects this visible world seems formed in love, the invisible spheres were formed in fright.' Invisibility connotes to him 'the heartless voids and immensities of the universe,' and stabs him with the thought of annihilation. This 'colorless all-color' suggests too the atheism from which he shrinks; it drives home the feeling that all the vivid tinges of nature herself can be but 'subtle deceits' laid on to conceal the blank charnel house within. As Ishmael heaps instance upon instance, the terrifying indifference of the universe to man's pursuits moves towards the 'vast skepticism and apathy' of existence, which Dreiser is always stressing.

We perceive an important distinction between Melville and Hawthorne when Starbuck reflects that the revelry in the forecastle after the grog, in contrast with 'the unfaltering silence aft,' forms an accurate image of life: 'Foremost through the sparkling sea shoots on the gay, embattled, bantering bow, but only to drag dark Ahab after it, where he broods within his sternward cabin, builded over the dead water of the wake, and further on, hunted by its wolfish gurglings.' When he looks at things thus as they are, the mate can feel nothing but the 'latent horror' in life. 'But 'tis not me! that horror's out of me!' Not even Starbuck, dwelling on the human kindness in his heart, can maintain that evil is entirely external to it. Nevertheless, the far range of Melville's symbols is carrying him into a different world from Hawthorne's. Hawthorne was concerned with depicting the good and evil within man's heart. Melville is not so concerned with individual sin as with titanic uncontrollable forces which seem to dwarf man altogether.

The extreme to which he pushes his symbols involves reversals of values that are not always easy to understand. He had praised Hawthorne most for his assertion of darkness; and in consequence of his own distrust of all optimisms, here light itself became dark. As an instance of the way he made his shifts, you find him first numbering among the sacred associations of whiteness, 'the white forked flame . . . held the holiest on the altar . . . by the Persian fire-worshippers.' Yet when he came to treat the relations between Ahab and Fedallah, he was thinking in terms of a Yankee *Faust,* and the Parsee's power had therefore to be made diabolic. Consequently, fire-worship became a sinister act that had left Ahab scarred for life; and in his final defiance of it Ahab shared in the heroic quality that Melville found in those who could say 'No! in thunder.' Yet observe what Ahab then declared: 'Light though thou be, thou leapest out of darkness; but I am darkness leaping out of light.' By exalting the dark half of the sphere, Ahab was not envisaging good, but a gloomier, more obscure evil. By this time neither light nor dark was good for Ahab, and his state was represented in the nocturnal fire of 'The Try-Works,' in another compressed image for the ship, which matches the inner world to the outer: 'Then the rushing *Pequod*, freighted with savages, and laden with fire, and burning a corpse, and plunging into that blackness of darkness, seemed the material counterpart of her monomaniac commander's soul.'

Amidst these protean changes of values you begin to ask what, if anything, remained good for Melville. The answer might be made through the creed of the Marcionites, another Gnostic sect, which he doubtless read about in Bayle, since he alluded to it in *White Jacket*. Marcion's utter separation of the stern and harsh God of the Old Testament from the New Testament God of love was fundamentally in accord with Melville's contrast between true Christianity and its distortion by the brutalities of a man-of-war. It was equally apposite, for that matter, to the contrast he had made between the ideal faith of Serenia and religion as practiced in the rest of *Mardi*. The fullest Charity, the expression of which he underlined in his copy of the thirteenth chapter of *First Corinthians,* was alone compatible with 'that unshackled, democratic spirit of Christianity in all things.'

In putting that phrase now finally in the full context of Melville's thought and feeling, we can best understand his conception of the matching of the forces in tragedy. However baffled he was to become in his head-on quest for truth, in his effort to win any final answer for man's relation to the universe, he was always to retain, even in the bitterness of *The Confidence Man,* a firm hold on the conception of a balanced society, on the desirable relation of man to man. His fervent belief in democracy was the origin of his sense of tragic loss at the distortion or destruction of the unique value of a human being. How high he set that value and how he instinctively linked it with Christianity are suggested by his annotation to a sentence in Madame de Staël's *Germany:* 'A man, regarded in a religious light, is as much as the entire human race.' Upon this Melville wrote: 'This was an early and innate conviction of mine, suggested by my revulsion from the counting-room philosophy of Paley.'[1] His continued assertion of the nobility, not of nobles but of man, was couched in religious terms from *Redburn* to *Billy Budd*. But the terms were equally democratic. He insisted that Israel Potter was a 'plebeian Lear or Oedipus.' Reviewing *The Oregon Trail*[2] in that pregnant winter of his many discoveries, he objected to what he considered Parkman's tone of cool superiority to the Indians. After making a reasoned and not idealized defense of the savage as he was, he concluded, with a burst of feeling: 'Let us not disdain, then, but pity. And wherever we recognize the image of God, let us reverence it, though it hung from the gallows.'

As Melville examined man's lot, he was impressed, no less than Hawthorne, by the terrifying consequences of an individual's separation from his fellow beings. The narrator of *Moby-Dick* is not his only Ishmael. The discouraged loneliness with which the young whaleman feels the name of the outcast wanderer to belong to him had already been voiced by Redburn, in his dread lest his hatred of the brutal crew should master his heart, and end by making him a 'fiend.' The same strain is to be re-echoed by Pierre, who discovers, as he breaks through the conventional shams of his mother's existence, that his devotion to truth has driven him out, 'an infant Ishmael into the desert, with no maternal Hagar to accompany and comfort him.' In addition, White Jacket is damned as a Jonah, and Israel Potter's name is taken as prophetic, since for more than forty years he 'wandered in the wild wilderness of the world's extremest hardships and ills.'

The one thing that could redeem 'the wolfish world,' the Ishmael of *Moby-Dick* found, was sympathy with another human being. Similarly, Pierre, at the crisis when he thinks that divinity and humanity both despise him, feels revived by the touch of Lucy's unselfishness, a feeling that Melville was able to express with something of the shattering force of Dostoevsky. He gave his fullest presentation of the transforming power of such feeling in the relation between Ishmael and Queequeg. When Ishmael recognized that 'the man's a human being just as I am,' he was freed from the burden of his isolation, his heart was no longer turned against society. That he rediscovered the sense of Christian brotherhood

1. Melville dated his acquisition of Madame de Staël's volumes March 4, 1862. This annotation has been erased, and can be read only because of the pressure left by Melville's pencil. What I have taken to be 'innate' is so compressed that it may actually be 'irate.'

2. In *The Literary World* (March 31, 1849).

through companionship with a tattooed pagan was the consequence of Melville's now matured perception of the ironic contradictions between appearance and fact.

His belief in the potential good of democracy was carried to the length of celebrating, in a passage in *Redburn,* the opening promise of America, the free mixture of bloods which would make us not a mere nation but a world. Yet, contemplating the actual, Melville saw the gap between our professions and our practice, as in the great wrong of slavery; in the tendency to sacrifice everything to the grasping individual will; in the difficulty of establishing adequate human contacts in our violently expanding life. When writing *Israel Potter,* he observed in Paul Jones a fascinating but terrible symbol for the American character: 'Intrepid, unprincipled, reckless, predatory, with boundless ambition, civilized in externals but a savage at heart, America is, or may yet be, the Paul Jones of nations.'

Melville's hopes for American democracy, his dread of its lack of humane warmth, his apprehension of the actual privations and defeats of the common man, and his depth of compassion for courageous struggle unite in giving fervor to the declaration of his purpose in writing *Moby-Dick:* a declaration in which he feels most profoundly the Shakespearean lineage of his intent and method. It comes in 'Knights and Squires,' where, summing up his motley cast of characters, he is conscious that he may seem to be endowing ordinary whalemen with too heroic gifts:

But this august divinity I treat of, is not the dignity of kings and robes, but that abounding dignity which has no robed investiture. Thou shalt see it shining in the arm that wields a pick or drives a spike; that democratic dignity which, on all hands, radiates without end from God; Himself! The great God absolute! The centre and circumference of all democracy! His omnipresence, our divine equality.

If, then, to meanest mariners, and renegades and castaways, I shall hereafter ascribe high qualities, though dark; weave round them tragic graces; if even the most mournful, perchance the most abased, among them all, shall at times lift himself to the exalted mounts; if I shall touch that workman's arm with some ethereal light; if I shall spread a rainbow over his disastrous set of sun; then against all mortal critics bear me out in it, thou just Spirit of Equality, which hast spread one royal mantle of humanity over all my kind! Bear me out in it, thou great democratic God! who didst not refuse to the swart convict Bunyan, the pale, poetic pearl: Thou who didst clothe with doubly hammered leaves of finest gold, the stumped and paupered arm of old Cervantes; Thou who didst pick up Andrew Jackson from the pebbles; who didst hurl him upon a war-horse; who didst thunder him higher than a throne! Thou who, in all Thy mighty, earthly marchings, ever cullest Thy selected champions from the kingly commons; bear me out in it, O God!

This last paragraph-long sentence is one of the summits of Melville's rhetoric: the formal progression of its almost architecturally balanced iterations rises to an eloquence of a purity and sublimity beyond what any other American writer has been able to command. Its crescendo completes his fusion of Christianity and democracy. His unexpected linking of the three heroes would not have surprised Hawthorne, who added to his admiration for Bunyan and for Jackson a warm understanding of 'the profound, pathetic humor' of Cervantes. Through such symbolical figures Melville discloses what wealth of suffering humanity he believed to be pitted in the dynamic struggle against evil. By this full-voiced affirmation of democratic dignity, even of divine equality, he reveals also with what assurance he felt that a great theme could be created from the common stuff of American life. Indeed, he lets us enter the very avenues through which he was then creating one.

6. The Fate of the Ungodly God-like Man

NOTWITHSTANDING the depth of his feeling for 'the kingly commons,' Melville knew the strength of the contrast between the great individual and the inert mass. He expressed it in Ahab's power to coerce all the rest within the sphere of 'the Leyden jar of his own magnetic life.' Melville himself was caught and fascinated by his hero. He asserted from the outset that he was dealing with 'a man of greatly superior natural force, with a globular brain and a ponderous heart . . . one in a whole nation's census—a mighty pageant creature, formed for noble tragedies.' To such lengths did he go in building up his old whale hunter to the stature of a Shakespearean king. But he was struck at the same time by the obverse side, and concluded his first adumbration of the still unseen captain by adding that 'all men tragically great are made so through a certain morbidness. Be sure of this, O young ambition, all mortal greatness is but disease.'

This electric attraction and repulsion runs through Melville's whole portrayal from the moment when, in this same chapter describing Ishmael's first boarding of the ship, Captain Peleg forewarns him that Captain Ahab is 'a grand, ungodly, god-like man . . . Ahab's above the common; Ahab's been in colleges, as well as 'mong the cannibals; been used to deeper wonders than the waves.' He hints to the awed sailor that Ahab has had moody and savage spells since the loss of his leg; but tells him not to be afraid, for though Ahab is not a pious good man like Captain Bildad, he is a swearing good one. 'Besides, my boy, he has a wife—not three voyages wedded—a sweet, resigned girl. Think of that; by that sweet girl that old man has a child: hold ye then there can be any utter, hopeless harm in Ahab? No, no, my lad; stricken, blasted, if he be, Ahab has his humanities.'

The implications of the contrasting terms, 'ungodly' and 'god-like,' come out only as we follow the captain's subsequent career. But their very choice shows Melville's sensitiveness to what was happening in his time. Anyone concerned with orthodoxy holds that the spiritual decadence of the nineteenth century can be measured according to the alteration in the object of its belief from God-Man to Man-God, and to the corresponding shift in emphasis from Incarnation to Deification. Melville did not use those terms, but he had been responsive himself to that alteration, from belief in the salvation of man through the mercy and grace of a sovereign God, to belief in the potential divinity in every man. That alteration centered around the Crucifixion. By Melville's time, and especially in protestant, democratic America, the emphasis was no longer on God become Man, on the unique birth and Divinity of the Christ, who was killed and died back into eternal life; but on the rebel killed by an unworthy society, on Man become the Messiah, become God. That celebration of Man's triumph involved also the loss of several important attitudes: that there was anything more important than the individual; that he might find his completion in something greater than himself; that the real basis for human brotherhood was not in humanitarianism but in men's common aspiration and fallibility, in their humility before God.

The relevance of these reflections to Ahab's tragedy emerges as we see how overwhelmingly he assumes the center of the stage. At the end of the account of what the captain found symbolized in Moby-Dick, of why he was intent on an audacious and immitigable revenge, Melville showed how this fixed resolve could sway all before it. There was none who could stand up against him in this crew, composed chiefly 'of mongrel renegades, and castaways, and cannibals—morally enfeebled, also, by the incompetence of mere unaided virtue or right-mindedness in Starbuck, the invulnerable jollity of indifference and recklessness in Stubb, and the pervading mediocrity in Flask.' But Ahab's absolute domination carried Melville even farther; it caused him to drop what had seemed to be one of his major themes—the relation between Ishmael and Queequeg, to abandon all development or even subsequent mention of Bulkington, the barrel-chested demigod whom he had introduced, at the Spouter Inn, as a natural seeker for truth. To a degree even beyond what Melville may have intended, all other personalities, all other human relations became dwarfed before Ahab's purpose.

Therefore, to grasp the meaning of this tragedy, it is necessary to examine Ahab's development in more detail than we did that of any of Hawthorne's characters. Not that he is more living than Hester Prynne, for the comparison reveals him to be not so much a varied human being as a state of mind. In one of the fragmentary comments in *The Confidence Man,* on the question of what is meant by an original character in fiction, Melville was virtually saying what he had intended in Ahab. He held that a writer could pick up plenty of singular characters by observation, but that the true original character was rare, that such a one, like Hamlet, was 'a revolving Drummond light, raying away from itself all round it,' and illuminating life as much as a new radical philosopher. Such a description of Hamlet shows Melville's inclination to the Coleridgean interpretation of the play, which exalts the hero and tends to ignore his social environment, as Shakespeare never did. In line with this interpretation is Melville's further remark that 'for much the same reason that there is but one planet to one orbit, so can there be but one such original character to one work of invention.' But with his belief that the creation of such a character depended on more than mere observation, on a depth of spiritual insight, Melville was none the less explicit that it could not spring merely from 'the author's imagination—it being as true in literature as in zoology, that all life is from the egg.' A concentrated view of Ahab will disclose that he was born from the matrix of Melville's age. He is an embodiment of his author's most profound response to the problem of the free individual will *in extremis.*

Melville's first detailed characterization of him stresses his apartness and his suffering, his 'infinity of firmest fortitude,' and yet the 'crucifixion in his face.' His driven mind has already lost all touch with pleasure of the senses. He can no longer relish his pipe, and tosses it moodily into the sea. He looks at the sunset, and reflects that it soothes him no more: 'This lovely light, it lights not me; all loveliness is anguish to me, since I can ne'er enjoy. Gifted with the high perception, I lack the low, enjoying power; damned, most subtly and most malignantly! damned in the midst of Paradise!' The critical danger involved in the separation between perception and feeling had been noted by Melville in another context, when he underscored Gloucester's comment on the type of man who is blind to the heavenly powers,

> that will not see
> Because he doth not feel.

This cleavage is at the root of Ahab's dilemma. He can see nothing but his own burning thoughts since he no longer shares in any normal fellow-feelings. His resolve to take it upon himself to seek out and annihilate the source of malignity, is god-like, for it represents human effort in its highest reach. But as he himself declares, it is likewise 'demoniac,' the sanity of a controlled madness. The control depends upon 'that certain sultanism of his brain,' which cunningly builds its power over the others into 'an irresistible dictatorship.' At the moment of the initial announcement of his vengeance, he rises to a staggering *hubris,* as he shouts, 'Who's over me?' Starbuck, powerless before such madness, can only think: 'Horrible old man! Who's over him he cries;—ay, he would be a democrat to all above; look how he lords it over all below!' Yet Starbuck is forced not simply to resent but to pity him, since he reads in the lurid eyes the captain's desperation. And in sleep, when alone the grip of the conscious mind has been relaxed, Ahab's tortured soul shrieks out in nightmares, in its frantic effort to escape from the drive of his obsession. At such moments Melville finds an image for his state in calling him a Prometheus whose intense thinking has created the vulture that feeds upon his heart forever. It is significant that Melville wrote·on the back inner cover of the last volume of his Shakespeare, 'Eschylus' *Tragedies,*' as though intending to read them. ·Prometheus, whose desire to help humanity was also misdirected and led him into crime, makes a not unfitting counterpart for Ahab, for the stark grandeur of Melville's creation is comparable even to that of Aeschylus.

Ahab's tragedy also runs the course of the tragedy of Ethan Brand, whom Melville regarded as typifying the man whose inordinate development of will and brain 'eats out the heart.' He read Hawthorne's story in the summer of 1851, too late for it to have affected the first conception of his hero, but possibly in time for it to have entered into the portrayal of Ahab's final damnation through his having lost hold, no less than Brand, 'of the magnetic chain of humanity.' Moreover, Ahab's career falls into the pattern that Hawthorne had handled many other times, since it is basically a tragedy of pride. The increasing glare in his eyes reminds you of Chillingworth. The manifestations of his arrogance become ever more excessive as he advances, 'both chasing and being chased to his deadly end.' He hates to be indebted to anyone else, even to the carpenter who makes him a new leg. His refusal of Starbuck's entreaties with the insistence that just as there is one God, there is one captain, finally mounts to the point where, denying his aid to the grief-stricken master of the *Rachel,* he declares: 'God bless ye, man, and may I forgive myself, but I must go.'

Melville typifies the fatal lengths to which Ahab has gone from normality by making him hurl the quadrant to the deck and trample on it. In this action he curses everything that elevates man's eye to the heavens and the sun; he scorns man's science, the light of his mind, as an idle toy. Incidentally, the drama of this gesture may have been suggested by that scene of *Richard II*—marked in Melville's copy of Shakespeare—where the King dashes the mirror to the ground.

Up to this point there would seem to have been small scope given to 'the humanities,' which Captain Peleg insisted were also to be found in Ahab. They rise to the surface in his relations with Pip, the conception of which reveals the most effectual connection between Shakespearean tragedy and *Moby-Dick.* To judge even from the incidental verbal echoes, *King Lear* was working more pervasively in Melville's imagination at this time than any other play. Many of the sailors' defiances of outer storms ring as close to the original as 'Split jibs! tear yourselves!' When Melville wanted to magnify the size of the ship and the perilous descent of the boats over its side for the lowering, he recalled the Shakespeare passage which creates the greatest sense of height, and said that 'the three boats swung over the sea like three samphire baskets over high cliffs.' At the time of their first meeting with another vessel, Ahab notes that when the two wakes cross, a school 'of small harmless fish,' which have been swimming for some days by the *Pequod's* side dart off to follow the *Albatross:* '"Swim away from me, do ye?" murmured Ahab, gazing over into the water. There seemed but little in the words, but the tone conveyed more of deep helpless sadness than the insane old man had ever before evinced.' It may not be merely fanciful to read in Ahab's pathetic attitude a recombination of Lear's twisted notion that

> the little dogs and all,
> Tray, Blanch, and Sweet-heart, see, they bark at me.

But a more significant analogy resides in the function that Melville evolved for Pip. One day, after his disastrous accident, the cabin boy wandered crazily up to the quarterdeck, from which a member of the crew started to drive him, only to have Ahab shout, 'Hands off from that holiness!' and then add: 'Here, boy; Ahab's cabin shall be Pip's home henceforth, while Ahab lives. Thou touchest my inmost centre, boy . . . Come, let's down.'

What strikes Ahab most in Pip's fate is that the 'frozen heavens' created and then abandoned him: 'Lo! ye believers in gods all goodness, and in man all ill, lo you! see the omniscient gods oblivious of suffering man; and man, though idiotic, and knowing not what he does, yet full of the sweet things of love and gratitude. Come! I feel prouder leading thee by thy black hand, than though I grasped an emperor's.' That gives us another glimpse of the attraction that some of the Gnostic sects held for Melville through their insistence on a tyrannous and savage Jehovah. That Ahab's sense of the evil in God corresponds to something Melville had himself experienced is plain enough in that letter he wrote to Hawthorne while working on the concluding sections of *Moby-Dick*. He had just been discussing 'Ethan Brand,' and went on to say: 'I stand for the heart. To the dogs with the head! I had rather be a fool with a heart, than Jupiter Olympus with his head. The reason the mass of men fear God, and *at bottom dislike* Him, is because they rather distrust His heart, and fancy Him all brain like a watch.'[1] To such an extent had the grounds for Channing's 'Moral Argument against Calvin-

---

1. More than twenty years later Melville marked in the copy of Shelley's *Essays,* which he bought in 1873, the following passage: 'Milton's Devil as a moral being is as far superior to his God, as one who perseveres in some purpose which he has conceived to be excellent in spite of adversity and torture, is to one who in the cold security of undoubted triumph inflicts the most horrible revenge upon his enemy.'

ism' entered into Melville's revolt from the old strict theology. Yet unlike
Channing's his attitude was ambivalent, since he continued to be absorbed with the problem of evil. How the terms of that ambivalence
fought in him and demanded a solution will have to be traced from
Pierre to *Billy Budd.*

An observant sailor finds the bond between Ahab and Pip to be that
the one is 'daft with strength, the other daft with weakness.' The captain drinks a restorative philosophy from the boy's devotion to him: 'Oh!
spite of million villains, this makes me a bigot in the fadeless fidelity of
man! and a black! and crazy!' The 'contraries' seem to have struck Ahab
much as they did Ishmael in his reconciliation to life through the comradeship of Queequeg. But at this juncture there is a crucial divergence
not only from the experience of Ishmael, but also from *Lear,* where the
central movement is the purgation of the headstrong and arrogant King.
In that scene on the heath where he finally becomes aware of the blindness in his former pomp, where he both sees and feels the plight of
other human beings, and prays for all 'poor naked wretches' whereso'er
they are, he is no longer a vain monarch but a fellow man.

No such purgation transforms Ahab. He perceives in Pip's attachment
the quality that might cure his own malady, but he refuses to be deflected from his pursuit by the stirring of any sympathy for others, and
warns the pitiful boy: 'Weep so, and I will murder thee!' In the fixity of
Ahab's eyes, domineering over the doubts and misgivings of all the crew,
there now lurked something 'hardly sufferable for feeble souls to see.' Yet
at moments when he thought no third glance upon him, he seemed
in turn awed by the eyes of the Parsee; or again, their two figures seemed
'yoked together, and an unseen tyrant driving them.'

The only other member of his crew who dares even to try to sway him
is Starbuck. But his failure is foreshadowed from the first description
of him as a steadfast, careful man who is full of awe, abiding firm in the
conflict with seas or whales or 'any of the ordinary irrational horrors
of the world,' yet unable to withstand 'those more terrific, because more
spiritual terrors, which sometimes menace you from the concentrating
brow of an enraged and mighty man.' Melville gave considerable thought
to the problem presented by a character like the mate's. He observed in
The Confidence Man how 'the moderate man' might be 'the invaluable
understrapper of the wicked man,' capable of being 'used for wrong, but
. . . useless for right.' To be sure, he marked in *The Seven Gables* an

opposite view of the problem, the singular strength that Hepzibah was able to show in her unequal struggle against the Judge, through the sheer 'moral force of a deeply grounded antipathy.' But the obverse aspect again struck Melville when he found in Edmund's 'infernal nature . . . a valor often denied to innocence'; and that face of the matter was uppermost in his handling of Ahab and Starbuck.

Yet the further contrast between Starbuck and Stubb shows the latter even less able to come within Ahab's sphere. When they reveal themselves through the symbolical meanings that they find in the design on the doubloon, Starbuck is a man of tragic foreboding who shrinks from the blackness of truth and hopes that 'in this vale of Death, God girds us round.' Stubb reads in its signs of the zodiac the successive acts of life's comedy. He is neither valiant nor craven, but happy-go-lucky. He accepts Ahab's purpose as 'predestinated,' but concludes that a laugh is always the wisest answer, and wonders 'What's my juicy little pear at home doing now?' Melville deliberately portrays in the three mates the graduated steps of decline from spiritual insight. For Flask is utterly lacking in reverence, fearless through ignorance. He sees in the doubloon 'nothing . . . but a round thing made of gold,' worth sixteen dollars to whoever raises a certain whale. That conception runs close to Blake's in 'A Vision of the Last Judgment': ' "What," it will be Question'd, "When the Sun rises, do you not see a round disk of fire somewhat like a Guinea?" O no, no, I see an Innumerable company of the Heavenly host crying, "Holy, Holy, Holy is the Lord God Almighty." ' Flask is entirely the man of unilluminated common sense, farthest from the madness that transfigures life.

Starbuck's righteousness carries him to the point of begging Ahab to turn the ship back from its ominous course. But though Ahab rides brutally over him and threatens his life, and though Starbuck knows they are all doomed unless he acts, he cannot face the thought of killing the captain even when he comes upon him defenseless in sleep. He makes one further effort to sway him, on that day of enchanted calm just before the white whale is sighted. The innocence of the blue air has seemed to dispel for a moment the torment in Ahab's soul, and tears well into his eyes. Starbuck senses his emotion, but is careful not to betray that he does. He moves beside Ahab as he leans over the rail, the mate of thirty beside the captain of twice his age.

Ahab starts to talk of his remembrance that on just such a mild day as this he struck his first whale, as a boy-harpooner of eighteen, and that since then he has spent almost forty years on the pitiless sea, in 'the desolation of solitude.' He thinks of the poor girl he has only lately married, and says to his mate: 'Close! stand close to me, Starbuck; let me look into a human eye; it is better than to gaze into the sea or sky; better than to gaze upon God. By the green land; by the bright hearthstone! this is the magic glass, man; I see my wife and my child in thine eye.' He thinks even that he can hear her telling the boy 'of cannibal old me.' But when Starbuck seizes the occasion to talk about his own wife and boy, and to urge that the ship be headed back for Nantucket, Ahab averts his glance. He declares that 'against all natural lovings and longings,' he is recklessly driven on by his 'hidden lord and master,' by the 'cruel, remorseless emperor' that commands him. 'By heaven, man, we are turned round and round in this world, like yonder windlass, and Fate is the handspike.' To such words, which admit an irreparable cleavage between Ahab's heart and his predestinated will, Starbuck can listen no more, and moves away in despair.

By his unrelaxing energy throughout the three days' chase, Ahab towers even higher above them all, for as he himself declares, 'Starbuck is Stubb reversed, and Stubb is Starbuck; and ye two are all mankind; and Ahab stands alone.' When he snaps his ivory leg again in being thrown from his boat on the second day, he is helped back onto deck by the mate, to whom he says, 'Ay, ay, Starbuck, 'tis sweet to lean sometimes, be the leaner who he will; and would old Ahab had leaned oftener than he has.' But again, unlike Lear, though he sees his dilemma, he is not really moved, for he adds that 'nor white whale, nor man, nor fiend, can so much as graze old Ahab in his own proper and inaccessible being.'

Starbuck is driven to a further agonized plea that, with Fedallah now dead, 'thy evil shadow gone—all good angels mobbing thee with warnings:—what more wouldst thou have? . . . In Jesus' name, no more of this, that's worse than devil's madness.' But the only answer he gets, after beseeching Ahab to avoid impiety and blasphemy, is: 'This whole act's immutably decreed . . . Fool! I am the Fates' lieutenant.' In that reckless hyperbole Ahab betrays again how he has misconceived any possible human purpose, since he has insanely taken upon himself the fulfilment of decrees that could properly belong only to Fate or to God.

Yet Starbuck persists in a final attempt. As Ahab prepares to have his boat lowered on the third morning, the mate clasps his hand: 'Oh, my captain, my captain!—noble heart—go not—go not! see, it's a brave man that weeps; how great the agony of the persuasion then!' But Ahab proceeds with his orders, while the voice of Pip, who has disappeared from the scene since the beginning of the chase, cries from a low cabin-window: 'O master, my master, come back!' Even after the captain's boat is launched, Starbuck sees that the white whale has changed his course, and is swimming directly away. He calls after Ahab that it is not yet too late to desist: 'See, Moby-Dick seeks thee not. It is thou, thou, that madly seekest him!'

Starbuck had not accepted the theory of Moby-Dick's 'intelligent malignity.' He had declared from the start that it was insane to undertake vengeance 'on a dumb brute that simply smote thee from blindest instinct!' But the evidence from the ships they have met 'contrastingly concurred to show the demoniac indifference with which the White Whale tore his hunters, whether sinning or sinned against.' No doubt concerning this last alternative, so strangely wrenched from *Lear,* touches Ahab in the least. His antagonist remains the incarnation of evil, and must, therefore, be destroyed. His pride in his purpose rises to the final terrifying pitch when he shouts to his boat crew: 'Ye are not other men, but my arms and my legs: and so obey me.' Such *hubris* challenges instant *nemesis.* Yet Ahab keeps on even after his darted harpoon has so maddened the whale that it has rushed full against the *Pequod* itself, and shattered its bow. As he sees his ship sinking, with himself not on it, the captain turns his body from the sun to seek his 'lonely death on lonely life.' But his last resolve, his last words are: 'Toward thee I roll, thou all-destroying but unconquering whale; to the last I grapple with thee; from hell's heart I stab at thee; for hate's sake I spit my last breath at thee . . . *Thus,* I give up the spear!'

Ahab's career, like that of the protagonists of many of the Elizabethan tragedies of revenge, has revealed him as both hero and villain. Ordinary men are no match for him. His superiorities of mind and will, of courage and conviction, have exalted him above the sphere of anything petty or ignoble. Yet it is repeatedly affirmed that he is a monomaniac, and that his fixed idea, his hatred of the whale as the symbol of malignity, has carried him into the toils of a diabolical bond. The contrasting halves of his nature cannot be summed up better than in the 'ungodly, god-like' of Captain Peleg's description.

The meaning of his tragedy is involved with his conception of the rigid Fate to which he is chained. This conception runs likewise through Ishmael's comments. The *Pequod* is described as 'the sometimes madly merry and predestinated craft.' In Moby-Dick's final desperate rush against its bow, he vibrated 'his predestinating head': 'Retribution, swift vengeance, eternal malice were in his whole aspect.' The problem of determinism was part of the residue of Puritanism which Melville inherited. Babbalanja had devoted one of his discourses to trying to make a fundamental distinction between Fate and Necessity: 'Confound not the distinct. Fatalism presumes express and irrevocable edicts of heaven concerning particular events. Whereas, Necessity holds that all events are naturally linked, and inevitably follow each other, without providential interposition, though by the eternal letting of Providence.' Melville himself became absorbed in such discussion, and recorded, for instance, how, on his passage to England in 1849 to see about the publication of *White Jacket,* he spent many evenings drinking whiskey and 'talking of "Fixed Fate, Free-will, foreknowledge absolute," etc.'[2] with a German scholar on board. In launching Ahab on his pursuit, he emphasized how, 'with little external to constrain us, the innermost necessities in our being, these still drive us on.' But though Babbalanja also declared himself a Necessitarian and not a Fatalist, neither he nor Melville was able to keep himself secure in that position.

One reason why Melville was driven to magnify the relentless power of Fate is to be found in his reaction against Emersonianism. Emerson was too easy in his distinction when he said, 'Our doctrine must begin with the Necessary and Eternal, and discriminate Fate from the Necessary. There is no limitation about the Eternal.' Briefly, then, in one of the key-passages in his essay on 'Fate': 'So far as a man thinks, he is free,' since thought partakes in the Eternal. 'But Fate is the name we give to the action of that . . . all various necessity on the brute myriads, whether in things, animals, or in men in whom the intellect pure is not yet opened. To such it is only a burning wall which hurts those who run against it.' But Melville apprehended in Ahab a man who thought, and yet conceived the white whale as an inscrutable wall shoved near him. The captain's insistence that 'Truth hath no confines' demanded that he thrust through the wall. Emerson would have agreed about the illimitability of truth, and, indeed, went on to say that Fate involves 'meliora-

---

2. In quoting this line from *Paradise Lost,* Melville was doubtless aware that the next line added: 'And found no end, in wandering mazes lost.'

tion.' For 'the one serious and formidable thing in nature is a will.' Emerson's hero is the man of will who moves others forward by it, since 'the direction of the whole and of the parts is toward benefit.' But Melville's hero of formidable will swept his whole crew to destruction.[3]

The result of Ahab's Fatalism is that his tragedy admits no adequate moral recognition. The catharsis is, therefore, partially frustrated, since we cannot respond, as we can in *Lear*, to Ahab's deliverance from the evil forces in which he has been immersed. He is held to the end in his Faustian bond to the devil. Moreover, unlike both the sixteenth- and the nineteenth-century Faust,[4] he never really struggles to escape from it. Although his tortured soul cries out in his sleep, during his waking hours his mind and will are dominant, and inflexible. When talking with Pip and Starbuck, he perceives the human consequences of his action. He is momentarily touched, but he is not moved from his insistence that his course is necessary. In his death therefore—a death that engulfs so many others—colossal pride meets its rightful end, and there can be no unmixed pity for him as a human being. There is no moment of release comparable, for instance, to one that Melville marked: when, at Antony's death, Cleopatra sees and feels herself as she is, and answers Iras' 'Royal Egypt! Empress!' with

> No more, but e'en a woman, and commanded
> By such poor passion as the maid that milks
> And does the meanest chares.

The effect of that reduction is to magnify. It endows Cleopatra with the 'august dignity' of common humanity, which Melville proclaimed in his crew. But he does not portray its full working in Ahab, since, though the captain sees, he does not amply feel. He is not caught out of himself and transfigured by sympathy. As a result, his madness is not divine like

3. This juxtaposition of some of the contrasting implications of Emerson's and Melville's texts is not meant to imply a direct reaction in *Moby-Dick* against the essay 'Fate,' since that was not printed until *The Conduct of Life* (1860)—though it had been read as a lecture at least as early as 1851. The diffused presence of transcendentalism in the work of Melville and Whitman shows that, by the end of the eighteen-forties, a man did not have to be thinking of a specific text in order to be conscious of the main doctrines of the movement. In both Melville and Whitman we can perceive a double process of assimilation and rejection of these doctrines, with the chief accent on the first by Whitman, on the second by Melville.

4. As another possible force affecting Melville's conception of tragedy, Marlowe's *Plays* were among the books he listed as having bought in London in 1849.

Blake's, or even like Pip's, since his burning mind is barred out from the exuberance of love. His tragedy is that of an unregenerate will, which stifles his soul and drives his brain with an inescapable fierceness.[5] He suffers, but unlike Hawthorne's Hester or Miriam, he is not purified by his suffering. He remains, like Ethan Brand, damned.

Thoughts like these may have been stirring in Melville when he said to Hawthorne: 'I have written a wicked book, and feel spotless as the lamb.' He thus instinctively transferred the effect of tragedy from the audience to make it apply to the author as well. While still in the throes of finishing it, he had also said that 'the hell-fire in which the whole book is broiled might not unreasonably have cooked it ere this,' and had added: 'This is the book's motto (the secret one), Ego non baptizo te in nomine —but make out the rest yourself.' The whole quotation, as Ahab howled it out while christening his 'malignant iron' in the harpooners' blood, was 'Ego non baptizo te in nomine patris, sed in nomine diaboli.' [6] The strain involved in portraying Ahab's demonic nature perhaps caused Melville to

5. The most comparable character in the literature of the time is Heathcliff. I have found no evidence that Melville read *Wuthering Heights* (1847), which was generally misunderstood and attacked by contemporary reviewers; but Emily Brontë's genuine wildness of imagination strikes an intensity akin to that of some of the scenes on the *Pequod*. Virginia Woolf has remarked that *Wuthering Heights* and *Moby-Dick* seem apart from all other novels in the way poetry pervades their entire structure.

6. On the back fly-leaf of the final volume of his Shakespeare, the volume containing *Lear, Romeo and Juliet, Hamlet,* and *Othello,* Melville jotted down some notes, apparently designed for a story involving a formal compact with the devil, cast in modern terms, since he was to have been met 'at the Astor.' He then added:

> Ego non baptizo te in nomine Patris et
> Filii et Spiritus Sancti—sed in nomine
> Diaboli.—Madness is undefinable—
> It & right reason extremes of one,
> —not the (black art) Goetic but Theurgic magic—
> seeks converse with the Intelligence, Power, the
> Angel.

Charles Olson, in his essay '*Lear* and *Moby-Dick*' takes these to be 'rough jottings for *Moby-Dick*.' 'Right reason,' in the Coleridgean and Emersonian terminology, is the highest range of intuitive intelligence, the gateway to divine madness. We recall that Melville had made the Serenians declare: 'Right reason, and Alma, are the same; else Alma, not reason, would we reject. The Master's great command is Love; and here do all things wise, and all things good, unite . . . The more we love, the more we know.'

Olson is particularly interesting in the way he brings out the contrast between 'Goetic' and 'Theurgic,' the traditional terms for black and white magic, for the demonic and sacred arts. The contrast involved here may clearly have some bearing on the difference between Ahab's diabolism and Pip's innocence; as may the general contrast between madness and

feel momentarily identified with it. But when the book was done, when he had written his vision of Ahab's madness out of his system, he could feel himself purged. Even though he had composed a tragedy incomplete when judged by Shakespearean standards, he had eased his thoughts by the act of creating so prodigious an artistic structure. He had experienced the meaning of catharsis, even though his protagonist had not.

Responsive to the shaping forces of his age as only men of passionate imagination are, even Melville can hardly have been fully aware of how symbolical an American hero he had fashioned in Ahab. The length to which the captain carried his belief in the fixity of Fate makes a searching comment on the theological decay that conditioned Melville's thought. He recognized the inadequacy of transcendentalism on most of the essential problems; but when he tried to reassert the significance of Original Sin, there was no orthodoxy that he could accept. When he examined the dying Calvinism in which he had been brought up, his mind could discover there only the Manichean heresy, which its founders had staunchly repudiated. Its determinism became for him the drastic distortion that he projected in Ahab's career, wherein there was no possibility of regeneration since there remained no effectual faith in the existence of divine grace. The severe, bleak, and uninspired Presbyterian church of Melville's experience had driven him inevitably into questioning even the goodness of the Biblical God.

On the other hand, he could find no security in throwing over all the restraints of dogma, and exalting the god-like man. If the will was free, as the new faith insisted, Melville knew that it was free to do evil as well as to do good. He could not rest happy with Emerson's declaration that

right reason, on the difference between both these characters and Ishmael and Bulkington, the seekers for truth. But in holding that these notes contain the key-idea for the development of *Moby-Dick*, Olson finds an 'extreme significance' in Melville's curtailing of the Latin in the book itself. Olson's point is that, 'Of necessity, from Ahab's world, both Christ and the Holy Ghost are absent . . . It is the outward symbol of the inner truth that the name of Christ is uttered but once in the book and then it is torn from Starbuck, the only possible man to use it.' But without seeking very far you can find the old Manx sailor saying, 'O Christ! to think of the green navies and the green-skulled crews!' and Ishmael remarking on 'the celebration of the Passion of our Lord.'

These notes project one phase of Melville's speculation, but it does not seem fruitful to try to make them a formula for Ahab's tragedy, which, as we have seen, is too richly complex to be so reduced. I have been stimulated by Olson's vigorous and imaginative essay to take issue with it on many other points of fact and interpretation, particularly concerning the relation between Ahab and Pip.

if he turned out to be the devil's child, why then he would live from the devil. For Melville had envisaged the fate of just such a man in Ahab. He had also seen in Ahab the destruction that must overtake the Man-God, the self-appointed Messiah. 'Man's self-affirmation leads to his perdition; the free play of human forces unconnected with any higher aim brings about the exhaustion of man's creative powers.' That sentence was to be written three-quarters of a century after *Moby-Dick*, by Berdyaev in *The Meaning of History;* but it bears unintentional relevance to what happened to Ahab. And the captain's career is prophetic of many others in the history of later nineteenth-century America. Man's confidence in his own unaided resources has seldom been carried farther than during that era in this country. The strong-willed individuals who seized the land and gutted the forests and built the railroads were no longer troubled with Ahab's obsessive sense of evil, since theology had receded even farther into their backgrounds. But their drives were as relentless as his, and they were to prove like him in many other ways also, as they went on to become the empire builders of the post-Civil War world. They tended to be as dead to enjoyment as he, as blind to everything but their one pursuit, as unmoved by fear or sympathy, as confident in assuming an identification of their wills with immutable plan or manifest destiny, as liable to regard other men as merely arms and legs for the fulfilment of their purposes, and, finally, as arid and exhausted in their burnt-out souls. Without deliberately intending it, but by virtue of his intense concern with the precariously maintained values of democratic Christianity, which he saw everywhere being threatened or broken down, Melville created in Ahab's tragedy a fearful symbol of the self-enclosed individualism that, carried to its furthest extreme, brings disaster both upon itself and upon the group of which it is part. He provided also an ominous glimpse of what was to result when the Emersonian will to virtue became in less innocent natures the will to power and conquest.[7]

7. The tendency that Melville prefigured in his creation of Ahab has also been described by Berdyaev in *The Fate of Man in the Modern World:* 'Liberty was discovered to be protection of the rights of the strong, leaving the weak defenceless. This is one of the paradoxes of liberty in social life. Freedom turned out to be freedom for oneself and slavery for others. He is the true lover of liberty who desires it for others as well as for himself. Liberty has become the protection of the rights of a privileged minority, the defence of capitalistic property and the power of money . . .' You do not have to accept Berdyaev's solution, the mysticism of the old Russia, of the Greek Orthodox church, in order to profit from the trenchancy of his analysis.

7. The Levels Beyond

BUT THE passages of *Moby-Dick* that stay with the reader longest are probably not the dialogue and soliloquies of the tragedy, since, even at their best, these are always liable to break into fragments from Shakespeare; and, at their worst, their romantic Satanism belongs to a mode as dead for us as the Gothic novel. The writing is more consistently alive on the Homeric than on the Shakespearean level, in the passages that rise to Melville's conviction, expressed in the chapter on 'The Tail,' that 'real strength never impairs beauty or harmony, but it often bestows it; and in everything imposingly beautiful, strength has much to do with the magic.' The mightiness of Melville's theme challenged him to magnify it as far as possible; and he mastered a type of imagery that, like the world-images in *Antony and Cleopatra,* enabled him to keep before the reader's imagination an illusion of sheer size.

One secret of this was to compare the whale to something even greater than itself, as when he wrote of one that had been harpooned: 'Yet so vast is the quantity of blood in him, and so distant and numerous its interior fountains, that he will keep thus bleeding and bleeding for a considerable period; even as in a drought a river will flow, whose source is in the well-springs of far-off and indiscernible hills.' Having thus apparently spent all his resources on extending the already enormous whale to remote and mysterious proportions, he would seem to have handicapped himself for the task of making his hero equal his prey. But Melville was at no loss when he wanted to heighten Ahab's stature. Consider, for instance, this conclusion to his defying worship of the fire: 'As in the hurricane that sweeps the plain, men fly the neighborhood of some lone, gigantic elm, whose very height and strength but render it so much the more unsafe, because so much the more a mark for thunderbolts; so at those last words of Ahab's many of the mariners did run from him in a terror of dismay.'

The reason for speaking of the Homeric level in Melville's narrative appears in these last two quotations, for both utilize the elaborate kind of simile that is called by Homer's name. It is hard to say how conscious

Melville was of the origin of this device. He had made one or two flat attempts to handle it in *Mardi;*[1] and his general interest in Homer was to be shown several years later by his frequent markings in Arnold's essay on how to translate him, and by his enthusiasm for Chapman's version.[2] But what Melville had learned in *Moby-Dick* that he had not known in *Mardi* came not from Homer, but from his own assimilation of the organic principle. He had learned how to make beauty out of natural strength. He had learned how to make it functional, for, unlike most borrowers, he did not let his Homeric similes remain mere ornaments. There could hardly be a more integral way of giving body to Ahab's *hubris* than by the image of the towering elm about to call down heaven's thunderbolt.

The controlled accumulation of such similes was the prime source for both his volume and variety in the narrative of the final chase, as we may gather from an abbreviated notation of the most striking of those that occur within half a dozen pages on the second day. Melville first drives home his point that there is nothing extraordinary in their being able to know where to expect Moby-Dick next, by a comparison with the timed appearance of 'the mighty iron leviathan of the modern railway.' A more compact simile in the very next paragraph picks up and prolongs this sense of speed and power: 'The ship tore on; leaving such a furrow in the sea as when a cannon-ball, missent, becomes a ploughshare and turns up the level field.'

At the renewed cry of 'there she blows!' Stubb shouts to the whale that he can't escape, for 'Ahab will dam off your blood, as a miller shuts his water-gate upon the stream!' Melville stresses how at such a moment the frenzies of the chase had again worked them all 'bubblingly up, like old wine worked anew. Whatever pale fears and forebodings some of them might have felt before; these were not only now kept out of sight through the growing awe of Ahab, but they were broken up, and on

---

1. E.g. 'As on the night-banks of the far-rolling Ganges, the royal bridegroom sets forth for his bride, preceded by nymphs, now this side, now that, lighting up all the flowery flambeaux held on high as they pass; so came the sun, to his nuptials with Mardi:—the hours going on before, touching all the peaks, till they glowed rosy-red.' The sense impressions here seem wholly conventional; we are not enabled to perceive anything fresh through the simile's extension.

2. In November 1858, Melville thanked Duyckinck for the gift of Chapman's *Homer,* and said that it would send Pope's 'off shrieking, like the bankrupt deities in Milton's hymn.'

all sides routed, as timid prairie hares that scatter before the bounding bison.'

The succession of land-images, which has given us the sweep of the train, of the cannon-ball, of the broad prairie, is now alternated with one in which all the thirty men are reduced to a single unit:

For as the one ship that held them all; though it was put together of all contrasting things—oak, and maple, and pine wood; iron, and pitch, and hemp—yet all these ran into each other in the one concrete hull, which shot on its way, both balanced and directed by the long central keel; even so, all the individualities of the crew, this man's valor, that man's fear; guilt and guiltiness, all varieties were welded into oneness, and were all directed to that fatal goal which Ahab their one lord and keel did point to.

The twist of that final phrase serves to fuse the two halves of the comparison, to make the men identical with the driving ship, no longer human but a projectile for Ahab's aim.

From that concentration Melville radiates out again to diversity. Any natural object can be made to subserve his immense action. 'The mastheads, like the tops of tall palms, were outspreadingly tufted with arms and legs.' As the white whale breached above the surface, the spray that he raised 'intolerably glittered and glared like a glacier.' The air rang out with thirty cries like 'the combined discharges of rifles.' No longer mindful of the tedious rope ladders, the men aloft 'like shooting-stars, slid to the deck.' This shorthand compression of Melville's images may make them seem too breathlessly mixed, but in their contexts they are all subordinated to the narrative, to whose advance they contribute their startling energy.

Their value in creating the dramatic movement is apparent when the launched boats are described as 'skillfully manoeuvred, incessantly wheeling like trained chargers in the field.' But here Melville wanted to dwarf everything—except Ahab's will—before Moby-Dick, who presently dashed two of these proud boats together 'like two rolling husks on a surf-beaten beach, and then, diving down into the sea, disappeared in a boiling maelstrom, in which, for a space, the odorous cedar chips of the wrecks danced round and round, like the grated nutmeg in a swiftly-stirred bowl of punch.'

The relevance of these comparisons may not in every case be as exact as in the simile of Ahab and the lightning-menaced elm. But their imaginative abundance is astonishing. They are no less notable for breadth; and the more sustained among them, for an heroic dignity. Yet Melville's breadth and dignity are more often Biblical than Homeric. To judge simply from the number of direct allusions, the Bible was the most deeply rooted element in his reading, the one most likely to assert itself when he wanted an illustration. But the influence it had left upon his mind was more than the memory of many characters and stories. It had empowered him to sustain Father Mapple's discourse, and, what is more, to strike such a tone for his general narrative, so naturally serious and pondering, that a full-length sermon, introduced within the first fifty pages, does not seem an obtrusion. It also seems natural that his whalemen from Quaker Nantucket should bear Old Testament names: that pious hard-bargaining Captain Bildad should be remindful of the Book of Job; that the man who prophetically warns Ishmael not to embark on the *Pequod* should be called Elijah; that Ahab should have inherited his name from one of the greatest of the kings of Israel, who, seduced by false prophets, went to his death in battle. Nor should it be forgotten that Captain Ahab's tragedy is Biblical in its last page and sentence. The 'Epilogue' opens with the quotation from Job, 'And I only am escaped alone to tell thee'; and ends with Ishmael's description of how he was picked up by 'the devious-cruising *Rachel,* that in her retracing search after her missing children only found another orphan.'

The allusions to the Old Testament are more frequent than those to the New, since they are more apposite to the fierceness of the theme. And the qualities I started to instance, of elemental breadth and dignity, are most reminiscent of the Psalms. As Melville himself declared, 'The Nantucketer, he alone resides and riots on the sea; he alone, in Bible language, goes down to it in ships.' And from his own share in that experience, as well as in the Biblical expression of it, Melville could make his language also rise to solemnity when he related 'how the great leviathan is afar off descried from the mast-head; how he is chased over the watery moors, and slaughtered in the valleys of the deep . . .'

But it is in the meditations of the instinctive young philosopher, Ishmael, that the Biblical element becomes an important factor in Melville's creative process, not through specific allusions, but by a pervasive interfusion. If I were forced to pick a single chapter as Melville's best writing, my inclination would be strong for 'The Pacific,' in which, in a few more words than those of the Gettysburg Address, Melville gave, as Lincoln was to give, the essence of his thought and poetry.

The thrice-repeated naming of the sea in the ample divisions of its opening sentence creates the illusion of movement. As in the case of Whitman's best lines, these irregular successions have been calculated to sweep up like waves: 'When gliding by the Bashee isles we emerged at last upon the great South Sea; were it not for other things, I could have greeted my dear Pacific with uncounted thanks, for now the long supplication of my youth was answered; that serene ocean rolled eastward from me a thousand leagues of blue.'

But this lulling rhythm is only a prelude to the symbolical meaning which, latent in all water, finds its great compendium here:

There is, one knows not what sweet mystery about this sea, whose gently awful stirrings seem to speak of some hidden soul beneath; like those fabled undulations of the Ephesian sod over the buried Evangelist St. John. And meet it is, that over these sea-pastures, wide-rolling watery prairies and Potters' Fields of all four continents, the waves should rise and fall, and ebb and flow unceasingly; for here, millions of mixed shades and shadows, drowned dreams, somnambulisms, reveries; all that we call lives and souls, lie dreaming, dreaming, still; tossing like slumberers in their beds; the ever-rolling waves but made so by their restlessness.

The daring license of that last phrase succeeds, for he has demonstrated here what he meant by saying at the outset of the book, that 'meditation and water are wedded forever.' He has reached the level where both abstraction and concretion may have full play; and though that is not a level which he, or many other artists, can sustain for long—but rather, a precarious point of equilibrium between two opposed forces—it gave rise to his most memorable utterance.

According to Baudelaire, a poet must be both somnambulist and hypnotist; and Melville has given that sensation here. For he speaks as though out of deep dreams and yet carries the reader with him by his incantatory rhythms. This combination helped him to break through the restrictions of space and time, and seemingly to resurrect the entire past in the embrace of his thought. But just as in the case of Thoreau's passage on the blended waters of Walden and Ganges, what kept Melville's flow from evaporating into mere revery was his solid hold upon immediate experience. This enabled him to include the past in the now and thus to gain universality—especially in the paragraph that follows:

To any meditative Magian rover, this serene Pacific, once beheld, must ever after be the sea of his adoption. It rolls the midmost waters of the world, the Indian Ocean and Atlantic being but its arms. The same waves wash the moles of the new-built Californian towns, but yesterday planted by the recentest race of men, and lave the faded but still gorgeous skirts of Asiatic lands, older than Abraham; while all between float milky-ways of coral isles, and low-lying, endless, unknown archipelagoes, and impenetrable Japans. Thus this mysterious, divine Pacific zones the world's whole bulk about; makes all coasts one bay to it; seems the tide-beating heart of earth. Lifted by those eternal swells, you needs must own the seductive god, bowing your head to Pan.

Melville has learned a great deal from Thomas Browne here, but the secret is now thoroughly his own. His symbolism is both abundant and controlled. The sea remains itself, and yet becomes the sky in the floating 'milky-ways of coral isles'; and thus it comes to include all of space, the whole galaxy of thought. 'Impenetrable' acts in a similar way in projecting outwards through successive layers of connotation, for it describes not merely the difficulty of trading with an Oriental country before the days of the open door, but the inscrutability of the Orient for a western mind; and since 'Japans' is plural, it is no longer just a geographical term, but another sign for the mystery of speculation. The sexual hyperbole of the Pacific as the undulating zone of the earth leads naturally into the philosophy of pagan well-being, into the worship of Pan.

The most characteristically Melvillian aspect is the intermingling of such an element with the Biblical, of allusions to Pan with the others to Abraham and St. John. For this is what had happened to the scion of Presbyterians when he discovered in Typee what he was to call, in a late, reminiscent poem,

Authentic Edens in a Pagan sea.

But just as that paradise had been only an interlude before the confronting of stern issues, so too this calm is broken by the figure of Ahab, in whose brain stirred few thoughts of Pan as he stood by the rigging, unconscious that he 'snuffed the sugary musk from the Bashee isles (in whose sweet woods mild lovers must be walking),' conscious only of 'the salt breath of the new found sea; that sea in which the hated White Whale must even then be swimming.' It is only a delusion to think of the Pacific as 'the tide-beating heart of earth.' Melville's fundamental contrast reasserts itself as Ahab rejects the land, rejects the senses for the mind, and love for hate. The momentarily peaceful surface of the sea is made to contrast with the surging violence of the captain himself, in this conclusion to the chapter: 'His firm lips met like the lips of a vice; the Delta of his forehead's veins swelled like overladen brooks; in his very sleep, his ringing cry ran through the vaulted hull, "Stern all! the White Whale spouts thick blood!"'

Ahab's savagery, not unlike that of a Hebrew prophet, has rejected the warmly material pantheism of the Greeks; but Melville's breadth has effected, not a fusion, but a unique counterpoint of both. The reason why the values of both Pan and Jehovah were not merely words to him, as they are to most men, is that he had relived them for himself in his own body and mind, and especially in his imagination. This means that he had cut through the dead tissues of the culture of his day, and had re-discovered the primitive and enduring nature of man. By virtue of the range of his own experience, he was able to recognize instinctively what remained for the poet of our still more conscious age to reduce to the theory that the artist 'is more *primitive,* as well as more civilized, than his contemporaries, his experience is deeper than civilization, and he only uses the phenomena of civilization in expressing it.' When Eliot wrote that about Wyndham Lewis in 1918, he had just begun to tap the vital springs of anthropology in Frazer's *Golden Bough,* where he was to find the myth around which to compose *The Waste Land.* Practitioners in the other arts had already made equivalent discoveries, as witness the renewal of painting and sculpture that came through Picasso's response to African art. In his own day Melville had enacted the same funda-mental pattern by 'sinking to the most primitive and forgotten, returning to the origin and bringing something back, seeking the beginning and the end.' Those words of Eliot's can serve to describe the most profound level of *Moby-Dick;* and it is significant of Melville's difference from Emerson that he did not conceive of art as an ever higher and more refined ascent of the mind. He wanted nothing less than the whole of life. He symbolized its vast and terrifying forces when he likened Ahab's 'darker, deeper' part to those hidden antiquities beneath the Hotel de Cluny, where man's 'root of grandeur, his whole awful essence sits in bearded state.' The flavor of that image is even more Biblical than Greek. It takes man beyond history to the source of his elemental energies.

⇒ XI ⇐

THE TROUBLED MIND

'My mind is troubled, like a fountain stirr'd;
And I myself see not the bottom of it.'
—marked by Melville in
Troilus and Cressida.

IN *Pierre* Melville conceived a tragedy the opposite of Ahab's. After having portrayed the disaster of an egocentric mind, he examined in his next hero the situation of a young idealist, who, with some distrust of his intellect but none of his heart, followed unswervingly his generous impulses. Full of sympathy, careless of himself, he also went to destruction. In working out his cast of characters Melville almost duplicated those of *Hamlet,* but the course of his tragedy ran opposite to it as well. For he made his hero remember this play in his hour of crisis, and remind himself that all meditation is worthless unless it leads to action. Whereupon Pierre, adopting the reverse of Hamlet's behavior, acted at once and decisively, and accomplished nothing but ruin.

Emerson believed that his America was to find its true genius in speculation akin to that of Shakespeare's hero; and Poe, in the exaggeration of ignorance, pronounced it the first 'thinking age' there had ever been. *Pierre* is an ironic commentary upon their views: one of the few major efforts of that period to produce a tragedy, its situation resulted from the contrary bias—reckless and unforeseeing impulsiveness. The driven confusions of Pierre's thought actually seem a better mirror of our eighteen-forties and fifties than would the skepticism which had drawn Shakespeare to Montaigne, and which had sicklied his Renaissance prince. To judge from their spasmodic writings, the trouble with most of Emerson's young transcendentalists was not that they had thought too much, but that, swept along by a clutter of diverse enthusiasms, they had never really learned, any more than Hawthorne's Holgrave, how to think at all. If they had possessed the intensity with which Melville was able to endow Pierre, they might finally have seen, with something of the horror of both that hero and his creator, the bottomless vortices that they had been skirting. Poe possessed such intensity, though of sensibility rather than of thought. Despite his brittle pretensions, his work has slight intellectual content, yet an excruciated consciousness of suffering. And when a poet arose who was not engaged in a war to the death with the barbarities of Jacksonian democracy as they struck the most high-strung individual that was exposed to them, but who celebrated the very forces that Poe fled from in his fantasies and grotesques, the content of *Leaves of Grass* was dependent even less upon intellect and not at all upon skepticism. Consequently, an American *Hamlet* would be a *Hamlet à rebours,* responsive to the dilemma that Melville was to note in Arnold's statement of 'The Function of Criticism at the Present Time': 'To act is so easy, as Goethe says; to think is so hard.'

In completing another large book within less than a year after *Moby-Dick,* Melville seems to have been compelled most by the problem, the satisfactory solution of which had impressed him as being that of the Master Genius of the Age in Hawthorne's symbolic sketch. For in that man's eyes had glowed such a warm light 'as never illuminates the earth save when a great heart burns as the household fire of a grand intellect.' In his letter about 'Ethan Brand' Melville had declared, to be sure, 'I stand for the heart. To the dogs with the head!' and the worst thing he found in Emerson was 'a defect in the region of the heart.' But Melville knew as well as Hawthorne that the two forces must be in equilibrium; and he knew that Pierre was fated for disaster when he threw away all pondering scruples and cried: 'The heart! the heart! 'tis God's anointed; let me pursue the heart!'

Pierre is the book wherein we might find the most evident traces of the interaction between Hawthorne and Melville. It is probably not merely a coincidence that, appearing a few months after *The Blithedale Romance,* it also undertook to satirize the New England reformers. It seems even more likely that the change in *Pierre* from the aristocratic past to the democratic present, which involved the ruin of a house, may have been suggested in part by *The Seven Gables.* However, in this first and last big attempt by Melville to present the problems of American society on land, he also drew his materials from the kind of life that had surrounded his Gansevoort forebears. He made Pierre's grandfather also a general of the Revolution, and endowed him with the balance of the heroic character, with both strength and beauty. He was 'fit image of his

God,' with the traits of both the war-like lion and the Christian lamb. Pierre himself at nineteen was the proper descendant of such stock. He was not the ethereal Hamlet, whom Coleridge's criticism had created in his own image, but something more like Shakespeare's 'glass of fashion and the mold of form,' since he took a vigorous pride in his landed estate, and also 'pressed the wide beauty of the world in his embracing arms.' In writing about Pierre's heritage, Melville seemed to assume, as Cooper had, that such privileged families would last forever, even in America, though his own experience had run directly counter to that conclusion. However, he did remark in the opening chapter that if the reader thought Pierre too fond and foolish in his family pride, he must remember that Pierre was still very young and unphilosophical: 'and believe me you will pronounce Pierre a thorough-going Democrat in time; perhaps a little too Radical altogether to your fancy.'

But his tragedy has really very little to do with political or social values. Unlike the devolution of the Pyncheons, the fate of the Glendinning family does not assert itself as a central theme. Pierre's mother dies from the shock of his having violated her will in his alliance with Isabel. But when he flees to the city, midway through the book, the patrician life of Saddle Meadows is left behind him. His social background becomes just background, something he can reject and ignore. Its semi-feudal magnificence bears little further relation to his career. Though by his death his line is blotted out, there is no explicit denouement of social loss or transformation. Pierre's world is gone, but, contrary to Shakespeare's method, nothing rises to take its place and assert continuity. Nor has Pierre succeeded in making any contact with the city around him. His radicalism is entirely a matter of personal conduct. From the moment he learns of the existence of his illegitimate half-sister, he determines to right the wrong done her by his dead father in the only way left open to him, by giving her his name. But though that involves a break with everything that had been expected of him, it means also a relation of hostility to the rest of the world. In the city, in the poverty for which he is unequipped, Pierre remains an adolescent, desperately trying to earn a living by writing a mature book. He has no time to think of himself in any coherent connection with society; he is submerged by the ghastly consequences that have followed his idealistic act.

Nor can his mind reach any satisfactory conclusion on the relation between good and evil. Melville shows that, once Pierre has thrown convention overboard, he has no religious dogma to support him, and that the more he analyzes his thoughts, the more he feels utterly alone in himself. Pierre has discovered the secret that Henry James, Sr., was to proclaim, that life is tragedy for such as are spiritually awakened, not merely morally righteous. But though Pierre perceives that only thus does life take on significance, and though Melville declared that 'in the Enthusiast to Duty, the heaven-begotten Christ is born'; nevertheless, the same problems that plagued Ahab rise for Pierre with renewed intensity. Things that have seemed certain shift before his eyes, and the solid ground sinks when he tries to advance on it. All confidence in God forsakes him, as the clarity of truth blurs into the ambiguous malice of evil. He becomes obsessed by the idea that he is helplessly caught by Fate, and Melville's incessant pounding upon this strain ends by robbing Pierre's struggle of much meaning. If the man destined to fail will fail despite any effort he makes, tragedy tends thereby to be robbed of catharsis. And when Pierre shouts, 'I am what I am,' these words do not come from the savage control with which Swift was inured to accept whatever might lie ahead. Pierre is headlong and defiant to the end. He naturally has not learned what Melville was to be impressed with, in reading Schopenhauer's 'Worldly Fortune' as an old man: the steadying effect of the knowledge that 'everything that happens—from the smallest up to the greatest facts of existence—happens of necessity. If a man is steeped in the knowledge of this truth, he will, first of all, do what he can, and then readily endure what he must.'

Schopenhauer's reflection depends on the distinction between Fate and Necessity, which Pierre has been too tormented to master, and which Melville as a tragic artist inevitably conceived in more emotional terms than those of the detached metaphysician. Pierre's life ends on his first night in the prison-cell to which he has been brought for killing his cousin Glen, in consequence of an insulting challenge. The final tableau where he follows Isabel in drinking poison has something of the air of the Capulets' tomb. But Pierre's immaturity as a tragic hero differentiates him not only from Hamlet but from Romeo. Pierre sees himself at the end as 'the fool of Truth, the fool of Virtue, the fool of Fate,' in something of the same helpless light as Romeo did midway through the play. But Pierre has no growth into Romeo's final recognition of the lasting values of love. He believes himself doomed to hell both in this world and the next, and kills himself in reckless despair.

LONG ISLAND FARMHOUSES, BY W. S. MOUNT

The book in which Melville tried to project this tragedy is about the most desperate in our literature, since Pierre's sufferings were very much his author's own. Melville could suggest a counsel of moderation in the pamphlet, 'Chronometricals and Horologicals,' which Pierre read in the stagecoach to New York. It emphasized the difference between the ideal and the actual by refuting the transcendental doctrine of Correspondence. It argued that heavenly wisdom is earthly folly, and that the only way God's truth and man's truth correspond is through their contradictions. The inference was that any idealist, 'who finding in himself a chronometrical soul, seeks practically to force that heavenly time upon the earth,' is doomed to failure and worse. 'A virtuous expediency, then, seems the highest desirable or attainable earthly excellence for the mass of men, and is the only earthly excellence that their Creator intended for them.'

Melville could formulate these distinctions, but his heart was not in them. Pierre's later glimpse of the pamphlet's author, Plotinus Plinlimmon, was thoroughly ambiguous, of a 'gracefully bowing, gently smiling, and most miraculously self-possessed, non-benevolent man.' To that careful coldness had his doctrine seemingly brought Plinlimmon. And Melville, by his recognition that 'Bacon's brains were mere watchmaker's brains, but Christ was a chronometer,' asserted his desire, almost in Blake's terms, for the older fullness of imagination and passion 'before man's brain went into doting bondage' and was 'bleached and beaten in Baconian fulling-mills.' However, the more he thought about the transcendentalists' variety of freedom, the less it recommended itself to him. At the time he had first heard Emerson, he had blurted out that such thinkers 'are all cracked right across the brow.' Now, when he surrounded Pierre in the city with a group of new-light Apostles, his objections became more specific. He was willing to grant that the transcendentalists were ordinarily 'theoretic and inactive, and therefore harmless.' But as he studied Pierre's sufferings in his poverty, he mocked at the cant of 'the "Compensation," or "Optimist" school' that there was no such thing as misery. As he watched Pierre also adopt the Apostles' notions of ascetic discipline of the body, he voiced robust contempt against all 'Shelleyan dietings': 'Feed all things with food convenient for them,—that is, if the food be procurable. The food of thy soul is light and space; feed it then on light and space. But the food of thy body is champagne and oysters; feed it then on champagne and oysters . . . Know this: that while many a consumptive dietarian has but produced the merest literary flatulencies to the world; convivial authors have alike given utterance to the sublimest wisdom . . .' And as he saw Pierre finally drained of his natural health, from having stayed cooped up day after day writing in a bleak and cheerless room, with no stove, a cup of water, and a dry biscuit or two, Melville broke out: 'Civilization, philosophy, Ideal Virtue! behold your victim!' [1]

1. Melville reacted in like fashion against the ascetic strain in Emerson's essay on 'The Poet.' The philosopher said: 'So the poet's habit of living should be set on a key so low, that the common influences should delight him. His cheerfulness should be the gift of the sunlight; the air should suffice for his inspiration, and he should be tipsy with water.' But the novelist added: 'This makes the Wordsworthian poet—not the Shakespearean.' When Emerson generalized further, on how those artists who had been deflected from 'the true nectar' to 'Devil's wine' had been punished by 'deterioration,' Melville wrote: 'No, no, no.— Titian—did he deteriorate?—Byron—did he?—Mr. E. is horribly narrow here. He has his Dardanelles for every Marmora.—But he keeps nobly on, for all that!'

It is quite possible that Melville may have remembered his impression of Emerson when making this sketch of a mystic in *The Confidence Man:* 'a blue-eyed man, sandy-haired, and Saxon-looking; perhaps five-and-forty; tall, and, but for a certain angularity, well made: little touch of the drawing room about him, but a look of plain propriety of a Puritan sort, with a kind of farmer dignity. His age seemed betokened more by his brow, placidly thoughtful, than by his general aspect, which had that look of youthfulness in maturity, peculiar sometimes to habitual health of body, the original gift of nature, or in part the effect or reward of steady temperance of the passions, kept so, perhaps, by constitution as much as morality. A neat, comely, almost ruddy cheek, coolly fresh, like a red clover-blossom at coolish dawn—the color of warmth preserved by the virtue of chill. Toning the whole man, was one-knows-not-what of shrewdness and mythiness, strangely jumbled; in that way, he seemed a kind of cross between a Yankee peddler and a Tartar priest, though it seemed as if, at a pinch, the first would not in all probability play second fiddle to the last.'

This philosopher, 'purely and coldly radiant as a prism,' sat opposite the cosmopolitan. When he talked, there shone 'such a preternaturally cold, gemmy glance out of his pellucid blue eye, that he seemed more a metaphysical merman than a feeling man.' When he argued that Beauty and Ill are incompatible, the cosmopolitan agreed, and said that he would thereafter trust the benignity of the burnished rattle-snake.

The more closely you investigate Melville's thought at every stage of his development, the less accurate seems Parrington's account of his 'pessimism' as 'a natural end and outcome of his transcendental speculations, once those speculations had come to intimate contact with life.' Not only did such contact antedate his speculations; but at no period, not even in *Mardi,* does it seem right to think of him as other than a critic of transcendentalism. Incidentally, the fact that Parrington apparently took his quotations from *Clarel* from Weaver's biography instead of reading them in the poem, caused him to run together the speeches of several different characters as though they were Melville's own.

Parrington's natural desire for a neat formulation also betrayed him somewhat in presenting 'Nathaniel Hawthorne: Sceptic,' for though he was not unaware of Hawthorne's religious nature, he failed to reckon with its full strength. His method was much more successful with 'Emerson: Transcendental Critic' and 'Whitman: The Afterglow of the Enlightenment.'

By this point Melville's scorn had begun to spread from transcendental-ism to all philosophy. At the bottom of his hopelessness, Pierre wrote in *his* book: 'Away, ye chattering apes of a sophomorean Spinoza and Plato . . . Explain this darkness, exorcise this devil, ye cannot.' And speaking, not through his hero, but in his own person, Melville also lumped Plato and Spinoza together with Goethe and the newer guild of 'self-impostors,' the 'preposterous rabble of Muggletonian Scots and Yankees, whose vile brogue still the more bestreaks the stripedness of their Greek or German Neoplatonical originals.' Years later, in marking his copy of Arnold's *Essays in Criticism,* he put his finger on the dispro-portion that had made him blur here all the essential differences between these thinkers: 'The provincial spirit, again, exaggerates the value of its ideas for want of a high standard at hand by which to try them. Or rather, for want of such a standard, it gives one idea too much promi-nence at the expense of others; it orders its ideas amiss; it is hurried away by fancies; it likes and dislikes too passionately, too exclusively. Its ad-miration weeps hysterical tears, and its disapprobation foams at the mouth. So we get the *eruptive* and the *aggressive* manner in literature.' Melville may by then have been able even to apply this passage to what had happened to his own writing in *Pierre.* For he had reflected too on the critic's famous passage on the cause of some of the violence in the modern spirit.[2]

But though he found much to admire and agree with in Arnold, who was almost his exact contemporary, Melville had been severely harassed by the dissolvent forces, to whose operation this least provincial of Eng-

2. Arnold's passage appeared in the essay on Heine: 'Modern times find themselves with an immense system of institutions, established facts, accredited dogmas, customs, rules, which have come to them from times not modern. In this system their life has to be carried forward; yet they have a sense that this system is not of their own creation, that it by no means corresponds exactly with the wants of their actual life, that, for them, it is custom-ary, not rational. The awakening of this sense is the awakening of the modern spirit. The modern spirit is now awake almost everywhere; the sense of want of correspondence be-tween the forms of modern Europe and its spirit, between the new wine of the eighteenth and nineteenth centuries, and the old bottles of the eleventh and twelfth centuries, or even of the sixteenth and seventeenth, almost everyone now perceives; it is no longer dangerous to affirm that this want of correspondence exists; people are even beginning to be shy of denying it. To remove this want of correspondence is beginning to be the settled endeavour of most persons of good sense. Dissolvents of the old European system of dominant ideas and facts we must all be, all of us who have any power of working; what we have to study is that we may not be acrid dissolvents of it.' Melville scored this paragraph, and underlined 'acrid dissolvents.'

lishmen could adjust himself more steadily. Moreover, Melville was far more passionate in his thought, and plunged into realms which the Oxford graduate had shied away from. By the mid-eighteen-eighties he was remarking how the *Essays* are 'diluted with that prudential worldly element, wherewithal Mr. Arnold has conciliated the conventionalists.' In his earlier annotations (1869) he had already struck upon some shallows. When Arnold said, 'And such is the fundamental constitution of human affairs, that the measure of right proves also, in the end, the measure of power,' Melville reacted just as he had against Emerson's cheery assumptions, and wrote: 'Even the truest will say untrue things, and the wisest say foolish things.' At the time when he had been caught in the throes of Pierre's misery, his reaction would have been much less temperate.

For that story gives the sense of having been wrenched from him in a mood when illusion after illusion was crashing in his mind, when, as the sub-title *The Ambiguities* suggests, even the distinctions between virtue and vice seemed to become obliterated and truth itself to become meaningless. He felt these things no less than his boyish hero. His own generalizations at crucial points in the narrative betray his hopelessness about the quest upon which he had embarked in *Mardi*. He had found the emptiness of art when a man is 'in a really profound mood; then all merely verbal or written profundities are unspeakably repulsive, and seem downright childish to him.' He had found too that there is 'no philosophy, that a mortal man can possibly evoke, which will stand the final test of a real impassioned onset of Life and Passion.' Worse still, having plunged, as he describes it, into the 'tremendous immensity' of his soul, having felt at last 'afloat in himself,' he had discovered that 'appallingly vacant as vast is the soul of a man.' Having struck through the pasteboard mask of appearance, he had found nothing in reality to sustain him.

These statements do not suggest the tone of tragedy, but of a psychological chaos in which discriminations between good and evil have inevitably been engulfed in the general wreckage of art and philosophy. Melville's effort to arrive at certainty by main force appears now as naïve as it was impossible. But the passion that drove him into the discovery of his ambiguities was peculiarly American. As we have had occasion to note more than once in this volume, our distance from the center of civilization has repeatedly caused our writers to question things that Europeans took for granted. Endless scrutiny of what belonged to the

American through his new circumstances, in contrast to what he was merely imitating from foreign custom, became a preoccupation for both Emerson and Thoreau, as the subtle differences between American and European characters formed later the main ground for Henry James. Melville's inordinate difficulty with thinking is partly illuminated by Ortega y Gasset's discussion of borrowed cultures in *The Revolt of the Masses:*

Half the 'gestures' of the Romans are not their own, they have been learnt. And the 'gesture' which has been learnt, accepted, has always a double aspect, its real meaning is oblique, not direct. The man who performs an act which he has learnt—speaks a foreign word, for example—carries out beneath it an act of his own, genuine; he translates the foreign term to his own language . . . America is younger than Russia. I have always maintained, though in fear of exaggeration, that it is a primitive people camouflaged behind the latest inventions.

Emerson had sensed something of the same problem, in his lecture on 'The Young American' (1844), concerning the gap between our education and our life: 'Our books are European. We were born within the fame and sphere of Shakespeare and Milton, of Bacon, Dryden, and Pope. Our college text-books are the writings of Butler, Locke, Paley, Blackstone, and Stewart; and our domestic reading has been Clarendon and Hume, Addison and Johnson, Young and Cowper, Edgeworth and Scott, Southey, Coleridge, and Wordsworth, and the *Edinburgh* and *Quarterly Reviews*. We are sent to a feudal school to learn democracy.' That passage radiates beyond my present concern in its relevance to major problems in our culture—a culture whose greatest weakness has continued to be that our so-called educated class knows so little of the country and the people of which it is nominally part. This lack of roots helps to explain the usual selfish indifference of our university men to political or social responsibility, as well as the tendency of our artists as they became more sophisticated, from the time of James to that of Eliot, to feel less at home on our shores. Inordinate cleavage between fact and theory has caused us to go to every extreme, has been the reason why, to offset our expatriates, we have often produced the blindest nationalists in art no less than in politics; and why the idealistic strain of our thought has often been so tenuous, so without bearing on the tough materialism of our daily practice. This cleavage may, indeed, have been more responsible than even Emerson was aware for the 'double consciousness' on which he commented, for the fact that the realm of his understanding and that of his soul seemed to have so little connection.

We remember that in his essay on 'Experience' he simply took this discrepancy as inescapable: 'Well, souls never touch their objects . . . Our relations to each other are oblique and casual . . . There is an optical illusion about every person we meet.' These are almost the thoughts of Pierre, but their tone is entirely different. For whereas Emerson could quietly accept the illusory nature of every event, and could grieve only that grief could teach him nothing, Melville was tortured at being immersed in the flux. Suffering had taught him much. He knew that it alone could bring a man to the meaning of Shakespeare and Dante. But at the time he was working on *Pierre,* he felt himself so flooded by the bitterness of experience as to be helpless before it.

His tone suggests the difference between his ambiguity and Hawthorne's. Although Hawthorne often left his reader with several choices as to the reasons for his characters' acts, this was a device to heighten our sense of the complexity of human motives. At crucial points he was generally careful not to allow uncertainty; even in such a story as 'The Birthmark,' where he had held two opposed interpretations in suspense, he handled his last paragraph in such a way as to leave no doubt in Melville's mind as to the nature of the moral. It is necessary to stress the deliberate intention of Hawthorne's device, since James developed it to greater lengths than he did any other, and his use of it has generally been misunderstood. The ambiguous characters with which he endowed, for instance, the governess and the former valet in *The Turn of the Screw,* are not owing to any obscurantism on his part, or to his unawareness of the unnamed sexual implications, but to a desire to create the dense illusion of the passage of life itself, the alternate disclosures and bafflements that you sense in your inevitably partial knowledge of any person or situation. After reading *The Wings of the Dove* you may take exception to the values that James emphasizes, you may feel that however poignant the sacrifice of Milly Theale, her life is too special to be broadly representative; but you can hardly deny that James was primarily a very deliberate and unconfused moralist.

In 'Benito Cereno' Melville built his effect out of ambiguity in the Jamesian sense. He made the tension depend on how the sinister situation on the Spanish ship slowly comes to penetrate the consciousness of the trusting and obtuse Yankee captain. The way the captain's mind sidles round and round the facts, almost seeing them at one moment only to be ingenuously diverted at the next, prefigures also something of Conrad's method in working up to a crisis. But at the time of *Pierre* Melville was incapable of manipulating any such studied device. He had already stated that there were depths in Ahab beyond the reach of his words; but he now realized more painfully that 'the strongest and fiercest emotions of life defy all analytical insight.' Yet no matter how hard it might prove to discern psychological causation, he was determined to 'follow the end-less, winding way,—the flowing river in the cave of man; careless whither I be led, reckless where I land.' In *The Scarlet Letter* Hawthorne had spoken of how, 'at some inevitable moment, will the soul of the sufferer be dissolved, and flow forth in a dark, but transparent stream, bringing all its mysteries into the daylight.'

The difference between the two images is symptomatic. It marks the divergence between Hawthorne's deliberate darkening of the shadows for the sake of intensified high lights, and Melville's involuntary horror at what he encountered as he penetrated the dark, and ambiguity dissolved into obscurity. The difference in emotional voltage behind the images, the difference involved in Melville's throwing himself helplessly open to the workings of his unconscious mind, accounts for the fact that it was in him and not in Hawthorne that Lawrence found expression of 'the extreme transitions of the isolated far-driven soul.'

Moreover, in spite of all wildness and incoherence, Melville was still grappling closely in *Pierre* with Shakespeare's 'contraries.' He may have been driven no less than his hero to the verge of collapse by the inscru-tability of existence. He may have been sick with doubts not only about the world, but even about the divine element within himself. But he was still translating Shakespeare into his own language and time. And his oblique American approach enabled him to see and confront ambiguities in *Hamlet* which no Englishman was then facing, and which were not to be apprehended again with such dynamic fierceness until after Freud's investigation of the Oedipus-complex.

This is what gives coherence and significance to the many parallels be-tween the novel and the play. These are to be traced through nearly all the characters: Lucy's pale innocence fails Pierre as Ophelia's did Ham-let; the well-named Reverend Mr. Falsgrave's cushioned voice of worldly policy is not unlike the platitudinizing of Polonius; Charlie Millthorpe plays a kind of Horatio; Glen Stanly confronts Pierre's seemingly mad violence with the decisiveness of Laertes. But the crucial relation here as in *Hamlet* is that of son and mother. Pierre's father has died when their only child was twelve, and his mother has grown to treat him more like a younger brother than a son. The current of tenderness between them, now that Mary Glendinning is 'not very far from her grand climacteric,' has unconsciously flowed almost into that of lovers.

Pierre's tragedy is caused by the shattering of the spotless image that he had preserved of his father. Isabel's arrival on the scene, her uncanny likeness to the sketch of his father as a young bachelor, her confused memories of her orphaned childhood are agonizingly pieced together by Pierre into the pattern of a liaison and desertion. Worse still, once 'the long-cherished image' of his father has been 'transfigured before him from a green foliaged tree into a blasted trunk,' once his youthful and middle-aged portraits are seen as unlike as those of Hamlet's father and uncle, every other image in Pierre's mind begins to fluctuate and alter. He knows without mentioning them to her that his mother will not endure the new facts; he sees her as no longer lovely, but haughty and selfish, determined to preserve privileged appearances at all cost. He has previously felt that Lucy's pure radiance was so unearthly that marriage with her would be almost 'an impious thing.' He can certainly tell her nothing about what has happened. He is thrown back entirely on his own resources, and quickly decides that he can take Isabel under his protection only by pretending that he has married her. But from that act results an ambiguity worse than all the others. Pierre has aspired to an inhuman ideal which he cannot sustain. Even at the outset he has felt that 'never, never would he be able to embrace Isabel with the mere brotherly embrace; while the thought of any other caress . . . was entirely vacant from his uncontaminated soul, for it had never consciously intruded there.' Yet, in spite of his belief that he is acting wholly unselfishly, he has broken away from a sister-mother to become involved with a sister-wife.

Since little is known about Melville's own childhood and youth, his biographers have drawn heavily on *Pierre;* and since Melville's father died when he was twelve, they have concluded that Mary Glendinning is to be taken as an exact likeness of Maria Gansevoort Melville. This interpretation neglects such items as that Melville was not an only child but the third among eight, that his mother was not left in sheltered affluence at her husband's death, that none of her sons killed her by marrying a half-sister or even by writing *Pierre*, in which she recognized no insulting portrait of herself, since she remained in correspondence with her son Herman until her death when he was beyond fifty. The travesty of trying to make fiction into autobiography is that it oversimplifies and thus distorts the creative process; it jumps without warrant from the life of the soul to that of outer events, for that is what is involved in the translation of symbolic fantasies into literal happenings. It is by no means impossible that Melville felt an incestuous attraction to one of his sisters, but we prove nothing by assuming that he did. It is apparent that the author of *Pierre* was tormented by the ambiguity of sexual relations as they revealed the impossibility of ideal truth. The search for certainty and authority may be understood as a phase of the search for a lost father. But since such connections are hard enough for a trained scientist to make when analyzing a living patient who furnishes him evidence for months, harder for even Freud with a dead man like Leonardo da Vinci, it is impossible for a literary critic to produce more than long-shot hunches in trying to get at an author's particular conflicts through his novels or plays. What the critic is in a position to know best are the complex transformations involved in any imaginative creation; and the slightest acquaintance with psychoanalysis should teach him how intricate is the technique required to interpret biographically the ambivalent symbols of even the simplest dream. This is not to maintain that a man's writing does not distill the essential qualities from his inner life; and it would be absurd to deny that a scientist could make a challenging, if hypothetical case-history out of what is known of Melville's biography and the indirect light cast upon it by his books.[3] But a generation of amateur efforts on the part of critics have served largely to explain away rather than to explain works of art. And in the case of Melville, it must be repeated, these have tended so far to deflect from any comprehensive study of the works, and to compensate with no reliable biography, owing to the loose liberties that have been taken with the known facts.

What a critic can gain from Freudian theory is a very comprehensive kind of description of human norms and processes, an incalculably great asset in interpreting patterns of character and meaning. What can be learned directly from *Pierre* is that much material had surged up into Melville's mind, of the sort that remains unconscious for most authors,

3. Such a study has been under preparation for some time by Dr. Harry Murray of the Harvard Psychological Clinic.

and was not allowed to ripple the surface of Victorian literature. It is no longer shocking to observe Melville's pained awareness of an Oedipus-relation, or even of the latent homosexuality in Pierre's boyhood attachment to his cousin Glen, for we now know that such elements are usual in a human being's evolution. Why their hidden memories rose to plague Melville during the writing of *Pierre* is fairly clear from the text itself. When Pierre starts feverishly to write, Melville comments that he had 'not as yet procured for himself that enchanter's wand of the soul, which but touching the humblest experiences in one's life, straightway it starts up all eyes, in every one of which are endless significancies. Not yet had he dropped his angle into the well of his childhood, to find what fish might be there; for who dreams to find fish in a well?'

But that is exactly what Melville himself had now done. In his determination to penetrate the mask of appearance even more deeply than he had in *Moby-Dick,* to drive even farther down to primary levels of experience,[4] he had found himself surrounded by corridors of 'endless significancies' opening in all directions, with only hazy vistas at their ends. He had made the very dangerous discovery he was to proclaim in *The Confidence Man,* that to portray a consistent character in fiction is to be untrue to life; that no matter whether shallow critics declare that an author 'should represent human nature not in obscurity, but transparency,' nevertheless he who says of human nature what 'is said of the divine nature, that it is past finding out,' thereby evinces a better appreciation of its mysterious contrasts. To be sure, he went on to firmer ground in that discussion, for he added that the greatest 'psychological novelists . . . challenge astonishment at the tangled web of some character, and then raise admiration still greater at their satisfactory unravelling of it.' Thus they prove their rare mastery of the truth that, despite all twistings and apparent confusions, 'the grand points of human nature are the same to-day they were a thousand years ago.'

Melville insisted on that universality also in *Pierre*. He explicitly stated

---

4. He wrote to Hawthorne in the fall of 1851: 'Lord, when shall we be done growing? As long as we have anything more to do, we have done nothing. So, now, let us add Moby-Dick to our blessing, and step from that. Leviathan is not the biggest fish;—I have heard of Krakens [the fabulous Scandinavian sea-monsters].' That harks back to his letter of the spring before, which had likened the miracle of his growth since his twenty-fifth year to that of 'one of those seeds taken out of the Egyptian Pyramids, which, after being three thousand years a seed and nothing but a seed, being planted in English soil, it developed itself, grew to greenness, and then fell to mould.'

that the tragedy of Memnon, ' "the flower of virtue cropped by a too rare mischance," ' was an ancient *Hamlet,* and thus implied that *Pierre* could be a modern one. Yet he encountered great difficulty in objectifying his own sufferings. Especially when Pierre started to be an author, Melville could not keep the boy of nineteen separate from himself at thirty-two, from the man who was finishing his seventh book in as many years, and who, to judge from the texture of its thought and writing, was not only discouraged but nearly exhausted. While still engaged with *Moby-Dick* he had cried out to Hawthorne: 'Try to get a living by the Truth—and go to the Soup Societies.' Now he had no hesitation in saying that Pierre, in his lonely room, was embarked on 'that most miserable of all the pursuits of a man.' He added too what the general misunderstanding of *Moby-Dick* was just teaching him: 'He shall now learn, and very bitterly learn, that though the world worship Mediocrity and Commonplace, yet hath it fire and sword for all contemporary Grandeur; that though it swears that it fiercely assails all Hypocrisy, yet hath it not always an ear for Earnestness.'

Melville could not keep the contours of his hero distinct from this heart-knowledge of his own. What Eliot has remarked about *Hamlet* might be applied to *Pierre,* that it gives the impression of being full of some 'intractable' stuff which its writer could not 'manipulate into art.' Although the sexual problems have become more explicit' in Melville's meditation over Shakespeare than in the play itself, further ambiguities are introduced by the contrast between Lucy and Isabel. This contrast corresponds to nothing in *Hamlet,* but goes back to the symbolic abstractions of Yillah and Hautia. Once again the difference between fair and dark is subjected to a variety of interpretations. The two seem to stand for ideal love and earthly passion, or as Isabel wretchedly says, they are Pierre's good and bad angels. But the contrast is not left so clear-cut as it is, say, in Shakespeare's *Sonnets.* For Isabel is obviously not evil. Pierre's presentiment at first seeing her is cast in the familiar Melvillian terms of the difference between the peaceful land in which Pierre has been living and the dangerous waters that lie ahead: 'He felt that what he had always before considered the solid land of veritable reality, was now being audaciously encroached upon by bannered armies of hooded phantoms, disembarking in his soul, as from flotillas of spectre-boats.' But Isabel is no Fedallah. She is a child of nature to whom the policy of the world is unknown. She feels rather than thinks, and it strikes her that she will always continue to be a child, no matter how old she lives to be. Yet there is an imploring anguish in her beauty, in her expression compounded 'of hell and heaven.' She has suffered desperately in being alone, and wants to absorb life, or rather, to be absorbed into it, for she feels that 'there can be no perfect peace in individualness.'

In the chaotic state of mind that led Melville to say, 'Let the ambiguous procession of events reveal their own ambiguousness,' the theme of 'Isabel and mystery' was diffused to insufferable lengths. Some of its less controlled elements may have been stimulated by Sylvester Judd's rhapsodic descriptions of his heroine Margaret, whose shadowy childhood memories are not unlike Isabel's.[5] But in spite of all such extravagant qualities as her preternatural 'magnetic power,' the crux of her relation to Pierre is unmistakable: she has bound him to her from the start by an attraction that is both spiritual and physical, and which will prove impossible for him to deny.

On the other hand, Lucy is all light. As Pierre tells her at the outset, she belongs 'to the regions of an infinite day.' But even in his inexperience before meeting Isabel, he senses something inhuman in such unrelieved whiteness, in the fact that Lucy is almost angelic in her lack of 'vulgar vigor.' The news of his supposed marriage throws her into a swoon, and then into a nearly mortal illness. But as she rallies, she is made still more unearthly by her grief. She determines to join Pierre and Isabel in the city, for she says that she can live only for him, that she asks no visible response, but trusts only that her love will triumph in heaven. A terrifying quality creeps into such virtue. She is sustained by her self-sacrifice, which is so complete that she does not even feel that she is making a renunciation. Her action, nevertheless, brings on the final tragedy. The very fact of her presence drives Isabel into jealousy and desperation. It also goads Lucy's brother to join Glen Stanly in taking drastic steps against Pierre, whom they now judge to be the worst of seducers. Moreover, when Lucy at last learns the secret, when she sees Isabel embrace Pierre and call him not husband but brother, she is killed by the shock.

It would be profitless to pursue all the ramifications of these symbols, since they are not really created into living characters, but are dispersed

---

5. Melville had borrowed *Margaret: A Tale of the Real and Ideal, Blight and Bloom,* from Duyckinck in the summer of 1850, when, incidentally, he had also borrowed Thoreau's *Week.*

in metaphysical clouds. Melville came nearest to condensing his meaning into dramatic form through the dream of Enceladus, the dream that Pierre had during the state of debilitated torpor produced by his final unsuccessful struggles with his book. In this dream Pierre remembered how, in the purple haze of distance, the mountain at Saddle Meadows had seemed to live up to its old name of the Delectable Mountain; but that if he went near, its unexpected crags and savage precipices, its stark and ruinous desolation justified its being called the Mount of the Titans. In addition to this fit symbol for the differences between anticipation and the event, Pierre remembered too how among these vast rocks was one formation that had struck him as looking like Enceladus, 'the most potent of all the giants, writhing from out the imprisoning earth,' and, though armless, 'still turning his unconquerable front toward that majestic mount eternally in vain assailed by him.' But in the dream this form was no longer frozen into rocky stasis. He sprang as leader of the Titans in their assault upon heaven, and 'despairing of any other mode of wreaking his immitigable hate, turned his vast trunk into a battering-ram, and hurled his own arched-out ribs again and yet again against the invulnerable steep.' In the moment when Pierre saw this leader's anguished face, he recognized it as his own. 'With trembling frame he started from his chair, and woke from that ideal horror to all his actual grief.'

Melville's comment was that Pierre did not wrest the final comfort from the fable that he might have, that just as Enceladus was the incestuous offspring of Titan and his mother Terra, herself the incestuous wife of her son Coelus,

even thus, there had been born from the organic blended heavenliness and earthliness of Pierre, another mixed, uncertain, heaven-aspiring, but still not wholly earth-emancipated mood; which again, by its terrestrial taint held down to its terrestrial mother, generated there the present doubly incestuous Enceladus within him; so that the present mood of Pierre—that reckless sky-assaulting mood of his, was nevertheless on one side the grandson of the sky. For it is according to eternal fitness, that the precipitated Titan should still seek to regain his paternal birthright even by fierce escalade. Wherefore whoso storms the sky gives best proof he came from thither! But whatso crawls contented in the moat before that crystal fort, shows it was born within that slime, and there forever will abide.

But such reflections could hardly have given much comfort to Pierre in his final headlong disasters. And though the meaning of the fable seems secure within its context, when you try to square its implications with the somewhat different incests in Pierre's life, or with the contrasting doctrine of Plinlimmon's pamphlet, you find yourself caught in multiplying the ambiguities still further. You can better discern what had been Melville's emotional center in his contrast between Lucy and Isabel through a minor passage in the dream. The pastures by the Delectable Mountain had been increasingly invaded by 'a small white amaranthine flower,' inodorous and sterile, and 'irreconcilably distasteful to the cattle.' It seemed to the disheartened tenants that this flower was immortal, since every year the pastures grew more glitteringly white. Only here and there you might still catch the sweet aroma of clumps of catnip, 'that dear farm-house herb.' Yet 'every spring the amaranthine and celestial flower gained on the mortal household herb; for every autumn the catnip died, but never an autumn made the amaranth to wane. The catnip and the amaranth!—man's earthly household peace, and the ever-encroaching appetite for God.'

Melville makes no clumsy parallel to Lucy's whiteness; and there are many guises in which Isabel, despite her longing for the immobility 'of some plant, absorbing life without seeking it,' is anything but a peaceful herb. Yet what had bothered Melville ever since he began to think about the differences between the sensuous instinctual life of the savages and the tortures of the aspiring mind and spirit became part of the contrast between the two girls. Pierre seems to need them both, but far below any conscious awareness, he is drawn most naturally to the dark life-giving forces of Isabel, the forces that were being so atrophied by the incessant pale American search for the ideal.

Although the Enceladus myth is one of the few symbols in the book that seem really under control, there is no denying the amount of extraordinary writing. It is hard always to be sure of its intention. Melville himself declared, 'I write precisely as I please,' and reiterated the conviction which had come upon him in *Mardi*, that genius is full of trash.[6] His manner is frequently so reckless that Shakespearean scraps get out of hand and go into hysterical seizures; and what may start as telling irony generally breaks down into facetiousness. The chief trouble is the lack of

6. He also checked, in *The Seven Gables*, Holgrave's remark, 'I begin to suspect that a man's bewilderment is the measure of his wisdom.'

any norm. Beside one of Arnold's sentences, 'It is comparatively a small matter to express oneself well, if one will be content with not expressing much, with expressing only trite ideas,' Melville was to write 'G.W.C.' which would refer most appropriately to George William Curtis, one of the milder young men of Brook Farm, subsequently the author of *Nile Notes of a Howadji* (1851) and *Prue and I* (1856), who as editor of *Putnam's* once counselled Melville to study Addison in order to improve his work. As Arnold held, and Melville noted, 'The problem is to express new and profound ideas in a perfectly sound and classical style.' What Arnold observed in the English writers of the day was the lack of any such balance. He put it down to the unfavorable atmosphere, to the want of a clarified tradition, a state that tended 'to make even a man of great ability either a Mr. Carlyle or else a Lord Macaulay.' Melville marked that sentence too, as well he might; for he had labored with far less semblance of any tradition. At least Carlyle's mannerisms, however lugged-in from the German, were intentional; whereas Melville in *Pierre* was often obviously at a loss how to handle the radical material he wanted to express.

He was capable of producing passages of an electric intensity, the passages that testify to what Lawrence meant by saying that Melville gave him the sense of being almost played out in 'his human-emotional self,' of being 'abstract, self-analytical and abstracted,' almost over the verge into pathology; but that on that verge he could portray the full fierceness of anguish. Such a passage is the one where Pierre receives Lucy's letter saying that she is coming to join them: and the swiftly varying prose reaches into every interstice of his tangled reactions:

He held the artless, angelical letter in his unrealising hand; he started, and gazed round his room, and out at the window, commanding the bare, desolate, all-forbidding quadrangle, and then asked himself whether this was the place that an angel should choose for its visit to earth. Then he felt a vast, out-swelling triumphantness, that the girl whose rare merits his intuitive soul had once so clearly and passionately discerned, should indeed, in this most tremendous of all trials, have acquitted herself with such infinite majesty. Then again, he sunk utterly down from her, as in a bottomless gulf, and ran shuddering through hideous galleries of despair, in pursuit of some vague, white shape, and lo! two unfathomable dark eyes met his, and Isabel stood mutely and mournfully, yet all-ravishingly before him.

Such a pitch could not possibly be sustained as a norm.[7] Melville was so helplessly open to his emotions that he sometimes could not find language distinguishable from that of the magazine-shocker: ' "Curses, wasp-like, cohere on that villain, Ned, and sting him to his death!" cried Pierre, smit by this most piteous tale.' Harder to place is some of the diction in the opening section, the many clichés, the heaped-up jargon of such needlessly ugly inventions as 'diamondness,' 'amaranthiness,' 'descendedness.' It is even harder to be certain what Melville intended in the first passages between Pierre and Lucy. They read in part like a forecast of the ejaculative idyll of young love that Meredith was to handle between his Lucy and Richard Feverel half a dozen years later. But often they give the impression that Melville was so tormented by the thought of what lay ahead for his hero that he could not help mocking his own lyricism. The result, from the author of *Moby-Dick,* was incredible: confused insecurity of intention could reduce his voice to an impotent echo of the *Lady's Book:* 'Love is both Creator's and Saviour's gospel to mankind; a volume bound in rose-leaves, clasped with violets, and by the beaks of humming-birds printed with peach-juice on the leaves of lilies. Endless is the account of Love'—and so on, without undercutting, to the end of the chapter.

The most powerful section in the book, the first night of Pierre and Isabel's arrival in the city, may owe its greater steadiness to Melville's having had a partial model in the flight of Clifford and Hepzibah. That is not to say that Melville's effect is not peculiarly his own, the quality of a heart-breaking nightmare wherein trusting inexperience is shattered against the hardness of a world in which only money opens doors.

At the outset of his hero's trouble, Melville addressed him: 'Ay, Pierre . . . for thee, the before undistrusted moral beauty of the world is forever fled; for thee, thy sacred father is no more a saint; all brightness hath gone from thy hills, and all peace from thy plains; and now, now,

7. Even more violent is the concluding sentence to Pierre's first verification of his presentiment of Isabel's identity: 'He could not stay in his chamber; the house contracted to a nut-shell around him; the walls smote his forehead; bare-headed he rushed from the place, and only in the infinite air, found scope for that boundless expansion of his life.'

Out of its context another final sentence, that of the chapter in which Pierre struggles towards his decision to act, is so extravagant in its verbal action that it is almost over the border into burlesque: 'The cheeks of his soul collapsed in him; he dashed himself in blind fury and swift madness against the wall, and fell dabbling in the vomit of his loathed identity.'

for the first time, Pierre, Truth rolls a black billow through thy soul! Ah, miserable thou, to whom Truth, in her first tides, bears nothing but wrecks!' That imagery goes back not only to *Moby-Dick* but also to *Mardi;* and Pierre enacts the 'utter wreck' that Taji dreaded and yet challenged. It is impossible to write tragedy if you feel an ambiguity in all distinctions between virtue and vice, if in your hopelessness about human misery. you can take joy only in the fact that 'death is a democrat.' Nevertheless, if *Pierre* is a failure, it must be accounted a great one, a failure in an effort to express as honestly as possible what it meant to undergo the test 'of a real impassioned onset of Life and Passion.' The importance of such an effort may be grasped in the contrast between two variations on the same theme. To instance the inevitability of man's fate, Emerson remarked: 'I seemed in the height of a tempest to see men overboard struggling in the waves, and driven about here and there. They glanced intelligently at each other, but 'twas little they could do for one another; 'twas much if each could keep afloat alone. Well, they had a right to their eye-beams, and all the rest was Fate.' To those to whom such easy acceptance seems inhuman, Melville's surcharged words about Pierre come with the relief of uninhibited passion: 'For in tremendous extremities human souls are like drowning men; well enough they know they are in peril; well enough they know the causes of that peril; nevertheless, the sea is the sea, and these drowning men do drown.'

⇒ XII ⇐

REASSERTION OF THE HEART

'The brave impetuous heart yields everywhere
To the subtle contriving head.'
   —marked by Melville in Arnold's *Empedocles on Etna*.

1. An Alien to His Contemporaries

'The more a man belongs to posterity, in other words to humanity in
general, the more of an alien is he to his contemporaries . . . People
are more likely to appreciate the man who serves the circumstances of
his own brief hour, or the temper of the moment,—belonging to it,
and living and dying with it.'—marked by Melville in Schopenhauer's
essay on 'Fame,' in *The Wisdom of Life* (1891).

WHAT happened next has generally been overdramatized. Professor
Weaver started it by giving only two chapters of his biography (1921),
hardly more than an eighth of the whole, to all Melville's career after
Moby-Dick, and by calling these 'The Great Refusal' and 'The Long
Quietus.' Such foreshortening was disproportionate, since not only
forty years of Melville's life, but also eight of the sixteen volumes of his
collected works were thus huddled together. Lewis Mumford did much
to redress the impression thereby created of Melville's collapse into misanthropy if not actual insanity; but the tone of his book (1929) can
be suggested by his handling of Melville's relation with Hawthorne.
He counted it as 'one of the tragedies' of Melville's life, and declared
that Hawthorne committed 'the unpardonable sin of friendship' by portraying Ethan Brand as a warning of what Melville himself must avoid
becoming. Even if Mumford did not know that Hawthorne's story had
already been printed several months before the two first met, he had no
excuse for saying that Brand was echoing Ahab's words, since he could
have had the evidence of Melville's letter discussing the story while *The
Whale* was still under way. Again Mumford assumed that Hawthorne's

488

indifference after *Moby-Dick* was dedicated to him drove Melville into the ironic gesture of inscribing *Pierre* to Mt. Greylock.[1] Actually the paragraph of apostrophe to 'Greylock's Most Excellent Majesty' seems playful rather than misanthropic; and as far as Hawthorne's opinion of *Moby-Dick* is concerned, we have not only his praise to Duyckinck, but also Melville's letter expressing complete satisfaction in what Hawthorne had written him. No comment of Hawthorne's upon *Pierre* has yet come to light, though it may be supposed that he referred partly to this book in his observation, at the time of Melville's visit to Liverpool, that 'his writings, for a long while past, have indicated a morbid state of mind.'[2] However, over against this should be remembered his tribute to the 'excellent novel or biography of *Israel Potter.*'

It is obvious that the two men were of very different temperaments, and it is more than possible that Melville finally felt disappointed that his longing to discuss 'ontological heroics' aroused no comparable ardor from the older man's reserve. But there seems no sign of a break between them. When Melville turned up in Liverpool in 1856, Hawthorne said: "I felt rather awkward at first; because this is the first time I have met him since my ineffectual attempt to get him a consular appointment from General Pierce. However, I failed only from real lack of power to serve him; so there was no reason to be ashamed, and we soon found ourselves on pretty much our former terms of sociability and confidence.'

On Melville's side, there is the evidence of his continued interest in Hawthorne's later works, in *The Marble Faun* and the various volumes of posthumous *Notebooks*. In May 1865, he recurred to a passage in 'The

1. It is hardly important, yet symptomatic, that Mumford said 'Monadnock' instead of 'Greylock.' For his book is full of such small mistakes that add up to a big one. He was particularly careless in summarizing the plots, with the result that, as R. S. Forsythe demonstrated in the case of *Pierre* (*American Literature*, November 1930), he generally twisted them badly.

Weaver had already said that Melville underlined the phrase 'this hellish society of men' in his Schopenhauer, when it happens to be in his copy of Shelley's *Letters*. Mumford went even more unaccountably out of his way in declaring that Melville wrote in *Pierre*, 'The novel will find the way to our interiors, one day, and will not always be novel of costume merely.' The remark is not to be found there, but if Mumford had remembered the much more unexpected source from which it actually came, he could have made the telling point of Emerson's perception in theory (1848) of what he then failed to recognize in the practice of *Moby-Dick* and *The Scarlet Letter*, no less than of *Pierre*.

2. This remark was naturally not included by Mrs. Hawthorne in her edition of *The English Notebooks*. A complete edition has now been prepared by Randall Stewart, and will soon be in print.

Celestial Railroad,' on the vanishing of man's life like a bubble, with the comment, 'Nothing can be finer than this.' The point of recording the date was that it marked the first anniversary of Hawthorne's death. It seems possible that Melville may also have had Hawthorne in mind while drawing one of the characters in *Clarel*, for some of the novelist's traits are those of the shy and musing Vine, 'opulent in withheld replies.' It is certain that Melville was still thinking of that sketch in the *Mosses* which had commanded his closest attention when he wrote a poem, left unpublished at his death, on 'Madam Mirror,' who registered

> the anguish
> Of the Real and the Seeming in life.

As a final instance of the many distortions which still remain to be corrected by Melville's next biographer, there is his remark to Hawthorne during their last days together in Liverpool, that he 'had pretty much made up his mind to be annihilated.' Mumford concluded, 'Melville would not commit suicide: that was a weak way out: but he might deliberately withdraw.' In the right reading of the context neither alternative is relevant. Hawthorne quotes the remark in his account of how, on a long walk, when they sat down to smoke their cigars, Melville,

as he always does, began to reason of Providence and futurity, and of everything that lies beyond human ken, and informed me that he 'had pretty much made up his mind to be annihilated'; but still he does not seem to rest in that anticipation; and, I think, will never rest until he gets hold of a definite belief. It is strange how he persists—and has persisted ever since I knew him, and probably long before—in wandering to-and-fro over these deserts, as dismal and monotonous as the sand hills amid which we were sitting. He can neither believe, nor be comfortable in his unbelief; and he is too honest and courageous not to try to do one or the other. If he were a religious man, he would be one of the most truly religious and reverential; he has a very high and noble nature, and better worth immortality than most of us.

What harried Melville was the same debate between faith and doubt that aged Clough so young, that determined the temper of Arnold's 'Obermann' and 'The Grand Chartreuse,' and that became one of the most pervasive elements in Victorian poetry. For Melville to give up idealism for materialism, to accept the doctrine of the annihilation of the soul at death, would be a hard decision; and as Hawthorne suggests, he never really made it. What he did come to accept, however, is indicated by one of his late quatrains, an alleged fragment 'of a lost Gnostic poem of the twelfth century':

> Found a family, build a state,
> The pledged event is still the same:
> Matter in end will never abate
> His ancient brutal claim.

Hawthorne was worried by Melville's poor health, as Mrs. Melville had been before he started out on this vacation in the hope of restoring it. His eyes had begun to trouble him severely at the time of *Moby-Dick*, and his general spirits were now such that Hawthorne felt him 'much overshadowed' since their previous meeting. And though Hawthorne's passage has no bearing upon this, the mood which produced *The Confidence Man* was one in which its author might indeed have thought of suicide. Yet, to balance the scales, there is an entry in Duyckinck's diary at the time when Melville would just have finished this book: 'In the evening at Mr. Shepherd's, in 14th str: . . . Good talk. Herman warming like an old sailor over the supper.'

The one certain place to look for signs of exhaustion in Melville's vitality is in his own creative work; and the structure of both *Israel Potter* and *The Confidence Man* shows them to have been produced by a man not at all able to write the kind of books he wanted to, but under a miserable compulsion. In the former he started out to portray the tragedy of exile, but when he came to the ex-soldier's destitution in London, his own sense of suffering was so great that he could not bear to dwell on Potter's, and slurred over what was to have been his main subject in a couple of short chapters. He had come to feel that 'just as extreme suffering, without hope, is intolerable to the victim, so, to others, is its depiction without some corresponding delusive mitigation.' He thus hit instinctively upon much the same considerations that had caused Arnold to withdraw his *Empedocles* from circulation only the year before. The poet had come to perceive, in that masterful preface of 1853 in defense of the classic attitude,[3] that any attempt at tragedy fails of catharsis in those situations where the protagonist's suffering finds no vent in action, 'in

3. There is no indication that Melville had read Arnold at this time. His markings in *Empedocles* date after its restoration to circulation, at Browning's request, in the edition of 1867.

which a continuous state of mental distress is prolonged, unrelieved by incident, hope, or resistance, in which there is everything to be endured, nothing to be done.' Arnold's conclusion was that 'in such situations there is inevitably something morbid, in the description of them something monotonous. When they occur in actual life, they are painful, not tragic; the representation of them in poetry is painful also.'

That formulation can serve to throw light on the failure of *Israel Potter,* wherein Melville had arrived at the antipodal state from that of the transcendentalists. For them tragedy, being the product of evil, was merely partial, hence was unreal, hence should not be written; for him it had become so real that it could not be written. In his situations that allowed no resolution the economic factor bulked larger than it did in Arnold's. In the case of a crippled soldier of fortune in *The Confidence Man,* he showed again how misery at first enlists our sympathy, but if too extreme it chills and repels it; how the utterly abject suffering of the really poor is something to whose existence the world will only blind itself. In 'Poor Man's Pudding' he raised the question, which has often been asked by European observers and which has become more pressing with time: whether our fierce individualism does not make our perhaps fewer victims of poverty 'suffer more in mind' than those in any other country.

Unrelieved mental suffering, not merely because of the problem of poverty, but because of the ambiguity of all appearances, had become so intense for Melville at the time of *The Confidence Man* that, as we have noted, there was no real progression to its theme, no possible resolution other than to break it off in the middle. The incessant hammering of his thoughts had drawn him far beyond the danger point, which he was to recognize and triple check long afterwards in one of Arnold's *Mixed Essays* (1883): the danger point reached even by Goethe, whose later works 'are wanting in the vigorous sensuousness, the concrete and immediate impression of things, which makes the artist, and which distinguishes him from the thinker.' The structure of *The Confidence Man* is no more than a manipulated pattern of abstractions; but the exhaustion of Melville's powers at this period should not be exaggerated. However mechanical the conception of this book, its style, as in the characterization of the mystical philosopher,[4] is hard and decisive, far more certain in its

4. Quoted above, p. 472.

aim than the style of *Pierre*. What bear out Hawthorne's praise of *Israel Potter* are such things as the rich portrait of Franklin as a kind of Biblical patriarch, a subtle Jacob. 'By nature turned to knowledge, his mind was often grave, but never serious . . . This philosophical levity of tranquillity, so to speak, is shown in his easy variety of pursuits . . . Jack of all trades, master of each and mastered by none—the type and genius of his land. Franklin was everything but a poet.' This shrewd evaluation should stand beside Melville's grimmer reckoning with that democratic sea-king Paul Jones: 'in one view, the Coriolanus of the sea; in another a cross between the gentleman and the wolf.' Together these sketches show how much Melville had reflected on the American character, and on what it needed most to bring it to completion.

There were still other manifestations of Melville's energy during these years, which contradict the allegations of those who have followed the first uncomprehending reviewers not only of *Pierre* but of *Moby-Dick*, and have hinted at the breakdown of his mind. He contributed a dozen or more stories to magazines before collecting some of them in *The Piazza Tales*. The introductory section, in which he relishes his piazza at Pittsfield, must have been suggested by Hawthorne's manse. The three most ambitious stories are all tragic. In addition to 'Benito Cereno' they are 'Bartleby the Scrivener' and 'The Encantadas.' 'Bartleby' is a tragedy of utter negation, of the enduring hopelessness of a young man who is absolutely alone, 'a bit of wreck in the mid-Atlantic' which is New York. 'The Encantadas' are mainly descriptive sketches of the ironically named Enchanted Isles, a group of such bleak desolation that they could exist 'in no world but a fallen one.' The most moving section recounts how an Indian woman, Hunilla, survived long desertion on one of these islands after the death of her husband and her brother, her sole companions there. As Melville celebrates her courage, 'nature's pride subduing nature's torture,' he accepts what had been impossible for him when writing *Pierre*: that good can come out of evil, as well as evil from good. He rises to his equivalent for Whitman's affirmation when he declares: 'Humanity, thou strong thing, I worship thee, not in the laurelled victor, but in this vanquished one.'

Nevertheless, *The Confidence Man*, if not a dead-end, marked at least the completion of a cycle. It added the final proof, if any was needed after *Pierre*, that Melville's books had no market; and though he seems to have begun to write verse within a year or so after his return from the

Holy Land in 1857, during the remainder of his life, almost half of the whole, he gave no sign of wanting to publish any more prose.[5] His poetry, though very illuminating for his inner biography, adds little to his stature as an artist. The casual nature of its form is partly accounted for by his having accepted the fatal symbol of the Aeolian harp. As he said in his preface to *Battle-Pieces:* 'I seem, in most of these verses, to have but placed a harp in a window, and noted the contrasted airs which wayward winds have played upon the strings.' He could hit upon an occasional lyric sequence, as in 'Shiloh,' 'Sheridan at Cedar Creek,' several of his. ballad refrains, and 'A Requiem for Soldiers Lost in Ocean Transports,' which last seems to echo 'Lycidas' in some of its undersea images. Moreover, his whole conception of war poetry shares in the breadth of *Drum-Taps*. Although there is no wavering in his devotion to the Union's cause, he can see Stonewall Jackson as a type of classic heroism. He also states that he 'never was a blind adherent,' and submits that reunion depends most on forbearance and Christian humanity from the North. Thus he envisages the significance of the conflict in terms which were not current among the Northern poets of progress in 1866, and which could be understood only by a man who had mastered the meaning of suffering: 'Let us pray that the terrible historic tragedy of our time may not have been enacted without instructing our whole beloved country through terror and pity.'

Clarel (1876), completed a considerable interval before its publication,

5. The official position of his family regarding his talents would appear to have been summed up in a letter from his young cousin Henry to his father, Peter Gansevoort. Henry had graduated from Princeton and was studying in the Harvard Law School when he heard Melville lecture in Boston late in 1857. He wrote: 'Herman Melville seems considerably improved in health and spirits by his interspersing the spice of variety with the reality of life. I met him at Mr. Griggs last Sunday evening. He was in a fine flow of humor which I enjoyed exceedingly. There is doubtless positive originality in him, Brilliancy but misanthropy, Genius but less judgement. He evidently mistakes his sphere. He has dropped the pen of candid narration for that of captious criticism. He does the latter well but he can do the former much better. I had the pleasure of listening to his lecture on Statuary in Rome delivered a week since. It was well conceived and executed but it lacked the force and beauty that characterise his early writings.'

Henry's father was entirely in accord with this opinion, and was surprised that Melville had not made his recent travels the subject of a book, 'which would be not only instructive to others, but very profitable to himself—Such a work would not make a requisition on his imagination.' It was this same Peter Gansevoort who was to provide the money for the belated appearance of *Clarel*, even though it contained sadly more criticism than narrative.

follows rather the course of Melville's doubts than that of any faith. It would be impossible to say, from the several thousand lines of discussion between its shadowy characters, precisely what Melville himself accepted, but some of his blacker visions of society are thereby accentuated. Rolfe, an outdoor man of action who knows also the 'ocean waste' of open thought, holds, in spite of his New World lack of reverence, that religion must endure as long as man's heart does. He questions the ultimate value of freedom of thought, even as he engages in it. His 'considerate, uncommitted eyes' foresee that all nations are prone to slide into degradation, that men

> Get tired at last of being free—
> Whether in states—in states or creeds.

But the most radical doctrines for Melville's America are voiced by Ungar, a scarred veteran of the Southwest, 'a wandering Ishmael,' a descendant of Maryland Catholics, with a strain of Indian blood, who, though no longer in the Church himself, has inherited the Catholic mind. He has a low opinion of Anglo-Saxon exploiters throughout the world; it is he who criticizes the brutalities of the new factory system.[6] He holds that in America,

> The vast reserves—the untried fields;
> These long shall keep off and delay
> The class-war, rich-and-poor man-fray
> Of history. From that alone
> Can serious trouble spring. Even that
> Itself, this good result may own—
> The first firm founding of the state.

Although Ungar glimpses that possible synthesis, he has little confidence in it. In his view, popular ignorance often increases as society 'progresses,' and masterless men who have foregone all recognition of evil within themselves, are easy prey for demagogues. He holds that only an awareness of Original Sin can give significance to man's struggle; and the last that is seen of him by Clarel, he is riding off with

> that strange look
> Of one enlisted for sad fight
> Upon some desperate dark shore.

The conclusion of the poem takes Clarel, the former divinity student, back to Jerusalem at Easter, but he has not succeeded in reconciling the

6. See above, p. 401.

doubts that drove him on this pilgrimage, and is near despair. Melville's
'Epilogue' dwells on how,

> If Luther's day expand to Darwin's year,

the problem of belief is thus only greatly aggravated by science. Still he
concludes in the vein—though without the verbal skill—of *In Memoriam:*

> Emerge thou mayst from the last whelming sea,
> And prove that death but routs life into victory.

The most explicit statement that Melville gave of the position he had
settled down to in his later years is in a letter to James Billson, an English
admirer who had sent him, in the mid-eighties, Thomson's *City of Dreadful Night*. This poem caused him to say: 'As to the pessimism, although
neither pessimist nor optimist myself, nevertheless I relish it in the verse,
if for nothing else than as a counterpoise to the exorbitant hopefulness,
juvenile and shallow, that makes such a bluster in these days—at least
in some quarters.' A similar attitude had shown itself in his reaction to
Arnold's expression, through Empedocles, of the weariness of the modern
spirit:

> But still, as we proceed,
> The mass swells more and more
> Of volumes yet to read,
> Of secrets yet to explore.

At the bottom of that page Melville had written: ' "The volumes," exclaims the Western critic. "What could a sage of the nineteenth century
teach Socrates? Why, nothing more than something about Cyrus Fields,
and the ocean telegraph, and the sewing machine, &." ' In that remark
Melville was such a Western critic as Thoreau had been; but the values of
Socrates tended to be in abeyance during the era when Mark Twain,
kindling to admiration of H. H. Rogers and other barons of success,
could write to Whitman on his seventieth birthday that he had lived
'just the seventy years which are greatest in the world's history.'

Melville had not needed the corruption of the post-Civil War era to see
through such shallow complacence. In the last stanza of his poem 'Commemorative of a Naval Victory,' he had given fuller utterance to what
it meant to be 'neither pessimist nor optimist':

> But seldom the laurel wreath is seen
> Unmixed with pensive pansies dark;

There's a light and a shadow on every man
  Who at last attains his lifted mark—
  Nursing through night the ethereal spark.
Elate he never can be;
He feels that spirits which glad had hailed his worth,
  Sleep in oblivion.—The shark
Glides white through the phosphorous sea.

The metre may break down in the seventh line, but the whole makes a sample of his verse at its best. It conveys his special perception of the unavoidable lurking terror in life.

Few voices in our eighteen-eighties had anything to say to such a man, though there is at least one evidence of affinity. In another letter to Billson he thanked him for sending Robert Buchanan's essay, 'Socrates in Camden' (1885): 'For more than one reason this piece could not but give me pleasure. Aside from its poetic quality, there is implied in it the fact that the writer has intuitively penetrated beneath the surface of certain matters here . . . The tribute to Walt Whitman has the ring of strong sincerity. As to the incidental allusion to my humble self, it is overpraise, to be sure; but I can't help that, though I am alive to the spirit that dictated it.' What Buchanan had said in the passage linking the two was: 'I sought everywhere for this Triton who is still living somewhere in New York. No one seemed•to know anything of the one great imaginative writer fit to stand shoulder to shoulder with Whitman on that continent.' But Buchanan had not really gone so far in his praise as Thomson had a decade before, when drawing the attention of Billson and others in his group to Melville. The poet had written in *The National Reformer,* which, conducted by Charles Bradlaugh, was read by the proletariat: 'I know but one other living American author who approaches him [Whitman] in his sympathy with all ordinary life and vulgar occupations, in his feeling of brotherhood for all rough workers, and at the same time in his sense of beauty and grandeur, and in his power of thought; I mean Herman Melville.'

Buchanan may have exaggerated slightly America's ignorance of Melville's continued existence, though not much, to judge from the bare notices at the time of his death. However, E. C. Stedman ('Pan in Wall Street') was acquainted with Melville, and wrote him in 1888, following some discussion regarding a possible contribution to Stedman's anthology, *Poets of America:* 'Moreover, as you said so much of Whitman, I will run the risk of showing you my chapter on him—not that it is of any great importance.' It is another commentary upon the isolation of the artist in America that Whitman and Melville, separated by only two months in the dates of their birth and by six in those of their death, both spending more of their time in the vicinity of New York than anywhere else, never came into contact. There seems to be no evidence that Whitman, after writing his light-hearted hack paragraph on *Typee* and *Omoo,* ever read Melville again; and even in Traubel's Boswellizing, which drew out the old man's memories of nearly everybody, down to the poetasters N. P. Willis and Aldrich and Stedman himself, there is no mention of the author of *Moby-Dick.*

The two might have found much in common. Although a great deal of *Moby-Dick* and *Pierre* might have been over Whitman's head, he would certainly have responded to Melville's warmth of feeling for Jack Chase, the heroic full-blooded foretopman in *White Jacket,* as well as to that book's exposure of undemocratic abuses. Moreover, he could have seen one of his chief convictions expressed in another of Melville's thumbnail sketches in *Israel Potter.* For Melville's interpretation there of Ethan Allen was that, 'though born in New England, he exhibited no trace of her character. He was frank, bluff, companionable as a Pagan, convivial, a Roman, hearty as a harvest. His spirit was essentially Western; and herein is his peculiar Americanism; for the Western spirit is, or will yet be (for no other is, or can be), the true American one.'

But even on this subject Melville diverged from Whitman—as in the preface to *John Marr and Other Sailors* (1888). He pictures Marr as an old man who has left the sea for the equal vastness of the prairies. But the sailor finds a great difference there in richness of spirit, and what he finds may make an oblique parable too of the limitations Melville felt in the bleakness of his own later years—though these were passed on East 26th Street. The pioneer settlers

were a staid people; staid through habituation to monotonous hardship; ascetics by necessity not less than through moral bias; nearly all of them sincerely, however narrowly, religious. They were kindly at need, after their fashion; but to a man wonted—as John Marr in his previous homeless sojournings could not but have been—to the free-and-easy tavern clubs affording cheap recreation of an evening in certain old and comfortable seaport towns of that time, and yet more familiar with the companionship afloat of the sailors of the same period, something was lacking. That something was geniality, the flower of life springing from some sense of joy in it.

When Marr tried to enliven a corn-husking by reciting a story of adventures at sea, 'an elderly man—a blacksmith, and at Sunday gatherings an earnest exhorter—honestly said to him, "Friend, we know nothing of that here." ' Such unresponsiveness from his fellow-men struck Marr as 'of a piece with the apathy of Nature herself as envisaged to him here on a prairie where none but the perished mound-builders had as yet left a durable mark.'

Whitman would not have admitted blank indifference in nature, still less Melville's frequent imputation of malign evil in men. The poet might have come nearest to understanding what Melville was driving at in his tragedies if he had read *Billy Budd,* which Melville, taking up fiction again after so long, dedicated 'to Jack Chase, Englishman, wherever that great heart may now be, here on Earth or harbored in Paradise.' The recrudescence of Melville's talents in the last years of his life was aided by his release from his customhouse job at the end of 1885. In addition to printing two volumes of verse, he left still a third gathered in manuscript, with epigraphs from Shakespeare ('Alms for oblivion'), from Hawthorne ('Youth is the proper, permanent, and genuine condition of man'), and, poignantly, from his own late sketch, 'Rip Van Winkle's Lilac' ('Yes, decay is often a gardener'). Among still other unprinted poems was his most sustained of all, 'The Lake,' which affirms an analogy to man's spirit in the perpetual rebirth of nature. In *Billy Budd, Foretopman,* he gave a last, coherent statement to the issues that had plagued his mind ever since the experiences of Redburn.

2. *Billy Budd, Foretopman*

'Home art gone and ta'en thy wages . . .
Quiet consummation have.'
   —marked by Melville in *Cymbeline*.

'Then in the circuit calm of one vast coil,
Its lashings charmed and malice reconciled
    . . . High in the azure steeps
Monody shall not wake the mariner.'
   —from Hart Crane's 'At Melville's Tomb.'

JUDGING from the dates on the manuscript,[1] Melville worked on this final story off and on from the fall of 1888 to the spring of 1891; and even then he did not feel that he had attained 'symmetry of form.' But though many of its pages are still unfinished, it furnishes a comprehensive restatement of the chief themes and symbols with which he had been concerned so long ago. And he had conceived the idea for a purer, more balanced tragedy than he had ever composed before.

He stated explicitly once again that his was a democratic stage, and affirmed the universality of passion in common men as well as in kings. Just as, when dealing with Ahab or with Israel Potter, he had remarked on the outer contrast between his material and Shakespeare's, so now he asserted that 'Passion, and passion in its profoundest, is not a thing demanding a palatial stage whereon to play its part. Down among the groundlings, among the beggars and rakers of the garbage, profound

1. The only edition of *Billy Budd* so far is that prepared by Raymond Weaver for *The Collected Works*, London 1924, and somewhat corrected by him in *The Shorter Novels of Herman Melville*, New York 1928. The problem of editing Melville's one extant major manuscript was an exacting one, since, in addition to the general difficulty of the novelist's handwriting, these particular pages contain many insertions by no means easy to decipher; and even the order of pagination is not always certain. It is not surprising that Weaver fell into many inaccuracies. A more thoroughly detailed study of the manuscript, which is now in the Harvard College Library, has led F. B. Freeman to undertake a new edition. By Freeman's courtesy I have had the great benefit of using this edition, which should soon be in print, and I have thus been able to adopt the true readings in two or three crucial passages quoted below. The need of making corrections both in Weaver's edition and in his biography should not cause us to forget that we are indebted to his enthusiastic and devoted pioneering for the first full-length study of Melville.

passion is enacted.' He chose for his hero a young sailor, impressed into the King's service in the latter years of the eighteenth century, shortly after the Great Mutiny at the Nore. By turning to such material Melville made clear that his thought was not bounded by a narrow nationalism, that the important thing was the inherent tragic quality, no matter where or when it was found.[2] As he said in one of the prefaces to his verse: 'It is not the purpose of literature to purvey news. For news consult the *Almanac de Gotha.*'

Billy is suggestive of Redburn in his innocence; but he is not so boyish, and not at all helpless in dealing with the other men, among whom he is very popular. He combines strength and beauty, and thereby shares in the quality of Jack Chase himself, as well as in that which Pierre inherited from his grandfather. But no more than Pierre does Billy have any wisdom of experience. Melville's conception of him is Blakean. He has not yet 'been proffered the questionable apple of knowledge.' He is illiterate, and ignorant even of who his father was, since he is a foundling, in whom, nevertheless, 'noble descent' is as evident as 'in a blood horse.' He is unself-conscious about this, as about all else, an instinctively 'upright barbarian,' a handsome image 'of young Adam before the Fall.' How dominantly Melville is thinking in Biblical terms appears when he adds that a character of such unsullied freshness seems as though it had been 'exceptionally transmitted from a period prior to Cain's city and citified man.' He had made a similar contrast between the country and the city in *Pierre;* and he had thought of unspoiled barbarism at every stage of his writing since *Typee.* Here he focuses his meaning more specifically and submits 'that, apparently going to corroborate the doctrine of man's fall, a doctrine now popularly ignored, it is observable that where certain virtues pristine and unadulterate peculiarly characterise anybody in the external uniform of civilization, they will upon scrutiny seem not to be derived from custom or convention, but rather to be out of keeping with these.'

2. Melville also refers to a similar story of a hanging for an alleged mutiny on board the U. S. brig-of-war *Somers* in 1842. Though Melville does not mention it, his cousin Guert Gansevoort was the Lieutenant on the *Somers* at that fateful time. As C. R. Anderson has suggested, in 'The Genesis of *Billy Budd*' (*American Literature,* November 1940), the retelling of 'The Mutiny on the *Somers*' in *The American Magazine* in June 1888 may very well have been what stimulated Melville to give his interpretation of the same theme.

This reflection dovetails in with many passages that struck Melville in Schopenhauer, the newly acquired volumes of whom, along with several in the Mermaid series of Elizabethan dramatists, quickened his interest most in these last years. He was impressed by Schopenhauer's frequent declaration that Christianity presents a 'significant truth in its claim that human nature is fundamentally corrupt. He also scored in *Studies in Pessimism* (1891): 'Accordingly the sole thing that reconciles me to the Old Testament is the story of the Fall. In my eyes, it is the only metaphysical truth in that book, even though it appears in the form of an allegory.' This preoccupation of Melville's with the Fall can be traced back to some of his markings in *The Marble Faun,* and even further. For he noted in *Henry V* the King's belief that the monstrous ingratitude of Cambridge and Scroop against his trust was like 'another fall of man.' He underlined likewise, in *Richard II,* the Queen's agonized question to the old gardener who had reported the evil news of her Richard's deposition:

> What Eve, what serpent, hath suggested thee
> To make a second fall of cursed man?

Melville also added there that this same thought was 'to be found in Shelley & (through him) in Byron. Also in Dryden.' As far as the last is concerned, Melville might have been thinking of *The State of Innocence, and Fall of Man,* Dryden's theatrical version of *Paradise Lost.* We shall find evidence that he was thinking of Milton directly while envisaging the tragedy of Billy Budd.

One thing to be noted is that whiteness is no longer ambiguous as it was in *Pierre,* or terrifying as in *Moby-Dick.* It has been restored its connotations of purity and innocence, such as it had in *Redburn,* such as were attributed to it more specifically when Melville remarked in *Typee* that 'white appears to be the sacred color among the Marquesans,' and when he caused the narrator of *Mardi* to be mistaken by the natives for the demigod, White Taji. The accretions and variations in Melville's symbolic handling of light and dark could form a separate essay in themselves. How ingrained a part of his imaginative process their contrast became can be judged from a single instance in those self-revelatory notes for the story about Agatha, which he sent to Hawthorne just after finishing *Pierre.* He conceived that this story of a girl who was to be deserted by her sailor husband should open with a shipwreck, and that 'it were well if some faint shadow of the preceding *calm* were thrown forth to lead the whole.' That, incidentally, is the theoretical corroboration of what had been his successful practice in *Moby-Dick*, the intensification of his dramatic effects by making them burst out of just such moments of delusive calm. The contrast between light and shade that he is cultivating here is a peculiarly subtle one, as effective as his symbolical use of the amaranth in *Pierre*. Filled with meditations, the girl reclines along the edge of a cliff, and gazes seaward.

Suddenly she catches the long shadow of the cliff cast upon the beach a hundred feet beneath her; and now she notes a shadow moving along the shadow. It is cast by a sheep from the pasture. It has advanced to the very edge of the cliff, and is sending a mild innocent glance far out upon the water. There, in strange and beautiful contrast, we have the innocence of the lamb placidly eyeing the malignity of the sea (All this having poetic reference to Agatha and her sea-lover, who is coming in the storm . . .).

This extraordinary way of presenting good and evil has not really carried us far from *Billy Budd,* where innocence is as inevitably foredoomed by black malice. Billy does not have the spiritual insight of Dostoevsky's Idiot, some share of which came to Pip in his madness. 'With little or no sharpness of faculty or any trace of the wisdom of the serpent, nor yet quite a dove, he possessed that kind and degree of intelligence going along with the unconventional rectitude of a sound human creature.' But his simplicity was completely baffled by anything equivocal; he had no knowledge of the bad, no understanding even of indirection. Honest and open hearted, he concluded everyone else to be likewise. In such an undeveloped nature the only overt flaw was a blemish in his physical perfection, a liability to a severe blockage in his speech under moments of emotional pressure. Melville deliberately recurred in this detail to his memory of 'the beautiful woman in one of Hawthorne's minor tales,' that is to say, to 'The Birthmark,' and thus resumed another element from his past. He found his hero's defect to be 'a striking instance that the archinterpreter, the envious marplot of Eden still has more or less to do with every human consignment to this planet.'

From the day when Billy was suddenly transferred by impressment from the homeward-bound merchantman *Rights-of-Man* to H.M.S. *Indomitable*—the names of the ships provide an ironic commentary on the act—he came into the sphere of Claggart, the master-at-arms, a type of character whose lineage also goes back to the beginning of Melville's experience. Melville dwells on his striking appearance, on the fact that his features were as finely cut 'as those on a Greek medallion,' except for a strangely heavy chin. His forehead 'was of the sort phrenologically associated with more than average intellect.' His silken black hair made a foil to the pallor of his face, an unnatural complexion for a sailor, and though not actually displeasing, seeming 'to hint of something defective or abnormal in the constitution and blood.' Everything in his manner and education seems incongruous with his present position as a naval chief of police and, though nothing is known of his life on shore, the sailors surmise him to be a gentleman with reasons of his own for going incognito. He is about thirty-five, nearly double Billy's age, and in character his opposite. His skill as master-at-arms is owing to his 'peculiar ferreting genius'; and as Melville probes his cold-blooded superiority, he is led to formulate its essence by way of an allusion to Plato's conception of 'natural depravity':

A definition which though savoring of Calvinism, by no means involves Calvin's dogma as to total mankind. Evidently its intent makes it applicable but to individuals. Not many are the examples of this depravity which the gallows and jail supply. At any rate, for notable instances,—since these have no vulgar alloy of the brute in them, but invariably are dominated by intellectuality,—one must go elsewhere. Civilization, especially if of the austerer sort, is auspicious to it. It folds itself in the mantle of respectability. It has its certain negative virtues serving as silent auxiliaries . . . There is a phenomenal pride in it . . .

But the thing which in eminent instances signalises so exceptional a nature is this: though the man's even temper and discreet bearing would seem to intimate a mind peculiarly subject to the law of reason, not the less in his heart [3] he would seem to riot in complete exemption from that law, having apparently little to do with reason further than to employ it as an ambidexter implement for effecting the irrational. That is to say: toward the accomplishment of an aim which in wantonness of malignity would seem to partake of the insane, he will direct a cool judgment sagacious and sound.

Melville's growing interest in this story seems to have lain in such elaboration of the types to which his characters belonged, since nearly all the longer passages of abstract analysis appear to have been added after

3. An earlier reading for 'heart' was 'soul's recesses.'

the first draft. In this formulation Claggart takes on some of the attributes of Ahab's monomania; he possesses also the controlled diabolic nature of a Chillingworth. Melville sums up his spiritual dilemma by saying that, 'apprehending the good,' Claggart was 'powerless to be it'; and though Iago is not mentioned, the two seem cast in the same mould. Melville had made an earlier sketch of this type in Bland, the subtle and insinuating master-at-arms in *White Jacket;* but a nearer likeness was Jackson, whose malevolence had so terrified Redburn. The extraordinary domination that this frail tubercular sailor had also managed to exercise over all the rest of the crew was due solely to his fiendish power of will. He was 'a Cain afloat,' with even more of contempt than hatred towards life; and as this quality burned still in his dying eyes, he seemed consumed with its infernal force.

Just as the presence of Redburn's virtue and health had served to stimulate Jackson's bitterest cruelty, so Billy affected Claggart. But Redburn had at least perceived something of what Jackson was, whereas Billy's open good-nature has not even that defense. In a passage that takes us back to a variant of his observations on the power of an Edmund and the helplessness of unaided virtue, Melville reflects that 'simple courage lacking experience and address and without any touch of defensive ugliness, is of little avail'; since such innocence 'in a moral emergency' does not 'always sharpen the faculties or enlighten the will.' In pushing farther than he had in *Redburn* his analysis of how antipathy can be called forth by harmlessness, Melville contrasted Billy's effect on Claggart with what it was on all the others. The Master of the *Rights-of-Man* had hated to lose him, since 'a virtue went out of him, sugaring the sour ones' in its tough crew. He is a natural favorite in any group, a fact that helps condition Claggart's perverse reaction. To characterize what Claggart feels, Melville has recourse to the quotation, 'Pale ire, envy, and despair,' the forces that were working in Milton's Satan as he first approached the Garden of Eden. Melville also jotted down, on the back of his manuscript, some remembered details about Spenser's Envy; [4] and in his depiction of Claggart's inextricable mixture of longing and malice, he would seem to be recurring likewise to the properties he had noted in Shakespeare's conception of this deadly sin. The necessity of elucidating Clag-

4. 'Spenser depicts her (Envy) as a ghastly hag forever chewing a venomous toad.' For Melville's view of Shakespeare's envy see above, p. 440.

gart's subtlety thus called to Melville's mind the major portrayals of evil that he knew. For all his intellectual superiority, Claggart, like Satan, is incapable of understanding the innocent heart. He cannot conceive of 'an unreciprocated malice'; and therefore coming to believe that Billy must also hate him, he is provoked into bringing about the boy's downfall by reporting him to the captain on a framed-up charge of plotting mutiny.

My account thus far of Melville's antagonists may make this work sound like a metaphysical discourse rather than a created piece of fiction. The abstract elements do break through the surface much more than they did in *Moby-Dick,* yet the characters are not merely stated, but are launched into conflict. A condensed scene brings out the ambiguous mixture of attraction and repulsion that governs Claggart's actions concerning Billy. This is one of the passages where a writer to-day would be fully aware of what may have been only latent for Melville, the sexual element in Claggart's ambivalence. Even if Melville did not have this consciously in mind, it emerges for the reader now with intense psychological accuracy.[5] The scene is where Billy at mess has just chanced, in a sudden lurch of the ship, 'to spill the entire contents of his soup-pan upon the new-scrubbed deck.'

[Claggart,] official rattan in hand, happened to be passing along the battery in a bay of which the mess was lodged, and the greasy liquid streamed just across his path. Stepping over it, he was proceeding on his way without comment, since the matter was nothing to take notice of under the circumstances, when he happened to observe who it was that had done the spilling. His countenance changed. Pausing, he was about to ejaculate something hasty at the sailor, but checked himself, and pointing down to the streaming soup, playfully tapped him from behind with his rattan, saying, in a low musical voice, peculiar to him at times, 'Handsomely done, my lad! And handsome is as handsome did it, too!' and with that passed on. Not noted by Billy as not coming within his view was the involuntary smile, or rather grimace, that accompanied Claggart's equivocal words. Aridly it drew down the thin corners of his shapely mouth.

5. E. H. Eby has remarked (*Modern Language Quarterly,* March 1940) on the extraordinary symbols of gestation that run throughout 'The Tartarus of Maids.' If, on one level, Melville was writing about the social injustices produced by the factory system, on another he was contrasting the biological burdens of women with the easy lot of the men in his companion piece, 'The Paradise of Bachelors.'

Everybody laughed as they felt bound to at a humorous remark from a superior, and Billy happily joined in. But entirely out of his observation was the fact that Claggart, as he resumed his way, 'must have momentarily worn some expression less guarded than that of the bitter smile and, usurping the face from the heart, some distorting expression perhaps, for a drummer-boy heedlessly frolicking along from the opposite direction, and chancing to come into light collision with his person, was strangely disconcerted by his aspect. Nor was the impression lessened when the official, impulsively giving him a sharp cut with the rattan, vehemently exclaimed, "Look where you go!" '

Preoccupied as Melville was throughout his career by the opposition between the generous heart and the ingrown self-consuming mind, he never made the merely facile contrast. He had presented the atheistic Jackson as 'branded on his yellow brow with some inscrutable curse; and going about corrupting and searing every heart that beat near him.' Yet he had concluded, through Redburn's own thoughts, that 'there seemed even more woe than wickedness about the man; and his wickedness seemed to spring from his woe; and for all his hideousness there was that in his eye at times that was ineffably pitiable and touching; and though there were moments when I almost hated this Jackson, yet I have pitied no man as I have pitied him.' These feelings were what kept Redburn from becoming an Ishmael. Such compassion for life, matched with the facing of evil in its fullness, makes likewise, as we have seen, the briefest description of the elements that composed Melville's tragic vision.

In Claggart again he does not portray a monster. For when the master-at-arms' 'unobserved glance happened to light on belted Billy rolling along the upper gun-deck in the leisure of the second dog-watch, exchanging passing broadsides of fun with other young promenaders in the crowd, that glance would follow the cheerful sea-Hyperion with a settled meditative and melancholy expression, his eyes strangely suffused with incipient feverish tears. Then would Claggart look like the man of sorrows. Yes, and sometimes the melancholy expression would have in it a touch of soft yearning, as if Claggart could even have loved Billy but for fate and ban.' Evanescent as that tenderness was, it shows that Claggart is not wholly diabolic, and that the felt recognition of its miserable isolation by even the warped mind partakes in the suffering of the Christ.

Thus Melville's vision tended always to be more complex than the posing of a white innocence against a very black evil. In *Moby-Dick*, and drastically in *Pierre,* the symbolical values of this contrast began so to interchange that they could not always be followed. In 'Benito Cereno' they became distinct again, but the embodiment of good in the pale Spanish captain and of evil in the mutinied African crew, though pictorially and theatrically effective, was unfortunate in raising unanswered questions. Although the Negroes were savagely vindictive and drove a terror of blackness into Cereno's heart, the fact remains that they were slaves and that evil had thus originally been done to them. Melville's failure to reckon with this fact within the limits of his narrative makes its tragedy, for all its prolonged suspense, comparatively superficial. In *Billy Budd* he has progressed far from any such arbitrary manipulation of his symbols. Furthermore, he has added another dimension through the character of Captain Vere, whose experienced and just mind puts him in contrast with both Billy and Claggart. Melville indicates how this captain, though not brilliant, is set apart from his fellow officers by 'a marked leaning toward everything intellectual,' especially for 'writers who, free from cant and convention, like Montaigne, honestly, and in the spirit of common sense, philosophise upon realities.' It reinforces our knowledge of what Melville meant by 'realities' to observe that this last phrase originally read 'upon those greatest of all mysteries, facts.'

The central scene of the drama takes place in Vere's cabin. The captain has an instinctive mistrust for Claggart, but deems it necessary to summon Billy to answer the charge just brought against him. A familiar strain of Melville's imagery asserts itself as Claggart fixes Billy with his eyes, which now become 'gelidly protruding like the alien eyes of certain uncatalogued creatures of the deep. The first mesmeric glance was one of surprised fascination; the last was as the hungry lurch of the torpedo-fish.' The unsuspecting sailor is so amazed by the suddenness of the accusation that he is speechless, seized by one of his paroxysms of stuttering. Desperate to break its spell and to assert his innocence, he strikes out, and the force of his blow over Claggart's temple is such that it not only fells him to the deck, but kills him. With a single insight Vere grasps the whole situation: 'Struck dead by an angel of God. Yet the angel must hang!' In the court-martial that he summons, he points out to his less intelligent and less rigorous officers that they must not let themselves be swayed by their feelings, that the recent great mutiny in the fleet will not permit now any swerving from the strictest discipline. He argues that they do not owe their allegiance to human nature, but to the king, that martial law can deal only with appearance, with the prisoner's deed; and he fears how appearances will affect the crew if a murderer is not executed. 'But I beseech you, my friends, do not take me amiss. I feel as you do for this unfortunate boy. But did he know our hearts, I take him to be of that generous nature that he would feel even for us on whom in this military necessity so heavy a compulsion is laid.' Yet the heart is 'the feminine in man, and hard though it be, she must here be ruled out.'

In such manner the struggle between Claggart and Billy is re-enacted on a wholly different plane within the nature of Vere himself. He has the strength of mind and the earnestness of will to dominate his instincts. He believes that in man's government, 'forms, measured forms, are everything.' But his decision to fulfil the letter of his duty is not won without anguish. He holds to it, however, and thereby Billy, who had been defenseless before the evil mind of Claggart, goes to defeat before the just mind as well. It does not occur to him to make any case at his trial. He is incapable of piecing things together, and though certain odd details that other sailors had told him about the master-at-arms now flash back into his mind, his 'erring sense of uninstructed honor' keeps him from acting what he thinks would be the part of an informer against his shipmates. So he remains silent, and puts himself entirely in his captain's hands.

The final interview between them, in which the captain communicates the death-sentence, is left shrouded by Melville as not having been witnessed by a third party. He conjectures, however, that Vere,

in the end may have developed the passion sometimes latent under an exterior stoical or indifferent. He was old enough to have been Billy's father. The austere devotee of military duty, letting himself melt back into what remains primeval in our formalized humanity, may in the end have caught Billy to his heart, even as Abraham may have caught young Isaac on the brink of resolutely offering him up in obedience to the exacting behest. But there is no telling the sacrament—seldom if in any case revealed to the gadding world—wherever, under circumstances at all akin to those here attempted to be set forth, two of great Nature's nobler order embrace.

Here the search for a father, if latent in all Melville's Ishmaels, and in all the questings of his homeless spirit for authority, is enacted in an elemental pattern. Following out the Biblical parallels that have been suggested at crucial points throughout this story, if Billy is young Adam before the Fall, and Claggart is almost the Devil incarnate, Vere is the wise Father, terribly severe but righteous. No longer does Melville feel the fear and dislike of Jehovah that were oppressing him through *Moby-Dick* and *Pierre*. He is no longer protesting against the determined laws as being savagely inexorable. He has come to respect necessity.[6]

He can therefore treat a character like Vere's with full sympathy. As the two emerge from the cabin, the captain's face is a startling revelation to the senior lieutenant, since it is transfigured for a moment with 'the agony of the strong.' In contrast Billy appears serene. He had been shocked to the roots of his being by his first experience of the existence of evil; but that tension has been relaxed by the mutual trust that he found in his captain. During his last night, when he is kept under guard on the upper gun-deck, his white jumper and duck trousers glimmer obscurely against the cannon surrounding him, 'like a patch of discolored snow in early April lingering at some upland cave's black mouth.' Other images of whiteness rise repeatedly through the final pages, as they alone can express Billy's essence.

He slept for several hours as peacefully as a child. 'Not that like children Billy was incapable of conceiving what death really is. No, but he was wholly without irrational fear of it, a fear more prevalent in highly civilized communities than those so-called barbarous ones which in all respects stand nearer to unadulterate Nature.' And it was as a barbarian that he received the ministrations of the chaplain, with a native courtesy though with no response to the awfulness of death to which the priest sought to awaken him. But this man possessed 'the good sense of a good heart,' and 'since he felt that innocence was even a better thing than religion wherewith to go to judgment, he reluctantly withdrew.' Though he realized that he could not convert Billy to dogma, he did not for all that fear for his future.

At the climax of the story, the 'fervid heart' asserts its transcendent power, in the one passage that takes on the full body of the great passages in *Moby-Dick*. At the scene of his execution,

Billy stood facing aft. At the penultimate moment, his words, his only ones, words wholly unobstructed in the utterance, were these—'God bless Captain

6. In that extremely popular nineteenth-century fantasy, Adelbert von Chamisso's *Peter Schlemihl*, which he owned in the translated edition of 1874, Melville checked the following statement and underscored its last phrase: 'Afterwards I became reconciled to myself. I learnt, in the first place, to respect necessity.'

Vere!' Syllables so unanticipated coming from one with the hemp [7] about his neck—a conventional felon's benediction directed aft toward the quarters of honor; syllables, too, delivered in the clear melody of a singing-bird on the point of launching from the twig, had a phenomenal effect, not unenhanced by the rare personal beauty of the young sailor, spiritualized now through late experiences so poignantly profound.

Without volition, as it were, as if indeed the ship's populace were the yehicles of some vocal current-electric, with one voice from alow and aloft, came a resonant sympathetic [8] echo—'God bless Captain Vere!' And yet at that instant Billy alone must have been in their hearts, even as he was in their eyes.

At the pronounced words and the spontaneous echo that voluminously rebounded them, Captain Vere, either through stoic self-control or a sort of momentary paralysis induced by emotional shock, stood erectly rigid as a musket in the ship-armorer's rack.

The hull, deliberately recovering from the periodic roll to leeward, was just regaining an even keel, when the last signal, the preconcerted dumb one, was given. At the same moment it chanced that the vapory fleece hanging low in the East, was shot through with a soft glory as of the fleece of the Lamb of God seen in mystical vision, and simultaneously therewith, watched by the wedged mass of upturned faces, Billy ascended; and ascending, took the full rose of the dawn.

In his steady handling here of his old distinctions between earthly truth and heavenly truth, between horologicals and chronometricals, Melville has gained a balance that was lacking to his angry defiance in *Pierre* and *The Confidence Man*. Vere obeys the law, yet understands the deeper reality of the spirit. Billy instinctively accepts the captain's duty, and forgives him. Melville affirms the rareness of such forgiveness by means of the double image in which the sudden raising of Billy on the halter becomes also his ascension into heaven, an identification even more complete in an earlier variant of the final clause: 'took the full Shekinah of that grand dawn,' that is to say, received the divine manifestation by which God's presence is felt by man. How carefully Melville is holding the scales, how conscious he is of the delicacy of the equilibrium he has created, is shown by the fact that the crew, swept in the moment of high tension into echoing Billy's words, reacts in the next with a murmur

7. An alternative reading: 'ignominious noose.'
8. Weaver omitted this word.

that implies a sullen revocation of their involuntary blessing, a murmur that is cut short by the command, 'Pipe down the starboard watch, boatswain, and see that they go.'

Appearances were against Billy even after his death. The only report of the event in an official naval chronicle recorded how Claggart, 'in the act of arraigning the man before the captain was vindictively stabbed to the heart by the suddenly drawn sheath-knife of Budd.' Praising the master-at-arms' fidelity to his thankless function, it reflected on 'the enormity of the crime and the extreme depravity of the criminal.' Yet one of Billy's shipmates kept his name alive in some fashion by a doggerel ballad on his tragic end. And Melville added, in a note to his manuscript, 'Here ends a story not unwarranted by what sometimes happens in this incomprehensible world of ours—Innocence and infamy, spiritual depravity and fair repute.' [9] The 'contraries' were still ever present to him, and in the pages dealing with the chaplain he broke again into what had been one of his themes in *White Jacket:* the incongruity that Christianity should lend the sanction of its presence to a battle cruiser. In his hatred of war he felt that the *Athéiste,* with which the *Indomitable* fell into engagement shortly after Billy's execution, was, 'though not so intended to be, the aptest name . . . ever given to a warship.' In that engagement Captain Vere received a mortal wound, and in his dying hours was heard to murmur the words, 'Billy Budd,' but not in 'accents of remorse.' Melville could now face incongruity; he could accept the existence of both good and evil with a calm impossible to him in *Moby-Dick*. In one of his *Battle-Pieces* he had already expressed the conclusion that

> No utter surprise can come to him
> Who reaches Shakespeare's core;
> That which we seek and shun is there—
> Man's final lore.

In creating *Lear* or *Macbeth* Shakespeare did not seek good and shun evil. He sought and shunned one and the same thing, the double-faced image of life. It is hardly too much to say that Melville's quatrain is

---

9. This note is one of the hardest passages to decipher. What I have taken to be an abbreviation for 'incomprehensible,' Weaver read as 'incongruous' and though that reading does not seem to correspond to the shapes of the letters, 'incomprehen' may be 'incompeten[t].' Weaver first printed 'infamy' as 'infirmary,' but since this was meaningless in the context, he changed it to 'infirmity' in 1928, though he then unaccountably omitted 'by what sometimes happens.' In his version 'repute' appears as 'respite.'

one of the most comprehending perceptions ever made of the essence of tragedy.

Throughout *Billy Budd* Melville gave testimony that he had grown into possession of what he had perceived in those lines. He showed too what he had meant by calling his age shallow. He knew, as he had known in *The Confidence Man,* that something more than mere worldly shrewdness was necessary for understanding such characters as those of his villain and hero. We have observed how often in his final story he reinforced himself at critical instances by Biblical allusions. His concern with both Testaments, pervasive throughout his work, now gave rise to his laconic statement that the great masters of legal policy, Coke and Blackstone, 'hardly shed so much light into obscure spiritual places as the Hebrew prophets.' Melville believed that he could probe Claggart's depravity only by means of the illumination gained in meditating on the Scriptural phrase, 'mysteries of iniquity.' And only by profound acceptance of the Gospels was he able to make his warmest affirmation of good through a common sailor's act of holy forgiveness.

At the time of Captain Vere's announcement of Billy's sentence, Melville remarked that it 'was listened to by the throng of standing sailors in a dumbness like that of a seated congregation of believers in Hell listening to their clergyman's announcement of his Calvinistic text.' At that point Melville added in the margin of his manuscript the name of Jonathan Edwards. The rectitude of Vere seems to have recalled to him the inexorable logic, the tremendous force of mind in the greatest of our theologians. Melville might also have reflected that the relentless denial of the claims of ordinary nature on which Edwards based his reasoned declaration of the absolute Sovereignty of God had left its mark on the New England character, on such emotionally starved and one-sided figures as Hawthorne drew, on the nightmare of will which a perverted determinism had become in Ahab. Without minimizing the justice of Vere's stern mind, Melville could feel that the deepest need for rapaciously individualistic America was a radical affirmation of the heart. He knew that his conception of the young sailor's 'essential innocence' was in accord with no orthodoxy; but he found it 'an irruption of heretic thought hard to suppress.'[10] The hardness was increased by his having also

10. Freeman's edition places this significant comment in its proper context for the first time. Weaver's inaccurate placing of it made it refer to the way that Christianity is distorted by a chaplain's lending its sanction to a man-of-war.

learned what Keats had, through his kindred apprehension of the meaning of Shakespeare, that the Heart is the Mind's Bible. Such knowledge was the source of the passionate humanity in Melville's own creation of tragedy.

How important it was to reaffirm the heart in the America in which *Billy Budd* was shaped can be corroborated by the search that was being made for the drift of significance in our eighteen-eighties and nineties by two of our most symptomatic minds. John Jay Chapman was already protesting against the conservative legalistic dryness that characterized our educated class, as fatal to real vitality; while Henry Adams, in assessing his heritage, knew that it tended too much towards the analytic mind, that it lacked juices. Those juices could spring only from the 'depth of tenderness,' the 'boundless sympathy' to which Adams responded in the symbol of the Virgin, but which Melville—for the phrases are his —had found in great tragedy. After all he had suffered Melville could endure to the end in the belief that though good goes to defeat and death, its radiance can redeem life. His career did not fall into what has been too often assumed to be the pattern for the lives of our artists: brilliant beginnings without staying power, truncated and broken by our hostile environment. Melville's endurance is a challenge for a later America.

N. B: ps 500 - 514 are reprinted in "C. 20 (Melvil Views", ed Richard Chase [and annotated by me there]

BOOK FOUR

✦

Whitman

⇛ XIII ⇚

ONLY A LANGUAGE EXPERIMENT

1. 'Words! book-words! what are you?'

ONE ASPECT of Whitman's work that has not yet received its due attention is outlined in *An American Primer,* notes for a lecture that he seems to have collected mainly between 1855 and 1860, using the paper covers of the unbound copies of the first edition of *Leaves of Grass* for his improvised sheets. This lecture, which, as he says, 'does not suggest the invention but describes the growth of an American English enjoying a distinct identity,' remained, like most of Whitman's lectures, undelivered and unpublished at his death. But he often talked to Traubel about it in the late eighteen-eighties, telling him that he never quite got its subject out of his mind, that he had long thought of making it into a book,[1] and adding: 'I sometimes think the *Leaves* is only a language experiment.' It will be interesting, therefore, to begin by seeing how much we can learn about Whitman just by examining his diction.

He understood that language was not 'an abstract construction' made by the learned, but that it had arisen out of the work and needs, the joys and struggles and desires of long generations of humanity, and that it had 'its bases broad and low, close to the ground.' Words were not arbitrary inventions, but the product of human events and customs, the progeny of folkways. Consequently he believed that the fresh opportunities for the English tongue in America were immense, offering themselves in the whole range of American facts. His poems, by cleaving to these facts, could thereby release 'new potentialities' of expression for our native character. When he started to develop his conviction that 'a perfect user of words uses things,' and to mention some of the things, he unconsciously dilated into the loose beats of his poetry: 'they exude in power and beauty from him—miracles from his hands—miracles from his mouth

---

1. It was issued as a separate book by Traubel in 1904.

. . . things, whirled like chain-shot rocks, defiance, compulsion, houses, iron, locomotives, the oak, the pine, the keen eye, the hairy breast, the Texan ranger, the Boston truckman, the woman that arouses a man, the man that arouses a woman.'

He there reveals the joy of the child or the primitive poet just in naming things. This was the quality in Coleridge that made Whitman speak of him as being 'like Adam in Paradise, and almost as free from artificiality' —though Whitman's own joy is far more naïve and relaxed than anything in Coleridge. Whitman's excitement carries weight because he realized that a man cannot use words so unless he has experienced the facts that they express, unless he has grasped them with his senses. This kind of realization was generally obscured in the nineteenth century, partly by its tendency to divorce education of the mind from the body and to treat language as something to be learned from a dictionary. Such division of the individual's wholeness, intensified by the specializations of a mechanized society, has become a chief cause of the neurotic strain oppressing present-day man, for whom the words that pour into him from headlines so infrequently correspond to a concrete actuality that he has touched at first hand. For Whitman it was axiomatic that the speakers of such words are merely juggling helplessly with a foreign tongue. He was already convinced by 1847—as he recorded in the earliest of his manuscript notebooks that has been preserved—that 'a man only is interested in anything when he identifies himself with it.' When he came to observe in the *Primer* that 'a perfect writer would make words sing, dance, kiss . . . or do any thing that man or woman or the natural powers can do,' he believed that such a writer must have realized the full resources of his physical life, and have been immersed in the evolving social experience of his own time.

Thus instinctively, if crudely, he reached the conviction that 'only the greatest user of words himself fully enjoys and understands himself,' a conviction surprisingly close to Eliot's, that Racine and Baudelaire, the two chief French 'masters of diction are also the greatest two psychologists' among French poets. Whitman thought that all the talk in Racine was 'on stilts,' and his sole mention of Baudelaire was to quote one of the few beliefs they shared, 'The immoderate taste for beauty and art leads men into monstrous excesses.' Noting that *Les Fleurs du Mal* appeared only two years after *Leaves of Grass,* Eliot has asked whether any age could have produced 'more heterogeneous leaves and flowers?'

WALT WHITMAN, BY MATTHEW BRADY

But his pronouncement that there was for Whitman 'no chasm between the real and the ideal, such as opened before the horrified eyes of Baudelaire,' did not blind him 'to Whitman's prodigious faculty 'in making America as it was . . . into something grand and significant,' 'of transmuting the real into an ideal.'

Feeling that he had discovered the real America that had been hidden behind the diction of a superficial culture which hardly touched native life, Whitman exclaimed with delight: 'Monongahela—it rolls with venison richness upon the palate.' He pursued the subject of how 'words become vitaliz'd, and stand for things' in an essay in his late *November Boughs* called 'Slang in America' (1885). He grasped there the truth that language is the 'universal absorber and combiner,' the best index we have to the history of civilization. In the *Primer* his cognizance that English had assimilated contributions from every stock, that it had become an amalgamation from all races, rejecting none, had led him to declare that he would never allude to this tongue 'without exultation.' In the few pages of his printed essay there is more exultation than clarity, particularly in his conception of slang. His starting point is straightforward enough, the statement that 'slang, profoundly consider'd, is the lawless germinal element, below all words and sentences, and behind all poetry, and proves a certain perennial rankness and protestantism in speech.' But when he equates slang with 'indirection, an attempt of common humanity to escape from bald literalism, and express itself illimitably,' we are reminded of Emerson's use of the term 'indirection' and need recourse to other passages in Whitman for the elusive connotations that he associated with this word.

When he said in his 1855 preface that the expression of the American poet was to be 'transcendent and new,' 'indirect and not direct or descriptive or epic,' he had just been enumerating the kinds of things the poet must incarnate if he was to be commensurate with his people: the continent's geography and history, the fluid movement of the population, the life of its factories and commerce and of the southern plantations. He appears to have thought that the expression of this surging newness must be 'indirect' in the sense that it could not find its voice through any of the conventional modes, but must wait for the poet who 'sees the solid and beautiful forms of the future where there are now no solid forms.' [2]

2. The explicit connection that Whitman made between 'indirection' and his use of symbols is dealt with at p. 575.

Here Whitman's belief in the way in which the organic style is called into being is seen to converge with his similar understanding of the origin of words. He might have had in mind either or both in his account of the creative process, in another early notebook: 'All truths lie waiting in all things.—They neither urge the opening of themselves nor resist it. For their birth you need not the obstetric forceps of the surgeon. They unfold to you and emit themselves more fragrant than roses from living buds, whenever you fetch the spring sunshine moistened with summer rain.—But it must be in yourself.—It shall come from your soul.—It shall be love.'

Living speech could come to a man only through his absorption in the life surrounding him. He must learn that the final decisions of language are not made by dictionary makers but 'by the masses, people nearest the concrete, having most to do with actual land and sea.' By such a route, illogical as it may be, Whitman came to think of slang as indirection, as the power to embody in a vibrant word or phrase 'the deep silent mysterious never to be examined, never to be told quality of life itself.' When he tried to make his meaning plainer by giving examples of how many 'of the oldest and solidest words we use, were originally generated from the daring and license of slang,' he showed that what he was really thinking of was something very like Emerson's first proposition about language—that words are signs of natural facts.[3] Whitman's examples are almost identical with those in *Nature:* 'Thus the term *right* means literally only straight. *Wrong* primarily meant twisted, distorted. *Integrity* meant oneness. *Spirit* meant breath, or flame. A *supercilious* person was one who rais'd his eyebrows. To *insult* was to leap against. If you *influenc'd* a man, you but flow'd into him.' Moreover, as Whitman continued, he expanded into Emerson's next proposition—that natural facts are symbols of spiritual facts—by launching from the word 'prophesy' into an enunciation of the transcendental view of the poet: 'The Hebrew word which is translated *prophesy* meant to bubble up and pour forth as a fountain. The enthusiast bubbles up from the Spirit of God within him, and it pours forth from him like a fountain. The word prophecy is misunderstood. Many suppose that it is limited to mere prediction; that is but the lesser portion of prophecy. The greater work is to reveal God. Every true religious enthusiast is a prophet.'

3. See 'The Word One with the Thing,' pp. 30-44 above.

In such a passage you come up against one of the most confusing aspects of Whitman, the easy-hearted way he could shuttle back and forth from materialism to idealism without troubling himself about any inconsistency. Thinking of *Children of Adam* or of what Lawrence cared for in Whitman, 'the sheer appreciation of the instant moment, life surging itself at its very wellhead,' we tend to deny that his bond with transcendentalism could have been strong. But it is significant that his earliest quotation from one of Emerson's 'inimitable lectures,' in a notice for *The Brooklyn Eagle* in 1847, is from 'Spiritual Laws' and begins, 'When the act of reflection takes place in the mind, when we look at ourselves in the light of thought, we discover that our life is embosomed in beauty.' Whitman's response to this kind of idealism was more than fleeting, as we may judge from his marginal note on an unidentified essay on 'Imagination and Fact,' which Bucke dated to the early fifties. The sentence that struck the poet reads: 'The mountains, rivers, forests and the elements that gird them round about would be only blank conditions of matter if the mind did not fling its own divinity around them.' Whitman commented: 'This I think is one of the most indicative sentences I ever read.'

The idealistic strain also runs through his conception of language. Although he asks in his 'Song of the Banner at Daybreak':

> Words! book-words! what are you?

and affirms in 'A Song of the Rolling Earth':

> The substantial words are in the ground and sea,

nevertheless he proclaims on the first page of his *Primer*: 'All words are spiritual—nothing is more spiritual than words.' This is the Whitman who could say, 'The words of my book nothing, the drift of it every thing,' the Whitman so concerned with the idea rather than the form that he could take flight into the vaguest undifferentiated generalizations about 'Democracy, ma femme,' or could write on occasion even of 'the body electric' with no sensuous touch of his material:

> O for you whoever you are your correlative body! O it, more than all else,
>   you delighting!

This is the Whitman who has seemed to linguists as though he was trying to get beyond the limits of language altogether. In the view of Sapir, subscribed to by Ogden and Richards, he sometimes is moving so entirely in terms of abstractions that he appears to be 'striving for a generalized art language, a literary algebra.' In this quality of his work Sapir regarded him as an extreme example of the transcendental drift, an artist whose 'expression is frequently strained, it sounds at times like a translation from an unknown original—which, indeed, is precisely what it is.' We recall that Emerson's most idealized passages of verse struck Chapman in much the same way.

Emerson

Thus Whitman seems to show the very dichotomy between the material and the ideal, the concrete and the abstract that we observed in Emerson's remarks on language. Nevertheless, when we look at their poems, it is obvious that Whitman often bridged the gap in a way that Emerson could not. The whole question of the relation of Whitman's theory and practice of art to Emerson's is fascinating, since, starting so often from similar if not identical positions, they end up with very different results. The extent of Emerson's influence has been obscured by Whitman's desire in his old age not to appear to have been too indebted to anyone. In his open letter to Emerson, which appeared in the second (1856) edition, though not subsequently, Whitman did not hesitate to address him as 'Master.' Speaking of 'that new moral American continent without which, I see, the physical continent remained incomplete,' he said: 'Those shores you found. I say you have led the States there—have led me there.' Long afterwards he told his disciples that he was referring to the experience of having read Emerson after receiving his tribute to the first edition of the *Leaves*, but a more likely account would seem to be the one he gave to J. T. Trowbridge. In this version, based on a conversation in 1860—though not printed until after Whitman's death—the poet 'freely admitted that he could never have written his poems if he had not first "come to himself," and that Emerson helped him to "find himself." I asked him if he thought he would have come to himself without that help. He said, "Yes, but it would have taken longer." ' Here Whitman dated the fecund reading to the summer of 1854 when he had been working at his trade of carpenter and had carried a book with him in his lunch pail. One day it 'chanced to be a volume of Emerson; and from that time he took with him no other writer.' As we know, he had been at least acquainted with Emerson's ideas for some years before that, and their working in him may well have been a slower fermentation. He gave his own characteristic expression to the process: 'I was simmering, simmering, simmering; Emerson brought me to a boil.'

It is not hard to find, for what they are worth, passages in Whitman running parallel to most of Emerson's major convictions about the nature of art. But it would always be salutary to head them with these two from 'Self-Reliance' and 'Song of Myself': 'Suppose you should contradict yourself; what then? . . . With consistency a great soul has simply nothing to do'; and

> Do I contradict myself?
> Very well then I contradict myself,
> (I am large, I contain multitudes.)

At the end of a long paragraph of appreciation of Emerson that Bucke places around eighteen-fifty, Whitman had already observed that 'there is hardly a proposition in Emerson's poems or prose which you cannot find the opposite of in some other place.' Nevertheless, the main contours of Emerson's doctrine of expression, as we have seen it develop, are unmistakable, and unmistakably Whitman's as well. They can both compress it into headlines: Emerson, 'By God, it is in me, and must come forth of me'; Whitman, 'Walt you contain enough, why don't you let it out then?' Again, whole essays of Emerson's, notably that on 'The Poet,' speak eloquently about the very things from which Whitman made his poetry.[4] The two share the same view of the poet as inspired seer, of his dependence for his utterance upon his moments of inner illumination. Yet looking back over forty years, though Whitman reaffirmed that his last word would be 'loyal, loyal,' he admitted that Emerson's work had latterly seemed to him 'pretty thin,' 'always a *make,* never an unconscious *growth,*' and 'some ways short of earth.'

Whitman's language is more earthy because he was aware, in a way that distinguished him not merely from Emerson but from every other writer of the day, of the power of sex. In affirming natural passion to be 'the enclosing basis of everything,' he spoke of its sanity, of the sacredness of the human body, using specifically religious terms: 'we were all lost without redemption, except we retain the sexual fibre of things.' In defending his insistence on this element in his poems (1856), he made clear his understanding of its immediate bearing upon a living speech: 'To the lack of an avowed, empowered, unabashed development of sex

4. See above, p. 29.

(the only salvation for the same), and to the fact of speakers and writers fraudulently assuming as always dead what every one knows to be always alive, is attributable the remarkable non-personality and indistinctness of modern productions in books.' Continuing in this vein he made almost the same observations about conventional society as were later to be expressed by Henry Adams, who, incidentally, found Whitman to be the only American writer who had drawn upon the dynamic force of sex 'as every classic had always done.' Both were agreed, though the phrasing here is Whitman's, that particularly among the so-called cultivated class the neuter gender prevailed, and that 'if the dresses were changed, the men might easily pass for women and the women for men.'

Emerson never gave up deploring the want of male principle in our literature, but one reason why it remained remote from his own pages is contained in his pronouncement (1834): 'I believe in the existence of the material world as the expression of the spiritual or real.' The continuation of his thought reveals the difference of his emphasis from that of the poet of 'Crossing Brooklyn Ferry': 'and so look with a quite comic and condescending interest upon the show of Broadway with the air of an old gentleman when he says, "Sir, I knew your father." Is it not forever the aim and endeavor of the real to embody itself in the phenomenal?' No matter how happily inconsistent Emerson might be on other matters, this basic position of the idealist was one from which he never departed. Whitman was far less consistent in his consideration of the relation between body and soul. He was impressed by a line of John Sterling's, which was also a favorite of Emerson's, 'Still lives the song tho' Regnar dies.' Whitman added this gloss to it: 'The word is become flesh.' Just what he implied in talking about language as incarnation, and how he diverged from Emerson, can be followed most briefly in his own words.

In the manuscript draft for the opening section of 'Song of Myself,' he announced the equalitarian inclusiveness that was destined always to be part of his desire:

> And I say that the soul is not greater than the body,
> And I say that the body is not greater than the soul.

However, that arbitrary equilibrium between the two is far less characteristic of his accents of most intimate discovery than his exultant reckless feeling in *Children of Adam* that the body 'includes and is the soul,'

And if the body were not the soul, what is the soul?

But in different moods, as in 'A Song of Joys,' he veers towards the other pole and seems loosely to approximate Blake in saying that the real life of his senses transcends his senses and flesh, that it is not his material eyes that finally see, or his material body that finally loves. However, he does not pursue this strain very long, and says more usually that the soul achieves its 'identity' through the act of observing, loving, and absorbing concrete objects:

We realize the soul only by you, you faithful solids and fluids.

This particular kind of material ideality, suggestive in general of Fichte's, remains his dominant thought, so it is worth observing how he formulated it in one of his notebooks: 'Most writers have disclaimed the physical world and they have not over-estimated the other, or soul, but have under-estimated the corporeal. How shall my eye separate the beauty of the blossoming buckwheat field from the stalks and heads of tangible matter? How shall I know what the life is except as I see it in the flesh? I will not praise one without the other or any more than the other.'

In commenting on the mixture of his heritage, Whitman once remarked that 'like the Quakers, the Dutch are very practical and materialistic . . . but are terribly transcendental and cloudy too.' That mixture confronts and tantalizes you throughout his poetry. He is at his firmest when he says that 'imagination and actuality must be united.' But in spite of his enthusiasm for the natural sciences as well as for every other manifestation of progress, he never came very close to a scientific realism. When he enunciated, in the eighteenth-seventies, that 'body and mind are one,' he had then been led into this thought by his reading of—or about— the German metaphysicians. And he declared that 'only Hegel is fit for America,' since in his system 'the human soul stands in the centre, and all the universes minister to it.' Following the Civil War, and increasingly *Spiritual* during the last twenty years of his life, he kept saying that in his *Leaves,* 'One deep purpose underlay the others—and that has been the religious purpose.' He often posed variants of the question, 'If the spiritual is not behind the material, to what purpose is the material?' Yet, even then, his most natural way of reconciling the dichotomy between the two elements, 'fused though antagonistic,' was to reaffirm his earlier analogy: 'The Soul of the Universe is the Male and genital master and the im-

pregnating and animating spirit—Physical matter is Female and Mother
and waits . . .'

No arrangement or rearrangement of Whitman's thoughts on this or
any other subject can resolve the paradoxes or discover in them a fully
coherent pattern. He was incapable of sustained logic, but that should
not blind the reader into impatient rejection of the ebb and flow of his
antitheses. They possess a loose dialectic of their own, and a clue of how
to find it is provided by Engels' discussion of Feuerbach: 'One knows
that these antitheses have only a relative validity; that that which
is recognized now as true has also its latent false side which will later
manifest itself, just as that which is now regarded as false has also its
true side by virtue of which it could previously have been regarded as
true.' Whitman's ability to make a synthesis in his poems of the contrasting elements that he calls body and soul may serve as a measure of his
stature as a poet. When his words adhere to concrete experience and yet
are bathed in imagination, his statements become broadly representative
of humanity:

> I am she who adorn'd herself and folded her hair expectantly,
> My truant lover has come, and it is dark.

When he fails to make that synthesis, his language can break into the
extremes noted by Emerson when he called it 'a remarkable mixture of
the *Bhagvat-Geeta* and the *New York Herald.*' The incongruous lengths
to which Whitman was frequently carried in each direction shows how
hard a task he undertook. On the one hand, his desire to grasp American
facts could lead him beyond slang into the rawest jargon, the journalese
of the day. On the other, his attempts to pass beyond the restrictions of
language into the atmosphere it could suggest often produced only the
barest formulas. His inordinate and grotesque failures in both directions
throw into clearer light his rare successes, and the fusion upon which
they depend.

The slang that he relished as providing more fun than 'the books of
all "the American humorists" ' was what he heard in the ordinary talk of
'a gang of laborers, rail-road men, miners, drivers, or boatmen,' in their
tendency 'to approach a meaning not directly and squarely' but by the
circuitous routes of lively fancy. This tendency expressed itself in their
fondness for nicknames like Old Hickory, or Wolverines, or Suckers,
or Buckeyes. Their inventiveness had sowed the frontier with many a

Shirttail Bend and Toenail Lake. Current evasions of the literal transformed a horsecar conductor into a 'snatcher,' straight whisky into 'barefoot,' and codfish balls into 'sleeve buttons.' But even though Whitman
held such slang to be the source of all that was poetical in human
utterance, he was aware that its fermentation was often hasty and
frothy, and, except for occasional friendly regional epithets like Hoosiers
or Kanucks, he used it only sparingly in his poems. Indeed, in some
notes during the period of the gestation of his first *Leaves,* he ad-
vised himself to use 'common idioms and phrases—Yankeeisms and vulgarisms—cant expressions, when very pat only.' In consequence, the
diction of his poetry is seldom as unconventional as that in the advice
he gave himself for an essay on contemporary writing: 'Bring in a sock-
dolager on the Dickens-fawners.' He gave examples of 'fierce words' in
the *Primer*—'skulk,' 'shyster,' 'doughface,' 'mean cuss,' 'backslider,' 'lick-
spittle'—and sometimes cut loose in the talk that Traubel reported. But
only on the rare occasions when he felt scorn did he introduce into his
poems any expressions as savagely untrammelled as

> This now is too lamentable a face for a man,
> Some abject louse asking leave to be, cringing for it,
> Some milk-nosed maggot blessing what lets it wrig to its hole.

By contrast his most characteristic colloquialisms are easy and relaxed,
as when he said 'howdy' to Traubel and told him that he felt 'flirty' or
'hunkydory,' or fell into slang with no self-consciousness, but with the
careless aplomb of a man speaking the language most natural to him:

> I reckon I am their boss, and they make me a pet besides.

> And will go gallivant with the light and air myself.

> Shoulder your duds, dear son, and I will mine.

> Earth! you seem to look for something at my hands,
> Say, old top-knot, what do you want?

One of Whitman's demands in the *Primer* was that words should be
brought into literature from factories and farms and trades, for he knew
that 'around the markets, among the fish-smacks, along the wharves,
you hear a thousand words, never yet printed in the repertoire of any
lexicon.' What resulted was sometimes as mechanical as the long lists in

'A Song for Occupations,' but his resolve for inclusiveness also produced dozens of snap-shot impressions as accurate as

The butcher-boy puts off his killing-clothes, or sharpens his knife at the stall
    in the market,
I loiter enjoying his repartee and his shuffle and break-down.

Watching men in action called out of him some of his most fluid phrases, which seem to bathe and surround the objects they describe—as this, of the blacksmiths:

The *lithe sheer* of their waists plays even with their massive arms.

Or this,

The negro holds firmly the reins of his four horses, the block *swags under-
    neath* on its tied-over chain.

Or a line that is itself a description of the very process by which he enfolds such movement:

In me the caresser of life wherever moving, backward as well as forward
    sluing.

At times he produced suggestive coinages of his own:

The blab of the pave, tires of carts, sluff of boot-soles, talk of the promenaders.

Yet he is making various approaches to language even in that one line. 'Blab' and 'sluff' have risen from his desire to suggest actual sounds, but 'promenaders,' which also sounds well, has clearly been employed for that reason alone since it does not belong to the talk of any American folk. 'Pave' instead of 'pavement' is the kind of bastard word that, to use another, Whitman liked to 'promulge.' Sometimes it is hard to tell whether such words sprang from intention or ignorance, particularly in view of the appearance of 'semitic' in place of 'seminal' ('semitic muscle,' 'semitic milk') in both the 1855 preface and the first printing of 'A Woman Waits for Me.' Most frequently his hybrids take the form of the free substitution of one part of speech for another—sometimes quite effectively ('the soothe of the waves'), sometimes less so (she that 'birth'd him').

Although it has been estimated that Whitman had a vocabulary of more than thirteen thousand words, of which slightly over half were used by him only once,[5] the number of his authentic coinages is not very large. Probably the largest group is composed of his agent-nouns, which is not surprising for a poet who was so occupied with types and classes of men and women. Unfortunately these also furnish some of the ugliest-sounding words in his pages, 'originatress,' 'revoltress,' 'dispensatress,' which have hardly been surpassed even in the age of the realtor and the beautician. He was luckier with an occasional abstract noun like 'presidentiad,' though this is offset by a needless monstrosity like 'savantism.' The one kind of coinage where his ear was listening sensitively is in such compounds as 'the transparent green-shine' of the water around the naked swimmer in 'I Sing the Body Electric,' or that evoking the apples hanging 'indolent-ripe' in 'Halcyon Days.'

His belief in the need to speak not merely for Americans but for the workers of all lands seems to have given the impetus for his odd habit of introducing random words from other languages, to the point of talking about 'the ouvrier class'! He took from the Italian chiefly the terms of the opera, also 'viva,' 'romanza,' and even 'ambulanza.' From the Spanish he was pleased to borrow the orotund way of naming his countrymen 'Americanos,' while the occasional circulation of Mexican dollars in the States during the eighteen-forties may have given him his word 'Libertad.' His favorite 'camerado,' an archaic English version of the Spanish 'camarada,' seems most likely to have come to him from the pages of the Waverley novels, of which he had been an enthusiastic reader in his youth. But the smattering of French which he picked up on his trip to New Orleans, and which constituted the most extensive knowledge that he ever was to have of another tongue, furnished him with the majority of his borrowings. It allowed him to talk of his 'amour' and his 'eleves,' of a 'soiree' or an 'accoucheur,' of 'trottoirs' and 'feuillage' and 'delicatesse'; to say that his were not 'the songs of an ennuyeed person,' or to shout, 'Allons! from all formules! . . . Allons! the road is before us!' Frequently he was speaking no language, as when he proclaimed himself 'no dainty dolce affetuoso.' But he could go much farther than that into a foreign

5. The reported figures, 13,447 and 6,978, are those of W. H. Trimble's unpublished concordance. The most useful work that has been done on Whitman's diction are several articles by Louise Pound, particularly 'Walt Whitman's Neologisms' (*American Mercury,* February 1925) and 'Walt Whitman and the French Language' (*American Speech,* May 1926).

jargon in his desire to 'eclaircise the myths Asiatic' in his 'Passage to India,' or to fulfil 'the rapt promises and luminè of seers.' He could address God, with ecstatic and monumental tastelessness, as 'thou reservoir.'

Many of these are samples of the confused American effort to <u>talk big</u> <u>by using high-sounding terms with only the vaguest notion of their</u> <u>original meaning.</u> The resultant fantastic transformations have enlivened every stage of our history, from the frontiersman's determination to twist his tongue around the syllables of the French settlement at Chemincouvert, Ark., which ended up with the name being turned into Smackover, down to Ring Lardner's dumb nurse who thought people were calling her 'a mormon or something.' In Whitman's case, the fact that he was a reader and so could depend upon letters as well as upon sounds overheard kept him from drifting to such gorgeous lengths. His transformations retain some battered semblance of the original word, which, with the happy pride of the half-educated in the learned term, he then deployed grandly for purposes of his own. Often the attraction for him in the French words ran counter to the identification he usually desired between the word and the thing, since it sprang from intoxication with the mere sound. You can observe the same tendency in some of the jotted lists of his notebooks, 'Cantaloupe. Muskmelon. Cantabile. Cacique City,' or in his shaping such a generalized description of the earth as 'O vast rondure swimming in space.' When caught up by the desire to include the whole universe in his embrace, he could be swept far into the intense inane, chanting in 'Night on the Prairies' of 'immortality and peace':

How plenteous! how spiritual! how resumé!

The two diverging strains in his use of language were with him to the end, for he never outgrew his tendency to lapse from specific images into undifferentiated and lifeless abstractions, as in the closing phrase of this description of his grandfather: 'jovial, red, stout, with sonorous voice and characteristic physiognomy.' In some of his latest poems, *Sands at Seventy,* he could still be satisfied with the merest rhetoric:

Of ye, O God, Life, Nature, Freedom, Poetry.

In his fondness for all his *Leaves,* he seems never to have perceived what we can note in the two halves of a single line,

I concentrate toward them that are nigh, I wait on the door slab,

—the contrast between the clumsy stilted opening and the simple close. The total pattern of his speech is, therefore, difficult to chart, since it is formed both by the improviser's carelessness about words and by the kind of attention to them indicated in his telling Burroughs that he had been 'searching for twenty-five years for the word to express what the twilight note of the robin meant to him.' He also engaged in endless minute revisions of his poems, the purpose of which is often baffling. Although sometimes serving to fuse the syllables into an ampler rhythm, as in the transformation of

Out of the rocked cradle

into one of his most memorable opening lines; they seem almost as likely to add up to nothing more than the dozens of minor substitutions in 'Salut au Monde,' which leave it the flat and formless catalogue that it was in the beginning.

In a warm appreciation of Burns in *November Boughs,* Whitman said that 'his brightest hit is his use of the Scotch patois, so full of terms flavor'd like wild fruits or berries.' Thinking not only of Burns he relished a special charm in 'the very neglect, unfinish, careless nudity,' which were not to be found in more polished language and verse. But his suggested comparison between the Scotch poet and himself would bring out at once the important difference that Whitman is not using anything like a folk-speech. Indeed, his phrasing is generally remote from any customary locutions of the sort that he jotted down as notes for one un-written poem. This was to have been based on a free rendering of local native calls, such as 'Here goes your fine fat oysters—Rock Point oysters— here they go.' When put beside such natural words and cadences, Whitman's usual diction is clearly not that of a countryman but of what he called himself, 'a jour printer.' In its curious amalgamation of homely and simple usage with half-remembered terms he read once somewhere, and with casual inventions of the moment, he often gives the impression of using a language not quite his own. In his determination to strike up for a new world, he deliberately rid himself of foreign models. But, so far as his speech is concerned, this was only very partially possible, and consequently Whitman reveals the peculiarly American combination of a childish freshness with a mechanical and desiccated repetition of book terms that had had significance for the more complex civilization in which they had had their roots and growth. The freshness has come, as it did to Huck Finn, through instinctive rejection of the authority of those terms, in Whitman's reaction against what he called Emerson's cold intellectuality: 'Suppose his books becoming absorb'd, the permanent chyle of American general and particular character—what a well-wash'd and grammatical, but bloodless and helpless race we should turn out!'

Yet the broken chrysalis of the old restrictions still hangs about Whitman. Every page betrays that his language is deeply ingrained with the educational habits of a middle-class people who put a fierce emphasis on the importance of the written word. His speech did not spring primarily from contact with the soil, for though his father was a descendant of Long Island farmers, he was also a citizen of the age of reason, an acquaintance and admirer of Tom Paine. Nor did Whitman himself develop his diction as Thoreau did, by the slow absorption through every pore of the folkways of a single spot of earth. He was attracted by the wider sweep of the city, and though his language is a natural product, it is the natural product of a Brooklyn journalist of the eighteen-forties who had previously been a country schoolteacher and a carpenter's helper, and who had finally felt an irresistible impulse to be a poet.

2. Vision and Attitude

'The hum of your valvèd voice'

WRITING about the American language as he had studied it at the time when Whitman should still have been a schoolboy but was actually a printer's assistant, Tocqueville gave several cogent reasons for the ways in which democracy had modified the English tongue. Disturbed by the barbarism of pseudo-learned coinages, he reflected that 'men living in democratic countries know but little of the language which was spoken at Athens or Rome, and they do not care to dive into the lore of antiquity to find the expression which they want. If they have sometimes recourse to learned etymologies, vanity will induce them to search for roots from the dead languages; but erudition does not naturally furnish them its resources. The most ignorant, it sometimes happens, will use them most.' There could hardly be a suaver shudder at such monstrosities then extant as 'homologize,' 'doxologize,' 'questionize,' 'compromit,' or 'happify.'

The quality that makes Tocqueville's book the most penetrating study of our society ever to have been written by a European, beside which Bryce's *American Commonwealth* seems merely competent, is his rare ability to ground philosophic generalizations on trenchantly observed and representative facts. This double gift empowered him to come to some of the root causes of Whitman's curiously blurred diction. The Frenchman discerned that 'the most common expedient employed by democratic nations to make an innovation in language consists in giving an unwonted meaning to an expression already in use.' He deplored the carelessness and ignorance behind these deviations, and the resulting inexactitude and ambiguity, since he held that 'without clear phraseology there is no good language.' But he also recognized the inextricable connection of the American tendencies with a characteristic merit and defect of a democratic people, its great, often inordinate liking for general ideas. As he developed this thought, Tocqueville might almost have been annotating some of Whitman's passages in advance:

Democratic nations are passionately addicted to generic terms and abstract expressions, because these modes of speech enlarge thought, and assist the operations of the mind by enabling it to include many objects in a small compass. A democratic writer will be apt to speak of *capacities* in the abstract for *men of capacity,* and without specifying the objects to which their capacity is applied: he will talk about *actualities* to designate in one word the things passing before his eyes at the moment; and, in French, he will comprehend under the term *éventualités* whatever may happen in the universe, dating from the moment at which he speaks.

You need hardly exercise invention to conceive Whitman kindling to this very word for an 'Orbic Chant for All Eventualitès,' since he would have remained unperturbed by Tocqueville's conclusion that these abstract terms 'which are used on every occasion without attaching them to any particular fact, enlarge and obscure the thoughts they are intended to convey; they render the mode of speech more succinct, and the idea contained in it less clear. But with regard to language, democratic nations prefer obscurity to labor.'

Whitman's indolence was among his chief resources in escaping from the nervous tensions of American life. But it also caused him complacently to ignore the implications of some of his very foolish statements, such as that the Old World 'is the region of the poetry of concrete and real things,' the New World 'is the region of the future, and its poetry must be spiritual and democratic.' He generally remembered to make his counterstatement that 'out from the well-tended concrete and the physical—and in them and from them only—radiate the spiritual and heroic.' But for anyone who took the function of thought seriously, great danger lay in undefined terms, each of which, in Tocqueville's analogy was 'like a box with a false bottom; you may put in it what ideas you please, and take them out again without being observed.' In Melville's case, as we have seen, the uncertainty that accrued to him from his age's unexamined and shifting repetition of the very words 'spiritual' and 'democratic' became one of the most disturbing ambiguities.

Tocqueville, with aristocratic bias, found the American habit of moving with one step from the individual to the broadest and vaguest universal to be owing to the lack of gradations and distinctions in society. His fear was not that democratic poetry would cling too close to trivial details or fly too near the ground, but rather that it would 'be forever losing itself in the clouds,' and that 'surcharged with immense and incoherent imagery,' it would 'range at last to purely imaginary regions.' The kind of result he dreaded was enthusiastically celebrated by Whitman:

> I will not make poems with reference to parts,
> But I will make poems, songs, thoughts, with reference to ensemble.

According to Tocqueville, 'American writers and orators often use an inflated style' because of a dilemma peculiar to democratic communities, where 'each citizen is habitually engaged in the contemplation of a very puny object, namely himself,' and where, on the occasions when he 'raises his looks higher, he perceives only the immense form of society at large, or the still more imposing aspect of mankind.' In critical consequence, 'his ideas are all either extremely minute and clear, or extremely general and vague: what lies between is a void.' Tocqueville granted, freely ignoring Bryant and being quite naturally unaware of the obscure first volumes of Poe, that the Americans had as yet no poets, though many poetic ideas.

The depth and force of imagination that could bridge the void by making the specific richly symbolic of the universal had not yet shown itself. Whitman's success in doing this, in such poems of his as did justice to both the parts and the whole, depended on the emotional attitude articulated near the opening of 'Song of Myself':

I believe in you my soul, the other I am must not abase itself to you,
And you must not be abased to the other.

Loafe with me on the grass, loose the stop from your throat,
Not words, not music or rhyme I want, not custom or lecture, not even the
  best,
Only the lull I like, the hum of your valvèd voice.

I mind how once we lay such a transparent summer morning,
How you settled your head athwart my hips and gently turn'd over upon me,
And parted the shirt from my bosom-bone, and plunged your tongue to my
  bare-stript heart,
And reach'd till you felt my beard, and reach'd till you held my feet.

Swiftly arose and spread around me the peace and knowledge that pass all
  the argument of the earth,
And I know that the hand of God is the promise of my own,
And I know that the spirit of God is the brother of my own,
And that all the men ever born are also my brothers, and the women my
  sisters and lovers,
And that a kelson of the creation is love,
And limitless are leaves stiff or drooping in the fields,
And brown ants in the little wells beneath them,
And mossy scabs of the worm fence, heap'd stones, elder, mullein and poke-
  weed.

That vision is the fullest expression of the sources from which Whitman's poetry rose, and consequently provides a central problem in appreciation. Readers with a distaste for loosely defined mysticism have plenty of grounds for objection in the way the poet's belief in divine inspiration is clothed in imagery that obscures all distinctions between body and soul by portraying the soul as merely the sexual agent. Moreover, in the passivity of the poet's body there is a quality vaguely pathological and homosexual. This is in keeping with the regressive, infantile fluidity, imaginatively polyperverse, which breaks down all mature barriers, a little further on in 'Song of Myself,' to declare that he is 'maternal as well as paternal, a child as well as a man.' Nevertheless, this fluidity of sexual sympathy made possible Whitman's fallow receptivity to life. The ability to live spontaneously on primitive levels, whose very existence was denied by the educated mind of his time, wiped out arbitrary conventions and yielded a broader experience than that of any of his contemporaries. And he did not simply exhibit pathological symptoms; he created poetry. It becomes essential therefore to scrutinize his vision [1] and the attitude towards life to which it gave rise. Such scrutiny can lead us both to his conception of the creative process, and to the reasons for his choice of themes and materials.

That he felt himself liberated by his vision into serene contemplation is manifest both in the relaxed rhythm of the lines describing the merging of body and soul, and in the firm movement of his declaration,

Swiftly arose and spread around me the peace and knowledge that pass all the argument of the earth.

The Biblical cadences are not stock rhetoric but have been rephrased into his personal accent. The shift in tense from 'arose' to the repeated 'I know' of the successive lines serves to frame the experience, to date his fuller life from its occurrence. It was an unfortunate revision that changed

And I know that the hand of God is the *elderhand* of my own.

Apparently through the desire to avoid repetition, Whitman has made his expression more standardized, and has lost something of the peculiar intimacy between the material and the ideal that was conveyed by his imaginative coinage.

It was not accidental or arbitrary that Whitman fell into mystical terms to express the birth of his inner sureness, for such terms belonged to the deepest emotional strain in his heritage, the Quaker faith of his mother's family. The obvious traces of Quakerism in the expression of his vision here may not seem many, although the sect's bare and simple separation between 'body' and 'soul' [2] may well have conditioned his way of talking about these as distinct entities, and have impelled his search for a harmony between them. Moreover, the humanitarian equality, which springs in his lines from his knowledge of peace, was a Quaker attribute

---

1. Whenever I use the word 'vision' in this section, I am referring specifically to the experience expressed in the quoted passage.

2. For a characteristic example, this account by a Quaker girl: 'One time being in meeting, and sitting very contentedly under my own vine and figtree, a call arose in my mind . . . My soul, and all within me, trembled at the hearing of it. Yea, my outward tabernacle shook.' For further material of the same sort see Rufus M. Jones, *Later Periods of Quakerism* (1921).

long before the Declaration of Independence. To be sure, Whitman's acceptance of anything so integral to the ideals of democracy can hardly be attributed to a single isolated influence, but it is remarkable how much in his make-up he himself attributed to the quietistic spirit.

He told Traubel that as 'a young fellow up on the Long Island shore' he had seriously debated whether he was not 'by spiritual bent' a Quaker; and though he granted in the next breath that *Leaves of Grass* would never have been written unless he had gone beyond that fence and looked back at the best Quaker qualities from outside, still those qualities remained part of him to the end of his life. When he wanted to describe his most stimulating relationship, he remarked how he and Emerson, when they met, were 'like two Quakers together' in their accord. He always dated his deepened perception of the meaning of suffering from his resolution to become a volunteer nurse during the Civil War—the experience that produced *Drum-Taps,* which he was the first to recognize as superior to his earlier work. In reviewing years later the grounds for this resolution, he said that he could never think of himself as firing a gun on another man, but that he had felt his 'greatest call'—and he indicated its source by adding in parentheses 'Quaker'—to go around and do what he could for the wounded and dying. The same strain persisted in many of his thoughts about his poems. From 1860 on he consistently adopted the unadorned 'third month,' 'fourth month,' etc. in place of the pagan names. He requested the publisher of his 1881 edition to have the paper and binding 'markedly plain and simple even to Quakerness.' And when he wanted to emphasize the more pervasive presence of religious poetry in his later volumes, he expressed it by saying that 'the "inner light" of the Quakers, the pure conscience' was 'rising over all the rest.'

Therefore, when we find him announcing in 1858 his plans for the further development of his book, 'the Spirit commanding it,' or declaring himself in a later note, 'lowly reverent to the voice,' these remarks, which might be stock utterances of romanticism, may be attributed to a more specific frame of reference. It is also notable that he outlined the meaning of 'prophecy,' in a passage on the death of Carlyle (1881), using practically the same words as he was to do in 'Slang in America,' and concluding: 'The great matter is to reveal and outpour the God-like suggestions pressing for birth in the soul. This is briefly the doctrine of the Friends or Quakers.' No matter how far Whitman's sensuality took him from anything remotely acceptable to believers in this doctrine, its presence as a shaping force in his background does much to account for his freedom from the pale cast of intellectualism that bothered him in Emerson. Quakerism had not been marked by the sharp debate over interpretation that had characterized Puritanism at every stage, or by the doctrinal development and breakdown into Unitarianism. In contrast with this intense activity of the mind, the Quakers' passivity had allowed the growth of an undisturbed depth of emotion—'the lull I like'—which could be of cardinal value to a poet whose strongest desire was to absorb the life of his time. The sympathetic kinship that Emerson felt with Quakerism in his liberated maturity had belonged to Whitman as his birthright.

The various things it meant for his development are symbolized in the figure of Elias Hicks. Writing almost sixty years after the event, Whitman could still picture the evening in 1829 when his father came home from work and said, as he threw down 'his armful of kindling-blocks with a bounce on the kitchen floor, "Come, mother, Elias preaches tonight."' Hicks, then an old man in the final months of his life, had become recognized as the leader of the liberal movement that had divided the sect after a long period of stability. Yet his 'revolt' was based simply on his extreme quietism, which, putting an even increased emphasis on the inner light as the sole agent of salvation, waived the necessity of any outward authorities or historical revelations and regarded Jesus himself as essentially human, as the perfect man. In later life Whitman was to keep Hicks' portrait always in his room, to talk about him repeatedly, and to give his failing strength in 1888 to the essay about him with which he closed *November Boughs* and which he then expected would be his final work. The reasons for Hicks' appeal to him can be summed up in his two introductory statements, that the Quaker leader had pointed 'to the fountain of all naked theology' as being 'in *yourself*,' and that he was the most democratic of all the prophets. Such attributes inevitably took on symbolic proportions for Whitman, and his appreciation of Hicks led him to the point of saying that 'above Shakespeare's plays, or Concord philosophy' there rises superior 'the intuitive blending of divine love and faith in a human emotional character—blending for all, the unlearn'd, the common, and the poor.'

The extent to which such a character had become interwoven with

Whitman's own emerging aspirations is suggested by his unforgotten impression of how Hicks' inner personality had been carried across to his audience by the magnetism of his eloquence. This impression had been greatly responsible for Whitman's early efforts to be an orator. More important still, when Whitman described the effect on the preacher of his surroundings: 'a curious, quiet yet busy life centred in a little country village on Long Island, and within sound on still nights of the mystic surf-beat of the sea,' he was virtually describing himself and the natural force that played the greatest part in conditioning his sense of rhythm.

If we turn again to Whitman's vision, it becomes apparent how many of its qualities cluster around its Quaker center. It hardly seems fanciful even to relate its looseness of expression to the Friends' ecclesiastical form-lessness, to their untrammelled freedom from sacraments. What prevented this from degenerating into mere individual license was their counter-stress on social values, on sympathy and mutual helpfulness. Whitman's mystic abandon was held in check by a similar concrete humanitarianism. And the placid benevolence that was so often the fruit of their trust in silence is as characteristic of him as his unconventionality and plainness. Even his fondness for gray clothes and for wearing his hat as he pleased, in-doors or out, were echoes of their practice. Such kinships lead us to the cardinal fact: when Whitman was describing the nature of the inner light in Hicks, and pointing out the likeness between it and Emerson's reliance on the Over-Soul, he was also giving his whole conception of the way in which the creative imagination works.

He repeatedly avowed that his poems were not productions of his con-scious intellect. Indeed, in his distrust of mere mental processes, he could go to the length of declaring, 'Intellect is a fiend.' [3] In his belief that 'the great thing is to be inspired as one divinely possessed,' he regarded his soul as distinct from his ordinary conscious personality, a conception that is reflected in his frequent habit of speaking of 'my soul and I.' He felt that his work was accomplished by submitting this everyday conscious-ness to the guidance of the same power as had given to Hicks his flow of persuasive words. In one of his notebooks he tried to describe the actual operation of this power, the way in which the inspiration for a poem rose out of a trance-like suspension of activity: 'a trance, yet with

3. I am indebted here to Clifton J. Furness, whose *Walt Whitman's Workshop: A Col-lection of Unpublished Manuscripts* (1928) throws light on every stage of Whitman's development.

all the senses alert—only a state of high exalted musing—the tangible and material with all its shows, the objective world suspended or surmounted for a while, and the powers in exaltation, freedom, vision—yet the *senses* not lost or counteracted.' The trend is similar to Wordsworth's account of his moments of mystical illumination, in which 'serene and blessed mood . . . we are laid asleep in body, and become a living soul.' In contrast, Whitman's twice repeated emphasis that the senses are 'not counteracted' marks his vision—and this is true also of the resulting poetry—as less pure, ranker, and more earthy than Wordsworth's.

Because he was thus physical, much that is most typical of Whitman is utterly foreign to Quakerism. A buoyant sense of bodily well-being was for him a necessary concomitant with inner serenity: the personality that he wanted to project in his poems was that of 'a live flush eating and drinking man.' As Mary Colum has observed, 'What was remarkable about Whitman was that he really soaked up something of all the ideas of his age.' But ideas did not come to him disembodied. The gestation of *Leaves of Grass* from 1840 to 1855 was, he said, 'not in the usual way of an author withdrawing, composing his work in a study, addressing himself to the literary formulation, consulting authorities, and the like, but in the way of first merging oneself in all the living flood and practicality and fervency of that period.' Only after such contact with all the common aspects of society was it 'just possible there comes to a man, a woman, the divine power to speak words.' Still, the inner experience remained crucial, for 'only to the rapt vision does the seen become the prophecy of the unseen.'

The attitude produced by that illumination was dominant throughout his work, and was in strong contrast to much European romanticism, to the pattern of qualities that Madame de Staël had seen in the emerging new literature, 'the sorrowful sentiment of the incompleteness of human destiny, melancholy, reverie, mysticism, the sense of the enigma of life.' That makes a fairly adequate description of what Poe had been impelled to express, and Whitman's criticism of him, not recorded until three decades after Poe's death, defines by implication his own aims. Though he admired Poe's courage in making his relentless diagnosis of what he considered to be 'this disease called humanity,' Whitman took issue with all his premises in finding him 'almost without the first sign of moral principle, or of the concrete or its heroisms, or the simpler affections of the heart.' Whitman recognized his 'intense faculty for technical and abstract beauty,' but judged him finally to belong 'among the electric lights of imaginative literature, brilliant and dazzling, but with no heat.' [4]

After idling by a pond on a bright February morning, in the kind of ramble that was so restoring to his half-paralyzed old age, Whitman wrote that the modern tendency 'to turn everything to pathos, ennui, morbidity, dissatisfaction, death' was not 'the born result' of nature at all but merely of the writers' own sick and distorted souls. What he felt 'amid this wild, free scene' was 'how healthy, how joyous, how clean and vigorous and sweet.' Such feelings made him say that 'the sanity of everything' was the atmosphere that he wanted to exude from his book. When nearly fifty he could still write to one of his Civil War comrades with unreflecting happiness: 'I sometimes think I am the particular man who enjoys the show of all these things in N. Y. more than any other mortal—as if it was all got up just for me to observe and study.' This abundant zest carried him through what would have seemed to another spirit the poverty and loneliness of the final twenty years of his life. It led him, in one of his notebooks, to date his real experiences under the heading 'Good Moments,' and gave him the porous fibre that could soak up so many diverging social and philosophic views with no worry about their incongruity.

His unwavering belief in Quaker intuition did not prevent him from feeling a strong enthusiasm, from his earliest days, for the contrasting strain of free-thinking rationalism, as voiced by Paine and Frances Wright, the latter of whom he had heard lecture when he was scarcely ten.[5] How Whitman managed to amalgamate their views with his mysti-

---

4. How far Whitman was capable of appreciating the tragic significance of Poe's career is generally forgotten: 'In a dream I once had, I saw a vessel on the sea, at midnight, in a storm. It was no great full-rigg'd ship, nor majestic steamer, steering firmly through the gale, but seem'd one of those superb little schooner yachts I had often seen lying anchor'd, rocking so jauntily, in the waters around New York, or up Long Island sound— now flying uncontroll'd with torn sails and broken spars through the wild sleet and winds and waves of the night. On the deck was a slender, slight, beautiful figure, a dim man, apparently enjoying all the terror, the murk, and the dislocation of which he was the centre and the victim. That figure of my lurid dream might stand for Edgar Poe, his spirit, his fortunes, and his poems—themselves all lurid dreams.'

5. He told Traubel that her book about Epicurus, *A Few Days in Athens* (1822), had once been daily food to him. How intimate a part of him it remained is shown by his assimilation—in his draft of notes for a poem called 'Pictures' (*c.* 1850)—of her idealized

cal tendencies can be explained only by the fact that he passed over their agnosticism in his enthusiasm for their political liberalism, for what he called their ardent belief in the 'substantial practice of radical human rights.' Their early sway over him prepared him for his whole-hearted championship of William Leggett, the left-wing Jacksonian of the eighteen-thirties, and caused him always to look for the source of valuable character not in leaders but in the bulk of the people. In this allegiance, as Arvin has demonstrated so carefully, Whitman's attitude differed again from that of most of the European apostles of romantic equality. The distinction was that Whitman did not 'espouse' the cause of the masses through any self-conscious gesture of identification. The relation was simpler and more natural, <u>for he was quite literally one of them himself.</u> As the son of a common man, as a casual worker in his own turn, he knew how the poor really lived.[6] In the fluctuating course of his political and economic opinions he is typical of the aspirations and

description of a master and his disciples. Several sentences project one of his leading conceptions of his own role:

Frances Wright	*Whitman*
A crowd of disciples were assembled, waiting the arrival of their master.	Young men, pupils, collect in the gardens of a favorite master, waiting for him,
Zeno advanced into the midst; he stood by the head and shoulders above the crowd; . . .	Till, beyond, the master appears advancing—his form shows above the crowd, a head taller than they,
His gait, erect, calm, and dignified; his features . . . seemed sculptured by the chisel for a colossal divinity: the forehead . . . was marked with the even lines of wisdom and age; but no harsh wrinkles . . .	His gait is erect, calm and dignified—his features are colossal—he is old, yet his forehead has no wrinkles,
Wisdom, undisturbable, fortitude unshakeable, self-respect . . . were in his face, his carriage and his tread.	Wisdom undisturbed, self-respect, fortitude unshaken, are in his expression, his personality.

These parallels have been noted by David Goodale, 'Some of Walt Whitman's Borrowings' (*American Literature,* May 1938).

6. An undated note describes what 'the divine average' has in millions of cases actually been: 'Did you ever think for a moment how so many young men, full of the stuff to make the noblest heroes of the earth, really live—really pass their lives, year after year, and so till death? Constant toil—ever alert to keep the wolf back from the door—no development—no rational pleasure—sleeping in some cramped dirty place—never knowing once a beautiful happy home—never knowing once in their whole lives real affection, sweetly returned, the joy, the life of life—always kept down, unaware of religion—no habitual rendezvous except the bar-room—unaware of any amusements except these preposterous theatres, and of a Sunday these and those equally preposterous and painful screamings from the pulpit.'

struggles of the working class in the America of his time. Through his confusions, his generosities and blurred enthusiasms, he advanced to an increasing awareness after the Civil War of how industrialization was radically altering the world of the small farmer and artisan he had known in his youth. He veered inevitably, though by no very coherent course, from individualism towards socialism.

He thought of himself both as the poet of the city and as the poet of nature, differing sharply in this from Wordsworth and Baudelaire. The English romantics had nearly all fled from the sordidness and squalor of the rising Coketowns, and America had reflected the tendency in Emerson's instinctive shying away to country solitude, and in Thoreau's taking his stand against further encroachments of complex mechanization. But Whitman's eager abandonment to sprawling New York in its iron age was even more remote from Baudelaire's haunted sense of the oppression of the metropolis upon the lonely individual, or from what the French poet's imagination had told him that Poe's America must have been—a barbaric immensity lit up by gas.

Whitman's confident vision led him to fulfil the most naïve and therefore most natural kind of romanticism for America, the romanticism of the future. He formulated directly what was often implicit in Emerson: 'The Poetry of other lands lies in the past—what they have been. The Poetry of America lies in the future—what These States and their coming men and women are certainly to be.' In his generalizations about the need for untrammelled expression of emotion in this new poetry, he could summon an ally no less authoritative than Sainte-Beuve, who held that 'to-day something else is wanted' than the most perfect work composed by recognized rules. 'For us the greatest poet is he who in his works most stimulates the reader's imagination and reflection, who excites him the most himself to poetize. The greatest poet is not he who has done the best; it is he who suggests the most; he, not all of whose meaning is at first obvious, and who leaves you much to desire, to explain, to study, much to complete in your turn.'

This passage, which Whitman did not quote until 1881, corresponds exactly to the doctrine of his prefaces from the start. Certain other aspects of that doctrine were foreshadowed by Tocqueville, even though he began from premises that Whitman would not have accepted. Tocqueville's logic held that the principle of equality, 'after having deprived poetry of the past, . . . robs it in part of the present.' In addition to the people's in-

stinctive distaste for anything ancient, he believed that the general simili-
tude of individuals in a democracy rendered any one of them alone an
inadequate subject for the poet. Nevertheless, an enormous vista remained open to the poet of democracy, since such nations, though they
care but little for what has been, 'are haunted by visions of what will be.'
Although the delineation of subtly differentiated characters was hardly
within his scope, the democratic poet could make a broad survey of Man
himself in the presence of nature and God, and could mingle the celebration of his future destiny with a diffuse celebration of the divine.
Tocqueville's distinction between an individual and Man accords with
Whitman's desire to project what he called 'a stock personality' that could
typify all men as his brothers. In another fragmentary note, which follows his frequent custom of generalizing his intention by putting it in
the third person, he said: 'Other writers (poets) look on a laborer as a
laborer, a poet as a poet, a President as a President, a merchant as a merchant—and so on. He looks on the President as a man, on the laborer as
a man, on the poet and all the rest, as men.' This conviction was given
fervor by the peace that he found through his vision, and so is bound up
with the last element in his resulting attitude that needs to be discussed.

It must not be forgotten how often Whitman made such a remark as
that he could not 'have written a word of the *Leaves* without its religious
root-ground.' But though he kept insisting that his 'interior and foundation quality' was 'Hebraic, Biblical, mystic,' he had gone still farther
than Emerson in throwing overboard church and dogma,[7] even the tenets
of Quakerism. The religion that remained to him was the very simplified kind of humanitarianism which can make an immediate passage
from man to God. He said that no one 'has ever yet been half devout
enough' in his worship of the sacredness of man:

Painters have painted their swarming groups and the centre-figure of all,
From the head of the centre-figure spreading a nimbus of gold-color'd light,
But I paint myriads of heads, but paint no head without its nimbus of gold-
    color'd light,
From my hand from the brain of every man and woman it streams, efful-
    gently flowing forever.

His perception of a natural halo in the spokes of sunlight that diverged

7. Emerson wrote in 1859 that 'the mind of our culture' had left Unitarianism behind.
'Nobody goes to church or longer holds the Christian traditions. We rest on the moral
nature, and the whole world shortly must.'

around the shadow of his head, or of anyone's head, as he leaned over the rail of a Brooklyn ferry, found its purest symbolical expression when he spoke, in one of his catalogues of occupations, of

the mechanic's wife with her babe at her nipple interceding for every person born.

A comparable emotional fullness, based on a stricter materialism, has been at work in many of Rivera's frescoes, as in his holy family in Detroit, where the figures are a young nurse who holds an infant in her arms while a doctor performs the circumcision. The white official cap and the infant's hair suggest the haloes, as the whole scene is handled in the light of the painter's belief in the beneficent power of science.

Whitman's reverence for Christ as his 'dear brother' was the theme of 'To Him that was Crucified.' It also provided the emotional substance for a much better poem, one of his very best, 'A Sight in Camp in the daybreak gray and dim,' which describes how, coming out of his tent, he saw three forms on stretchers under blankets, and turning back the folds of woolen from their faces, he found in that of the third

a face nor child nor old, very calm, as of beautiful yellow-white ivory;
Young man I think I know you—I think this face is the face of the Christ himself,
Dead and divine and brother of all, and here again he lies.

But when Whitman turned from contemplating the transfiguration of common humanity through sacrifice to celebrating the rare individual, the poet as prophet, he could expand into the pride that annihilates all valid distinctions between the actual and the ideal. In the midst of his pondering on man as 'how awful, how beautiful a being,' he suddenly asked: 'Why has it been taught that there is only one Supreme?' More disturbing, when he incorporated these notes for a lecture on religion into his poetry, he transferred the supremacy to himself:

The supernatural of no account, myself waiting my time to be one of the supremes,
The day getting ready for me when I shall do as much good as the best, and be as prodigious.[8]

8. The intimate union between Whitman's religious and sexual impulses can be seen once more in the immediate continuation of this passage:

By my life-lumps! becoming already a creator,
Putting myself here and now to the ambush'd womb of the shadows.

This religious assurance, unleashed from all control in dogma or creed, must be called no less than terrifying in the lengths to which it was to go in proclaiming the individual as his own Messiah. For this tendency, so mildly innocent in Emerson, so confused and bombastic in Whitman, was to result in the hardness of Nietzsche, in the violence of those characters of Dostoevsky's who have been uprooted from all tradition and find no law but themselves, in such demonic nihilism as that of Kirilov in *The Possessed*. Nietzsche, reading Emerson's *Essays* when he was thirty, found him the most fecund in thoughts of any writer of the century, and heartily subscribed to his criticism of the feeble spirit of the times and to his insistence on regeneration. But how overwhelmingly different in their contexts are the implications of 'Life is a search after power' and 'Leben ist Wille zur Macht'; or 'We have never seen a man' and 'Niemals noch gab es einen Übermenschen.' When the doctrine of the Superman was again transformed, or rather, brutally distorted, the voice of Hitler's megalomania was to be heard sounding through it.

For the course of such development Whitman is responsible only to the degree that his inordinate complacence could let him address Christ by saying, 'We few equals indifferent of lands, indifferent of times.' It is significant that a good deal of stilted rhetoric but none of his readable poetry came from that mood. Despite Whitman's willingness to speak as the prophet of all religions, affirming the fundamental lack of difference between them, and despite his propensity to ever vaster inclusions, the lines that round off the account of what his vision brought him betray something else: that the source of his real poetry was not in the grandiose or orotund but in the common and humble:

> a kelson of the creation is love
> And limitless are leaves stiff or drooping in the fields,
> And brown ants in the little wells beneath them,
> And mossy scabs of the worm fence, heap'd stones, elder, mullein and poke-
> weed.

As a conclusion to the whole passage and to its affirmation of the brotherhood of man, this may seem to trail off into an unexpectedly minor key. Yet the fact is that even though Whitman did not want to be personal,

but to write poems 'with reference to ensemble,' to make his voice that
of the general bard of democracy, the evidence of the poems themselves
shows that he was at his best, not when he was being sweeping, but when
contemplating with delicacy and tenderness some object near at hand.
He spoke once of the harvest of his work as 'a windrow-drift of weeds
and shells,' and though this favorite symbol of Emerson's may be too
fragile a description for Whitman's substance, it suggests why he chose
the smallest, if most universal, sign of nature's fertility as the title for
his book. The role played by the grass as the central symbol in 'Song of
Myself' is worth dwelling on. For it gave this poem, his earliest major
effort and by far the most important of the dozen poems that made up
his first edition, a much more consciously planned structure than it is
usually credited with. The uses of this symbol can also serve to summarize
the various implications of the poet's attitude that rose from his experience
of loafing on the summer earth.

(margin handwritten note: "Song of Myself")

He had been feeling his way to this symbol from the opening pages of
his first notebook, where he wrote: 'Bring all the art and science of the
world, and baffle and humble it with one spear of grass.' That approach
to the mystery of growing life is to be found in the romantic movement
as far back as Blake, or even in the aphorisms of Lavater. Emerson
shared in the organic conviction that each particle of matter is an immensity, each leaf a world. In his delight in the humblest natural forms,
he asked, 'What is there that is not a miracle?' Carlyle also used Whitman's very symbol by asking, near the opening of *Heroes and Hero-
Worship*, '. . . through every blade of grass, is not a God made visible?'[9]
Whitman made the range of such feeling more explicit in the easy progressions of his longest poem, from its beginning lines:

> I celebrate myself, and sing myself,
> And what I assume you shall assume,
> For every atom belonging to me as good belongs to you.

> I loafe and invite my soul,
> I lean and loafe at my ease observing a spear of summer grass.

9. The format of Whitman's first volume—planned and printed by himself—is somewhat similar to that of the then current best seller, *Fern Leaves from Fanny's Portfolio*. If
Whitman received a hint for his symbol from that unlikely source, that is another indication of his generously undiscriminating tendency to respond to every stimulus of his time,
good or bad.

That announced theme is returned to presently, to be expanded in his vision, which forms the fifth short section of the whole. (It is interesting to note that just as Keats took a special relish in writing 'plumb' for 'plum,' Whitman seems to have felt that his coined spelling of 'loafe' somehow made the experience more expressive.) The line that opens the section immediately after the vision,

> A child said *What is the grass?* fetching it to me with full hands,

gave the poet the opportunity to introduce the chief variations on his theme, which are recurred to repeatedly thereafter. His series of answers to the child starts characteristically by attributing to the grass his own qualities:

I guess it must be the flag of my disposition, out of hopeful green stuff woven.

Next he calls it 'the handkerchief of the Lord,' and then sees it as the sign of fecundity, as itself a child, 'the produced babe of the vegetation.' It is likewise a symbol of the equality among the various regions of the earth, and among the various races—'growing among black folks as among white.' Finally, it springs up as 'the beautiful uncut hair of graves,' and is a token of the cyclical progression of life, and of its triumph over death.

The theme is not expanded again to any such length, but this development of it permeates the rest of the poem and provides a substantial background of reference for each repetition. An indirect fulfilment of the symbol comes in the first of the detailed pictures in the poem, which composes the ninth section, the scene of the idyllic abundance of the haying, with the mow being packed with the fragrant dried timothy. When Whitman states, in the seventeenth section, that if his thoughts 'are not yours as much as mine they are nothing,' he concludes the paragraph with this sentence:

> This is the grass that grows wherever the land is and the water is,
> This the common air that bathes the globe.

Beyond the middle of the poem he begins a section (the thirty-first) by reaffirming,

> I believe a leaf of grass is no less than the journey-work of the stars;

and two sections later he reiterates,

> now I see it is true, what I guess'd at,
> What I guess'd when I loaf'd on the grass.

In one of the descriptions of the ideal natural man he wants to be, he delights in 'behavior lawless as snow-flakes, words simple as grass.' And in the closing section of all (the fifty-second), he sums up once more what has been everywhere latent:

> I depart as air, I shake my white locks at the runaway sun,
> I effuse my flesh in eddies, and drift it in lacy jags.

> I bequeath myself to the dirt to grow from the grass I love,
> If you want me again look for me under your boot-soles.

He thus suggests how all the things that he is, equalitarian democrat, sensualist, transcendental optimist, mystic, and pagan, are dissolving into the elements, into light, air, cloud, and dirt, and the green life springing up from it.

3. Three Analogies for a Poem

Oratory

'In me it begins to talk'

BEYOND the experiments that Whitman made with words, and the attitude to which these gave utterance, lies the central question of why he devised his peculiar form. The result has been evaluated in innumerable ways: it has been commended for its freedom and blamed for its monotony; it has been viewed as an extension of the possibilities of poetry, and also as no poetry at all, as a muddy encroachment on the domains of prose. It seems most fruitful, therefore, to begin with an account of what Whitman himself believed he was doing, to try to grasp his evolving sense of what he meant by a poem, complicated though that meaning is by his three chief recurrent analogies for his 'songs': with oratory, with Italian music, and with the sea. Any one of these analogies may seem confused enough; together they would appear inevitably and absurdly incompatible. Nevertheless, Whitman persisted in feeling connections between them.

In looking now at his notebooks, which, starting in 1847, belong mainly to the period between then and the first *Leaves,* it is often impossible to tell whether passages of loosely rhythmical prose were originally conceived for a speech or as a draft towards a poem. As a result of going over these notes and arranging them for publication, Bucke believed it certain that Whitman's first intention, some years before *Leaves of Grass* had been thought of, was to publish his ideas by lectures. The example of Emerson may again have given him a challenge, for in a passage written about 1848, one of the earliest in which his material was grouping itself into the catalogue sequence, an item reads: 'And there, tall and slender, stands Ralph Waldo Emerson, of New England, at the lecturer's desk, lecturing.' But Whitman's deep concern with oratory can be dated back to his active membership in debating societies when he was sixteen, to his well-known habit, which had developed by then and which lasted to his old age, of shouting declamatory pieces, or lines from Shakespeare, to the accompaniment of the waves as he walked along the shore. The two strongest personalities that impressed his boyhood both moved him as public speakers. Not only did his reminiscences of Hicks always dwell on the Quaker's force of natural eloquence, but also when he came to recite, in 'A Song of Joys,' the joys of the orator, he was still very close to Frances Wright's idea of the qualities essential to that great role.[1] His

1. She said, in *Views of Society and Manners in America* (1821), that an orator should possess 'animation, energy, high moral feeling, ardent patriotism, a sublime love of liberty, a rapid flow of ideas and of language, a happy vein of irony, an action at once vehement and dignified, and a voice, full, sonorous, distinct, and flexible, exquisitely adapted to all the varieties of passion or argument.' To be sure, this description is so generalized that it can be duplicated in many other expressions of the stock ideal of the time. Yet in view of Whitman's enthusiasm for her, of his saying that 'her very appearance seemed to enthrall us,' the shaping of his own version of that ideal may most probably be traced to her effect. Witness the similarity to her description in some of these lines:

O the orator's joys!
To inflate the chest, to roll the thunder of the voice out from the ribs and throat,
To make the people rage, weep, hate, desire, with yourself,
To lead America—to quell America with a great tongue . . .
To speak with a full and sonorous voice out of a broad chest,
To confront with your personality all the other personalities of the earth.

continued devotion to the most popular art form of his day is clear from the terms in which he phrased his late tribute to Father Taylor as the 'one essentially perfect orator' he had ever heard, as 'this first-class genius in the rarest and most profound of humanity's arts.'

It seems most natural, therefore, that he should have conceived of 'the idea of strong live addresses directly to the people, adm. 10c.' as a means of 'promulging the grand ideas of American ensemble.' He affirmed somewhat later (1858) that a revolution in our oratory was needed to eliminate the artificial ornaments of declamation as commonly studied. When he reaches the theme of his peroration, 'Washington made free the body of America . . . Now comes one who will make free the American soul,' you are able to sense some of the ferment of emotion that had transformed this man from a writer of newspaper paragraphs and of fourth-rate romantic verse.[2] The simplicity for which he argued, a style designed *always to hold the ear of the people,* was what Lincoln was actually moving towards at this very time. But Whitman's gradual releasing of his deepest nature through experimentation with the cadences of public speech antedated by many years his earliest knowledge of Lincoln.[3] He told Burroughs that between the ages of twenty and thirty, while he was working on various papers, he had sometimes gone into the country 'delivering political addresses.' His brother George remembered that the social agitation that had led Walt from orthodox Democrat to Barn-

2. How banal this verse was and how indistinguishable from that of the general run of the day is worth recalling by a few lines from 'Ambition' (1842), probably as good as any of the small sheaf of poems that he wrote before beginning the experiments that led to *Leaves of Grass:*

> O, many a panting, noble heart
>   Cherishes in its deep recess
> The hope to win renown o'er earth
>   From Glory's prized caress.

> And some will win that envied goal,
>   And have their deeds known far and wide;
> And some—by far the most—will sink
>   Down in oblivion's tide.

3. Lincoln found his own liberation from conventional rhetoric only through the slow deepening of his experience. At the start he relied on such commonplace, if effective, devices as in this passage from his address to the Young Men's Lyceum of Springfield (1837) on 'The Perpetuation of Our Political Institutions': 'All the armies of Europe, Asia, and Africa, combined with all the treasure of the earth (our own excepted) in their military chest, with a Bonaparte for a commander, could not by force take a drink from the Ohio or make a track on the Blue Ridge in a trial of a thousand years.'

burner and finally to Black Republican had caused him to write 'what mother called barrels of lectures.' The earliest of these to be reported was at a big meeting of Democrats in the New York City Hall Park in 1841, where he urged the party not just to nominate a great individual but to fight for a body of principles. However, the summary in the *Post* shows nothing of the quality of the speech, and no whole text has been preserved earlier than his address to the Brooklyn Art Union ten years later.

This consists of an ardent adaptation of the Emersonian doctrine of the function of the natural creator. Its most interesting passage is at the end, where Whitman links the artist's work with the struggle for freedom, and incorporates, with no marked break in the rhythm, some lines from one of his first attempts at free verse.[4] Otherwise the speech is fairly conventional in its rhetorical stops, and limp in its structure. It obviously needed the presence of a speaking personality to lend it any effectiveness, an observation that would apply also to his two principal efforts as an orator that have been preserved, and upon which any assessment of his gifts in this art would have to be based. 'The Eighteenth Presidency,' his contribution to the campaign of 1856 in support of the Republican candidate Frémont against Buchanan, minces no words in its anti-capitalistic position, in its direct plea to workmen and workwomen, farmers and mechanics, as the source of power. 'Death of Abraham Lincoln,' which he delivered several times in the years after 1879, is pretty discursive, and though tender in its feeling, reaches nowhere the depth of 'When lilacs last in the dooryard bloom'd.'

Contemporary evidence, based almost entirely on the period after he was badly handicapped by his paralysis, gives no great testimony to Whitman's powers as a speaker. Granting him an indefinably easy manner and a simple range of tone, the consensus indicates that his voice was too high pitched for strength and was frequently almost inaudible. There are no reports to suggest that he ever lived up to the early ideal that he set himself: 'From the opening of the Oration and on through, the great thing is to be inspired as one divinely possessed, blind to all subordinate affairs and given up entirely to the surgings and utterances of the mighty tempestuous demon.' He devoted dozens of notes to his own instruction, on

4. This poem, which, with some alterations, was finally called 'Europe, the 72d and 73d Years of These States,' deals with the revolutions of 1848. It was the only poem in the 1855 *Leaves* to have appeared previously.

the necessity of practicing 'the elementary sounds' continually so that he might gain a limpid and resonant voice, on the necessity too of subordinating all gestures to 'a few irresistible ones.' All this advice finally centers on the figure as he steps onto the platform: 'Suddenly the countenance illumined, the breast expanded, the nostrils and mouth electric and quivering, the attitude imperious and erect—a God stands before you . . .' Here Whitman went even farther than Emerson in his literal acceptance of the romantic view of the sublime as it blended with the idea that the natural man was endowed with the faculty of spontaneously inspired speech.

Whitman kept reiterating his desire to be 'a wander speaker' in order to educate the people, and was seriously considering in 1858, and again five years later, the prospect of making his living by this means. Even in 1879 he had not wholly abandoned the notion of going up and down the land seeking whom he might 'devour with lectures.' Yet in the face of the fact that none of these intentions was ever fulfilled, it is apparent that he was far less capable than Emerson of attaining success in what they both agreed with their time in regarding as the art pre-eminently fitted for democracies. It might be argued that their lack of ability to meet the standard tastes of the day was in some correspondence with the degree to which each felt himself surcharged with a quality of feeling that exceeded any conventional modes. But if the *persona* that became free through Whitman's declamatory incantation was too lyric to make a forceful orator, by the same token his poetry never got clear of its rhetorical sources.

Ordinarily he made only the loosest distinctions between the two forms, and even by the time of his final preface, 'A Backward Glance O'er Travel'd Roads' (1888), he could describe the style of *Drum-Taps* as having been his 'new and national declamatory expression.' To be sure, after he had published the first *Leaves,* he recognized that a speaking style 'requires many different things from the written style,' and he had come to feel then that his way of repeating passages from *Richard III* and *Julius Caesar,* as well as 'the habit of forming the rhythmic style' of his poems, had tended to make the emphases of his speeches too monotonous, to keep them from being as 'abrupt' and 'crackling' as they should be. But it does not seem to have occurred to him that the influence in the other direction might be equally damaging. In his own copy of the 1860 edition of his poems, he inserted this note:

Lecture
(Not character, nor life worthy the name without religion,
Nor State nor man nor woman without religion).

But his indecision between the two mediums was still prevailing, for he later crossed out the word lecture, and incorporated the straggling lines, virtually unchanged, into the next revision of 'Starting from Paumanok.'

We enter even more intimately into the process by which a speech could become one of his poems, in a curious composition into which he inserted his own stage directions:

Was it thought that all was achieved when Liberty was achieved? (Shaking
the head—no—no—no.)
Make a large part of lecture-meaning consist in significant gestures.
When liberty is achieved—when rage no more the red and circling rivers,
with death in every eddy.
When the exiles that pined away in distant lands and died have borne the
fruit they died for . . .

In the 1856 *Leaves* this theme has been worked up into a poem which, except for an occasional simple enunciation,

The great speakers and writers are exiled, they lie sick in distant lands,

is, in its dithyrambic sweep, almost as bombastic as its title, 'Liberty Poem for Asia, Africa, Europe, America, Australia, Cuba, and the Archipelagoes of the Sea.' [5]

From such samples it might seem that any connections between Whitman's poetry and its forensic base constituted his heaviest liability. Yet it remains equally true that his richest feelings were aroused by the sound and action of the voice, in a way that he tried often to describe, especially in his *Primer*. He believed that you could realize the full beauty of a word only on those rare occasions when you heard it pronounced with modulation and timbre, and that such power of speech was the subtlest property of organic well-being, dependent alike on the flexible structure of the throat and chest, and on 'a developed harmonious soul.' The lurking, yet compelling charm of the voice was the ultimate token of personality. It was not something that could be taught, but was bound up inextricably with the growth of experience, and its final ripening could come only after 'the chaste drench of love.' It is no wonder, therefore, that he

5. This was subsequently toned down: 'To a Foil'd European Revolutionaire.'

reached the conclusion that the best poetry 'perhaps waits to be rous'd out yet, or suggested, by the perfect physiological human voice.'

In such a way he arrived again at the bodily and spiritual oneness which he wanted his poems to convey, and which made him declare of his book, 'who touches this touches a man.' He implied a great deal in his repeated use of the word 'vocalism,' in his desire that it should be 'limpid' and 'inspired' in both his speeches and poems. What he meant is developed in a poem with the word itself for title, though it was at one time called 'To Oratists.' Here he declares that 'the divine power to speak words' comes only as a product of the most vigorous assimilation of life, and rounds again to the point:

All waits for the right voices;
Where is the practis'd and perfect organ? where is the develop'd soul?
For I see every word utter'd thence has deeper, sweeter, new sounds, impos-
sible on less terms.

The formulation gropes after the main forces that moved him in his *Leaves*. He wrote in the manuscript draft of the very first lines of 'Song of Myself':

I am your voice—It was tied in you—In me it begins to talk.
I celebrate myself to celebrate every man and woman alive;
I loosen the tongue that was tied in them,
It begins to talk out of my mouth.[6]

In these lines he experienced his birth as a poet, for the vibration of emo-
tion *in* the voice was his first step towards poetic rhythm. His demand for the direct presence of speaking tones in poetry would put him in accord with the revolt of modern poets against the artificial muffling of such tones by Tennyson and Swinburne. Here Eliot and Frost are on common ground, and even Valéry has declared: 'Le lyrisme est le genre de poésie qui suppose la voix en action—la voix directement issue de ou provoquée par—les choses que l'on voit ou que l'on sent comme présentes . . . La présence de la voix explique la littérature première.' Whitman underwent

6. In view of the close identification Whitman made between the word and the voice, it is significant that these lines are immediately followed in the manuscript by

I celebrate myself to celebrate you:
I say the same word for every man and woman alive.
And I say that the soul is not greater than the body,
And I say that the body is not greater than the soul.

this sensation on the most elementary level, as witnessed by the way he speaks in the *Primer* of the poet's words as 'miracles from his hands—miracles from his mouth,' and particularly by the way in which many of his notes show him making use of language in the fashion of the primitive conjuror: 'Perfect Sanity. Divine Instinct. Breadth of Vision. Healthy Rudeness of body, Withdrawnness. Gayety. Sun-tan and air sweetness.' His belief that he could summon up a state or quality simply by articulating its name went to such lengths that all he felt it necessary to do here was to rearrange this list slightly, and to add 'such are some of the words of poems' in order to make two lines in his self-descriptive 'Song of the Answerer.' [7]

Actually Whitman's language approximates only intermittently any customary colloquial phrasing, though the success of some of his best shorter poems, 'As I lay with my head in your lap camerado,' or, probably the most skillfully sustained of all, 'When I heard at the close of the day,' is owing to their suggestion of intimate conversation. This fact raises the ambiguous problem of just who his audience was. Recurring to Eliot's categories, it seems clear that, unlike Emerson and Thoreau and other keepers of journals, Whitman was not engaged in talking to himself; nor, unlike the novelists, was he opening an intercourse with society. His undelivered speeches can hardly be said to be addressed to anyone. He asserted that 'the place of the orator and his hearers is truly an agonistic arena. There he wrestles and contends with them—he suffers, sweats, undergoes his great toil and ecstasy.' That would make a good description of Webster's activity, but has only casual bearing on the growth of Whitman's rhetoric. For this came out of no real struggle with others, and is, consequently, even as rhetoric, an odd hybrid, since its sinews have not had the normal toughening. And although his rhythms, in their almost total avoidance of run-on lines, are consistently based on the parallelism of sentence structure so familiar to the orator, and employ too the orator's reiteration of words and phrases, still they ceased to be mechanical and took on life only after Whitman had

---

7. Divine instinct, breadth of vision, the law of reason, health, rudeness of body, withdrawnness,
  Gayety, sun-tan, air-sweetness, such are some of the words of poems.

I have received many suggestions at this point from Jean Catel, whose study, *Rhythme et Langage dans la 1re Edition des Leaves of Grass* (1930), makes use of considerable material from primitive anthropology.

realized that animation 'may be shown in a speech by great feeling in voice and look—interior gesture which is perhaps better than exterior.'

Such interior gestures were the bridge by which he passed from declamation to lyricism. Whitman ordinarily assumed that in his songs he was talking to everybody, and liked to think of his voice withering the pretensions of the thinly cultivated and radiating out to all the common people of these States. Yet even he granted at times that he wasted no ink, that his words were only for those few who had gone through enough experience to be able to apprehend them. And when he signed himself, 'from me to you, whoever you are, we twain,' he reached the audience he has actually held. For though he deliberately broke through all barriers of class to a degree that has hardly yet been surpassed, the fact remains that he has never spoken to wide groups. In his best poetry his favorite oratorical figures, the questions and exclamations, the apostrophes and parenthetical asides, have all become personal: they imply the presence not of many but of one:

As I lay with my head in your lap camerado,
The confession I made I resume, what I said to you and the open air
    I resume.

Even the broad humanity of his tribute to Lincoln, which reaches out to include the whole continent, even this is cast in the most intimate form of a 'thought of him I love.'

Whitman had wanted to devise a wholly new speaking style, far more direct and compelling 'than any hitherto . . . and acting as Consuelo's free and strong Italian style did in the singing of the respectable village church.' Consuelo, the heroine of George Sand's novel, remained for forty years his favorite heroine in literature, a symbol for the simplest devotion to inspired art. But the difference between the effect of her lyricism and that of either his speeches or poems was that her freedom of voice expressed itself in traditional popular forms, and thereby was able to move the whole congregation. In his self-conscious determination to be new, he threw away the only poetic medium that might have spoken to the people at large, the ballad or folk-song. He left such ballads and hymns to be the basis of Whittier's popular appeal, and seemed to think that he could gain universality by making his chants psalms for a new Bible. But though some cadences of the Hebrew testaments resulted from his assumption of the prophet's role, he thought far more frequently of his work as songs, untuneful as all of them are. Consuelo's was not the only voice he would have liked to equal, for when he listed, near the end of his life, the men and women whose utterance had moved him most, they were 'the contralto Alboni, Elias Hicks, Father Taylor, the tenor Bettini, Fanny Kemble, and the old actor Booth.' His attraction to the theatre and especially to the opera brings us to the second chief analogy he developed when he was thinking not of the message of his poems, but of their structure.

THE OPERA

'Easily written loose-finger'd chords'

HIS EVENINGS at the Bowery Theatre or the old Park, or at the opera houses in Astor Place or Castle Garden, provided beyond question the fullest aesthetic experience of his life. By virtue of being on the free list as a writer for the papers, he was able, from the late eighteen-thirties, to go continually, and so to satisfy his eagerness to have his impressions of Shakespeare reinforced by immediate embodiment. He read each play through again the day before the performance, and could never conceive of anything finer than the energy of Junius Booth's voice as he gave himself up to Richard III, Lear, or Iago, or to Sir Giles Overreach in Massinger's *New Way to Pay Old Debts*. His passion for music followed soon after, and became the more compelling in the years during which the initial *Leaves* were taking shape. At the time of his visit to New Orleans (1848), where opera had first been introduced into America, performances took place four times a week. In New York he heard all the leading soloists, orchestras and bands of the day, and recorded his pleasure in most of them. In 'Proud Music of the Storm' (1868), he listed some of his favorite operas. Gounod's *Faust* and Mozart's *Don Juan* were among them, but the bulk were Italian, Verdi's *Ernani*, *Rigoletto*, and *Il Trovatore*, Donizetti's *Lucia*, and Rossini's *William Tell*. He had tried to phrase his sensation of what this music did to him, in the passage on sounds in 'Song of Myself':

> A tenor large and fresh as the creation fills me,
> The orbic flex of his mouth is pouring and filling me full.

One of the summits of his experience was listening to Marietta Alboni on every occasion she sang during the season of 1853, probably twenty times in all. But he had felt an even richer reward three years before in the 'fresh vigorous tones' of Bettini: 'None have thoroughly satisfied me, overwhelmed me, but this man. Never before did I realize what an indescribable volume of delight the recesses of the soul can bear from the sound of the honied perfection of the human voice. The *manly* voice it must be, too,' for the woman's in comparison was 'but as the pleasant moonlight.' Whitman's congested description of his almost unendurable pleasure in the performances of these two great artists was one of the passages in his notebooks that was taken over, virtually entire, into 'Song of Myself.'[8] Its very lack of control is eloquent evidence of what these voices were doing to him, moving him towards his own style of expression in a way that no reading ever did.

For his belief that poetry was not something written but uttered, he may well have been indebted to the vogue of Ossian and to the romanticization of the heroic bard as the equivalent of the Biblical prophet. But he observed that the 'Address to the Sun' was misty and windy, 'how full of diffused, only half-meaning words,' and warned himself not to 'fall into the Ossianic, *by any chance.*' The mode to which he conceived his own poems to belong is made unmistakable by the fact that he did not use the word 'write' in connection with them, but described his activity variously as 'singing,' 'warbling,' 'carolling,' 'trilling,' and 'chanting.' Moreover, he told Trowbridge, in the same conversation in 1860 in which he phrased his debt to Emerson: 'But for the opera I could never have

---

8. 'I want that tenor, large and fresh as the creation, the orbed parting of whose mouth shall lift over my head the sluices of all the delight yet discovered for our race.— I want the soprano that lithely overleaps the stars, and convulses me like the love-grips of her in whose arms I lay last night.—I want an infinite chorus and orchestrium, wide as the orbit of Uranus, true as the hours of the day, and filling my capacities to receive, as thoroughly as the sea fills its scooped out sands.—I want the chanted Hymn whose tremendous sentiment shall uncage in my breast a thousand wide-winged strengths and unknown ardors and terrible ecstasies—putting me through the flights of all the passions —dilating me beyond time and air—startling me with the overture of some unnamable horror—calmly sailing me all day on a bright river with lazy slapping waves—stabbing my heart with myriads of forked distractions more furious than hail or lightning—lulling me drowsily with honeyed morphine—tightening the fakes of death about my throat, and awakening me again to know by that comparison, the most positive wonder in the world, and that's what we call life.' The rearrangement is to be found in section twenty-six of 'Song of Myself.' For an admirably concise summary of Whitman's debt to the opera, see Louise Pound, 'Walt Whitman and Italian Music' (*American Mercury*, September 1925).

written *Leaves of Grass.*' He was fully aware that his rapt identification
with this music had been the root cause of his emancipation from what
he called the 'ballad-style' of poetry, which seems to have meant to him
all poetry encumbered by rhyme and metre. His closest approach to contact with authentic ballads had been through Scott's *Border Minstrelsy,*
of which he possessed in youth a well-thumbed copy. In his own early
efforts, such as 'The Inca's Daughter' (1840), he betrayed that he was not
handling a form with any living growth in his surroundings, but
merely a stale journalistic convention. Among the pieces that he liked
to launch forth in his 'vocalism' were 'the wild tunes and refrains' he had
heard from the blacks down South; but only the minstrel shows had
then perceived in these the source of a native art. And although Whitman, from his earliest days as a reporter, could make a distinction between 'art-singing' and 'heart-singing,' and assert, in the vein of Herder,
that 'no human power can thoroughly suppress the spirit which lives in
national lyrics, and sounds in the favorite melodies sung by high and low,'
he was never to possess the gift of supplying these.[9]

However, he did have several notions for the development of a native
opera—that it should be much simpler than the European, that it should
put three or more banjos into the orchestra for the accompaniment of the
tenor, and give 'far more scope to the persons enacting the characters.' Towards the end of his life, musicians among his friends claimed that the
thematic method of his poems was more akin to Wagner than to the
Italians, but he knew himself that he had been 'fed and bred' by the
earlier school. Certainly he has nothing like the musical connections be-

9. Whitman made this distinction in an enthusiastic review of the country style of the
Cheney family, a quartet of singers from New Hampshire, as being 'good and fitting to
our own nation' in contrast to 'the stale, second-hand, foreign method.' This review appeared in *The Broadway Journal* (1845), of which Poe was then in charge. It carried an
editorial note presumably by Poe himself, and if so, the only record that has been preserved of his opinion of the younger writer: 'The author desires us to say, for him, that
he pretends to no scientific knowledge of music. He merely claims to appreciate so much
of it (a sadly disdained department, just now) as affects, in the language of the deacons,
"the natural heart of man." It is scarcely necessary to add that we agree with our cor-
respondent throughout.'

Whitman cited Herder explicitly in his final (1888) preface: 'Concluding with two items
for the imaginative genius of the West, when it worthily rises—First, what Herder taught
to the young Goethe, that really great poetry is always (like the Homeric or Biblical canti-
cles) the result of a national spirit, and not the privilege of a polish'd and select few;
Second, that the strongest and sweetest songs yet remain to be sung.'

tween themes and sequences that the symbolists deliberately patterned on Wagner, even as late as *The Waste Land*. In one of his frequent explanations of his own work he said (1860): 'Walt Whitman's method in the construction of his songs is strictly the method of the Italian Opera, which, when heard, confounds the new person,' since, showing on the surface no 'analogy to his previous-accustomed tunes,' it 'impresses him as if all the sounds of earth and hell were tumbled promiscuously together.'

• He was undoubtedly talking big in claiming any strictness for his compositions. Yet in referring to their alternating *recitative* and *aria*, he meant the kind of contrast that is used most effectively in 'Out of the cradle endlessly rocking,' between the narrative sections and the rising song of the bird. It is possible also to see likenesses to music in the varied repetitions of some of his catalogues, or to go farther and note that his method in a poem is to present a main motive, which is repeated, amplified, and recapitulated. Or you can make rough analogies of his climactic effects with operatic 'crescendo,' 'fortissimo,' and 'diminuendo.'[10] Indeed, the quietness of the closing lines of his vision may well be judged an instance of his approximation to the last device. But in general it does not seem profitable to push such analogies any farther than he did when, in blithe ignorance of exact musical technique, he spoke of his

Easily written loose-finger'd chords—I feel the thrum of your climax and close.

He often longed to rival Bettini and to fold

> or seek to fold, within my chants transmuting,
> Freedom's and Love's and Faith's unloos'd cantabile.

He seems to have believed that he could summon directly the music of the storm or that of 'the mystic trumpeter,' but his rejection of all the resources of verbal melody, of the intricacies of rhyme and assonance that enabled Dryden or Tennyson to carry off *tours de force* of musical analogy, often left his lines as flat as

> Tutti! for earth and heaven,

or as scratchy and banal as the phrasing of this tribute, where he falls into the jargon of the hack reviewer:

10. The most sensitive technical analysis of Whitman in terms of such musical analogies is that by Basil De Sélincourt, *Walt Whitman: A Critical Study* (1914).

The teeming lady comes,
The lustrous orb, Venus contralto, the blooming mother,
Sister of loftiest gods, Alboni's self I hear.

It might seem that Whitman was the extreme example of the nineteenth-century poet who fooled himself, in ways far more disastrous than
Swinburne or Mallarmé, into thinking that he could rival the effects of
music, only to end by merely making his poems vaguer. Yet in the genetic
account of his work, it is indisputable that operatic singing first awoke
him, in the America of Tyler and Polk, to the range and vibration of
feeling that could be projected into art. And though he can set his reader's
teeth on edge by proclaiming himself a 'chansonnier'—one thing he trans-
parently is not in any language—what he wanted to call forth was a kind
of 'world-emotion,' lyric yet universal, as he had responded to it in
Bettini.

That he was not just the victim of an impossible confusion between
different arts is borne out by another glimpse into his creative process. In
old age he told a friend that 'it would be strange indeed if there were no
music at the heart of his poems, for more of these were actually inspired
by music than he himself could remember.' Moods 'awakened by music
in the streets, the theatre, and in private' had blended into poems apparently far removed from their original stimulus. Especially while he
was 'brooding over poems still to come,' he knew himself subtly touched
and challenged by his memories of Alboni. Indeed, he had never been
able to write a bird song, not that of the mocking-bird in 'Out of the
cradle endlessly rocking,' or that of the hermit-thrush in his tribute to
Lincoln, without being continually attended by his 'recollection of the
deep emotion' that had affected him in the great soprano's singing. Which
statement, in view of the fact that his most moving expressions of what
bird songs meant to him merge them instinctively with moonlight, is
oblique evidence that his own voice, despite his professed preference for
Bettini, is less often 'manly' than it is gentle and tender. Burroughs remarked that 'there is something indescribable in his look, in his eye, as
in that of the mother of many children'—a remark that seems to echo
Whitman's almost obsessive repetition that his ideal of beauty was not
that of the young girl, but of 'the mother of many children, middle-aged
or old.' Much in Whitman's temperament came to him directly from his

own placid generous-hearted Van Velsor mother, from his far more intimate devotion to her than to his father.

His bird passages are again evidence of how he listened. In his later years especially he loved to try to catch in words the effect of natural sounds. In many of his 'specimen days' down by Timber Creek he made an effort to describe quail notes or the 'reedy monotones' of locusts or the whirr of flocks migrating at midnight. But he was successful only in an occasional evocative phrase, 'the flup of a pike leaping out,' or the 'chippering-shriek of two kingfishers.' For the most part he was wholly content with 'indolently absorbing the scene.' The result, even in his best poems, was that he developed no skill that could create his impression of the 'warbling' of the hermit-thrush with any of the exact and exquisite purity of modulation with which the effect of its 'water-dripping song' is conveyed, for instance, in *The Waste Land*.

But that Whitman's songs as a whole, in spite of being unsingable, have music 'at their heart' is confirmed by the growing number of them that have been set by composers. The most successful of these, such as Holst's 'Dirge for Two Veterans,'[11] are persuasive evidence for Aaron Copland's conviction that, for the musician, the type of poem which furnishes the greatest stimulus is one whose significance is not too exact or complete. This lets the musician feel that there is still something for his technique to add to the realization of the emotion. In a period like ours, when music and poetry are no longer in the close alliance they were for the Elizabethans, the musician may naturally regard a poem as a libretto. In that he is not too far from Whitman, who believed that the main function of his unfinished lines was to call up in his reader a state of creative feeling from which further music might spring.

11. A bibliography by Bella Landauer (1937) lists 244 compositions, among them being Percy Grainger, 'Marching Song for Democracy'; Roy Harris, 'A Song for Occupations'; Paul Hindemith, 'This is Thy hour, O soul'; Charles Ives, 'Who goes there? Hankering, gross, mystical, and nude'; Vaughan Williams, 'Darest thou now, O Soul?' There are also such orchestral pieces as Ernest Bloch, 'America: An Epic Rhapsody,' dedicated to Whitman and Lincoln with the quotation 'O America, because you build for mankind, I build for you'; and John Alden Carpenter, 'Sea Drift, A Symphonic Poem.'

THE OCEAN

'The solid marrying the liquid'

WHITMAN'S analogy of his form with music escaped being just a made-up notion precisely to the extent to which his responses to the opera instructed him in the physical basis of rhythm. It is palpable, as Mary Austin argued,[12] that our conventional poets believed that the source of poetry was in England, and behaved as though rhythm was a matter of instructed imitation. The followers in this country of Byron and Keats had shown no more realization than our preceding century of followers of Pope that poetic rhythm was an organic response to the centers of experience—to the internal pulsations of the body, to its external movements in work and in making love, to such sounds as the wind and the sea. Emerson perceived the deficiency, and Poe, in the intensity of his suffering, transformed the hackneyed romantic cadences into a dreamworld haunted with the reality of tragedy. But Whitman's desire to give up borrowed cadences altogether came from his crude re-living of the primitive evolution of poetry.

If poetry's origin is to be found in the dance, in the rise and fall 'of consenting feet' (in Gummere's phrase), the phases of its progression may be thought of in the following closely connected order: first, movement; then, sound (or melody); then, sense (or words). As a half-educated journalist, Whitman was farthest away from the springs of elemental life, and so operated in his first writing almost solely on the level of sense. Then, through his fascination with music and with oratory, he began to stir to the richer impulses of sound and movement. These came to fruition in his own lines because there lay, behind the aroused interests of his adolescence and maturity, an experience of natural rhythm that carried him back to his earliest awareness as a child. In the account he gave of his ancestry he remarked that his family on both sides had' lived for generations near enough the sea 'to hear in still hours the roar of the surf.' He remarked also that his own first adventures were going down to the beach, and watching the men as they cut salt-hay or went clamming or fishing. It is no wonder that he added, 'The first time I ever

12. In *The American Rhythm* (1923).

wanted to make anything enduring was when I saw a ship under full sail and had the desire to describe it directly as it seemed to me.' That symbol of the beauty of movement, which Greenough recognized as so appropriate to the age, belonged peculiarly to Whitman.

When he spoke of his 'liquid-flowing syllables,' he was hoping for the same effect in his work as when he jotted down as the possible genesis for a poem: 'Sound of walking barefoot ankle deep in the edge of the water by the sea.' He tried again and again to describe what he wanted from this primal force, and put it most briefly when he said that if he had the choice of equalling the greatest poets in theme or in metre or in perfect rhyme,

> These, these, O sea, all these I'd gladly barter,
> Would you the undulation of one wave, its trick to me transfer,
> Or breathe one breath of yours upon my verse,
> And leave its odor there.

Here he is akin to Thoreau who, with equal ignorance of musical technique, found his surest inspiration in his physical response to natural harmonies. Whitman's full cognizance of the organic basis of rhythm, which he developed in hints in more than a dozen poems, is condensed, so far as he was capable of condensation, in one of his *Specimen Days*:

Even as a boy, I had the fancy, the wish, to write a piece, perhaps a poem, about the sea-shore—that suggesting, dividing line, contact, junction, the solid marrying the liquid—that curious, lurking something, (as doubtless every objective form finally becomes to the subjective spirit,) which means far more than its mere first sight, grand as that is—blending the real and ideal, and each made portion of the other. Hours, days, in my Long Island youth and early manhood, I haunted the shores of Rockaway or Coney island, or away east to the Hamptons or Montauk. Once, at the latter place, (by the old lighthouse, nothing but sea-tossings in sight in every direction as far as the eye could reach,) I remember well, I felt that I must one day write a book expressing this liquid, mystic theme. Afterward, I recollect, how it came to me that instead of any special lyrical or epical or literary attempt, the sea-shore should be an invisible *influence*, a pervading gauge and tally for me, in my composition.

He apprehends here, as he did in his vision, a mingling of immediate sensuous amplitude and of mystery. In his description of the junction of the sea and the land as 'the solid marrying the liquid,' he instinctively adopts the sexual symbolism which is nearly always at the root of his most living utterance. Whether or not he was conscious of this symbolism —as Lawrence or any other poet who had felt the influence of Freud would have been—when he called attention to the meaning of the Indian name for Long Island in 'Starting from *fish-shape* Paumanok where I was born,' he neglected no opportunity to convey 'the mad pushes of waves upon the land.' These reinforce the effect of many of the poems about his 'electric self,' as they compose the undertone for the bird's song in 'Out of the cradle endlessly rocking,' which awakened the boy on the beach to the meaning of love. Often Whitman's imagery is even more direct, as when he speaks of

> The souse upon me of my lover the sea, as I lie willing and naked.

In other moods he thinks of the unfathomable power that lies behind the fragile arc of foam, and as his symbol varies, we are reminded of the many fundamental things which Melville found expressed by the sea as he contrasted its 'unshored harborless immensities' with the land's peaceful margin of safety, or reflected with terror on the violence and death that lurked beneath the illusory calm of the surface. Melville developed his meditations much more profoundly than Whitman, but his starting point for them was the hitherto unplumbed realms of his being, which were sluiced open by the lulling rhythm. Melville suggested the process in many of his descriptions of standing the mast-head, as when he said, 'To and fro I idly swayed in what seemed an enchanted air . . . in that dreamy mood losing all consciousness, at last my soul went out of my body.' Such reverie was very familiar to Whitman.

Coleridge's principle that the reconciliation of opposites is essential for the creation of any great art lies behind Melville's belief that beauty must be united with strength, as well as behind Whitman's desire that the sea should endow him with its 'cosmic elemental passion' just as much as with its delicacy and whispering 'soothe.' Whitman made his special application of this principle fairly explicit in the course of developing, on another occasion, what he meant by the word he italicized above, the indirect *influence,* the invisible flowing-in of the waves upon his composition: 'Its analogy is *the Ocean*. Its verses are the liquid, billowy waves, ever rising and falling, perhaps sunny and smooth, perhaps wild with storm, always moving, always alike in their nature as rolling waves, but hardly any two exactly alike in size or measure (metre), never having the sense of something finished and fixed, always suggesting something beyond.' He touches there on the widely contrasting aspects of the sea, the calm and the tempest that both correspond to his desire, but he also reveals a marked difference from Coleridge in his conception of how these might be transferred to his verse. For Coleridge, tracing the origin of metre 'to the balance in the mind effected by that spontaneous effort which strives to hold in check the workings of passion,' recognized verse as a product both of emotion *and* its control, a harmony that sprang from the resolution of the antagonism between them. Whitman seemed to sense this tension at the base of art when he spoke of the pressure of 'the whole bubble of the sea-ooze against that unspeakable something in my own soul which makes me know without being able to tell how it is that I know.' But he did not try to make his verse reflect the overcoming of that tension. He evaded the problem by throwing over the discipline of metre altogether in his eagerness 'to let nature speak, without check, with original energy.' The sea did not remain a challenge to him to master his own rhythm. He wanted to absorb its elemental power by identifying himself with it.

In this breakdown of the distinctions between man and nature can be read also the reason for the deliquescence and disintegration in his work of the controls of traditional poetic movement. As Mary Austin concluded after analyzing his rhythms, he 'was sensitive to the bigness of things, which he mistook for universality, moved about a great deal, speculated freely, and was unclear in his conclusions: the American type.' But as she was likewise aware, his confused revolt resulted in an enormous positive gain. By turning to oratory he showed his instinctive recognition that this art had been always closer to the masses in America than any verse had been. He was not quite conscious of what we have now found demonstrated by many of the work songs and sea-chanteys of his day, that their rhythm, which rises directly from 'the tug and heave of constructive labor,' is more authentic than something Longfellow read in a book and tried to copy. Nevertheless, Whitman's scores of descriptions of men and women engaged in everyday occupations are the product of his fertile discovery of the physical grounding of rhythm, which came to him first in the rising and falling of the waves:

> The boatmen and clam-diggers arose early and stopt for me,
> I tuck'd my trowser-ends in my boots and went and had a good time;
> You should have been with us that day round the chowder-kettle.

But Whitman's cadences here do not reflect primarily the purposeful activity but his enjoyment of relaxed buoyant existence.

This conclusion seems borne out generally by his verbs of motion. Arvin has asked whether any other verse has ever so abounded in such verbs and participles, but when he asserts that 'to float' and 'to flow' are less characteristic of Whitman than 'to arise' and 'to stride on,' he makes the poet's activity sound more severely energetic than the texture of the poems themselves will substantiate. This is not to gainsay in the least Whitman's whole-hearted acceptance that 'all the forces of the Universe . . . are pulsating, progressing,' or that such a poem as 'Song of the Open Road' announces a dynamic philosophy of forward movement, struggle and triumph. But the key-attitude that made Whitman a lyrical poet rather than an orator caused him to choose such a theme as that of crossing Brooklyn Ferry, and to celebrate the passage rather than the arrival. He revealed why he delighted to conjure with the original name of his city when he said that 'Mannahatta means the place around which the hurried (or feverish) waters are continually coming or whence they are going.' His poem of the crossing might almost seem intended as an illustration of Coleridge's belief that the reader of poetry 'should be carried forward, not merely or chiefly by the mechanical impulse of curiosity, or a restless desire to arrive at the final solution; but by the pleasurable activity of mind excited by the attractions of the journey itself.' Indeed, taking literally what was for Coleridge only a metaphor, Whitman was so pleased with his journeys, and with exciting a similar attitude in his reader, that often he did not bother to write his poems but just left them heaps of materials.

He was himself aware of the kinds of movement that called forth his poetry when he listed as important influences in the 'gestation' of the *Leaves* not merely his 'still excitement' as he spent whole afternoons or evenings crossing and recrossing the river, but likewise 'how many exhilarating jaunts' sitting beside the driver on top of a Broadway omnibus. Moreover, at the very time of his first experiments with his free medium (1848), he came upon a magazine article on Indian epic poetry from which he copied a description of style that he was to try to adhere to throughout his work: 'A great poem must flow on "unhasting and unresting." ' How natural it became for him to think in such terms is shown by his parallel ideal for oratory, 'a determined, not hurried, not too pouring style of vocalism, but yet animated and live with full swelling, serious life.' The determination, the act of will, is relaxed in his ripest creations, which did not spring from desire to reform but from realization, not from the protesting zeal to improve society but from the discovery of the previously unexpressed abundance of ordinary American life. In such moods he felt that 'merely to *move* is then a happiness, a pleasure—to breathe, to see, is also,' and that all he wanted was to abandon himself to the moment, letting it 'float on, carrying me in its placid ecstasy.'

Jean Catel has remarked, after detailed scrutiny of Whitman's rhythm and language, that his epithets of movement reveal the very kind of limber indolence that was so characteristic of his own body. How characteristic this could be was proclaimed by *The Brooklyn Eagle* when it fired him in 1848 because of his liberal free-soil political convictions, but put it on the grounds that he was slow, 'heavy, discourteous and without steady principles . . . a clog upon our success.' And refuting the charge of a rival paper that he had been dismissed because he had kicked a prominent politician downstairs, the comment concluded with an authoritative air: 'He is too indolent to kick a musketo.'

Irrespective of the caricature here, a similar index to the range of his plastic skill in creating movement is provided in the concluding passage of 'Song of Myself':

> I effuse my flesh in eddies, and drift it in lacy jags.

Such effusion conditions the slow-paced action that his loose rhythm can encompass best:

> I recline by the sills of the exquisite flexible doors.

There he does not even suggest movement so much as the muscular satisfaction in the suspension of movement, in happy contrast with

> From Paumanok starting I fly like a bird,
> Around and around to soar to sing the idea of all.

That may be unfairly chosen since the intrusion of his own figure exaggerates the grotesque failure to create a living image. Yet he usually fails when his verbal imagery is violently active, and only when it is more supple succeeds in endowing his poetry with the sensuousness that Coleridge held indispensable to insure a 'framework of objectivity.' Such a framework, in turn, is essential for 'that definiteness and articulation of imagery, and that modification of the images themselves, without which poetry becomes flattened into mere didactics of practice, or evaporated into a hazy, unthoughtful day-dreaming.' A poet can provide this kind of framework only from materials to which his own senses have responded, and Whitman's intermittent power is called forth most surely by the movement of such a situation as that in which a woman says 'to the limber-hipp'd man near the garden pickets':

> Stand at my side till I lean as high as I can upon you,
> Fill me with albescent honey, bend down to me,
> Rub to me with your chafing beard, rub to my breast and shoulders.

On the other hand, the situations where he makes his flattest statements, assertions unrelieved by any contours of developed sensation, are those in which his voice rises to a shrill declamatory pitch in its urge for an indiscriminate drive forward:

> Victory, union, faith, identity, time,
> The indissoluble compacts, riches, mystery,
> Eternal progress, the kosmos, and the modern reports.

The register within which he can project movement into his imagery, and not merely proclaim its existence, is suggested most surely by the kinetic gestures in two lines of 'Song of Myself':

In me the caresser of life wherever moving, backward as well as forward sluing,

and

> I moisten the roots of all that has grown.

Even the male vigor of *Children of Adam,* when it pauses long enough from delirious enumeration of parts of the body to develop its description, avails itself predominantly of delicate verbs:

The curious roamer the hand roaming all over the body, the bashful withdrawing of flesh where the fingers soothingly pause and edge themselves.

His most memorable epithets of movement become such caresses, as when he speaks of the 'billowy drowse' of the sea, of 'the elastic air,' of 'serene-moving animals teaching content'; or when he develops one of his many paeans to the 'apple-shaped' earth rolling through space, in lines that catch the impalpable drift of the night air:

> Earth of the slumbering and liquid trees!
> Earth of departed sunset—earth of the mountains misty-topt! [13]
> Earth of the vitreous pour of the full moon just tinged with blue!

The more you examine his way of expressing his reception of all life, his feeling that he could represent an object adequately only by identifying himself with it, the more you are struck by his constant repetition of almost the same phrasing:

Myself effusing and fluid, a phantom curiously floating, now here absorb'd and arrested.

From his counterbalancing desire also to embrace what had absorbed him sprang his typical groupings of lines, long paragraphs without a main verb and yet with a distinct structural wholeness. He seems to have felt that his identification with the object made a verb unnecessary, that present participles or infinitives with a vocative urge could best convey immediate reality—a continuous present enfolding both past and future. By this means his notes for declamation were given the suppleness, or, to adopt one of his favorite words, the nonchalance of expression that he wanted, as in the following whole poem with its sustained movement of pressure towards a climax:

Me imperturbe, standing at ease in Nature,
Master of all or mistress of all, aplomb in the midst of irrational things,
Imbued as they, passive, receptive, silent as they,
Finding my occupation, poverty, notoriety, foibles, crimes, less important than
    I thought,
Me toward the Mexican sea, or in the Mannahatta or the Tennessee, or far
    north or inland,

13. This reminiscence of the passage in *Romeo and Juliet,*

> Night's candles are burnt out, and jocund day
> Stands tiptoe on the misty mountain tops,

is one of the few signs in Whitman of his reading of Shakespeare. It seems probable that 'multitudinous' and some of the richest sounding archaic words in *Leaves of Grass*—'ostent,' 'vagrom,' 'alarum,' 'rondure,'—were suggested to Whitman by the plays. See Rebecca Coy, 'A Study of Whitman's Diction' (*University of Texas Studies in English*, Vol. xvi, 125-37).

A river man, or a man of the woods or of any farm-life of these States or of
the coast, or the lakes of Kanada,
Me wherever my life is lived, O to be self-balanced for contingencies,
To confront night, storms, hunger, ridicule, accidents, rebuffs, as the trees
and animals do.

At this point, in completing the account of the genesis of his form, it is
possible to demonstrate the course by which such a verse paragraph grew
to the firmness of shape that it did not have in the inchoate notebook
drafts. The distinguishing factor, Whitman's confidence that he had
found the right approach to handling his material, comes out into the
clear in a little-known poem, 'The Sleepers,' which was among the dozen
in his first *Leaves*. This poem is not very decisive in its effect, as might
be expected from the declaration with which it starts:

I wander all night in my vision . . .
Bending with open eyes over the shut eyes of sleepers,
Wandering and confused, lost to myself, ill-assorted, contradictory,
Pausing, gazing, bending, and stopping.

There follows the recital of all the recumbent figures whom he sees, 'the
white features of corpses . . . the sick-gray faces of onanists . . . the insane in their strong-door'd rooms, the sacred idiots, the new-born emerging from gates, and the dying emerging from gates . . . all, all sleep.'
As the poet moves among them he believes that by passing his hands
soothingly a few inches above the worst-suffering and most restless, he
can bring them peace; or again, that he can sleep close with each in turn
and become their dreams. Thus merged with the night, his series of flick-
ering pictures expands into a few that take up whole paragraphs: of a
swimmer being drowned; of a ship being wrecked—a reconstruction of
his memory of the *Mexico* as it was broken to pieces on Hempstead beach
in 1840; of Washington in a stock-attitude after the defeat at Brooklyn;
of what Whitman's mother had told him about an Indian squaw who
had come to their house one day selling rushes for bottoming chairs. He
is seemingly unaware of the fact that he is no longer describing sleepers,
and he does not wittingly present these scenes as dreams. At the end he
links all his figures together by swearing that the great and the weak 'are
averaged now,' that one is no better than another since 'the night and
sleep have liken'd them and restored them.' And he adds, in language
that might easily be Dreiser's,

They pass the invigoration of the night and the chemistry of the night, and
   awake.

Whether or not Whitman made a conscious effort in this poem to
fathom the substance of his dream life, his intoxication with the mystery
of night whirled him into the desire to 'go gallivant' with the summer
darkness, and caused him to declare: 'I am a dance.' In that phrase he
enunciates the sensation of wholeness that has descended over him: his
words are no longer fragmentary as they were in his notebooks, but have
become, in a sense, comparable to those of the primitive ritualistic
singer, the full gesture of his united body and spirit. And this 'dance' carried him far beyond the limits of his conscious self into groupings of
association of the sort released most readily in dreams. This is particularly true of one passage near the beginning of the poem, rejected in his
latest editions, where the confused but powerful sexual symbolism reads
very like the half-comprehended memories of night that you have at the
instant of awaking:

O hotcheek'd and blushing! O foolish hectic!
O for pity's sake, no one must see me now! my clothes were stolen while I
   was abed,
Now I am thrust forth, where shall I run?

Pier that I saw dimly last night when I looked from the windows!
Pier out from the main, let me catch myself with you and stay—I will not
   chafe you;
I feel ashamed to go naked about the world.
And am curious to know where my feet stand—and what is this flooding
   me, childhood or manhood—and the hunger that crosses the bridge
   between.

The cloth laps a first sweet eating and drinking,
Laps life-swelling yolks—laps ear of rose-corn, milky and just ripened;
The white teeth stay, and the boss-tooth advances in darkness,
And liquor is spilled on lips and bosoms by touching glasses, and the best
   liquor afterward.

This sense of flooding abundance and fertility is comparable to Melville's
realization, in the chapter on 'Dreams' in *Mardi,* of the stirring of inner
resources theretofore not suspected by the daily levels of his mind—the
chapter from which we dated his full birth as an artist. Whitman tried

later to describe the sensation he had had when first composing 'Song of Myself,' how it had seemed to him afterwards as though the poem had risen from a kind of trance, how 'in contemplating it, he felt, in regard to his own agency in it, like a somnambulist who is shown, during his waking hours, the giddy heights and impossible situations over which he has passed safely in his sleep.' This description of how his moments of creation seemed beyond the scope of his will's control would apply even more accurately to the just quoted lines of almost automatic writing.

If measured by Baudelaire's demand that the poet should be hypnotist and somnambulist combined, Whitman was very often only the latter. One of the great dilemmas of nineteenth-century poetry may be attributed to the cleavage between these two halves of the role. At one extreme is Swinburne, who is a master of purely hypnotic sound that is reinforced by no psychological or spiritual depth. Near him is Tennyson, in whose 'finest verbalism' Whitman could feel a warning to himself for what he had rejected, even though he generally regarded the Laureate complacently as merely 'the poetic cream-skimmer of our age's melody, *ennui* and polish.' But by going himself to the opposite pole Whitman had virtually deprived his pages of all that Yeats was later to demand again, the disciplined resources of words and metre 'exact enough to hold a subtle ear.'

Yet his somnambulism was a great asset since it let him be swept into the currents of the unconscious mind, and so made it possible for him to plumb emotional forces far beyond the depth of most other writers of his day. His first full-length efforts to project these forces into words, as in 'The Sleepers,' brought him to the recognition that 'by curious indirections only can there be any statement of the spiritual world.' He had come to realize that his bare notebook rhetoric was not adequate to comprehend the range of experience. He made more explicit how he had grown aware of other meanings of meaning beyond mere sense:

Common teachers or critics are always asking 'What does it mean?' Symphony of fine musician, or sunset, or sea-waves rolling up the beach—what do they mean? Undoubtedly in the most subtle-elusive sense they mean something—as love does, and religion does, and the best poem;—but who shall fathom and define those meanings? (I do not intend this as a warrant for wildness and frantic escapades—but to justify the soul's frequent joy in what cannot be defined to the intellectual part, or to calculation.)

Something like this feeling was the usual result of the transcendental conception that the idea is always greater than any expression of it. Such feeling could dissipate into fondness for atmosphere and suggestion, as when Whitman remarked that 'grandest poetic passages are only to be taken at free removes, as we sometimes look for stars at night, not by gazing directly toward them, but off one side.' However, the check that he gave himself in his parenthetical expression shows his solid understanding of the worst romantic excesses, and serves to develop his continually repeated statement that he wanted in his poems such 'subtle indirection' as came to him from the movement of the sea. This indirection is the kind of extension of experience that the symbol is designed to make; and in Whitman's best articulated poems such symbols give cohesion to his three analogies. His declaiming chant becomes one with his longing for music that will rival the sibilance of the waves, 'rolling in without intermission, and fitfully rising and falling.' Such fusion is achieved in his handling of many different themes, but a single example can bring together all the elaborations of my effort to give a normative description of a Whitman poem. This is one of several poems that take a beach for their setting, though here the subject is not the sea:

On the beach at night,
Stands a child with her father,
Watching the east, the autumn sky.

Up through the darkness,
While ravening clouds, the burial clouds, in black masses spreading,
Lower sullen and fast athwart and down the sky,
Amid a transparent clear belt of ether yet left in the east,
Ascends large and calm the lord-star Jupiter,
And nigh at hand, only a very little above,
Swim the delicate sisters the Pleiades.

From the beach the child holding the hand of her father,
Those burial clouds that lower victorious soon to devour all,
Watching, silently weeps.

Weep not, child,
Weep not, my darling,
With these kisses let me remove your tears,
The ravening clouds shall not long be victorious,
They shall not long possess the sky, they devour the stars only in apparition,

Jupiter shall emerge, be patient, watch again another night, the Pleiades shall
    emerge,
They are immortal, all those stars both silvery and golden shall shine out
    again,
The great stars and the little ones shall shine out again, they endure,
The vast immortal suns and the long-enduring pensive moons shall again
    shine.

Then dearest child mournest thou only for Jupiter?
Considerest thou alone the burial of the stars?
Something there is,
(With my lips soothing thee, adding I whisper,
I give thee the first suggestion, the problem and indirection,)
Something there is more immortal even than the stars,
(Many the burials, many the days and nights, passing away,)
Something that shall endure longer even than lustrous Jupiter,
Longer than sun or any revolving satellite,
Or the radiant sisters the Pleiades.

Here Whitman's distinction between recitative and aria falls in with
the natural division between the opening description and the words of the
father to his child, which begin with the fourth stanza. The recitative
itself is enclosed in the 'frame' structure of which Whitman was so fond,
its last three lines repeating with variation and extension the substance
of the first three, and thus serving to set off the whole. The central passage between ('Up through the darkness,' etc.) is an apt instance of what
Whitman believed he could gain by imitating the effects of the ocean.
These seven lines possess 'both continuity and independence,' in De Sélincourt's phrase, and can readily be conceived as a succession of wave-crests,
some larger, some smaller, which attain at least a momentary climax in
the rippling firmness of the last. The liquid sound of the word 'Pleiades'
has been exquisitely heightened by the similar vowels and consonants preceding it; while the masterful ascent of Jupiter, creating a symbol of
radiance for the whole poem, is accentuated by the slow rhythm.

    There is a possible bit of evidence as to how a poet receives his sugges-
tions and then transforms them in one of Whitman's prose accounts of
an October night when he had again been struck by the magnificence of
Jupiter, and had remembered these lines from an old Hindu poem:

Clothed in his white garments,
Into the round and clear arena slowly entered the brahmin,
Holding a little child by the hand,
Like the moon with the planet Jupiter in a cloudless night-sky.

That this 'specimen day' was in 1876, five years after he had written 'On the Beach at Night,' would have little bearing on the probability of his having known the Hindu lines much earlier, or on the possibility of their having been the starting point for his other association between the ascending planet and the man with the child.

The aria rises from a distinctly theatrical situation, since the likelihood of a child's weeping at the dark clouds seems fairly strained. But as is often the case in opera, once the implausibility is granted, the emotion that is developed from it is affecting and genuine. The symbol of the burial clouds and the light that emerges triumphant above them is given its human implication in the quiet suggestion of illimitability, which is beyond the understanding but within the perception of the small girl. This kind of dawning of elemental consciousness is the state that Whitman could portray most convincingly, since it is akin to the simple half-mature feelings in which he himself habitually lived. His gift in portraying them depends on the broad generous effect rather than on any sustained craftsmanship. He can fall into the flattest stock response to the stars as 'silvery and golden,' only to rescue himself by the majestic sweep of 'the vast immortal suns and the long-enduring pensive moons.' Again, his clumsy lapse into such an archaic poeticism as 'considerest thou' is redeemed by the delicate insight that, without mentioning the sea, can blend its soothing, whispering voice with the father's. He thus adds further evidence of nature's constant laws, the permanence of the sea to the permanence of the stars. This constancy is also the strongest sign by which the Father—and he is mankind's as well as the child's—persuades that the soul endures beyond all natural phenomena. The way Whitman's lines continue to suggest the regular recurrence of waves, and make at the close a thematic repetition that joins his aria and recitative by as much melody as his lack of metre can command, is an indication of the wholeness of poetic conception to which his analogies had brought him.

4. 'Rhythm in its last ruggedness and decomposition'

'Had Walt Whitman lived out of phase, desire to prove that all his emotions were healthy and intelligible, to set his practical sanity above all not made in his fashion, to cry "Thirty years old and in perfect health!" would have turned him into some kind of jibing demagogue; and to think of him would be to remember that Thoreau, picking up the jaw-bone of a pig with no tooth missing, recorded that there also was perfect health. He would, that he might believe in himself, have compelled others to believe. Not being out of phase, he used his *Body of Fate* (his interest in crowds, in casual loves and affections, in all summary human experience) to clear intellect of *antithetical* emotion . . . and haunted and hunted by the now involuntary *Mask,* created an *Image* of vague, half-civilized man, all his thought and impulse a product of democratic bonhomie, of schools, of colleges, of public discussion. Abstraction had been born,-but it remained the abstraction of a community, of a tradition, a synthesis starting, not . . . with logical deduction from an observed fact, but from the whole experience or from some experience of the individual or of the community: "I have such and such a feeling. I have such and such a belief. What follows from feeling, what from belief?" . . . Whitman makes catalogues of all that has moved him, or amused his eye, that he may grow more poetical. Experience is all-absorbing . . . Impulse or instinct begins to be all in all. In a little while, though not yet, it must, sweeping away catalogue and category, fill the mind with terror.'

—YEATS, *A Vision*

THE EVOLUTION of many of Whitman's poems can be traced from his first notation of what he liked to call 'the spinal idea' to the culminating point where he felt confident that the scattered lines, drafted frequently on scraps of paper or backs of envelopes, would 'always fall properly into place.' The conscious construction often amounted to no more than is suggested by one of the titles he considered for his final volume—'Life Mosaic of Native Moments.' The unity of his longer poems, as of Blake's *Prophetic Books,* is often arbitrarily designed rather than plastically composed. And the question still remains in many minds whether such constructions are poetry at all.

The two fundamental ways of regarding the poet, either as inspired genius or as craftsman, may divide American poetry between the descendants of Whitman and of Poe. For Poe, in spite of gross crudities and lapses in taste, was the first man in this country to declare that practice must not be separated from 'the theory that includes it'; and it was his strict if brittle insistence on the principles of art that helped free Baudelaire and the French symbolists from the effluvia of romanticism, and so cleared the way in turn for the emergence of Pound and Eliot. Therefore, having evolved the account of Whitman's poetry in his own terms, it is time now to let the opposition speak.

Two decades ago Pound held that thirty well-written pages might be winnowed from *Leaves of Grass,* but he has lately said that he can no longer find them. Eliot's dissatisfaction with the free verse of the imagists, several of whom hailed Whitman as an ancestor, led him to develop his own theory that 'poetry is right when it hesitates between two modes,' that what constituted the extraordinary resilience of, for example, the poets of the early seventeenth century, was 'the constant evasion and recognition of regularity.' The utter absence in Whitman of the periodic tension between withdrawing from and returning to a metrical norm produced an uninterrupted flow, which Eliot could reckon with only by characterizing Whitman as an occasional master of prose. It may be worth mentioning that the passage he once used to demonstrate this conviction, the description of 'an old-time sea-fight' in 'Song of Myself,' *was* originally prose, for it has recently been shown that Whitman's lines are based practically verbatim on John Paul Jones' own account of his engagement with the *Serapis*.[1] Pound has assessed Whitman's particular problem more closely, and has reached conclusions not unlike those we have found borne out by Whitman's diction and by his search for a form:

Whitman's faults are superficial, he does convey an image of his time, he has written *histoire morale,* as Montaigne wrote the history of his epoch. You can learn more of nineteenth-century America from Whitman than from any of the writers who either refrained from perceiving, or limited their record to what they had been taught to consider suitable literary expression. The only way to enjoy Whitman thoroughly is to concentrate on his fundamental meaning. If you insist, however, on dissecting his language you will probably find that it is wrong NOT because he broke all of what were considered in his day 'the rules' but because he is spasmodically conforming to this, that

1. See David Goodale, 'Some of Walt Whitman's Borrowings' (*American Literature,* May 1938).

or the other; sporadically dragging in a bit of 'regular' metre, using a bit of literary language, and putting his adjectives where, in the spoken tongue, they are not. His real writing occurs when he gets free of all this barbed wire.

Both Pound and Eliot, however, sought from the start another goal, exactitude of presentation, and found two of their masters in Rémy de Gourmont and Henry James. James had written at the age of twenty-two an unfavorable review of *Drum-Taps* (1865), which he concluded with an apostrophe 'from the intelligence to the bard.' His dissatisfaction caused him virtually to anticipate the formula of de Gourmont, which Pound was to single out for approval: 'Le style, c'est de sentir, de voir, de penser, et rien plus.' If both James and his followers would grant Whitman the power of seeing, they would deny him not merely that of thinking, but in any strict sense that of feeling as well. Pound's conviction is that you can move a reader only by the clarity of emotion which is inseparable from precision of thought. In Eliot's terms, 'every precise emotion tends towards intellectual formulation,' and he would agree with James' objections to Whitman's stylistic innovations, that they were false since unnecessary for the expression of such an uncomplicated sensibility. Eliot would also agree with James' dictum that 'prose, in order to be good poetry, must first be good prose.'

But Whitman—who was to say of James' novels, they are 'only feathers to me'—waived the whole question by announcing that the time had arrived to 'break down the barriers of form between prose and poetry.' He granted the value of 'rhyming metre' in preserving folk-poetry from generation to generation before the time of writing or print. He granted too that there were still illustrious poets 'whose shapes the mantle of such verse has beautifully and appropriately envelopt.' But he was none the less confident that henceforth this medium was to be restricted to light verse, or as he humorlessly phrased it, to the inferior realm of 'persiflage and the comic.' On the other hand, 'the truest and greatest *Poetry,* (while subtly and necessarily always rhythmic, and distinguishable easily enough), can never again, in the English language, be express'd in arbitrary and rhyming metre, any more than the greatest eloquence, or the truest power and passion.' He felt that the restrictions of formal verse could not fit the great modern themes, the enlargement of the people's experiences, the advance of science, the new facts of industry; that for these—and except for the exalted pitch it might be Edmund Wilson talking about 'the dying technique' of verse—the muse must resume 'that other medium of expression, more flexible, more eligible,' soaring 'to the freer, vast, diviner heaven of prose.'

You recall, in sharpest contrast, the conclusion of Richards' psychological investigation—and in spite of the examples of Proust and Joyce, the bulk of the evidence still seems to be on his side—that 'metre for the most difficult and most delicate utterances is the all but inevitable means.' But as far as Whitman's own practice was concerned, he followed his contention to the point even of sometimes making his poetry and prose interchangeable. In the preface to his first *Leaves* he came nearest to defining his own quality when he said of the poet's function, 'The time straying toward infidelity and confections and persiflage he withholds by his steady faith . . . he spreads out his dishes . . . he offers the sweet firmfibred meat that grows men and women. His brain is the ultimate brain. He is no arguer . . . he is judgment. He judges not as the judge judges but as the sun falling around a helpless thing.' [2] When Whitman decided to break up his preface and to incorporate much of it into 'By Blue Ontario's Shore' (1856), these sentences became three lines:

The years straying toward infidelity he withholds by his steady faith,
He is no arguer, he is judgment, (Nature accepts him absolutely,)
He judges not as the judge judges but as the sun falling round a helpless
    thing.

The first line is strengthened by dropping the trivial words after 'infidelity,' but some of the most lyric images are also sacrificed between this line and the next. The final sentence in the prose epitomizes the essence of Whitman's poetry and makes ridiculous any further efforts to establish formal distinctions between his two mediums. About as much as you can say is that his cadences come alive as poetry only when he feels his subject matter intensely.

Many of his prose descriptions, despite titles that might belong to his poems, 'Entering a Long Farm-Lane' or 'The Common Earth, the Soil,' are actually so diluted and hazy in feeling that they have little of the lyric immediacy of Thoreau. On the other hand, several of Whitman's direct accounts of his experiences in the war-hospitals have a poignance almost equal to that of the short pieces in *Drum-Taps:* 'I often come and

2. In this case the dots do not indicate omissions; Whitman used them himself instead of dashes.

sit by him in perfect silence . . . One time as I sat looking at him while he lay asleep, he suddenly, without the least start, awaken'd, open'd his eyes, gave me a long steady look, turning his face very slightly to gaze easier—one long, clear, silent look—a slight sigh—then turn'd back and went into his doze again. Little he knew, poor death-stricken boy, the heart of the stranger that hover'd near.'

The mature Henry James found in Whitman's letters to Pete Doyle (reviewing them in 1898) qualities similar to those here, 'the beauty of the natural,' 'the man's own overflow' in 'the love of life.' The expression of emotion is less self-conscious in the letters[3] than in the hospital sketches. In those to the young streetcar conductor, as James said, 'there is not even by accident a line with a hint of style—it is all flat, familiar, affectionate, illiterate colloquy.' James had long since outgrown the patronizing tone that had started his review of *Drum-Taps* with 'It has been a melancholy task to read this book,' and, according to Edith Wharton, now read Whitman aloud 'in a mood of subdued ecstasy.' What he could find even in the poet's letters were 'a thousand images of patient, homely American life . . . an audible New Jersey voice.' But neither these letters, nor his descriptions of the cases in the wards, would finally be mistaken for his poems. The passages quoted come as close as any, and

3. One sustained example is a letter to one of his army friends, which, since it also gives the fullest expression of the much disputed question of what he meant by comradeship, is worth quoting as a whole:

April 15, 1870.

Dear Benton Wilson,

Dear loving comrade, As I have just been again reading your last letter to me of December 19, last. I think I wrote to you on receiving it, but cannot now remember for certain. Sometimes, after an interval, the thought of one I much love comes upon me strong and full all of a sudden—and now as I sit here by a big open window, this beautiful afternoon, every thing quiet and sunny—I have been and am now, thinking so of you, dear young man, and of your love, or more rightly speaking, our love for each other —so curious, so sweet, I say so *religious*—We met there in the Hospital—how little we have been together—seems to me we ought to be some together every day of our lives— I don't care about talking, or amusement—but just to be together, and work together, or go off in the open air together—Now it is a long while since we have been together—and it seems a long while since I have had a letter. Don't blame me for not writing oftener. I know you would feel satisfied if you could only realize how and how much I am thinking of you, and with what great love, this afternoon. I can hardly express it in a letter— but I thought I would just write a letter this time off-hand to you, dearest soldier, only for love to you—I thought it might please you.

Nothing very new or different in my affairs. I am still working here in Atty Gens office —same posish—have good health—expect to bring out new editions of my books before long—how is the little boy—I send my love to him and to your wife and parents.

yet their matter-of-fact firmness lacks the flow that he could command as the fruition of having explored his analogies.

It is the kind of flow that you feel here:

I see in my mind the hired men and master dropping the implements of
    their labor in the field and wending their way with a sober satisfaction
    toward the house;
I see the well-sweep rise and fall;
I see the preparatory ablutions and the table laden with the smoking meal.

Yet this is not from the catalogues of 'Salut au Monde,' but is Thoreau's prose account—which I have arranged as free verse—of what had occurred to him when, during one of his rambles, he heard 'a farmer's horn calling his hands in from the field to an early tea.' Such dilating rhythm, suitable for the affirmation of the variety and plenitude of existence, was not limited to Whitman, but was the common property of the era which believed that, by breaking through the conventional restrictions of art, the writer could be invigorated by the elemental force of nature. 'Ablutions' might give the passage away as not being Whitman's, since it is a latinate word used accurately; and yet this word also marks how hard it was, even for a man as close to the soil as Thoreau, to throw off literary formalism and gain full realistic grasp of the commonest acts in the words that people really used for them.

Sometimes, as we have seen in the conclusion of Whitman's vision, the celebration of earth's abundance fell into a minor key, owing partly to the transcendental belief in the symbolical quality of even the tiniest natural object, partly to the inherent difficulty that this individualistic age found in any direct act of possession of complex social forces. Thoreau expressed his delight in being at the pond by means of images that are both common and isolated, and once again in falling cadences that could almost be arranged like Whitman lines: 'I am no more lonely than a single mullein or dandelion in a pasture, or a bean leaf, or sorrel, or a horse-fly, or a humble bee. I am no more lonely than the Mill Brook, or a weathercock, or the north star, or the south wind, or an April shower, or a January thaw, or the first spider in a new house.' Here, despite his declaration that he did not intend to write an ode to dejection, Thoreau's tone is not unlike the elegiac wistfulness of the Lake poets. What motivated their elegy was the sense of the impending loss of a rural world. This sense runs through the nineteenth century from Wordsworth to the local colorists, and reaches its amplest American expression in Mark Twain's reminiscences of the vanished Mississippi of his youth;[4] but such a sense was not ordinarily dominant in the Emersonian mood of confidence of our eighteen-forties and fifties. The transcendentalists' destruction of the divisions between poetry and prose came out of their robust assurance that all divisions were out of date. That this assurance could cause severe confusions in the craft of writing is witnessed by Melville's vertiginous floundering, even in *Moby-Dick,* between verbal harmonies that can excel the diapason of Thomas Browne, and the fulsome rhetoric of ham Shakespeareanism, in neither case very clear in his own mind whether he was pursuing the discipline of verse or of prose. It was only after some of the consequences of indiscriminate expansion on all fronts began occasionally to be perceived in the years following the Civil War that a writer like Sarah Jewett, whose ear had been trained on Flaubert as well as on the laconic precision of Maine speech, could note that without defined standards of what constituted the limits of a given art 'we confuse our scaffoldings with our buildings.'

But much the most searching examination of the general problem presented by Whitman's form was made by a man who, born twenty-five years after the author of *Leaves of Grass,* became the period's most thoroughgoing student of language and rhythm. Gerard Manley Hopkins devised his 'sprung rhythm' 'because it is the nearest to the rhythm of prose, that is the native and natural rhythm of speech, the least forced, the most rhetorical and emphatic of all possible rhythms, combining, as it seems to me, opposite and, one would have thought, incompatible excellences, markedness of rhythm—that is rhythm's self—and naturalness of expression.' He felt compelled to his innovation by the vogue of such emptiness as Swinburne's 'perpetual functioning of genius without truth, feeling, or any adequate matter to be at function on,' by this poet's in-

4. I am thinking especially of the magnificent opening chapters of *Life on the Mississippi,* and likewise of such occasional passages of reminiscence as this, in his *Autobiography,* of his uncle's place near Florida, Missouri: 'I can see the farm yet, with perfect clearness. I can see all its belongings, all its details; the family room of the house, with a "trundle" bed in one corner and a spinning-wheel in another . . . the vast fireplace, piled high, on winter nights, with flaming hickory logs from whose ends a sugary sap bubbled out, but did not go to waste, for we scraped it off and ate it; the lazy cat spread out on the rough hearthstones; the drowsy dogs braced against the jambs and blinking; my aunt in one chimney corner, knitting; my uncle in the other, smoking his corn-cob pipe . . . half a dozen children romping in the background twilight; "split"-bottomed chairs here and there, some with rockers; a cradle—out of service, but waiting, with confidence.'

creasing failure in his later work to recognize that 'words only are only words.' At the other pole was Wordsworth; but he, notwithstanding his 'spiritual insight into nature,' was, in Hopkins' view, a transparent instance of the chief fault in English poetry after Milton, its weakness in rhetoric. By rhetoric Hopkins meant something far more exact than Whitman did, even though they are on common ground in the younger poet's declaration, 'My verse is less to be read than heard . . . it is oratorical, that is the rhythm is so.' Rhetoric had seemed valuable to Whitman, as to Emerson, only at those moments when it flamed into eloquence and lost the necessity for any restraining rules. To Hopkins it meant 'all the common and teachable element in literature, what grammar is to speech, what thorough bass is to music, what theatrical experience gives to playwrights.'

Yet Bridges believed that he detected Whitman's influence, as he read the draft of 'The Leaden Echo and the Golden Echo' which Hopkins had sent him in 1882. Hopkins' answer is one of the most clarifying documents in the history of the development of modern poetry. He doubted the influence, since all he had ever read of Whitman were three poems, 'Come Up from the Fields Father,' 'To the Man-of-War Bird,' 'Spirit that Form'd this Scene,' and a few quotations in a review. He knew that this did not preclude the possibility of a strong impression on his style, since 'they say the French trace their whole modern school of landscape to a single piece of Constable's exhibited at the Salon early this century.' And he confessed what he 'should not otherwise have said, that I always knew in my heart Walt Whitman's mind to be more like my own than any other man's living. As he is a very great scoundrel this is not a pleasant confession. And this also makes me the more desirous to read him and the more determined that I will not.' He must have been referring to Whitman's homosexuality and his own avoidance of this latent strain in himself. For when he later sent Bridges his sonnet, 'Harry Ploughman,' where this feeling rises closest to the surface in his pleasure in the liquid movement of the workman's body, he hoped that there was not 'anything like it in Walt Whitman, as perhaps there may be, and I should be sorry for that.'

But despite the compelling and dangerous attraction that his Jesuit training taught him to cast out, he believed Bridges to be quite mistaken in supposing imitation in his poems. He granted that both Whitman and himself wrote 'in irregular rhythms,' but there the likeness ended. For

Whitman intended no other than a free rhythmic prose, a 'rugged,' or as he called it in 'Spirit that Form'd this Scene,' a 'savage' art and rhythm, which would fit its neglect of conventional technique to the vast Platte Cañon of Colorado, where this poem had been written in 1881. It was always Hopkins' contention against Bridges' incredulity that his 'sprung rhythm' was 'the most natural of things,' since 'it is the rhythm of common speech and of written prose, when rhythm is perceived in them.' It was indisputable, too, that Whitman's native instinct had rediscovered something similar to what Hopkins believed he had found by learning Anglo-Saxon: that before the language had bent itself to classical influence, and had still depended in its poetry wholly on speech stresses and on a variable number of unstressed syllables between, it was 'a vastly superior thing to what we have now.' Still there was all the difference in the world between Whitman's occasional unconscious approximations and Hopkins' deliberately planned and highly wrought effects, for 'in a matter like this a thing does not exist, is not *done* unless it is wittingly and willingly done; to recognize the form you are employing and to mean it is everything.'

However—and here is one of the flashes that can illuminate a whole period of cultural development: 'Extremes meet, and (I must for truth's sake say what sounds pride) this savagery of his art, this rhythm in its last ruggedness and decomposition into common prose, comes near the last elaboration of mine . . . The above remarks are not meant to run down Whitman. His "savage" style has advantages, and he has chosen it; he says so. But you cannot eat your cake and keep it: he eats his offhand, I keep mine.'

Both these extremes had been called into being by the inordinate expansiveness of the age. It had distended the language that men used away from the formal denotations of the eighteenth century, and had admitted such a range of connotations to meet new demands that the exact sense of any single one of them was hard to pin down. Whitman, as we have seen, luxuriated in such unlimited possibilities for suggestion, just as he spoke of 'the middle range of the nineteenth century' as 'a strange, unloosen'd, wondrous time.' But Hopkins' way was a hitherto unparalleled concentration. In his dissatisfaction with the vague poeticisms of Tennyson and Morris, he held that the true 'poetical language of an age should be the current language heightened.' Although Whitman would have agreed that the only sound basis for poetry was ordinary speech,

Hopkins carried the practice of his theory, in this respect as in all others, to far more rigorous lengths. Appalled by the flux of contemporary art, he argued with Bridges on the merit of 'terseness': 'it is like a mate which may be given, one way only, in three moves; otherwise, various ways, in many.'

When Hopkins said that he wanted to bring some of the resources of music into his poems, he did not mean Whitman's indefiniteness of association, for Hopkins spoke as a trained musician, an accomplished composer of fugues, who aimed to utilize in his language the most telling correspondence between sound and sense, and to give his compositions in verse an ordering comparable to the intricacies of counterpoint. In his comprehension of the significance of technical expertness in every art, he showed how different a thing tradition could be for a nineteenth-century European than for a typical American. With a no less complete rejection of contemporary practice than Whitman's, he did not therefore throw over other men's work altogether but dredged his way back to earlier values, which he assumed as his birthright, to Milton's rhetoric and the harmonies of Purcell. When Bridges taxed him with obscurity, he kept insisting that he was clearing the ground for a new popular style. The first essential was a return to strictness in the use of words, and it is manifest to us to-day that his compact method of joining them together compels them 'to be understood as he meant them to be, or understood not at all.'[5] In his intense precision of design, or 'inscape' as he named it, he is in revolutionary opposition both to Whitman's happy diffuseness and to Bridges' conventional decorum. He is likewise opposed to the belief of the late-century French poets that the symbol suggests far more than it can state, or—as Eliot has defined it for his own practice—to the belief that the symbol can be at once 'consciously concrete' and 'unconsciously general.'

However, inasmuch as Hopkins' most matured poems are so subtle and recondite as to require repeated reading, and even then some of them might still be imperfectly comprehensible without his own prose arguments, it is obvious that as the author of a popular style he fell even farther short than Whitman. Yet they both were insistent on the centrality of man. You would expect as one of Whitman's key declarations: 'In the centre of all, and object of all, stands the Human Being, towards

5. Robert Graves and Laura Riding, *A Survey of Modernist Poetry* (1928), p. 90.

whose heroic and spiritual evolution poems and everything directly or indirectly tend, Old World or New.' It might appear much less likely that an isolated Jesuit priest would declare, in a sonnet called 'To what serves Mortal Beauty?'

> To man, that needs would worship block or barren stone,
> Our law says: Love what are love's worthiest, were all known:
> World's loveliest—men's selves.

Hopkins was like Whitman in his ingenuous delight in the variegated surfaces of daily existence, in 'all trades, their gear and tackle and trim.' Moreover, writing during the days of the French Commune, he said, 'I must tell you I am always thinking of the Communist future . . . I am afraid some great revolution is not far off. Horrible to say, in a manner I am a Communist.' For he could see that their ideal was just. 'I do not mean the means of getting to it are. But it is a dreadful thing for the greatest and most necessary part of a very rich nation to live a hard life without dignity, knowledge, comforts, delight, or hopes in the midst of plenty—which plenty they make. They profess that they do not care what they wreck and burn, the old civilization and order must be destroyed. This is a dreadful look out but what has the old civilization done for them?'

This would chime in exactly with what Whitman thought about Europe. But he had great confidence that the United States, 'the born offspring of Revolt,' was different from any other country. He believed that here alone 'all forms of practical labor are recognized as honorable,' and consequently he could hope that the average bulk of mankind, 'a magnificent mass of material, never before equal'd on earth,' would continue to go forward in natural progress. However, after the Civil War, he began to know more fully that there was 'nothing more treacherous' than the attitude 'of nearly all the eminent persons' here towards the advance of democracy. He drafted a scheme for 'Songs of Insurrection' to warn against 'the more and more insidious grip of capital.'

He tackled the problem most sharply in notes for another undelivered lecture, on 'The Tramp and Strike Questions' (1879). The panic of 1873, with its aftermath of hard times, which reached their crisis four years later in the great railroad strike, the first occasion when federal troops fired on American workers, had compelled Whitman to think of our conditions in some of the same terms as Hopkins. He now realized that the critical issue was the struggle for adequate distribution of wealth, since 'beneath the whole political world, what most presses and perplexes to-day, sending vastest results affecting the future, is not the abstract question of democracy, but of social and economic organization, the treatment of working-people by employers, and all that goes along with it— not only the wages-payment part, but a certain spirit and principle, to vivify anew these relations.' At the time when most respectable citizens were deploring the violence of the strikers, Whitman asserted that 'the great American revolution of 1776 was simply a great strike, successful for its immediate object,' but whether a lasting success still remained to be tested. For 'if the United States, like the countries of the Old World, are also to grow vast crops of poor, desperate, dissatisfied, nomadic, miserably-waged populations, such as we see looming upon us of late years— steadily, even if slowly, eating into them like a cancer of lungs or stomach —then our republican experiment, notwithstanding all its surface-successes, is at heart an unhealthy failure.'

That these two so different poets had the same misgivings concerning the state of society shows how central such issues were. The conditions they foresaw and the question of how to deal with them remain the cardinal problems for the writer to-day. And their solutions, Whitman's drift towards socialism and Hopkins' conversion to Catholicism, are still the two extremes that are embraced, by Malraux and Eliot, by Auden and Hemingway (who, so far as I know, has not discussed in print the grounds for his faith). In his letter about the crisis dramatized for him by the Commune, Hopkins continued that as civilization

. . . at present stands in England it is itself in great measure founded on wrecking. But they [the people] got none of the spoils, they came in for nothing but harm from it then and thereafter. England has grown hugely wealthy but this wealth has not reached the working classes; I expect it has made their condition worse. Besides this iniquitous order the old civilization embodies another order mostly old and what is new in direct entail from the old, the old religion, learning, law, art, etc. and all the history that is preserved in standing monuments. But as the working classes have not been educated they know next to nothing of all this and cannot be expected to care if they destroy it. The more I look the more black and deservedly black the future looks, so I will write no more.

But Hopkins' comprehension of the desperate conditions of mankind not only made the substance of his poem 'Tom's Garland: upon the Unemployed'; it also served to heighten the tension that you feel almost everywhere in his work. His rejection of much that Whitman had included, his closing the doors against the open road, did not mean ease. His subject, which grew ever more obsessive, was struggle, the unending necessity to fight against inner division. His moments of triumph came when he could portray the fusion of man's energies at their full exertion, a harmony between discipline and spontaneity. He delighted in the movement of the windhover, in its unexampled splendor as it mounted above the earth:

> I caught this morning morning's minion, kingdom of daylight's dauphin,
>   dapple-dawn-drawn Falcon, in his riding
> Of the rolling level underneath him steady air, and striding
> High there, how he rung upon the rein of a wimpling wing
> In his ecstasy!

The difference from the movement of Whitman's man-of-war bird is overwhelming. However similar Whitman's exuberance in the wings matching the gale (similar enough for Hopkins to have possibly received the hint for his theme from it [6]), his eagle's muscles are flaccid by contrast:

> Days, even weeks untired and onward, through spaces, realms gyrating,
> At dusk that look'st on Senegal, at morn America,
> That sport'st amid the lightning-flash and thunder-cloud,
> In them, in thy experiences, had'st thou my soul,
> What joys! what joys were thine!

It is no adequate comparison of powers thus to put the opening of what Hopkins called 'the best thing I ever wrote' beside the conclusion of one of Whitman's merely average productions.[7] Still Hopkins might have justly contended that any group of Whitman's lines would show the same logical consequences of extreme protestantism, of his downright statement that formal verse was as outmoded as sacraments and dogma. Whitman also declared that he had an instinctive 'aversion to the church notion of an atonement,' because of 'its essential vulgarity, its wanton

6. The likelihood becomes greater in view of the proximity between the publication of Whitman's poem in the London *Atheneum* in 1876, where Hopkins said that he read it, and the composition of 'The Windhover' in the following spring.

7. A much more energetically imaginative poem on a similar subject is Whitman's 'The Dalliance of the Eagles.'

treachery' to what he believed to be the 'high and imperative' recognition that man was made to be free. To the Catholic this would furnish the most compelling evidence why Whitman's rhythms had naturally fallen into the final looseness of decomposition. Whitman said that he could not read Tolstoy's *Confession,* since he had never been worried by the question of whether he should be saved or lost. Yet in his desire to keep all doors open, he was willing to grant that the 'introspective, sin-seeking' element in the Russian 'may better represent the present day than I do.' However, his complacence did not leave his view of freedom so undeveloped that he thought any road as good as another or that the individual's impulse constituted the only law. When he surveyed the instances of usurping individualistic lawlessness in the era of the robber barons, he had reached his main position in *Democratic Vistas* (1871): that the crucial task for the American future was some reconciliation of the contradictory needs for full personal development and for 'one's obligations to the State and Nation,' to 'the paramount aggregate.' Although this conception of the One and the many would not have satisfied Hopkins, when Whitman went on to say that 'most people entirely misunderstand Freedom,' which we can attain only 'by a knowledge of, and implicit obedience to, Law,' he at least approached Engels' disciplined comprehension of freedom as 'the recognition of necessity.' [8]

It is wholly obvious to us now that Bridges was wrong in his notion that Hopkins' work was a case of 'unexampled liberty.' His reaction against flabbiness had driven him rather to an excessive control, which finally amounted to constriction. The 'terrible pathos' that became his habitual tone sprang never from doubt, but from the bitterest anguish, from the absence of movement in a life driven in on itself, from the unflinching scrutiny of his weakness before the perfection of God. But what is expressed has hardly any of the resolution of tragedy, since all action has been reduced to suffering. In his unsurpassable courage to endure, his world finally became as narrow as the cell in a monastery.

8. Despite the wandering course of his argument in *Democratic Vistas,* Whitman was entirely aware of the critical issue for democracy: 'Must not the virtue of modern Individualism, continually enlarging, usurping all, seriously affect, perhaps keep down entirely in America, the like of the ancient virtue of Patriotism, the fervid and absorbing love of general country? I have no doubt myself that the two will merge, and will mutually profit and brace each other, and that from them a greater product, a third, will arise. But I feel that at present they and their oppositions form a serious problem and paradox in the United States.'

His poems were not published by Bridges until 1918, three decades after Hopkins' death, but since his technical discoveries have had a chance to become generally known, especially during the past dozen years, they have provided the greatest single stimulus to the development of the craft of poetry. It is not surprising, however, that the poets who have profited from them most have used them to express attitudes far more akin to Whitman's. Auden and the other young radical poets have tried to develop sprung rhythm into a vehicle for public speech, for drama that will restore to poetry a wider social range. On the other hand, if we think of style rather than content, it is hard to say just whom Whitman has affected fruitfully. As a warming and sustaining voice he has heartened American artists of many kinds, Louis Sullivan and the painters grouping around Robert Henri, E. A. Robinson as well as Sherwood Anderson. He has helped them to break through the aridity of our academic culture to handle life with passion. But his kind of rhythm seems to have been suited almost exclusively to his own temperament; it has so little 'teachable element' to be transmitted that in other hands all virtue has tended to go out of it. Waiving the inevitable failures of his immediate disciples who had no more life of their own than a ventriloquist's dummies, it is hard to see whose style he has benefited during our poetic renaissance of the past thirty years. Pound said in 1916, 'I make a pact with you, Walt Whitman.' He had detested him long enough; he would come to him 'as a grown child' finally comes to 'a pig-headed father.'

Out of the unique flavor of his distaste for all concerned, Yvor Winters has maintained that, unlike Hart Crane who developed Whitmanian themes in verse deeply influenced by Eliot, Pound's relation to Whitman is one of form. His 'long line is in part a refinement of Whitman's line; his progression from image to image resembles Whitman's in everything save Whitman's lack of skill.' The *Cantos,* into which all manner of disparate material is introduced casually, 'are structurally Whitmanian songs, dealing with non-Whitmanian matter.'

Jeffers has voiced the negation to Whitman's triumphant optimism, in free verse which, superficially like that in the *Leaves,* actually is built much more deliberately into grave metrical patterns that reckon both with stresses and, as Jeffers has said, with 'the quantities of the unstressed syllables.' The conspicuous case of Whitman's influence is Carl Sandburg who, instead of holding with Jeffers that the republic is perishing in luxury and corruption and that 'humanity is the mould to break away from,' has responded whole-heartedly to Whitman's desires for this country. His biography of Lincoln is the only one to equal Whitman's depth of feeling for the land that the President came from; and his contacts with our saltiest life have yielded the devoted collection of our folk-songs. In his own poetry Sandburg has followed Whitman's lead by opening up new material from the Middle West, from the soil of cornhuskers, from the fierce violence of the smoke and steel of Chicago. He has thereby also stimulated ensuing poets to a wider scope, as MacLeish acknowledged by dedicating to him *Frescoes for Mr. Rockefeller's City*. But save on a few occasions, such as 'Psalm of Those Who Go Forth,' where his rhythms are made accurate by his own knowledge of physical labor, his descriptions are left even rougher than Whitman's, raw material not worked up, impressions hardly created. The difficulty in sharing very completely in just what is being said is owing most to the cloudiness of his mysticism. Whitman's faith, though incapable of exact definition, sprang from his profound acceptance of natural order, but Sandburg's is not so grounded, since he sees man's life as anarchy, swept by uncontrollable forces. Yet he is not a thoroughgoing tragic naturalist like Dreiser, for though repelled by the city's brutality, he is at the next moment celebrating its beautiful energy. His confused state of mind is a symptomatic response to our social chaos, but it can scarcely find the source of the life in Whitman's rhythms, the deep confidence in organic wholeness.

We are now in a position to test the validity of Coleridge's organic principle in a more comprehensive context than when we were faced with the preliminary necessity of outlining what it meant to Emerson and Thoreau as they started to build their styles upon it. Whitman, with no Yankee restraint, could push the analogy between art and nature to the farthest limits of recklessness and confusion. He could sometimes fail altogether to distinguish between unlikes, as when he asserted with rapt fatuity, during his western jaunt in 1879, that in the presence of the prairies 'a poem would be almost an impertinence,' since the prairies themselves were 'first-class art.' Yet, at his best, he penetrated to the core of Coleridge's principle, and demonstrated what it could mean by his own creation. However the idea came to him, whether from Emerson or from some magazine article on recent philosophy or aesthetics, or from his own intuitive discovery, he said, in an undated note, that his chief aim had been 'to construct a poem on the open principles of nature.' This was his response to the age's assurance that a work of art was a living growth. In his late dissatisfaction with Emerson's constriction, he was reasserting what he had said in his first preface, that 'the cleanest expression is that which finds no sphere worthy of itself and makes one.' He believed his poems to have the rounded profuseness of ripened fruit, and to prove, with like functional form, that 'anything is most beautiful without ornament.' His scattered remarks about beauty in art always led to the point that its 'fruition . . . is no chance of hit or miss' but as 'exact and plumb as gravitation,' the product of man in his fullest development, of 'beautiful blood and a beautiful brain.' He came to think not just of separate poems but of his whole book as an organism, and to contemplate the finished work with the hope that the whole was more than the abstract sum of its parts, a concrete entity incapable of dissection. This integrity remained his final goal—

> The journey done, the journeyman come home,
> And man and art with Nature fused again.

But despite his hope for this goal, his work is not a craftsman's. Unlike Thoreau's, it does not fulfil Maritain's conception of the good poet as an expert artisan. It comes much closer to that of the casual day-laborer, or of the 'jour printer' who said that his 'favorite symbol' for art 'would be a good font of type, where the impeccable long-primer rejects nothing.' His desire to be inclusive above all robbed him of the severe choice between alternatives, which the craftsman knows as his greatest difficulty and reward. This is not to lose sight of the fact that Whitman rejected decorative ornament on grounds the same as Greenough's, and would have agreed with Sheeler's reaffirmation of the same truth, that 'the shapes of the early barns of Bucks County—the barns perhaps even more than the houses—were determined by function; one sees that, feels it.' But Whitman did not dwell long enough on such a corollary as the painter added in his next sentence, 'The strong relationship between the parts produces one's final satisfaction'—not long enough to make it the primary agent in his poems.

Those who have turned to Whitman as one of their masters have believed the aim of art to be the expression of the artist's personality. They have stressed what they have learned from him as Henri did in saying that 'before a man tries to express anything to the world he must recognize in himself an individual, a new one, very distinct from others.' This painter's assertion that the unique spontaneous moment must be projected with technical bravura is the kind of thing James was deploring in the final heavy words spoken by 'the intelligence' to the bard of *Drum-Taps:* 'It is not enough to be rude, lugubrious, and grim. You must also be serious. You must forget yourself in your ideas. Your personal qualities—the vigor of your temperament, the manly independence of your nature, the tenderness of your heart—these facts are impertinent. You must be *possessed,* and you must strive to possess your possession. If in your striving you break into divine eloquence, then you are a poet.' James was at that time still sufficiently the conventional Anglo-Saxon to disapprove of the morals of the French novelists, and to prefer George Eliot to any of them. Yet Flaubert could phrase the craftsman's objection to the exalted seer, in fewer words: 'The author in his work ought to be like God in the universe, present everywhere but visible nowhere . . . The man is nothing, the work is everything.'

Although Whitman furnishes plenty of leads for the kind of interpretation that Henri and other romantics of gusto have made of him, his dominant intention was not to proclaim Rousseau's 'moi seul' but 'the divine average,' not 'je ne suis fait comme aucun de ceux que j'ai vus,' but 'what I assume you shall assume.' You can see him groping for his own kind of subordination, his own perception of the meaning of the union of opposites, when he says in the 1855 preface that the soul has 'measureless pride' in its own identity, but likewise 'sympathy as measureless as its pride and the one balances the other and neither can stretch too far while it stretches in company with the other. The inmost secrets of art sleep with the twain. The greatest poet has lain close betwixt both and they are vital in his style and thoughts.' Although he possessed no trace of the true opposite of pride, the humility that could lose sight of self altogether in the act to be performed, he could at least see one lesson in Dante —even if he never learned it—the challenge of his economy to 'diffuse moderns.' When he wrote a long letter to O'Connor [9] in the last winter

9. This letter was first printed in its entirety in the Random House edition of Whitman's *Complete Poetry and Selected Prose and Letters,* edited by Emory Holloway (1938). This edition is particularly notable for the number of letters and fugitive prose pieces that it makes available for the general reader. Whitman readers have long been indebted to Emory Holloway, especially for *The Uncollected Poetry and Prose of Walt Whitman* (1921), and for his inclusive edition of *Leaves of Grass* (1925) which contains all the variorum readings.

of the Civil War, explaining why he thought his forthcoming *Drum-Taps* an advance over his earlier work, he came closer to meeting James on common ground than that young reviewer would have believed possible. Whitman declared that the new book was 'more perfect as a work of art, being adjusted in all its proportions, and its passion having the indispensable merit that though to the ordinary reader let loose with wildest abandon, the true artist can see it is yet under control.' He granted that he was 'perhaps mainly satisfied with *Drum-Taps* because it delivers my ambition of the task that has haunted me, namely, to express in a poem (and in the way I like, which is not at all by directly stating it) the pending action of this *Time and Land we swim in,* with all their large conflicting fluctuations of despair and hope . . .' Nevertheless, after much discussion of its subject, he returned again to the effort to say more exactly why he felt this volume's superiority: 'because I have in it only succeeded to my satisfaction in removing all superfluity from it, verbal superfluity I mean. I delight to make a poem where I feel clear that not a word but is indispensable part thereof and of my meaning.' The drift of this letter, in its insistence on the proportions of form as well as on the voicing of his own age, makes explicit all that he implied by calling himself 'an American constructor.'

5. 'Landscapes projected masculine, full-sized and golden'

The Genre Painting of W. S. Mount

As a critic of the exhibition of the Brooklyn Art Union in 1851, Whitman showed the characteristic American attitude towards painting by assuming the conception and the content to be more important than the execution. Much of his space was given over to arguing that a vigorous augmentation of power would come to the work of our isolated painters if they were joined together in a close group, 'ardent, radical and progressive.' When he spoke of specific pictures, he was struck chiefly by the fact that such a one as Walter Libbey's 'Boy with a Flute,' the coloring and design of which he described with careful detail, was in marked contrast with what would have been a European's handling of the subject. Abroad 'the stamp of class' would have been upon this country boy; he would have been portrayed 'as handsome, perhaps, but he would be a young boor, and nothing more.' To Whitman's eyes 'the character of Americanism' in this canvas consisted in the spirited well-being of the figure, in such 'exquisitely fine' details as the natural grace of his hands holding the flute. There was nothing to prevent this boy 'becoming a President, or even an editor of a leading newspaper.' The Whitman who smiled over that thought was already headed in the direction of becoming the Whitman who told Pete Doyle that it had been his main object 'to get a real human being into a book.' And although he did not draw an analogy between his form and painting as he did with music, certain aspects of the advance of native realism in our pictures do, in fact, run closely parallel to his aims, and can help us finally to place his work in its amplest cultural context.

The most enduring strain in our mid-nineteenth-century painting can be seen now to have extended back to the earliest tradition active in our colonial art, that of the firm and incisive Dutch school which was dominant in Europe at the time when our first settlers were coming over.[1] It continued as the standard for our seventeenth-century portraits, and no school could have been better suited to the single demand which was made by the sitters, for solid likeness. The colonial stress on serviceability, which had to be met by any art that was to survive, is to be found as well in the most living branch of our early literature, the writing of history, in the skilled craftsmanship of William Bradford or of those biographies of Cotton Mather's where he forgot his conspicuous learning in his concentration on the simple record. The cumulative value of the fidelity to visible fact was to have its best demonstration, so far as painting is concerned, long after the specific impetus from the Netherlands had been forgotten—in the extraordinary achievement of Copley who, in spite of the scantiest opportunity for professional training, possessed so much authority and distinction in contrast with the softness of Reynolds.

By the time of Whitman many other influences had drifted in, and our first landscape school, the Hudson River group, had been distended

1. This point has been made by Alan Burroughs, whose *Limners and Likenesses: Three Centuries of American Painting* (1936) is the most comprehensive history of our painting yet to have been written.

by Bierstadt to the Rocky Mountains. One critic's awe before such inflated work (1853) is akin to Whitman's loosest expansiveness: 'The future spirit of our art must be inherently vast like our western plains, majestic like our forests, generous like our rivers.' But the quieter desire, to record life as it was, still prevailed, and could be seen at its homely best in William Sidney Mount (1807-68), whom Whitman's review took as a standard of comparison for his young Brooklyn painters. Mount had been born at Setauket, Long Island, a dozen years earlier than Whitman, and up to the age of seventeen had been, as he said, 'a hard-working farmer's boy.' His longing to be an artist had then necessarily followed the customary apprenticeship of that day as he engaged with an older brother in painting signs. Some of his first independent canvases attracted the critical approval of Washington Allston who, in urging that he take Van Ostade and Steen for his models, recognized the realistic vein in which the young man's strength lay. But though Mount is to be classified among our genre painters, he avoided the excesses to which that school often went in its sacrifice of all plastic interest to a humorous or sentimental situation. He was as far from that extreme as he was from the age's susceptibility to romantic vagueness. He declared as his downright program: 'I shall endeavor to copy nature as I have tried to do with truth and soberness. There has been enough written on ideality and the grand style of Art, etc. to divert the artist from the true study of natural objects.'

In 'Eel Spearing at Setauket' he was not preoccupied with making an illustration of a quaint regional custom, for though he noted with scrupulous precision every detail of his boat, even to the clothes worn by the boy in the stern and the old Negress in the bow, the effect of the canvas is produced by the deftness of its design. This depends on the triangle formed by the rising lines of the boy's paddle and the woman's spear, their partial repetition in delicate reflections in the still water, and the harmonious interrelation between the subdued tones of this foreground and the sloping green hill of the distant shore. Not that Mount, as an occasional drinking companion of the Duyckincks and Melville, was lacking in humor or in a relish for the humorous in the scenes he often chose. This quality has full play in 'Coming to the Point,' whose familiar incident was described by a newspaper as 'an image of pure Yankeeism' wherein both of the horsetraders 'seem to be "reckoning," whittling, both delaying. The horse, which is the object of their crafty equivocations, stands tied as "sleek as a whistle," waiting for a change of owners.' But even here Mount's main concern is with the representation of amply modelled bodies in light and shade. His record of the native flavor is akin to the best strain in Whittier and Lowell, who wrote of the rural and the near at hand, not because the local was odd, but because it was broadly human.

Mount was most like Whitman in 'Long Island Farmhouses,' for there everything depends on accuracy of vision. The children grouped around the back door where a woman sits at work are hardly more important to the composition than the chickens and turkeys in the front yard. The subject is a full impression of a wide-shingled house, unpainted but stained by the elements, dappled by faint shadows from a spreading tree, and set into a rhythmic arrangement with a more distant house, with a cluster of outbuildings, and with the straggling lines of rail fences that lead the eye to a glimpse of the Sound. The reliance for color upon a simple tonality of dominant tans and greens against a graying sky makes for an effect as single and undistracted as that of Whitman's three-line 'Farm Picture':

> Through the ample door of the peaceful country barn,
> A sunlit pasture field with cattle and horses feeding,
> And haze and vista, and the far horizon fading away.

It is not fanciful or arbitrary to think of Whitman's poems in relation to the development of open-air painting. He reminded himself in his notebooks to make 'living pictures,' and frequently he gave his shorter poems such titles as 'A Paumanok Picture,' or 'A Sight in Camp,' and composed them as objective sketches of cavalry crossing a ford, or a group of children around a knife-grinder in a city street, or even as full-length portraits like that of the eighty-year-old father of the early Republic, 'the frequent gunner and fisher,' whose massive vigor still includes him among the children of Adam. The first sign of this method is in a notebook about 1850, the earliest notebook that contains not merely outlines and plans but a whole poem. This is called 'Pictures,' and uses Whitman's simplest type of structure by listing all the things he has 'seen,' from the time of the Egyptian prophets and of the master and his disciples in Athens down to 'this is Chicago, my great city.' Whitman never printed it, and showed the grounds for his dissatisfaction by writing at the top, 'Break all this into several Pictures'—which he did by scattering variants of passages through a number of poems during the next thirty years. The belief enunciated in the final line, that

Every rod of land or sea affords me, as long as I live, inimitable pictures,

had already played an important part in Whitman's efforts to master concreteness of statement. He anticipated Hopkins' objection to Swinburne, that 'he does not see nature at all . . . at any rate there is no picture,' by his determination to free himself from the cheaply colored melodrama of his first newspaper stories. He began to know, as Hemingway has known, that the only way to tell the truth about his feelings was to objectify them. This was the quality in *Leaves of Grass* that was to impress John Sloan no less than it did Henri. As Sloan has said: 'A poetic painting of a fog or a moor is just about the limit in "no-thingness." Poetic in the "ic" sense. Poetic in the sense of Whitman is something else entirely. He was dealing with things, things used as symbols.' You can observe Whitman working for this quality in his very first notebook.[2] The effort sprang from his emerging perception:

I will not be a great philosopher, and found any school, and build it with iron pillars, and gather the young men around me, and make them my disciples, that new superior churches and politics shall come.—But I will take

2. Consider this attempt to present the problem created by the fact of poverty: 'I am hungry and with my last dime get me some meat and bread, and have appetite enough to relish it all.—But then like a phantom at my side suddenly appears a starved face, either human or brute, uttering not a word. Now do I talk of mine and his?—Has my heart no more passion than a squid or clam shell has? I know the bread is my bread, and that on it must I dine and sup. I know I may munch, and not grit my teeth against the laws of church or state . . . The orthodox proprietor says This is mine, I earned or received or paid for it,—and by positive right of my own I will put a fence around it, and keep it exclusively to myself . . . Yet—yet—what cold drop is that which slowly patters, patters with sharpened poisoned points, on the skull of his greediness, and go whichever way he may, it still hits him, though he see not whence it drips nor what it is?'

The language may still be raw, but Whitman has at least begun to be able to suggest the physical pressures that enter into a state of emotion. This marks a great advance not merely over the banal sentimentality of his hack novel, *Franklin Evans; or The Inebriate* (1842), but likewise over the lifeless abstractions with which he had tried to express, in one of his 'Sun-Down Papers' for *The Long Island Democrat* (1840-1), a serious vision of the majesty of truth: 'Kneel, then, oh! insect of an hour, whose every formation is subject enough for an eternity of wonder—and whose fate is wrapped in a black shroud of uncertainty—kneel on that earth which thou makest the scene of thy wretched strife after corruptible honors—of thy own little schemes for happiness—and of thy crimes and guilt—kneel, bend thy face to the sand, spread out the puny arms with which thy pride would win so much glory—and adore with a voiceless awe, that Unknown Power,' etc.

each man and woman of you to the window and open the shutters and the sash, and my left arm shall hook you round the waist, and my right shall point you to the endless and beginningless road along whose sides are crowded the rich cities of all living philosophy, and oval gates that pass you in to fields of clover and landscapes clumped with sassafras, and orchards of good apples, and every breath through your mouth shall be of a new perfumed and elastic air, which is love.—Not I—not God—can travel this road for you.[3]

These distinctions were of the greatest significance to him, for he put them, in briefer phrasing, near the opening of 'Song of Myself.' His insistence that 'you shall not look through my eyes either, nor take things from me,' his desire to present reality to his readers directly and not through the medium of himself, mark how he went beyond the Emersonian manner of hanging a veil of idealism between the facts and his audience. Such considerations seem to have conditioned his resolve for 'a perfectly transparent, plate-glassy style,' which is not really in conflict with his repeated emphasis on 'indirection,' since the value of the symbol remains, and the only warning that Whitman gives himself is to be sure to avoid making his poems 'in the spirit that comes from the study of pictures of things—and not from the spirit that comes from the contact with real things themselves.'

The values of his imagery are primarily visual and tactual, for his eye was more accurate than his ear, and it was the long passage in 'Song of Myself' on the enigmatic release of touch, 'quivering me to a new identity,' which ended with the declaration that from its ache and recompense had come his power to project his landscapes, 'masculine, full-sized and golden.' He was not thinking there of painting, but directly of the forces of nature. When he did draw an analogy for his 'pictures,' he was most likely to take pride that in his *Leaves* 'everything is literally photographed,' since he could thus believe that he was putting his work in line with the technical discoveries of his age.

3. Thoreau said to Emerson (1845): 'Philosophers are broken-down poets.' Emerson elaborated substantially the same thought in one of his late lectures (1870): 'The poet sees wholes and avoids analysis; the metaphysician, dealing as it were with the mathematics of the mind, puts himself out of the way of the inspiration, loses that which is the miracle and creates the worship. The poet believes; the philosopher, after some struggle, has only reasons for believing.'

The Realism of Millet and of Eakins

Yet, in his later years particularly, he did think of his work in relation to painting. He said that 'the *Leaves* are really only Millet in another form.' When he visited Quincy Shaw's collection in Boston in 1881, he spent 'two rapt hours' there, for he found in 'The Sower' above all 'that last impalpable ethic purpose' which was his touchstone for great art. Before then he had known only occasional prints, though the vogue of Millet (1814-75) in this country dated back to William Morris Hunt's enthusiastic discovery while himself an art student in France in the late eighteen-forties. Hunt had helped keep the painter from starving by buying several canvases, 'The Sower' among them. On his return to America in 1856, he had brought these to Boston, along with Corots and Rousseaus, and his generous efforts provided there the first market for the Barbizon group at a time when they were hardly acknowledged in France. That day when Whitman first saw some of these pictures gave him the sense that he finally understood the French Revolution, the titanic force of those masses who, long crushed to earth in poverty, had become 'the stronger and hardier for that repression—waiting terribly to break forth.' After that he talked so often about Millet as 'my painter,' as 'a whole religion in himself,' that Bucke drew up a long list of mechanical parallels between the two men. Their authentic kinship lay in the similarity of their inspiration. Whitman would have agreed with the painter's simple statement that 'Art began to decline from the moment that the artist did not lean directly and naively upon nature.' What the poet saw in the pictures was not the obvious manipulation of sentiment which makes Millet so soft to twentieth-century eyes, so much less searching a revolutionary painter than Daumier. On the other hand, Whitman was not blinded, as were most of the painter's romantic contemporaries, into mistaking the choice of somber material for unnecessary brutality and ugliness.

It was natural that an American like Hunt should have been among the first to recognize that Millet's subjects were 'real people who had work to do.' It was natural for Sarah Jewett to perceive that the French painter's 'Washerwoman at Her Tub' was endowed with a dignity of classic proportions. Such perception entered into her own presentation of New England country-folk, as when she showed a fisherman's widow like Almiry Todd to be not only the drolly downright and loquacious figure who weighted down the stern of a dory, but also, in an unperceived moment while she walked up the rocky shore path, as massive in her grief as Antigone 'alone on the Theban plain.' Whitman took similar pleasure in the fact that the painter 'did what he found right at hand . . . the peasants at his doors.' His response met the artist on his own ground, for Millet had insisted that though he saw the sweat that went into the gaining of the daily bread, his aim was 'to paint the soul.' In Whitman's view this was what gave Millet his 'unique majesty of expression,' the power to portray the people as heroic as they were.

The profound reality that Whitman felt in Millet was coherent with what he wanted in our literature. In some notes for a lecture, under the heading, '*beauty,* series of comparisons,' he phrased his ideal as 'not the beautiful girl or the elegant lady . . . but the mechanic's wife at work,' 'not the vaunted scenery of the tourist, picturesque, but the plain landscape, the bleak sea shore, or the barren plain, with the common sky and sun.' When he objected to the intrusion of ornament, he also added that the human form 'must never be made ridiculous' or 'caricatured.' When Hamlin Garland talked to him enthusiastically about the local-color school of Cable, Harris, and Mary Wilkins as the forerunner of powerful native art, Whitman took strenuous exception. He objected because these writers did not seem 'content with the normal man,' whereas in all his coming and going among the camps of the Civil War he had been everywhere struck with 'the decorum'—a word he liked to use—'of the common soldier, his good manners, his quiet heroism, his generosity, even his good, real grammar.' Those typical qualities of the farmer and the mechanic were obscured by emphasis on regional peculiarities, and Whitman was firm in saying that the novel or drama claiming to show our life 'is false if it deals mainly or largely with abnormal or grotesque characters.' In his final year he wrote an essay on 'American National Literature' wherein he summed up the three prevailing traits to be found in groups of American men as 'Good-Nature, Decorum, and Intelligence.' These were substantially what he had already told Garland to be necessary if 'the really heroic character of the common American' was to be adequately depicted. Though Whitman did not make the point, a quiet humanism, a devoted tenacity to broadly representative qualities, were what distinguished Mount from the run of genre painters, and Sarah Jewett from most of the other local colorists.

In concluding his tribute to Millet, Whitman had asked, 'Will America ever have such an artist out of her own gestation, body, soul?' He gave two of his very latest passages of verse to phrasing his response to Inness' poetic vision of 'The Valley of the Shadow of Death,' and he would doubtless have felt some sympathy with the Swedenborgian strain that caused that painter to say that 'Art is the endeavor on the part of the mind to express through the senses ideas of the great principles of unity.' But Whitman knew at closer hand work from another school. A favorite topic of conversation at Camden posed the merits of the increasing number of portraits and drawings of the poet. About the canvas finished by Eakins in the spring of 1888 Traubel felt a little uneasily that it had caught Whitman in the mood of 'I have said that the soul is not more than the body,' rather than 'I have said that the body is not more than the soul.' It made him think 'of a rubicund sailor with his hands folded across his belly about to tell a story.' Whitman agreed that it might give him a touch 'too much Rabelais instead of just enough.' But he liked it the best of all the portraits, for in contrast the Alexander was too idealized and the Gilchrist lacked 'guts.' 'I never knew of but one artist, and that's Tom Eakins,' he said, 'who could resist the temptation to see what they thought ought to be rather than what is.' That was the Whitman who told Traubel: 'Be sure to write about me honest; whatever you do, do not prettify me; include all the hells and damns.' But when he thought that 'we need a Millet in portraiture—a man who sees the spirit but does not make too much of it—one who sees the flesh but does not make a man all flesh—all of him body,' he veered closer to Traubel and said that Eakins 'almost achieves this balance—almost—not quite: Eakins errs just a little, just a little—a little—in the direction of the flesh.'

In these last years Whitman greatly enjoyed the company of the painter, who used to come over from Philadelphia to see him. A quarter of a century the poet's junior, Eakins (1844-1916) had already encountered many of the problems of being an artist in America. He shared Whitman's feeling of solidarity with ordinary people, but when he proceeded to paint from what he knew, that a naked woman 'is the most beautiful thing there is—except a naked man,' he quickly found himself hounded by the genteel tradition's high priests of taste. He lost his job as teacher at the Pennsylvania Academy, just as Whitman had lost his clerkship in the Department of the Interior for writing 'an indecent book'; and his work was condemned until after his death to an even greater obscurity of reputation than had befallen *Leaves of Grass.* Whitman sensed something of what his friend was up against when he said that Eakins was not 'appreciated by the artists, so-called—the professional elects: the people who like Eakins best are the people who have no art prejudices to interpose.'

Eakins, on his part, admired especially the poet's power of concrete observation, and used to say, 'Whitman never makes a mistake.' He would naturally have responded to such swiftly accurate notations as

> The opium-eater reclines with rigid head and just-open'd lips,

or

> The runaway slave came to my house and stopt outside . . .
> Through the swung half-door of the kitchen I saw him limpsy and weak.

Yet the divergences in the scope of their realism mark them unmistakably as belonging to different generations, and can serve to place Whitman as effectively as would a contrast between his method and that of Zola as used by Frank Norris and Dreiser, or as would an analysis of the poet's even wider separation from the restricted theories of realism developed by Howells and James.

The painter came from much the same kind of stock as Whitman, with a Dutch Quaker strain on his mother's side, though Scotch-Irish rather than English on his father's. Eakins' father, a skilled writing-master who taught the old copperplate hand in the Philadelphia schools, seems to have passed on to his son an early interest in mechanical dexterity. His schoolboy curiosity in natural science never left him, and gave him an equipment of exactitude such as Whitman never possessed. He studied anatomy with a passionate closeness, he later followed Muybridge in pioneer experiments of taking moving-pictures of a horse, and it is apparent from his choice of doctors' clinics for the subjects of his most ambitious canvases that nothing absorbed him more than a surgical operation—unless it was a boxing match.

When he landed in France at twenty-two, to spend the only years that he ever lived away from Philadelphia in working under Gérôme, he was already a man of gravely independent tastes. In one of his regular accounts of his expenditures he remarked on his purchase of a volume of Rabelais, 'a writer, priest, doctor of medicine, and hater of priesthood. He wrote a very fine book which I bought and am now reading.' He also reported to his father his discovery of the nude form as the painter's central subject and discipline. He took the job of being an art student with such single-minded thoroughness that he seems to have had little time to find out about contemporary painting. Though he was later to admire Courbet and Manet, his letter home about the Universal Exposition of 1867 bore no sign that he was aware of the furore caused by their refusal and by their separate exhibit in a shed outside the grounds. Most of his space was given over to describing the machinery, and he showed himself a good American by declaring that our great locomotive was 'by far the finest there.'

He was not much concerned with aesthetic discussion, and even shied away from words that seemed pretentious, preferring to say 'workshop' instead of 'studio,' 'painter' instead of 'artist,' 'naked' instead of 'nude.' The nearest approach he ever made to defining a philosophy of art was in another long letter to his father. This is notable for its expression, with the uncomplicated directness of a Hemingway, of a position from which he was never to swerve. It has much bearing too on a further phase of the organic style, on what primary analogies between art and nature have continued to mean when freed from transcendental philosophy. 'The big artist,' Eakins wrote, in terms also not unlike those in Marin's letters,

does not sit down monkey-like and copy a coal-scuttle or an ugly old woman like some Dutch painters have done, nor a dung pile, but he keeps a sharp eye on Nature and steals her tools. He learns what she does with light, the big tool, and then color, then form, and appropriates them to his own use. Then he's got a canoe of his own, smaller than Nature's, but big enough for every purpose . . . With this canoe he can sail parallel to Nature's sailing. He will soon be sailing only where he wants to . . . but if ever he thinks he can sail another fashion from Nature or make a better-shaped boat, he'll capsize or stick in the mud, and nobody will buy his pictures or sail with him in his old tub. If a big painter wants to draw a coal-scuttle, he can do it better than the man that has been doing nothing but coal-scuttles all his life . . . In a big picture you can see what o'clock it is, afternoon or morning, if it's hot or cold, winter or summer, and what kind of people are there, and what they are doing and why they are doing it.[4] The sentiments run beyond words. If a man makes a hot day he makes it like a hot day he once

4. Compare the drift of this passage with those from Thoreau and Hemingway quoted on p. 85.

WALT WHITMAN, 1887, BY THOMAS EAKINS

saw or is seeing; if a sweet face, a face he once saw or which he imagines from old memories or parts of memories and his knowledge, and he combines and combines, never creates—but at the very first combination no man, and least of all himself, could ever disentangle the feelings that animated him just then, and refer each one to its right place.

Though Eakins put light first in his list of 'tools,' he was, unlike Monet, not interested in painting it for itself but only as it could reveal form. His typical subjects were more homely than those of most of the impressionists: men and women absorbed in daily events, his boyhood friend Max Schmitt in a single scull, a woman singing, his sister in a skating costume, his father and himself hunting reed-birds, shad-fishermen on the Delaware mending their net. He painted each event in its detailed action, with a dislike of idealization, a belief that beauty consisted in fitness, an insistence on firmness and solidity. He had not been taught his subjects in Gérôme's studio but had grown into them by himself. He came increasingly to believe—in this he went to the opposite pole from his contemporary Whistler—that the elimination of decoration for dynamic fundamentals was bound up with a painter's mastery of his own environment, his country's 'life and types.'

He was squarely in line with Emerson and Thoreau when he said that 'nature is just as varied and just as beautiful in our day as she was in the time of Phidias.' But he was more akin to Whitman in that early letter to his father:

I love sunlight and children and beautiful women and men, their heads and hands, and most everything I see, and some day I expect to paint them as I see them, and even paint some that I remember or imagine . . . but if I went to Greece to live there twenty years I could not paint a Greek subject, for my head would be full of classics, the nasty, besmeared, wooden, hard, gloomy, tragic figures of the great French school of the last few centuries, and Ingres, and the Greek letters I learned at the High School, and my mud marks of the antique statues. Heavens, what will a fellow ever do that runs his boat, a mean old tub, in the marks not of Nature but of another man that run after Nature centuries ago?

As Lloyd Goodrich has put it: while La Farge and Kenyon Cox worked from a wider range of culture and taste in towards their own somewhat derivative creation, Eakins 'worked from the core of reality out into art.'[5] Though his paid commissions were few, owing partly to his refusal to flatter, partly to the scandal over the loss of his teaching position in 1886, he chose among his acquaintances the subjects who interested him most, and before he was through he had made a record of American types that has not been surpassed by any of our novelists. These portraits ran into several hundred, starting with the sitters nearest at hand, his father at his desk or with friends playing chess; baseball players, sportsmen, and hunting companions; his sister at the piano, with a child on the floor; his fiancée with a cat in her lap; many of his students, and other painters, sculptors, and engravers; art critics, also, and collectors and dealers. Unexcelled for the light they throw on our professional men are his diverse studies of chemists, inventors, engineers, professors in the the University of Pennsylvania and its Medical School, journalists, lawyers, and musicians. The leaders in the Catholic Church attracted him because they were intelligent men and not too other-worldly, and because of the color of their vestments. His canvases of them included James Wood, the first Archbishop of Philadelphia, Cardinal Martinelli, Monsignor James F. Loughlin, the Very Reverend John J. Fedigan—an index in their faces as in their names of the racial history of their Church in this country. Eakins painted many of his friends' wives, knitting or practicing music, though he liked them best in party dresses, the open sleeves of which were the nearest the age would let him come to their bodies. The few society ladies were not pleased with their likenesses; it would be interesting to know what Mrs. McKeever, the mother of a prizefighter, thought of hers.

His favorite device for making the closest identification he could with the actual was to surround his sitters with whatever objects concerned them most. The portrait of Frank Cushing, a pioneer ethnologist, let the painter represent some Indian relics from the New Mexican pueblos. Mrs. Frishmuth is in the midst of the collection of musical instruments that she gave to the Pennsylvania Museum. The celebrated physicist Henry Rowland holds his diffraction grating for spectrum analysis. In this case even the frame is decorated with lines of the spectrum and with mathematical formulae—a point where the heaping of sheer details becomes as distracting to the spectator as it does in Whitman's catalogues.

---

5. I have been greatly indebted to Goodrich's admirable monograph, *Thomas Eakins: His Life and Work* (1933).

But we have not yet quite completed Eakins' catalogue of American life, which runs parallel to Whitman's in attaining, as Henri saw, 'the reality of beauty in matter as it is.' He included Civil War veterans, and Rear-Admiral Sigsbee who had been commander of the *Maine,* manufacturers and merchants and a member of the firm of John Wanamaker. His first important commission had been from the Union League of Philadelphia for a portrait of President Hayes shortly after his inauguration (1877). But when the painter did not give them an exalted pillar of Republicanism with the proper red plush drapery, but instead a man in ordinary clothes seriously at work at his desk, and with his face flushed because the day was warm, the gentlemen of the Union League were profoundly shocked. They did what they could. They at first refused the canvas, but finally paid the four hundred dollars that they had originally agreed to. Then they destroyed or perhaps only hid it. It has never been seen since.

Even the foregoing recital shows that though Whitman and Eakins are alike in taking democratic character for their main theme, the poet broadly celebrates the sacredness of every human being, whereas the painter scrutinizes the traits of the specific individual before him. Eakins was matter-of-fact, not expansive, the trained artisan doing his job. He was less imaginative than Whitman, and gave a downright account of his conscious processes: 'You can copy a thing to a certain limit. Then you must use intellect.' The painter was not given to philosophical speculation, and was in less open revolt than the poet against the cultural limitations of his day. Although none knew better than Eakins that 'respectability in art is appalling,' he spent little breath in protest, but felt adjusted to an ordinary community from which he could draw the raw materials for his art. His conception of the world was less spacious than Whitman's, and his work sometimes shows it in a certain rigidity in his figures and a lack of vibrancy in color. He may at times have been more the scientist than the artist, but he was generally saved from a tendency to dryness by his desire for the 'solid, springy, and strong,' and by his eagerness not only for form but for action: 'Don't copy. Feel the forms. Feel how much it swings, how much it slants.' Though the low-toned range of his palette was in keeping with the quiet seriousness of his temperament, its dark monotony has been exaggerated by some critics. The most striking quality in his portrait of Whitman is the mellowness produced by the simple contrasts in clear pigments, between the grays of his hair and beard, the darker gray of his suit, the ruddy face, and the white Byronic collar with its narrow edging of lace—in which detail Eakins seems to have caught a special taste of the bard's. He caught something more important in the expression of the shaded, generous, but finally inscrutable eyes.

In so far as the effects of one art can approach those of another, Eakins is most like Whitman in 'The Swimming Hole,' where one of his favorite relaxations provided the material for this natural arrangement of the naked bodies of some of his students and himself against a summer landscape. The design is one of his most concentrated, and almost matches those of the Italian Renaissance in constructing a rhythmical pyramid. The base runs from a swimmer in the water to another thigh-deep at the edge, and is extended by the downward thrust from the legs of a third man stretched out on the bank. The axis rises from the head of this last man to the head of a standing figure who is watching another dive. The descending line of this latter body carries the eye back down into the water again. The massive, almost sculptural handling of all the bodies shows what Eakins meant by saying, 'The more factors you have, the simpler will be your work.' What would have appealed most to Whitman was the free flexible movement within the composition, and the rich physical pleasure in the outdoor scene and in the sunlight on the firmly modelled flesh.

Whitman's work, in turn, approaches the powerful construction of Eakins in his sketch, 'Twenty-eight young men bathe by the shore,' in 'Song of Myself,' or in his more detailed portrayal of the funeral of a Broadway stage-driver:

Cold dash of waves at the ferry-wharf, posh and ice in the river, half-frozen mud in the streets,
A gray discouraged sky overhead, the short last daylight of December,
A hearse and stages, the funeral of an old Broadway stage-driver, the cortege mostly drivers.

Steady the trot to the cemetery, duly rattles the death-bell,
The gate is pass'd, the new-dug grave is halted at, the living alight, the hearse uncloses,
The coffin is pass'd out, lower'd and settled, the whip is laid on the coffin, the earth is swiftly shovel'd in,
The mound above is flatted with the spades—silence,

A minute—no one moves or speaks—it is done,
He is decently put away—is there any thing more?

He was a good fellow, free-mouth'd, quick-temper'd, not bad-looking,
Ready with life or death for a friend, fond of women, gambled, ate hearty,
  drank hearty,
Had known what it was to be flush, grew low-spirited toward the last, sick-
  en'd, was help'd by a contribution,
Died, aged forty-one years—and that was his funeral.

Thumb extended, finger uplifted, apron, cape, gloves, strap, wet-weather
  clothes, whip carefully chosen,
Boss, spotter, starter, hostler, somebody loafing on you, you loafing on somebody, headway, man before and man behind,
Good day's work, bad day's work, pet stock, mean stock, first out, last out,
  turning-in at night,
To think that these are so much and so nigh to other drivers, and he there
  takes no interest in them.

An interesting thing to observe here is how the poet, after giving the
facts with swift directness, adds, as a final stanza to complete the man's
likeness, one of his most original experiments with language. He weaves
into a pattern the equipment and lingo of the driver's job as they blended
into the routine of a day. The whole portrait furnishes an instance of the
kind of brooding care Whitman continued to give to his poems long after
their first composition. It appeared in the 1855 *Leaves* as the fourth section of 'To Think of Time,' and was the realistic earthward element in
that poem's affirmation of the conquest of death by the soul. In 1871 the
poet decided that this concrete illustration of how 'the perpetual successions of shallow people are not nothing as they go' needed more adequate framing, and so wrote, as an opening stanza:

> A reminiscence of the vulgar fate,
> A frequent sample of the life and death of workmen,
> Each after his kind.

He had previously made other changes. In the first revision in 1856 he
had merely added the specific word 'Broadway,' and had tightened up the
next to last line by dropping three 'or's' between its phrases. However,
in 1860 he introduced several important new details. The 'trot to the
cemetery' became 'steady' in place of 'rapid,' thus bringing it into con-

sonance with the kind of movement that the rhythm here conveys. In
addition he made the scene more visual by inserting, in the lines immediately succeeding, 'new-dug,' 'pass'd out,' and 'the mound above is flatted
with the spades.' He also added the word 'silence' and thereby created the
very sense of that minute's pause. In the second line of the next stanza
'played some' was sharpened to 'gambled.' But he was not wholly satisfied with his characterization, for, turning again to this poem in 1881,
he dropped what had been the opening words of this same line for
twenty-six years, 'Witty, sensitive to a slight.' He also excised two other
phrases which struck him then as needless: 'other vehicles give place'
after 'a hearse and stages' in what had originally been the third line, and
'able to take his own part' after 'not bad looking.' In its final form Whitman's portrait is hardly that of an individual, but of what he would have
called 'a stock type.' He would have considered its merits to consist in its
suggestion of universal traits, in its being a genuine 'sample of the life
and death of workmen.' That he took it for granted that a stage-driver
was 'old' at forty-one makes an ironic comment on 'the vulgar fate,' on
the premature exhaustion that the rigorous demands upon workmen can
entail.

For the distinguishing gesture, the particular emphases of look and
bearing that are the main preoccupation of the portrait painter, Whitman
had no sustained gift, any more than he had for the detailed characteriza-
tions of the novelist. Thoreau gave himself the severer discipline of
drawing type-characters in something of the manner of the seventeenth
century, and sketched in his journal (c.1845) a likeness of Hugh Quoil,
an old Irishman who had fought at Waterloo, had fallen on bad times,
and had drunk himself to death while living in a shack in Walden
woods. Thoreau deliberately tried for more flavor of actual speech than
Whitman did, and portrayed a more specific person, but to the same
end of generalizing on common humanity. Once again their basic
rhythms are more than a little akin: 'He has gone away; his house here
"all tore to pieces" . . . He was here, the likes of him, for a season, standing light in his shoes like a faded gentleman, with gesture almost learned
in drawing-rooms; wore clothes, hat, shoes, cut ditches, felled wood, did
farm work for various people, kindled fires, worked enough, ate enough,
drank too much. He was one of those unnamed countless sects of philosophers who founded no school.'

Whitman was clearly right in feeling that his work had more in common with Millet than with Eakins. The reasons can be condensed by suggesting the comparison between Whitman's portrayal of the Civil War and that made by Winslow Homer, whom Eakins considered the best painter of his day, and the only one whose aims were like his own. Homer thought far less creatively about style than Eakins did, and was more exclusively concerned with objectively literal recording. His goal was honest actuality, not the union of it with imagination which remained Whitman's cardinal aim. The result might be that the poet's figures were sometimes blurred around the edges, but they unquestionably took on the heroic stature that both Millet and Whitman wanted, and of which Homer's careful illustrations had no trace. Yet as Whitman contemplated reverently the magnificent endurance of Millet's peasants, he knew his own experience to be crucially divergent in one fundamental: 'As to the old feeling of pride in the rustic because he was rustic—Burns, Millet, Whittier: I do not share that pride myself: whatever it may be it is not modern.'

'AND WHAT SHALL THE PICTURES BE THAT I HANG ON THE WALLS?'

YET IN his haphazard way of placing himself with relation to the advance of his own art during the century, it was Burns to whom Whitman devoted one of his few critical essays (1882). What attracted him most was the proof that Burns provided 'of the perennial existence among the laboring classes, especially farmers, of the finest latent poetic elements in their blood.' He defined the Scotchman's quality by saying that his racy and warm-colored portrayal of concrete natural life had outvied 'the best painted pictures of the Dutch school.' But despite Whitman's enthusiasm for his broad handling of figures of flesh and blood, Burns' unleavened earthiness, his want of 'spirituality,' caused the American to conclude that he was 'not to be mention'd with Shakespeare—hardly even with . . . Emerson,' in meeting the final test of the poet, the ability to intimate man's 'last, victorious fusion in himself of Real and Ideal.'

A more likely comparison with Whitman would be Wordsworth, but concerning him Whitman made only such brief comments as that he 'lacks sympathy with men and women.' Notwithstanding this acceptance of the then current notion of 'the lost leader,' which apparently kept Whitman from any close reading of him, there is no document more allied to Whitman's prefaces, in the conception of the function of the poet as 'a man speaking to men,' in the stress on natural emotion ('who rejoices more than other men in the spirit of life that is in him'), even in the phrasing, than Wordsworth's preface to *Lyrical Ballads*. The correspondences between many of their key passages are all the more interesting for being independent reactions: Whitman: The poet 'is the equalizer of his age and land . . . The time straying toward infidelity . . . he withholds by his steady faith,' etc.; Wordsworth: 'His own feelings are his stay and support . . . The poet binds together by passion and knowledge the vast empire of human society, as it is spread over the whole earth, and over all time.' They are especially akin in the broad connections they saw between poetry and science. When Whitman said, 'In the beauty of poems are the tuft and final applause of science,' he was phrasing loosely one of Wordsworth's most famous dicta: 'Poetry is the breath and finer spirit of all knowledge; it is the impassioned expression which is in the countenance of all Science.' Whitman, advancing with the century, went much farther than Wordsworth in his confidence (1855) that 'exact science and its practical movements are no checks on the greatest poet but always his encouragement and support.' He accepted eagerly the new material that the geologist and the astronomer might furnish him, and asserted (1888) that 'whatever may have been the case in years gone by, the true use for the imaginative faculty of modern times is to give ultimate vivification to facts, to science, and to common lives.'

When Whitman exclaims, in 'The Mystic Trumpeter' (1872), 'Enough to merely be! enough to breathe!,' he is catching, if in less memorable words, some of the vibration that runs through Wordsworth's freshest work. 'There was a child went forth' is virtually a variation on the theme of 'One impulse from a vernal wood'; and, in turn, a line from 'Song of Myself,'

A morning-glory at my window satisfies me more than the metaphysics of
     books,

might easily have gone on Wordsworth's title page as an epigraph. But beyond any specific similarities both exemplify the dominant trend of art during their century. They both represent man and nature as deeply interrelated, for reasons given by Whitehead's explanation, in *Science and*

the Modern World, of the origin of romanticism.[6] As a result of the conception held by the scientists of the late seventeenth century that the universe was a mechanism, the conclusion had been drawn that man must
have been introduced into it from outside, and that he was wholly apart
from nature and alien to it. But by the end of the eighteenth century a
sensitive man like Wordsworth, stimulated by the newer associationist
psychology, had already come to feel the falsity of this assumption. He
perceived the physical world to be an organism, and he knew that man
is integrally connected with what he sees, hears, and feels, that what he *is*
cannot be separated from the impressions made by external nature upon
his sensibility. Belief in this intimate bond between the landscape and
man's emotions motivates all Wordsworth's art, wherein his sonnet to
Toussaint L'Ouverture is a cornerstone. But such belief was not limited
to the Lake poets, since Wordsworth's contemporary Turner built equally
upon it, and its implications were extended further by Bastien-Lepage
and the plein-airists, and again by the impressionists. Moreover, what was
visioned as a romantic dream has been upheld by modern thought.
Whitehead affirms that human feelings and inanimate objects are inter-
penetrated, that Wordsworth was right in bearing emphatic witness 'that
nature cannot be divorced from its aesthetic values.'

Wordsworth's particular tendency was to represent people living close
to nature and drinking in its healing power as a restorative to the soul-
less life of towns. Against any such limitation of range Whitman stood
strongly opposed, declaring that 'other poets have formed for themselves
an idea apart from positive life, and disdainful of it—but for me I ask
nothing better or more divine than real life, here, now, yourself, your
work, house-building, boating, or in any factory.' Again in contrast with
Wordsworth, and in even greater contrast with Emerson, Whitman was
moving from transcendentalism back to a kind of materialism, though,
as we have seen, by no consistent course. 'We start from real, active men,
and from their life-process also show the development of the ideological
reflexes and echoes of this life-process'—the plural pronoun and the
learned vocabulary, but not the thought, betray that this is not Whitman's. Marx and Engels were advancing there to one of their basic conclusions: that 'it is not consciousness that determines life, but life that

6. *In Axel's Castle,* Edmund Wilson showed how Whitehead's explanation, which is
substantially that of Lovejoy and other contemporary intellectual historians, can also throw
light on the symbolists.

determines consciousness.' Whitman's willingness to agree with this may hardly be proved by his celebration, in 'Song of Myself,' of 'exact demonstration':

> I accept Reality and dare not question it,
> Materialism first and last imbuing.

However, the notes that Marx jotted down for his first thesis on Feuerbach could scarcely have phrased more explicitly the acceptance of life that Whitman always demanded as the requisite for valid art: 'The chief defect of all hitherto existing materialism . . . is that the object, reality, sensuousness, is conceived only in the form of the *object* or *contemplation* but not as *human sensuous activity, practice,* not subjectively.'

But Whitman would at no period have satisfied a strict Marxist for more than ten minutes. Indeed, not even Traubel's pertinacity could keep him pinned down to a steady commitment to socialism from one day to the next. Trusting utterly the subjective world that the impressions of his senses brought him, he insisted to the end that the complete meaning and value of this world lay in both the obvious surface and the latent mysterious suggestion. What he wanted his songs to convey was not the bare object alone but the atmosphere that surrounded it, or, as he said in his greatest poem, the winds that would perfume Lincoln's grave. We have previously observed the synthesis that he was capable of making in his language between the concrete experience and its symbolic range. We are now in a better position to understand the secret of the baffling intermittence of his powers. In this characteristic he is again like Wordsworth, of whom Arthur Symons remarked, 'What goes on is a kind of measured talk. Every now and then an ecstasy wakes out of it . . . He wrote instinctively . . . he wrote mechanically, and . . . he wrote always.' But we can define the reasons for Whitman's successes more adequately than by simply attributing them to a discontinuous inspiration. He introduced his catalogues as deliberate illustrations of his belief that the true use of the imagination was to give 'vivification to facts.' In his assurance that his interminable lists could be the briefest conveyors of fresh knowledge he was almost utterly mistaken.[7] We learned the reasons when examin-

---

7. An occasional exception is when he does not just assume that all the items in his list are equal, since each is entitled to one vote, but, acting as a constructor, composes his series of snap-shots into a unit by means of functional repetition:

> The sprawl and fulness of babes, the bosoms and heads of women, the folds of their dress,
>   their style as we pass in the street, the contour of their shape downwards,

ing his diction, reasons that Emerson condensed by saying, 'Things added to things, as statistics, civil history, are inventories. Things used as language are inexhaustibly attractive.' That furnishes an exact index both to Whitman's failures and to his triumphs. Despite his 'Hurrah for positive science!' he was never rigorous enough to arrive at anything like comprehension of its methods; and though he talked about being 'the bard of Scientism,' his notes for such pieces as 'Poem of Chemistry' give promise of nothing more than a monotonous recital of the surface information he could have picked up in a magazine. Swinburne was judicious when he pointed out that there were in Whitman two men 'of most inharmonious kinds; a poet and a formalist.' Whitman's feeling was at his richest when he declared that 'the earth is sufficient.' But he could make poetry of this feeling only when he gave due weight to both halves of his proposition that 'imagination and actuality must be united.'

His secret for doing this—it is now clear—depended upon the adequacy with which he could translate man into nature. This involved, for instance, finding the right symbol to condense what he meant by

> Earth of chaste love, life that is only life after love.

He developed it thus:

> The hairy wild-bee that murmurs and hankers up and down, that gripes the full-grown lady-flower, curves upon her with amorous firm legs, takes his will of her, and holds himself tremulous and tight till he is satisfied.

Here he was so humanly accurate that we are not bothered by his poet's version of pollination. More passionate than Wordsworth, Whitman

> The swimmer naked in the swimming-bath, seen as he swims through the transparent green-shine, or lies with his face up and rolls silently to and fro in the heave of the water . . .
> The wrestle of wrestlers, two apprentice-boys, quite grown, lusty, good-natured, native-born, out on the vacant lot at sundown after work,
> The coats and caps thrown down, the embrace of love and resistance,
> The upper-hold and under-hold, the hair rumpled over and blinding the eyes;
> The march of firemen in their own costumes, the play of masculine muscle through clean-setting trowsers and waist-straps,
> The slow return from the fire, the pause when the bell strikes suddenly again, and the listening on the alert,
> The natural, perfect, varied attitudes, the bent head, the curv'd neck and the counting;
> Such like I love—I loosen myself, pass freely, am at the mother's breast with the little child,
> Swim with the swimmers, wrestle with the wrestlers, march in line with the firemen, and pause, listen, count.

could create this 'sanity of atmosphere,' as he called it, most limpidly and unerringly when he was dealing with sex, 'the enclosing basis' of all his work. He needed to draw on all the resources of what he implied by 'indirection' if he was to go beyond the diffused iteration of the parts of a woman's body, and to discover the universal in the immediate:

Bridegroom night of love working surely and softly into the prostrate dawn,
Undulating into the willing and yielding day,
Lost in the cleave of the clasping and sweet-flesh'd day.

Here his range depends upon his translation of his lovers into primal organic forces, upon making them blend with the rhythmic succession of darkness and light.

This power of giving mythical proportions to his material was best sustained in his tribute to Lincoln. The controlling idea for his other poems about the Civil War, as he had outlined it in his letter to O'Connor only three months before the President's assassination, was the time's 'large conflicting fluctuations of despair and hope,' 'the unprecedented anguish of wounded and suffering,' and yet also, sounding through lulls in the chaos like the steady beat of a drum, the 'clear notes of faith and triumph.' That confidence was now put to its severest test, and the result was 'When lilacs last in the dooryard bloom'd.' Like all of *Drum-Taps* this was written so much under the stress of a dominant emotion that it was not revised, except in the slightest details, after its first printing in 1865. In this period of his most intense feeling Whitman also reverted to the hackneyed cadences and imagery of his first newspaper verse in producing 'O Captain! my Captain!' That this ballad, wholly untypical of his poems, should have been the only one to have found its way to the great world of grammar school readers is ample and ironic comment on how far Whitman's authentic idiom was from even the rudimentary means by which a wide audience is reached.

In his later reminiscent lecture about the President (1879), he said that 'to the complete limning of this man's future portrait' there will be needed 'the eyes and brains and finger-touch of Plutarch and Aeschylus and Michel Angelo, assisted by Rabelais.' His poem enlisted no such powers, but was composed as an elegy 'for the sweetest, wisest soul of all my days and lands.' Whitman was not concerned with the expression of merely personal emotion; he wanted to give it an objective existence as broad as the country over which the coffin passed on its journey to Illinois. We are able to glimpse in a different context some of the original impressions that lay behind his symbols here—a rare thing with Whitman's poems, since he kept no regular journal. He had written down, a month before, what he had experienced on the day of Lincoln's second inauguration. He noted that the President looked very worn and tired, the lines 'of vast responsibilities . . . and demands of life and death, cut deeper than ever upon his dark brown face; yet all the old goodness, tenderness, sadness, and canny shrewdness, underneath the furrows. (I never see that man without feeling that he is one to become personally attach'd to, for his combination of purest, heartiest tenderness, and native western form of manliness.)'

In another paragraph Whitman wandered along about the weather, which he thought to have been unusually bad during the past several months, and wondered whether there might not be some strange correspondence between its tempestuous violence and the upheaval of war. Then he noted that in the afternoon, just before the President had come out on the portico of the Capitol, the deluging rain of the morning had let up, leaving the air 'so calm, so bathed with flooding splendor from heaven's most excellent sun, with atmosphere of sweetness; so clear, it show'd the stars, long, long before they were due.' This led him on to remember that, in spells of sharpest contrast with the storms, 'nor earth nor sky ever knew spectacles of superber beauty than some of the nights lately here. The western star, Venus, in the earlier hours of evening, has never been so large, so clear; it seems as if it told something, as if it held rapport indulgent with humanity, with us Americans.' He ended his account of the day by saying that he had been looking up at the 'dark blue, the transparent night' when he had heard a bugle sounding tattoo in one of the army hospitals, where the wounded were 'lying in their cots, and many a sick boy come down to the war from Illinois, Michigan, Wisconsin, Iowa, and the rest.'

There is no description of Lincoln in the poem itself, for it is entirely given up to 'sane and sacred death.' Yet Whitman asked, in lines whose rhythmical repetitions were all but Biblical,

> O what shall I hang on the chamber walls?
> And what shall the pictures be that I hang on the walls,
> To adorn the burial-house of him I love?

And the pictures that ensued, of 'growing spring' on the farms with 'the gray smoke lucid and bright,' of the breast of a river with 'a wind-dapple here and there,' of Manhattan's spires and Ohio's shores, were crowned with the light of 'the most excellent sun so calm and haughty . . . enveloping man and land,' both South and North. The poet may there have been unconsciously repeating a phrase, the broad sound of which had appealed to him. But he made an explicit reference back to his feelings on the day of the inauguration in the section that began:

> O western orb sailing the heaven,
> Now I know what you must have meant as a month since I walk'd,
> As I walk'd in silence the transparent shadowy night,
> As I saw you had something to tell as you bent to me night after night.

Those lines may be adulterated with some of the least satisfactory elements of the poem, in the use of 'orb,' an orator's word, which seems always to have pleased Whitman as it rolled from his mouth; and particularly in the pathetic fallacy. But as he continued the passage, the poet freed himself from the stilted fancy of the star's bending to him, and saw it in its own motion:

> As my soul in its trouble dissatisfied sank, as where you sad orb,
> Concluded, dropt in the night, and was gone.

What has taken place through the fusion of Whitman's materials is that the planet whose radiance had so impressed him a month before has become for him now 'O powerful western fallen star!' It has become the symbol, in its disappearance into the dark, for the President himself.

Whitman does not handle his subject primarily by objective descriptions, but by thematic use of three primary symbols—the lilac, the star, and the song of the thrush—which are repeated with the most subtle ordonnance that he ever managed. They are introduced in the brief opening section:

> When lilacs last in the dooryard bloom'd,
> And the great star early droop'd in the western sky in the night,
> I mourn'd, and yet shall mourn with ever-returning spring.
>
> Ever-returning spring, trinity sure to me you bring,
> Lilac blooming perennial and drooping star in the west,
> And thought of him I love.

They are then successively extended in the next three sections. The 'black murk' that engulfed the star is immediately equated with the 'harsh surrounding cloud that will not free my soul.' The lilacs 'fronting an old farm-house near the white-wash'd palings' are lent a special relevance by their 'heart-shaped leaves of rich green.' They have come to Whitman from his Long Island childhood, and their use in the poem may unconsciously have been suggested to him by his having been at home in Brooklyn on the day of the assassination, alone with his mother. ('. . . we heard the news very early in the morning. Mother prepared breakfast— and other meals afterward—as usual; but not a mouthful was eaten all day by either of us. We each drank half a cup of coffee; that was all. Little was said. We got every newspaper morning and evening . . . and pass'd them silently to each other.') The delicately colored blossoms grew close to nearly every country home. The bush was right by the windows at Whitman's birthplace at West Hills, and its absence in Mount's Long Island scene is exceptional. In fact the lilac is almost as native a symbol as the common grass itself.

The 'thought of him I love' is given symbolic concretion by being merged with song, with the note of the solitary hermit-thrush from the swamp-cedars, which had always meant so much to Whitman. Here its painful ecstasy becomes 'death's outlet song of life,'

> for well dear brother I know,
> If thou wast not granted to sing thou would'st surely die.

Thus it merges also with the poet's song of grief, through the release of which he finds his way back to acceptance and peace.

The fifth and sixth sections present the picture of the coffin in its night and day journey past depots and streets and over the breast of the land, met everywhere by solemn crowds. Standing among these in his imagination, as the train slowly passes, the poet bestows his 'sprig of lilac.' But not 'for you, for one alone,' he says, as he again develops this symbol's theme. He would bring signs of the rebirth of the year to no one man but to all in his chant 'for you O sane and sacred death.' It is notable that, in deep fulfilment of his instinct for universality, Whitman nowhere in the poem mentions Lincoln by name, not even in the next section (the eighth) where, in the middle of his song, he introduces his reminiscence of the star a month ago. Then he completes his round of symbols for the second time by telling the thrush to sing on in the swamp, that he will come there presently, but that the star, 'my departing comrade holds and detains me.'

At this point he breaks off to ask,

> O how shall I warble myself for the dead one there I loved?
> And how shall I deck my song for the large sweet soul that has gone?
> And what shall my perfume be for the grave of him I love?

Having bid the sea-winds from both east and west to meet on the prairies, he asks, in like form, his question about the pictures, and decks the burial house with them in the twenty lines of his eleventh and twelfth sections. He then turns once more to the thrush, to its 'reedy song, loud human song.' The poet's voice now matches that of the bird, as, in the longest section, he launches into his aria to 'the sure-enwinding arms of cool-enfolding death,' and urges, 'when thou must indeed come, come unfalteringly.' But before this, in addition to declaring his carol a brother to that of the thrush, he has felt all three of his symbols coalesce into an organic whole:

> O liquid and free and tender!
> O wild and loose to my soul—O wondrous singer!
> You only I hear—yet the star holds me, (but will soon depart,)
> Yet the lilac with mastering odor holds me.

He has blended the impressions of his different senses, of hearing, sight, and smell, as they do blend in an individual's full impression of a moment. Moreover, in 'liquid' he has suggested the kind of touch and movement that most appealed to him, just as in 'wild and loose' he has characterized the kind of form he felt at home with, and in 'free and tender' the emotional range he could encompass best. The symbolists were to carry much farther the merging of sensations, to the point of transference of one into another, as of color into sound or smell. But Whitman's greatest act of pioneering was in helping the modern sensibility feel at home in the natural world. He was able to suggest the interdependence of man and nature since his 'trinity' of symbols sprang from the forces of earth, no matter what spiritual implications they could rise to in his hymn to rebirth through fertility. In the closing lines of the poem the three are resumed again, but it is the poet's 'powerful psalm' of tribute that now emerges transcendent over the others:

Lilac and star and bird twined with the chant of my soul,
There in the fragrant pines and the cedars dusk and dim.

One other strain had been given development in the penultimate section. The 'unprecedented anguish of wounded and suffering' that Whitman had declared to be central to the design of his war poems had found very little foreshadowing in the optimistic glow of the earlier *Leaves*. Among other war poets of the day, despite Lowell's set rhetorical piece in the Commemoration Ode for the Harvard dead, only Melville stressed the tragic purification through terror and pity that could be gained from the disaster of war. Whitman showed humanity as broad as Melville's in his concern for equal treatment for the South. He expressed it in 'Reconciliation':

Word over all, beautiful as the sky,
Beautiful that war and all its deeds of carnage must in time be utterly
 lost . . .
For my enemy is dead, a man divine as myself is dead . . .

In his grief for Lincoln he understood where the real anguish lay:

I saw the debris and debris of all the slain soldiers of the war,
But I saw they were not as was thought,
They themselves were fully at rest, they suffer'd not,
But the living remain'd and suffer'd, the mother suffer'd,
And the wife and the child and the musing comrade suffer'd,
And the armies that remained suffer'd.[8]

8. The kind of experience out of which these lines rose was described by Whitman in some of his letters during the war, especially in those to his mother, who always called out her son's most honest statements of emotion: 'Mother, it was a dreadful night (last Friday night)—pretty dark, the wind gusty, and the rain fell in torrents. One poor boy— this is a sample of one case out of the 600—he seemed to be quite young, he was quite small (I looked at his body afterwards), he groaned some as the stretcher bearers were carrying him along, and again as they carried him through the hospital gate. They set down the stretcher and examined him, and the poor boy was dead. They took him into the ward, and the doctor came immediately, but it was all of no use. The worst of it is, too, that he is entirely unknown—there was nothing on his clothes, or anyone with him to identify him, and he is altogether unknown. Mother, it is enough to rack one's heart— such things. Very likely his folks will never know in the world what has become of him. Poor, poor child, for he appeared as though he could be but 18. I feel lately as though I must have some intermission. I feel well and hearty enough, and was never better but my feelings are kept in a painful condition a great part of the time. [This was in March 1864 and his own health broke down badly three months later.] Things get worse and worse, as to the amount and sufferings of the sick, and as I have said before, those who

In the capacity to suffer revealed in this poem, Whitman moved farthest away from the superficial innocence of evil with which Yeats has
charged him. It had not needed the war to open his eyes. He had remembered what Elias Hicks said, 'There is no worse devil than man.' In
1860 he had begun a poem with the line,

I sit and look out upon all the sorrows of the world, and upon all oppression
    and shame,

and had composed it entirely of such sights. But the war alone held him
to a consistent tragic sense. In his later years he might still speak of 'this
bad—this nineteen-twentieths of us all,' but he generally entertained such
thoughts only that he might add what had occurred to him 'after reading
Hegel':

I saw the little that is Good steadily hastening towards immortality,
And the vast all that is call'd Evil I saw hastening to merge itself and become
    lost and dead.

The habit of philosophizing grew on him, and he made explicit 'L. of
G.'s Purport' in some of the last verses that he wrote:

Not to exclude or demarcate, or pick out evils from their formidable masses
    (even to expose them,)
But add, fuse, complete, extend—and celebrate the immortal and the good.

That was a happy mood for an old man: he told Traubel that it was a
comfort to him that the Lord finds a place for all, for the bedbug, the rat,
the flea, even for Matthew Arnold. That last admission marked Whitman's extreme limit in inclusiveness, for Arnold always gave him the
impression of hating 'to touch the dirt—the dirt is so dirty'; whereas
Whitman insisted, 'Everything comes out of the dirt—everything: everything comes out of the people, the everyday people, the people as you find
them and leave them: not university people, not FFV people.'

have to do with them are getting more and more callous and indifferent. Mother, .when
I see the common soldiers, what they go through, and how everybody seems to try to
pick upon them, and what humbug there is over them every how, even the dying soldier's
money stolen from his body by some scoundrel attendant, or from [the] sick one, even
from under his head, which is a common thing, and then the agony I see every day, I
get almost frightened at the world. Mother, I will try to write more cheerfully next time—
but I see so much. Well, good-bye for present, dear mother,
                                                      Walt.'

The strength of Whitman's democratic faith made the strength of his poetry, but his inability even to discern the meaning of Arnold's analysis of the age is one sign of how different a level from Melville's Whitman's mind habitually moved on.[9] Melville found many passages in Arnold to support his own discriminations between good and evil. In *Billy Budd* he worked towards a resolution of the tragic problem of life in the very years when Whitman was benevolently dismissing its existence. The Whitman who is most nearly meaningless is the one who could declare at the start of his career and repeat on occasion to the end:

I am myself just as much evil as good, and my nation is—and I say there is in fact no evil.

This indiscriminate acceptance becomes real only when it is based on an awareness of the human issues involved, when it rises out of tenderness over man's struggle and suffering, and says:

I moisten the roots of all that has grown.

The endurance of Whitman's spirit through his long career is like the 'sturdy, passive acceptance of things' that Dreiser has sought. And of all our writers since Whitman, Dreiser seems the chief heir of the qualities the poet liked most to dwell on: sympathy, solidarity—obscured though these often may be by the naturalistic novelist's entanglement in clumsy and wordy despair over man's helplessness. The other great force in our literature since Whitman who penetrates so deep into the soil of democracy is Mark Twain. But the Civil War was hardly his problem, as he turned his back and went off roughing it. Yet he had known the pre-war world, and in his memories of it alone could he shake himself wholly free from the professional funny man his audience wanted, and project, if only through the eyes of a small boy, an epic of the mid-century's human splendor, as well as of its cruelty and violence—all things that Whitman had also absorbed and expressed.

9. Traubel recorded Whitman's objections to Arnold, 'that he brings to the world what the world already has a surfeit of: is rich, hefted, lousy, reeking, with delicacy, refinement, elegance, prettiness, propriety, criticism, analysis.' The blindness was mutual. When someone asked Arnold, at the end of one of his lectures in this country, what he thought of Whitman, his only answer was: 'What did Mr. Longfellow think of Whitman?'

⫸ XIV ⫷

MAN IN THE OPEN AIR

'We have had man indoors and under artificial relations—man in war, in love (both the natural, universal elements of human lives)—man in courts, bowers, castles, parlors—man in personal haughtiness and the tussle of war, as in Homer—or the passions, crimes, ambitions, murder, jealousy, love carried to extreme as in Shakespeare. We have been listening to divine, ravishing tales, plots inexpressibly valuable, hitherto (like the Christian religion) to temper and modify his prevalent perhaps natural ferocity and hoggishness—but never before have we had *man in the open air,* his attitude adjusted to the seasons and as one might describe it, adjusted to the sun by day and the stars by night.'

—Whitman

1. The Need for Mythology

'We need a theory of interpretation or Mythology.'

—Emerson's *Journal* (1835)

Where the age of Emerson may be most like our own is in its discovery of the value of myth. The starting point is in Emerson's 'History,' the opening essay in his first collection. He believed that history can be re-created only by a man for whom the present is alive. He had reached his initial premise of 'the identity of human character in all ages' as a schoolmaster of nineteen. But his example then was the conventional one: 'There is as much instruction in the tale of Troy as in the Annals of the French Revolution.' In his mature work the emphasis was to be reversed. He was still concerned with 'the universal nature which gives worth to particular men and things.' But his chief desire was to translate the Then into the Now. In the academic sense, his interest was unhistorical. He was never satisfied with studying process. His belief that 'the use of history is to give value to the present hour' was a natural corollary to his conception of time: that when we come to the quality of the moment

626

we drop duration altogether. The opening sentences of *Nature* were a protest against being history-ridden: 'Our age is retrospective. It builds the sepulchres of the fathers. It writes biographies, histories, and criticism. The foregoing generations beheld God and nature face to face; we, through their eyes. Why should not we also enjoy an original relation to the universe?'

His essay on 'History' was thus compelled by his deepest needs. The compensation of the isolated villager lay in Emerson's assurance that 'civil and natural history, the history of art and of literature, must be explained from individual history, or must remain words.' His idealism and his individualism, his religion and his politics joined when he said: 'I believe in Eternity. I can find Greece, Asia, Italy, Spain and the Islands,—the genius and creative principle of each and of all eras, in my own mind.' Yet he had, as always, the counterpoise to his extreme subjectivity. If all public facts were to be individualized, all private facts must be generalized. On the last page of his essay he declared that every history should be written in a wisdom that looks on facts as symbols. And though he gave only the shadowiest indication of an awareness of the intricate forces that had conditioned the activities of men in any epoch, he held fast to his conviction of the artist's responsibility to 'employ the symbols in use in his day and nation to convey his enlarged sense to his fellow-men.'

We recall that Emerson also found 'the cardinal fact' about Thoreau to be that he had learned to regard 'the material world as a means and symbol.' Thoreau's greater concentration carried him to explicit statement of the connections between symbol and myth. In his affirmation both of the moment and of all time, he often differed from Emerson only in his special philological twist: 'The life of a wise man is most of all extemporaneous, for he lives out of an eternity which includes all time.' He believed that mythology best expressed that eternal quality, and developed his meaning characteristically when reflecting on the beauty of some trout. He could hardly trust his senses as he stood over them, 'that these jewels should have swam away in that Aboljacknagesic water for so long, so many dark ages;—these bright fluviatile flowers, seen of Indians only, made beautiful, the Lord only knows why, to swim there! I could understand better for this, the truth of mythology, the fables of Proteus, and all those beautiful sea-monsters,—how all history, indeed, put to a terrestrial use, is mere history; but put to a celestial, is mythology always.'

He made the same distinctions even in less poetic moods. Delighted with the kinship between folk-tales of widely separated races, he took this for 'the most impressive proof of a common humanity.' [1] Moreover, he relived the process of myth-making for himself. He believed that 'as men lived in Thebes, so do they live in Dunstable to-day.' If mythology was more primitive than history, the nature that had inspired the myths was still flourishing. He could walk out into a world 'such as the old prophets and poets, Menu, Moses, Homer, Chaucer, walked in.' He felt certain that he could establish this identity between past and present, because he had seized upon the living principle of nature: 'If I am overflowing with life, am rich in experience for which I lack expression, then nature will be my language full of poetry,—all nature will *fable,* and every natural phenomenon be a myth.' When he looked at the result rather than the process, he said: 'A fact truly and absolutely stated . . . acquires a mythologic or universal significance.'

Those sentences bring us back to the chief propositions about the organic style. They reassert the fusion between the word and the thing. They suggest again how Grimm and others could arrive at mythology through the study of the origins of language. Emerson knew that 'language is fossil poetry.' Thoreau could back up that truth with a specific example. In studying a dictionary of the Abenaki tongue, he perceived how language provides an index to the primitive and hence real history of any race. 'Let us know what words they had and how they used them, and we can infer almost all the rest.' The Indians had left records there of what they had seen and felt and imagined, what they were.

Thoreau's major concern was with what men are. If symbols from the past could give expansion to life, his intense localism kept him aware that most people discern the heroic past only, that they read Plutarch but

1. After going by boat from Boston to Hull (1851), Thoreau remarked: 'I heard a boy telling the story of Nix's Mate to some girls, as we passed that spot, how "he said, 'If I am guilty, this island will remain; but if I am innocent, it will be washed away,' and now it is all washed away." This was a simple and strong expression of feeling suitable to the occasion, by which he committed the evidence of his innocence to the dumb isle, such as the boy could appreciate, a proper sailor's legend; and I was reminded that it is the illiterate and unimaginative class that seizes on and transmits the legends in which the more cultivated delight. No fastidious poet dwelling in Boston had tampered with it,— no narrow poet, but broad mankind, sailors from all ports sailing by.'

ignore John Brown. In the short essay on history that he wrote for *The Dial* and used again in his *Week,* the leading idea was: 'Critical acumen is exerted in vain to uncover the past; the *past* cannot be *presented;* we cannot know what we are not. But one veil hangs over past, present, and future, and it is the province of the historian to find out, not what was, but what is. Where a battle has been fought, you will find nothing but the bones of men and beasts; where a battle is being fought, there are hearts beating . . . Ancient history has an air of antiquity. It should be more modern.'

Thomas Mann has said almost the same things about myth. He has called it the mode of celebrating life whereby the moment becomes infinitely larger than itself, and the individual existence escapes from its narrow bounds and finds sanction and consecration. Writing about 'Freud and the Future,' he stated that 'life in the myth, life, so to speak, in quotation, is a kind of celebration, in that it is a making present of the past, it becomes a religious act, the performance by a celebrant of a prescribed procedure; it becomes a feast. For a feast is an anniversary, a renewal of the past in the present.' That is akin to Emerson's sense of what he could find in the Now, and celebrate as ecstasy. If the Now is eternal, the role of the prophet, the poet becomes the same in all incarnations and Emerson becomes Saadi, becomes a representative man.

Mann has found corroboration for his belief wherever he has turned, as did one of his 'past masters,' Nietzsche.[2] In his essay on Lessing, Mann set out to revitalize the meaning of 'classic' by giving it a mythical significance, because 'the essence of the myth is recurrence, timelessness, a perpetual present.' He has spoken in almost the same terms of why he has been drawn to re-create the legend of Joseph: ' "At any time": therein lies the mystery. For the mystery is timeless, but the form of timelessness is the now and here. . . . For the essence of life is presentness.' Freud has taught him that the infancy of a human being recapitulates the infancy of the race, and that myths are collective dreams. That Whitman arrived instinctively at the first of these truths is shown by the significance he could give to his own adolescent experience in such a poem

2. An integral link between Emerson's conception of history and Mann's is provided by Nietzsche's view that 'Only the supreme power of the present can interpret the past . . . Otherwise men depress the past to their own level . . . The voices of the past speak in oracles; and only the master of the present and the architect of the future can hope to decipher their meaning.'

as 'There was a child went forth.' Without ever formulating it into a theory, Melville illustrated the second truth in his chapter on 'Dreams' in *Mardi,* in his discovery of 'all the past and present pouring in me.'

The reasons why we have felt again to-day the need for the reinforcement of myth could take us too far afield into a diagnosis of modern culture. We have inevitably been even more burdened than Emerson's contemporaries by the accretions of another century of the historical method. To Lawrence the merely critical mind had become so desiccating that he could find his renewal only in the realms of the unconscious, and declared that the great myths 'now begin to hypnotize us again, our own impulse towards our own scientific way of understanding being almost spent.' Twenty years ago Eliot spoke of how *The Golden Bough* 'has influenced our generation profoundly.' What he discovered in anthropology is what Mann has also found, the reassertion—for an age almost overwhelmed by its sense of historical tendencies—of the basic dramatic patterns in the cyclic death and rebirth of nature and of man. In the primitive and the remote Eliot first regained contact with sources of vitality deeper than his mind. But unlike Lawrence, he was not satisfied with the primitive for its own sake. The problem still remained to integrate its vitality with the complex life of the present. In the year after *The Waste Land,* Eliot wrote a short essay on *'Ulysses,* Order, and Myth': 'In using the myth, in manipulating a continuous parallel between contemporaneity and antiquity, Mr. Joyce is pursuing a method which others must pursue after him . . . It is simply a way of controlling, or ordering, of giving a shape and a significance to the immense panorama of futility and anarchy which is contemporary history.'

Even this glimpse of the myth-making faculty of our modern writers reveals a difference from Emerson's discovery of the paradox that 'always and never man is the same.' Emerson's innocent celebration of our common nature is radically unlike Mann's understanding of the disease latent everywhere in society, of man's corruptibility. Hawthorne is more like Eliot in his sense of the weight of the past, in his discernment of human traits which are constant beneath varying guises, and especially in his discovery of the lasting bond between the ages in man's capacity for suffering. His awareness of 'the haunted mind' also points towards our concern with the subconscious. But Hawthorne, alone of the five writers who have been the subject of this volume, did not conceive of his work in any relation to myth. He did not seek for universal analogies, but gained his moral profundity by remaining strictly a provincial and digging where he was. When he spoke of how 'all men must descend' into 'dark caverns . . . if they would know anything beneath the surface and illusive pleasures of existence,' he showed where his consciousness of suffering had brought him. He was at the threshold of the descent into myth, he was using almost Mann's words in the 'Prelude' to *Joseph and His Brothers*. By the very fact of not consciously intending it, Hawthorne thus furnishes a striking if oblique example of Emerson's and Thoreau's major reason for valuing myth: the way it reveals the inevitable recurrence of the elemental human patterns.

2. *Representative Men*

WHAT Emerson conceived to be 'the symbols in use in his day and nation,' which he must use in turn if he was to express the meaning of its life, can be read most clearly in *Representative Men*.[1] Notwithstanding his satisfaction in his New England setting, he repeatedly declared that nature must be humanized, that its beauty 'must always seem unreal and mocking, until the landscape has human figures that are as good as itself.' His selection of such figures—Plato, Swedenborg, Montaigne, Shakespeare, Napoleon, Goethe—is by itself ample evidence of his freedom from any restrictions of nationalism. He knew that an American renaissance needed the encouragement of great writers and thinkers. His timelessness took for granted his country's immediate share in the whole cultural heritage.

One inevitable stimulus to the form of this book was Carlyle's *Heroes and Hero-Worship* (1841). But even before that appeared, Emerson had reached his own position that 'there is properly no history, only biography,' a position that Thoreau, in his confidence, carried to the point of saying, 'Biography, too, is liable to the same objection; it should be autobiography.' Carlyle's book was more than a stimulus: it provided the assumptions against which Emerson made a quiet but fundamental counterstatement. The difference between the titles is significant. 'Great

1. Though not published until 1850, the substance of the book had first been delivered as lectures in the winter of 1845-6, and again in England in 1847-8.

men,' said Emerson, 'the word is injurious'; and his grounds for objection to Carlyle were both religious and social. The source of his own title was probably Swedenborg, whom he celebrated for daring to take the last and boldest step of genius, to provide a theory of interpretation for the meaning of existence. Emerson quoted triumphant evidence of this from *The Animal Kingdom:* 'In our doctrine of Representations and Correspondences we shall treat of both these symbolical and typical resemblances, and of the astonishing things which occur, I will not say in the living body only, but throughout nature, and which correspond so entirely to supreme and spiritual things that one would swear that the physical world was purely symbolical of the spiritual world.' Swedenborg's correspondences were in harmonious keeping with Emerson's belief that what made one man more representative than another was the degree to which he was a receptive channel for the superincumbent spirit. Emerson held Carlyle's greatest blemish to be his inadequate understanding of spirituality. As Henry James, Sr. phrased it: 'Moral force was the deity of Carlyle's unscrupulous worship,—the force of unprincipled, irresponsible will.' As a result he had glorified the strong men of history, in a sequence that devolved from Odin to Cromwell to Frederick of Prussia, and thus helped prepare the way for our contemporary fatal worship of force. Though Emerson did not phrase himself with James' terseness, he grew to realize the drastic importance of Carlyle's defect.

What Emerson wanted to say was that 'no individual was great, except through the general.' He could go so far as to speak of the 'inflamed individualism' that separated the man of power from the mass of his fellows. But he had not gone far enough to satisfy himself. As soon as he had sent *Representative Men* to press, he regretted that 'many after thoughts, as usual . . . come just a little too late; and my new book seems to lose all value from their omission. Plainly one is the justice that should have been done to the unexpressed greatness of the common farmer and laborer.' Thoreau had developed that same strain when writing his essay on Carlyle (1847). Balancing Thoreau's belief that history must be written as though it had happened to the writer was his equally strong conviction that if so written it would not be the history of reigns but of peoples. The trouble even with Carlyle's *French Revolution* was that there were no chapters called 'Work for the Month,' 'State of the Crops and Markets,' 'Day Labor'—'just to remind the reader that the French peasantry did something beside go without breeches, burn châteaus, get ready knotted cords, and embrace and throttle one another by turns.' In consequence of this lack, Carlyle did not speak to 'the Man of the Age, come to be called workingman.'

Thoreau thus phrased in its simplest form the theory of history that he believed must prevail in America. On the basis of such a theory Parker held Prescott's dramatic pageants to amount to no more than rhetorical *tours de force,* the product of a superficial aristocrat. In Parker's solid if somewhat naïve objections we come to the democratic core of New England transcendentalism. For Parker believed that an American historian must write in the interest of mankind, in the spirit of the nineteenth century. He must be occupied with the growth of institutions, not with glamorous spectacles. 'He must tell us of the social state of the people, the relation of the cultivator to the soil, the relation of class to class. It is well to know what songs the peasant sung; what prayers he prayed; what food he ate; what tools he wrought with; what tax he paid; how he stood connected with the soil; how he was brought to war; and what weapons armed him for the fight.'

Through this view of history Emerson's age found its myth. Whitman joined to the full in the objections to Carlyle. Though he valued the challenge of Carlyle's attack on democracy, and wrote his own *Democratic Vistas* (1871) partly as an answer to *Shooting Niagara* (1867), he believed the worship of heroes to be poisonous. He was sure that 'always waiting untold in the souls of the armies of common people, is stuff better than anything that can possibly appear in the leadership of the same.' Even when talking about Lincoln he said that 'man moves as man, in all the great achievements—man in the great mass.' Thoreau did not share Whitman's confidence in mass movements, and said that California was '3000 miles nearer to hell,' since its gold was a touchstone that had betrayed 'the rottenness, the baseness of mankind.' Yet even Thoreau could respond to the myth of the age when he looked (1851) at a panorama of the Mississippi. He saw in his imagination 'the steamboats wooding up, counted the rising cities, gazed on the fresh ruins of Nauvoo . . . I saw that this was a Rhine stream of a different kind; that . . . the famous bridges were yet to be thrown over the river; and I felt that *this was the heroic age itself,* though we know it not, for the hero is commonly the simplest and obscurest of men.'

Emerson penetrated to the heart of this myth in his conception (1846) of 'the central man,' the creative source of all vitality. He imagined himself in talk with him, and that the voice of the central man was that of Socrates. 'Then the discourse changes, and the man, and we see the face and hear the tones of Shakespeare . . . A change again, and the countenance of our companion is youthful and beardless, he talks of form and color and the riches of design; it is the face of the painter Raffaelle.' Next it is Michel Angelo, then Dante, afterwards Jesus: 'And so it appears that these great secular personalities were only expressions of his face chasing each other like the rack of clouds.' The Orphic poet who spoke at the end of *Nature* had voiced a kindred parable of the continual renewal of man's heroic energy. Emerson felt that in *Representative Men* he had only managed to suggest this under a few shadowy guises. Looking back at this book a dozen years later, he said that he had sensed when writing it that Jesus was the 'Representative Man' whom he ought to sketch, but that he had not felt equal to the task. What he might have tried to present is suggested by a few sentences in his journal several years before (1842): 'The history of Christ is the best document of the power of Character which we have. A youth who owed nothing to fortune and who was "hanged at Tyburn,"—by the pure quality of his nature has shed this epic splendor around the facts of his death which has transfigured every particular into a grand universal symbol for the eyes of all mankind ever since.' That is similar to Melville's conception of democratic tragedy, and also to what Hawthorne had perceived in Sodoma's picture of Christ bound to a pillar—the union of suffering and majesty. But it is unlikely that Emerson would have concentrated long on the tragic aspect. Even in his journal he went on to say, 'This was a great Defeat; we demand Victory,' and to insist on the mind's conquest of Fate.

Where he was at his best in *Representative Men* was in translating Plato into Concord, in giving a portrait of Socrates as a 'plain old uncle . . . with his great ears, an immense talker,' 'what our country-people call *an old one*.' Emerson's concern in this book with man's common nature also gave him an insight into the value of tradition that we would hardly expect from him. Elsewhere, as in 'Self-Reliance,' he often said, 'Where is the master who could have taught Shakespeare? . . . Every great man is a unique.' But here he saw that 'the rude warm blood of the living England circulated in the play, as in street-ballads.' He went even farther and declared: 'What is best written or done by genius in the world, was no man's work, but came by wide social labor, when a thousand wrought like one, sharing the same impulse.' Unhappily Emerson, as we have seen, could not make much out of that perception. The 'genius of humanity' that he announced to be his real subject could become very amorphous, most devastatingly so in his vague treatment of his modern figures, Napoleon and Goethe. It was no accident that his passage on the different incarnations of 'the central man' ended with these sentences: 'Then all will subside, and I find myself alone. I dreamed and did not know my dreams.'

3. American Demigods

CARLYLE, who kept urging Emerson to carve an American hero out of the facts of the nineteenth century, drove through (1849) to an imaginative conception of a possible American myth of the frontier: 'How beautiful to think of lean tough Yankee settlers, tough as gutta-percha, with most *occult* unsubduable fire in their belly, steering over the Western Mountains, to annihilate the jungle, and bring bacon and corn out of it for the Posterity of Adam . . . There is no *Myth* of Athene or Herakles equal to this *fact.*'

The circumstances of Thoreau's 'heroic age' called out many independent efforts to create a mythology that would express it, conscious and instinctive, exuberantly playful and highly serious. Between them they give the collective portrait that Whitman wanted, the likeness of 'man in the open air.' Whitman's poetic phrase symbolizes the fact that this age of the rise of the common man was still mainly agrarian. The writers tended to show that even in their looks. All of Emerson's pictures could be those of a village parson. Melville as an old New Yorker still continued to look like a sailor, though not the 'rubicund sailor' to whom Whitman seemed akin in Eakins' canvas. Thoreau struck a surprised admirer as being indistinguishable from 'a respectable husbandman,' and Hawthorne, though in appearance less a man of the country than the others, retained in his language the marks of his 'ineradicable rusticity.'

Since they were still close to the soil, analogies with the great nature myths came naturally to most of them, though their awareness of these as analogies differentiate their creations from those of a primitive age. What Greenough found is relevant to their problem: 'Though the country was young, yet the people were old, . . . as Americans we have no childhood, no half-fabulous, legendary wealth, no misty, cloud-enveloped background.' This fact may have determined in part why humor has been such a natural expression for our national character. Max Eastman's hypothesis about our particular enjoyment of laughter starts with some of the same facts that Greenough observed. He finds that we believe in being humorous more than most civilized peoples 'because we have had the energy and the abounding spirits of a young nation, and yet our childhood fell in a day of skepticism instead of animal faith.'

None of our major writers of the mid-century worked primarily in comic modes. Yet even Emerson said, in his essay on 'Heroism': 'The great will not condescend to take anything seriously; all must be as gay as the song of a canary, though it were the building of cities or the eradication of old and foolish churches.' Though Emerson did not know it, the 'frolic health' he wanted in our poets was the best description of the mood that produced the tall tale. Thoreau turned, half-humorously, to the possibilities of a new western mythology to take its place beside that of the Greeks: 'Who knows what shape the fable of Columbus will at length assume, to be confounded with that of Jason and the expedition of the Argonauts. And Franklin,—there may be a line for him in the future classical dictionary, recording what that demigod did, and referring him to some new genealogy. "Son of —— and ——. He aided the Americans to gain their independence, instructed mankind in economy, and drew down lightning from the clouds."'

Melville's gusto enabled him to create modern myths befitting 'the honor and glory of whaling': 'Any man may kill a snake, but only a Perseus, a St. George, a Coffin, have the heart in them to march boldly up to a whale.' And if any Englishman should seriously maintain that St. George's dragon *was* 'a crawling reptile of the land' instead of the great monster of the deep, so much the worse for that hero's legend. Melville's democratic scrutiny was also levelled on the contemporary recipients of the Order of St. George: 'Let not the knights of that honorable company (none of whom, I venture to say, have ever had to do with a whale like their great patron), let them never eye a Nantucketer with disdain, since even in our woollen frocks and tarred trowsers we are much better entitled to St. George's decoration than they.'

Melville's chief use of the mock-heroic, unlike the eighteenth century's, was not to satirize. Believing in the potentialities of his age, he wanted to magnify it beyond the scope of the past. He spoke of Hercules as 'that antique Crockett and Kit Carson.' His own accents were at times closer than he probably realized to those of Crockett himself. When Melville wanted to rise to the heights of his theme he shouted, 'Give me Vesuvius' crater for an inkstand! Friends, hold my arms!' That might have been the gamecock of the backwoods warming up to proclaim that he was 'half-horse, half-alligator, a little touched with the snapping turtle,' who could whip his weight in wild-cats—'and if any gentleman pleases, for a ten-dollar bill, he may throw in a panther—hug a bear too close for comfort, and eat any man opposed to Jackson.'

The created heroes of the tall tales provided a substantial western fact for Carlyle, though not one whose value that prophet could recognize. Nor does Emerson, nor, for that matter, do any of our serious writers appear to have given attention to William Trotter Porter's *Spirit of the Times* (1831-61). Yet that 'Chronicle of the Turf, Agriculture, Field Sports, Literature and the Stage,' edited in New York, boasted that its circulation of forty thousand or more went to readers 'from Hudson's Bay to the Caribbean,' and that its contributions of native oral humor came from men of all sorts, army officers and country gentlemen, lawyers and frontiersmen, all 'gifted with good sense and knowledge of the world,' fond of whisky and story-telling. The Boston *Times* asserted as early as 1840 that Porter had 'done more to develop and foster the humorous genius of his countrymen than any man alive.'

Our concern with this material here may be only with the way it fills out the contours of the myth of the common man. The legend of Davy Crockett (1786-1836) shows how the myth-making faculty of the day could start with an actual man and transform him to fabulous proportions. The most extraordinary of the frontier humorists among Porter's contributors was George Washington Harris (1814-69), the creator of Sut Lovingood. He brings us closer than any other writer to the indigenous and undiluted resources of the American language, to the tastes of the common man himself. The unprinted stories that legend attributes to Lincoln were probably not very different from those Harris put into the mouth of his mischief-making hero, a tough young frontier Till Eulenspiegel.[1]

1. This comparison is Walter Blair's, to whose *Native American Humor* (1937) I am indebted for much material. My debt is even heavier to Constance Rourke's *American Humor* (1931), especially to her treatment of Crockett. A selection from the Crockett

Elected to Congress from the canebrake of Tennessee for no better reason than that he was a great bear-hunter, Crockett took himself seriously, but he was really a grotesque frontier joke. When he turned against Jackson for not being loyal enough to what Davy conceived to be the frontier interests, Whig politicians were quick to exploit this opposition. They encouraged him to go around the country making anti-Jackson speeches and let him sit on the same platform with Daniel Webster. The hands of clever journalists are discernible in the sketches of his legendary prowess that now began to appear under his name. Somebody said that he ought to be the next president, and he believed it. He boasted and strutted, and showed to the full his capacity for blatant egotism and resentful meanness. As Parrington has remarked, Davy the politician, whose greatest asset for electioneering was the shrewd instinct when to pay for his constituents' liquor, was a huge figure for comedy; but Davy the wastrel character, the reckless hunter who slaughtered the resources of the frontier, was 'a hard, unlovely fact' typifying a stage of our civilization.

Instead of rising to the presidency, he failed of re-election to Congress. Staggered at first, he soon wrote characteristically, or so at least the legend wove: 'As my country no longer requires my services, I have made up my mind to leave it.' He determined to say good-bye to Tennessee and follow manifest destiny to the Mexican border. 'I have a new row to hoe, a long and rough one; but I will go ahead.' He added: 'I told my constituents they might all go to hell, and I would go to Texas.' So he went, to live up to his legend, and was killed at the Alamo. And out of his farce sprang the materials for an American tragedy.

That tragedy was not written, but after Crockett's death the humor and imagination of the Southwest continued to dwell on him and made him into a more universal figure. Crockett *Almanacs,* illustrated with clumsy woodcuts, appeared all over the country (1835-56), and their jokes and stories show how much that we have connected with Mark Twain really belonged not to any one man but to the frontier soil.[2] The

Almanacs has been edited by Richard M. Dorson (1939). I have also made use of Lucy Hazard's *The Frontier in American Literature* (1927).

2. Among the stories that Samuel Clemens used to tell in his old age was how he and young Tom Blankenship, the original for Huck Finn, once wanted some money and had a coonskin, which they took and sold to Selms the grocer for ten cents. Then they went

poetry of folklore also touched Crockett's legend. The bears and buffaloes are made to rejoice at his death 'bekos the rifle of Crockett is silent forever.' Then he came to life again in even bolder stature. One of the almanacs began his story by picturing him as a baby giant fed by buffalo's milk. Another affirmed that as a boy he had carried home five cubs in his cap. In still another he twisted off the tail of a comet. Once he went up Niagara Falls on the back of an alligator: 'The alligator walked up the great hill of water as slick as a wild cat up a white oak.'[3] Always a wanderer, he became in the end a demigod, a frontier Prometheus:

One January morning it was so all screwen cold that the forest trees were stiff and they couldn't shake, and the very daybreak froze fast as it was tryin' to dawn. The tinder box in my cabin would no more ketch fire than a sunk raft at the bottom of the sea. Well, seein' daylight war so far behind time I thought creation war in a fair way for freezen fast: so, thinks I, I must strike a little fire from my fingers, light my pipe, an' travel out a few

around back, climbed in a window, stole the skin, and repeated the sale. And so again, many times over. Telling that story brought back Clemens' boyhood to him very vividly. But as Bernard DeVoto has pointed out, it had already been told in Crockett's *Autobiography* before Sam Clemens was born. Thus men lived in the forms of the myth.

3. Similar frozen-faced exaggeration had been part of our tradition at least as far back as Franklin. When confronted in London (1765) with a mass of misinformation and falsehoods about America, instead of denying them he ironically vouched for their truth by capping them with others of his own invention. In a letter to a newspaper he spoke of the cod and whale fishing in the upper Lakes, and added: 'Ignorant People may object that the upper Lakes are fresh, and that Cod and Whale are Salt Water Fish: But let them know, Sir, that Cod, like other Fish when attack'd by their Enemies, fly into any Water where they can be safest; that Whales, when they have a mind to eat Cod, pursue them wherever they fly; and that the grand Leap of the Whale in the Chase up the Fall of Niagara is esteemed, by all who have seen it, as one of the finest Spectacles in Nature.'

Another aspect of tall talk, the peculiar rhythm of western 'flyting' had struck a European traveller as early as 1808: 'In passing two boats next to mine [anchored at Natchez], I heard some very warm words; which my men informed me proceeded from some drunken sailors, who had a dispute respecting a *Choctaw* lady. Although I might fill half a dozen pages with the curious slang made use of . . . I prefer selecting a few of the most brilliant expressions . . . One said, "I am a man; I am a horse; I am a team. I can whip any man *in all Kentucky,* by G-d." The other replied, "I am an alligator, half man, half horse; can whip any man *on the Mississippi,* by G-d." The first one again, "I am a man; have the best horse, best dog, best gun, and the handsomest wife in all Kentucky, by G-d." The other, "I am a Mississippi snapping turtle: have bear's claws, alligator's teeth, and the devil's tail; can whip *any man,* by G-d." This was too much for the first, and at it they went like two bulls . . .' This was reported by Christian Schultz, Jr., *Travels on an Inland Voyage.*

leagues, and see about it. Then I brought my knuckles together like two thunderclouds, but the sparks froze up afore I could begin to collect 'em, so out I walked, whistlin' 'Fire in the mountains!' . . . Well, arter I had walked about twenty miles up the peak o' Daybreak Hill I soon discovered what war the matter. The airth had actually friz fast on her axes, and couldn't turn round; the sun had got jammed between two cakes o' ice under the wheels, an' thar he had been shinin' an' workin' to get loose till he friz fast in his cold sweat. C-r-e-a-t-i-o-n! thought I, this ar the toughest sort of suspension, an' it mustn't be endured. Somethin' must be done, or human creation is done for. It war then so anteluvian an' premature cold that my upper and lower teeth an' tongue war all collapsed together as tight as a friz oyster; but I took a fresh twenty-pound bear off my back that I'd picked up on my road, and beat the animal agin the ice till the hot ile began to walk out on him at all sides. I then took an' held him over the airth's axes an' squeezed him till I'd thawed 'em loose, poured about a ton on't over the sun's face, give the airth's cog-wheel one kick backward till I got the sun loose— whistled 'Push along, keep movin'!' an' in about fifteen seconds the airth gave a grunt, an' began movin'. The sun walked up beautiful, salutin' me with sich a wind o' gratitude that it made me sneeze. I lit my pipe by the blaze o' his top-knot, shouldered my bear, an' walked home, introducin' people to the fresh daylight with a piece of sunrise in my pocket.

The distinctively American thing about such legendary figures, East- man has maintained, is not their size. 'All mythical heroes have been ex- aggerations, but they have been serious ones. America came too late for that. Her demigods were born in laughter; they are consciously prepos- terous; they are cockalorum demigods. That is the natively American thing—not that her primitive humor is exaggerative, but that her primi- tive exaggerations were humorous.' That generalization would apply to Paul Bunyan and Pecos Bill and many others. But it does not seem to leave enough room for the deep strain of lyric poetry which runs through that final anonymous transformation of Crockett. And behind the ex- travagant high spirits of some of our folk heroes, you can occasionally catch a more serious expression. Mike Fink (1770?-1823?), 'the last of the boatmen,' the king of the Ohio River outlaws before the coming of steam, vaunted himself on his prowess with women and whisky. Yet between his fits of 'flyting,' he sometimes lapsed into sadness: 'What's the use of im- provements? Where's the fun, the frolicking, the fighting? Gone! All

gone!' A boat song that kept alive his fame is a mournful elegy for a
vanished past:

> Hard upon the beech oar
> She moves too slow!
> All the way to Shawneetown,
> Long while ago.

Johnny Appleseed was never a boaster at all. In life he had been John
Chapman (1775?-1847), a New England Swedenborgian who had conceived it to be his mission to sow fruit trees through the Middle West,
and had spent nearly half a century travelling by canoe and on foot,
reading aloud from the Bible and leaving orchards behind him. The
Indians thought of him as a great medicine man. After his death from
pneumonia following a long hard trip to a distant orchard, he became a
frontier saint, almost a god of fertility.

No one can tell for sure the birthplace of John Henry, though his
death came while building a tunnel for the railroad just after the Civil
War. The songs that have grown up around him are work songs, their
rhythms responsive to the rise and fall of the hammer. Some of the
stanzas are funny and some obscene, but the pattern is unmistakable,
though not consciously designed by its makers. John Henry, backed by
his white boss in a contest against the new steam drill, won the bet but
died from the strain. His story is a symbol of many things, primarily
of the tragedy of the black man subjected to the power of the white; of
the losing battle of the worker in those desperate stages of industrialism
when he blindly felt that survival depended on matching his strength
against that of the encroaching machine. The death of John Henry coin-
cided with the exploitation of the West, as that of Paul Bunyan with the
gutting of the forests. The recent attempts to retell their legends show
by their factitiousness that the folk art of an industrialized society, like
that of Chaplin or Disney, must spring from new sources and new
techniques of its own.

No cosmic reflections about mythology disturbed Sut Lovingood or
his creator. Harris, who had been born in western Pennsylvania, spent his
life in Knoxville, Tennessee, where he was first apprenticed to a jeweler.
He showed natural skill and considerable technical inventiveness, and by
the age of twenty-one he was captain of the *Knoxville,* the first steamboat

plying regularly out of the city. He also kept up his workshop, and advertised that he was equipped to execute orders for jewelry and wood-engraving, every variety of turning in steel, iron, and brass, and racing cups. He was also postmaster for a spell. A jack of many trades and master of several, he was a craftsman of the kind Thoreau admired. He wrote papers for *The Scientific American,* and from 1843 on was one of the most popular contributors to *The Spirit of the Times.* The first of his sketches about Sut Lovingood appeared in the same year as *Walden.*[4]

Harris took the by then traditional framework for the tall tale, and, because he possessed a keen eye and ear, could use it as a means to portray the frontier life with both realism and fantastic extravagance—the union of incongruities most natural to American humor. Sut, who tells all the stories to Harris, is not yet twenty but has a definite philosophy of life: 'Men were made a-purpus jus' to eat, drink, an' fur stayin' awake in the early part of the nites: an wimen were made to cook the vittles, mix the spirits, an' help the men do the stayin' awake. That's all, an' nothin' more, unless it's fur the wimen to raise the devil atwix meals, an' knit socks atwix drams, an' the men to play short cards, swap hosses with fools, an fite fur exercise, at odd spells.'[5] The world that is refracted through Sut's hard and knowing eyes is that of the practical joker who enjoys violence and cruelty, and often ends his situations in complete social disruption. He delights to put lizards in a parson's pants, or to turn loose a hornet's nest at a prayer meeting; and he strews unconscious bodies around the scene of a fight with as much gusto as Fielding. He is specially pleased with the result when the victims are the sheriff or the circuit-rider, who, with Yankee peddlers or anyone from Massachusetts, are the chief objects of Sut's lawless distaste. He can see no sense in preaching: 'Oh, it's jus' no use in their talkin', an' groanin', an' sweatin' theirselves about it; they must jus' upset nature ontu her head, an' keep her thar, or shut up. Lets taste this here whisky.' What Sut enjoys most

4. The one book collected by Harris from his magazine contributions was *Sut Lovingood* (1867). A new edition, including some uncollected pieces, is now under preparation by F. J. Meine.

5. Since Harris' spelling in dialect has been the chief bar to his being as widely read as he deserves, I have simplified that spelling somewhat in the direction of normal usage. 'Yearly' for 'early,' 'kerds' for 'cards,' etc. are not essential to his effect, and can be very confusing on a first reading.

are social gatherings, quilting parties and dances, and horse races, even though what he contributes to make a lively time livelier generally turns the occasion, as in the case of Sicily Burns' wedding, into the most 'misfortunate' one 'since ole Adam married that heifer what were so fond of talkin' to snakes.' [6]

Sut's life at home with his folks was of a squalor unalleviated and unashamed, but he could admire a hero when he saw one, particularly Wirt Staples, the blacksmith's cousin. Even at the top of Wirt's boast of what he would do to the 'ole false apostil' of the law, you couldn't think for the life of you that he had overbragged a single word:

His britches were buttoned tite round his loins, an' stuffed 'bout half intu his boots, his shirt bagg'd out abuv, an' were as white as milk, his sleeves were rolled up to his arm-pits, an' his collar were as wide open as a gate, the mussils on his arms moved about like rabbits under the skin, an' ontu his hips an' thighs they play'd like the swell on the river, his skin were clear red an' white, an' his eyes a deep, sparklin', wickid blue, while a smile fluttered like a hummin' bird round his mouth all the while. When the State-fair offers a premium fur *men* like they now does fur jackasses, I means to enter Wirt Staples, an' I'll git it, if there's five thousand entrys.

There is 'the central man' of the Smoky Mountains to stand beside Emerson's. He is a blood brother to Bulkington, whose appearance so struck Ishmael at the Spouter Inn. That mariner 'stood full six feet in height, with noble shoulders, and a chest like a coffer-dam. I have seldom seen such brawn in a man. His face was deeply brown and burnt, making his white teeth dazzling by the contrast; while in the deep shadows of his eyes floated some reminiscences that did not seem to give him

6. Sut's recipe for a successful party is a pleasant one to remember, and also provides an instance of Harris' skill in building up rhetoric. In this case I haven't tampered with the spelling: 'Hit wer the bigges' quiltin ever Missis Yardley hilt, an' she hed hilt hundreds; everybody wer thar, 'scept the constibil an' suckit-rider, two dam easily-spared pussons; the numbers ni ontu even too; jis' a few more boys nur gals; that made hit more exhitin, fur hit gin the gals a chance tu kick an' squeal a littil, wifout runnin eny risk ove not gittin kissed at all, an' hit gin reasonabil grounds fur a few scrimmages amung the he's. Now es kissin an' fitin am the pepper an' salt ove all soshul getherins, so hit wer more espishully wif this ove ours. Es I swung my eyes over the crowd, George, I thought quiltins, managed in a morril an' sensibil way, truly am good things—good fur free drinkin, good fur free eatin, good fur free huggin, good fur free dancin, good fur free fitin, an' goodest ove all fur poperlatin a country fas'.'

much joy. His voice at once announced that he was a Southerner, and from his fine stature, I thought he must be one of those tall mountaineers from the Alleghenian Ridge in Virginia.' When the *Pequod* sets sail, Melville dwells on the fact that Bulkington is at the helm. Though he had just landed in midwinter from a four years' dangerous voyage, he has unrestingly pushed off again. 'Know ye, now, Bulkington?' Melville symbolizes in him the natural seeker for 'the open independence' of truth's sea, and his last words to him are: 'Bear thee grimly, demigod! Up from the spray of thy ocean-perishing—straight up, leaps thy apotheosis!'

Wirt Staples was troubled with no such tragic thoughts. His temper could be described in Rabelais' words: 'a certain jollity of mind pickled in a scorn of fortune.' Wirt is the common man in his full stature, but he is not quite what Jefferson had foreseen. Still less is he the representative of the race that Noah Webster had hoped to educate by his spelling book, a sober, dignified and well-trained folk, neither peasants on the one hand, nor corrupt aristocrats on the other, but developing the refinements of a wise culture. Wirt roars like a bull, or—in a shift of the animal imagery of which Harris was so fond since it brought man close to nature—when Wirt has had about eight drinks, he hoists his tail and sets his bristles ready for the sheriff, whom he presently knocks out with a leg of venison. The language Harris put in his mouth makes an epitome of what Mencken has found recorded in the American's speech: 'his bold and somewhat grotesque imagination, his contempt for dignified authority, his lack of aesthetic sensitiveness, his extravagant humor.'

Harris' gifts go beyond the difficult one of being able to translate to the printed page such tales as he had heard. Sut may say, 'I ladles out my words at random,' and he may repeat over and again the same comic-strip situations for his exploits; but his inventiveness is astonishing, particularly in the kind of similes that, irrelevant to his narrative, hand you gratis a compressed scene or character-sketch: 'He watched fur openins to work off some kind of devilment, just as close as a ole woman what were wunst unsanctified herself watches her daughters when a circus or a camp meetin' am in heat.' Harris possesses on the comic level something of what Melville does on the tragic, the rare kind of dramatic imagination that can get movement directly into words. This brings a wonderfully kinetic quality to whole situations, to Bart Davis' dance or to the ructions caused in Lynchburg market by an escaped bull. The ability to use every possible verbal gesture of action alone could create this whirlwind description of a preacher attacked by hornets: 'I seed him fotch hisself a lick . . . with both hans ontu the place where they brands Freemasons an' mustangs, an' he shot his belly forwards an' his shoulders back'ards, like ontu a woman shuttin' the nex' to the top drawer of a beauro; an' he come outen that pulpit back'ards a-tarin', his hans a-flyin' round his hed like a pair of windin' blades.'

The panorama of life that flashes by in Sut's yarns may well remind you of Josh Billings' definition of our humor: 'Americans love caustick things: they would prefer turpentine to colone-water, if they had tew drink either. So with their relish of humor; they must have it on the half-shell with cayenne.' But in many casual passages, without consciously intending it, Sut catches more surely the quality of homely existence. In his picture of Wirt's woman he completes his version of the heroic myth, as he celebrates the abundance he has glimpsed and so knows to be possible: 'She ain't one of your she-cat wimmin, always spittin' an' groanin', an' swellin' their tails 'bout their virtue. She never talks a word about it, no more nor if she didn't have any; an' she has as true a heart as ever beat agin a shift hem, or a husband's shirt. But she am full of fun, an' I mout add as purty as a hen canary, an' I swear I don't b'leve the woman knows it.' This makes the prelude to his description of her cooking, for Sut understands the connection between good food and a husband's love, and gives his own kind of hymn to fertility:

Wirt's wife got early supper, a real circuit-rider's supper, where the woman of the house were a rich b'lever. There were chickens cut up, an' fried in butter, brown, white, flakey, light, hot biskit, made with cream, scrambled eggs, yaller butter, fried ham in slices as big as your hand, pickled beets, an' cowcumbers, roastin' ears, shaved down an' fried, sweet taters, baked, a stack of buckwheat cakes, as full of holes as a sifter, an' a bowl of strained honey, to fill the holes . . . I gets dog hungry every time I see Wirt's wife, or even her side-saddle, or her frocks a-hangin' on the clothesline.

4. Full Circle

'Make-belief is an enervating exercise of fancy not to be confused with imaginative growth. The saner and greater mythologies are not fancies; they are the utterance of the whole soul of man and, as such, inexhaustible to meditation. They are no amusement or diversion to be sought as a relaxation and an escape from the hard realities of life. They are these hard realities in projection, their symbolic recognition, co-ordination and acceptance. Through such mythologies our will is collected, our powers unified, our growth controlled. Through them the infinitely divergent strayings of our being are brought into "balance or reconciliation." The "opposite and discordant qualities" of things in them acquire a form; and such integrity as we possess as "civilized" men is our inheritance through them. Without his mythologies man is only a cruel animal without a soul—for a soul is a central part of his governing mythology—he is a congeries of possibilities without order and without aim.'

—RICHARDS, *Coleridge on Imagination*

THOREAU's ability to create myth ran on a deeper level than his amused fancies about Franklin. Those fancies were the instinctive product of his sense of the age's plenitude. He would have liked Mann's description of myth as 'the holiday garment,' 'the recurrent feast which bestrides the tenses and makes the has-been and the to-be present to the popular sense.' Thoreau's own superabundant life let him find a river god in a logger on the Penobscot, it let him read in Homer about 'such a fire-eyed Agamemnon as you may see at town meetings.' He was following there one of Emerson's most fruitful leads. The birth of a first son (1836) had given Emerson's life at Concord its final consecration. He felt that he had at last reached the solidity of life's fundamental pattern: 'A wife, a babe, a brother, poverty, and a country, which the Greek had, I have.' Emerson continued these thoughts in a passage that he later incorporated into 'History': 'Our admiration of the Antique is not admiration of the old, but of the natural. We admire the Greek in an American ploughboy often.' Thoreau might have said that, but there turned out to be this crucial distinction: there was a great deal of admiration of the antique in Thoreau's practice, in the precision and toughness of language that the Greeks and Romans had taught him to be his goal. Emerson's heart, as Santayana has said, 'was fixed on eternal things,' his Now was that of the metaphysicians, and—despite his earnest desire that it should be otherwise—had very little relation to an actual present or past. Thoreau possessed more of the past, not through his mind, but as an experienced linguistic discipline. Therefore he inevitably possessed a more concrete present as well.

He re-created a basic myth because he was able to assimilate his conscious analogies into re-enacting what Emerson had perceived but could not put his muscle into, the union of work and culture. As Odell Shepard has discerned, 'This man who read his Homer in a hut by a woodland lake can show us better, perhaps, than any other teacher we have yet had how to coordinate whatever is peculiarly American with the tradition of the ages.' The day after Thoreau had settled by Walden he felt that he had found 'the very light and atmosphere in which the works of Grecian art were composed, and in which they rest.' He was glad on summer nights to sit on the shore of his Ithaca, 'a fellow-wanderer and survivor of Ulysses.' But the reason why his allusions did not become merely literary, the reason why he accomplished his rare coordination, lies in the way he reacted to his reading. Cato's *De Re Rustica* did not remain quaint for him. He described it thus (1851): 'A small treatise or Farmer's Manual of those days, fresh from the field of Roman life, all reeking with and redolent of the life of those days, containing more indirect history than any of the histories of Rome of direct,—all of that time but that time,— *here* is a simple, direct pertinent word addressed to the Romans. And where are *the Romans?*' Thoreau's answer was that the Romans are ordinarily 'an ornament of rhetoric,' but that 'we have here their *New England Farmer,* the very manual those Roman farmers read . . . as fresh as a dripping dish-cloth from a Roman kitchen.' It was as if he read the letters of Solon Robinson, and how much was paid to Joe Farrar 'for work done.'

Thoreau thus became an actor in the great cyclic drama, but did not give up his New England accent. He had not perceived more than Emerson of the New England character. For Emerson had caught its essence when observing the struggle between 'sage and savage' in Ezra Ripley (1834): 'These old semi-savages do from the solitude in which they live and their remoteness from artificial society and their inevitable daily comparing man with beast, village with wilderness, their inevitable acquaintance with the outward nature of man, and with his strict dependence on sun and rain and wind and frost, wood, worm, cow and bird, get an education to the Homeric simplicity, which all the libraries of the Reviews and the Commentators in Boston do not countervail.' Thoreau had the immeasurable benefit of such thought from the day he listened to *The American Scholar*. He could give it sturdier expression. His words ring with the authority of having experienced both halves of his comparison when he says that Minott tells his long stories with the same satisfaction in the details as Herodotus. In his sympathy with the seasons as well as with the farmers' often grim effort to wrest subsistence from them, Thoreau learned that 'the perennial mind' did not die with Cato, 'and will not die with Hosmer.' This mind was nothing rarefied; it was an integral part of the functioning of the human organism. What interested Thoreau most in literature was the expression of this mind, the insight it gave into collective existence: 'it is the spirit of humanity, that which animates both so-called savages and civilized nations, working through a man, and not the man expressing himself.' Thoreau had come to that fundamental understanding while studying the Indians, just as Mann came to it at the close of his essay on Dürer, in whose deep humanity he had found 'history as myth, history that is ever fresh and ever present. For we are much less individuals than we either hope or fear to be.'

Thoreau's accent is no less that of a New Englander for betraying an awareness of both the Romans and the Indians. Living in an age of waning Christianity, he became convinced that there was no important difference between his countrymen's religion and that of the ancient world: 'The New Englander is a pagan suckled in a creed outworn.' Thoreau's light-hearted worship of Pan set the tone for his *Week*. But much of his praise of Jupiter in place of Jehovah was designed simply to shock, and some of it is merely frivolous, gaining its license from the accepted fact of the Christian background. He struck his most autochthonous vein when he noted the difference between English and American time, how here he could penetrate almost immediately to a savage past. He was not a savage himself, more the villager than the hunter, but he felt in his world no unbridgeable gap between these roles. His sense of closeness to the Indian strengthened his hold on the primitive, and kept him from writing Victorian idylls. He was most nearly an antique Roman when he said: 'Superstition has always reigned. It is absurd to think that these farmers, dressed in their Sunday clothes, proceeding to church, differ essentially in this respect from the Roman peasantry. They have merely changed the names and number of their gods. Men were as good then as they are now, and loved one another as much—or little.'

The source of vigor in Thoreau's New England festival was his knowledge that 'the husbandman is always a better Greek than the scholar is prepared to appreciate.' The old customs still survive, even while antiquarians grow gray in commemorating their past existence. 'The farmers crowd to the fair to-day in obedience to the same ancient law, which Solon or Lycurgus did not enact, as naturally as bees swarm and follow their queen.' Thoreau's quality there, as we have found it in *Walden*, is more cultivated than wild. It is more lyric and pastoral than heroic, though this, like the question of whether he belonged to the village or to the forest or to the borderline between, is simply a matter of degree. He saw the classical present in his own surroundings just as Sarah Jewett was to do when she envisaged the Bowden family reunion in its procession across the field to the picnic grove as though it was a company of ancient Greeks going to worship the god of the harvests: 'We were no more a New England family celebrating its own existence and simple progress; we carried the tokens and inheritance of all such households from which this had descended, and were only the latest of our line.' Unlike Thoreau's, Miss Jewett's tone is generally elegiac. Robert Frost has more of Thoreau's dramatic immediacy, but since the forests have now receded and the cities have encroached on the farms, Frost's scope as a poet of nature has inevitably been contracted to the more purely personal.

The heroic quality is absent from *North of Boston*, if by that quality you mean what Thoreau could sense in Whitman, that he was 'something a little more than human.' Thoreau was not blind to the element of brag, but when he called on Whitman in Brooklyn (1856), he felt at once, 'He is apparently the greatest democrat the world has ever seen.' It is hardly necessary to dwell on Whitman's creation of myth, since it is so explicit throughout the whole breadth of his work. He looked at the past in a more reckless mood than Thoreau: 'As if the beauty and sacredness of the demonstrable must fall behind that of the mythical! As if men do not make their mark out of any times! As if the opening of the western continent by discovery and what has transpired since in North and South America were less than the small theatre of the antique or the aimless sleepwalking of the middle ages!' That was the opening blast of his 1855 preface, though he presently added:

> In the name of the States shall I scorn the antique?
> Why these are the children of the antique to justify it.

Whitman set out more deliberately than any of his contemporaries to create the kind of hero whom Emerson had foreshadowed in his varying guises of the Scholar and the Poet. Looking back over his career in his final preface, he said that *Leaves of Grass* had been impelled by his desire to realize his own personality, both physical and spiritual, in the midst of its momentous surroundings, 'to exploit that Personality, identified with place and date, in a far more candid and comprehensive sense than any hitherto poem or book.' He had said long before, 'I have but one central figure, the general human personality typified in myself.' He had felt from the time of his first *Leaves* that if his book was to be true to its American origin, it must be 'a song of "the great pride of man in himself."' What saved Whitman from the last extreme of egotism was his insistence on the typical and his boundless store of fellow-feeling. His one quarrel with Thoreau was his 'disdain for men (for Tom, Dick, and Harry): inability to appreciate the average.'[1] If the poet had discovered himself to be at the creative center of life, with all its potential energies radiating out from him, this discovery was the property of all. Whitman wanted his book to compel 'every reader to transpose himself or herself into the central position, and become the living fountain.' He took his final pleasure in reflecting: 'I have imagined a life which should be that of the average man in average circumstances, and still grand, heroic.'

His work inevitably assumed cosmic proportions. He said that from the press of his foot to the earth sprang 'a hundred affections' that eluded his best efforts to describe them. But the language of his poems does not

---

1. The difference between their temperaments could hardly have been revealed more characteristically than in their first meeting. Thoreau reported: 'I did not get far in conversation with him,—two more being present,—and among the few things which I chanced to say, I remember that one was, in answer to him as representing America, that I did not think much of America or of politics, and so on, which may have been somewhat of a damper to him.' Years later Whitman generalized: Thoreau 'couldn't put his life into any other life—realize why one man was so and another man not so: was impatient with other people on the street and so forth . . . We could not agree at all in our estimate of men—of the men we met here, there, everywhere—the concrete man. Thoreau had an abstraction about man—a right abstraction: there we agreed.'

suggest contact with the soil so much as with the streets of Brooklyn. When he thought of the past, his instinctive analogy was:

Lads ahold of fire-engines and hook-and-ladder ropes no less to me than the gods of the antique wars.

When he envisaged his 'stock personality' in its most godlike stature, he made it come to life by breaking into slang:

> Earth! you seem to look for something at my hands,
> Say, old top-knot, what do you want?

Otherwise his cult of himself as the bearded prophet could lead into pages of solemn straining for effect. The dichotomy that we observed in both his diction and his content expresses itself again in the contrast between Whitman's actual and ideal selves. Tocqueville foresaw his problem when he observed that the poet of democracy, having given up the past, thus ran the risk of losing part of the present in his excessive preoccupation with the future destinies of mankind. Lawrence's distinction between the poetry of the future and the poetry of the present is likewise partly relevant. Lawrence held that the first may possess the crystallized perfection of things to come, whereas the second, lacking this, seeks to catch the present in all its confusion, and is 'plasmic.' Whitman possessed none of the power of thought or form that would have been necessary to give his poems of ideal democracy any perfection, and to keep them from the barrenness of abstraction. He created his lasting image of the common man and 'the pending action of this Time and Land we swim in' when he remained the instinctual being who found no sweeter fat than stuck to his own bones.

He was never conscious of the dichotomy, but he described its consequences in his surprised and hesitant admission as an old man that Thoreau, though not 'so precious, tender, a personality' as Emerson, was 'one of the native forces' and so possibly 'bigger.' The heroic stature that Whitman recognized in Thoreau was the result of Thoreau's having lived up to his own dictum that 'it is the faculty of the poet to see present things as if . . . also past and future, as if distant or universally significant.' By so doing Thoreau made actual the classical present instead of merely perceiving it like Emerson. Whitman had neither Thoreau's lucidity nor firmness. By cutting himself loose from any past, he often went billowing away into a dream of perfectibility, which tried to make the human literally divine and was hence unreal. But because he was more porous to all kinds of experience, he gave a more comprehensive, if confused, image of his fluid age than Thoreau did.

The cult of perfection was an inevitable concomitant of the romantic cult of the future. The attitude behind both received its most searching contemporary analysis from Hawthorne. He sensed that Emerson's exaltation of the divinity in man had obliterated the distinctions between man and God, between time and eternity. Although no theologian, Hawthorne did not relax his grip on the Christian conception of time. This had been obscured by Thoreau and Whitman no less than by Emerson in their exhilaration over the fullness of the moment. Hawthorne knew that he lived both in time and out of it, that the process of man's history was a deep interaction between eternity and time, an incessant eruption of eternity into time. And he knew the tragic nature of such conflict. In spite of the capacity of man's soul to share immediately in eternal life, his finite and limited nature made it inevitable that nothing perfect could be realized in time.[2] Hawthorne's understanding of human destiny ran counter to all the doctrines of progress. It made him cling fast to the quality of actual existence even though he was aware of its impermanence; it made him insist that 'all philosophy that would abstract man from the present is no more than words.' It made him profoundly conscious that the moments of greatest human import were the moments of moral crisis, for then men and women entered most nearly into the eternal nature even as they were aware of their limitations.

Such a reading of destiny came to Hawthorne through his resistance to what he could not deem otherwise than transcendental fads. It enabled him to criticize, in *The Blithedale Romance,* one phase of the contemporary myth, the quest for Utopia. However inadequately worked out some of his social criticism may be, there is no questioning the acuity with which he saw the weaknesses of Brook Farm. He could not help feeling that its spirit was essentially that of a picnic, of an escape to a woodland paradise. As he watched the community's competition with the outside market-gardeners, he soon realized that with relation to 'society at large, we stood in a position of new hostility, rather than new brotherhood.'

2. Cf. above, pp. 254-5. Our present awareness of this strain of thought has been increased by the rediscovery of Kierkegaard, and by Karl Barth's 'theology of crisis.'

These views might well have seemed captious to George Ripley, who gave his heart's blood to prove that such experiments could lead the way to a more just organization of society as a whole. Where Hawthorne's criticism runs no risk of being obscurantistic is in his portrait of Hollingsworth, man the reformer. There Hawthorne could make articulate his understanding of what happened when a man failed to distinguish between time and eternity, between his fallibility and his longing for the ideal. Hollingsworth was desperately earnest in his scheme for reforming criminals 'through an appeal to their higher instincts,' but he had no faint inkling of the complexity of man's nature. He was warped by his single thought, to which he would brook no opposition, and was interested in other people only to the extent that they accepted his plan. He became an incarnation of the terrible egotism that mistakes its own will for the promptings of God.

Emerson had more opportunity to study reformers than Hawthorne, since they were always swarming around him, but he never saw the problem they presented with such deadly lucidity. He found many of them bores, but he was partial to their trust in uplift, and relied on compensation to atone for their want of balance. When Thoreau and Whitman thought of a reformer, they, like Emerson, remembered the heroic affirmation of John Brown, of whom Hawthorne said: 'Nobody was ever more justly hanged. He won his martyrdom fairly and took it firmly.' But both Whitman and Thoreau could have learned something from the example of Hollingsworth. Their images of the rising common man are far more compelling than anything Hawthorne conceived through Holgrave. But Whitman's belief in the poet as his own Messiah escaped Hollingsworth's tragedy only by the counterpoise of his generous warmth. And although Thoreau evaded the literal-minded apostles of improvement, his weakest element lay in the impossible perfection he demanded from mankind. ('I love my friends very much, but I find that it is no use to go to see them. I hate them commonly when I am near them.') So far as there was a defect in his valiant self-reliance, it emerged when he turned his back on other men, and sought for truth not in the great and common world but exclusively within himself.

What Hawthorne found through his descent into the caverns of the heart was the general bond of suffering. His discovery gave Melville his only clue through the labyrinth of the age's confusions. He plunged deeper into the blackness than Hawthorne had, and needed more complex images to express his findings. He developed one by likening Ahab's buried life, 'his whole awful essence,' to the mystic grandeur of an ancient statue far beneath the modern surface of existence. The primitive spoke to Melville with different meanings than it did to Thoreau. He might joke about Hercules as an antique Crockett, but he did not so often think of the presentness of the past as of the pastness of the present, of its illimitable shadowy extensions backward to the roots of history, to the preconscious and the unknown. 'Ten million things were as yet uncovered to Pierre. The old mummy lies buried in cloth on cloth; it takes time to unwrap this Egyptian king. Yet now, forsooth, because Pierre began to see through the first superficiality of the world, he fondly weens he has come to the unlayered substance. But, far as any geologist has yet gone down into the world, it is found to consist of nothing but surface stratified on surface. To its axis, the world being nothing but superinduced superficies.' That is akin to Mann's reflection on the bottomless well of the past, on the incertitude of the researcher as he lets down his plummet into unfathomable depths. But the author of *Pierre* did not possess Mann's humanistic patience. He had become identified with his hero's agony: 'By vast pains we mine into the pyramid; by horrible gropings we come to the central room; with joy we espy the sarcophagus; but we lift the lid—and no body is there! appallingly vacant as vast is the soul of a man!'

Such a mood could lead only to nihilism. But the passion with which Melville made his demands upon life had given him previously an instinctive awareness of the significance of myth. He had commented in *Moby-Dick* on the loss of poetic mythology 'in the now egotistical sky.' He had sensed the primal vitality of the stories that are preserved in the popular memory, and that help keep alive the hidden strivings of the human spirit by giving them concrete shape. He had sensed too the destructive quality of the enlightened mind if by its criticism it served merely to divorce man from his past by dispelling the reality of the myths, by reducing them to a remote and naïve stage of racial development. Though Melville did not articulate his theory of history, he affirmed its values by finding figures of tragic stature on board a whaler, and in Ahab all the majesty of a Biblical king. Melville knew that beyond the bright circle of man's educated consciousness lay unsuspected energies that were both magnificent and terrifying. He wanted to rouse his country to its 'contemporary grandeur.' His detailed recording of the whaling industry sprang from his comprehension that the living facts of ordinary existence were the source of whatever heroic myths Americans could live by.

His choice of material was hardly thus deliberate, but by taking the segment of human activity that he knew best, he re-enacted through it the major significances of myth. He had been attracted to whaling as the great adventure of his day, around which had clustered such widely current legends as the one Emerson had reported in his journal (1834) after a trip from New Bedford to Boston: 'A seaman in the coach told the story of an old sperm-whale, which he called a white whale, which was known for many years by the whalemen as Old Tom, and who rushed upon the boats which attacked him, and crushed the boats to small chips in his jaws, the men generally escaping by jumping overboard and being picked up. A vessel was fitted out at New Bedford, he said, to take him. And he was finally taken somewhere off Payta Head by the *Winslow* or the *Essex*.' That was the subject for an adventure story, but the way Melville transformed his version shows the principal function of myth, its symbolizing of the fundamental truths. In his narrative of whaling Melville could see how this industry typified man's wresting a livelihood from nature and extending his power over the globe by peaceful commerce rather than by war. He could trustingly visualize the whale ship as a means of communication, battering down ancient prejudices, opening doors in the Orient, even, as we have noted, leading the way to the liberation of South America from autocratic domination and to the establishment 'of the eternal democracy' there.

But that was scarcely Melville's main theme. The dark half of his mind remembered what effect the white man had left on the South Sea islands; and as he meditated too on the brutal savagery in the conquest of the whale, his imagination stirred to the latent possibilities in the story Emerson had heard. He grasped intuitively the process that Whitehead has described: 'We inherit legends, weird, horrible, beautiful, expressing in curious, specialized ways the interweaving of law and capriciousness in the mystery of things. It is the problem of good and evil. Sometimes the law is good and the capriciousness evil; sometimes the law is iron and evil and the capriciousness is merciful and good.' Melville could not say directly whether the law was good or evil. He had been born into a world whose traditional religion was in a state of decay, and whose grim Jehovah often struck him as being only the projection of man's inexorable will to power. But as Melville responded to the Christian belief in equality and brotherhood, he poured out his praise to 'the great God absolute, the centre and circumference of all democracy.'

Melville did not achieve in *Moby-Dick* a *Paradise Lost* or a *Faust*. The search for the meaning of life that could be symbolized through the struggle between Ahab and the White Whale was neither so lucid nor so universal. But he did apprehend therein the tragedy of extreme individualism, the disasters of the selfish will, the agony of a spirit so walled within itself that it seemed cut off from any possibility of salvation. Beyond that, his theme of the White Whale was so ambivalent that as he probed into the meaning of good and evil he found their expected values shifting. His symbols were most comprehensive when they enabled him to elicit 'what remains primeval in our formalized humanity,' when they took such a basic pattern as that of his later discernment of Abraham and Isaac in Captain Vere and Billy. When the Pacific called out the response of his united body and mind, he wrote the enduring signature of his age. He gave full expression to its abundance, to its energetic desire to master history by repossessing all the resources of the hidden past in a timeless and heroic present. But he did not avoid the darkness in that past, the perpetual suffering in the heart of man, the broken arc of his career which inevitably ends in death. He thus fulfilled what Coleridge held to be the major function of the artist: he brought 'the whole soul of man into activity.'

Chronology

1803 Emerson born, at Boston, May 25.
1804 Hawthorne born, at Salem, July 4.
1817 Thoreau born, at Concord, July 12.
1819 Whitman born, at West Hills, Long Island, May 31.
      Melville born, at New York City, August 1.
1821 Emerson graduated from Harvard, and spent the next seven years school-teaching and studying in the Harvard Divinity School.
1825 Hawthorne graduated from Bowdoin, in the same class with Longfellow and Franklin Pierce, and went back to live in Salem.
1828 Hawthorne published anonymously *Fanshawe, A Tale.*
1829 Emerson accepted the call to become pastor of the Second Church of Boston, and was married to Ellen Tucker.
1831 Emerson's wife died.
1831 Whitman was working as a printer's devil on Long Island and in
-34 Brooklyn.
1832 Emerson resigned his pastorate, and went to Europe for a year. He began his career as a lecturer on his return.
1834 Emerson made his home at Concord.
      Because of his family's lack of resources after financial reverses and the death of his father, Melville had to leave the Albany Academy and become a clerk.
1835 Emerson married Lydia Jackson.
1836 Emerson published *Nature.*
1836 Whitman taught school on Long Island, and worked for various
-41 papers.
1837 Hawthorne published *Twice-Told Tales,* a collection of the stories he had been writing during the past nine years.
      Emerson delivered *The American Scholar* as the Phi Beta Kappa address at Harvard.
      Thoreau graduated from Harvard, and started his journal.
      Melville shipped as a sailor on a merchantman for Liverpool.
1838 Emerson delivered his Divinity School Address.
      Thoreau taught school at Concord, read his first lecture before the Concord Lyceum, and made his first trip to Maine.

Hawthorne became engaged to Sophia Peabody.

1838
-41
Melville was teaching school at Greenbush, New York, and Pittsfield, Mass.

1839 Thoreau made his week's trip on the Concord and Merrimack rivers with his brother John.

1839
-40
Hawthorne was a measurer at the Boston Customhouse.

1840
-44
The Dial.

1841 On January 3, Melville shipped out of New Bedford for the South Seas on the whaler *Acushnet.*

Emerson, *Essays: First Series.*

Hawthorne was at Brook Farm, from April to November.

Whitman began contributing prose and verse to newspapers and magazines in New York.

1842 Hawthorne married, and settled at the Old Manse in Concord for the next three years. He also published a second edition of *Twice-Told Tales.*

Melville jumped ship at the Marquesa Islands, and lived a month among the cannibals in the Taipi valley before escaping to Tahiti.

1843 Whitman, *Franklin Evans, or The Inebriate,* a temperance tract masked as a novel.

Melville was mustered into the navy at Honolulu, on the frigate *United States.*

1844 Emerson, *Essays: Second Series.*

Melville landed in Boston in October, and was discharged from the navy.

1845 Thoreau began living at Walden Pond on the 4th of July.

1846 Melville, *Typee.*

Thoreau spent a night in the Concord jail.

Hawthorne published *Mosses from an Old Manse,* and became a surveyor in the Salem Customhouse.

1846
-48
Whitman worked for *The Brooklyn Eagle* until he lost his position for his free-soil principles.

1847 Emerson's first volume of *Poems.*

Melville published *Omoo,* married Elizabeth Shaw, daughter of the Chief Justice of Massachusetts, and settled in New York.

Thoreau returned from Walden to Concord in the fall.

1847
-48
Emerson made a second visit to Europe.

1848 Thoreau wrote 'Civil Disobedience.'

Whitman took a several months' trip to New Orleans.

1849 Thoreau, *A Week on the Concord and Merrimack Rivers.*

Hawthorne lost his position in the Customhouse.

Melville published *Mardi* in the spring, *Redburn* in the fall, and went to London in October to arrange for the publication of *White Jacket,* which came out the next winter.

1850 Emerson, *Representative Men.* He made the first of his long lecture tours through the West, going down the Ohio and up the Mississippi to St. Louis, and coming back by stage and rail.

Thoreau went to Canada for a week.

Whitman printed "Blood-Money," his first free-verse, a poem on the slavery issue.

Hawthorne published *The Scarlet Letter,* and went to live in Lenox.

Melville removed to Pittsfield, and wrote his essay on "Hawthorne and his *Mosses*" shortly before meeting him.

1851 Hawthorne published *The House of the Seven Gables* and *The Snow-Image.*

Melville, *Moby-Dick.*

1851 Whitman worked irregularly for newspapers, and at house-building
-54 with his father. He began to compose *Leaves of Grass.*

1852 Hawthorne returned to Concord, published *The Blithedale Romance* and his campaign biography of Franklin Pierce.

Melville, *Pierre.*

1853 Thoreau's *Yankee in Canada* began to appear in *Putnam's Magazine.*

1853 Hawthorne was consul at Liverpool.
-57

1854 Thoreau, *Walden.*

1855 Melville, *Israel Potter.*

On the 4th of July Whitman issued *Leaves of Grass,* containing a dozen poems, much the most important being "Song of Myself."

Four chapters of Thoreau's *Cape Cod* were printed in *Putnam's.*

1856 Emerson, *English Traits.*

Whitman, *Leaves of Grass,* second edition, with twenty more poems.

Melville published *The Piazza Tales,* finished *The Confidence Man,* and left for a trip to the Holy Land. On his return he lectured in various cities (1857-60) on "Statuary in Rome," "The South Seas," and "Travelling."

1858 Part of Thoreau's *Maine Woods* was printed in *The Atlantic.*

1858 Hawthorne was living in Italy.
-59

1859 Thoreau and Emerson both spoke in defense of John Brown.

1860 Emerson, *The Conduct of Life*.

Whitman, *Leaves of Grass*, third edition, with over a hundred more poems, including "Out of the cradle endlessly rocking," *Children of Adam*, and *Calamus*.

Hawthorne published *The Marble Faun*, and returned to The Wayside in Concord.

Melville sailed to San Francisco with his brother Thomas, captain of the clipper-ship, *Meteor*.

1861 Thoreau made a trip to Minnesota for his health.

1862 Thoreau died at Concord, May 6.

Whitman became a volunteer nurse in the army hospitals in Washington.

1863 Hawthorne, *Our Old Home*.

1864 Hawthorne died at Plymouth, N. H., on May 19, while on a trip for his health with Franklin Pierce. He was buried in Concord.

1865 Whitman held a clerkship in the Indian Bureau, Department of the Interior, in Washington, until he was dismissed as an indecent writer. He published *Drum-Taps*, including his tribute to Lincoln, in the fall.

1865 Whitman remained in Washington except for brief visits to Brooklyn.
-73   He again had a position as a government clerk.

1866 Melville's poems, *Battle-Pieces*. He was appointed district inspector of Customs in New York, a post he held through 1885.

1867 Emerson's second and final volume of poems, *May-Day*.

1870 Emerson, *Society and Solitude*.

1870 Whitman, *Democratic Vistas*.
-71

1871 Whitman added "Passage to India" and about thirty-five other poems to *Leaves of Grass*.

1872 Emerson's house burned, and he made his third and final visit to Europe.

1873 Whitman suffered an attack of paralysis and removed to Camden, where he lived for the rest of his life.

1875 Emerson, *Letters and Social Aims*.

1876 Emerson made the last entry in his journal.

Melville published his long narrative poem, *Clarel*.

Whitman added "Prayer for Columbus," "To a Locomotive in Winter" and several other poems to *Leaves of Grass*.

1879 Whitman delivered the first of his Lincoln lectures, visited his brother Jeff in St. Louis, and went as far west as Denver.

1881   Emerson died at Concord, April 27.

The first edition of *Leaves of Grass* to be issued by a regular publisher, Osgood in Boston. Six months later Osgood was threatened by the Massachusetts Society for the Suppression of Vice, and the edition was abandoned.

1882   Whitman, *Specimen Days,* issued in Philadelphia.

1888   Whitman, *November Boughs.*

Melville, *John Marr and Other Sailors,* published privately.

1891   Melville, *Timoleon,* again published privately in twenty-five copies. He had been at work on *Billy Budd* off and on from 1888 until April, 1891. He died at New York on September 28.

Whitman, *Good-Bye, My Fancy.*

1892   A collected edition of *Leaves of Grass* was brought out by David McKay, Philadelphia. Whitman died at Camden on March 26.

Index

674

Pattee, F. L., 174n
Paul, Saint, 385n
Peabody, Elizabeth, 321n, 357
Pearson, Norman H., 361n
Pecos Bill, 640
Perry, Bliss, 15
Perugino, Pietro, 353
Petrarch, 385n
Phidias, 16, 607
Pierce, Franklin, 189, 267, 316, 317, 319, 489
Pindar, 102, 149
Plato, 3, 4, 14, 14n, 59, 62, 102, 103, 105, 125, 186, 187, 198, 385n, 405, 439, 473, 504, 631, 634
Pliny, 231n
Plotinus, 4, 68
Plutarch, 15, 19, 71, 122, 618, 628
Poe, Edgar Allan, 8, 8n, 10, 57n, 74, 136, 144, 202; praise of Hawthorne, 205-6, 208; 213, 219; on subconscious mind, 233; 234, 242-3, 247, 295, 302-3, 387, 467-8, 534; Whitman on, 540-41, 541n; 543, 560n, 564, 579
Poetry, confusion of with oratory, 22-3; with religion, 23-6, 42-4; Emerson's conception of, 42-4, 50-55, 59; Emerson's practice of, 44-9, 52-3, 55-64, 113-15; Hawthorne's indifference to, 200n; Melville's, 401, 490, 493-7, 512; Whitman's conception of, 543-4, 549-77, 580-81, 614; Whitman's practice of, 517-625 *passim;* Tocqueville on American, 543-4, 651
Polk, James K., 562
Politics (*see* Society), Thoreau's, 77-9; Hawthorne's, 323-37, 360; Melville's, 382-3; Whitman's, 541-3, 616, 633
Pope, Alexander, 18, 207, 208, 461n, 475, 564
Porter, William Trotter, 637
Pound, Ezra, 305, 356; on Whitman, 579-80, 592
Pound, Louise, 529n, 559n
Praxiteles, 244, 263
Proclus, 50, 385n
Prescott, Col. William, 18
Prescott, William H., 197, 200, 202, 208, 214, 633
Propertius, 356
Proudhon, Pierre Joseph, 77n
Proust, Marcel, 10, 172, 581
Psychology, Coleridge's concern with, 7; Hawthorne's, 294-5, 305-12, 337-51; Melville's, 445-53, 467-87, 500-514

Psychoanalysis, 337, 479
Ptolemy, 106
Purcell, Henry, 587
Puritanism, in N. E. culture, 40, 56, 72, 199, 215-18, 278, 321, 322; Emerson and, 103, 104, 116; Hawthorne and, 190, 192, 193, 199, 205, 215-18, 235, 271, 273, 278, 306, 310, 322, 337, 341; psychology of, 312, 407; Melville and, 407, 435, 455
Pyrrho, 385n
Pythagoras, 137

Quakers, Emerson's kinship with, 9; 202; in 'The Gentle Boy,' 215-18; Whitman and, 269, 525, 536-41, 544; 342, 343, 400, 428
Quarles, Francis, 101, 105, 110n
Quincy, Josiah, 18

Rabelais, François, 35, 291, 377, 409, 604, 605, 618, 644
Racine, Jean Baptiste, 231n, 314, 518
Radcliffe, Mrs. Anne, 201
Raleigh, Sir Walter, 111
Ransom, John Crowe, 291n
Raphael, 142, 634
Read, Herbert, 270
Reed, Sampson, 13, 14
Rembrandt van Rijn, 281
Renan, Ernest, 423, 423n
Reni, Guido, 230, 352-5
Reynolds, Sir Joshua, 409, 597
Rhythm, Emerson's, 46ff, 53; Thoreau's, 83-6, 92-8; Melville's, 119-32, 385-8, 390-95, 421-31, 460-66, 484-7; Whitman's, 564-9, 584-93; Hopkins' and Whitman's compared, 584
Richards, I. A., 31, 129, 522, 581, 646
Richardson, Samuel, 202n
Richelieu, Cardinal de, 231n
Richter, Jean Paul, 94, 120n, 227, 291, 385n
Riding, Laura, 587n
Rig Veda, 175
Rimbaud, Arthur, 69, 395
Ripley, Rev. Ezra, 71-2, 195, 213, 361, 647
Ripley, George, 12n, 251n, 333n, 653
Rivera, Diego, 545
Robinson, Edwin Arlington, 347, 592
Rogers, H. H., 496
Romains, Jules, 21n
Rossini, Gioachino, 558
Rourke, Constance, 172, 173, 637n
Rousseau, Jean-Jacques, 231n, 345, 377, 595

"A Century ago, the image contrived to embody the most fruitful contemporary ideas was that of the authentic American as a figure of heroic innocence and vast potentialities, poised at the start of a new history. This image is the title of the book."

[R. W. B. Lewis, "The American Adam"]

"Here's for the plain old Adam, the simple genuine self against the whole world"

[R. W. Emerson, Journals]

Melville   184 - 190
                284 - 291
                402 - 466